TELEVISION:
The American Medium In Crisis

TELEVISION:
The American Medium In Crisis

Edited by Lauren R. Sass

Assistant Editor: Debbie Sontag

Facts On File
119 West 57th Street, New York, N.Y. 10019

TELEVISION:
The American Medium
In Crisis

© Copyright, 1979 by Facts On File, Inc.
Published by Facts on File, Inc.
119 West 57th Street, New York, N.Y. 10019

Library of Congress Cataloging in Publication Data

Main entry under title:

Television: the American medium in crisis.

    Includes index.
    1. Television broadcasting—Social aspects—United
States—Addresses, essays, lectures. 2. Television
broadcasting—United States—Addresses, essays,
lectures. I. Sass, Lauren R., 1953-   II. Sontag,
Deborah, 1956-   III. Facts on File, Inc., New York.
PN1992.6.T44   791.45'01'3   79-12103
ISBN 0-87196-367-1

9 8 7 6 5 4 3 2 1

PRINTED IN THE UNITED STATES OF AMERICA

Contents

Preface

"I believe television is going to be the test of the modern world, and that in this new opportunity to see beyond the range of our vision we shall discover either a new and unbearable disturbance of the general peace or a saving radiance in the sky. We shall stand or fall by television — of that I am quite sure."

So observed E. B. White in 1938, on the eve of television's infancy. In the subsequent four decades, we have witnessed both television's magic and its menace; we remain suspended in its glow, crouched before the screen, awaiting a clearer picture. For in time, what began as a flickering new medium of communication has grown into a $6 billion-a-year industry, a voracious national habit and complex topic of controversy.

Television provides our society with talk-show host heroes and bionic sex symbols, light opera and soap opera, investigative documentaries and situation comedies. We rely upon it for the morning weather report, the evening news bulletin and, at any time of day or night, for a look at history in the making. Television has succeeded, moreso than any other medium, in fulfilling the mandate of pleasing *most* of the people *all* of the time.

The problems now facing television are largely the result of its pervasiveness. According to the latest figures, 74 million households (96%) have at least one television, and the set is "on" an average of six-and-a-half hours a day. "TV Guide," the pocket-size weekly, has the largest circulation and the highest advertising income of any magazine in publishing history. Not even baseball or apple pie, those two enduring standards of Americanism, can rival the popularity of television. Ours is a culture inextricably bound to the video experience: living color and vertical hold, Nielsen ratings and Mr. Whipple. Despite the familiar appellations — "boob tube," "chewing gum for the eyes," "plug-in drug" — that suggest that TV-watching is tantamount to home-style hypnosis, narcotic addiction or sheer boredom, the fact is that television possesses the raw power to persuade, inspire, delight, disgust, enrage or amuse us.

Yet, even in the best of all possible global villages, we must ask ourselves if television can meet so many expectations — to be our fourth estate, dramatic stage, babysitter, sports arena, classroom, campaign trail, program sponsor, public servant — without running the risk of misleading, violating or simply dictating our society's values. The television debate is now taking place in an age when it is difficult to isolate those changes that can be laid to the media from those that are based in other areas of American life. Nevertheless, while all the social upheaval that has occurred *since* the advent of television certainly has not occurred *because* of it, television's impact is undeniable. It is not a question of whether, but how television is affecting the quality of our lives. Ultimately, that matter should be determined by us, for without people, in the words of Edward R. Murrow, television "is merely lights and wires in a box."

March, 1979 Lauren R. Sass

Politics: Focus On Style or Substance?

In 1966, TV Guide magazine asked historian Arthur Schlesinger Jr. to offer an assessment of television's impact on American politics. Assuming that the available evidence was inconclusive and contradictory, Schlesinger himself was unable to firmly decide whether the medium was strengthening or weakening the workings of our system. He did however, note that "If television would recognize an affirmative obligation to elevate the level of our politics, and applied as much thought and talent to this as it does to selling detergent, it might play a great role in making our democracy more rational and responsible."

As early as the 1940s, television was staking out its political territory, turning its eye on Washington and focusing on the news-making events taking place there. In 1947, the opening of Congress (the 80th) was telecast for the first time. The following summer, the three major networks combined their facilities to provide the first nationwide coverage of a political nominating convention, and in 1949 the country watched the inauguration of President Harry Truman.

Since those landmark broadcast dates, television has become a principle vehicle of political organization and mobilization in America. Most notably in the course of campaigning, nominating conventions and all election-related activities, the television camera plays an increasingly critical role. Repeated studies indicate that Americans get more news, including election information, from TV than from newspapers and magazines combined. In fact, the 30-second to one-minute advertising spot (generally wedged between two highly-rated light entertainment programs) has become the most precious time in an office-seeker's busy schedule.

Television's utility as a political tool — its broad outreach, its vivid persuasiveness, its immediacy — has even spawned a new breed of political practitioner, the media consultant, whose business is to manipulate the candidate's image for maximum voter response. The high fees charged by these specialists, combined with the exorbitant cost of air time, has made it almost mandatory for candidates for statewide or national office (or local office in major cities) to be wealthy or to have access to major sources of money.

The exception to the brief and costly commercial glimpses of candidates has been the televised debate. The first series of televised debates between presidential candidates, in 1960, was between then- Vice President Richard Nixon and Sen. John F. Kennedy. It wasn't until 16 years later that the second round of debates took place, between the incumbent Gerald R. Ford and Georgia Gov. Jimmy Carter. The Ford-Carter debates were organized and funded by the non-profit League of Women voters and covered by the networks as a "news event" (thus circumventing the Federal Communication Commission's "equal time" provision.) In the election that followed the Kennedy-Nixon debates, voter turnout reached a percentage peak that broke all previous records — 64.5%. In the 1976 election, voter turnout dropped to a three-decade low. Curtis Gans, director of a Washington-based group studying voter apathy, claims a correlation exists between the decline in political participation and the degree to which television has saturated our daily lives.

Despite all the law-making that goes on behind closed doors, Congressional investigating committees have traditionally been open to the press and solicited the audience television provides. The first televised hearings took place in 1951, when the Kefauver Committee's investigation into organized crime was aired. The hearings, conducted in New York City, were a huge broadcast success, drawing a daily audience of about 30,000,000 and establishing a precedent for reporting of its kind. The 1954 televised Army-McCarthy hearings have been widely credited with ending the witch-hunting career of Wisconsin Sen. Joseph McCarthy. More recently, the 1973 Senate Watergate Committee's hearings, chaired by former Sen. Sam Ervin, afforded the television viewer detailed testimony on one of the most massive conspiracies involving the federal government.

Despite widespread agreement that televised hearings are a useful method of informing the public of the total dimensions of certain issues, some critics feel that the televising of such proceedings contributes an unnatural air of theatricality that is inappropriate, if not disruptive, to the conduct of serious matters of state. This argument has arisen repeatedly in discussing televising regular sessions of Congress. In October 1977, after 30 years of consideration, the House of Representatives voted to install a closed-circuit television system and to make the unedited footage available for broadcast. However, the issue of who would control the cameras remained unresolved. House Speaker Thomas (Tip) O'Neill opted to keep them under House supervision rather than turn over coverage to a commercial network. O'Neill and other House members expressed concern that networks could not be relied upon to avoid focusing on the spectacular, thereby giving a false impression of the legislative process. Addressing this issue, former television newsman Daniel Schorr warned that "Television lumbers into a complicated situation like King Kong, altering the landscape by its sheer weight and force. Brushing aside complexities and seizing upon a few concrete images, it often provides its own version of events, simplified and sometimes modified."

It is that same threat of television's "weight and force" that has kept video cameras out of the courtroom since 1965. In that year, the Supreme Court held that the activities of television crews in the Billie Sol Estes trial in Texas had deprived Estes of a fair trial. The word "circus" was used to describe the courtroom atmosphere. In the years immediately following the high court's ruling, only Colorado allowed filming in court to continue — under limited conditions. However, since 1977, with the technological advances that have produced more unobtrusive equipment, Alabama, Florida, Georgia, Montana, Texas and Washington have joined Colorado in permitting televised trials. The American Bar Association has yet to take a formal stand on the matter.

Television has boosted this country's overall political and social awareness by supplying the public with a greater body of shared information. However, although television can widen public acquaintance with issues and proceedings, it may, at the same time, oversimplify or misrepresent them.

THE ANN ARBOR NEWS
Ann Arbor, Mich., December 30, 1975

WITH another presidential election year about to begin, the news media can expect to be under the gun until the votes are counted in November.

It is difficult enough trying to be absolutely fair and objective in the news columns of the newspaper about all the political contests, but it is impossible to have all of your readers believe you are. One reason is because mistakes in judgment are made under the pressure of deadlines and space limitations. A more important reason for the credibility lapse, however, is the reader's own partisanship. It is hard for him to judge objectivity when he lacks it himself where a candidate or party is concerned.

The News has a drawerful of letters from officials of political parties commending us for impartial handling of election information over the years, but we are sure many members of their parties don't share their impressions. The "professionals" are in a better position to judge such performances, of course.

One problem for the communications business in election years is the unfair and sweeping generalization that all the media are "liberal." We'd be happier if more people would remember that it was Spiro Agnew who said it loudest and most often

During the 1950's and earlier the charge was that the newspapers had a conservative bias and favored Republicans. That was certainly true in regard to presidential endorsements, and some newspapers were guilty of political bias in their news columns. Thankfully, there are only isolated cases of that today.

* * *

TELEVISION'S entrance into the communications field in the 1950's brought considerable change. Some of the early mistakes of the fledgling medium caused problems for all the media. But a too suspicious public made matters worse when viewers began watching for voice changes and "twitching eyebrows" to detect signs of slanting on the part of TV news personnel.

The News recognizes its responsibility of being fair to all candidates and parties and will strive for objectivity during the coming election year. Part of that responsibility to our readers, however, involves the use of good judgment in how much space to devote to politics. The average reader isn't as interested in the subject as the candidate or party worker. We'd like to find the happy point in presenting election information where the voter-reader becomes informed and before he becomes glassy-eyed. It's not easy

The Hartford Courant
Hartford, Conn., July 25, 1976

So much has been blamed on television to date, one more indictment will not blow the tube. The fact that a serious study has concluded that television viewers learn practically nothing to aid them in making political decisions probably will surprise no one. Especially television viewers. Millions of them must have already reached a similar conclusion, expressed not in words but in boredom and ennui.

Nonetheless, an analysis of network newscasts during the 1972 general election, undertaken by faculty members at Syracuse University and reported in Psychology Today magazine, is important for its sharp emphasis on the lack of substantive value in presentations which preempt so much of the electorate's time. It is important now because with primary contests over and only one convention extravaganza to go, there is still time for networks to prepare to explore and define issues and devote less attention to crowd shots and pompon girls between August and November.

Thomas Patterson and Robert McClure, associate professors of political science at Syracuse, have come up with some impressive documentation, derived, they say, from auditing every televised political commercial and every week-night evening newscast of ABC, CBS and NBC from September 18 to November 6, 1972, augumented, would you believe, by 2,000 interviews, each an hour long, talking with the same voters, at the start, in the middle and at the end of the Nixon-McGovern campaign.

As a network average, the authors found only three per cent of available news minutes were given to reporting the candidates' stand on issues such as inflation, welfare, busing, crime, drugs, withdrawal from Vietnam and amnesty for deserters. The coverage given any single candidate's position on an issue was, they said, so minimal as to be meaningless.

Television, newest comer in communications, still regards itself as primarily a provider of entertainment and is thereby depriving its eagerly captive audience of millions of people of vitally needed, in-depth information. To the networks, political contests are another form of horse race. Sad it is to put the fate of candidates and the nation's destiny in the hands of touts.

The Syracuse team found that newspapers were far more effective than television in informing voters on the issues, but what is at stake here is far more important than merely arguing relative merit. The whole matter of government, of conflict between liberal and conservative points of view, of voter involvement, personal obligations, value judgments, collective security and well-being has grown complex and overpowering in this huge, diverse country. As a result, there is need for all informative communications to operate at full potential, either separately or in benign collusion.

Television viewers are not stupid people who respond only to the flashier aspects of the political scene; the hecklers, the balloons, the motorcade, the bumped head. The study found that by six-to-one, viewers would prefer fewer crowd shots, two-to-one would prefer fewer rally films, three-to-one would prefer more candidate interviews, and two-to-one more "talking about the candidates" by experts and voters.

It is high time that the television industry made itself relevant to the democratic society in which it operates, and it is high time also that democratic society does something to change the networks' impression that a horse race is all the viewers want or need.

Szep's View:

I'VE BEEN WATCHING THESE POLITICAL CANDIDATES ON TV FOR THE PAST 10 YEARS

EACH YEAR THEY ALL TELL ME HOW MUCH BETTER MY LIFE WILL BE IF I VOTE FOR THEM

BUT MY LIFE HAS NOT GOT BETTER IF ANYTHING . . . IT'S GOT WORSE

THERE MUST BE SOMETHING WRONG WITH MY TV

CLICK

Reprinted by permission of McNaught Syndicate.

The Boston Globe

THE WALL STREET JOURNAL

New York, N.Y., March 31, 1976

The National Broadcasting Company deserves some kudos for its decision this week to sell Governor Ronald Reagan a half hour of prime time to discuss his views on the world and nation. Earlier, NBC, along with ABC and CBS, had refused to sell Mr. Reagan the time.

For this refusal they offered a variety of reasons. But clearly they were reluctant to put on a show that would probably have a far smaller audience than the situation comedies and crime shows that make up standard prime time fare. NBC's decision was easier since it has been trailing in the ratings

game, and had a particularly vulnerable time spot to offer Mr. Reagan. But that does not detract from the decision. A way was found, and the speech will be available to interested viewers.

Clearly the television networks have an obligation to play an important part in the electoral process. They not only have the general responsibility of any news media, but their constituent stations have special obligations under the broadcasting act. For all practical purposes, the stations have been granted by the federal government a right to print money, in the form

of regularly renewed franchises on the TV spectrum, allocated in a way to protect profitability. The theory is that in return they will operate in the public interest, particularly by airing news and public affairs.

The precise boundaries of this obligation may be hard to define or codify into law, and no doubt problems were created by the rather short notice Mr. Reagan gave, and by potential demands from other candidates. But certainly airing the views of a major presidential candidate in the midst of an election year is very much in the public interest. Something would have been quite

amiss if Mr. Reagan had been unable to buy time.

We have no doubt that if Mr. Reagan had asked for 60 "image" spots of 30 seconds each, he would have had little problem with the networks. Instead, he asked for time to present his views in some depth. This should lead to more intelligent discussion, something the networks would serve the electoral process by promoting.

In all, NBC's decision has salvaged the embarrassment of the networks' early replies. We hope it sets a standard for the rest of the electoral campaign.

The Knickerbocker News

Albany, N.Y., October 28, 1976

If the presidential campaign this year has been a disappointment—and few would deny it has been—the media deserve some of the blame, along with the candidates.

Specifically, we find fault with the Washington press corps, including some of the network TV reporters, for their infatuation with all the news that titillates and their apparent aversion to reporting on issues of substance. Both President Ford and Jimmy Carter have issued dozens of position papers on their policy ideas. These papers have scarcely been reported. But look at the saturation coverage of Carter's relatively insignificant Playboy interview.

Because of what and how they report, the media tend to shape the

campaign. The candidates quickly learn that thoughtful statements on important issues earn them fewer headlines and less TV time than low-road, cheap-shot campaigning. Since they need those headlines and that TV exposure to get elected, it's no wonder their campaigns end up being pedestrian and uninstructive.

Many members of the Washington press corps—print as well as electronic—no longer consider it fashionable to report what candidates say in speeches. They would rather tell you who they think is going to win—which we are all going to find out next Tuesday anyway—or provide you with stories about campaign strategy. Now, strategy is interesting; there's no doubt about that. But it seems to us less consequential than telling voters,

for instance, about the candidates' positions on the environment.

This newspaper recently published an article detailing the differences between Carter and Ford on environmental questions (which are clearly among the most important questions our nation faces). But it wasn't written by a reporter. It was written by an environmentalist. On this issue, as on many others, both candidates have records that can be examined, even if they try to hide from the press as Ford has done. The TV networks would do us all a better service if they would dig into a few issues like this one instead of treating us to those pointless two-minute shots of the candidates getting off and on airplanes.

One Washington reporter has ob-

served that his colleagues immediately stick their notebooks in their pockets whenever a candidate addresses himself to moral issues. Surely, what these candidates have to say about moral issues is of some concern to the American public.

If the voters this year are as apathetic about the campaign as they are reported to be, maybe it's because they don't know about some of the very real differences between Carter and Ford on issues that have an immediate and direct impact on their lives—such as Carter's superior stance on consumer matters, for one example. And the reason they don't know? Because, in too many instances, the media have concentrated more on superficiality than substance.

The Dallas Morning News

Dallas, Texas, October 16, 1976

TWO THIRDS of all Americans, so it is estimated, get most of their news from television. A fair question to ask, during this presidential campaign, is how much they are learning about the choice to be made on Nov. 2.

Hoping for some indication, members of The News' editorial page staff on Thursday, Oct. 14, monitored the evening news programs of the three networks, ABC, CBS and NBC. The melancholy conclusion arrived at was that two thirds of all Americans are not learning much about the choice they must make.

It is possible to push the conclusion too far. The monitoring occurred on one day chosen at random. Yet consider some pertinent facts.

NBC devoted the first minute and 40 seconds of its broadcast to news of the Watergate special prosecutor's clearing of President Ford on charges of having misused campaign finances. In a following 90 second sequence, Jimmy Carter was pictured urging voters in Rochester, N.Y., not to believe Republican charges leveled at him. He also commented to newsmen on the special prosecutor's action and

on Ford's decision to schedule a press conference. There followed a 25-second report on the Democrats' registration drive.

That was it—the sum total of coverage afforded the presidential campaign—if one excepts later sequences dealing with Eugene McCarthy (38 seconds), and Democratic charges that grain price supports were raised to help the Republican ticket (20 seconds). Ford himself turned up in a news clip that showed him exposing a muscular arm to receive his swine flu shot.

On the CBS Evening News, the special prosecutor story ran for 95 seconds. A story about Carter's widening margin in the Gallup poll consumed 3 minutes—90 seconds of it devoted to replaying tapes of the second debate.

Carter, in a 75-second sequence about his appearance in Rochester, was shown speaking for just 15 seconds. The vice-presidential candidates were shown preparing for their Houston debate. The film footage of Dole and Mondale, however, depicted neither man as saying anything very significant. A 30-second piece on the McCarthy campaign and an Eric Sevareid commentary

on voter apathy rounded out CBS' contribution to public understanding.

ABC did better. Its campaign coverage came to 10-and-a-half minutes. An additional 5 minutes, 47 seconds was devoted to a Barbara Walters interview with Secretary of State Kissinger. But then what? Fully 2 minutes, 44 seconds dealt with the special prosecutor story. News of Carter was allotted 1 minute, 9 seconds. For the 30 seconds Carter himself was on film, he talked only of the prosecutor and of campaign generalities. Other stories dealt with Mondale (2 minutes, 4 seconds), and the polls in Illinois and California (19 seconds).

More than a question of simple time is involved here, of course. The question, really, is how time is used, in presenting issues or in merely recounting the progress of events.

On almost every occasion, the networks glossed over issues to talk of events. Surely, in Rochester, Carter said something about the issues; but from the television news, no one would know it. (In point of fact, Carter talked about taxes and loopholes, among other

things.) Neither did Ford's positions come through—save for his gaffe in the second debate, thoughtfully rerun for us by CBS, as though we had forgotten.

It is a dissatisfying way, is it not, to cover an election for the world's most important job. Granted that such coverage is characteristic of television. "After a while," as one network correspondent recently quoted by Newsweek puts it, "you get lazy. You start to look for the sexy, easy-to-tell story rather than going into complicated background that would really be helpful to people."

The question nevertheless must be asked: How are two thirds of Americans to form intelligent judgments about the presidential choice afforded them when the networks choose to talk not of issues but of the passing scene? They ought to be serving us meat. Instead, the menu features pablum.

It is distressing when one thinks of what is at stake on Nov. 2. What is equally distressing is that the networks—if Thursday, Oct. 14, was any indication— seem unaware of the fact that they are supposed to be covering an election, not a horse race.

THE MILWAUKEE JOURNAL

Milwaukee, Wisc., June 5, 1978

If even the "best laid plans" can go awry, then it's hardly any wonder that federal regulations don't always work out as expected. For years, the government has tried to use an "equal time" law to make broadcasters treat political candidates equitably. And it has imposed a "fairness doctrine" in an attempt to assure that opposing views on public issues are aired on TV and radio. But things haven't panned out well.

On the surface, it might appear that the equal time law would simply keep political coverage in balance, preventing a station from favoring one candidate or party over another. However, a literal view of the law has allowed tiny splinter groups to demand equal footing with the major parties in such events as televised debates. Thus many broadcasters have shied away from those events, depriving voters of coverage that should have been available.

The fairness doctrine has been similarly perverted. If certain groups — often small but very militant — didn't like a station's reporting on a controversial issue, they could demand that the Federal Communications Commission intervene. Unfortunately, rather than go through the trouble of proving that their coverage already was fair, broadcasters sometimes chose to cave in to the pressure groups or simply to

quit covering the controversy entirely. Either way, the public was the loser.

Sen. Proxmire of Wisconsin, in a laudable effort to correct these problems, proposes to repeal the equal time provision and the fairness doctrine. In effect, Proxmire's bill would give broadcasters freedom to control the content of their programs, just as newspapers control what goes into their columns.

Some will ask what assures fairness if the government doesn't set standards for broadcasters. The most likely prospect is that radio and television, in general, will be guided by journalism's traditions of impartiality, fair play, professional detachment. Yes, a few stations may abuse the new freedom, just as someone abuses every freedom, but that is likely to be the exception.

What is important to remember is the potential benefit. It's probable that the amount of significant public affairs broadcasting will increase and that both quality and balance will improve once television and radio are free to cover events on the basis of their genuine worth, rather than being cramped by arbitrary rules and bureaucratic interpretations of fairness and equity.

The Washington Star
and Daily News

Washington, D.C., March 31, 1976

Ronald Reagan finally was allowed to buy a half hour of prime television time for his presidential campaign but that should not be the end of the controversy.

With television so important an element in political campaigns — if not the single most important element — it ought to go without saying that candidates should have access to the medium.

In Mr. Reagan's case, the candidate thought his campaign could very well end if he couldn't take his case to the public on national television. His campaign is suffering from a shortage of money, which the Reagan camp believed could be cured by a nationally-televised appeal. Beyond that, Mr. Reagan thought that the best way to sharpen the issues between him and President Ford was via a nationwide television speech.

It wasn't as if Mr. Reagan asked for free time, although the argument often is made that candidates should be given free television time. He asked to buy a half hour — at a cost of $100,000 — on any of the three networks during the evening hours when the chance is greatest of attracting the widest audience.

What held it up? A Reagan aide said one network contended that Mr. Reagan is not a national candidate. If such an argument was in fact made, it ranks among the dumber statements to come out of televisionland.

The aide said another network claimed that it would have to sell time to other candidates if it sold time to Mr. Reagan. Well, what's wrong with that? If it is assumed that all the candidates of both parties who still are running in the primaries would want to buy a half hour — which isn't likely — that would amount to something like five hours. Divided among the three networks that would be less than two hours per network.

The real problem is that the networks are too concerned with their Neilson ratings. They're afraid that putting on a political speech in prime time will mean a loss of viewers for that time slot and a drop in those precious ratings which seem to control every decision of consequence in the commercial television industry.

It isn't that the networks favor the candidacy of President Ford, as one of the Reagan operatives charged. It's purely a business decision — a matter of dollars and cents; network executives fear that political programming, even though paid for by the candidates, will ultimately mean a loss of revenue because of a drop in viewer ratings.

NBC finally agreed to sell a half hour to Mr. Reagan, noting however that the decision was an exception to its general policy of not making time available to candidates while state primaries still are in process. ABC and CBS stuck to their refusal to sell the time. While NBC deserves commendation for its action, we suspect that the poor rating for the show Mr. Reagan's speech replaced had a good deal to do with its reversal.

We believe that Ronald Reagan, or any other legitimate presidential candidate, has a right to take his campaign to the public by national television, if that's the way he believes is the most effective — during the primary season as well as during the general election campaign. Perhaps Congress will want to see if some new rules for access to the airwaves by political candidates are in order.

It is incredible that during a year in which the leader of the free world is to be elected, a network executive can give the public reruns of comedy shows and cops and robbers but deny the public an opportunity to measure the presidential candidates.

THE DAILY HERALD

Biloxi, Miss., March 31, 1976

Ronald Reagan may rather be president, but, for now at least, he's right.

Right, that is, in his contention that the three major television networks ought to sell him air time in which to conduct part of his campaign for the nation's highest office.

Reagan has succeeded in obtaining approval of at least one network NBC, for a half-hour broadcast tonight. The other networks have treated Reagan's request for time with aloof silence. Reagan contends the three networks should sell him the time "in the interest of fairness and justice, as well as the people's right to know."

He's right also in his contention that his Republican opponent can usually get network time whenever he requests it, simply because Gerald Ford is the incumbent President of the United States. Mr. Ford's message to the people, once he's requested and gotten national television time, need not be wholly non-political. In fact, little that Mr. Ford does or says between now and the Republican Convention — or the November election, for that matter — can be objectively divorced from politics.

Perhaps the networks' position, which they have failed to publicize adequately, may have merit in that Mr. Reagan may have requested air time that has previously been committed. Arranging national television time involves more than simple acquiesence to a request. Whatever the case, the networks should get themselves out of the scapegoat roll in which Mr. Reagan has miscast them by explaining exactly what their position is.

The former California governor has already gotten a good measure of exposure by making a flap of the incident. But that exposure, while it may be considered a political asset, doesn't convey whatever message it is he's compiling for the voters' benefit.

National political candidates should not be barred from utilizing the national networks as a medium for carrying their campaigns to voters. Network policies that prohibit such advertising messages should be modified, not just for the benefit of Mr. Reagan, but for all who aspire to national offices.

ST. LOUIS POST-DISPATCH
St. Louis, Mo., October 11, 1976

Due to a failure of Congress to distinguish between public and commercial television when it passed the Federal Election Campaign Act of 1971, public broadcasters now are being threatened with the prospect of chaos in the campaign period before elections. Under the FEC act, broadcasting stations are required to provide "reasonable access" to political candidates. Now in a New York case where Senator Buckley asked for advertising time, the Federal Communications Commission has ruled that the law applies equally to commercial and public broadcasters.

Currently no paid commercials appear on public television. In lieu of advertising, corporations may "underwrite" programs, in which case they receive both audio and video credits. As for political programing, public television's record has been a responsible one. In addition

to debates and interviews that public stations carry, national public television is making available a large number of 30-minute programs to acquaint the American people with presidential candidates from, among others, the American Party, the Libertarian Party, the American Independent Party, the Socialist Workers Party and former Senator McCarthy's independent movement.

If public television stations are forced to accept paid political announcements, the lower rates they would charge would ensure a glut of political messages that could play havoc with programing. The principle of public broadcasting would be severely compromised if the medium is made to accept advertising, whether commercial or political. If the FCC does not reconsider its decision, Congress should repair the deficiency in the law.

Portland Press Herald
Portland, Me., March 9, 1976

That old nemesis of the networks, the equal time provision, is causing new headaches in this presidential year.

It's never been worked out to universal satisfaction and there seems little likelihood that any wholly satisfactory solution ever will be found. But there's a new slant to the old problem this year.

The Federal Communications Commission has labeled a presidential press conference as a bonafide news event and as such television may cover it without providing equal time to other candidates.

As might be expected, the President's press conference last month ignited a new flame under the old fuel. One columnist, not generally regarded as one of the President's greatest admirers, was bitter about the injustice of it all.

"The President utilized his session with the press, which was carried live by all the networks at no cost to him, to criticize his GOP rival, Ronald Reagan, on several specific campaign issues. He clearly addressed his nationwide audience not merely as a presidential incumbent but also as a political candidate worried about saving his skin," she wrote.

It could be assessed that way. But there was another side to it. It will be remembered that President Ford called that press conference to announce his plan for overhauling the command level of the intelligence system. After making his statement, he opened the session to questions.

Everything he said in that conference about Ronald Reagan or the political campaign was in

response to questions from reporters. This was prior to the primary season, and more than once reporters tried to prod him into saying he expected to win in New Hampshire. More than one reporter pressed the President about his Florida comment and the differences between his position and that of Ronald Reagan.

The President's clumsiness in answering those questions may have been more beneficial for Reagan than for him.

The purpose of the news conference was entirely legitimate and the networks exercised responsible news judgment in covering it live. But political strategists also know that whatever the announced purpose of the session, any presidential conference opened to questions by reporters is certain to get into

politics when the President is in the midst of a campaign.

Is there any satisfactory solution to the problem? Are presidential press conferences to be prohibited during an election year? Are the television networks to be excluded? It would be impossible to outlaw political questions because a president's view on any subject can be a political issue during a campaign.

We think the FCC ruling is right. What a president has to say to the people is legitimate news. It's an incumbent's advantage, to be sure, but campaign or not the President is still the President and the people have a right to see and hear him when he has an announcement of significance. What happens after that announcement is controlled by the press.

The Honolulu Advertiser
Honolulu, Hawaii, May 23, 1977

There is much to be said in favor of the Federal Communications Commission's decision to ask Congress for abandonment of the "equal time" provision in the case of candidates for the presidency and vice presidency of the United States.

The law has become limiting and self-defeating in many ways. As it stands, the "equal time" provision means any candidate for one of these offices whose name appears on a ballot may claim the same amount of time given any other candidate.

News programs alone are exempt. Documentaries are not. Such shows as "Meet the Press" or "Face the Nation" are not. Thus, in a presidential election, although the public might be interested in only two candidates, the Republican and the Democrat, conceivably they might have to watch and listen to the Vegetarian, Anti-Saloon League, Anti-Cigarette League, and assorted other candidates whose names on a ballot in some states is simply a reaffirmation of free elections.

THE FCC ALSO voted (4-3) to ask Congress to limit equal time in all elections to candidates whose party polls 2 per cent of the vote, or who

achieve a certain respectable number of petition signatures to get onto the ballot.

The problem with equal time lies in the nature of the electronic media. Radio and television are limited by the number of broadcast hours in a day. Within the framework of that period devoted to news and public service, the limitation is even more severe.

BECAUSE OF these factors, and the nature of radio and television, using public airwaves, these media have been subject to restrictions by the Federal government. Print media are protected by the First Amendment.

Newspapers do not give equal space to all candidates. Nor do magazines. Good newspapers try to be fair, but in the printed media the editor makes the judgment as to the importance of a story.

Obviously a speech by Jimmy Carter in Honolulu during the 1980 political campaign for the presidency would be more important than one delivered by Alonzo Whosis of the Wonder Workers party. But if the equal time rule is invoked on

electronic media except for news programs, both have to be treated the same.

That is the basic dilemma of the FCC. The equal time provision has become bent in recent years by such end-arounds as the presidential debates of the elections of 1976 when the government evaded the issue by letting the League of Women Voters "sponsor" the debates.

Eugene McCarthy tried unsuccessfully to achieve equal time in that series. He failed, for the simple reason that there was no method by which it could be properly done. The strictures of TV prevented it.

And so equal time has become relatively meaningless. Radio and television have grown up in the years since the rule was established. They are far more responsible now than they were 20 years ago.

SOME OF THE OLD methods of regulating the electronic media, then, seem to have become outmoded. The equal time rule has those earmarks, and Congress ought to give the FCC's request serious consideration.

The Oregonian

Portland, Ore., July 15, 1976

Democrats have been whooping it up at the party's National Convention in New York City's Madison Square Garden. But there have been clear indications that the American electorate is not overly impressed by the lack of suspense in the political performance dominated by Jimmy Carter and his legions of delegates.

A telephone survey of Portland area residents by The Oregonian Tuesday night indicated that more television viewers tuned in on the All-Star baseball game in Philadelphia than on the convention session in New York. The A. C. Nielsen TV rating service reported Wednesday that surveys indicated the All-Star game on the ABC network drew more than twice the audience of the convention broadcast on both CBS and NBC networks.

One of the beneficiaries of the audience preference was President Ford. He threw out the "first ball" of the All-Star game — twice — to American and National League catchers Thurman Munson and Johnny Bench, at the time that Sen. Hubert Humphrey was speaking to the convention. The Nielsen ratings indicate that he had more than twice the number of viewers as had Sen. Humphrey.

The way the President did it was also of interest. He signs his signature with his left hand and performs other functions from the port side. But Tuesday night he threw first with his left hand, then with his right. Was this a silent commentary on Democrat Jimmy Carter's tendency to balance his views on public policies?

THE BLADE

Toledo, Ohio, October 12, 1976

CITIZENS who enjoy the escape from television commercials afforded by public broadcasting could be in for a rude jolt during election campaigns. Under pressure from Sen. James Buckley, some public-television stations in New York state are allowing him time for his re-election-campaign advertisements — a move with ominous portents.

Actually, Senator Buckley is not to blame; he is merely taking advantage of a federal law that has been on the books for five years. It requires broadcasters to provide "reasonable access" to political candidates, and, according to a ruling of the Federal Communications Commission, the law makes no distinction between commercial and noncommercial stations. It was not until the New York conservative demanded the right to advertise on the public-television stations in his state that the issue came to light.

Now that it has, public-television spokesmen are alarmed, and properly so. Charles W. Lichenstein, a vice president of the Public Broadcasting Service, says the "implications are absolutely wide open and very disturbing." That is true for the public stations' audiences as well.

The intrusion of commercial-type advertising into the realm of public broadcasting would represent a major departure from a fundamental principle underlying the creation of these outlets. And once the erosion is begun, how far would it go? Perhaps not very, as a practical matter: the size of the audiences might be deemed insufficient to warrant the expenditure of much money on ads. Yet the steady improvement in and expansion of public broadcasting, both television and radio, could be expected to make it an increasingly inviting target.

Plans already are afoot as a result of the New York situation to urge Congress to change the law specifically to exempt public stations from the reasonable-access requirement — if, in fact, that provision should be retained at all. One problem is that, with Senator Buckley having shown the way, other lawmakers now may want to leave the statute intact and use it themselves.

That might prove to be a political boomerang, however. The citizens who provide the tax dollars and the contributions to support the commercial-free public stations could not be expected to feel friendly toward politicians who sabotaged it for the sake of trying to sell themselves.

The Cleveland Press

Cleveland, Ohio, October 9, 1976

Any move to dilute public broadcasting as free of commercial influences should be viewed with deep concern, and so this newspaper hastily runs up a warning flag on the attempt of James Buckley to obtain time for political messages on PBS stations in New York.

We also trust that Howard Metzenbaum will veto any effort by his campaign advisers to seek commercial time on Channel 25 in Cleveland and sister stations in Ohio.

In each case, our concern is not with the party affiliation or qualifications of the candidate. What could be at stake, unless this caper is nipped at the outset, is the entire future of non-commercial television. For if a political candidate succeeds in obtaining air time, what is to stop special-interest organizations — or private business — from insisting that they be permitted to do the same?

This potential crisis arises from the fact that a provision of the Federal Communications Act requires that non-commercial broadcasting stations provide "reasonable access" to candidates for federal office.

That stipulation has never before been invoked and, indeed, was not known by many people in the broadcast industry to exist at all. But there it is, and as long as it remains on the books, it is a threat to public broadcasting. In fact, violation of the "reasonable access" rule could deprive a station of its license.

Assuming that the Federal Communications Commission doesn't have the authority to nullify the provision, we can only hope that some member of Congress will introduce corrective legislation as soon as possible.

In the meantime, we regret that the stations in New York, the dangers notwithstanding, gave in so easily to Buckley. If a showdown is forced in Ohio, we would hope that the PBS stations here would at least take the case to court while putting the heat on Congress to make public broadcasting immune to the "reasonable access" rule.

The Detroit News

Detroit, Mich., December 1, 1978

Television seems at times to be the tail that wags the dog. Offering a case in point, a Republican spokesman admits that the television networks will decisively influence the choice of where to hold the 1980 Republican National Convention.

When the Republican National Committee's site selection team visited Detroit this week, its members were outnumbered, 16 to 8, by TV network representatives. An NBC special events producer traveling with the Republicans explained, perhaps with excessive modesty: "We're strictly in an advisory position."

However, Ody J. Smith, search committee vice chairman, spoke more candidly: "I wouldn't call it a veto, but if the networks said they absolutely couldn't go somewhere, and were able to document it, I don't think we would go."

True, Detroit could be the beneficiary of the networks' influence, since a single convention room in Cobo Hall offers three times the amount of space the networks say they need to cover a national political convention. Though delighted that Detroit enjoys this advantage, we find somewhat disturbing the fact that Detroit probably would not be in the running at all for the GOP convention if the city didn't meet the standards established by television producers.

The selection of a convention city is a news story. Theoretically, TV networks merely report news events; they don't create or control them. In practice, TV often determines, in fact often dictates, the format, the character and the unfolding of political events — usually by merely announcing its presence; sometimes, as in the present case, by stating the conditions under which it will agree to attend.

Politicians have always angled for good notice in the press, of course, but it took television to turn politics into thoroughgoing show business. More and more, political events occur not because of their inherent importance but because the television camera will be present.

Political debates no longer merely take place; they are made for TV. Thanks to his superior stage presence and the magic of the lighting director, the network newsman often dominates the politicians he interviews. And as we now see, network producers may decide where political parties shall conduct their business. It's a good thing that World War II took place before the popularization of TV; the networks, lacking communications satellites at first, might have arranged to move the theater of war to the continental United States.

Little wonder that so many young people complain of "cut-and-dried" politics and "phony" politicians. At times it does seem, indeed, that America's public affairs have been prepackaged for display on prime time.

Naturally, the Republicans want maximum exposure for their quadrennial convention, and this of course entails finding out what facilities the networks — and the newspapers and the magazines — need in order to do a decent job. That information can be obtained, however, without making CBS, NBC, and ABC de facto members of the Republican National Committee.

In the end, the TV networks and the other media will always find a way to cover a national political convention, even if it takes place in an igloo in the Arctic. The medium is the message only if the makers of news allow it to be.

The Des Moines Register

Des Moines, Iowa, September 7, 1976

Recent Gallup Poll releases have confirmed the potential value of extended national convention TV exposure to the party's nominee.

In the last four campaigns, Republican and Democratic candidates have jumped an average of 5.5 percentage points in public favor in the first polls after the conventions.

The average is seven percentage points if two atypical Democratic years are excluded. These years are 1964 (Lyndon Johnson was the choice of 65 per cent of the voters before the convention and had no place to go) and 1968 (it's a wonder Hubert Humphrey didn't drop 20 points instead of rising two after all that coverage of the disasters in the streets of Chicago).

President Ford rose from 33 per cent to 39 per cent in the poll taken the week following the rousing Republican performance in Kansas City. Those six points have inspired Republicans but that is about par. Had he risen any less, the prospect for November would be bleak, indeed.

Consider George McGovern in 1972. He jumped 10 percentage points the week after the Miami convention even though his you-can't-boss-me followers used up the convention's prime time playing games with the vice-presidential nomination and forced McGovern to speak after the nation had gone to bed.

The post-convention glow begins to fade the following week — the average drop has been 2.5 per cent for Republican nominees, 4.5 for Democrats. President Ford's drop in the second Gallup Poll following the convention was three points.

But the net gain remains. Future convention planners in both parties will, we suspect, be looking for devices to milk the free coast-to-coast air time for even better and longer-lasting gains.

THE STATES-ITEM

New Orleans, La., October 9, 1976

Throughout the 1976 presidential campaign, beginning with the Democratic and Republican primaries, the American people have been treated to a media performance that has obscured important national issues while paying microscopic attention to candidates' verbal gaffes.

This is not the first time that the media have dwelled on the candidates' fumbles and stumbles. George Romney became a historical footnote because of the inordinate attention to his offhand remark that he had been brainwashed by American generals in Vietnam. Sen. Edmund Muskie, the Democratic front-runner for President in 1972, became a media casualty for weeping in the snow over an insult to his wife in New Hampshire.

As a consequence of media preoccupation with candidates' missteps, an almost hysterical atmosphere pervades this presidential campaign in its closing weeks. The selection of the next president might well be determined, not on the basis of records, individual capabilities, the state of the nation, and the candidates' stands on issues, but on the basis of which candidate makes the last verbal error. To be sure, it is the media's responsibility to scrutinize the candidates carefully, but the attention should focus on important issues and leadership abilities.

Can anyone really believe that Jimmy Carter intended to offend his black supporters when he spoke of "ethnic purity"? Yet the pack journalism that pounced upon the two words diverted Mr. Carter's campaign and those of his competitors away from genuine discussion of important issues for days. Magnification of the significance of Mr. Carter's Playboy remarks also detracted attention from the important questions of inflation, unemployment, the cities' troubles and the energy problem.

The journalistic mining that turned up former Agriculture Secretary Butz' offensive, private racial slur in another publication produced another flurry of sensationalism without prompting serious discussion of farm and food policies.

Can anyone really believe that President Ford is not aware of Soviet domination of Eastern Europe? Clearly he did not intend to say what he said in the second debate. At the same time, have not the media accepted too passively Mr. Ford's Rose Garden "campaign," a carefully calculated effort to avoid the political hazards of an active campaign?

The media's role should be to encourage serious discussion, to help the candidates clarify their positions for the benefit of the voters, not to perpetuate misstatements and confuse the electorate.

The media, including ourselves, have catered too much of late to the trivial and superficial in politics.

More than any other medium, television has pre-empted the national political stage. Yet its pack journalism and microscopic attention to the sensational make it almost impossible for candidates to be themselves and present their true dimensions to the voters. Candidates are forced to become mechanical people, actors, to survive.

Preoccupation with imagery rather than substance also pervades political advertising. Instead of candidates in the flesh, the electorate is offered one-dimensional media ghosts, facile creations of public relations craftsmen.

It is time for the media to acknowledge their vastly expanded importance in the political process, to reassess their manner of coverage of candidates and their campaigns. We must recognize that we can be a bridge between the candidates and the electorate or an obstacle.

The Virginian-Pilot

Norfolk, Va., October 27, 1976

You watch "All in the Family" and you get President Ford.

You watch "Kojak" and you get Jimmy Carter.

You watch "The Waltons" and you get Senator Harry F. Byrd Jr.

You watch "Maude" and you get Admiral Elmo R. Zumwalt Jr., who is a candidate for Mr. Byrd's Senate seat.

You watch "Hee Haw" and you get Representative G. William Whitehurst, plus Representative Robert W. Daniel Jr., plus Delegate J. W. (Billy) O'Brien, Mr. Daniel's opponent.

You watch "The Cross Wits" and you get Delegate Robert E. Washington, who is challenging Mr. Whitehurst.

You watch "Doc" and you get Delegate Robert W. Quinn. You watch "The Merv Griffin Show" and you get Paul Trible. Mr. Quinn and Mr. Trible are contending for the Congressional seat vacated by Representative Thomas N. Downing's retirement.

All of the foregoing are actual "adjacencies" that have been purchased in Tidewater. The political spots threaten to crowd the detergents and deodorants off the tube this week.

This is the homestretch. This is the time when the candidates spend the last penny. And they're spending it to buy time on the tube, to force their way into the dens and family rooms and living rooms where the voters are.

The candidates are eager to let us know how much they care for us and how hard they'll work for us. They look purposeful, they carry coats slung over their shoulder, they smile, they ask us to help them.

All of which is nothing new. Library shelves are filled with books and studies on the subject. "The Selling of the President," the book by Joe McGinnis on the merchandising of Richard Nixon in 1968, was something of a best-seller even. "It is not surprising," Mr. McGinnis wrote, "that politicians and advertising men should have discovered one another. And, once they recognized that the citizen did not so much vote for a candidate as make a psychological purchase of him, not surprising that they began to work together."

He quotes a memorandum written for Mr. Nixon that takes a condescending, but essentially realistic view of the American voter as television viewer.

"Voters are basically lazy, basically uninterested in making an effort to understand what we're talking about," the memo said. "Reason requires a high degree of discipline, of concentration; impression is easier. Reason pushes the viewer back, it assaults him, it demands that he agree or disagree; impression can envelop him, invite him in, without making an intellectual demand. . . . When we argue with him we demand that he make the effort of replying. We seek to engage his intellect, and for most people this is the most difficult work of all. The emotions are more easily roused, closer to the surface, more malleable. . . ."

So the candidate is packaged by specialists. He borrows familiar rituals and positive symbols. (A classroom of children reciting the Pledge of Allegiance fades into a political spot for Mr. Whitehurst.) Because the American people are turned off by politics and politicians, the current gimmick is to put the message into the mouth of the man in the street, the bearded kid, the housewife, the ordinary person.

It is easy to blame television, when the fact is voters are "basically lazy, basically uninterested . . . ." The media specialists of today are not any more crass or cynical than the bosses of yesterday. Democracy is an imperfect process. And the politicians of today are better, perhaps, than the politicians of yesterday. They're playing for higher stakes.

But the circumstances of 1976 have served to reinforce the trend. The campaign finance laws have made it harder for candidates to raise money, so they are cutting down to essential expenditures, i.e., television. And apathy and cynicism in the electorate, plus the decline of the old political party structure, tend to shrink the focus of politics to the dimensions of the TV screen. For better or worse, and the experts are unsure which, that's where the action is in politics. But you can't cancel a Congressman after 13 weeks and you can't throw away a President like a tube of toothpaste.

Los Angeles Times
Los Angeles, Calif., August 11, 1976

Ronald Reagan is on record as favoring a series of television debates between the presidential contenders this fall, but Jimmy Carter and President Ford have been unwilling to commit themselves definitely to even one joint appearance with the opposing nominee.

The nonpartisan League of Women Voters is determined to force the issue. It has begun the circulation of petitions to demonstrate public support for three network confrontations between the major party candidates for President and one between the nominees for Vice President.

We support the league's effort, although it shouldn't require petitions to convince Carter and Ford that they ought to accept the challenge. A recent Gallup Poll found that 68% of Americans want the debates. In addition to that, 1976 is the first year the taxpayers will be footing each of the candidates' bills through $20 million in public financing. For that reason, if for no other, they ought to be held more accountable to the voters.

This is also the first presidential year in which the equal-time provisions of the Federal Communications Act will not apply. A recent interpretation permits television coverage of the debates as bona fide news events if they are held under the sponsorship of a nonbroadcast organization, and the League of Women Voters is willing to assume that role. In the past, the networks have been reluctant to accept debates because of the now-inoperative requirement that they had to give equal time to all minor-party candidates.

Carter and his rival will spend huge sums of money on advertising this year. The Democrat has set his budget at more than $8 million, most of it for TV, and the Republican will spend as much or more. The past has shown that such media exposure—always under the direct control of the candidate—is more likely to emphasize image than issues, and we can expect more of the same this year.

It seems to us that if the nominees are going to spend public money to say whatever they like of themselves and their opponent—with no opportunity for rebuttal—they have an obvious responsibility to accept free network time for an exchange in which they would have to justify their claims.

There have been no TV debates between presidential contenders since the Nixon-Kennedy appearances in 1960. More than 75 million persons saw the four encounters, and the percentage of voter turnout that year was the highest for a national election in this century. A reprise this year might just reverse the lamentable decline of voter enthusiasm in the 16 years since.

We can think of no reason why either Carter or Ford would want to evade a direct discussion of the issues with his opponent, except the fear that his public positions—or criticism of his rival—might not stand up to such a test.

They could save the League of Women Voters a lot of work and expense by declaring, and promptly, that they are willing to accept the league's proposals.

Who will speak up first?

MANCHESTER NEW HAMPSHIRE UNION LEADER
Manchester, N.H., September 5, 1976

Who says politics is a divisive, inherently partisan beast which promotes only rancor and discord across our land? (We think we just made that up but it does have a certain ring to it, yes?)

What but politics could bring the likes of Eugene J. McCarthy and Lester G. Maddox together? 'Tis true, the left-leaning Minnesotan and the conservative Georgian are teaming up for a court battle in hopes of gaining access to the upcoming Presidential debates or, failing that, gaining equal television time.

The prospect of the debate itself, starring Gerry Ford and Jimmy Carter, leaves us cold. Political debate certainly has its place but modern-day television isn't it. We're afraid most viewers will succumb to the "star quality" of the participants rather than to the substance of the issues discussed.

That's not to say these two men have any great star quality. It's just that most people, ourselves included, probably will spend most of the time watching the two men's faces instead of listening to what they say. Will Gerry Ford have five o'clock shadow? Will Jimmy Carter's grin turn to a grimace? Will they sweat?

Had the Abraham Lincoln-Steven Douglas debates been broadcast on TV, poor Abe may have been doomed to life as an Illinois lawyer. Instead, the quality of his reasoning propelled him into the White House, even though he first lost the U.S. Senate seat for which the two men were fighting.

Alas, such are the realities of present-day politics. Television is both the medium and the message on the national level and the two candidates and their parties must make the most of it — another practical reason why the articulate, well-composed Ronald Reagan would have had the better chance for election on a GOP ticket.

The Washington Star
Washington, D.C., September 3, 1976

Well, we'll be having those debates. Gerald Ford and Jimmy Carter will, in some fashion, confront each other on national television and talk about the issues of the 1976 presidential campaign.

Which issues? That was an issue in itself; the first area of skirmish between the contestants. The President wanted to begin by talking about national defense, where his insider's knowledge and incumbent's prestige give him the advantage. The governor would rather have opened with a few exchanges on the quality of leadership in Washington, which would offer him a comparable chance to look good and one-up his opponent. The agenda now calls for an initial debate September 23 on the economy and domestic issues.

What remains to be seen is how well the debates will serve their ostensible purpose.

Back in the innocent dawn of the television era, it was thought that the tube would make it impossible for politicians to fool even some of the people some of the time. Seeing and hearing them so directly, voters would be able to tell good guys from bad guys. No longer would anybody be taken in by false smiles and weasel words.

That turned out to be as much an illusion as the idea that if women could vote there would be no more wars.

Now we know that televised politics is simply a latter-day version of the image politics that has been going on in one form or another since the days of primitive priest-kings trying to outdo each other in displays of magic and ceremonial splendor. For the citizen viewer, a video debate between presidential candidates presents a choice of facades which may or may not have much to do with the national policies that make a difference to people, either as individuals or as members of a community.

Techniques for measuring TV impact are notably imprecise. The experts cannot even say for sure who's doing better than whom when two pols face each other before the cameras, much less why. Furthermore, post-mortems on yesterday's bombs and successes are not reassuring to those who would like to believe either sound reasoning or sound intuition matter much in deciding who makes it and who doesn't.

Did Sen. Joe McCarthy really lose his powers of intimidation because five o'clock shadow gave his jaws an uncongenially sinister look on the TV screens of America during the Army-McCarthy hearings? Did Lyndon Johnson's attempts to come across as dignified and historic on TV instead of like the earthy Texan he was cancel out his force as a leader? Who can say?

If the Kennedy-Nixon debates of 1960 set a precedent, nobody's going to learn a great deal about national alternatives from the coming Ford-Carter confrontation. Perhaps nobody expects to.

Some Republicans worry about their man's nimbleness in the give and take of debate. Some Democrats are afraid their champion can shed his reputation for lofty vagueness only by alienating too many groups with his specifics. Neither factor is likely to be decisive.

Glibness might as easily turn out to be a negative as inarticulateness. After World War II, British voters rejected Winston Churchill, perhaps the greatest political speaker of modern times, for a man he had immortalized as "a sheep in sheep's clothing": Clement Attlee. Dwight D. Eisenhower, whose syntax so amused journalists, made the witty and sophisticated Adlai Stevenson seem a little trivial when he dismissed a Stevenson nifty by saying the nation's problems were no laughing matter. And think of poor Hubert Humphrey.

What the debate audiences will be looking for, after all, is not intellectual superiority or verbal flair but a sign — some indefinable aura of nerve and authority that transcends answers to particular questions. Chances are that seeing Ford versus Carter on TV won't clarify anything about detente or the economy for anybody. Chances are, too, that it will obscure at least as much as it reveals about the two personalities presenting themselves. All we can say with any confidence is that it should be a good show and help a lot of people make up their minds. For better or worse.

Roanoke Times & World-News
Roanoke, Va., September 2, 1976

Those tempted, on the strength of early polls, to make book on the 1976 presidential race would do well to wait. Latest opinion surveys show the gap between President Ford and Jimmy Carter narrowing rapidly after the Republican convention. And now comes "Son of Great Debates," which could upset the betting entirely.

Certainly the original—and to date, the only—televised debates between presidential candidates made a tremendous difference in the 1960 election's outcome. Before John Kennedy and Richard Nixon met to answer panelists' questions on camera, the then Vice President had a healthy lead; he was perceived as cool and experienced, in contrast with the Democratic nominee who was widely regarded as callow if not shallow.

The first debate altered that perception. Mr. Nixon, who had an unfortunate tendency to perspire under the hot lights, was poorly made up for the appearance; he looked uncomfortable, on the spot. This, combined with his early effort to grin ingratiatingly, gave him—in the words of one Southern governor—"the look of the accused."

The handsome Mr. Kennedy was nothing if not telegenic. He was also cool, unruffled, and on the attack against Mr. Nixon, who was forced into defending some Eisenhower administration positions he might have preferred to abandon. In later debates, Mr. Nixon rallied to acquit himself well against his challenger; but he never shook off the ill impression of that first encounter. John Kennedy could not have won without the debates.

Knowledge that the debates are something of a dice game has deterred other candidates since then—especially incumbent presidents. As an underdog, Mr. Ford's position is different. He evidently believes he has more to gain than lose from confronting Mr. Carter. And the ex-Georgia governor seems more than willing. The first round of the Ford-Carter debates, promoted by the League of Women Voters, is due this month.

What the candidates say may matter much less than how they come across to the viewers. Each would like to appear calm, cool, in command—in a word, presidential. Aware that in the past Jimmy Carter has shown flashes of temper, Gerald Ford may be counting on a breakthrough in this category. He may also hope that the Democrat will come to the debates less prepared than a President who, conventional wisdom says, has all the facts.

Mr. Carter, however, has a nimble mind and will be on guard. Perhaps the chief danger to his hopes is seeming too eager. If he jumps too hard on the President, he risks rousing sympathy for him; Mr. Ford is a man most people instinctively like, whatever their political preferences.

At this stage, it seems unlikely either man will pin the other, struggling, to the wall. Neither is by nature a rousing speaker or a forceful point-maker. In their efforts to present a collected, unruffled front, they risk casting a spell of profound boredom over their national audience—and persuading millions of voters to stay home on November 2. Who then could confidently predict the outcome?

The Boston Globe
Boston, Mass., September 1, 1976

Nothing is so flexible as a law that the government wants to ignore. The Federal Communications Commission proved that point last fall by twisting beyond recognition its own "equal time" rule to allow televised debates limited to the major party presidential candidates. And the Federal Election Commission proved the same point this week by ruling that the League of Women Voters could sponsor debates between Gerald Ford and Jimmy Carter, could solicit supporting funds from business and labor "political action committees" and that the entire business would not be treated as an illegal private contribution to either party's campaign.

The debates in fact are a contribution by the League, its donors and above all the TV networks to the two-party system. That system and the debates are good for the country but the powers that be have taken a dishonest approach to making them possible — in contrast to what happened in 1960, when Congress straightforwardly suspended the law.

In an ideal world the public would also hear a confrontation between Lester Maddox and Eugene McCarthy, lively and forceful exponents of genuinely different views of the nation, and would also be given a debate between, say, the Libertarian and Socialist Worker candidates. But in the real world the meaningful event is between Ford and Carter, and its usefulness depends in large part on the format.

President Ford wants each 75-minute session to be limited to a single topic, and he wants the first to focus on defense policy. Those rules would help him look tough and hawkish and presidential at the beginning of the campaign, which, according to his aides, is the image he seeks.

Governor Carter emphasizes that the debates should be free-swinging, which would enable him to demonstrate his deftness, articulation and balance against an opponent who is often clumsy with words.

Strategy aside, the public's interest would be best served by a debate as nearly free of "commentators" as possible. Although reporters are often helpful in reminding candidates that they are straying from the truth, the public considers itself capable of forming its own opinion about a man's honesty.

If newsmen are to be excluded, the format will need drama to keep 75 minutes on one subject from seeming interminable. We suggest that, after brief opening speeches of five to seven minutes, the candidates question each other directly — with questions of no more than two minutes and answers of no more than five. Mr. Ford may not like having to scrap. Mr. Carter may not like having to get tough instead of smile. But, if each man is trying to pin the other down, instead of trying to duck a reporter's question gracefully, the candidates will be much less likely to waffle.

The programs will probably need a moderator. Here, too, how about a non-newsman, say Judge John Sirica, who is a Republican respected by Democrats, or Leon Jaworski, or former ambassador John J. McCloy? If the debates are not to be a loophole-inspired media event, let's make them as much as possible the kind of genuine news event the FCC said should be exempt.

The Dallas Morning News
Dallas, Tex., August 19, 1976

A RECENT poll by the Gallup organization shows that the American people strongly favor a nationally televised debate between the nominees of the two major parties. We believe that a repeat of the 1960 series would be a good thing for the country and for the democratic process.

The debates of 1960 were launched in expectation that such face-to-face confrontations would become a regular fixture in presidential elections. And they did, in fact, prove to be extremely popular with the public. It was estimated that 75 million Americans watched Richard Nixon and John F. Kennedy argue the issues of that campaign.

Nixon, intellectually incisive and a skilled debater, made points and those who heard the debates on radio felt that he swept the field. But Kennedy, the Irish charmer, made friends among the television audience. Though opinions are still mixed, the consensus was that the lesser-known JFK probably made a net gain, enough to win the whisker-close election.

Since that time, for one tactical reason or another, it has been impossible to get both candidates to risk a TV debate. Some critics claim the debates are only beauty contests, putting too much emphasis on the photogenic face, the glib and facile performance.

There is something to that, but it is not all of the story by a long shot. The debate airing of stands on issues may be superficial compared with, say, a scholarly, point-by-point comparison of the two tickets' position papers. But very, very few ordinary voters go to that length to determine exactly how the candidates differ on their plans for the country.

The significant comparison should be between debates and the ordinary network TV news coverage of the campaign. Americans today get most of their news from television, which requires no effort or indeed literacy on the viewer's part. But comparing candidates' stands on issues is an information task that TV news coverage does most abysmally.

Television network news is oriented to present campaigns as a combination of sports events and entertainment spectaculars, the sort of dramatic, picturable fare that the television medium does best. We see many shots of roaring crowds, handshaking candidates, smiling wives, tote boards for survey results and election night vote totals.

This sort of coverage may fit the TV needs for visual excitement—though we suspect most viewers have seen it so often that it has become tiresome to many—but it does little to inform the voters on how the candidates would make decisions, if elected. And that is crucial information.

A survey during the 1972 campaign showed that newspaper readers are much better informed voters than those who watch only television. But among the latter, it was found that even the candidates' own short commercial spots did a better job of informing voters on the issues than the news coverage.

Televised debates, as compared to the horse-race style of coverage, may be dull and untheatrical, as some charge. But whatever they lack in visual appeal may be compensated for by the fact that one of the debaters is going to have a major effect on all the viewers' lives in the next four years. And dull or not, the 1960 test showed that Americans will watch and learn from the encounters.

Voter participation in national elections has dropped steadily in the 16 years since the Nixon-Kennedy debates and that is a trend that we should reverse. More Americans might turn out on election day if they knew what, as well as whom, they are voting for.

RAPID CITY JOURNAL—

Rapid City, S.D., October 21, 1976

The third and final nationally televised debate involving presidential candidates Ford and Carter is scheduled for Friday night.

Many voters in sports-minded America will be at high school stadiums watching football rather than at home watching politics. They can't really be faulted for that. For the average, politically unsophisticated viewer, the first two debates were dull.

Recognizing that people probably can't be talked into watching the debate if their minds are made up to do something else, we still feel there are numerous good reasons for tuning in.

The debates, and particularly the third debate, are history in the making, events to be remembered like the Kennedy-Nixon debates of 1960 and the Lincoln-Douglas debates of a century before that.

Head-to-head public confrontations between potential leaders of the nation apparently are exclusive to the United States and its unique political process. Where else could it happen?

Television itself, in presenting the debates, offers another indication that it no longer is the "vast wasteland" it once was described as being. The debates are representative of its maturation as a communications medium. TV is perhaps performing the type of role its creators envisioned for it.

Pollsters currently are calling the race nearly even. Ford was given a slight edge in the first debate and Carter a somewhat wider margin in the second. But in both earlier rounds there was trivia that fogged the real issues, and after each there was magnification of mistakes by one candidate or the other.

The fate of the election should not hinge on the candidates' television demeanor and the debates should not be judged as entertainment is judged.

Nevertheless, the debates have been instructive. The final round on Friday, if not approached with unusual expectations, can add to voters' perspective of both candidates, whose philosophies and records transcend 90 minutes before the TV cameras.

The Courier-Journal

Louisville, Ky., September 2, 1976

ONE VOTER in eight is listed right now as undecided between Gerald Ford and Jimmy Carter, and some of the remaining seven are tentative and unenthusiastic in their choices. Those voters, in particular, had better cherish the three nationally broadcast debates scheduled to begin this month.

That's because the planned debates may be, by default, commercial TV's major effort to clarify the issues of the 1976 campaign. Judging from what accompanied the Kennedy-Nixon debates in 1960, the networks may be strongly tempted to regard this as their "serious" coverage, enabling them to spend the rest of the time on frills.

Polls indicate that most Americans rely heavily on the TV evening news for information. Yet 1960 showed that once presidential candidates commit themselves to broadcast debates, there's a strong pull on network news directors to ignore the whys and wherefores of a farm-embargo issue, for instance, and to get back to TV's more usual coverage of politics as melodrama, instead of as a selection process.

The assumption that watching the candidates debate issues raised by panels of journalists, or by each other, will help voters in making their selection is not universally held. Some observers recall that the 1960 "Great Debates" did little to clarify national issues. They indict the networks, the ad agencies that ran the campaigns and the strategies of Messrs. Kennedy and Nixon themselves for turning such encounters into an "image-making" sideshow.

The same thing could happen again, unless the newsmen who start each round of responses and rebuttals propose incisive questions and follow them up adequately, and unless time is reserved for candidates to cross-question each other. Nothing is so revealing as the kind of response one candidate makes to a direct challenge from another — as occurred, for instance, in televised "candidate forums" sponsored by the League of Women Voters during the primaries, or in the Democratic Issues Forum in Louisville last year.

The voter who hopes to make a rational choice nine weeks hence might also keep in mind that nothing restricts the candidates to the three, 75-minute debates negotiated through the League. If the President and Governor Carter agree to share other platforms, they will be free to confront each other further on issues of their own or their hosts' choosing.

The voter, in the end, is paying the bill. What's more in his or her interest: Is it spending a good part of the $40 million in public financing on 30-second commercials? Or is it prepping the candidates for and staging what could be (especially if more time and forums were available) a modern equivalent of the Lincoln-Douglas encounters of 1858?

Unfortunately, multiple occasions for direct debate could very well not develop. An opinion of the Federal Election Commission on sponsorship cleared the way for the League's efforts. But that ruling, if good law for the moment, was bad policy for the future. It demanded that the League preserve its non-partisan standing by refusing any contributions for the debate expenses from corporations and unions. Then it turned the question upside down, saying the League would be free to take money from political-action groups that these same unions and corporations are wont to create to make their imprint on campaigns.

Further complicating the prospects for a "Jerry and Jimmy Show" are threats of legal action from independent Eugene McCarthy and conservative Lester Maddox. One could foresee splinters in the major parties (like the Bull Moose candidacy of Teddy Roosevelt in 1912 and Henry Wallace's ill-fated Progressive Party in 1948) that would require three-man debate in order to satisfy public curiosity about the full range of electable candidates. But the discretion of the League of Women Voters in inviting only two debaters this time around seems justifiable in terms of voter interests in 1976.

All the disorder of this last-minute debate about the debates suggests that politics needs more freedom for maneuver. Congress may feel, after November, that it needs to legislate in this area. However, it should not attempt a comprehensive law, the kind it felt it had to produce in reaction to the parties' fund-raising abuses. Comprehensiveness can create new problems.

What would be best is not a debate law, as such, but action by Congress to move legal problems out of the way of full and frank discussion of national problems by the people who say they're best equipped to handle those problems.

THE DAILY HERALD

Biloxi, Miss.,
October 7, 1976

In denying requests from Eugene McCarthy and Lester Maddox this week for broadcast time equal to that given the major party candidates in the presidential debates, the Federal Communications Commission has shown just how flimsy the fairness doctrine is.

Both Maddox and McCarthy argued unsuccessfully that the presidential debates are not bona fide news events as is required by the FCC rules to qualify them from exemption from the equal time rule.

To buttress their claim, Maddox and McCarthy noted that the candidates had input in arranging the debates, and the 30-minute audio interruption during the first meeting in Philadelphia proved the meeting was not a bona fide news event.

The FCC held that when the audio portion of the debate was lost, no broadcaster was shown to have exercised any control over the suspension, or requested the candidates to halt.

The fact that the candidates waited for the technical problems to be resolved does not remove the event from the equal time exemption, it said.

"The complainants have not demonstrated that the networks' coverage of their campaign has been unreasonable," the FCC decision said.

"The networks contend that neither McCarthy nor Maddox represent significant viewpoints on the issue of who should be elected president."

The FCC is unable to argue convincingly that the fairness doctrine is either fair or equal.

The decisions on whether or not to telecast the Ford-Carter debate, and whether to allow any other candidates, and if so, which ones, similar television time, should have been left to the networks.

CASPER STAR-TRIBUNE

Casper, Wyo., September 19, 1976

The complications surrounding the Ford-Carter debates have provided a classic example of the problems caused by government regulation of the broadcasting industry.

Saturday CBS president Richard Salant walked out of a meeting with the League of Women Voters, the organization sponsoring the debates, because he could not come to terms on the ground rules proposed for the first debate scheduled for Thursday evening in Philadelphia.

It was not the first meeting which has ended in an impasse.

The League wants to run the ballgame, the networks primarily want to treat the debates as unstructured news events and the representatives for the candidates want to protect their interests and insure that nothing occurs which would embarrass their charges.

The debates could have run on network television without a sponsor if it were not for the infamous Fairness Doctrine, that vague concept with which the Federal Communications Commission attempts to dictate to broadcasters how they will treat political candidates.

Getting a sponsor such as the League was supposed to have

enabled the networks to get around a requirement which would have forced them to provide "equal time" for the 100 or so independent candidates who are getting their names on Presidential ballots in a number of states.

The Doctrine is supposed to insure that political candidates are treated fairly in campaigns but more and more, broadcasters will admit, it is becoming a tool of censorship for the federal government.

Television for years has been limited in its treatment of news events, many times reporting controversy at standards far below those it is capable of as the most powerful visual medium ever invented by man. But when reporters work under a cloud of possible FCC retaliation from a Washington office they understandably remain timid.

Last week American Independent Party nominee Lestor Maddox applied the old argument when vying for a spot on the television debates.

The decision to leave off him the television screen, he said, "would not only violate the FCC Fairness Doctrine and campaign disclosure laws but would also represent a denial of freedom of speech."

Admittedly, determining what is fair play and applying fair standards almost requires heavenly intervention. It is a tremendously difficult task.

But broadcasters in increasing numbers in recent years have been clamoring for the right to try. Court tests of the Fairness Doctrine more often than nought have shown that the FCC doesn't have a monopoly on wisdom.

Establishing the ground rules for the debates has become so bogged down in bickering that at one time last week the League was insisting that television cameras not be pointed at the audience because showing the reactions of those attending might upset the candidates.

Nonsense.

It is not for the League, the network executives or the representatives of the candidates

to structure a news event in this matter.

Let the event unfold as it may. Free and open debate is basic to the American concept of free thought. If those involved let structure and organization substitute for substance than it will be the American public who will suffer.

Either the public will lose the televising of the debates all together or viewers will be subjected to the same kind of bland presentation which all too often has the been rule, rather than the exception for broadcast news.

Hands off the news, organizers. Give the viewing public the facts as they fall. The candidates' views and their reaction to stress, not the television lights, should determine who is the better candidate. Let the voters decide.

THE KANSAS CITY STAR

Kansas City, Mo., September 22, 1976

The wonder of the Ford-Carter debate tomorrow night is that it and the two subsequent encounters between the presidential rivals will take place at all. The recital of obstacles that had to be brought down could run on and on. First there was the surprise acceptance of the idea by an incumbent President. No one in his make-the-rules position ever before had agreed to such a campaign confrontation. Mr. Ford simply could have said no, and that would have been that. Instead he wanted head-to-head meetings with Jimmy Carter, seeing them as possibly advantageous and perhaps even crucial to his underdog's chances.

Then there was the matter of settling on a proper sponsor—in this case the respected League of Women Voters. After that there were the format, physical arrangements and rules of the contest to work out. The television networks remain unhappy with three restrictions the league has imposed on coverage of the debates—the screening of the questioners, the use of a single, "pooled" camera feed instead of each network having its own, and prohibiting the networks from showing audience reaction.

We do not see keeping the camera's range confined to the two candidates and the newsperson panelists as a loss to the event. On the contrary, it is what the President and the former governor say that especially matters, not how their words are visually received by the theater audience. The TV executives are thinking in show-business terms. But this is no frivolous "Queen

for a Day" affair. Audience reactions—considering the preconceived attitudes that those in the seats may bring with them—could distort the proceedings and unfairly influence TV watchers throughout the country.

As for the format of having three panelists ask the questions, we are not convinced that this is the best possible way to conduct a debate whose stakes potentially are so great. Another way, obviously rejected, would be for the two contestants to engage in a Lincoln-Douglas style debate with a prestigious moderator such as the president of a major university. What will be seen will more nearly resemble "Meet the Press" or "Face the Nation" than a straightforward exchange of arguments by the candidates.

But there can be a direct clash on the issues nonetheless. For the first time viewers can observe and compare the political and philosophical differences between Jerry Ford and Jimmy Carter. For some, a personal judgment of how they present themselves will be almost as important as what they actually say. The TV forum does offer this indisputable advantage.

Whether one begins to emerge with an edge over the other may be reflected in future national polling. Certainly there will be some impact—perhaps even decisive—on the showdown voting in November. The Nixon-Kennedy debates in 1960 made political history. The direct Ford-Carter rivalry that begins tomorrow night at a theater in Philadelphia could be equally momentous in its effects.

The San Diego Union

San Diego, Calif., September 23, 1976

The televised debate tonight between President Ford and Gov. Jimmy Carter brings this type of presidential campaign event before Americans for the first time in 16 years. There is no reason why such debates should not become a regular campaign institution, every four years. If communications technology permits millions of voters to sit in on a debate by presidential candidates, it should be used.

It's obvious, however, that the means of staging the debates and getting them on the television screen is still a problem. There have been compromises with principle, and with the law, in order for the 1976 debates to get on the air.

The Federal Communications Commission found an expedient way to get around Section 315 of the Communications Act, the so-called "equal time" rule. Following it to the letter would seem to require that broadcasters give all minor-party or independent candidates for president an equal shot at the audience if they provide time for a debate between the Democratic and Republican candidates.

The way out was for the FCC to declare that if the debate were sponsored by a third party—in this case the League of Women voters—television could cover it as a news event. Some of the excluded candidates are challenging the right of the FCC to wink at its own rule, and they have a point. The bigger point is whether the rule should exist at all—whether government's attempt to impose fair-

ness on the electronic media is compatible with the free-speech, free-press concepts of the First Amendment.

The Ford-Carter debates also have bumped up against the Federal Election Commission, which found it expedient to rule that the League's sponsorship of the debates does not constitute a campaign contribution to the candidates which otherwise would be prohibited under the new election laws. The roles of both the FCC and the FEC in these debates illustrates the inhibiting effect that government regulations can have on a political process that is supposed to be free.

Finally, with the debates classified as "news events" from the regulatory standpoint, the networks find themselves unable to treat them exactly that way. In demanding that cameras not reveal reactions of the audience, and in stipulating other conditions for televising the event, the League and the candidates clearly were seizing a prerogative that belongs to the editors and production people behind the cameras.

As the two major candidates square off in their first debate tonight, the subject will be domestic issues. The legal and ethical questions raised in arranging the debates suggest an issue for the next Congress. Regulatory codes which are supposed to protect the public interest are in fact making it difficult to give the public this kind of valuable opportunity to size up candidates for president.

The Seattle Times

Seattle, Wash., September 21, 1976

THE objections raised by the three commercial television networks to the League of Women Voters' ground rules for the debates between President Ford and Jimmy Carter amount largely to petty bickering, considering the immense stakes involved in the debates themselves.

Network executives argued against the league's restraints on audience-reaction pictures and its attempts to limit the amount of broadcasting paraphernalia on grounds the networks would be robbed of their "editorial freedom" to report the debates.

But Mrs. Ruth C. Clusen, the league's national president, said the ground rules were established in hopes of providing as fair and impartial a setting as possible, one that would be free of distractions either to the candidates or the viewers.

"Our position," Mrs. Clusen said, "is that this was arranged by us with the cooperation of the candidates. We have worked out the arrangements and the networks are invited."

That seems fair enough. The networks are free to cover the debates as a "news event," thus exempting them from legal obligation to afford equal amounts of broadcast time to all candidates.

For far too long, the commercial TV people have manipulated the scheduling and format of various public events—including professional football games and the national political conventions—to suit their convenience.

Whether pictures of the debate should include audience-reaction views or include a variety of scenes from other than "pool" cameras--two points over which the networks have been haggling—is far less important than the Ford-Carter confrontation itself.

That the networks would quibble over such matters to the point of threatening a boycott is symptomatic of the long-standing tendency among commercial broadcasters to stress "images" at the expense of substance in political reporting.

Whether the boycott actually would occur was a question of little moment, since the Public Broadcasting System—mindful of its responsibility to perform in the public interest—said it would provide live coverage according to the league's rules.

Richmond Times-Dispatch

Richmond, Va., September 22, 1976

The television networks, and especially CBS, have been loudly bemoaning what they claim is censorship and violation of the rights of a free press in the rule forbidding "cutaway" shots of the audience during tomorrow night's presidential candidates' debate.

"We are being required to distort the event," cries CBS news president, Richard S. Salant, "by ignoring...that there is an audience there."

The TV officials are reaching a long way, indeed, to find a basis for complaint on this score.

The purpose of the debate is to give the people of this nation an opportunity to see and hear Gerald Ford and Jimmy Carter present their views on issues of the day.

The reaction of any particular individual in the audience not only is irrelevant to the basic aim of the debate, but could also be misleading and unfair.

If the networks were permitted to cut away from the speaker and show, say, the one member of the audience who was then yawning, the impression left on the viewer at home could be that the candidate who was speaking was putting his listeners to sleep. In other words, the cameramen could editorialize, and rather powerfully, by their selections of audience shots. And editorializing during the debate proceedings certainly would not be in accord with the whole purpose of the Ford-Carter confrontation.

It is good that all the networks will carry the debate, since it is in the interest of the public that the event be given as wide coverage as possible. The "serious reservations" with which CBS will participate are not justified by the sensible requirement that the cameras focus on the two candidates for president of the United States, and on the questioners, and not on the people in the audience in Philadelphia's Walnut Street Theater.

The Morning Star

Rockford, Ill., September 23, 1976

It's a little difficult to find much sympathy for the national television networks who balked briefly at covering the Ford-Carter presidential debates because of "restrictions" placed on the coverage.

The key item in these restrictions is a rule which will prohibit the TV cameras from showing audience reaction to individual comments during the debate.

The only thing good to be said for showing the audience reaction is that it could add "color" to the telecast. That's another way of saying the shots of the audience could make the debates more entertaining to the viewing public.

Since the purpose of the debates supposedly is to give the American public more information in advance of the very serious business of selecting a president, there would seem to be little defense of a plan to make the show entertainment.

On the other hand, there could be a very real danger in showing audience reaction.

A television director, an anonymous man working behind the scenes in a control room, could pick and choose small sections of the audience or even individuals to flash on screens across the nation.

By selecting what he shows and when, this director could give those watching at home an unfair and biased picture of how the live audience is reacting to the two candidates.

A minor point?

Possibly. But of such minor things are elections too often won or lost.

There would seem no reason to risk such impact only in the name of adding "entertainment" to the program.

THE ATLANTA CONSTITUTION

Atlanta, Ga., September 21, 1976

With the great presidential debate just three days away, spokesmen for both President Gerald Ford and Jimmy Carter seem far more interested in form rather than substance.

Ford's man claims the President has the image of being weak. Carter's people say they are working to erase their candidate's perceived posture of being wishy-washy.

No wonder both sides are having image problems. Ford keeps crowing about what he's done for the economy. With the unemployment rate standing at 7.5 percent-plus and inflation rolling ever onward and upward, the sound of President Ford patting himself on the back for economic achievement has a hollow ring.

Then there's Carter who sometimes seems to be awash in images and image makers. He offically opened his campaign at FDR's Little White House. He evokes the memory of Harry Truman by praising his name and setting forth on a whistle-stop tour of the country in Truman fashion. And he drops the names of Kennedy and Johnson here and there. His television commercials show him loping across a field of peanuts.

However, when Carter's imagery is pushed aside, some complain that it's hard to get a handle on where he stands on substantive issues. His campaign organizers say, of course, that all his stands are clear as a bell. But he seems to have trouble enunciating them. Over the weekend the Associated Press ran out an interview seemingly quoting Carter as saying his tax reform package would sock the great American middle class as well as the rich with extra taxes so the poor would have to bear little of the burden. That is not what he said at all, said Carter after the interview was published. That's easy to believe, except it has happened so often on other issues that he has become known in some circles as Clarify Carter.

So both Carter and Ford are heading into the television debates with images that could use some propping up. But they also are reported to be doing their home work on the hard questions of inflation, unemployment and federal spending. Hopefully, most American voters will do less looking and more listening to Thursday night's debates. Then perhaps we can get down to a campaign of issues rather than images.

Chicago Tribune

Chicago, Ill., September 21, 1976

Plans for the opening debate Thursday between President Ford and Jimmy Carter have set off a preliminary battle that may be angrier than the main event.

One of the ground rules for the four debates is that television cameras would not be allowed to focus on the studio audience and show its reactions to the candidates' words. Richard Salant, president of Columbia Broadcasting System, is hotly protesting this rule as "prior censorship" and an infringement on the right of news media to make independent judgments on what to cover. Mr. Salant sent a strongly-worded telegram to the candidates saying that such a rule "would create the most dangerous precedents, not only at home but abroad, where we have consistently resisted all attempts to control our coverage."

The League of Women Voters, which is sponsoring the debates, says the rule will be changed only if both candidates favor changing it. People in both camps were concerned that audience-reaction shots might distract or influence millions of viewers at home, and at this writing neither have changed their minds.

The whole issue seems to us a bit synthetic for two reasons. One is that these debates are not just news stories in the usual sense. They are unique, planned events whose purpose is to expose the candidates' views directly to the voters at large; to give the public a long, concentrated look at Mr. Ford and Mr. Carter as they are, with the absolute minimum of interruption or interpretation by anyone else. Its value is that it allows a straightforward, two-way relationship between the candidates and the viewers.

In these circumstances, the objection to audience shots makes good sense. Why should somebody's instant reaction be included in the package, so that it is part of the overall impression people get of the candidates?

Better still, no compelling reason to have a studio audience at all. Without one, the issue would not have come up. The history-making Kennedy-Nixon debates of 1960 did not include an audience.

Since most of the audience, apart from reporters, is to consist of members of the League of Women Voters, it seems to us they could settle the issue themselves by confining their attendance to those whose presence is essential. Like reporters, this select group would presumably refrain from photogenic emotional outbursts and thus offer no temptation for the TV cameras to focus on them. The issue could then be resolved without challenging the position of the TV networks.

Los Angeles Times

Los Angeles, Calif., September 21, 1976

The League of Women Voters has made a muddle of the rules for the televised presentation of the presidential candidates Thursday.

It has given the candidates much too much power over the event, and has placed restrictions on the television coverage that will do nothing to enhance the presentation.

We share, first of all, the misgivings of the networks about the prohibition of camera coverage of the audience itself. If this is in fact a news event, as had been argued to evade the restrictions on political programs, then all the media should be equally free to cover the events as their wisdom dictates. We can share the unease of many with the way cameras sometimes wander at major events, dawdling over the inopportune sleeper, ridiculously costumed people and other diversions from the thrust and content of the event. But to impose regulations to limit that is to take a step down the risky road to total control over which camera looks at what.

Nor has the league made a persuasive case for limiting the coverage to the pool cameras of a single network. We liked the alternative, for the pool to be supplemented by a few additional cameras for each of the other networks, introducing some flexibility in the coverage and assuring more diversity for the audience. There would certainly be objections from the newspapers of the nation if their coverage were restricted to the eyes and ears of the staff of a single newspaper or wire service.

Perhaps of greatest concern, however, was the willingness of the League of Women Voters to allow the two candidates to screen prospective members of the panel that will ask the questions Thursday night. It is reassuring that qualified people have emerged from this process. But that is a decision that the league should properly have insisted on exercising independently.

The Courier-Journal

Louisville, Ky., September 21, 1976

THE EXTENT to which the staffs of presidential candidates have tried to rig the campaign debates that start Thursday should be no surprise to those who have watched the meteoric rise of "media experts" in recent political history. But the success of those arranging the Carter-Ford debates in dictating where the TV networks may point their cameras is a disturbing development.

The networks, being competitive and recognizing the vast public interest in these debates, have accepted — with varying degrees of protest — the instruction that they train their cameras only on the candidates and panelists. No "audience reaction" pictures will be permitted.

In theory, this is a sensible idea. Constant motion as cameras pan the audience for hostility, enthusiasm, amusement or boredom would be out of keeping with the tone of the event and, more importantly, might unfairly influence the public at home. But there is greater danger in dictating how reporters, whether they work for TV, radio or newspapers, must tell their story. The public should judge carefully the motives of those who would manipulate news coverage by imposing prior restraints.

Obviously, the press sometimes must accept restrictions on news coverage when such factors as the public safety are involved. At other times, to lessen the possibility that its coverage can be exploited by those trying to get on camera, it is quick to impose cautionary guidelines on itself. But more dangerous than excesses, in a nation that is healthiest when its people get all the news rather than just the parts that government or somebody thinks it should know, is suppression.

In practice, the news in the Carter-Ford debates is in what the candidates say, not in how a hand-picked studio audience instructed to silence seems to react. Still, what makes the debates news events is their unpredictability. What if Mr. Ford were to make a momentous policy disclosure? What if Mr. Carter were to say he really did mean to increase taxes on all family incomes over $15,000, as the Republicans have been charging?

Wouldn't audience reaction, pleased or displeased, be part of the story if an audience is present?

As news events, the debates can't be controlled in every detail by the candidates, beyond necessary ground rules. Nonetheless, the controversy over audience-reaction pictures is a reminder that what made this year's debates possible was a new interpretation of the federal "equal-time" rule that circumvented a policy that otherwise might have made it necessary to invite the Prohibition and Vegetarian candidates to share the studio.

Congress and the Federal Communications Commission might as well face the issue: the presidential contests are between the candidates of the two major parties. The equal-time law (as in 1960) should be altered to allow program content to reflect that fact.

The Topeka Daily Capital

Topeka, Kans., September 22, 1976

Scheduled TV debates between President Ford and challenger Jimmy Carter will be important in deciding who will be president for the next four years.

A majority of Americans should watch them and they should be presented in a way that permits viewers to make up their minds about the knowledge and ability of the candidates and the soundness of their political views.

Therefore, it is good news that all four TV networks wil carry the debates, despite disagreement about rules set by the sponsoring League of Women Voters and the candidates.

The debates could not be presented by networks because Congress would not repeal equal time laws. If networks sponsored them, they would have to include all "presidential candidates," and that includes scores of persons.

So the League-sponsored debates will be covered as news events by networks. TV officials objected to some League rules, saying they amount to "prior censorship," a limitation on freedom of the press — in this case, the electronic media.

The strongest objection was to the ruling (requested by both Ford and Carter) that networks not pan around the audience for reactions. A hand-picked group of about 500 will be present.

After a stormy session Saturday, NBC, CBS, ABC and the Public Broadcasting System have said they will cover the first debate at 8:30 p.m. Topeka time Thursday.

Press and broadcast media should not be limited in coverage of news. So networks had a good argument against the restriction.

Still, "panning around the audience" for reaction could result in unfair coverage of the debates. The audience will be selected and could be slanted toward one candidate or the other. The people would not be identified to viewers but their reactions might affect those of millions of voters.

Voters' judgment shouldn't be influenced by a TV director or reactions of a hand-picked audience in Philadelphia.

THE ARIZONA REPUBLIC

Phoenix, Ariz., September 22, 1976

Getting the first Ford-Carter television debate on the airwaves has churned almost as much acrimony and debate as the confrontation of the candidates.

The three television networks and the debates' sponsoring group, the League of Women Voters, got locked in a king-size argument over ground rules of Thursday night's telecast. At one point, TV appeared to be so unhappy it might boycott the event, and deprive tens of millions of Americans a ringside seat at this historic showdown.

Happily, the networks recognized the newsworthiness involved, and will cover the event under protest. To do otherwise would have been unthinkable.

Yet, the broadcasters were on solid ground when they unsuccessfully protested the League's prohibition against cameras showing the audience.

It was a political restriction as much as anything. The candidates apparently don't want to run the risk of a camera picking up a spectator yawning or snickering during an answer.

The League limitation obviously takes away some of the freedom of one segment of the free press.

As for the League's insistence on picking the panelists who will ask the President and Carter questions, TV was on shaky ground. Although the League's sponsorship is simply a ruse to avoid equal time requirements of federal law (and which would require TV appearances by dozens of presidential pretenders), the show is still a League show.

Picking panelists for this is no different than the League picking guest panelists for its annual banquet without consulting the media.

Just how balanced and fair the questions will be is something that can't be judged until after the show is over.

Moderator Edwin Newman, a veteran NBC reporter-commentator and author, is tactful, erudite and poker-faced. He is not given to raising eyebrows when interviewing political celebrities with whom he might disagree.

Panelist Frank Reynolds, an ABC television reporter, has liberal colors. Panelist Joseph Gannon, of the Wall Street Journal, is more toward the other end of the ideological spectrum. Elizabeth Drew, a Washington reporter and author, has done devastating reports on the Nixon years, and can be depended on to hurl pungent questions at both candidates.

Seeing the candidates together, sparring over similar issues, voters will be convinced of which candidate looks presidential, seems more prepared, appears better equipped temperamentally to lead.

BUFFALO EVENING NEWS
Buffalo, N.Y., September 21, 1976

We can't agree with the three pouting TV networks that the ban against TV cameras focusing on studio audience reactions during Thursday night's first Ford-Carter presidential debate is a "dangerous precedent," as CBS News calls it.

The overriding purpose served by the debates is to allow the two major candidates to explain their views on public issues to millions expected to be watching in their homes. It is the substance of those ideas, and reactions of the candidates to the issues posed, rather than the reactions of a couple of hundred people in the studio, which are significant.

The studio audience shots would be a show-biz distraction from the main event and rife with possibilities for camera editorializing. So both the candidates and the debate-sponsoring League of Women Voters wisely stood pat on the arrangements and gave the networks "the option to cover or not cover." With the invitation put like that, the three networks have all grumblingly decided to cover. Did anyone think they would boycott the premier news event of the season?

THE MILWAUKEE JOURNAL
Milwaukee, Wisc., September 21, 1976

The League of Women Voters has performed a valuable service in arranging the presidential debates. So it is unfortunate that a dispute occurred over network television coverage.

The networks are reluctantly going along with the League's rule barring cameras from cutting away for audience reaction shots, and with the League's decision allowing the candidates to participate in selection of the journalists who will ask questions. The camera controversy is rather minor. The League's fear that cutaways could have a distorting effect may not be unreasonable, especially when the debate format is still rather experimental.

Far less trivial is the networks' complaint about the candidates exercising what seems, in effect, an indirect veto of journalistic interrogators. As it turns out, the panel for the first debate is fine. But the League is wrong to consult the candidates — if only because this risks the appearance of manipulation.

The League is a good group. It ought to pick the panels in future debates without soliciting names or reaction from the candidates.

DESERET NEWS
Salt Lake City, Utah, September 24, 1976

Whatever points President Ford and Governor Carter made or failed to make in their historic first debate, one principle came through loud and clear: The value of the American system of free, competitive enterprise.

There was much arguing before the event over the sponsor's rule that there be, in effect, n o competition between the networks in covering the debate. The Deseret News agreed with the principle that shots of audience reaction and other diversions should be banned. But limiting coverage to one "pool" camera and audio equipment instead of allowing each network to use its own facilities seemed pointless.

Obviously, it was worse than pointless. Thursday night's breakdown of the pool audio equipment left the two candidates standing awkward and helpless for nearly half an hour. It was an anachronistic travesty in this age of electronic genius.

It's not as though we hadn't learned the lesson before. Russia and China in their attempted monolythic societies have demonstrated again and again the inherent weakness of one-man, one-mind rule.

In the subsequent debates over what America's competitive free society should be like, let's at least use competitive broadcast facilities.

NEW YORK POST
New York, N.Y., September 20, 1976

Demands by the TV networks for the right to exhibit selective shots of the audience during the prospective presidential debates have created an unwarranted, diversionary dispute. We believe both the representatives of the candidates and the League of Women Voters, official sponsor of the events, are on sound ground in rejecting the "cutaway" formula.

What the country wants to see and hear is the direct combat between President Ford and challenger Jimmy Carter. No matter how skilled and conscientious the cameramen, random shots of the studio onlookers could inject a distracting, even prejudicial element.

The invited guests are not the jury in these contests; that function will be exercised by the public. If the screen depicts isolated closeup portraits of assent or hostility among some of the onlookers, there can be interminable controversy about whether the glimpses shown were designed to sway the millions viewing the encounters in their homes.

Indeed, it would be preferable to exclude any studio gathering—as in the 1960 Kennedy-Nixon debates—than to let the audience get into the act.

In short, the debate is the thing, not the incidental presence of those few citizens favored with admission to the scene. It is unthinkable that plans for these eagerly awaited exchanges could be even momentarily threatened by spurious argument about audience coverage. Let the debates proceed without further backstage discord.

ARKANSAS DEMOCRAT
Little Rock, Ark., September 21, 1976

The first Ford-Carter debate will be seen and heard Thursday night on all networks, but by now not many people can think of the debates as just a public political event. The arrangements have been largely private, and the networks have only reluctantly agreed to conditions laid down by the candidates and the sponsoring League of Women Voters.

The league and the candidates have cobbled and carpentered the production pretty much to suit themselves—even to the extent of telling the press what it can and can't do and say.

The league, for instance, let the candidates pick the three panelists, the people who'll be questioning the candidates. The networks objected to that. Above all, they wanted some details of the choosing: Who was picked by whom, and who got turned down?

Then there's the filming of the debates. The league told the networks that the candidates didn't want any filming of audience reaction. That means the cameras can't pan the crowd—made up of league-chosen spectators and newsmen in equal numbers—to see how immediate onlookers react to the exchanges between the candidates. There was also the question of pooling. The networks wanted cameras of their own in addition to the pool cameras. They were turned down.

The candidates evidently fear that audience reaction to a well-scored point or to a disastrous bumble could affect the judgments of the millions who will be watching the debates on home sets. Since the race has been tightening ever since Mr. Ford's nomination, there is a feeling that the debates could make or break the chances of one man or the other. Certainly, the candidates were within their rights bargaining with one another on the format and on the dates and places of the debates, but the debates are a momentous political event and the people deserve more than what amounts to a contrived context.

As the networks put it to the league, this is a journalistic event, and the details of choosing the panelists as well as on-the-spot audience reaction are part of the event. That is to say, the debates are news and the press should be able to cover all relevant aspects of it so that the people have a broader understanding of what's happening.

The trouble with the league's management of the debates is that the league is private and answerable to nobody. That isn't true of the candidates. They are public figures. Their debates may very well decide the Presidency. If they are allowed to be selective about a news event of such magnitude, limiting the press' knowledge of details and coverage, then they are denying the people things they have no right to deny.

Such privacy as the candidates can claim in setting up the televised exchanges ends where the public interest begins. The public has an interest in knowing all about the panelists and how people watching the debates at first hand react. By interposing a private judgment against revelation of these details, the league has done the American people no service.

Private arrangements of public events can go only so far. In the case of presidential debates, such arrangements should be kept to a very minimum. The league, in future debates, should open up the news doors now closed.

St. Louis Globe-Democrat

St. Louis, Mo., September 21, 1976

Both sides—the presidential candidates and the television networks—are wrong in their wrangle over the debates between President Ford and Jimmy Carter which are scheduled to start Thursday night.

Ford and Carter are wrong in attempting to establish rigid ground rules that would prohibit the television networks from showing audience reaction to the debaters. And the networks are wrong in pretending that such reaction glimpses are vital to their news coverage of the debates.

Ideally interested Americans will want to watch the debates with a close eye on Ford and Carter and all ears attentive to what each contestant has to say. Viewers will be watching the President sharply to see if he handles himself effectively under fire. They will be observing Carter closely to see if he answers questions directly or if he dances around on an issue, leaving listeners in doubt.

Each candidate enters the debates untested and with a great deal at stake. If one should prove devastatingly superior to the other, it will be extremely difficult for the other to recover.

The networks' role in carrying the debates should be to perform a public service, not to be intrusive. Panning away from the participants for views of the audience while the speakers are making their points would be distractingly poor journalism.

Views of the audience between questions or after either contestant has scored a particularly solid point should be welcomed by everyone.

It is stuffy for the debaters to forbid all reaction.

It is fortunate that the three major networks have agreed for the time being to present the opening debate.

All concerned should realize that the American people are the ones to be served in the debates. Selfish wishes must be set aside.

ST. LOUIS POST-DISPATCH

St. Louis, Mo., September 22, 1976

The commercial television networks were right in principle in saying that, if the debate Thursday between the major presidential candidates is a bona fide news event, they should have been allowed to cover it as they saw fit—which, to them, meant showing audience reaction as well as the candidates themselves. But they would have been wrong in judgment—had they been given editorial discretion—if they had chosen to focus their cameras on individual reactions to candidate performance, which could have the effect of diverting attention from the substance of the debates and magnifying a possible biased perception of the candidates' remarks.

As it turned out, the networks yielded under protest to the ground rule against covering audience reaction. With the networks having made their rhetorical point on editorial freedom and the League of Women Voters, sponsor of the debates, having stood firm at the candidates' insistence, the character of television coverage of the first debate seems to have

been set. Whether the other two debates will follow the same format is yet to be determined.

In reaching decisions on future debates, the various parties might bear certain factors in mind. The League and the candidates should be aware that the news media rightly cherishes its editorial freedom. And the media—although the debates have been ruled bona fide news events by the FCC (and thus not subject to the equal time rule for all candidates)—should recognize that the debates, like many news events, are being staged and are thus subject to control by the producers. This control is evidenced by the fact that members of the audience are invited and do not represent a cross section of the public.

The important point for all parties to bear in mind is that the main purpose of the debates is to help the public to make up its mind about the candidates' characters and positions and not to put on a show for the benefit of television or the candidates.

The Morning Union

Springfield, Mass., September 1, 1976

The big flap about whether the TV cameras should be turned on the studio audience during the televised debates between President Ford and Jimmy Carter makes it appear the commercial networks are more interested in a "show biz" format than in service to the voting public.

CBS News President Richard Salant declared that a ban on audience shots would be "prior censorship" of the news. But the response of the candidates to questions, not the reaction of the audience to their answers, is what the series is designed to bring to the nationwide audience.

The League of Women Voters, sponsor of the debates, was justified in imposing the ban on audience shots. Both candidates were concerned that facial expressions or other reactions of those in the studio might distract or influence viewers at home.

If that were so, and it may be to some extent, the intent of the series would indeed be subverted. But just as a time-consuming sidelight that has no bearing on the debates as such, the audience shots should be banned. The Public Broadcasting system, to its credit, has not insisted that the studio audience be shown.

The Miami Herald

Miami, Fla., September 21, 1976

OFFICIALS of the commercial television networks, especially CBS, have been in high dudgeon over some conditions and restrictions placed on their coverage of the upcoming Ford-Carter debates.

But their high-sounding invocations of press freedom ring hollow in this case, for their arguments in favor of audience-reaction shots have more to do with show business than with the First Amendment.

We believe that the candidates and the sponsoring League of Women Voters are on firm ground in not wanting the affair colored by reactions from the studio audience. In any case, the debates are theirs and the American people's, not the networks'.

The networks have become so accustomed to running things — stage managing everything from political conventions to football games — that perhaps they've lost sight of their legal status as common carriers who operate over the public's air waves but don't own them any more than truckers own the roads.

As for the debates, we hope the candidates and the League will stand eyeball to eyeball with the networks on this issue until the CBS eye blinks.

The Providence Journal

Providence, R.I., September 21, 1976

The debate between the three major commercial television networks and the League of Women Voters is not entirely a whiffle ball contest, but it comes dangerously close. Let's take a closeup without any "cutaways".

The networks, incensed that the league is set against camera shots of the audience during the forthcoming presidential debates, have threatened to pick up their equipment and go home. Both candidates support the restriction, believing that so-called "cutaway" shots might tend to be diversionary and unfairly influence the viewers at home.

As petty as the dispute may seem, network officials are by no means altogether off limits. For them and for others in the business of reporting the news there is a principle involved. Simply put, it is that journalists covering bona fide news events must be free to report without undue interference. Restrictions placed upon a free press are always a serious matter, governed by the First Amendment.

Indeed, screening of the three panelists chosen by the networks is far more serious

in our view than the ultimate point of contention that brought negotiations to an impasse. At the same time, it should be noted that the debates are hardly news events in the ordinary sense. Rather, they are staged encounters with very high stakes resting on the outcome. Every effort has been made to ensure fairness and equity to the two sides and to eliminate anything that might create an unfair advantage. That, we think, is precisely as it should be.

Under the circumstances, making "cutaways" a major issue comes under the category of over-reacting. Except as a theatrical device and a prop for TV news prerogatives, the reactions of a theater audience have no positive value or proper place in a presentation whose legitimate aim is to inform, not to entertain, the voting public.

In the 1960 debates, the networks ran the show. If they are miffed at being outside looking in, subordinate to the league which volunteered to sponsor the event as a way around the equal-time provision, their pique is one of those audience reactions the public can easily do without.

DAILY ☒ NEWS

New York, N.Y., September 21, 1976

The television networks had conniptions because they will not be permitted to flash quickie shots of audience reaction during the debates between President Gerald Ford and Jimmy Carter.

Richard Salant

The most outspoken of the video news moguls has been Richard Salant of the Columbia Broadcasting System.

Salant sees the First Amendment being swept from its foundations if TV cameras are forced to focus exclusively on Mr. Ford, Carter and their selected questioners.

The notion that some sacred free-press principle will be destroyed by the restriction is grossly exaggerated, to say the least. The purpose of the debates is public education. The viewers are expecting a frank discussion of issues, not media events with a distracting dash of "Candid Camera" thrown in.

What Salant and his colleagues really were clamoring for was the right to dress up the debates with some of their own special show-biz touches. We don't blame Mr. Ford and Carter for arguing that the networks should stick to reporting, and not try to jazz up the proceeding with irrelevant shots of onlookers.

After all, the candidates were not asking for a limitation any more stringent than those the networks apply to most of their own panel shows, from which audiences are entirely excluded.

The Boston Herald American

Boston, Mass., September 21, 1976

To prohibit photographers from taking audience reaction shots at the Ford-Carter debates is a mistake.

In the first place, applause or disapproval among those in Philadelphia's Walnut Street Theater is not going to decide who wins or loses Thursday night. And even if audience reactions can be a bit contagious, seasoned troupers like Gerald Ford and Jimmy Carter have been around the kitchen long enough not to be afraid of a little heat.

CBS News President Richard Salant was understandably perturbed. In a telegraphed complaint to the candidates, he said that ". . . to require us, as the price of coverage, to agree to a restriction such as this—to require us to ignore an integral part of a news event and pretend it does not exist—would constitute not only an act of prior censorship but would strip us of the right to make those independent news judgments central to a free and vigorous press."

Such a ridiculous restriction makes the debates something less than great from a journalistic point of view.

We agree with Spiro Agnew that a raised eyebrow can be a distracting influence, but is is silly to black out audience reaction in Philadelphia, even if it includes a few scowls.

The Washington Star

Washington, D.C., September 21, 1976

It's no secret that the television networks preferred to stage and set the conditions for the Ford-Carter and Dole-Mondale debates, not to cover them as "news events" under rules set by the candidates and the League of Women Voters. But they lost the fight to do so. And their rather strained battle against camera restrictions seems the last gasp of bad losers.

When CBS News president Arthur Taylor was making the network case for a suspension of Section 315 of the Federal Communications Act — which Congress denied — he went so far as to warn Congress of "substantial danger" in the League of Women Voters' format. The danger, Mr. Taylor thought, was that "a live audience . . . in an informal setting (. . . however nonpartisan in theory the audience might be) could provide distraction from the substance of the debates or give supporting or negative emphasis to one participant or another."

That was on August 26. By September 18, last Saturday, the networks were taking a different view, apparently contradictory of the first. Mr. Richard Salant, president of CBS News, stalked out of a meeting of debate co-ordinators where one issue on the agenda was how the networks would cope with that "substantial danger" of which Mr. Taylor had warned: the danger that audience reactions at the Walnut Street Theater in Philadelphia might subtly influence the reactions of millions watching in their living rooms.

To forfend that danger, it had been agreed — and at this writing is still agreed — that the cameras will focus only on the two candidates, as they did in 1960, and ignore the invited audience.

Thus there will be no clever, potentially manipulative panning of cameras to catch audience reactions. The networks now profess to see this rule as a hindrance of their freedom to cover a news event as they choose. "A matter of journalistic principle and ethics of very great magnitude is at stake," said Mr. Salant, rather solemnly.

It would appear that Mr. Salant and Mr. Taylor need to call another huddle and co-ordinate signals. If Mr. Taylor was right about the dangers of a live audience, those dangers would stand to be compounded by the license Mr. Salant demands. As between the two CBS positions — and CBS seems to be the leader in threatening to boycott the proceedings — we prefer Mr. Taylor's. It is not only sensible, it is also unembellished with bogus free press issues.

Anyone who has watched live television coverage of political speechmaking — especially at national conventions — knows how the roving camera eye sometimes becomes an instrument of silent comment, a mute Greek chorus, on what is being said. It can record this smile, that scowl, and the other case of glazed-over eyes. It would be difficult to say just what subtle influence such silent commentary has upon the reactions of a television audience; it is probably considerable. No obvious manipulative intent, we hasten to add, need be evident. However random or aimless the camera, there is "substantial danger" that it can lead to prefabricated reactions for millions of viewers.

Especially far-fetched, in our view, is the breathless contention that the rule against wandering camera eyes constitutes a form of "prior censorship" of the news. The networks offering that argument confuse news with theater, for the story is not the reaction of a select audience, it is what the candidates say and how they say it.

Mr. Salant's attitude, and that of the other network spokesmen, is unreasonable. Television certainly is free to cover random news events as it pleases. But in a formal setting, whose rules have been carefully worked out to minimize bias against either candidate, it is entirely reasonable for the newsmakers to set the terms of the coverage. Restrictions on camera work are not capricious, but anyone who dislikes them may simply refuse coverage. That option is of course open to CBS News Thursday evening.

NEW YORK POST

New York, N.Y., October 22, 1976

A fall television special that started a few weeks ago is going off the air after tonight's episode. Unlike some lesser productions that are being dropped soon, it has had consistently high ratings.

The third and last of the Presidential campaign debates between President Ford and Jimmy Carter will start at 9:30 on Channels 2, 4, 7, and 13. It may, for "undecided" voters, be the encounter which makes up their minds.

There have inevitably been conflicting estimates about public perceptions of the debates, but there is no serious question that they have been intermittently informative and even occasionally dramatic. After 16 years of neglect, the televised Presidential debate has been successfully revived and it should become a standard feature of all future campaigns.

Whether it does may depend considerably on how many Americans watch tonight. The conscientious sponsors of the debates — the League of Women Voters and its supporters—have worked hard to encourage such voter involvement. Their concluding production deserves a record degree of recognition.

THE EMPORIA GAZETTE

Emporia, Kans., October 7, 1976

THIS week's 90-minute dual press conference, ballyhooed as the second in a series of debates between the candidates for President, proved two points. First it underscored plainly what critics have said all along — the appearances are not debates. Second, it raised some doubt about the value of such face-to-face confrontations.

During the first 150 years of the nation's history, debates probably were needed. The only way voters could see or hear the candidates was in person.

Today, the candidates appear in most homes — in living color and high-fidelity sound — at least once a day as families watch the evening television news. The statements and actions of the candidates also are reported frequently on radio broadcasts and covered at length in daily newspapers.

Rarely does a candidate say anything in a debate that he has not been quoted as saying before.

There is some question about the propriety of the debates.

Should the President have to prove himself as a prime-time father image in order to be reelected? Must he have the television charisma of Barbara Walters in order to govern properly?

Surely not.

One of the commentators pointed out that there is some danger in allowing the President to stand before the cameras and respond to probing questions about the nation's foreign policy for long periods. The challenger is free to say all sorts of outrageous things and not cause much stir abroad. Yet the President is the spokesman for the United States and he must be careful not to let something slip that might offend allies or incite enemies. His comments about foreign policy are not taken lightly by leaders of the other nations around the globe.

Finally, there is the sheer boredom of it all. The tedious arguments do not resolve anything; rarely do they shed new light.

If the Great Debates cannot be eliminated entirely they at least ought to be shortened to 60 minutes. — R.C.

Chicago Tribune

Chicago, Ill., September 26, 1976

If there were any real winners in Thursday night's big debate, one of them certainly was the Public Broadcasting System, which provided a running translation for the deaf in sign language and was thus quite prepared for the sound blackout.

Unfortunately few listeners other than the deaf were able to translate the translation or read the candidates' lips, but if we all study up before the next debate, then maybe it won't have to be suspended just because of some trouble with television wiring.

Which leads to some other winners, namely Eugene McCarthy and the other minority candidates. They tried in vain to be included in the debate under the Federal Communication Act's equal time rule for television. They were turned down on the ground that this was a public forum, a legitimate news event in itself, and that television was merely covering it.

But as our television critic, Gary Deeb, aptly points out, a legitimate news event does not stop just because something goes wrong with TV. That is like saying that the tail wags the dog. This aspect of the problem may not seem particularly important in connection with the present campaign. But it does seem to us either that somebody owes Mr. McCarthy a better explanation or that Congress and the FCC should rethink the television equal time rule.

The Des Moines Register

Des Moines, Iowa, September 29, 1976

President Ford was smart to insist that he and Jimmy Carter stand during the debates, to profit from his three-inch height advantage. Most voters seem concerned more with looks than with substance.

According to a CBS News-New York Times poll, most of those questioned said the candidates' style and presentation had been most important in forming their impressions of the debate. Although most politicians and analysts considered the debate a draw on the issues, or gave a slight advantage to Carter, the poll respondents preferred Ford. He was considered the winner by 37 per cent, Carter by 24 per cent.

As Richard Nixon learned in 1960 — and as he practiced thereafter — image, not substance, is what counts on TV. But it is unfair to blame "imagery" on TV alone. The voters, nonvoters, candidates and news media must share the blame.

Too often we look for the offbeat trivia, the family life, the sports ability, the religious persuasion (or put-on). Too seldom we look for leadership, for commitment, for action. That most people questioned said style and presentation were most important to their perception is a sad reinforcement of "image" politics and another blow to issues.

THE INDIANAPOLIS NEWS

Indianapolis, Ind., September 23, 1976

The presidential debates already have been derided for testing more of the style than the substance of the two candidates.

Events may prove this prediction wrong, but even in that unlikely occurrence, the exercise will be valuable. A word is warranted here about the role of style in the presidency.

Ever since John Kennedy redefined the word "charisma" for Americans, the appearance of being presidential has ranked almost as high in the public mind as the fact of being so. President Ford has staked his campaign strategy upon this assumption. The 1960 debates, which have recently become the hottest re-runs in town, are used to substantiate the claim that Kennedy "won" by coming across to viewers as being more presidential.

Looking back, it is important to note that style came into its own about the time television did. The 1960 debates made a particular impact precisely because they were televised and not reproduced in print. Television itself has functioned to ensure the primacy of style to the American presidency.

And style has become one criterion of the presidency. Since mass communications have become an integral part of politics, stage presence has become almost as important as world presence.

Tonight's debate must be viewed in this context. Even if the issues are glossed over or even if the average viewer forgets most of what is said, the evaluation of style must be made.

What a president does, however, is still much more important than how he appears. Although the debates will provide a legitimate public relations service, we hope that is not all they will do.

The Arizona Republic
Phoenix, Ariz., September 21, 1976

It wasn't exactly television's finest hour.

For 28 minutes the most powerful elected official in the world and the man who wants his job stood there, each behind his own podium, able to be seen but not able to be heard by 120 million TV viewers who wondered what was going on.

It may have been the longest half hour in the lives of Gerald Ford and Jimmy Carter. It certainly took years off the lives of Walter Cronkite and David Brinkley and all the valiant media people who were trying so desperately to hold an audience that probably would have preferred an old movie. A generation brought up on Sesame Street must have wondered how anything so dull could get on the screen.

The clear loser in the debate was American technology. The nation that could put a man on the moon was unable to bring sound into the living room.

And yet the first of the four campaign debates was a victory for American-style democracy. Nowhere else in the world could a nation watch the chief of state and his chief opponent submit themselves to the questioning of news reporters.

It would stretch the imagination to conceive of Premier Hua Kuofeng of Red China or Prime Minister Indira Gandhi of India submitting to such an inquisition. Only President Marcos of the Philippines could handle himself in such an encounter, and he wouldn't dignify his opposition by debating with it.

Field Marshal Idi Amin of Uganda would probably feed his opponent to the crocodiles. Yitzhak Rabin of Israel might take on an opponent, if the opponent weren't an Arab. Giscard d'Estaing of France would stack the deck with friendly reporters.

Queen Elizabeth of the United Kingdom would grace such a platform, but she couldn't speak for the government, and Prime Minister Harold Wilson would feel much more at home answering questions in the House of Commons. Prime Minister Aleksei Kosygin who claims to represent 99.64 of his people, couldn't find an opponent in all of Russia.

But if the chief spin-off of the first presidential campaign debate was an enhancement of the American political system, the more immediate result was a slight closing of the gap between front runner Jimmy Carter and incumbent Jerry Ford.

Most polls showed President Ford made a better impression on the voters than Carter did. Even if the margin was close,* and the number of undecideds remains large, any forward movement on Ford's part must be considered a plus for the Republican candidate.

The next round in the most carefully prepared public fight since Dempsey met Tunney will be staged October 6. The subject will be foreign affairs, a field in which President Ford should have a clear advantage because of his experience and because of currently favorable developments in Rhodesia and the Middle East.

While it may not hold for the future, the first debate did seem to reinforce the images both candidates had already established.

Carter came across as a warm human being, definitely interested in poor people and apparently a firm believer in Harry Hopkins' old political axiom: "Tax and tax, spend and spend, elect and elect."

President Ford came across as better informed on the day-to-day problems of government, a sincere man who doesn't think a country can spend itself into prosperity.

Neither of the two had enough charisma to arouse a spark in the breast of a firefly.

Probably Jerry Ford best summed up the question for this year's voters when he said, "The real issue is whether you should vote for his (Carter's) promises or my performances."

The voters should make that choice, and then go to the polls in large numbers on Nov. 2. Relatively few people in this troubled world get such an opportunity.

The Ann Arbor News
Ann Arbor, Mich., September 23, 1976

A SUSPICION that will be in the minds of a lot of Americans as they watch the first Ford-Carter television show tonight was expressed a few days ago by a veteran of U.S. politics, W. Averell Harriman.

"I'm not sure," said Harriman, "I was able to persuade him that everything that was said was of no importance."

Harriman used that phrase, we assume carelessly, in evaluating his effort to explain the U.S. presidential campaign to Soviet Communist Party leader Leonid I. Brezhnev.

Harriman is a former U.S. ambassador to the USSR who is working for Jimmy Carter. Presumably, if Harriman literally believed that everything the candidates say holds "no importance," he wouldn't be working for either of them.

★ ★ ★

STILL, the emphasis Ford and Carter and their public relations advisors are placing on appearance does encourage the idea that what they say may not matter much.

The candidates' image-makers have concentrated on such items as the height of the podiums they will speak from, and lighting to minimize the President's receding hairline without making Carter look fat-faced. There was even a suggestion that Ford should be compelled to stand in a four-inch hole so viewers wouldn't notice that he's taller than Carter.

Happily, no one has had the gall to suggest that the candidates' joint appearances should be filmed and edited before being broadcast, as is the case with most televised material.

Because it's live, what the candidates will say about issues will matter. They will also be talking about themselves, with no chance for a retake.

★ ★ ★

JOHN F. KENNEDY didn't win the 1960 election because Richard M. Nixon looked sweaty and unshaven in their first joint appearance.

Those who listened instead of just looking heard the contrast between a grim, humorless candidate, and a candidate who expressed an adult sense of humor and perspective in most of his comments, whether he was talking about serious issues or former President Truman's use of a cuss-word. The same contrast would have been on view again in 1968 if Nixon and Senator Humphrey had made joint appearances.

Joint television appearances won't be, and shouldn't be, a substitute for separate campaigning before live audiences. But these appearances will be important, even though the image-builders who plan them show a low regard for voters.

Register-Republic
Rockford, Ill., October 10, 1976

Harry Truman wouldn't think much of the whole thing.

Abe Lincoln and FDR probably wouldn't be very impressed either.

There's a certain magic gone from presidential campaigns and it's suggested that those nationally-televised debates may be partially to blame.

The missing ingredient is a matter of style, the style that the Trumans, Lincolns and Roosevelts brought to campaigning in simpler days.

Truman pulled one of the most stunning political upsets of history by "giving 'em hell" from the back platform of a train at hundreds of whistle stops.

Roosevelt won four terms, largely through the magic of his fireside chats.

Lincoln took a big leap forward in his climb to fame on a rough platform in Freeport.

All of them probably would have been very ill at ease in one of 1976's Great Debates, facing countless millions of faceless listeners, almost never looking at their opponent, dueling with facts and figures which can become almost incomprehensible to most Americans.

It's doubtful that Harry Truman could have given 'em hell in front of a TV camera. It's doubtful Roosevelt could have been folksy standing in the glare of those TV floodlights. It's doubtful Lincoln could have handled a Douglas knowing millions of people were sitting home comfortably watching to see who "sweated a lot" who seemed the most composed or who "had a sneer on his face."

It just may well be that this year's Ford-Carter debates are the best way to help the nation select a president. But it sure isn't as much fun as Truman's way or Lincoln's way or Roosevelt's way.

And listening to the public reaction, there certainly is a question about how effective Carter and Ford are being.

In too many cases, the public is saying things like:

—"The debates are not as valuable as I thought they might be."

—"The debates haven't changed my mind."

—"They're not as interesting as I feel they could be."

—"They are a waste of time."

—And, "I don't believe the debates will have any effect."

Even this may be for the best. Considering the awesome power of television to reach millions of Americans at one time, it probably is best that today's candidates debate on the factual level rather than an emotional one.

Wouldn't it be awful if a man could be elected president simply because he was the best television pitchman?

This is one case where too much excitement could be deadly.

Des Moines Tribune
Des Moines, Iowa, September 20, 1976

The electronic short-circuit that silenced Gerald Ford and Jimmy Carter during last week's televised debate was not only an embarrassment to the networks, it may have punctured their case against Eugene McCarthy, who has been trying unsuccessfully to be heard on the debates.

McCarthy, running as an independent candidate, renewed his plea for a hearing after the technical breakdown interrupted the first Ford-Carter confrontation. Not entirely in jest did McCarthy ask the Federal Communications Commission (FCC) for time to respond — 45 minutes with sound and 15 minutes of silence.

The networks have been fending off McCarthy by insisting that they are only giving national exposure to a "public forum" put on by the League of Women Voters. The debate, in other words, is being treated like any other news event of national significance. The FCC has gone along with that explanation.

With eight minutes left in last week's debate, the networks lost their sound. The debate, for all practical purposes, ended then, although 500 persons were in the audience at Philadelphia's Walnut Street Theater. Ford and Carter stood silently for 27 minutes until sound was restored, then concluded with three-minute summary statements.

McCarthy scored an interesting point with his complaint that the debate was really staged by and for the TV networks — that if it had been truly a public forum incidentally being broadcast, it would have continued with questions and answers during the networks' silence.

However that may be, McCarthy can argue credibly that he is a "major" or "serious" candidate entitled to equal time on TV and radio: Polls show him getting support from six to 10 per cent of respondents, which could be enough to tip the election from Carter to Ford.

Arkansas Gazette.
Little Rock, Ark., October 3, 1976

Some people in both the press and politics have been highly annoyed at the arrangements for the Ford-Carter debates on TV. The League of Women Voters stands accused by various critics of being arbitrary and contrary in setting up the rules, as these relate to the method of choosing questioners from among the press, the ban on viewing of audience response, and so forth. But we see no significant interference with freedom of the press in the way these performances were set up; the theater response can be reported amply by those present, and the interrogators empaneled all seem to be competent news people.

We must admit, however, to a twinge of annoyance at the very *necessity* of making all those stage arrangements, those touchy decisions as to how the images of these men will be projected to possibly 100 million viewers. Such preparations and judgments are inherent in the technology of the electronic age which dominates us more and more. In the images it brings us, nuance and emphasis can be highly important — more important, sometimes, than reality. Perhaps the arrangers of these exchanges should have allowed an occasional sweep of audience reactions there in the theater, but, to their credit, they have done their best to guard against any artificiality, diversions or distortions of emphasis which might flow from the medium itself, and tried to focus altogether on the candidates, in a sterile setting.

Nothing like this can be perfect, and everyone cannot be satisfied, for this is — in one way of looking at it — a packaged product, as almost everything is packaged nowadays. Perhaps, since this is the Bicentennial, when we are re-enacting the old times, the candidates should schedule just one additional debate, and do it the old-fashioned way. Maybe they should go down to Galesburg, Illinois, on a bright October day and there, where the seas of corn stretch to broad horizons, stand where Lincoln and Douglas stood and speak till each of them has nothing more to say.

It would be a fascinating experiment — no stage setting, no arrangements, no questions, nothing but the men on the platform in the outdoors. For one thing, it would be a test of endurance. Messrs. Lincoln and Douglas could speak extemporaneously for two or three hours (and then rebut at length later on), and certainly presidential endurance is as much of an issue as some of the trivia which has been dragged into the current race. It would show us, too, how much these gentlemen have in their heads to unreel, given all the time in the world, without prompting. In the old days, sometimes the great flashes of eloquence and intellect would come only after an hour of droning that put even screaming babies to sleep.

The people, of course, could simply come as they wished, and the reporters, and the camera crews, and we all would learn about it soon enough in fine detail, and there could be a dinner on the grounds afterward. When Messrs. Lincoln and Douglas first debated at Ottawa, Ill., 12,000 came, and stirred up such a dust that the candidates could barely be seen. Today the scene could be watered down in advance, and the affair would have the advantage of economy, and rustic informality.

We're indebted to debates not only for ventilating the views of candidates (which may require more time than we now assign to debates), but also for reminding us, in retrospect, not to take their pronouncements as final truth. It was stunning, for example, to hear John Kennedy in the recent ABC-TV rerun of the Kennedy-Nixon debates selling the "missile gap" as the transfixing issue, when in fact it was a figment of the imagination. One also can read the record of the Lincoln-Douglas debates and be no less stunned. The issue (and it was real) was whether a black person could be a citizen of this nation with full civil rights, and we all know that Mr. Lincoln was in the affirmative, on the side of both right and history. What we forget sometimes is his dismaying, disproved argument on those long-ago platforms in Illinois that there was "a physical difference between the two (races) which, in my judgment, will probably forever forbid their living together upon the footing of personal equality; and inasmuch as it becomes a necessity that there must be a difference, I, as well as Judge Douglas, am in favor of the race to which I belong living in a superior position."

So we must always take time to wonder, whether we hear the candidates outdoors or on The Tube, how the words they speak today will read in the next century, or even — at the speed things are moving — in the next decade. Not much has been said thus far in the current contest, we expect, that will loom very large upon the screen of history.

The Houston Post
Houston, Tex., October 28, 1976

Before the days of television, Americans thronged to the parade route or the football stadium or the city auditorium, taking the children along, to see and hear the President of the United States or the leading candidates opposing him for election. It was an instinctive wish to get the feel of the man — the stance, the character, whatever the intangibles of personality that do not quite come through in written or even in radio speeches. Anyone who ever saw Gen. Dwight Eisenhower and Gen. Douglas MacArthur riding through a city in an open car in a parade can remember seeing and sensing the difference in the two men. Both had written admirable, heroic chapters in our history. Both had unique qualities of magnetism and leadership. But they were remarkably different.

The television debates, both those of 1960 and those of 1976, served this purpose. Whether it was any of the bouts between the presidential candidates, or the one between the vice presidential candidates, the quality and fabric of each man gradually came through. Each to his own tastes: Each of us felt greater kinship with one of the candidates than the other, or perhaps some recognition that this man was the one we could most comfortably support during the next four years.

To this degree, the so-called debates had value. Maybe they will be the last such encounters ever televised. Maybe they will become an almost inevitable part of our national electioneering. If they do, then we should work to make them more rewarding. The League of Women Voters and the journalists who shaped the questions worked hard to make the most of the series. But many of us came away oddly dissatisfied. Too often the questions aimed at a specific issue or a specific statement of policy by the candidate inspired answers that were pat or a repetition of campaign oratory.

If in future elections the candidates are to be televised on national prime time, we should search for a different format, one that would enable the speaker to open out and broaden his remarks, to explore the big issues, to discuss the big public concerns, to free themselves and their audiences of the political cliches of slash and cut. These were not truly debates in the sense of two well-informed men talking to each other. A true political debate can be exciting and challenging. In the last days before the German elections, the leading candidates started a debate that was to have lasted two hours; it ran to four on the sheer impetus of excitement. Most of the large television audience stayed the whole course.

Our question-and-answer programs had much of the limitation and little of the excitement of a political debate. The speakers were caught in the point-counterpoint rhythm of a high school debating team without the chance to address each other in wit, sparkle, challenge and riposte. And, in the end, many viewers came away feeling that they had learned almost nothing new about the nation, its problems or the possible solutions. Perhaps we can do better next time.

Anchorage Times

Anchorage, Alaska, October 27, 1976

IN RETROSPECT, it's curious now how badly the presidential debates are being rated by the television commentators, the Washington columnists, the traveling White House press corps and the campaign reporters, the national magazines and various editorialists hither-and-yon around the country.

When the debates were first agreed to, and in the planning stages that led up to the three encounters between Jerry Ford and Jimmy Carter, there was an almost universal euphoria about the pending events. At last, the argument was, there would be a meaningful dialog between the candidates instead of the usual campaign froth of long-distance claim and counter-claim.

The voters, it was said, would truly be able to judge.

WELL, IT DIDN'T work out that way.

Maybe it was the format of the debates that helped make them so dreadfully dull. Maybe it was the artificially staged setting, which was fine in the first round at Philadelphia but grew increasingly tiresome as the TV cameras focused on the participants through the California and Virginia debates.

Maybe it was the tendency of the candidates to repeat and repeat again the same phrases from their cross-country stumping that turned people off. Maybe it was the inclination to generalize and overstate that dampened the viewing, as when Mr. Carter flatly said the great depression was caused by Herbert Hoover.

But mostly, perhaps, the failure of the debates to excite the voters must be laid on the doorstep of the press—that segment of society that led the cheers when the events were first scheduled.

AS PART OF the press, we hate to make this judgment. But we feel obliged.

In our view, the great weakness of the debate was that the reporters who served on the panels simply did not do a proper job of questioning and of following up. Again, maybe the format and restraints imposed on them make it dif-ficult to do a proper interviewing job.

The last debate was the worst from a press standpoint. It was almost shameful. Mr. Carter was asked pitty-pat questions of little consequence to which he was able to make sweeping and campaignish replies. The questioning of Mr. Ford was sharper, but was offset by the questioning of one panelist who appeared so biased against the President that his attitude was rude and offensive.

It's true, we think, that the presidential candidates did not come through the debates in much of a shining fashion. But the press came through in a shabby fashion. It should be ashamed of itself.

AKRON BEACON JOURNAL

Akron, Ohio, October 25, 1976

BARRING a bombshell, the presidential campaign is over.

It ended Friday night in Williamsburg, Va., with the finish of the third "debate" between President Ford and Gov. Carter. That series, plus the forum with vice presidential candidates Dole and Mondale, gave the American voter the chance to study the men who want to lead the nation for the next four years as well as the opportunity to consider the issues.

There were no splendid pyrotechnics, no miracles. The nationally televised debates, arranged by the League of Women Voters Education Fund, drew mixed reviews. Partisans saw their candidates winning; post-debate polls gave different rounds to different men.

Some remember the technical problems in the first debate; some argue that none of the confrontations were in debate format (which, of course, is incorrect); some suggest they were merely media events, where substance was lost to form; some considered the series boring; some complained that the splinter candidates were unfairly excluded. And yes, some say this was a pretty good way to let the country do a little comparison shopping for national candidates.

All in all, we were impressed.

Television is the auditorium for presidential campaigns in the 1970s: It is the back of the whistlestop train, the front row seat for most Americans interested in "meeting" the candidates. It is the vehicle that delivers the office-seeker to the living room.

The debates will have a major impact on the election. Neither Ford nor Carter has done much of anything else to arouse public interest. Both have their political records, position papers, obligatory campaign trips. Both have been interviewed and ana-lyzed and lauded and attacked in print.

But it strikes us that the public will be greatly affected in the final decision by simply looking at the men and deciding which one "feels right," which one offers the greater image of sincerity and whatever undefinable qualities are considered desirable in a President.

And America was looking. As many as 53 percent of all households with television sets tuned in on at least some of the debates. News coverage of them afterward rippled out the impact, magnifying the importance of the forums.

Right or wrong, most of us are preoccupied with the character of the man, not the statistics he recites. Many who watched probably can't remember a word Carter said about inflation or unemployment, or what Ford said about the federal tax system or the Congress. But most of us retain impressions about the candidates: which one looked nervous or flustered; which seemed assured; which appeared the more "presidential."

Some saw Ford as a leader; others saw Carter as the man. Likewise, with Dole and Mondale, there was a basis for judging leadership qualities — the judgment no doubt based more on tone than on statements, but nevertheless helping to clarify opinions.

The television forum was an earnest attempt to remove the middle-man and let the public see for itself. The League of Women Voters and the candidates deserve gratitude for the effort.

Whatever happens on Nov. 2, it seems safe to say that the debates were a major factor — probably one of the biggest — in helping voters make their choices.

The News and Courier

Charleston, S.C., October 27, 1976

When the televised presidential debates first were in prospect, we joined others in endorsing the concept for the potential it held for promoting a better informed electorate. The debates, we said then, could be enlightening, providing voters an opportunity to learn more about the candidates and their thinking on the issues.

As it turned out, the debates weren't as instructive as hoped. The reasons why were several. One had to do with the candidates themselves. The way Gerald Ford and Jimmy Carter reeled off figures and dates showed that both had boned up for the debates. Seldom, however, did either respond precisely to questions from the panels. Their answers were long and looping. Both repeated what they had said over and over in the course of the campaign, but neither was really articulate when it came to positions, policies and programs. The single debate between the vice presidential candidates came much closer to a clear enunciation of what the tickets and the parties stand for and offer.

Then, too, television, despite its unmatched capability of bringing political candidates up close to millions of people, distorts factors on which voter assessments ideally are based. As TV critic Sander Vanocur has noted, it puts a premium on on-camera performance and personality. Those are qualities which can figure into judgments on who would make the better president, but they are not the most important qualities. Popular attention was so fixed on performance — on judging who won and who lost in each debate — that it ignored what little of substance that was said. When the debates were over, Mr. Ford was still plodding, and Mr. Carter still was vague.

Whether the 1976 debates will have even half the impact on the outcome of the election that the 1960 debates had is an open question. As a learning process for voters, they did not measure up to potential. They may have been helpful in that they stimulated some people to think harder about the options the ballot offers in November. Acquisition by the Smithsonian Institution of the stage sets from the three debates says something, though, about what's to be remembered most about the Ford-Carter debates.

TULSA WORLD

Tulsa, Okla., January 19, 1976

HOUSE Speaker CARL ALBERT puts on his partisan hat to complain about the television networks' treatment of Democratic Party speeches, in comparison with their handling of Republican PRESIDENT'S requests for air time.

ALBERT knows better. He has been in politics long enough to understand the distinction between a PRESIDENT'S speech to the nation—even if it has some partisan color—and a purely party approach. But he has armed himself with a Library of Congress study showing the networks favor occupants of the White House.

He concludes that the networks give "rigorous" examination to the Democrats' request for time, but "have exercised little or no news judgment when considering PRESIDENTIAL requests for air time for television addresses."

It's probably true that the tv networks seldom deny a PRESIDENT air time when he asks for it. That is part of the unofficial power of his office—regardless of whether he is a Democrat or Republican. In the same vein, when a PRESIDENT calls a news conference at the White House, reporters flock in. They don't know what he is going to say, but it is always considered news—and may be big-headline news.

The Chairman of the Democratic National Committee can call a news conference without any such impact.

And even the Speaker of the House or the Majority Leader of the Senate, despite their importance in Government, cannot command the attention of the media so completely as can the PRESIDENT.

It is a built-in distinction, and the television networks are never going to disregard a PRESIDENT'S request unless it has an unrelieved political flavor. The reason is that almost everything a PRESIDENT says can be given some partisan interpretation, particularly if he is a candidate. But he is still PRESIDENT —and that allows him maximum leeway.

ALBERT knows this, of course. It is almost as if he feels duty bound to issue his protest from time to time—to make a record, or to remind the networks that they are under official surveillance.

The best thing the Speaker and his conorts can do to equalize the air time is to elect a Democratic PRESIDENT. They're trying to do just that—and if they succeed, we won't hear much from them about the networks unfair treatment of their party.

The Dallas Morning News

Dallas, Texas, January 24, 1976

House Speaker Carl Albert contends that in giving a great amount of TV play to speeches by presidents, but not so much to those of congressional luminaries, the television networks are abdicating their task of exercising news judgment.

It's just too easy for a president to get on the tube, argues the speaker, and it's the networks' fault.

Certainly there is a danger of manipulation if any president overdoes his requests for TV time. But possibly one reason that a televised presidential speech is regarded as more important than a congressman's speech by both the networks and the people is that the former is so much more likely to be carried out by subsequent action.

Though there have been exceptions, Americans have come to believe that when a president takes to the televised speaking stand, something is going to happen, some effort is going to be made, some activity is going to result.

Sad to say, there is no such expectation when congressmen speak. Congressional talk rarely seems to be followed up by effective action.

How many times have we heard empty promises that spending is going to be controlled, inflation is going to be reduced, the energy shortage dealt with and so on and so on? How many bold pledges have we heard that Congress is going to return to a full leadership role, taking initiative, assuming responsibility and directing the course of policy?

Yet the most noteworthy instance of initiative by Congress last year was when it slipped through an automatic pay raise system for itself. And for that maneuver, let us recall, broad media coverage was the last thing leading congressmen wanted.

We'd suggest that Speaker Albert and his legislative colleagues ask themselves: Is the greater attention paid presidential words by newsmen and public due to the networks' abdication of their news judgment responsibility? Or is it due to Congress' abdication of its leadership responsibility?

ST. LOUIS POST-DISPATCH

St. Louis, Mo., January 24, 1976

On the basis of statistics provided in a study done for him by the Congressional Research Service, Speaker Carl Albert of the House of Representatives understandably has complained that the commercial television networks abdicate their news judgment when a president requests air time. The study showed that only once in the last 10 years had CBS, NBC or ABC denied broadcast time to the president in the 45 times he asked for it, whereas the Democratic congressional leadership was given air time only three times out of the 11 times they requested it in the last seven years. Even when President Ford was turned down by CBS and NBC on Oct. 6, 1975, the rejection was not based primarily on news judgment but on the ground that, because Mr. Ford was by then a declared presidential candidate, the networks might have to give equal time to other candidates.

Regardless of whether Mr. Albert is right in his questioning of the networks' news judgment, he is right in deploring the failure of the networks to provide adequate access to spokesmen who oppose the president. The Congressional Research Service study, by citing public opinion polls before and after presidential television addresses, showed that the Chief Executive is able to use television as a powerful instrument to swing popular opinion in favor of his policies. Even if presidential policies are right, they should have to meet the test of winning public support through debate and not merely through manipulation from what has been called the president's "electronic throne."

Because of the imbalance in access to air time, Congress is about to consider a bill to establish a "right of reply" for the congressional opposition. Rather than invite this kind of governmental intrusion into programing (which could impinge on free press rights), the networks would be well advised to voluntarily correct the balance. And Congress itself could provide a remedy, without dictating programing, by simply opening some of its sessions to television coverage.

The Washington Star

Washington, D.C., January 26, 1976

A Library of Congress research report, compiled at the behest of House Speaker Carl Albert, attempts to show that the networks are biased in favor of the President in competition between the White House and Congress for television coverage.

According to the report, and an accompanying statement by Mr. Albert, the networks are patsies for presidential requests for air time while members of Congress usually get a fast shuffle when they put in a bid for special time.

Mere statistics on pre-emptions of air time for presidential addresses, messages and press conferences versus the same for spokesmen for the Democratic congressional majority would indicate Mr. Albert has a point. But statistics are not the only factor in this dispute.

The overriding issue is news value. Network officials seldom turn down a presidential request for air time because a presidential address is almost per se a newsworthy event. The public has a right to be made aware of the thoughts and judgments of the President on matters of national and world importance. He has, after all, been put there to provide leadership and preside over the nation's affairs; he is the single most important official in the free world.

That is not to say that Congress is unimportant. But it is, after all, a collection of 535 House and Senate members, none of whom as individuals can be compared to the President. Moreover, these 535 individuals have opinions and political outlooks that vary. Although the Democrats have a large majority in both houses, members of that party possess widely disparate views.

Senator Edward Kennedy's position on a given issue is highly unlikely, for instance, to tally with that of Senator James Allen of Alabama. Nor, for that matter, are Mr. Albert and the leader of the House Democratic Caucus, Phillip Burton, likely to see eye to eye on all issues; nor Senate Majority Leader Mike Mansfield and his assistant, Senator Robert Byrd.

So it is difficult to present a consensus view of Democratic congressional opinion. Yet the television networks have made attempts to give the party out of the White House a chance to speak its piece. For example, Senator Edmund Muskie, on behalf of the Democrats, last week answered President Ford's State of the Union address. But it is unreasonable to expect congressional Democrats to be given air time every time the President is on.

The argument over presidential access to television is largely political. Democrats on Capitol Hill don't complain when a Democrat is in the White House. Likewise, the Republicans don't complain about it when a Republican is in the White House but do when a Democrat is.

If Congress is serious about increasing its television exposure, it has a ready opportunity. Opening Senate and House floors to the cameras, as the networks have been urging for years, would get congressional speechmakers more TV time than all the complaining about presidential access to the medium.

The Detroit News
Detroit, Mich., February 4, 1977

PRESIDENT CARTER's use of the "fireside chat" technique was one of his better efforts at communicating directly with people, and he would be well advised to build on it.

Unlike the inaugural address, in which Mr. Carter's tendency to swallow his lines and time his pauses badly was manifest, the Wednesday night speech was delivered in the conversational manner that shows the new president at his best. Indeed, the whole performance supplied an important focus for the early agenda of the new administration.

In a sense, it is always a shame to concentrate on the techniques a president employs, rather than what he says and the leadership he offers. The country, however, is still taking the measure of the man in the White House, and his skill as a communicator will be important in determining how well he can lead.

The energy issue is emerging quickly as the standard by which the early Carter years may well be judged. The effects of the stalemate on energy policy are bearing down on us this winter, and Mr. Carter's most important early test will be how well he can lead us through the shortages and the frustrations to assure a society that works. Although it will be April before the full energy program is laid before Congress, the administration seems to be taking hold of this problem with an air of quiet competence.

In fact, the phrase "quiet competence" is one that comes to our minds a good bit as we watch the new president move forward in these early stages. And after the upheavals of the last few years, and some sense of drift on issues such as energy policy, tax reform and welfare reform, it feels good to watch the way he is going about his business.

Oregon Journal
Portland, Ore., February 4, 1977

President Carter's first fireside chat with the American people was important, not so much for what it said, but for what it symbolized.

The value of symbols in the political leadership he has assumed is not lost on the new president.

The fireside chat itself reached back to the Franklin Roosevelt era when FDR talked with his countrymen by radio. The fire and the sweater were obvious reminders of how a person can endure a winter evening with the thermostat set at 65 to conserve energy. The informal setting added further to Carter's determination to move the presidency away from the monarchial airs it has acquired over the years and back to the citizenry.

But perhaps most important of all is the message Carter sent to the people that he is resolved to stay in touch with them and not allow himself to be isolated by his office.

There may be no one way to avoid isolation, and many devices could be tried to stay in communication with the greater public beyond the immediate White House guard. An informal fireside chat is one method, although it is primarily one-way communication from the president to the people to let them know what is on his mind. The one Wednesday night should be just the first of many.

Other tactics will have to be used to turn the flow of communication in the other direction, from the people to the White House. Carter has referred to some of the thoughts he has had along this line, too, such as phone calls around the country, or setting aside a period of time to take phone calls, or opening the White House on occasion to the citizen coming in off the street.

There are methods, and not all will work. But the new president is to be encouraged to try them. Such a casual relationship with his countrymen at large will help the President shape his programs and achieve his goals, such as energy conservation, full employment in a stable economy, a restructured government, clearly worded regulations, welfare overhaul, and mutual trust between people and government — all worthy policies which he ticked off in his first fireside chat with the nation.

Sentinel Star
Orlando, Fla., February 6, 1977

PRESIDENT Carter began his fireside chats with the American people in familiar fashion, a soft-spoken recap of his campaign speeches which left us wondering what he had said, if anything.

Yet the talking picture continues to be the most powerful communication medium ever devised. And the public reaction to these periodic visits into the living room may be far more important than what the President actually tells us while he's on the screen.

The crackling fire, the sweater, the warm words spoken in a numbing three-word drone creates the image of a benign, humble but confident man full of love for God and country and totally dedicated to the leadership role he has won.

Neither an orator of John F. Kennedy's stature nor a spellbinder like Franklin D. Roosevelt, Carter nonetheless uses the talking picture with alarming effectiveness. And his first fireside performance provided some useful hints as to what this country can expect in the years to come.

JIMMY CARTER will attempt to lead us with soft sell of signs and symbols.

Rather than deal specifically with a single topic as Roosevelt did in his fireside chats, Carter chose a rambling dissertation that allowed him to say a little about a lot.

The underlying theme of it all, carefully wrapped in hopeful words and benevolent expressions, was to ask the American people to lower their expectations. Having been in office a couple of weeks, it was time to raise the possibility at least that he might not be able to do all the things he said he would, as quickly as he suggested he might.

For example Carter calmly noted that the economic problem could more easily be solved by public cooperation than by government action. Unsaid was that his initial dose of economic elixir isn't going down too well.

HIS PROPOSED $50 rebate has already been eaten up by increased heating costs due to cold weather. The business tax credits on investment and Social Security payments are being generally viewed as too little to stimulate meaningful expansion. And his $1.1 billion job plan is in so much trouble with organized labor that the Democratic Congress is already trying to double it.

At the same time Carter told America he doesn't have an answer to the energy problem either. Despite all the government involvement in the energy mess in the last five years, Carter's message was simply that Americans must use less energy and be prepared to pay more for it.

This doesn't mean that Carter doesn't have plans and programs. He does. And there's every indication he will try to push them through. But his success will depend on how well he can rally Americans behind his cause.

That's why we will continue to see him involved in the low-key but powerful manipulation of the talking picture to forge this relationship. When he comes to chat he will do so in the interest of building an image. And our task will be to distinguish illusion from reality.

The Philadelphia Inquirer
Philadelphia, Pa., February 4, 1977

It took a little getting used to at first. When the television camera zoomed in for a side view of that man in a sweater sitting casually by the fire in his library, it was hard to believe this was the President about to address the nation from the White House. At first blush, it might have been just another commercial.

Then the camera angle shifted to a head-on view and the man started talking. There was no doubt about it being President Carter — and the more he talked the more we liked both what he said and the way he said it. The fireside format isn't for everyone, but it is made to order for the plain-spoken, down-to-earth Jimmy Carter from Plains, Ga.

His first words were "Good evening" rather than "My friends," but the similarity to the famous fireside chats of President Franklin D. Roosevelt was unmistakable. For FDR, however, the medium was radio. President Carter has the added dimensions of television. For millions of families it was like having President Carter in their own living rooms — for no particular reason except to just sit down and talk a spell, the way friendly neighbors do when they come calling.

As for substance, it didn't quite measure up to the style. There was virtually nothing new or startling in what he had to say — but that is precisely the point of a fireside chat. It is not the proper setting for momentous announcements and we hope it isn't used for such. It is, however, a good way to level with the people on matters of national concern. We believe Mr. Carter did that — and did it well.

He did announce that he had signed the Emergency Natural Gas Act approved by Congress just a few hours earlier. The emergency legislation won't end the gas shortage or meet long-range energy needs, but it will provide temporary price and allocation flexibility to help the nation get through this winter.

For television viewers who had faithfully turned their thermostats down to 65 or lower, President Carter did appear just a bit too comfortable by the fire as he talked about energy problems. He might at least have buttoned up that sweater.

On other matters, the President showed refreshing candor in recalling a number of the campaign promises he had made — something that public officials rarely do after they are elected. He assured the American people he has not forgotten those promises and intends to keep them. For more about that, we will have to stay tuned.

Not the least of the pleasing things about Mr. Carter's chat was its brevity. He talked 25 minutes. The best thing about a good neighbor who comes calling is knowing when to leave.

Fireside chats should not be a substitute for frequent news conferences and periodic reports to Congress — and apparently are not intended to be — but they can be a useful part of presidential communication with the people. We hope President Carter keeps them up — and keeps them short.

THE ARIZONA REPUBLIC
Phoenix, Ariz., February 4, 1977

Reviews of President Carter's first "fireside chat" will not be kind. Not that Mr. Carter didn't mean well.

But, for content, his 30-minute radio-TV talk was nothing more than an updated and re-worked campaign speech.

He called at least three times for "sacrifice." He promised an energy policy. He believes people are better off working than collecting welfare. Etc.

It was mostly more of Mr. Carter's dependence on symbolism, rather than substance — the easy-going President sitting before a crackling fire, wearing a sweater instead of a pin-stripe suit.

If Mr. Carter asks the networks to cancel regular programming for another chat with the American people, he had better come up with something more stirring.

Pittsburgh Post-Gazette
Pittsburgh, Pa., February 4, 1977

IT WAS a portrait worthy of the brush of Norman Rockwell. Beside a cozy fire in the White House library sat President Carter, legs crossed, wearing a yellow sweater, blue shirt and red tie. But for the absence of slippers, a pipe and a dog, the scene might have been set by Hollywood. But the boys from Peachtree Street do their own image building and they haven't done badly, as Gerald Ford could testify.

Aside from its visual effects, the President's first "fireside chat," a term taken from the radio performances of Franklin D. Roosevelt, was impressive. He remained wholly in character—low-key, informal and apparently sincere. The substance of his message offered little that is new. It simply reiterated and emphasized promises made earlier.

In calling for personal sacrifices in dealing with an ailing economy, Mr. Carter went to the roots of our problems, including the energy crisis. For too long we have been incredibly wasteful of finite resources and now our sins have overtaken us.

It is one thing to preach sacrifice and another to practice it. Sacrifice is usually something for the other fellow to make. But the President wisely attempts to set an example. He promised to reduce the White House staff by about a third. He has ordered an end to ostentatious and unnecessary use of limousines by White House staff and he has asked Cabinet officers to apply the same rules to their departments. In doing this, the President recognizes that if the American people are expected to sacrifice, they should see an example of thrift in their bloated government.

The President is to be commended for his desire to give occasional personal accountings to the people. Instead of having to be reminded by others of his campaign pledges, he is recalling them himself and telling us what he is doing or proposes to do about them.

That is good politics. In taking them into his confidence, he brings the people closer to their government, for too long in bad odor.

It is possible for Mr. Carter to sit beside the fire too often. Every political leader runs the risk of overexposure. The President made a good start Wednesday evening, however, and so long as he has something worthwhile to say and says it with his accustomed candor and humility, he shouldn't wear out his welcome at our firesides.

Arkansas Gazette.
Little Rock, Ark., February 4, 1977

In trying to be jus' folks on the biggest stage of all, President Carter succeeded quite well, with his first "fireside chat." It was a low-key performance—bland, one might say—but it carried some reassurances which the country needs and made some emphases which lend encouragement. If it did not stir the blood with Rooseveltian eloquence, at least there was a measure of simple warmth in it, and renewal of the promise that the isolation of the White House from the people has ended.

Indeed Mr. Carter, in his unprecedented presidential sweater, gave us a view of informality we've never seen before in that building. As a craftsman of media symbolism, he's setting out to form an image of the "common" presidency—accessible, visible, folksy, in almost continuous communication with the populace. Some observers suspect this will not work as well as he hopes, that he'll bore the public before long, and that the presidency has to keep a certain dignified distance to maintain respect, to preserve a mystique of superior wisdom. But we welcome Mr. Carter's brash experiment of a highly communicative presidency, without airs, and he may very well prove the skeptics wrong, as he did in getting elected in the first place.

Of course the political motivation in this has to be recognized as well: Not only accessibility but power is in the cards. He's starting at once to keep his line open direct to the public, which is to say, over the heads of both Congress and any opposition which may be out there, Republican or otherwise. Congress in effect has been served early notice that it's dealing with a man who operates on the whole scale of public opinion, not merely in the give-and-take of compromise and inside barter between the powers on Capitol Hill and the power in the White House. There is ever so gentle a warning that the new chief executive will "go public" with his demands if Congress denies him his way. And the unmistakable evidence that Congress heard this was its hurried passage of his emergency natural gas bill, so that he could sign the measure into law just before the TV appearance.

Such a public presidency can make for either progress or fractious difficulty, depending on what vision of dominance Mr. Carter may have, and how well he oils the frictions with Congress which may develop. He has started, in this first appearance, on a befitting tone of modesty, coupled with firmness, which we hope will continue. He is being very careful, while calling for public sacrifices, not to inflate the public's expectations, and this can be all to the good if his view of what *should* be attained proves high enough when he gets down to all the particulars.

★   ★   ★

In any case, a country which had fallen upon such agonizing energy and employment troubles in two week's time certainly deserved to hear from its President. As to both admonitions and proposed remedies, his words were mostly laudable, though the test will be in the specifics of remedy which are yet to come. There was encouragement in his primary emphasis on stricter energy conservation, and the prominent mention of solar power development, not far behind the better use of coal and, in the sequence of his talk at least, ahead of nuclear power. And his pledge of greater attention to safety in any expansion of the latter was most welcome. Most importantly, though, he has set a firm timetable of 90 days for creation of his legislative program to get at the long-range energy problems, so we'll know the measure of it before long. In the meantime, conservation needs to become a national passion.

Of course the economic blows of this cruel winter are also testing the new administration severely in its first three weeks. The stunning energy-shortage unemployment and the drain on households of swelling fuel bills call for some alterations in Mr. Carter's economic recovery program. These unexpected factors also will require higher social outlays later on, especially to provide direct employment. And while income-tax rebates are a proper part of his stimulative package, as a spur to production, he ought to curb any notion of sizable permanent tax cuts, lest the government come up far short of the revenue it needs for the effective and humane programs which now are called for, in public-service jobs, health, aid to the poor and other areas.

Anyway, the fireside chat, as this first one was conducted, is a fitting part of the exercise of leadership, and we refuse to denigrate it because Jimmy Carter didn't match the lofty eloquence of Franklin D. Roosevelt, his model in this technique. Though much of it was simply a restatement of campaign positions, he was talking common sense for the most part, which is more comforting these days when not embellished with grandiloquence, which the public has come to equate with hokum.

EVEN BEFORE Jimmy Carter took the oath as the nation's Chief Executive, Rep. John J. Rhodes (R-Ariz.), the minority leader in the House of Representatives, was petitioning the three television networks for equal time under the Federal Communications Act's "fairness doctrine."

Representative Rhodes has taken to heart Mr. Carter's suggestion that, in the tradition of Franklin D. Roosevelt, he may resort to the fireside chat as a means of acquainting the American people with his views and legislative recommendations. The first was Wednesday night.

THE CINCINNATI ENQUIRER
Cincinnati, Ohio, February 5, 1977

If there are to be frequent fireside chats in the future, the Arizona lawmaker believes, Republican spokesmen ought to have an equal opportunity to be heard.

The Rhodes appeal, it seems to us, is strengthened by a combination of circumstances. For one thing, the nation has entrusted both the executive and the legislative branches to Democratic control for the first time in eight years. For another, the margins of Democratic control of Congress are reminiscent of those that prevailed in the early days of the New Deal. For yet another, Senate Democrats are already at work in an effort to

undermine the filibuster, one of the traditional devices by which the minority managed to focus public attention on its views.

There is an element of risk to the country and to the Carter administration as well in having the policy-making skids so well greased —a risk that would be offset in part by a widening of the public debate on the major issues before Congress.

Mr. Carter certainly has a right to speak directly to the American people through revived fireside chats.

But the opposition party surely must have the right to comparable access.

Portland Press Herald
Portland, Me., February 4, 1977

President Carter's initial fireside chat went rather well largely because it was nothing more than that—a fireside chat.

It was an informal, neighborly, pleasant little get-together that stirred little controversy because it offered little that was new or specific.

The platitudes were plentiful. Mr. Carter said he had learned in two weeks that "there are many things a president cannot do" by quick, easy action.

Obviously, he knew that long before he moved into the White House.

"If we are a united nation, then I can be a good

president. But I will need your help to do it," he said.

Mr. Carter can be a good president and, like all presidents, he needs the help of the people. But after two weeks in office he should also realize that he may be enjoying greater unity right now than he will at any other time in the coming four years.

The fireside chat, as President Roosevelt demonstrated, is more image builder than anything else. Whether this generation of Americans will respond to that approach as did the people of the Roosevelt era remains to be seen.

THE SUN
Baltimore, Md., February 4, 1977

Mr. Carter's chat with the American people Wednesday night was longer on personality than on hard substance. There were a few nuggets of new presidential information. There was a long defense of the Carter economic stimulus package and an exhortatory discussion of the energy crisis. But for the most part, the talk was an effort to establish and convey an administration tone and style markedly different from anything that has gone before. By the fireside, legs casually crossed, sat our cardiganed President discussing a wide range of subjects in flat, unemotional, conversational tones. The new, non-imperial President was having a heart-to-heart with those who elected him.

Running throughout the talk was the theme of shared faith, co-operation and sacrifice by all Americans, along with a dose of presidential humility. Fully a score of times Mr. Carter mentioned Congress, always in flattering terms, speaking, for example, of "Congress and the administration as partners in leadership." Here was an effort to preserve and prolong the honeymoon with Capitol Hill, a honeymoon already frazzled by the Sorensen debacle, congressional leaders' pique over administration failure to consult and the continuing criticism of the economic stimulus package. Here also was an attempt to replace the White House-Congress stalemate of the Nixon-Ford years with the hoped-for productivity of the Carter years.

It should be remembered, however, that the President Carter who now speaks at length of shared leadership and consultation with Congress is the Candidate Carter who made clear his belief in a strong presidency. Months before his nomination he was telling reporters he would use fireside chats to build up the kind of popular backing he would need to insure the success of his programs on Capitol Hill.

Mr. Carter's first by-the-fire chat marks a further refinement in the presidential use of the electronic media that began with Warren G. Harding and was developed into a fine art by Franklin D. Roosevelt. What Mr. Roosevelt achieved by radio, Mr. Carter obviously is attempting through the more compelling device of television. The new President showed a good command of the eye-to-eye, one-to-one relationship that TV offers. His first fireside chat was a sort of let's-get-better acquainted visit, with frequent use of the second-person singular in addressing his audience, bringing issues down to a very personal "you" level. This worked well when Mr. Carter's only purpose was to make himself better and more intimately known. Yet to be shown is how well he will do as he sits by the fire to drum up a floodtide of national support when very tough decisions are at hand or a balky Congress has to be brought into line.

BUFFALO EVENING NEWS
Buffalo, N.Y., February 4, 1977

An impressive performance, all in all. That is our reaction to President Carter's first televised chat with the American people from a White House fireside. The informal setting and the calm, friendly tone of Wednesday night's appearance refreshingly avoided the tense government-by-crisis atmosphere that has afflicted so many past White House addresses in the television era.

We disagree, to be sure, with the President's description of the substance of some of his programs, particularly his praise of the economic proposal he has put before Congress as "the best-balanced plan we can produce for the overall economic health of the nation."

The economic package has been carefully concocted, all right. But the fairest, surest way to stimulate the economy is not, in our view, through a combination of one-shot $50 rebates for all and permanent reductions tailored strictly to the lower brackets and omitting entirely the millions of taxpaying families with combined incomes over $17,500 a year. The better alternative to both these gimmicks surely is to reduce everyone's tax liability in the same proportion — giving this an immediate economic stimulus effect by lowering weekly withholding rates.

For all of this, though, President Carter in this chat was most helpful and reassuring in the way he sorted out priorities and got down to specifics.

Nor would we quarrel with what seem to be his top three priorities for orderly action early this year: First, stimulating the economy, which will take prompt and considered congressional action; second and meanwhile, reorganizing the federal bureaucracy, which will take prompt enabling legislation followed by sweeping executive action and ending with point-by-point congressional acquies-

cence or veto; and third, the immediate drafting of a comprehensive national energy policy.

Somewhat less urgent at the moment, he indicated, were welfare and tax reform, although both will be confronted this year. Much further down the list, obviously, is a national health insurance plan, which he supported during the campaign but didn't mention Wednesday. But he rightly did give a higher priority to straightening out the troubled medicaid program; obviously, this nation is not ready to take on such a massive new medical-care delivery commitment as that for national health insurance until it can better prevent all the abuses and rip-offs which are making such a shambles of the much more modest existing programs of medicaid.

Just as the President indicated a kind of general order in which he hoped to deal with national problems, so he also forthrightly put due dates on when the public could expect more concrete decisions in the future: April 20 for submission of a national energy policy to Congress, a first draft of welfare-reform plans "within 90 days," a tax-reform plan "before the end of this year."

That's a healthy sign, as were his recognition of the limits of any president's power and his reiteration of efforts to slim down staff sizes and kingly perquisites, which have already become a kind of popular Carter trademark nicely punctuated by his sweatered informality.

In all of this, as with his expressed hope to be able to use a growing sense of national unity to surmount the energy crisis, particularly through a conservation that will require certain sacrifices, President Carter calmly touched the right bases in a candid, sensible way.

WINSTON-SALEM JOURNAL
Winston-Salem, N.C., February 4, 1977

The hard news was skimpy, but the performance effective nonetheless: President Carter, fulfilling one of his campaign promises, spoke to the nation Wednesday night in the first of his "fireside chats." He looked and acted relaxed, dressed informally, and actually sat beside a fire. In the comfortable atmosphere of the White House library, he talked comfortably about the energy crisis and a number of other issues. Despite the teleprompter, despite the studied nonchalance, Carter came across with the small-group sincerity that served him so well during the campaign.

Of course, the timing of the first fireside chat helped. Carter has been in office just two weeks, hardly long enough to arouse violent opposition to his administration. Had he attempted to begin his talks a year or two from now, Carter could not have gotten away with the broad-brush comments and generalized exhortations that comprised most of Wednesday's effort. The "honeymoon" period enjoyed by every president is still in effect for Carter, and he was wise in using it to backstop his remarks.

When that period ends — and it will end soon enough — the fireside chats will more closely resemble adversary proceedings. The most important subject Carter had to deal with on Wednesday was the energy crisis, which is not yet a political hot potato. There is bipartisan teeth-chattering around the country, and thus bipartisan agreement that something must be done. Fierce arguments about how that something should be accomplished may develop eventually, but that time has not arrived. When it does, and when other controversies over Carter's administration take shape, the fireside chats will become more specific and more politically one-sided. The Republican party will no doubt respond — and rightly so — with their own chats, and the aura of goodwill that pervaded Carter's Wednesday performance will fade in his future efforts. Certainly the original fireside chats — Franklin Roosevelt's radio broadcasts of a generation ago — were not universally well received, because the man and his policies were not universally well liked.

No matter, for the moment. Carter has reestablished a useful technique for presidents to communicate with the nation. One remembers, despairingly, the countless televised addresses by Lyndon Johnson on the Vietnam War, and those by Richard Nixon on Vietnam and Watergate. Such speeches were agonizing to watch, in terms of both content and conduct. It is refreshing to again be able to watch a president talk on non-divisive issues in a non-divisive manner. If he can maintain the positive approach he demonstrated on Wednesday, even as the issues harden and opposition mounts, then Carter can use the fireside chats not just to his personal advantage, but to the nation's advantage as well.

The Virginian-Pilot
Norfolk, Va., February 4, 1977

President Carter's opening fireside chat—if he doesn't like the term, as press secretary Jody Powell has said is the case, why did he speak from a White House fireside?—was more important for what it portends than for what it amounted to. It established a line of communication from the White House to the American people. Mr. Carter is likely to find good use for the line from time to time. He hooked it up Wednesday night to congratulate Congress for its quick passage of his Emergency Natural Gas Act, which he had just signed, as well as to renew some campaign pledges, rephrase a few Inaugural pronouncements, and admonish us to love one another and work together. But let us wait.

The Carter version of the fireside chat demands comparison to the original—to those that President Franklin D. Roosevelt delivered by radio during the Depression and World War II, the first of them on Sunday evening, March 12, 1933, just eight days after his assumption of office. "Those radio 'visits' by the President of the United States into the American living room were a triumph of the dramatic art that no other public figure has ever matched," wrote Cabell Phillips in "From the Crash to the Blitz: 1929-1939," a continuation of Mark Sullivan's celebrated "Our Times" series, which left off at the mid-Twenties. The Phillips book appeared in 1969. Mr. Roosevelt's dramatic-art record among public figures remains secure.

So deftly done were those long-ago chats, Mr. Phillips continued, "so subtle were the histrionics and so free of pretensions or obvious guile, that one could feel the presence of Roosevelt as one listened to his words. In this first fireside chat he spoke as a wise friend speaks to his neighbors, telling them in simple, believable words why their banks were closed and what was being done to get them open again. He did not patronize his listeners with platitudes and false promises. The banking system was truly in a bad way, he said, and some people were going to be hurt before the damage could be repaired. But there would be fewer victims now than if the crisis were allowed to run its course, and when the banks would reopen in a few days they would be stronger than before.

"It was a masterful performance. It helped to restore the people's confidence and built a bridge of intimacy between them and the President. . . ."

Cold weather and a lack of fuel, not hard times and a money shortage, moved President Carter to counsel courage and forbearance. He wore a sweater, and of course much has been made by the commentators of that un-Presidential-like garment. It is possible, though, that F.D.R. wore a smoking jacket or dressing gown; his audience could not see him and his trappings, including the old-fashioned that supposedly he placed near the microphone for easy sipping and certain inspiration. An inclination toward informality links the Plains deacon and the Hyde Park squire. Style separates them.

But if Jimmy Carter did not meet Franklin D. Roosevelt's standard of broadcast theater, after his fashion he did quite well. Precision distinguishes his speaking. He wastes no words. He has not acquired authority but he has established sincerity. And, with his stress on humility, he seems likely to escape the arrogance that in time eroded Mr. Roosevelt's assurances.

In any event, Mr. Carter's first fireside chat was pleasant and instructive. The occasion is likely to come when he will visit in our living rooms not to praise Congress but to challenge, goad, and pressure it. For that let us wait.

The San Diego Union
San Diego, Cal., February 4, 1977

Sizing up President Carter's first "fireside chat" may depend on what one was expecting.

Those old enough to remember Franklin D. Roosevelt's intimate radio addresses — the original fireside chats — are probably disappointed. Jimmy Carter is no FDR in front of a microphone. But who is? No President since FDR has been able to make the sound of his voice so winning.

It's unfair, perhaps, to make such a comparison, although Mr. Carter invited it when he decided to speak on television from a chair in front of the fireplace in the White House library.

The casual and informal style Mr. Carter tried to bring to the occasion was flawed. His rather rapid, nervous monotone did not exude as much warmth as might have been intended by the cozy setting. We'll chalk that up to inexperience and the demands of technology. This was the new President's first attempt at this kind of communication with the public. And could FDR have been as charming if he were following a teleprompter and trying to keep eye contact with a camera lens?

The important thing is what Mr. Carter was trying to convey to us, what he was trying to accomplish. The talk itself was a summary of the principal goals he has before him at this early point in his Administration. In that respect it contained many echoes of his campaign speeches, though delivered with the confidence that comes from speaking from the White House.

Aside from the special emphasis on energy problems which the current fuel crisis justifies, and the specific details of his economic program, the talk did not add much to what we already know about Mr. Carter's aspirations.

The need for conservation and sacrifice to stop wasting energy has been stated before by practically everyone, and exactly what the President expects of us remains to be found in his energy program promised by April 20. As for the economy, Mr. Carter recapped the benefits of his tax and employment proposals, but dismissed with only a few reassuring words the heart of the controversy in Congress — whether his program will really produce the inflation-free economic growth he envisions.

Will Rogers remarked after a Roosevelt fireside chat that FDR had explained banking in such simple terms that "even bankers understood it." Perhaps Mr. Carter will tackle the justification for his economics in a later report.

Just as FDR used radio, a President today can use television to appeal directly to the people for support, especially when he wants a reluctant Congress to follow his lead. It's too soon to say how often Mr. Carter will need to go over the head of Congress to arouse a show of public support for endangered legislation. When he does, we think he will have to come on stronger than he did Wednesday night.

With his frequent use of the pronouns "we" and "us" the President sought to establish a bond with his audience. He spoke with candor and humility of the role he sees for himself as a leader. It was a decidedly low-key appeal for unity, cooperation and understanding. We're left with the feeling, however, that it will take a more forceful and persuasive tone of leadership to achieve some of the ambitious goals he reviewed in his first report from the White House fireside.

The Boston Globe
Boston, Mass., April 18, 1977

Jimmy Carter is leading the television industry around by the nose, dominating the networks with an ease beyond the dreams of more ordinary politicians. The President is getting away with it not because he is whipping news departments into line. He is using no muscle at all. What he is using is his own knowledge of the media. He knows how to make an offer, the networks can't refuse, even when they should.

A case in point was NBC's decision to build a show around a day in the Carter White House.

A camera crew was given an unprecedented opportunity to witness history in the making: to watch an actual cabinet meeting unfold, to hear the national security adviser's briefing, to stand by as President Sadat of Egypt called on the White House, to eavesdrop at that precious moment when Carter asked his distinguished guest if he cared to visit the restroom.

The only condition imposed was that the President could order the cameras from the room whenever he wanted to or whenever the conversation became too sensitive. There was no record of what Carter and Sadat actually said to each other after the initial pleasantries were exchanged, no record of what Brzezinski said once the briefing was under way. The President thus maintained control — at all times — over what NBC recorded.

NBC, of course, had the editing rights over a those moments its cameras did record. The problem was that the real editing was done before their cameras even arrived. It was done when the White House drew up the President's agenda for John Chancellor Day at the White House.

Carter was able to smile his way through his schedule, listening to Grieg, lunching with Mondale, joking with his cabinet, conferring with a congressional delegation on sugar quotas, discussing a trivial aspect of his congressional relations with political advisers. There would be no surprises from NBC.

At only one point did the light of inner bliss depart from Carter's eyes. That was when Jody Powell informed him of an apparently unfounded attempt by a little-known columnist to link his son Chip to a supposed scandal in Georgia state government. The warmth vanished from Carter's eyes. Suddenly, they became an icy blue. It was perhaps the most revealing moment of the entire show.

The rest was pure public relations, devoid of controversy and light, embarrassingly devoid of substance.

Such a show could be dismissed as mere entertainment were it not for the timing. Chancellor's show signaled the start of what is to be a Carter television blitz that will have a significant, if not telling, bearing on the success of Carter's energy program.

A news conference followed yesterday. Another is scheduled for Thursday. There will be an address to the Congress Wednesday and Monday a fireside chat — all in prime time. When the blitz is over it would not be surprising if Carter's popularity remains abnormally high despite the deeply controversial nature of his proposals. Television has all too readily acquiesced in the construction of that popularity.

It was ironic that Chancellor in an attempt to add a touch of criticism asked the President whether that popularity was the result of accomplishment or the deft use of symbolism. Carter handled the question without breaking stride. Perhaps he recognized it was a question the television industry had better ask itself.

THE SAGINAW NEWS
Saginaw, Mich., February 7, 1977

There was nothing original about it, little of great news value and only one thing startling to some when President Carter took to television last week for a fireside talk to the nation.

For those of us of enough age, it revived memories of Franklin D. Roosevelt's fireside chats carried by radio back in the 1930s.

But let us say at the outset we appreciated the warmth and easy informality of Mr. Carter's chat. And no marks at all against the beige cardigan sweater worn by the President. It was, after all, in the style of the man we know we elected to the White House. And certainly appropriate garb considering much of the subject of his talk — and where the White House thermostat is set these days of energy shortage.

Beyond that, what mattered as much as what the President said, was his presence. Here again was Jimmy Carter quickly making good on another campaign promise — to stay in touch with the people, to speak candidly of mutual problems, to invite public input and certainly to move away from any image of the imperial presidency.

Not everybody appreciated this performance, to be sure.

We did. And for pretty uncomplex reasons. We found Mr. Carter reassuring as he discussed again his agenda for making his administration and our government more responsive to the public's concerns and more accountable for their actions.

The overriding message was that the Carter administration, at least, isn't going to be above the people, but part of the people. There were no grand promises. Even some acknowledgment that some things weren't going to be easily done. And that some mistakes might even be made. But no mistakes buried.

Mr. Carter brought a spark of quiet determination to his talk and without pomposity.

There is, of course, palpable political gain to be drawn from these televised fireside chats — Carter style, 1977.

Yet we believe the public will appreciate being taken into confidence so long as it perceives it to be straight talk, particularly when there is nothing to sell. And so long as Mr. Carter also keeps his promise to speak frankly of the errors along with the efforts and the successes.

The Providence Journal
Providence, R.I., February 4, 1977

With exercises in symbolism such as the artful fireside talk to the nation Wednesday night, President Carter has embarked on something of a high-risk approach to his new job.

He may succeed in projecting his presidency in gentle, muted tones, with his appealing invitation for Americans to join in a spirit of national unity. Given too much of this low-key strategy, however, many Americans will begin to ask what the Carter administration is all about. If he should confuse substance with style, Mr. Carter may find himself losing headway before he's fairly begun.

In terms of substance, the President's first two weeks have been fairly impressive. He moved quickly to cope with the natural gas emergency; he opened discussions with the Soviet Union; he sent Vice President Mondale on a useful get-acquainted trip to meet allied leaders; and he symbolically trimmed back on White House staff, limousines and other attributes of a swollen presidency.

With these actions duly publicized, Mr. Carter hardly needed to go to the country with what essentially was little more than a replay of his now-familiar campaign pledges. Too many of these folksy talks, given at a time of no compelling national crisis, could exhaust Mr. Carter's political capital and bore the country to death.

The nation likes plain talk from its presidents, and Mr. Carter is going to great lengths to convey a plain-spoken tone for his administration. Plain talk does not mean platitudes, however, and Mr. Carter's repeated gauzy phrases about presidential modesty and national unity may wear thin in short order. Most Americans, it may be said, want a strong and effective president; but they do not want a preacher in the White House and they do not want presidents to talk down to them.

As Mr. Carter digs into the hard problems ahead, he may shed some of his political evangelism and go to the country only in some especially acute crisis, or if Congress is thwarting him and he needs a show of grass-roots support. He is still learning, after all, and some shakedown excesses can be overlooked.

Too much television exposure (to say nothing of those planned open-line telephone chats, as if the President were some local radio talk-show host) will stir some feelings that our new leader is going overboard with his public-relations efforts. There probably is nothing wrong with a president's wearing a cardigan sweater while he talks to the nation, and after he urged lowered thermostats the sweater even had a quaint sort of charm. Yet to some viewers it seemed a needlessly contrived bit of stage-managed artifice, and the country hardly needs government by gimmickry.

Some of Mr. Carter's basic judgments and priorities so far are commendable, and he can reap a harvest of public support with TV appearances — provided he has something specific to say and doesn't indulge in Oval Office overkill. His scaled-down view of the presidency, his serious invocation of a new spirit of national sharing and even sacrifice, and his sense of generally lowered expectations — all these qualities respond to the national mood. But Americans are looking for leadership, not showmanship, and one of Mr. Carter's jobs will be to learn the difference.

Chicago Tribune
Chicago, Ill., February 4, 1977

President Carter's first televised "fireside chat" [the 45-year-old label seems destined to stick] leaned more toward informality than information. To skeptical viewers, there was more than a hint of corn in his studiedly casual presentation, and, that sweater was a little too folksy to be real. Mr. Carter's campaign goals, it is clear, are still goals; they have not come perceptibly closer since his inauguration.

Mr. Carter's talk, in fact, might be dismissed as mere public relations, except that in the circumstances public relations is anything but mere. On the contrary, it may be the most important part of his job during the first few months of his administration.

A pressing need for this country right now is a new working relationship between public and government; a clearer mutual understanding of the responsibilities of each and the way they should interact. The American people need to define to our own satisfaction just what a President is—whether he is primarily a commander-in-chief, or a representative whose task is to carry out the popular will.

Mr. Carter's talk Wednesday, like previous ones, showed that he leans more toward the second interpretation than the first. Questions of style aside, we think he is leaning in the right direction, and can count on strong public approval for it.

Throughout his 25-minute overview of national problems and goals, Mr. Carter kept sounding his keynote: Government must have less control over the national life, the people must have more. Government must become more responsive, more open, and [perhaps most of all] smaller. This may not please people who voted for Mr. Carter on the campaign assurance that a Carter administration could solve our problems. Nor will the shift be painless; particularly in meeting the energy crisis, it will mean sacrifice on our part.

These parts of Mr. Carter's talk illustrated the theme:

● The place to start cutting back government is at the top. The President therefore is reducing the White House staff by one-third and requesting cabinet members to do the same with their staffs. A ceiling will be put on the number of people employed by federal agencies.

● "The energy shortage is permanent." It will not be solved by government orders or technological wizardry; it is up to the American people to meet it by learning to waste less energy.

● The deadening tide of government regulation will be pushed back. New federal rules must be examined and cleared by department heads; they must be written in understandable English [a historic breakthrough, if it happens]; and each new regulation will bear the name of its author.

● Viet Nam veterans will have priority in job training programs. [That is not only fair in itself, but is politically skillful; Mr. Carter needs to offset the bitter criticisms over his pardon of draft evaders.]

The common ground of all these proposals is to change the nature of federal government and the way it is perceived —to make it less of a monolithic, faceless controller of lives, more of an organization made up of men and women who judge, react, and even talk like standard human beings.

We have severe doubts over some of Mr. Carter's proposals—for example, his income-tax rebate. But what seems to be his main goal—reducing government to human scale, making it genuinely a representative of the people—seems to us beyond criticism. If his down-home style somehow helps to bring that about, it's fine with us.

The Boston Globe
Boston, Mass., July 22, 1978

Television has moved beyond the days when the good guys always wore white hats and rode distinctive horses, but it is still a medium that's most effective when characters are clearly drawn and the plot crisp and easy to follow. President Carter held his prime-time press conference debut Thursday night with neither his persona nor his policies in clear focus. And it showed.

The timing of this broadcast, a pilot for a series of evening news conferences aimed at drawing the widest possible viewing audience, could hardly have been worse. A trusted adviser, Dr. Peter Bourne, had been forced to resign earlier in the day because of the clearly improper prescription of a drug for an aide using a fictitious name. So the President opened his performance with a brief, somewhat obscure recapitulation of the affair and a statement that he wouldn't answer any questions about it. Hardly an upbeat, attention-grabbing beginning.

Yet, in a way, it was the dramatic highlight of the conference. Throughout, Carter's delivery was uncharacteristically halting, not at all typical of the presentations he has repeatedly made during daytime press conferences. And it wasn't just the delivery. The content itself portrayed a somewhat halting series of Administration policies and perspectives.

The Soviet Union's treatment of dissidents was unacceptable, yet the Administration response had been "very moderate." Proposed congressional changes in capital gains taxation would violate some of the "principles" of the Administration's tax-reform efforts, yet no veto was threatened directly. Ambassador Young's statements on US political prisoners were "unfortunate", yet "he's opened up new areas of communication and mutual trust." National health insurance principles will soon be enunciated, but a program cannot now be enacted.

When they are sufficiently elaborated to take into account the nuances of international diplomacy and domestic political realities, each of these Carter positions is fully defensible, for all their semming ambiguity.

Yet television is not a medium of nuances and ambiguities. Time restraints limit what a person on television can say. Living room interruptions limit what those viewing can hear and see. As a result, television sharpens contrasts while converting complexities into a grey blur. For a President seeking to demonstrate assured leadership in an unsure time, prime-time television may not be the path to high ratings.

The Detroit News
Detroit, Mich., July 23, 1978

It turns out the President is just as predictable in prime time as he is in soap opera time on the tube.

He's not planning any "vendetta" against the Soviet Union — something we already knew. He said Andrew Young's recent comments about the existence of "political prisoners" in the United States were "unfortunate" — which is about what he had said before — but praised the UN ambassador as a "very valuable asset to our country." And he repeated his threat to veto a tax bill proposing a capital gains tax cut that does not meet his criteria of simplification and fairness.

So, in effect, the President used his press conference, as other presidents have done before him, to lobby for his points of view rather than to provide much new information or even background for White House reporters.

But by doing so in prime time rather than in the afternoon soap opera periods in which he usually holds his press conferences, he presumably won a larger audience than usual. However, the returns are not yet in on whether his performance will provide him with political dividends by reversing his downward trend in the public opinion polls.

Whatever the public reaction, we think the President missed several opportunities to strengthen his positions on controversial issues.

Mr. Carter did reiterate the national commitment to the enhancement of human rights around the world but he weakened his case by also emphasizing his hope for better relationships with the Soviet Union without citing greater Soviet consideration for human rights as a precondition to such improvement. He could have even warned the Soviet Union that detente cannot be preserved by oppression.

His contradictory comments no doubt could be explained on the grounds he was speaking in the first instance to the American public and in the second to the Soviet Union but the net effect was to cloud his policy toward both human rights and the USSR.

The President did make clear his disagreement with Young, said he didn't think the ambassador would make the same mistake again but then said he had no plans to require prior approval of Young's remarks in the future.

Even though Young's "political prisoners" comment marked only one of a number of occasions on which the ambassador has embarrassed the President and the U.S. government, the President's rebuke was so soft and so qualified by his own praise for his UN envoy that it will do little to still Young's critics in Congress or the public.

In lobbying against the capital gains tax cut, the President missed an opportunity to explain that the administration now is willing to accept a compromise that would benefit chiefly homeowners and investors in risky enterprises.

An assistant treasury secretary, Donald Lubick, had told the House Ways and Means Committee prior to the press conference that such a compromise would be "much more preferable" than the rival capital gains tax plans by Reps. William Steiger, R-Wis., and James Jones, D-Okla., which the White House claims would benefit chiefly millionaires.

In this case the President seemed to be defending a position that his administration already had abandoned. And he lost the chance to gain goodwill from those homeowners who will benefit from the new proposal. Tax experts and congressmen seem to agree some cut in the capital gains tax will be approved by Congress despite Mr. Carter's continuing attack on it.

While this newspaper continues to be critical of many of Mr. Carter's actions and statements, we do give him high marks for his willingness to appear regularly before the press — the Thursday night conference was his 35th since he took office — and we continue to hope his performance and his public support will improve.

After all, he is President of all the people and will remain so for at least two and a half more years.

ARKANSAS DEMOCRAT

Little Rock, Ark., May 11, 1977

Was President Carter acting out an image-building charade during his first hundred days in office? Maybe. A pre-inauguaral memo covering a lot of things he has done makes it likely. But it's funny that some people think it makes Mr. Carter a phony — and it's even funnier that Sen. George McGovern should be leading the critical chorus.

McGovern has a bone to pick. In accusing Mr. Carter of empty symbolism, he's exploiting the shock brought on by the memo to underline his complaint that the new president has abandoned or postponed his promised liberal social programs.

That's as may be, but McGovern shouldn't be complaining of the Carter image-building. After all, the senator invented the new way of running for president that Mr. Carter — as another nobody from nowhere — improved on so stunningly. The soul of the new technique is to exploit an "outsider" status on national TV. McGovern's 1972 successes helped make him spokesman for the ADA today. Is it any wonder that Mr. Carter is continuing in the White House what he found to be so useful in the 1976 primaries?

But has it all been a charade, the 100 days — a performance based on a set script furnished him by his pollster Patrick Caddell? Were those apparently natural performances — visiting the homes of the humble, conducting fireside chats and quizzes, cutting White House frills, even appealing dramtically for new approaches to welfare and energy, all the product of Caddell's brain?

Well, most of these things are down in the 51-page memo written last December, but some were also in the Carter list of campaign pledges — and if there hadn't been a Caddell, would the 100-days performance been much different? Not if what we have seen of the Carter style has any meaning.

What he has done has mirrored the man we met in the primaries. As for the 100 days, what would have served the new president better during the months he was finding his presidential feet and seeking congressional support for his programs than to build on the old homey approach to the electorate?

And if we're a little more skeptical now of the Carter smile and style, there's no reason to think, as McGovern does, that the man is all image or that he has suddenly changed from liberal to conservative.

Conservatives might well hope he has done so but the odds are against it. Social programs lie at the heart of the Carter presidency. And if an uncertain economy and lack of revenues have pushed their enactment back, the delay hardly amounts to the betrayal of   principle of which McGovern accuses Carter. The new president is in fact, keeping these programs — welfare reform, national health insurance, election-day registration — to the forefront, even though action will have to wait.

. Conservatives, meanwhile, can take some heart from Mr. Carter's evident toughness on defense and security, his unwillingness to pillory the FBI and the CIA and his disinclination to go hog-wild on federal make-work schemes. He has promised to balance the budget, too. If this also is image-making, it is not a kind that conservatives will complain of — regardless of what the new President does to please the McGoverns.

The Washington Star
and Daily News

Washington, D.C., May 5, 1977

The reliance of Presidents on the clever devices of polltakers and public relations agents — whom the conventional wisdom sees as valuing "style" over "substance" — has been old hat since the late President Eisenhower hired a Hollywood actor to improve him for television.

That was about a quarter century ago, not long as the presidency goes. Indeed, the coincidence of this foolishness with the rise of television to political importance is not accidental. It is difficult to think of recent pre-television Presidents — Harry Truman, Franklin D. Roosevelt, not to mention Herbert Hoover — with such tacticians hovering at their elbows, although none was lacking in old-fashioned press agents.

In any event, we have not quite accustomed ourselves to these influences at the White House and it cannot have been a kindly hand that slipped copies of Mr. Caddell's December memorandum to President-elect Carter into certain reportorial pockets this week.

Even in the age of illusions, we tend to consider that there is something vaguely discreditable — or at least best left to the intimacy of the file cabinet — in the advice Mr. Caddell handed out, at least insofar as it seems to prod Mr. Carter to rely on appearances. Admonitions like "Too many good people have been beaten because they tried to substitute substance for style" and suggestions for the "ostentatious use" of prominent preachers and singers (no novelty at the White House, goodness knows) are bound to raise eyebrows. And raise them far higher, we might add, when the intended beneficiary of the advice has put great emphasis on candor and studied sincerity.

Yet Mr. Caddell's basic political point, we gather, is that "governing with public approval requires a continuing political campaign," which is hardly a revolutionary notion. True, the notion offends a certain streak of American political prudery, which is founded on the notion that statesmanship and politics can and should be hermetically separated. But presidential leadership, our history suggests, consists largely in the continuous fashioning of alliances and coalitions among dozens of factions and interest groups. These coalitions are not self-generating, nor is government by consent possible without them.

If we experience a certain chill of unease in reading these snippets from the memos of a President's mini-Machiavel, it is probably because they prompt us to wonder how much of that President's public behavior wells up from deep springs of character and how much is an act. Not, again, that character and theatricality are necessarily opposites in politics. When a newly-inaugurated president walks down Pennsylvania Avenue, it may be for more than one reason: that somebody suggested it for reasons of appearance, and that the notion appealed to the new president's sense of democratic propriety.

The true danger lies, as always, in extremes. Every one of Mr. Caddell's advisory maxims can be stood on its head. If there is an easier way for good men to founder in politics than by "substituting substance for style," it is by the opposite substitution. If it is true that one can't govern with public approval without "a continuing political campaign," it is equally true that the smell of ulterior political motivation in every presidential maneuver soon palls and produces resistance and cynicism.

It strikes us that Mr. Carter is not likely to suffer much from the publicity given Mr. Caddell's memorandum. He tends to come across as a politically serious man who does do his homework and who does wish to improve the citizen's sense that the White House is in touch. And in the last resort, after all, there is no known way in which a political adviser can create an illusion of solidity from thin air. In politics, tinsel wears thin in a hurry.

The Providence Journal

Providence, R.I., May II, 1977

A long memorandum from Jimmy Carter's campaign pollster has come to light, giving some fresh insights into this unusual presidency and the nature of American politics today.

The memo, drafted for Mr. Carter before the inauguration by his oracular young taker of the public pulse, Patrick H. Caddell, advises the incoming President how best to perform in his first weeks. He advised Mr. Carter to conduct a "continuing campaign" and to concentrate more on style than on substance.

What is immediately telling, obviously, is that the new President seems to have embraced Mr. Caddell's script with enthusiasm. The first weeks of the Carter presidency were laden with symbols — a walk, a sweater, a phone-in, a town meeting — and not with a great deal else. Now deeply immersed in issues, the President has eased away from this self-conscious devotion to his image. But when one views his current high standing in the public opinion polls, it seems clear that the strategy of style had its desired effect.

In certain respects, the Caddell advice was shrewd. Mr. Carter had campaigned on promises to de-mythologize the presidency and to keep in touch with the voters. To an extent, his early symbolic gestures did this. The new President also needed, as Mr. Caddell noted, "to gain personal credibility and restore the trust of the people" — to reassure the skeptics and broaden his base of support.

But the Caddell memo also reflects a disturbing trend — building up images at the expense of confronting reality — that increasingly marks American politics. In every big-time political campaign, the public relations consultant and the "media adviser" have become pivotal figures. They shape strategy, and channel candidates' energies, by what they deem most saleable in the political marketplace. The candidate has become a package; the public is asked to choose, not between two views of leadership, but between two rival advertising strategies.

Mr. Caddell is perceptive and talented, but his view of ideal political conduct seems twisted or even backward. "Too many people," he wrote to Mr. Carter, "have been beaten because they tried to substitute substance for style." Mr. Caddell evidently would put style first, but in fact the two cannot be separated. Presidential successes depend heavily on persuading public opinion, which in turn hinges considerably on reactions to how a President conducts himself.

While there has been nothing intrinsically wrong with Mr. Carter's novel stylistic gestures, they hardly form the stuff of real presidential leadership. Mr. Carter, now deeply immersed in the hard work of his new job, probably knows this. One hopes that Mr. Caddell does, as well, and that Mr. Carter will not insist on charting his course by the samplings of public opinion that Mr. Caddell's polls conjure up.

THE CINCINNATI ENQUIRER

Cincinnati, Ohio, June 5, 1977

CAN A PRESIDENT, like an entertainer, run the risk of overexposure? It may be too soon to speculate, but President Carter may be putting himself too much in the public eye via television, radio, phone-ins and the like.

He cannot by any means be accused of the seclusion that was a hallmark of much of Richard Nixon's tenure in the White House. But a danger exists, perhaps, at the other end of the spectrum. Mr Carter may be making himself too familiar to the American people. The result could be diminished public interest in the presidency. And this would be unfortunate.

Just where lies the ideal exposure balance is unknown. But it is a balance, perhaps, the President and his advisers ought to seek.

None could argue, of course, with frequent press conferences, though even this format, particularly with its televised "show-biz" format, could be overdone. Whether all press conferences should be televised is a matter of debate. Washington's most distinguished correspondent, James Reston of the *New York Times*, stopped participating in press confer-

ences after they came under the klieg lights of television. He maintained he didn't want to be an actor.

An appropriate media mix might feature occasional untelevised press conferences confined to correspondents regularly assigned to the White House (as opposed to the battalions at the video extravaganzas). We would be the last to suggest Mr. Carter renege on his pledge of an open presidency. But we believe he would be well advised to consider the pitfalls of too much exposure—whether, for example, it might not lower public interest in him and his office.

The Miami Herald

Miami, Fla., December 28, 1977

While there is nothing new about politicians using the media for political purposes, this is the first time TV has been employed tellingly in diplomacy. The results have been resoundingly positive.

The virtue of the new diplomacy is its openness. Events unfold and decisions are made in full view. The people know more about what is going on. Technology has provided a short cut out of the diplomatic darkness where so many important international decisions traditionally are made.

Diplomacy in the sunshine also has caused more people to become interested in foreign affairs, although at a relatively superficial level. It gives them what Flora Lewis of *The New York Times* calls a "sense of vicarious participation," which partly explains its power. It enables the people of the world to share a common experience.

Yet, there are also negatives. The media could get too caught up in the race to catch the global audience and distort the significance of some events.

They could become prey to or captive of skillful manipulators. These dangers are not new but are magnified by the new technology.

With so much riding on broadcast events, there is a chance that a slip of the tongue could have greatly magnified reprecussions. Recall what his unfortunate choice of the word "brainwashed" did to George Romney's presidential hopes.

And what of the leader whose program is good but whose "presence" isn't? We wonder what viewers would have thought of Abraham Lincoln had TV cameras been at that Pennsylvania battlefield as he stood, a tall, angular, unhandsome figure, and read his Gettysburg Address from the back of an envelope.

For good or ill, diplomacy by mass media is here to stay. And while it increases public access to history in the making, it also increases the public's need to distinguish illusion from reality, presence from substance.

THE drama of the Mideast peace talks now being played before an international television audience has a significance that goes beyond the subject at hand. What the world is witnessing is a new technique in diplomacy made possible by the technology of mass communications. It is mass diplomacy.

Egyptian President Anwar Sadat has with intuition and skill captured the interest, and the good will, of the people of other nations. He has won for Egypt a much improved image and a better bargaining position at the peace table.

Television made it all possible. It has made Mr. Sadat a familiar and sympathetic figure in the households of the world.

Through TV, he has leaped over the heads of national leaders to reach the masses, capitalizing on his talents and personality to sell himself and his programs.

Israeli Prime Minister Menahem Begin had little choice but to emulate him. Mr. Begin, too, has become a prominent television personality.

The Saturday OKLAHOMAN & TIMES

Oklahoma City, Okla., April 24, 1977

HIS unlimited access to network television gives President Carter a little-mentioned but potentially dangerous advantage in the public discussion of such complex subjects as the energy crisis.

The potential danger was starkly apparent in network television's enormous amplification of Carter's energy views on three separate occasions within a single week.

Persons having opposing views are not excluded by any of the various forms of mass communications, of course. But theirs is a diffused and sometimes technical response which doesn't have anything like the aggregate impact on public awareness that Carter exercises with his charm-school network productions.

There's nothing inherently wrong in a president's use of network television and radio to get his ideas across to a national audience in matters affecting the national interest. Other occupants of the White House have done the same thing.

President Carter took office with a promise to communicate freely with the people and make his ad-

ministration responsive to the national interest as he sees it. But experience attests the tendency of all presidents to equate the national interest with their own political interests. The ready availability of network television to further them in this purpose is a potentially dangerous thing. Instead of using television to bring himself closer to the popular mood, a charismatic president is apt more often to employ it to make public opinion conform to his own predilections.

Not even Congress, which is constitutionally a coequal branch of the government, can cope effectively with a president as skilled as Carter in exploiting the various organs of mass communications. Its members can express differences and have them widely circulated, of course, but who other than the chief executive can preempt prime time on all three networks to give his voice a stentorian quality not vouchsafed any other individual or institution in the nation?

The case for the opposition isn't improved by evidence that the public is increasingly becoming audio-

attuned and too often draws what fragmentary information it possesses from the broadcast spoken word. A subject as esoteric as the economics of oil and gas production isn't likely to be widely understood, no matter how exhaustively and accurately its complexities are publicly explored by spokesmen for the industry.

As one example, how many persons in the big consuming states — or even in Oklahoma and other producing states — understand the distinction between "old" and "new" oil which has such crucial relevance to Carter's energy proposals? Carter would allow "new" oil, now selling for $11.28 a barrel, to be priced at $13.50 a barrel. James Schlesinger, Carter's chief energy adviser, calls this a "very generous inducement" for producers to go out and find new sources.

The trouble is that the proposed regulations define "new" oil as oil drilled more than 2 1/2 miles from an existing onshore well. A. V. Jones, president of the Independent Petroleum Association of America, points out that it isn't possible to

draw many 5-mile circles in Oklahoma, Texas or Louisiana that haven't had an oil well drilled in them at some time.

The administration's distinction between "new" and "old" oil gives producers little or no incentive to undertake costly secondary or tertiary recovery efforts in existing fields where the oil remaining often exceeds the amounts already withdrawn. Fully as discouraging as a disincentive would be the enormous costs of drilling to deeper levels in existing fields with no prospect of recovering costs in higher prices.

These are considerations given short shrift by administration energy "experts" and the congressmen from consuming states who heavily outnumber their better-informed colleagues from the producing states.

In order for the people to understand what is involved, they would need a familiarity with oil and gas economics they aren't likely to acquire through 30-minute presidential appearances on network television. Therein lies the potential danger.

The Cleveland Press
Cleveland, Ohio, March 9, 1978

In an effort to bring government closer to the people, the U.S. House of Representatives voted overwhelmingly last fall to permit television coverage of House debates.

Now the House may be on the verge of undermining that decision by insisting that the cameras and microphones be manned by House employees rather than outside broadcasters.

Reflecting the views of House Speaker Thomas P. O'Neill, a subcommittee headed by Rep. Gillis W. Long, D-La., has recommended that the House run its own TV show — if, indeed, that show ever goes on the air.

For the subcommittee also noted that, because of bad lighting and acoustics, some members looked and sounded pretty dismal during a TV trial run last year.

The argument against professional coverage that keeps popping up is that network TV might call the shots, as it does at football games, telling the House when to take "timeouts" for commercials and thereby interfering with the legislative process.

Such reasoning seems farfetched, however, when you consider that congressional committee hearings, presidential press conferences, joint sessions of Congress and the proceedings of 40 state legislatures have been televised without interruption.

Beyond that, it seems to us that broadcast professionals would do a better job — at less expense to the taxpayers — than a crew of staff members employed by the House.

The Providence Journal
Providence, R.I., January 16, 1978

The House of Representatives, its veteran leaders wary as a pack of old bears, is deciding somewhat grumpily to try out a system for televising its proceedings. A long overdue move, and all that. Trouble is, the House nabobs are designing a system that they will control, that will work mostly to their own advantage and that will offer little flexibility in presenting news for TV as it actually occurs on the House floor.

It may be some small gratification that the House elders finally are accepting the idea that TV should cover the business of the House chamber. The idea, after all, has been floating around in various heads and pigeon-holes for something like 30 years. But now that House sentiment has shifted in favor of opening things up to TV coverage, it is a bit silly and even self-defeating to insist that the House alone can produce good TV coverage of its activities.

The broadcasting industry has argued that a network pool operation could be put in place to provide coverage of all floor action, both to House offices on a closed-circuit system and to radio and TV stations around the country, which could use it or not as they chose. But many House members, notably Speaker Thomas P. O'Neill Jr., firmly oppose this approach. They fear, evidently, that a pool camera run by the networks might swing about when business was slow to focus on a member grabbing a snooze or appearing otherwise less than dignified.

The leaders' concern about the House image is justified enough: the image has brightened in the last few years with internal reforms and procedural shakeups, but it still could use some improvement. What seems unlikely to improve the public's impressions of the House is a strictly controlled, stage-managed TV coverage. Granted, there would be gavel-to-gavel coverage of the rostrum and the minority and majority tables, and these tapes would be available for networks to use as they chose. Yet this system would restrict networks to only the pictures that House leaders wanted them to see.

At best, televised coverage of House proceedings is unlikely to zoom to the top of the Nielsen ratings. As any follower of the *Congressional Record* can attest, the chamber spends much of its time on procedural matters or esoteric debate on complex issues of little general interest. When there is something of real news interest going on, though, networks should have the freedom to record it and broadcast it — without the nervous hand of the House hierarchy imposing rigid controls.

Furthermore, it well could be that high-quality, professionally directed TV coverage could improve the public's view of the House, rather than detract from it. One has only to recall the electrifying impeachment debates of the House Judiciary Committee in 1974 to sense how effectively TV can educate the public about the workings of Congress. If a member knows that he or she may be on camera, they may chose to prepare themselves more diligently for debate.

Would free-swinging TV coverage encourage congressmen to grandstand and preen for the cameras more than usual? Perhaps at first, but after a time such antics could generate their own backlash and in any event the networks would be able to sift the newsworthy material out of the hours of daily tape.

Independent TV coverage of the House offers so many potential benefits, to both the American public and the House members themselves, that it deserves a fair test on its own. If serious problems crop up, drop the idea; but at least give it a chance — and if the House for whatever reason needs its own internal system, why not give access, as well, to the commercial networks (with their modern, unobtrusive cameras and comfortable lighting)?

Speaker O'Neill, sorry to say, doesn't see things this way. He wants the Rules Committee, when it recommends an option to him next month, to endorse his idea of an in-House system. But if it's the House image he is concerned about, Mr. O'Neill probably could do nothing to improve that image more readily than to open the House doors to television that is free from the uneasy hand of the House itself.

The News American
Baltimore, Md., March 30, 1976

THE NATION'S lawmakers, most of whom seem exceptionally qualified as public performers when they take to the stump seeking votes, have revealed a sudden terror of the live television camera if it is in the chamber of the House of Representatives.

After allowing the networks to install four unobtrusive TV cameras in the upper gallery so that all Americans might see, if they wished, how their elected representatives conduct the business of state, the House Rules Committee, by a vote of 9 to 6, has shelved and effectively killed its own proposal that would have permitted live TV and radio coverage of sessions. Unless they are present in person, ordinary Americans may not be allowed to witness floor proceedings.

The reasons for the rejection were explained by members of the committee. Cameras and microphones would reveal the customary large number of absentees; they would show some solons dozing; they would provide an advantage to those who are superior orators. Said Rep. B. F. Sisk, D.-Calif., the cameras would record representatives "pulling our ears or picking our noses, and we all recognize that isn't a pleasant sight to behold."

A point that is overlooked is that with live TV coverage there would be fewer absentees, there would be more decorum in the House and poor speakers would learn how to become better communicators — as they should do, anyway.

What is most important, however, is the arrogance implicit in the decision. The occupants of that House Chamber were sent there by the 220 million Americans whom they are supposed to represent. Not all of us can crowd into the gallery whenever we wish to know what's going on.

That Chamber belongs to us, not to them.

Oregon Journal
Portland, Ore., December 29, 1977

Congress has been slow to recognize that television is an important element in modern communications. But next year the House finally is going to allow the cameras to air proceedings on the floor.

Questions, however, already are forming over how the televising will be done. Whose hands will be on the cameras? Who will decide what will be covered and what will not?

House Speaker Thomas P. O'Neill recently declared, "The worst thing you could do would be to turn over to the broadcasting companies control of what is going on in the legislature."

He would be right, of course, if he means the kind of control networks have acquired over professional sports, often determining even such things as timeouts, game times, or where games are to be played.

But he's dead wrong if he means the networks and stations are not to operate their own cameras and determine for themselves what they believe should be shown to their audiences.

Yet that appears to be what the speaker has in mind. A committee has recommended a plan that the speaker seems ready to adopt that would keep the television in the hands of the House.

Three cameras would be limited to spots on the floor where the official debate takes place. They will be operated by employees and will not shift from debate to anything else going on. Apparently the House fears showing the homefolks a dozing congressman.

Another comparison with broadcasting and professional sports comes to mind. That is the established practice of the announcer being an employee of the team and not the station. He is beholden to the team, not the audience. He is more propagandist than reporter.

Television stations that want to cover the House should do their own work, not take what the House hands them in the way the House wants it packaged. That's the way it functions in the Oregon Legislature and it is successful. So here is another case where the Congress could learn from the Oregon Legislature.

The Des Moines Register

Des Moines, Iowa, October 30, 1977

Putting Congress on television — not just occasional hearings, but full coverage of action on the floor — is an idea that has been talked about for several years. Now it seems to be close to reality, but under rules that are disturbing.

Sessions of the House of Representatives may be appearing on home screens as soon as January. The Senate seems to favor allowing cameras to record its deliberations next year on ratification of the Panama Canal treaties, although there are no plans for other Senate coverage.

Some fear the presence of cameras will encourage grandstanding by congressmen trying to wow the home folks, and that coverage might embarrass anyone who happens to be absent during a quorum call, vote or important debate. But the public can recognize self-serving antics as well as the need for congressmen and senators to conduct business away from the floor.

It is unfortunate that congressional leaders seem to feel it necessary, in the name of preserving decorum, to restrict the type and extent of coverage allowed. Representative Jack Brooks (Dem., Tex.), chairman of a special committee that recommended TV coverage, has announced that House employees will control the cameras. He made it clear they would not show members of Congress in an unfavorable light.

That is censorship. Journalists and small groups of the public already can see and hear whatever happens in the two chambers. TV would only extend that opportunity to the millions of Americans to whom Congress is accountable. Brooks and others who favor controlling the coverage need to be reminded that the First Amendment does not stop at the foot of Capitol Hill.

Americans should have free access to Congress by whatever media are available. Television can be an effective link between congressmen and constituents, and it deserves an unfettered chance to prove its worth.

PORTLAND EVENING EXPRESS

Portland, Me., April 12, 1978

Except for perhaps a slight inclination toward long-windedness, Portland city councilors have apparently adapted easily and unselfconsciously to televised broadcasts of their regular public meetings.

We aren't surprised. That's usually what happens when deliberative bodies choose to open their proceedings to all media, broadcast as well as printed.

Politicians have mixed feelings about the broadcast media. They recognize that radio and television are important aids in election campaigns, but they tend to get nervous about the prospect of being scrutinized by microphone and camera while engaged in their public duties.

Whenever a proposal is made to televise lawmakers in action, the fear is expressed that individual politicians will be tempted to "play to the cameras."

This didn't happen in the case of the Maine Legislature when cameras were allowed in to the House and Senate several years ago, and it hasn't happened in the case of the Portland City Council.

Furthermore, it isn't likely to happen if Congress ever gets around to allowing cameras to televise formal proceedings of the legislative branch in Washington. The House has already given tentative approval for such telecasts, but apparently is still hung up over the question of who should control the cameras, Congress or the broadcasters.

But even at the risk of a little showboating on the part of a politician or two, the more exposure given to the governmental process in action, the better for both the government and the governed.

So what if some of the councilors in Portland get a little longwinded.

That, too, can be instructive.

Register-Republic

Rockford, Ill., February 9, 1978

Members of Congress are trying to figure how to get their faces on the nation's television screens — without being made to look bad in the process.

The debate involves plans for live television coverage of House of Representatives sessions — and turns on such issues as who will man those cameras and what they will be allowed to show.

From the beginning, there have been some questions about the whole plan for live television coverage.

First, there is the problem that almost all sessions are so terribly dull few will bother to watch.

And, second, there is the possibility of congressmen, aware of those cameras, endlessly delaying the legislative process while they primp, pose and orate strictly to create a TV image.

However, there could be some very real value in live telecasts of Congress if the cameras will "tell it like it is." We suspect it would be a valuable education to the public if they could watch their congressmen in action the way they really are.

Now, a House subcommittee has bowed to the pressure of House Speaker Thomas P. "Tip" O'Neill and proposed a plan to assure that will not happen.

Worried that the cameras might show how few congressmen actually attend floor sessions or that they might show congressmen sleeping at their desks, the subcommittee has proposed that the TV cameras be operated by House employees and not by professional newsmen. Beyond that, they have proposed that the cameras be limited to showing what is going on in only three isolated locations in the House chambers.

Such a plan obviously would guarantee complete censorship of the TV coverage and kill whatever value the coverage might provide the public.

Rep. John Anderson, R-Ill., speaking for the House Republicans, has challenged O'Neill and the subcommittee's proposal.

Anderson called the proposal "a sad commentary on the confidence the majority leadership has in . . . its own performance."

If congressional sessions are to be televised as news events, they obviously have to be handled by news professionals without censorship.

If the House members want to use them for their own public relations images, let them hire PR men and purchase commercial time to show the film.

The position taken by O'Neill and the subcommittee is beyond defense.

The Topeka Daily Capital

Topeka, Kans., February 12, 1978

A mild case of vanity may serve a good cause in Congress if it keeps television out of the Capitol.

A plan to begin coverage of the House of Representatives in June apparently has been put off by at least a year because many House members are getting cold feet over bald spots on the head, shadows under the eyes and, for some, "disappearing" altogether.

The problems foreseen by many of the members are marginal at best, and they may be using these excuses not to get into a long debate over the worth and effectiveness of televising the routine business of Congress.

Those Americans who have witnessed legislative action know that much of the floor activity of Congress is tedious and poorly attended. Most of the real action in Congress occurs in hearing rooms and caucuses. For these reasons it is doubtful that enough Americans would watch Congress in action to make the project worth the time, effort and money required.

But the reasons members of the House gave for delaying the plan — the Senate hasn't even considered televising sessions — is that the lighting in the House chamber would be less than flattering to most members and would make any black members of Congress "disappear," according to Rep. Shirley Chisholm, D-N.Y.

Speaker Thomas O'Neill, D-Mass., also worries that television floor directors and camera crews would begin scheduling Congress' time to fit their own activities, leading to floor votes and debates hanging in air as a commercial advertisement croons the glories of some brand of deodorant.

Most likely no commercial television enterprise would be interested in taking on congressional coverage day after day, anyway. So the job would be left to public television, and commercials wouldn't be a problem. But no matter who manages the telecasts, somebody has to pay the cost.

And it's difficult to see where daily live coverage of Congress would attract enough viewers to justify the cost of crews, equipment and air time.

The State

Columbia, S.C., February 2, 1978

NOT MANY politicians get to be U.S. senators by being camera shy, so other factors must influence the Senate's refused to televise the debates on the Panama Canal treaties.

The excuse cited by Senate Majority Leader Robert Byrd involves "technical problems," mostly over lighting. The television lights work just fine, but they make the senators too hot. Surely, Mr. Byrd is reasoning that the floor of the Senate will be hot enough as it is during the canal debates, but the senators could leave their wool suits at home and adjust to the warmth for the public's benefit.

Senator Byrd added that the lights are too bright and in poor locations. "The lighting I experienced was very distracting to me at my desk," he explained. Maybe the Senate is simply not used to sunshine.

No senator has mentioned it, but perhaps some see political dangers in televising the debates. The canal treaties have become an explosive public issue, and some senators may be worried about the intense scrutiny and pressure that television cameras could inspire.

But they may have overlooked the wholesome effect that television could have on the ratification process. The Army-McCarthy hearings and the various Watergate hearings have demonstrated that television can promote acceptance, if not approval, of controversial political decisions.

Through television, a nationwide constituency can see the agonizing process involved in resolving a question of great significance. Not every member of that constituency will agree with the course taken, but everyone will have seen, dimming the chance that some will cry foul after the matter is settled.

ST. LOUIS POST-DISPATCH

St. Louis, Mo., February 11, 1978

Congress is shying away from televised coverage of its floor proceedings as though it has a bad case of stage fright. After a 90-day televised test filming which itself came only after much delay, the House of Representatives has shelved, perhaps until next year, a plan for gavel-to-gavel television coverage. The reason given was that technical problems with lighting have not been worked out — the cameras don't show the members in a flattering light. Meanwhile, the Senate has taken the timid step of allowing radio coverage of its Panama Canal treaty debates.

A further sign of House shyness was provided by a vote of the Rules Committee to recommend giving the House, rather than a pool of commercial networks, control over broadcast coverage of floor proceedings whenever such broadcasts start. This would be like requiring newspaper reporters to rely on notes taken by House employees. Unless House employees have control, the members are obviously afraid that cameras might focus on sleeping lawmakers or on other embarrassing occurrences on the floor. That, however, is a proper risk of being covered by a free press. Television coverage of Congress should not be an officially produced program designed to show the voters only what the lawmakers want them to see.

AKRON BEACON JOURNAL

Akron, Ohio, February 8, 1978

THE HISTORIC debate on the Panama Canal treaties that began today in the Senate already has produced one victory for the public.

It has helped penetrate barriers to live coverage by the electronic news media of House and Senate sessions. However, important decisions remain that will have a bearing on the extent, flexibility and credibility of that coverage.

Today's opening debate on the treaties was the first Senate session ever to be broadcast live to radio listeners, with National Public Radio doing the job. In the Akron area, WKSU-FM, 89.7, has gavel-to-gavel coverage.

This breakthrough comes at a time when the House is about to open its sessions routinely to television cameras. Yet to be resolved, though, is who will control those cameras.

Essentially, there are three options:

● The House could contract with the three major networks plus Washington's public broadcasting station for coverage of all floor action. All radio and television stations wanting feeds would have access.

● The House could arrange a similar contract with only public broadcasting.

● The House could run the cameras with its own employes and make the material available, unedited, to accredited radio and television stations.

House Speaker Thomas P. O'Neill Jr. will have the final say. He is known to favor the third option.

But that alternative has drawbacks that would make it a less than adequate substitute for the others.

The biggest deficiency is that it would provide the public with a sanitized version of House proceedings, designed to put members in the best possible light.

The system Speaker O'Neill is believed to favor calls for three color cameras pointed at the speaker's rostrum and the majority and minority tables. There would be no shots of the galleries, or legislators at their desks, or any activity in the chamber other than of the member speaking at any particular time.

This prospect appeals to many representatives who worry about being captured in unflattering moments by cameras controlled by the networks or public television. The networks and public television view the concept with considerable disdain.

For all its importance, Congress still remains a mystery to many people. Most of what we know about its operations has been learned from civics books. Frequent coverage by the electronic media could change that dramatically.

The whole country can benefit from the chance to watch and hear Congress at work.

The Washington Post

Washington, D.C., February 14, 1978

ONE OF THE ARGUMENTS often made against broadcasting sessions of Congress is that the intrusion of microphones and cameras would change the nature of the proceedings. It seems clear, after three days of radio coverage of the debate on the Panama Canal treaties, that the presence of microphones does change what happens on the Senate floor. But the change, at least so far as we can see, weighs heavily in favor of broadcasting.

The sound in the Senate last week was that of a debate. Real, live senators were on the floor to challenge statements made by their colleagues. The accuracy of "facts" was questioned, interpretations were disputed, points were scored. Speakers seldom were allowed to drone on endlessly; some had to fight off questioners to get their speeches completed. Even absent senators appeared to think the debate meant something. Many tuned in in their offices.

Contrast that, if you will, with the sound of the Senate during some other historic "debates." All too often it has been the sound of a series of long and boring speeches listened to, as far as an observer could tell, by practically no one. Misstatements went unchallenged. Tourists went away shaking their heads at the Senate's claim to be "the world's greatest deliberative body."

Though we can't prove it, our suspicion is that the microphones made the debate. Neither supporters nor opponents of the treaties wanted any portion of the public to get a one-sided version of what the dispute is about. Thus, each side was making an effort to see that any argument was refuted as quickly as possible. And that, we submit, is just the point. Far from encouraging showboating, the microphones seemed to concentrate senatorial minds and create conditions conducive to a spirited exchange of opposing views. By broadcasting this debate live, public radio is doing a service not just to the public but to the Senate as well.

THE BLADE

Toledo, Ohio, November 2, 1977

THE odds reportedly are greatly improved that the U.S. House will approve a long-resisted proposal that its floor sessions be televised. The chances that the American public will get an accurate picture of what the lawmakers do are, however, worse than ever.

Congressmen — at Speaker O'Neill's urging — are expected to go along with a compromise plan that would put House employees rather than network or station personnel in charge of directing the cameras. That is aimed at relieving members' fears that they might be caught napping during a debate or that a representative might be shown

delivering an impassioned oration to a sea of empty seats. Pan shots would be barred, and the cameras would have to focus directly on the person speaking.

If it is show business the congressmen want, they would do better to go really professional and call in Hollywood experts to build a special set peopled with extras to simulate a screenwriter's notion of what a legislative session is supposed to look like. That certainly would be no sillier than an arrangement carefully contrived to keep the citizen audience from seeing

what actually goes on in the House chamber.

All of this bears out our long-held view that there is little useful purpose to be served in televising floor sessions in any case. The real work of lawmaking is done primarily in the committees and subcommittees, and under extraordinary circumstances — such as the Watergate hearings — those are interesting and informative enough to justify live telecasts. Otherwise, the legislative process is highly unlikely to produce anything that would keep the citizenry glued to its sets.

The Seattle Times

Seattle, Wash., December 30, 1977

WHILE details of television coverage of the U.S. House of Representatives, beginning in January, have yet to be agreed upon, it is evident the public will not be getting what it might want — or needs.

Three options for placing and operating cameras in the House chambers are being considered by the Rules Committee.

One would put them in the hands of a pool of the three major networks and the Washington public broadcasting station.

A second would put them under the control of public broadcasting.

The third would have House employes running the cameras, under tight restrictions, with

the product available, unedited, to accredited radio and television stations.

The last is expected to be the committee's choice, if only because it is favored by Speaker Thomas O'Neill, Jr., a longtime foe of any televising of House sessions.

He and others see television — if it must be there at all — as an "in house" function, its primary purpose not to give the public direct access to House proceedings, but simply to record House debate and voting and to pipe them into members' offices via a closed-circuit system — or file it away in libraries.

What the public needs and

would be more likely to get from news media and crews, public or private, is a questioning, probing, lively portrayal of the House at work.

House action for the most part won't be all that exciting. But there is interest in it, as evidenced by a 1975 Roper poll showing that 68 per cent of a national sample wanted at least some TV coverage of congressional debates; or by the public response to the 1974 broadcasts of the House Judiciary Committee's impeachment debates.

But all this has been lost on those fearful of what the public might see.

O'Neill's right-hand man in developing the TV ground rules

has been Texas Democrat Jack Brooks, who says networks should not be given control of the cameras because "these people think they should interpret what's going on. That would lead to possible distortion."

Lack of distortion, of course, has seldom been an overriding consideration in such congressional output as the paper barrage of self-promoting press releases or the Congressional Record. And it could be argued that whatever emerges from three computer-operated cameras, aimed solely at the Speaker's rostrum and the majority and minority tables on the floor, is distortion per se.

The Idaho STATESMAN

Boise, Idaho, June 22, 1978

The House has decided that its own employees will man the cameras that provide television coverage of House proceedings — if, in fact, the good representatives choose to allow coverage at all.

What bilge this is! What hypocrisy! It's sort of like the unhappy situation in which federal workers are the only ones not bound by law to contribute to Social Security. And the situation isn't much better at the White House.

The White House decides whether television cameras will be allowed on the grounds, when they will be allowed, and how they will be used, right down to settings and camera angles. If the president doesn't think he is being shown in his best light, or doesn't want pictures taken at all, out go the cameras.

Tourists can take their cameras just about anywhere they please. They whip out their Instamatics and shoot with abandon. But network cameramen, the ones whose job it is to film the daily affairs of government for the entire nation, supposedly protected by constitutional amendment, face red tape and closed doors in attempting to do their work.

It's interesting to note the distinctions in freedom of the press accorded by various government agencies. Local television people, not just here but in cities around the nation, can take take all the pictures they want in front of city halls, court buildings, statehouses, etc. No red tape, no written permission, just walk up and start shooting.

But at the White House and the nation's Capitol, the very seats of our democracy, freedom of the press is conditional, restricted, sometimes non-existent. Something is wrong. This can't be what the founding fathers had in mind.

The Democratic majority wants the House to decide where to point the congressional cameras. We were under the impression that the network experts did a fairly good job of deciding where to point their cameras. The nice part was that they sometimes pointed them in directions that made the pointees squirm, thereby making the news abundantly clear to the public. You knew precisely what was going on because you could see it with your own eyes. With politicians running the cameras it's likely to be a lot different. We'll see plenty of self-serving, complimentary footage, but we won't see much squirming, and it won't be nearly as easy to tell what's going on.

Networks should be allowed to shoot what they want. There are enough ads on the evening news already.

Honolulu Star-Bulletin

Honolulu, Hawaii, August 24, 1978

The news media have been taking a beating in the courts of late on such questions as closure of judicial proceedings, searches of newspaper offices and confidentiality of news sources.

That makes all the more welcome the endorsement by the chief justices of the state supreme courts of television, radio and photographic coverage of criminal trials.

Considering the subject at their annual meeting, the chief justices said they thought televising trials would strengthen the credibility of the judicial system. Anyway, they pointed out, public demand made the innovation inevitable.

Trials are supposed to be public affairs; television can make them more public than ever before. And we go along with the chief justices in believing that the televising can be done without detracting from the decorum of the courtroom.

What about Congress?

The Senate made history in February when it consented to radio coverage of the debate on the Panama Canal treaties. But television cameras were excluded.

Subsequently the House permitted radio networks to carry live and taped audio pickups of House proceedings. As for television, the House has approved it in principle but hasn't worked out all the details.

In June it voted to have its own employees — not commercial or public network broadcasters — control the cameras. This is likely to result in much tamer coverage than if the networks were permitted to handle it.

House Speaker Thomas O'Neill says he expects televising to begin in the House next year. No forecast is available for the Senate.

Meanwhile the cameras have been rolling at the Canadian Parliament with good results. Nor have there been problems at the Hawaii Legislature.

If the state chief justices approve of television in the courtroom, Congress looks silly dragging its heels.

The members are afraid of making fools of themselves in front of their constituents. But they look more foolish trying to hide.

The Courier-Journal
Louisville, Ky., December 27, 1977

THE STRONGEST spur to televised sessions of the House of Representatives may have been the impression its Judiciary Committee made on America during the 1974 Nixon impeachment hearings. Such names as Barbara Jordan, Peter Rodino and Charles Wiggins became household words to a degree most other congressmen could envy but never expect to share.

But citizens expecting that sort of show next year, when House Speaker O'Neill decides how and when to bring broadcast sessions to the public for the first time, are in for a disappointment.

There are two reasons for this, the first being that most of what occurs on the House floor is fairly routine. And that body's severe time limitations on debate, necessary in part because there are so many members, make it normally even less interesting than the talkier and more profound Senate. The second reason is the control the Speaker plans to maintain over the pictures and sounds available to TV and radio stations.

The Speaker is dead set against opening House doors to network cameras, analysts and announcers. He believes the traditional atmosphere of the House would be turned into the kind of circus observable at national party conventions. Doubtless he also fears that few Americans would believe congressmen work if they saw how few are sometimes in the chamber, or caught a glimpse of someone snoozing or reading the newspaper.

Therefore, unless persuaded otherwise before February 15, Mr. O'Neill plans to set up a committee to run a TV/radio operation. Three cameras, remotely controlled by House employes, will be aimed only at those "officially" taking part in debate.

Most members support Mr. O'Neill on this. But their objections, including the one that the United Nations operates its own cameras and receives interesting and coherent coverage, are silly. The House, which passes U.S. laws and is totally supported by U.S. taxpayers, isn't the U.N.

What the House could do, in preparation for what lies ahead, is clean up its act. If the Speaker were to permit a network pool to run the cameras, as some congressmen propose, the House might be forced to improve the quality of its proceedings. That has happened in many of the 44 states that allow broadcast coverage of its legislative sessions.

Speaker O'Neill is furthering public understanding of the democratic process as he ushers his politically minded colleagues into the age of electronic communication. But he still is unconvincing in his argument that the House itself should control the way the public gets its look.

SENATOR SOAPER SAYS: By the time you've discovered life's best highways, you're too old to drive.

San Francisco Chronicle
San Francisco, Cal., November 13, 1977

THE HOUSE OF REPRESENTATIVES late last month voted, 342-44, to authorize the televising of its sessions. This has raised questions on both sides: will our congressmen turn into instant grandstanders for the cameras, or will the public, through viewing debates, become more knowledgeable about the legislative process and thus be able to cast a more intelligent vote next year.

The debate was somewhat succinctly put by Congressmen Leo Ryan (Dem-San Mateo) and Claude Pepper (Dem-Fla.). Ryan is opposed to the plan. He said: "We are now about to change this body from a forum into a theater. And when this place becomes a theater, it is no longer a place for men and women to debate the issues." The generally acknowledged fact that Ryan is himself one of the leading grandstanders of the 95th Congress does not, we feel, blunt the point of his observation.

Pepper responded: "We used to come in stagecoaches: now we come in planes and cars. The public gallery is allowed to see us as we are. The people back home have the same right."

Pepper's argument is rather attractive, and in a sense echoes the comments of Senator James Allen (Dem-Ala.), who said with regard to the possibility of televising the Senate debate, probably early next year, on the Panama Canal treaties: "It might not improve the Senate's image, but if not, that is the Senate's fault, and not the fault of TV coverage."

But there are the possibilities of mischief in the televised coverage of legislative proceedings. The Canadian House of Commons has recently granted such coverage, and that, reports from Ottawa say, has resulted in what has become known as the "Commons Shuffle." When a member rises to speak, the reports say, his colleagues move in to fill the empty seats around him.

Senator Alan Cranston (Dem-Calif.) answers this potential source of criticism by saying: "We should open it up and show it like it is, empty seats and all. Television will definitely help the people get a better idea of how our system works, and it may even improve attendance." He may well be correct.

But the questions remain. For any visitor to Washington who has gained access to the public galleries of the House and Senate and watched the solons at work, the reaction is for the most part one of boredom. The discussions are desultory, and the minor haggling over obscure amendments is generally enough to dissuade the most ardent patriot from staying overlong in the uncomfortable gallery seats.

There is also the question of just how many viewers would prefer watching congressional sessions rather than, say, the Gong Show. A more serious question is how the 535 superegos on Capitol Hill would react to the editing of the day's tapes of sessions. This would particularly apply if the Public Broadcasting System, which lives for the most part on congressional subsidy, were to be the major disseminator of the televised sessions.

Congressman John Young (Dem-Tex.) raised that point last year, when he asked: "Just what protection do we have against the cameras showing only one side of an argument? None. I want some guarantees against that before I support the bill."

The contrary view to that is contained in a report of the Twentieth Century Fund Task Force on Broadcasting the Legislature, which found that the experiences of states — currently 44 allow at least partial televising of their legislative sessions—and foreign countries shows that conduct of debate is improved and the efficiency of the legislative sessions is increased by the cameras.

HOUSE SPEAKER THOMAS O'NEILL said last March that "I can't give you a date on which we're going to televise the House. I can tell you the House is going to be televised in the long run."

Since the televising of legislative proceedings has been accepted in 44 states and has neither subverted their legislatures nor brought the luminaries thereof into disrepute, we think Congress would be justified in chancing the TV experiment. The sky surely wouldn't fall.

THE CHRISTIAN SCIENCE MONITOR
Boston, Mass., January 31, 1978

There may come a day when American TV viewers will have to choose between watching "Happy Days" on one channel or a lively U.S. Senate debate on, say, the need to hike social security taxes on another. Or even worse, the prime-time choice may be between "Charlie's Angels" and Rep. Tip O'Neill's version of "We're No Angels" in the House chamber. But don't start chewing on your TV guide just yet. The first live coverage of House proceedings is not expected to get under way until this spring at the earliest. Congressional leaders seem so reticent about the prospect of becoming instant TV celebrities, they are going out of their way to make certain any televised coverage of their debates and proceedings remains tightly under their control — and, intentionally or not, the result is apt to be as dull as the umpteenth viewing of a TV rerun.

The Senate is even more cautious. It promises to jump the gun on the House by allowing its floor debate on the Panama Canal treaties to be broadcast live — but on radio only. Sen. Robert Byrd, the majority leader, says he personally favors televising Senate debates but that a few "mechanical difficulties" remain to be ironed out.

Some of the "non-mechanical" difficulties that have made Congress until now somewhat loath to beam its deliberations into American living rooms: the House normally is only a third to a half occupied; lawmakers frequently saunter around the chamber and now and then gather in small groups to map political strategy (or make plans for dinner), giving those speaking somewhat less than rapt attention; and congressmen are not above taking a nap now and then during a debate.

Recognizing that many Americans may not grasp the intricacies and importance of such goings-on in the legislative process, Speaker O'Neill's solution is a straightforward one: keep the cameras aimed at the speakers only, one on the majority table, one on the minority table, and one on the Speaker's rostrum.

This approach is not likely to put House debates high in the Neilsen ratings, but it at least will give the public greater TV exposure to the lawmaking process than it has now. Evening newscasts no doubt will pick up only bits and pieces of important debates, but even minimal coverage may stir new public interest in issues that directly affect the lives of many Americans "turned off" by government and public officials in the past. Polls have indicated considerable public interest in having TV coverage of Congress. The televised Watergate and presidential impeachment hearings drew large audiences. Floor debates, given the House's restrictions on coverage, will likely have less impact. But if the experiment succeeds in "turning on" only a few of the nation's too many apathetic voters, it is worth a try.

Democrat and Chronicle

Rochester, N.Y., May 6, 1978

EVEN as the U.S. Congress inches nervously up to live television coverage of some of its proceedings, the House of Commons in Canada is already looking back on six months' experience and liking what it sees.

According to the Speaker of the House, James Jerome, the nature of Parliament has been altered for the better.

Says Jerome: "I don't think there is any doubt that the effect has been all positive. There is the strongest evidence that television has really awakened an unprecedented interest in Parliament."

Noting a decline in disorderly conduct, he adds wryly: "It would be regrettable if it were to disappear altogether because then it would become too much of a sewing circle."

Generally the experience has been an encouraging one. Congress please note

DESERET NEWS

Salt Lake City, Utah, May 3, 1978

What TV newsman Roger Mudd told a Salt Lake City audience this week ought to sound highly familiar.

Congress, he declared, should permit live television coverage of its proceedings to help restore the balance of power that is now tipped toward the White House.

That's precisely what this page has been saying for years. So have plenty of other newspapers around the country even though such a move would be a break for their competitors in electronic journalism.

Why so much support for putting Congress on the tube?

Because it would increase attendance by lawmakers and improve the quality of debate on the floor of both houses of Congress.

Because it would help make those in power more responsive to questions about their actions and to the needs of the public.

And because it would give the public an invaluable lesson in just how this nation's lawmaking machinery works.

How can we really be sure that such benefits would actually be realized?

Because this is precisely what has happened in the past six months since even such a tradition-bound body as the Canadian Parliament permitted live TV coverage of its proceedings.

And because this is what has happened in the 44 states — up 100% in only five years — where TV cameras are permitted to record what goes on in the legislature.

What about fears that the cameras would catch lawmakers off-guard in undignified attitudes or encourage grand-standing?

That has seldom happened. Just ask Speaker James Jerome of the Canadian House of Commons. He is so satisfied with the results of live TV coverage that he declares: "I have no hesitation in recommending it to Congress."

Such coverage, Speaker Jerome adds, has "awakened unprecedented interest" in how a nation's laws are made. Or is that what Congress is afraid of?

Des Moines Tribune

Des Moines, Iowa, January 19, 1978

While the U.S. House of Representatives considers — with some trepidation — what kind of television coverage of its proceedings it will allow, the Canadian House of Commons is demonstrating how successfully a more flexible and sophisticated system can be run.

Like its American counterpart (assuming the plan supported by House Speaker Thomas P. O'Neill Jr. and Texas Democratic Representative Jack Brooks is adopted), the Canadian House retains ultimate control over the TV system and uses its own employees to operate the cameras.

The Canadian lawmakers decided, however, that if they were going to appear on nationwide television they should spend $4.8 million for a system that uses nine cameras (compared with just three in the O'Neill-Brooks plan) and hire several dozen professionals from the Canadian Broadcasting Corp. as employees of the House of Commons to run the cameras. (O'Neill and Brooks would require that cameras be manned by one or two regular House employees.) CBC employees designed and set up the Canadian system.

The most important difference between the Canadian and proposed American coverage is the extent of coverage allowed. The Canadian camera operators can show other views in the chamber, including members' reactions to a speaker. The O'Neill-Brooks plan would have computer-run cameras rigidly aimed at only three points: the speaker's rostrum and the tables of the majority and minority leaders.

The Canadian House coverage appears to be popular with legislators as well as viewers, although some constituents have been surprised at the rowdy behavior of their representatives.

The O'Neill-Brooks plan is better than nothing, but we agree with the Canadian TV adviser who observed that the American plan "sounds like a department store surveillance system."

The Washington Star
and Daily News

Washington, D.C., October 24, 1977

The Canadian Parliament last week began regular live television coverage of its proceedings. This effort to foster public enlightenment about the legislative process deserves a close watch by U.S. congressmen, on the chance that Capitol Hill might be encouraged to emulate Parliament Hill.

In some instances, television coverage here has focused great amounts of public attention on issues before congressional committees — just recently in the Bert Lance case and, a while back, in the Watergate and impeachment proceedings. But the House and the Senate, while they have come close at times, get cold feet about allowing the TV cameras to focus on floor debate in either chamber. A pending proposal to open the House to live TV and radio coverage in January appears to be a victim of the congressmen's souring on the general idea of reform, marked by the recent rejection of sterner ethics rules. The TV plan has been consigned to "study" by a subcommittee.

Objections to television in the Capitol include fears that some legislators will ham it up for the audience back home rather than stick to serious business, and that the cameras might focus on embarrassing details — empty seats or dozing members. Unfortunately, the question has never been put to a true test, which would require a sustained experiment in the televising of floor debate. Such an experiment, of course, might take the decision out of the congressman's hands should the public, as is possible, make up its mind that the congressional drama is a fine alternative to soap opera.

The Canadian example, at this stage, might not win congressional friends for the cause of TV coverage. From the glimpse we got of the televised doings in Ottawa, there was a good deal of boisterous hamming during the House of Commons question period when the prime minister and his cabinet try to fend off the opposition. Mr. Trudeau and his associates were in the disadvantageous position of answering for all of the nation's ills their opponents could think of to mention.

While there is no strictly comparable proceeding in the U.S. system, it might not have been lost on congressional observers that some lively Republicans could have a fine time badgering the smug Democratic majority in the course of televised debate. But this is a superficial and partisan way of viewing the matter.

The decisive consideration should be whether TV broadcasting of legislative proceedings is a useful way of informing the public. Congressmen, as the victims of much public misunderstanding, could benefit incidentally by letting people in on more of the Congress's business.

The Courier-Journal

Louisville, Ky., April 27, 1978

The radio broadcasts of the Senate's Panama Canal debate, though often tedious, drew a surprisingly large number of listeners and generated much interest in the issue.

In fact, the public response to the first live broadcast of a floor debate in Congress changed the minds of some senators who were at first skeptical of the idea.

Treaty opponents felt the programs helped spread their message. The dramatic speech in which Senator McIntyre of New Hampshire castigated the New Right brought letters from across the country.

The unavoidable conclusion is that the public is interested not only in legislative decisions but in the way those decisions are reached and in the personalities of the people who make them. Kentucky Educational Television's impressive following during this year's General Assembly confirms that view.

The obvious question is why Congress has been so slow to permit regular television and radio coverage of its proceedings.

As the KET broadcasts demonstrated, television is capable, at least, of offering a view of the legislative process that no other medium can provide. The extended coverage of the House debate on the Equal Rights Amendment is one unforgettable example. Many Kentuckians saw for the first time how the public business is transacted and what sort of people pass the laws under which we all must live.

Forty-four states, including Indiana, allow the cameras to peek into legislative chambers. So far none of the dreadful consequences predicted by opponents of the idea have come to pass. Showboating and long-windedness have not noticeably increased. Pictures of legislators picking their noses or engaging in other unseemly behavior have not been transmitted into living rooms.

Indeed, deportment and dress have become more dignified. Georgia even got rid of its spittoons.

The Canadian Parliament has been televised for the past six months with similar results. The daily questioning of government leaders by the opposition party has proved especially popular. The quality of debate is said to have improved while raucous behavior has disappeared.

So what's the matter with Congress? Politicians are forever telling us to learn more about government and the issues it confronts. The public pays the congressmen's salaries, owns the building in which they meet, and is helped or hurt by what they do. Why shouldn't we have a direct view, via television, of what's going on?

The House may grudgingly make concessions to the electronic age by letting television in next year. Even then, the purpose may be to show Congress in a favorable light rather than an honest one. Under a plan favored by Speaker O'Neill, House employees would control the cameras and members would be shown only when speaking.

That would not only guarantee unimaginative coverage but turn the film into an electronic press release. Viewers could at least count on objectivity if the cameras were managed by a pool of commerical and public networks.

In spite of the good reviews for its canal debate, the Senate has no plans for future broadcasts.

The excuses for delay include legal and technical problems, which, while real, are not insurmountable. A more likely cause for the foot-dragging is that with the election drawing near, many congressmen are worried about what sort of TV image they will project.

Experience suggests such fears are exaggerated, if not groundless. Meanwhile, the voting public is being denied a close-up view of what its national legislature does.

St. Petersburg Times

St. Petersburg, Fla., January 14, 1978

The television industry as you know is in shock. Its most recent ratings are down, after unbroken years of rocketing up. But the U.S. Congress will be on the air soon. And if the script as outlined by its leaders isn't rewritten fast, TV's lagging soaps and cop shows by comparison could start looking great.

Up to now, House and Senate both have barred not only TV but radio, any kind of recording device, still pictures and every other aspect of media coverage except for the note-taking reporter. So when the House of Representatives last Oct. 27 voted to let TV cameras into its sessions, starting this spring, the action was hailed as historic.

And taken at face value that's what it was. After years of debate on the issue, the vote was 342 to 44 to admit cameras and recording devices and let them run gavel to gavel. The House at last was about to go totally public, and there was talk that even the Senate might follow.

BUT WAIT.

The ground rules for this show were left to the discretion of congressional leaders. In practice that meant Speaker Thomas P. O'Neill, D-Mass., who is widely regarded as the toughest and most effective House boss since the late Sam Rayburn of Texas.

But O'Neill is not known for his expertise in broadcasting. And the rules he prescribed laid firmly to rest any hope TV may have had of hitching its wobbling wagon to the stars of the 95th Congress.

IN FACT, under the direction of Speaker O'Neill, the Capitol Hill Show might be lucky to get a moment or two on the evening news, let alone a spot of its own. Nothing but a talking head format will do for O'Neill. Cameras will be fixed, eyeballing nothing but positions prepared for formal debate.

The broadcast industry's cameramen and other technicians will be welcomed in the chamber only as tourists. Equipment will be manned and monitored by employees of the House, few of whom know anything more about show biz than O'Neill but all of whom are experts at pleasing their bosses in Congress.

The whole boring thing will be taped, and if a network is short of anything livelier, it can snip out and air whatever it wants. On an average day, broadcasts from the House on that basis should generate audience appeal equal to that of the daily test pattern.

BUT PLEASE stand by, fans of sit coms and games and talk shows and even wrestling matches, because all hope for this show still isn't lost. Because before O'Neill finally lays down the law, he must consider a report, not yet drafted, from the House Committee on Rules.

Some Rules members think that when the House voted to open itself to broadcast, that is just what it meant. And the committee currently is considering a final appeal from broadcasters to leave telecasts from the House to the discretion of industry pros.

Mightn't they sometimes air shots of members slumped in their seats, scratching, jawing, yawning, or even sleeping off a hard night before on the town? Couldn't they be sneaky enough during a momentous speech to pan around and disclose to the voters that only a handful of members had shown up to hear it? There could always be another fist fight on the floor, and wouldn't an outsider be likely to think that was news?

WE SURELY hope so. And we firmly believe that if given the chance, television can convey to the average American his first real sense not just of the dignity and responsibility and hard work of the world's greatest lawmaking body, but also of its bustle and drama and excitement and humor.

Our lawmakers worry a lot lately about improving their ratings. Televising the House, warts and all, could be their big chance. And aside from that, just for the sake of us soap-sated viewers, let's all hope Tip O'Neill isn't permitted to blow it.

THE DENVER POST
Denver, Colo., December 28, 1977

THE IDEA of televising sessions of Congress—allowing the public to witness the legislative process—is a good one.

Forty-four state legislatures have already taken such a route and so have the parliaments of several countries.

So it appeared encouraging when the Senate reported it was considering televised broadcasts of its debate on the Panama Canal treaties next year. And then the House went even further by agreeing to allow TV coverage of floor action during regular sessions.

However, there is a significant catch in the House's move that could well doom a good idea.

The House system, reportedly being considered by Speaker Thomas P. O'Neill, D-Mass., calls for cameras aimed at spots on the House floor where "official" debate is supposed to take place. There would be no televising of other sections of the chamber—of the gallery, for example, or of House members dozing, doodling or looking bored.

In fact, the automated cameras being considered would be operated by employees of the House. What kind of a picture of the House members at work would the public be given under such circumstances?

Certainly it would be an incomplete, unreal one, so stilted that it would be guaranteed to turn off viewers by the millions.

Why not allow the commercial and public networks to broadcast the congressional sessions the way they now do presidential press conferences and addresses before joint sessions of Congress? What's acceptable to the president, in this regard, ought to be acceptable to Congress.

If the House is going to open its proceedings through television to the public that elected it—as it most assuredly should—then it ought to do it right.

Arkansas Gazette.
Little Rock, Ark., February 7, 1978

Members of the U.S. House of Representatives are beginning to have some doubts about permitting their regular meetings to be broadcast "live"—or reasonably live—on radio and TV. And well they might, for if someone is looking for a good capsule definition of "asking for it," this would be it.

As a result of these second thoughts, the tentatively approved broadcasts, which were to have begun this June at the latest, now are not likely to be seen and heard until next year, if ever.

All the world's a stage, but this would be a little much, we think. The justifying theory is fine—to give the people a little more of an insight into how their laws are made and unmade. But the kind of viewer who would spend much time looking at this sort of thing would be the kind who would look at anything, and, so far from being satisfied with all his uncoerced non-stop viewing this kind tends to be crankier and more critical than the non-viewer who merely flips off, or doesn't flip on in the first place.

The risks to the on-camera lawgivers are so many and so obvious that we should have thought that the broadcasting of sessions of the House would never have even been seriously considered. Test runs on closed circuit systems have revealed one of the principal problems, the overhead lighting system that exists in the House chamber. In consequence, some of the Honourable Members are worried about their reflecting pates, while almost all are worried to some degree or other by the so-called "raccoon effect," excessive shading under the eyes and at the chin. Black members, especially, fear that they will become as "invisible" in appearance as they are in numbers and essential influence

But if the lighting were perfect there still would be risks. Skinheads aside, what of the member whose "rug" sometimes takes on a life of its own and leaps from the wearer's poll at the most embarrassing times? For members without hair problems, there

would be far fewer opportunities to snoozle away in your seat with your mouth open, a natural enough yielding to nature, considering the anesthetic effect of most of the spoken words that find their way eventually into the Congressional Record. And even taking into consideration the circumstance that most Americans do not know the name of their Congressman, much less what he looks like, there are always a few cranks out there who do, and simple absenteeism from the chamber will be more fraught with risk than it is now.

Finally—and we think inevitably—a variant of Gresham's Law will dictate that the worst will drive out the best with the more thespian inclined of the Members exercising a disproportionate share of the floor time, unless "Mr. Speaker" can wield an even quicker gavel than he does now. These buckos will be able to bore with the best of 'em of course. The only difference—a big one—is that they will do it louder.

THE SACRAMENTO BEE
Sacramento, Cal., February 5, 1978

Not for a moment do we suggest that everything that goes on in the U.S. Senate and House is worth televising or worth viewing. That could mean more of Congress on the tube than most people could bear. In 1977, to give you an idea, the House was in session for 881 hours and 37 minutes.

We think, however, the television networks should have the right to train their cameras on the workings of both houses and to transmit what they considered newsworthy to the American public.

The issue is current for several reasons. One is that the Senate leadership is willing to allow live radio but not television coverage of the floor debate on the Panama Canal treaties.

The radio pickup will mark the first broadcast ever of a Senate debate. This, standing alone, is commendable. The Panama Canal dispute, complex and emotional as it is, should be given all possible national exposure before the fateful vote is taken.

Sen. Robert C. Byrd, D-W.Va., the majority leader, professes to favor televised coverage but insists mechanical problems stand in the way. There also is suspicion that, beyond the intrusion of TV

gear and the glare of lighting for the cameras, some senators are fearful members might be shown to be inattentive or sleeping. Or maybe not even there for home-state folks to see.

The House is toying with the idea of televising its proceedings, with cameras manned by its own employees who would control what goes out to the viewer. This, protested Rep. Lionel Van Deerlin, D-Calif., a onetime television commentator, would be like requiring newspaper reporters to rely for their stories on notes taken by House employees.

The television networks did an objective job — and an important one — in televising congressional committees at work, from the Army-McCarthy hearings in 1954 to the more recent Watergate and impeachment hearings. We don't know how much of floor proceedings they would care to cover with cameras — our guess would be very little — but that's not the point. The essential issue is whether news professionals can turn on their cameras, as well as microphones, at their discretion and under their control. There can be no other way in the American scheme of things.

The Afro American
Baltimore, Md., February 11, 1978

Rep. Shirley Chisholm, D.-N.Y., stood alone on the vote—but she was right.

Mrs. Chisholm cast her lone vote against the recommendation of a House subcommittee which wants Congress, rather than the commercial networks, to control radio and television coverage of the House.

The 3-1 recommendation to the House Rules Committee suggests the congressmen want to have the final word on what the public sees and hears from their chambers.

It's something like having the government in control of newspapers and broadcast systems.

Rep. Chisholm favors coverage being controlled by the Public Broadcast Service Network or a pool involving PBS and the commercial networks.

The public would have fuller confidence in coverage handled by media people instead of news of the Congress, by the Congress and for the Congress.

THE DAILY HERALD

Biloxi, Miss., January 27, 1978

Should congressional newsmakers also become news managers?

We think not. But that's the way the U.S. House of Representatives is headed. The House is finally about to allow televised coverage of proceedings after some three decades of aimless debate.

Already, 44 state legislatures and the Canadian House of Commons have taken the big step from the Dark Ages into a presumed Age of Enlightenment — where citizens can watch their legislators in action.

Televised proceedings have had many pleasant side-effects.

✓ Speeches are said to be shorter and to the point, at least in Canada. And profanity is not as prevalent.

✓ Legislators appear to be more image-conscious. Solons are dressing up. Fewer are seen dozing at their desks. Or munching lunch with their feet propped up. Or sharing guffaws over a private joke.

✓ Fears of "grandstanding" by showhorses for the camera appear unfounded, at least in Florida. Public TV cameras there focus on legislative workhorses, as well as the traditional view "showboaters" at the speaker's podium.

The House of Representatives should know all this. They should also know better than to try to control TV cameras covering themselves. Such a plan is in the works.

Government cameras manned by government technicians would focus on government leaders in only a few government-approved areas of the House chamber. According to this plan, which is supported by Speaker Tip O'Neil and a large number of members, cameras could focus on the podium but not other parts of the chamber or galleries.

Congressmen could continue to snooze comfortably off-camera. Activity on the floor and in the gallery would go unrecorded by government cameras.

You'd be seeing what the House wants you to see.

It's starting to sound like a televised Congressional Record, isn't it? That's the feeble reason many of its supporters are citing. They point up the "need" to preserve a TV record of proceedings for posterity. It's bound to be a boodoggle. The House was in session for 881 hours and 37 minutes last year. Who needs a televised Congressional Record that drones on and on like a stuck record?

Happily, there are two other plans. One would ask a reluctant Washington public TV station to share its tapes with commercial TV networks. Neither side likes this plan, from standpoints of economics and labor union restrictions.

The third plan merits approval. Networks would "pool" their coverage. That's jargon for taking turns. The film would be made available to all accredited television and radio stations. Importantly, too, cameramen could focus on anything in the chamber.

Congressmen must remember that the First Amendment guarantees freedom of the press. That includes TV. Newspaper reporters do not rely on notes taken by House employes. Broadcasters should not have to rely on government-produced videotapes either.

Newsmakers should not become news managers.

The Boston Herald American

Boston, Mass., June 17, 1978

To televise, or not to televise? That is the question asked and argued for years by lawmakers in Washington and Ottawa. In both capitals it now has been answered in the affirmative, albeit tentatively and with varying results.

In Washington the House of Representatives has agreed to try television next year, provided a deal can be made with broadcasters who want to control coverage and not be spoon-fed by House technicians. The Senate has deferred action indefinitely.

To get the feel of airwave exposure, the house this week dipped its toe into electronic waters by allowing live radio broadcasts of regular proceedings. Although Tennessee's Rep. Albert Gore Jr. called it an "historic occasion," historians are likely to take a lesser view.

Only 16 members were on the floor. Only one station reported the proceedings, and for only five minutes. Another station tried and failed, running into that ageless bete noire of the electronic age, dead microphones. About the only comment of substance during those "historic" moments was a reminder from House Chaplain Edward Latch that we live in "troubled time," a fact with which House members should be somewhat acquainted.

The importance of all this, however, is that the House isn't afraid to open new avenues of information, and give the public a closer look at what it's up to. This is all to the good. It has worked for the better in Canada, where TV's eyes have been peeping at Parliament in Ottawa since October. The people's report card gives the experiment high marks for improving debate, encouraging backbenchers to speak up, reducing oratorical extravaganzas and cutting down on incidents of bad manners.

A Canadian commentator said it's "better than soap opera," which strikes us as a mixed compliment. But he heartily approved of the new electronic outlet, and expressed the hope the lawmaking process would be permanently pictured by television.

Cameras in congressional chambers, like cameras in our courts, are, when properly operated, a sound and sensible means of strengthening the people's right to know.

When producers and participants concentrate on history rather than histrionics, the televising of legislative proceedings can add a new dimension to a free and responsible press.

THE ARIZONA REPUBLIC

Phoenix, Ariz., May 4, 1978

THE House of Representatives, which voted earlier this year with fear and loathing to have television cover its proceedings but has yet to let the TV cameras in, should take heart from the experience of Canada's Parliament.

The House of Commons let them in six months ago. There was a great deal of fear and loathing in Commons, too, but now the vast majority of the members are enthusiastic about the experiment and plan to continue it.

Like the House of Representatives, the House of Commons debated for a long time whether it should demand control of the cameras or let the TV crews go about their business in their own way, without interference.

The members were afraid, as the congressmen are, of being made to look ridiculous on the screen, with the cameras focusing on empty seats or dozing MPs.

They finally decided to have the crews operate under the supervision of a staff member of Commons.

Only once has TV embarrassed a member. It caught him picking his nose. Otherwise, the cameras have concentrated on the action.

The program has proved more popular than anyone anticipated. The rating services have yet to assess how many Canadians watch it, but a broadcaster reports that whenever anything goes wrong, say with the sound, "the switchboard lights up."

The quality of debate in Commons has vastly improved, the members agree, and so has their own deportment. The latter happened after former Prime Minister John G. Diefenbaker admonished his fellow MPs for drowning out speakers by heckling, shouting and thumping desks.

Students in his rural Saskatchewan constituency told him they were shocked by such behavior, Diefenbaker declared. The students said they would be expelled from school if they ever acted as the MPs were doing.

Television also has caused the present prime minister, Pierre Elliott Trudeau, to get a haircut.

Being on television has enhanced the reputation of several MPs, notably of Joseph Clark, leader of the opposition Progressive Conservative Party.

Clark was relatively unknown when he became leader two years ago. His sharp questioning on TV of Trudeau and members of Trudeau's cabinet has made him a national figure.

"I don't think there is any doubt that the effect (of television) has been all positive," says James Jerome, the speaker of the House of Commons. "There is the strongest evidence that television has awakened an unprecedented interest in Parliament.

"We're talking here of a coast-to-coast, deep-seated and sustained demand."

Congress take heed.

EDITORIAL

WCBS-TV
NEW YORK

WHO'S CALLING THE SHOTS?

The House of Representatives is soon going to allow gavel to gavel television coverage of its sessions. Granted, not every congressional session will have the dramatic urgency of the Watergate hearings, but even being able to observe what goes on in Congress on an ordinary day is important.

It's on those ordinary days that decisions are debated in Congress that affect your life, decisions about how your tax dollars are spent, what kind of energy policy the country will have, whether you'll be paying more money in taxes or less; things like that.

That's why the presence of television cameras will be so valuable. The big unanswered question is whose hand will be on the camera--professional broadcasters or Congress itself? Some in Congress including House Speaker Tip O'Neill want house employes to run the television operation.

But the purpose of television coverage is to allow the public to keep an eye on Congress. So should Congress itself be deciding what the public can see? Obviously, that would undermine the whole idea.

We think it would be much more in the public's interest to let the three television networks pool their resources and cover congressional sessions as they routinely cover such governmental events as presidential press conferences and state of the union messages.

Opening Congress to television cameras can bring government closer to the people, but not if Congress is calling the shots.

Presented by Sue Cott, Manager of Editorials
January 17, 1978 at 6:55 PM

The Cincinnati Post

Cincinnati, Ohio, May 24, 1978

The Ohio Supreme Court should move ahead now to change its archaic rule that prohibits the use of cameras during court proceedings.

Years ago, before the advent of new technology, it made sense to keep noisy, flashing cameras out of the courtroom. But modern technology has changed all that.

Today's news cameras take pictures with available light, without the use of flash bulbs or bright lights and without disrupting the decorum of the court.

Chief Justice C. William O'Neill of the Ohio Supreme Court appointed two committees last month — one from newspapers and the other from broadcasting — to study the issue and make recommendations.

These recommendations are expected to come within the next few weeks. O'Neill says he will then ask for comments from judges around the state and various bar associations.

Allowing cameras in the courtroom will give Ohioans an opportunity to see as well as read about how justice is administered.

At least 13 states already have some form of rules that allow cameras in the courtroom. Ohio should do the same.

THE ARIZONA REPUBLIC

Phoenix, Ariz., December 4, 1978

UNLESS signs are all wrong, the day will come when cameras are permitted in Arizona courtrooms. But don't hold your breath waiting for that event. And don't expect any great improvement in the administration of justice when it occurs.

Other states have allowed news photographers to take pictures of actual courtroom scenes. They have been used, sparingly to be sure, in newspapers and on television. So far the skies haven't fallen.

The matter came up at the annual Arizona judges conference, held last week at Rio Rico. Chief Justice James Duke Cameron of the Arizona Supreme Court said there had been some movement in the direction of lowering the barriers in the courtrooms. He indicated that the court would investigate the matter.

The Conference of Supreme Court Justices, a national organization, has suggested that state courts explore the matter. The American Bar Association has recommended that state courts permit pictures to be taken of judges, juries, witnesses and attorneys.

Television audiences brought up on Perry Mason will find actual trials duller than dishwater. The profit-minded networks will never display uncut films of trials. While hour-long programs are devoted to sex and violence, few TV news programs would give more than 30 seconds to a criminal or a civil trial. Only the most sensational portions would be shown.

On the other hand, the public probably would benefit by being given even abbreviated glimpses of what happens during an actual trial. They would be able to compare how cases are tried in real life as against the hyped-up TV and movie versions.

Still cameras would be less likely to disturb the decorum of the court, and print reproduction of actual courtroom scenes would have some educational value.

The issue is worth exploring.

Just as an uneasy equilibrium has been reached between a free press and a fair trial, we think a way can be found to bring the austere courts closer to the people without destroying the judicial atmosphere that courts must have.

EVENING EXPRESS

Portland, Me., December 19, 1977

We suspect it will be some time before the suggestion that television cameras be permitted in Maine courtrooms is accepted.

Maine's newest Superior Court judge, Daniel Wathen of Augusta, made the proposal during a judicial seminar at Ellsworth last week.

Judge Wathen, who was appointed to the Superior Court by Governor Longley in September, said televised trials would go a long way toward reducing public criticism of judicial decisions.

He said if people in general could receive the same information that judges and juries get in the courtroom during a trial, they would have a better understanding of how the judicial process works, how verdicts are reached and sentences decided upon.

Still, many people both in and outside the judicial community have grave reservations about bringing television into the courtrooms, and their doubts are not entirely without justification.

The recent experiment in Florida in which the trial of a 15-year-old boy accused of murder was televised was not a very good argument for TV in the courtroom.

In addition to some rather flamboyant tactics by the defense lawyer, people watching at home got actively caught up in the process. Many, including some lawyers, began telephoning both defense and prosecuting attorneys to offer advice on courtroom tactics and jury selection.

In addition, the cameras and technicians involved in the broadcasts proved confusing and disruptive to the trial proceedings at times.

We can appreciate Judge Wathen's thinking in wanting to improve the public's understanding of the judicial process.

Nevertheless, the whole issue of television in Maine courtrooms should be much more thoroughly discussed before it is tried here.

THE PLAIN DEALER

Cleveland, Ohio, August 20, 1978

Ohio's courts should open their doors to newspaper photographers, radio broadcasters and television cameramen.

The Ohio Supreme Court is considering a well-reasoned set of rules that would lift the courtroom ban on photographic and broadcast equipment in the state's trial and appellate courts.

The court's approval of the changes, which could come as early as this fall, could give the public a better understanding of the judicial system.

Ohio's rule barring cameras in the courtroom dates to 1954, the year of Dr. Sam Sheppard's murder trial. Although the trial was not televised, his conviction was overturned in 1966 by the U.S. Supreme Court on the ground that extensive publicity had prevented Sheppard from getting a fair trial.

The year before, the Supreme Court, in reversing the swindling conviction of Texas financier Billie Sol Estes, said that trial "by television is . . . foreign to our system."

But television is now an accepted fact of American life. Recognizing this, 14 states already have taken steps to open their doors to broadcast and photographic coverage.

The reaction in those states has been overwhelmingly favorable. Colorado has allowed electronic coverage since 1956 and no verdict there has been reversed because of it. After the Florida murder trial of 15-year-old Ronney A. Zamora was televised last fall, the presiding judge called the experiment a success.

Claims that the presence of electronic equipment in the courtrooms will be disruptive lack merit.

When the Supreme Court decided the Billie Sol Estes case, television equipment was bulky and intruded on courtroom decorum. But today's equipment is compact, unobtrusive and portable.

The right of privacy is another reason cited for barring cameras from the courtroom. However, an individual's right of privacy is limited. When one becomes identified with an event of public interest, it is not an invasion of his right to privacy to give publicity to his connection with that event.

In addition, the rules proposed by the Ohio Supreme Court would allow the presiding judge to prohibit filming of victims or witnesses "if the court determines that there is reasonable cause for such objection." The rape victim, for example, certainly would not have to be subjected to close-up camera coverage.

Two other reasons cited by those opposed to electronic coverage — that it will make it more difficult to obtain witnesses and that it will place unneeded pressures on the trial participants — have not been borne out in those states where such coverage is permitted.

The record in those states shows that a balance can be struck between the defendant's Sixth Amendment right to a fair trial and the First Amendment guarantee of a free press. They need not be mutually exclusive.

Most cases receive little media attention, and permitting camera and tape recorder coverage will not change that fact. The judge's ordinary instructions that the jurors not read the papers, listen to radio news or watch television news during the trial would continue to be sufficient in most trials. In a highly notorious case, it might be necessary to sequester jurors — just as is done now.

A major national survey released earlier this year found that most people are either uninformed or misinformed about the operations of courts and that public confidence in state and local courts is extremely low. Three-fourths of the 1,931 adults questioned conceded they knew very little or nothing about courts.

During the Senate and House committee hearings on Watergate and impeachment, television did much to make the democratic process intelligible by its dignified and discreet coverage. Electronic coverage might be able to do the same for Ohio's courts.

Lincoln Journal

Lincoln, Neb., June 17, 1978

There is a true element of surprise, and encouragement, in the 22-15 vote of the Nebraska District Judges Association defeating a resolution for opening court rooms to photographers and telecasters.

The surprise is not that Douglas County Judge Rudy Tesar's motion failed. This was, after all, the first time the proposition formally had been advanced before the district jurists and the weight of tradition is inevitably against change.

What lifts the eyebrows is that 14 judges supported Tesar. That is cause for cheer, and a positive stimulant for the issue to be kept alive before the state's judiciary.

There's convincing evidence around the nation that the discreet presence of cameras in the courtroom do not disrupt the conduct of a trial or poison the environment against the parties at bar.

It may be there still are judges who, when someone mentions cameras in a courtroom, automatically conjure big and clumsy box-like articles and a joker in jodhpurs with riding crop, running about giving directions. Time and technology have advanced far beyond that primitive, neodramatic scene.

If there is a fear that Nebraska jurors might be influenced by cameras, in a trial setting, the thing to do is experimentally limit such coverage to trials before a judge only, or arguments before the Nebraska Supreme Court.

Tesar is on the mark when he says the public would benefit from a wider, more graphic look at what goes on in a public courtroom.

St. Petersburg Times

St. Petersburg, Fla., May 16, 1978

Like a television station whose picture has gone bad, the Florida Supreme Court is asking the public to stand by on courtroom viewing. The difference is that the court's one-year experiment on cameras in the courtroom is by all accounts running smoothly, with no technical difficulties.

We see no reason for the interruption that will result from the court's refusal to extend the pilot program while evaluating its effect. By a narrow 4-3 majority, the court concluded its "orderly consideration of the issues" could be impeded by permitting live and still cameras in Florida courtrooms beyond the June 30 deadline set a year ago.

IT ESCAPES us why the review would be made any less orderly by simply extending the strict rules that allow unobtrusive camera work during court proceedings. Dade County Circuit Judge Paul Baker, one of many trial judges skeptical about the pilot program before the Supreme Court ordered it last year, termed it a success after presiding over the much-publicized Ronnie Zamora

murder trial. The program was widely praised at a Florida Bar conference in Orlando in January.

"After one calendar year judges, lawyers, jurors, witnesses, news reporters and the viewing public have grown accustomed to cameras in court," Justice Joseph Boyd wrote in a dissenting opinion. "The temporary termination of such activity, with the probability of its renewal within a few weeks, would tend to disrupt and frustrate the program which at this time appears to be generally accepted in this state."

LIKE THE minority, which also included Chief Justice Ben Overton and Justice James Adkins, we believe the interruption will be more disruptive than continuation of the program pending the court's final decision.

But we remain optimistic that the full court, in reviewing its pilot program and considering arguments on both sides, ultimately will conclude that justice is served just as well, and probably better, when the public is better able to watch.

The Evening Bulletin

Philadelphia, Pa., February 27, 1978

Televising certain courtroom proceedings is an idea whose time has come.

Both Attorney General Griffin Bell and the likely future president of the American Bar Association recently endorsed allowing broadcast coverage of arguments in federal appeals courts. Already a handful of states are experimenting with television coverage of jury trials.

Television and still cameras have traditionally been banned in most courts, and that prohibition received support in 1965 when the U.S. Supreme Court reversed the swindling conviction of Texas financier Billie Sol Estes, whose trial had been televised. The high court ruled then that television could interfere with the right to a fair trial and could subject the defendant to "a form of mental — if not physical — harassment resembling a police lineup or the third degree."

That was undoubtedly true in 1965, when television involved bulky cameras, endless coils of wire and glaring lights. But today's TV equipment, not to mention that of radio, is compact and relatively unobtrusive. Cameras could be in fixed positions and could record courtroom activities with almost no disruption or distraction.

But that doesn't meet another frequent argument against televising courtroom proceedings: That attorneys, witnesses, maybe even judges would grandstand in

front of the cameras, or that the participants would be inhibited before them. Reportedly, U.S. Chief Justice Warren Burger is vehemently opposed to having Supreme Court proceedings televised, one reason being that he believes some of the justices would play to the cameras.

It cannot be shown whether the contentions about grandstanding are valid until there is more experimentation with televising courtroom proceedings. It is just as likely, we think, that the television eye could inspire people to do their best. Another likelihood is that television has become so commonplace that its presence in the courtroom would make little difference in anyone's behavior.

Overall, we believe there are educational and informational advantages to allowing cameras in the courtroom. We're glad the head of the Justice Department and the soon-to-be head of the bar association have endorsed the idea for federal appellate courts. That's a good place to begin and to watch the effects. Also, those few states which have experimented with television in the courtroom should make known what has happened there.

There needs to be greater public access to and understanding of the inner workings of the justice system, and television in the courtroom is one way to provide that.

ALBUQUERQUE JOURNAL

Albuquerque, N.M., February 28, 1978

Two vital and indispensable rights of the American people — the fair and impartial trial and the free and responsible press — have demonstrated that they can exist simultaneously in the same arena.

Recent tests under rigidly controlled and mutually acceptable conditions tend to confirm that modern technological extensions of traditional journalism — photo-journalism and electronic journalism — also can function in the courtroom without prejudice to prosecutors, defendants or civil litigants.

The landmark case was the murder trial of 15-year-old Ronny Zamora in Miami — a trial covered simultaneously by more than 60 news organizations from all parts of the world. It also is believed to have been the first trial ever covered in its entirety — from jury selection to verdict — on live television.

Paul Baker, trial judge in the Zamora case, acknowledged that he had some misgivings before the trial, but after the trial he declared: "The press policed themselves beautifully. I have no complaints . . . whatsoever . . . I never made a request that was argued with, or not complied with."

With much of the spade work already achieved — notably in the state courts of Florida, Washington, Alabama, Colorado and Georgia — it is neither surprising, presumptive nor innovative that the justices of New Mexico's Supreme Court should be talking about the experimental admission of cameras and cameramen to New Mexico courtrooms.

The experiences of other states with cameras and microphones in the courtroom should provide a sound basis for ground rules in New Mexico. Thereafter, the courts may proceed cautiously in expanding the privilege or, as experience indicates, providing safeguards.

The greatest safeguard springs from the fact that the editor, cameraman and newscaster are no less committed to the fairness or impartiality of a trial than the judge who conducts the trial or the individual who invokes the protection of the court. In fact, all are on the same team, for they draw their extraordinary powers, privileges and immunities from the same source — the Constitution of the United States.

Democrat Chronicle
Rochester, N.Y., June 15, 1978

THE TIME is coming closer when television coverage of court trials will no longer be unusual.

That will represent quite a turnaround since the U.S. Supreme Court 13 years ago reversed the conviction of Billy Sol Estes. In that case, it was determined, the televising of the trial created such a carnival atmosphere that Estes was denied the due process of law.

Today 13 states have now authorized, subject to various conditions, the televising and broadcasting of certain court proceedings.

A lot of things have changed in 13 years.

Television, thanks to technical improvements, is now much less intrusive and distracting.

Experience has shown that public scrutiny of governmental processes is generally healthy.

Proponents say in fact that a public presence in the courtroom helps assure the defendant of a fair trial.

"Government in the sunshine" has seized the imagination of public and politicians alike.

THE AMERICAN BAR Association is also changing its attitudes.

President William B. Spann Jr. recently told the West Virginia State Bar Association that judges and bar associations need to do a better job of explaining their problems to the public.

Although warmer to appellate proceedings coverage than to coverage of trial courts, Spann was yet generally favorable.

"The public needs to be involved," he said, "and visual communication, television in particular, is one of our best mediums for doing so if fair and intelligent standards can be worked out for its use and strictly adhered to.

"Two hundred years ago Thomas Jefferson said: 'If we think the public not enlightened enough to exercise a wholesome discretion, the remedy is not to take it from them but to inform their discretion by education.' "

The public is a whole lot smarter than it's often given credit for.

The Chattanooga Times
Chattanooga, Tenn., November 30, 1977

When it comes to covering legal issues as they are argued in the nation's courtrooms, television journalists are less than equal to their print media competitors. The reason is simple: Although they can sit in on trials and hearings, the broadcast journalist may not bring his microphone or television camera into most courtrooms. But things could be changing.

In a recent issue of Judicature, published by the American Judicature Society, U.S. Dist. Judge Jack B. Weinstein, and Diane L. Zimmerman, an assistant professor of law at New York University, argue for more access to the courts by broadcast journalists.

We can understand why most judges would not permit a broadcast journalist to creep about the courtroom during a trial with his camera. But television was allowed to cover — from a fixed position — the murder trial of young Ronnie Zamora in Miami recently with no apparent problems. Even the judge in that case lauded the experiment.

It would be even easier for television to cover hearings at the appellate levels, including the U.S. Supreme Court, where lawyers argue from one location. It would have been "fascinating," said authors Weinstein and Zimmerman, for the public to have witnessed the arguments for and against abortion and capital punishment when those issues were considered by the High Court.

Highly sophisticated equipment, much of it requiring less light than before, plus the dictates of the First Amendment, should be sufficient to encourage a change regarding broadcast journalists' rights to cover important stories involving the law. Now is as good a time as any to start.

EVENING JOURNAL
Wilmington, Del., August 7, 1978

The often tedious process of opening up the courtrooms of this country moved significantly forward last week when supreme court justices from across the nation voted overwhelmingly to endorse radio, television and photographic coverage of court proceedings.

The significance is more symbolic than substantial at this point since the resolution expresses only the feelings of the annual Conference of Chief Justices. But given the influential role chief justices play in state court operations, we find the vote encouraging.

Opening up the courts to photographers and broadcasters has long had our support. The courts of this country remain among the most remote and least understood of our governmental institutions. This lack of understanding, we believe, is a major contributor to the anti-judge, anti-court feelings we experience all too frequently.

Photographic equipment, and the machinery of television and radio broadcasting have improved considerably since the U.S. Supreme Court ruled, a little more than a decade ago, that Billie Sol Estes was denied a fair trial because of the presence of cameras in the courtroom.

It is our conviction that permitting photographic and broadcast coverage of courtroom proceedings would contribute to a better understanding of the courts. Obviously guidelines would have to be worked out to ensure that media coverage would not interfere with the administration of justice. But such guidelines are well within reach.

Chief Justice Daniel L. Herrmann of the Delaware Supreme Court encouraged an experiment in television coverage of a Superior Court trial last spring. After seeing the results the chief justice decided not to make any change in the current ban of cameras and other electronic equipment from the courts at this time.

The decision to proceed slowly on this matter is frustrating, but it may be the wisest course. Chief Justice Herrmann noted that the U.S. Supreme Court is likely to review television's effect on courts in the celebrated Florida murder trial of 15-year-old Ronny Zamora. The youngster's trial was televised. The chief justice wants to wait, for a year at least, to see what happens.

In the meantime we urge the establishment of a special committee of news media representatives, lawyers and judges to study the matter and develop guidelines for use of cameras and broadcast equipment in courtrooms.

The Philadelphia Inquirer
Philadelphia, Pa., March 2, 1978

Chief Justice Warren Burger best knows how he might act if Supreme Court proceedings were televised, but we have more confidence in his brethren than he evidently does.

Justice Burger was quoted recently as saying that court's proceedings would not be televised as "long as I am here" because the justices "would ham it up." It is not known to whom the chief justice was referring; perhaps, the other eight justices might demand a bill of particulars.

Regardless, the chief justice is raising a straw issue.

Rather than providing an unwanted stage for frustrated actors, televising court proceedings would provide a wonderful educational opportunity for millions of Americans as they watched critical issues being debated by skilled advocates before the nation's highest tribunal.

U. S. District Court Judge Jack Weinstein of the Eastern District of New York wrote recently, "Would it not have been fascinating to both the public and law students, for example, had the arguments before the Supreme Court on abortion and capital punishment been recorded for TV and radio? The public debate on the issues would have been conducted on a much higher level had the sophisticated argument on the diverse considerations been seen and heard across the country."

The educational value of television and radio has been demonstrated with the televising of the Watergate proceedings and, presently, with the broadcasting by the public radio network of the U. S. Senate's Panama Canal treaty debates.

Television and still cameras have been barred from many courtrooms for decades. The initial fear was that popping flashbulbs or even clouds of white powder from old-fashioned cameras would disrupt proceedings. Not until 1964, however, was the ban justified on constitutional grounds.

Importantly, however, in that 1964 Supreme Court decision, the late Justice John Harlan recognized that the "day may come when television will have become so commonplace" that its presence in the courtroom would not "disparage the judicial process."

Notwithstanding Justice Burger's concerns, many jurists, such as Judge Weinstein, believe that day has come. In fact, Florida recently permitted the televising of a controversial murder trial, which was viewed by millions of persons.

In a report assessing that trial, the trial judge, Paul Baker, concluded, "The conduct of the Zamora trial in this pilot experience must be viewed as a success." Undoubtedly, Chief Justice Burger and his eight colleagues would behave just as well as did the participants in the Florida trial.

THE INDIANAPOLIS NEWS
Indianapolis, Ind., November 30, 1977

Gradually, but inevitably, courtrooms are being opened to cameras — both still and motion — and the public thereby is gaining access to more of its own important business.

The latest experiment in Columbus, Ga., has been appraised by the judge as a "total success." It was Georgia's first televised murder trial, one in which the defendant was found guilty and sentenced to die. The judge, who was reported to be skeptical of using cameras in the courtroom, said: "The coverage didn't distract from the trial at all."

The murder victim's mother agreed. She said: "I didn't even realize they (the photographers) were here when I testified."

Guidelines established last May by the Georgia Supreme Court said the parties in a trial should agree to photographic coverage before cameras and microphones could be installed in the courtrooms:

Only one witness, the defendant's sister, requested not to be photographed, televised or tape recorded. Pictures of the jury were disallowed at the request of the panel. None of the television stations used live coverage or carried any of the court sessions in their entirety. But all used portions in their news programs. One radio station broadcast live from the courtroom for a part of the trial.

Precedent for the Superior Court pictures was established by the Georgia Supreme Court, and on the strength of this recent success other Georgia courts are expected to follow suit.

Georgia has joined Washington, Alabama, Florida and Colorado in permitting full media access to its legal process. Other states, including Indiana, should do likewise.

The State
Columbia, S.C., May 13, 1978

FOR MORE than 40 years, the American Bar Association has held a canon to the backs of photojournalists, forbidding cameras and broadcasting equipment in courtrooms.

But today, there seems a possibility that the canon might be removed or modified.

The ABA adopted Canon 35 in the wake of the controversy caused by the sensational Bruno Hauptmann trial in 1935 for the kidnap-slaying of the Lindbergh baby. During that trial, smoke from the photographers' flash hung like a pall over the room while photographers, sometimes pushing and shoving each other, indiscriminately stuck their lenses in the faces of witnesses. The judge lost control of the courtroom.

The canon, adopted in 1937 and amended in 1952 to include television, reads in part: " . . . The taking of photographs in the courtroom, during sessions of the court or recesses between sessions, and the broadcasting or televising of court procedings . . . should not be permitted."

However, times have changed, the nature of photojournalism has changed, photographic technology and equipment have changed, and it appears that the minds of many of the nation's lawyers and justices are beginning to change. Several states, Florida most notably, are in the process of conducting year-long experiments, under strict guidelines, allowing cameras in the courtrooms.

And now the national president of the ABA, William B. Spann Jr., has called for a partial lifting of the ban on cameras in federal courts at the appellate court level. He puts special emphasis on the Supreme Court, because cases there "often involve important constitutional issues about which the American public needs to receive information."

We agree wholeheartedly with Mr. Spann. Permitting cameras in the appellate federal courtroom under proper conditions would allow Americans to see a key branch of their government in action and to be privy to the arguments and debate of important issues.

Arguments in the *Bakke* case involving the use of quotas to fight discrimination, for example, would have been of great interest to many Americans. But tradition and the revised Canon 35 prevented cameras from recording the give and take in the Supreme Court.

Appellate court arguments are relatively short and are conducted exclusively by legal professionals, according to Mr. Spann. Therefore, there would be no problem of witnesses or jurors hamming it up or feeling intimidated by the camera.

For these same reasons, we still have reservations about opening the trial courts to the camera. Florida's strictly regulated experiment in opening all courts to cameras and television will end in July, and we would prefer to reserve judgment until those results are in.

The lifting of the ban on cameras in federal appellate courtrooms will be presented to the ABA House of Delegates this August. We urge careful consideration of the proposal. It would better acquaint the American public with a branch of government few ever see but which affects the lives of many. That, in the long run, should serve justice.

THE MILWAUKEE JOURNAL
Milwaukee, Wisc., June 3, 1978

From Madison to Amarillo, from Sacramento to St. Petersburg, the debate is joined: Should Americans be admitted to the courtrooms of the land, by camera? Should they also be admitted electronically to that highest sanctuary of the law, the US Supreme Court?

Thirteen years ago the high court reversed the conviction of Billie Sol Estes because the televising of his trial had created a carnival atmosphere and deprived him of due process of law. Since then, cameras have been banned from most US courtrooms.

Now the TV eye, still camera and radio microphone are beginning to return to the trials. Thirteen states allow them in the courtroom, either on an experimental or a permanent basis. Wisconsin recently began a one year test of this coverage.

The idea will get a major review this summer when the American Bar Association considers the courtroom camera issue. The draft of an ABA committee report reads: "Television, radio and photographic coverage of judicial proceedings is not per se inconsistent with the rights to a fair trial." We agree.

Opponents argue that audio-visual equipment may make defendants and witnesses nervous; encourage some judges to play for the camera and prompt some attorneys to strut and declaim. However, none of these arguments seems to outweigh the public value of full media coverage. The uneasiness of witnesses and defendants is neither novel nor an excuse not to testify. Electioneering judges and pompous lawyers will posture for the media no matter how the trial is covered — with ballpoint pens, sketch pads or TV eyes.

Besides, electronic coverage has come a long way since the bulky TV cameras, blinding lights and writhing cables of the Estes trial. Today's cameras are small, quiet, unobtrusive. They operate with available courtroom light. Standards should be set to keep them from intruding on private conversations between, say, a defendant and his lawyer.

As cameras continue to move into state courtrooms, we think they also should be admitted to federal courts and particularly to the Supreme Court. Chief Justice Warren Burger emphatically opposes the idea. But Justice Potter Stewart reportedly favors opening oral arguments to TV coverage. So do William Spann Jr., the ABA president, and Benjamin Civiletti, deputy US attorney general.

The potential public value here would be immense. Americans could see, hear and weigh arguments in landmark cases — capital punishment and abortion being only two of them. Here is absorbing public drama that vitally affects us all, yet it now may be seen and heard by only a handful.

The camera belongs in the courtroom, from lowest to highest. Close public scrutiny of public functions, including trials, is both essential and healthy in an open society.

The TENNESSEAN
Nashville, Tenn., January 25, 1979

HISTORIC hearings were held in the criminal courts here Tuesday and Judge John Draper made history by allowing the proceedings in his court room to be photographed.

The hearings concerned unprecedented challenges to the governor's powers to grant pardons and commutations. They rose out of the confused condition created when former Gov. Ray Blanton granted 52 pardons and commutations during his last week in office and Gov. Lamar Alexander blocked release of some of the inmates.

The events of the past week aroused intense public interest and when the matters reached the courts Judge Draper decided the people were entitled to as full and accurate account of the proceedings as it was possible to provide.

It was the first time that live news cameras were permitted to photograph actual criminal court proceedings here. As a result, dramatic scenes of the hearings appeared in newspapers and on television. Interested citizens — and there were hundreds of thousands of them — were given the next best thing to being in the courtroom.

Judge Draper acted in the public interest in allowing the cameras to be present. The people are keenly interested in the operations of the courts. They would be pleased to see photographs of more court cases, not just those of unusual historical significance.

The Wichita Eagle
Wichita, Kans., April 24, 1978

Judge Tyler Lockett has told the Wichita Bar Association that news cameras inevitably will be allowed inside courtrooms. It is a question of when attorneys and judges will allow it, he said.

We suggest that there will never be a better time than the present.

The judge wisely points out that cameras won't make much difference in how people appear before the court or how court business is conducted.

There may have been some reason for banning cameras when flash powder disrupted the event being photographed and often singed the eyebrows of the photographer.

Banning the cameras perhaps was justified when they were big, black boxes that were an intrusion on the dignity of the court.

However, banishment of cameras no longer is justified for any reason.

Cameras are small and unobtrusive. Films are so efficient that pictures can be taken with the light that exists in the courtroom. Shutters are quiet and in no way detract from the court's decorum.

Even television cameras can be operated unobtrusively if they are placed behind screens. Television equipment is smaller than it once was. Modern TV equipment also makes it possible to record scenes without supplemental lighting.

The public has a right to know what is happening and that right includes pictures as well as words.

A few judges recognize this. Others do not, on the mistaken assumption that photography somehow cheapens or that it creates a carnival atmosphere.

The Congress and various state legislatures have shared these views and have banned picture coverage, but that is changing.

Newspaper and television cameras are poking their lenses into legislative chambers in 44 states, including Kansas, about double the estimated total of just five years ago. In Canada, activities in the House of Commons also have been televised since the fall of 1977.

So far, the U.S. Congress has managed to buck the trend, though that might change sometime next year.

It is a trend that will benefit the people in the long term. But it carries a serious responsibility. Cameramen obviously must maintain the dignity of the courts and the legislatures at all times.

Cameras are useful to record what is happening, but they must not become part of the action.

THE CHRISTIAN SCIENCE MONITOR
Boston, Mass., May 23, 1978

TV lawyer Perry Mason had an uncanny knack for making a guilty party break down and confess on the witness stand, thereby proving the innocence of his wrongly accused clients, week after week. In real life, few courtroom dramas are resolved that neatly, although many Americans may not be aware of this, since much of what they know about the criminal justice system is limited to impressions gleaned from such TV exaggerations. The legal profession and the courts in experimenting with cameras in the courtrooms have an important opportunity to provide laymen with an accurate picture of how the U.S. legal system operates. Public access to trials is one of the bulwarks of a democratic society, and a better informed citizenry will help ensure that fairness and justice prevail in the courtroom.

The introduction of TV and other cameras into courtrooms, however, will need to continue to be handled with the greatest of caution and respect for the rights of accused and accuser alike. Television too often tends to dominate and dictate the events it covers, and this must not be allowed to happen in the courts. In the 13 states where cameras are being allowed, under varying restrictions, court administrators are taking care not to let their presence interfere with due process. In Alabama, for instance, all concerned parties — prosecutor, defendant, witness, and judge — must consent.

Properly regulated, cameras in the courtroom need not be a distraction. Technological improvements and "pooling" make their presence far less noticeable than was the case 13 years ago, when the U.S. Supreme Court reversed the conviction of Billie Sol Estes because the televising of his trial created such a carnival-like atmosphere as to deprive him of due process. It was this trial that prompted the ban on cameras in most courtrooms throughout the U.S.

Theoretically, trials already are open to the public, although it is physically impossible for most people with jobs and other responsibilities to actually take time out to attend them in person. Cameras can be their eyes and ears, giving an added dimension to the print journalist's written accounts. However, that also places a tremendous burden of responsibility on editors and reporters in the electronic media to hold sensationalism in check and not to distort testimony with misleading film editing. This will be particularly difficult in a medium with severe time limits for covering complicated cases.

While there may be some merit to arguments that TV cameras may encourage some lawyers to "ham it up" or make some jurors self-conscious, these clearly do not apply to appellate proceedings, especially those of the U.S. Supreme Court. As American Bar Association president William B. Spann points out, cases before the high court "often involve important constitutional issues about which the American public needs to receive information."

At the trial-court level, there are cases from which cameras should be barred. In Florida, exceptions have been made, for example, in a case involving undercover police informers, and again in a trial with testimony from relocated government witnesses. The sitting judge should decide for or against cameras in each case individually. But in general the impetus should be toward opening up trials to the public, and responsible TV coverage seems a logical way to achieve this.

The Birmingham News

Birmingham, Ala., May 23, 1978

Cameras have been banned from almost all courtrooms for 13 years—ever since the Supreme Court ruled that the atmosphere created by television at the Billie Sol Estes trial deprived the defendant of due process of law.

Tonight on public television Birmingham viewers will have a chance to see television return to the courtroom in highlights of the televised murder trial of 15-year-old Ronnie Zamora. The experiment at the Florida trial showed that TV could be informative and instructive rather than disruptive in opening the judicial process to the public.

The presiding judge in the Zamora case called the experiment a success due mainly to the cooperation of press personnel. Besides a new respect for the sensitive nature of court room proceedings demonstrated by the press since the Estes trial, there have also been technological refinements which make the camera less obtrusive.

Today, unlike the scene at the Estes trial, there is no noise from television equipment. Remote cameras are much smaller, and film and tape can be made in existing courtroom light. The judge at the Zamora trial said lighting—high intensity bulbs placed in existing ceiling fixtures—were neither distracting nor uncomfortable.

Similar experiments recently in at least 13 states including Alabama with the use of either TV or still cameras have encouraged a national movement to bring the cameras back on a permanent basis.

A major determination on the issue should come this summer at the meeting of the American Bar Association when revisions of the 1968 standards on fair trial and free press will be discussed.

Supporters of cameras in the courtroom argue that the public's presence would be increased helping assure the defendant a fair trial.

Another major issue is whether the cameras can be exploited by the the performers distracting from the the serious business at hand—whether it encourages judges—particularly elected judges, to play for the camera. And, does it create anxiety in defendants and witnesses?

Obviously there are situations when a camera would always be out of place such as in a small courtroom or when jurors express discomfort at the idea. Chief Justice Warren E. Burger has let it be known that he is emphatically opposed to televising United States Supreme Court proceedings.

Generally, increasing the public's insight into our governmental processes is desirable. Obviously, more thought should be given the issue and more experiments conducted so fairness for all those in the courtroom drama will be protected.

The Dallas Morning News

Dallas, Tex., March 16, 1978

Improving technology in television equipment probably means greater TV coverage of trials in the future.

Based on this fact of life, Robert Thomas, president of the Dallas Bar Association, wants the new court facility to be prepared. Architects have been asked to plan into the building facilities for electronic coverage of trials.

Certainly it would be cheaper to do that now than to renovate the building later. The present courthouse was planned with electronic coverage in mind. Facilities exist there, although judicial rules and court decisions have prohibited live coverage for more than a decade.

Times do change, though. Recently a committee of the American Bar Association proposed new rules to expand trial coverage. And a recent experiment in Florida bolstered arguments that live coverage need not be disruptive.

When the U.S. Supreme Court ruled in the 1960s that Billie Sol Estes had not received a fair trial because of live TV coverage, equipment was much more primitive. Bright lights were necessary then, and cameras were bulky. Today's equipment is much more compact and sophisticated.

By building in facilities for coverage from the start, the county can save money. And it can put itself in the forefront of the movement to broaden public understanding of the judicial system.

The Miami Herald

Miami, Fla., May 30, 1978

AN EXPERIMENT that has given thousands of Floridians their first look at how a real courtroom operates will end at 11:59 p.m. on June 30. After that hour, cameras will no longer be permitted inside Florida courtrooms, where for 11 months they have recorded judicial proceedings live for print and television audiences.

We hope the June 30 "blackout" will be only an interruption, not the termination, of what we consider a conspicuously successful experiment. If the Florida Supreme Court agrees after hearing arguments from both sides, it may well reopen courtrooms to still and TV cameras — possibly permanently.

The court voted 4 to 3 on May 11 to terminate the pilot program, begun last June at the request of television stations WPLG in Miami and WJXT in Jacksonville. Parties favoring cameras in the courtroom have until June 15 to submit written arguments to the court. Opponents will then have 30 days to respond, and advocates will then have 15 days in which to reply.

We can think of no substantive reason why Florida's courtrooms should not be permanently opened to cameras. The initial fears that cameras might disrupt courtroom solemnity have not materialized, thanks to equipment that is small, quiet, and capable of operating without banks of harsh lights.

The advantages, however, have materialized. Both in routine trials and in such highly publicized proceedings as the Miami murder trial of Ronny Zamora, the public has been able to view criminal justice as it really is, not as fiction portrays it.

Thus the public has seen that not all lawyers are facile, or even competent. That jurors sometimes doze. That judges may be cranky or patient beyond belief. That defendants may appear chastened or stolid. That witnesses may stammer but seem believable, or glib but seem to be lying.

There is, to our knowledge, no evidence that the judicial process has been demeaned or that any defendant's right to a fair trial has been jeopardized by cameras in the courtroom. On the contrary, The evidence suggests that Florida's experiment has enabled the public to see, warts and all, a process vital to democratic government and an informed citizenry.

We therefore urge the Florida Supreme Court to re-open courtrooms to cameras as soon as possible. And unless it hears compelling reasons why it should not do so, we urge the court to make the re-opening not experimental, but permanent.

EDITORIAL

WCBS-TV
NEW YORK

CAMERAS IN THE COURTROOM

Last September many Americans watched a murder trial on television. No, not on "Perry Mason"; it was a real murder trial of a 15-year-old boy in Florida. For many it was the first time they had seen what goes on in a real courtroom.

That's because Florida is one of a handful of states that allow television cameras in their courts. Some other states are considering doing so, among them, we're happy to say, New Jersey. And we'd be even happier if New York and Connecticut were considering letting television in their courts.

The tools of the trade of broadcasting journalism are cameras and microphones. When these are denied access to courtrooms, broadcasting journalists are treated as second class citizens. The pencil press brings its pencils to the courtroom, the electronic press should be allowed to bring it's equipment as well.

But it isn't just in the interest of broadcast journalists to have cameras in the courtroom; it's really in the interest of the people, because in a democracy people need information about how their government works.

Television cameras are already in many state legislatures and at public hearings held by executive agencies. But the branch of government least visible to the vast majority of Americans is the judicial.

Sure, the public is welcome at trials. But how often have you gone to watch one? And now especially, when the judicial system is being criticized for dispensing turnstile justice, when judges are often attacked for sloppy performances, it is important that citizens get a first hand look at their courts, so they'll know what changes should be made.

We believe television cameras in the courtroom can uniquely give them that first hand look.

Presented by Sue Cott, Manager of Editorials
June 8, 1978 at 6:55 PM.

NIXON CONCEDES IN TV INTERVIEW
HIS BAD JUDGMENT ON WATERGATE

Former President Richard M. Nixon conceded in a nationally televised interview May 4 that he had "let the American people down" by making misleading statements on the Watergate affair and not meeting his constitutional duty to see that the laws of the country were enforced. But he insisted that he not committed any criminal or impeachable offense. He had impeached himself by resigning, he said. "I brought myself down. I gave 'em a sword. And they stuck it in, and they twisted it with relish. And I guess if I'd been in their position, I'd have done the same thing."

The interviewer was British television celebrity David Frost, who challenged Nixon repeatedly with accusatory questions laced with quotes from the presidential tape recordings of the Nixon Administration. Frost, 38, had a reputation in England of being a probing interviewer, but he was known to American TV audiences primarily as a political satirist and the host of an interview program featuring show-business personalities.

Frost asked Nixon if he would admit to something stronger than "mistakes"—commission of a crime, or abuse of power or failure to fulfill totally the oath of office, or even making the public suffer "two years of needless agony." "I think that people need to hear it," Frost said, "and I think unless you say it you're going to be haunted for the rest of your life." He had made mistakes, Nixon said, and some he regretted the most came from his public statements. Some of those statements were misleading, he said, "misleading in exaggerating."

But, Nixon continued, "People didn't think it was enough to admit mistakes, fine. If they want me to get down and grovel on the floor, no. Never...." What he had done was fail to meet his responsibility to see that the laws of the nation had been enforced, he said. To the extent that he did not meet that responsibility, he said, "To the extent that within the law, and in some cases going right to the edge of the law in trying to advise Ehrlichman and Haldeman and all the rest as to how best to present their cases—because I thought they were legally innocent—that I came to the edge and, under the circumstances, I would have to say that a reasonable person could call that a cover-up. I didn't think of it as a cover-up. I didn't intend it to cover up. Let me say, if I intended to cover up, believe me, I'd have done it. You know how I could have done it? So easily? I could have done it immediately after the election, simply by giving clemency to everybody, and the whole thing would have gone away."

The program itself was a commercial venture, the first of a projected series of telecasts culled from nearly 29 hours of taped sessions with Nixon near his home in San Clemente, Calif. The first interview, whose broadcast time with commercials ran 90 minutes, was carried by 155 local stations signed up by Frost into a temporary national network. The interview also was carried by 10 foreign broadcast systems. Nixon's fee for the interviews reportedly was $600,000 plus a percentage of profits, possibly 10%, that was expected to put his take over the million dollar mark. Frost too reportedly would earn over a million dollars.

ST. LOUIS POST-DISPATCH
St. Louis, Mo., May 27, 1977

Richard Nixon, in four nationally televised interviews with David Frost, has now had his day in the court of public opinion—at a handsome profit to himself, but without offering any evidence to cast doubt on the unofficial judgments of Congress and the people that forced him from office nearly three years ago. The judgments had to be unofficial because his resignation avoided the impeachment trial in the Senate, which would have been sure to come; and the pardon by President Ford avoided prosecution in a criminal court.

This being the case, what Mr. Nixon had to say about the pardon was perhaps the most significant response in the fourth interview. After observing that he agonized over the pardon because his acceptance of it would be taken as an admission of guilt in connection with multiple crimes, he said he finally decided to sign the acceptance on the advice of his attorney that he could not get a fair trial. Whatever merit that argument had (and there was probably some basis for making it), it seems to us that it had far less validity for a defendant of Mr. Nixon's status than it would for many sensationally publicized cases involving defendants without the resources and the powerful friends that Mr. Nixon still had.

Any court that tried Mr. Nixon would have been scrupulous to be fair to a former president. He would have had the advantages of the law's presumption of innocence, skilled attorneys to plead his case and a judge to warn the jury against considering press publicity. (After all, three of Mr. Nixon's own former cabinet members—Attorney General John Mitchell, Commerce Secretary Maurice Stans and Treasury Secretary John Connally—were acquitted by criminal court juries despite sensational publicity.)

If Mr. Nixon, as he so persistently and self-righteously maintains, felt himself to be innocent, why wasn't he willing to seek vindication by subjecting his case to the courts, as his associates had to do without the choice of a pardon? The best that can be said for him is that at least he shunned the ultimate abuse of power by not taking the suggested course of pardoning himself and all others connected with the Watergate scandal.

The over-all impression created by the four interviews was that the former president was still projecting the old Nixon techniques and habits of mind in trying to sway his television audience. In the fourth interview American interference in the constitutional processes of Chile was held justifiable becase the democratically elected Allende regime might export Marxist revolution. He implied that the ruthless Pinochet dictatorship that succeeded Allende was preferable because it was "non-Communist." Spiro Agnew was an "honest" man despite having pleaded no contest to income tax evasion. As in Mr. Nixon's warped view of the law in his own case, a defendant's claim of subjective honest intent absolves him of criminal culpability.

In Mr. Nixon's vainglorious, self-pitying view of his world, his troubles are still seen as stemming not from misconduct but from mistakes in judgment, too much compassion for his friends (most of whom he abandoned), the vindictiveness of his enemies in the press and hypocritical liberals, and the virulence of anti-war demonstrators who, as a threat to the nation, were equated with the armies of the Confederate states in the Civil War. We believe the television "jury" will recognize these arguments for what they really are—sheer sophistry.

"CORRECT! CONTESTANT NIXON, YOU NOW HAVE THREE HUNDRED AND SIXTY THOUSAND DOLLARS!!—FOR ANOTHER FIVE HUNDRED DOLLARS, ANSWER THIS QUESTION..."

Reprinted by permission of the Los Angeles Times Syndicate.

Arkansas Gazette.
Little Rock, Ark., May 9, 1977

Reactions to the first Frost-Nixon interview have ranged, nationally, across a wide spectrum of feeling, from loathing to pity to sympathy for the former President in his first real public appearance since his abdication.

In most of central Arkansas, however, there is *no* reaction to determine, all three commercial TV stations having elected not to put on the Frost-Nixon interviews at all. This is one of the strangest combinations of decisions made in the history of Arkansas television. Here in Little Rock, the biggest city and crossroads of the state, an event of national significance and certainly of wide national interest was adjudged a non-event by all station managers. These station executives imposed a blackout upon a population of perhaps a million people within viewing range. One enterprising radio station, KXLR, did air the show but the only television availability was on North Little Rock cable, which, incidentally, has made a pretty good argument in this case for cable television.

The blackout stirred wide displeasure, including that of Governor Pryor, who summed up the issue succinctly, if with understatement, when he said of the Frost-Nixon show that no matter how painful the memory of Watergate the people of Arkansas "should have the opportunity to see it."

We could not agree more with the governor. We think it is incumbent upon at least one of the commercial stations to show the full series of interviews — beginning, of course, with the first, on Watergate, the one that was blacked out in Arkansas last week. The alternative is for the educational station at Conway to move in and do its thing, as it has on occasion in the past.

Governor Pryor said that the ETV had made preliminary inquiries last week but had run into technical difficulties. These could be overcome, we are sure. The lapses provided for commercials could be filled in somehow, or simply left in. Here is the opportunity for ETV to shine, as it rather often does.

The decisions made by the stations here were strange, as we have said, but not entirely unfathomable. One TV executive talked of beating a "dead horse," suggesting that he was afraid of the reaction of the small but loud contingent of remaining Nixon supporters. Another motive might have been financial — the fear that the ratings wouldn't support the commercials adequately — but the Nielsen ratings turned up a national audience of no less than 50 per cent! The one thing that seems clear is the timorousness of our commercial TV management.

The question here is not whether David Frost conducted the first interview correctly, or whether Richard Nixon was lieing and propagandizing in his grand old style, as we happen to believe he was. Nor do most of us have any idea what the other interviews will be like, although we suspect that they will probably give Nixon more historical credit than he deserves. Rather, the issue is as plain as Governor Pryor indicated: When a former president of the United States emerges from seclusion after years of silence, what he says is of much interest and historic import, even if only for footnotes. It does not matter here how he conducts himself or if money ($600,000) provides the motive for the series. Organized television has a responsibility to make the shows available. We hope that Arkansas ETV will fill the void.

ALBUQUERQUE JOURNAL
Albuquerque, N.M., May 6, 1977
"Now just a moment."

That was Richard Nixon's response to a question by David Frost during the first of four television interviews. We echo the thought. Now, just a moment, Mr. Nixon.

Obviously, three years in exile at San Clemente have taught Nixon very little. He obviously hopes to win sympathy but instead has reopened old wounds while shedding little additional light on his role in Watergate and its traumatic followup.

Why, we should all ask, can a former president who was almost impeached, who resigned and then accepted a presidential pardon for whatever crimes he might have committed, earn more than $1 million on television while his close aides who did much less were discredited, jailed or still face jail sentences.

Much of what Nixon said during the Frost interview is flatly contradicted in 7,200 pages of evidence gathered by the House Impeachment Commiteee which showed "clearly, conclusively and finally that Richard Nixon obstructed the Watergate investigation and that he abused the powers of his office as president and failed to comply with lawful subpenas."

Nixon said he would not "grovel" before the American people when he finally admitted he "went right to the edge of the law. . .A reasonable person could call that a cover-up. I didn't think of it as a cover-up."

We're not asking that Nixon grovel, but rather that he clear the record by forthrightly disclosing his entire role in the Watergate affair rather than continuing to stonewall it.

Nixon said he "made mistakes of heart rather than head." He also said, "I let down my friends, I let down my country, I let down our system of government." You betcha, Mr. Nixon. And somewhere in doggie heaven, Checkers must be howling.

The Salt Lake Tribune
Salt Lake City, Utah, May 6, 1977

It's possible to complain that still-missing answers to the Watergate scandal did not finally emerge Wednesday during the David Frost-produced television interview with former President Richard Nixon. However, the public was provided, for the first time, an opportunity to glimpse a singular impact of "Watergate" — the affect on Mr. Nixon, the fallen President.

The full historic meaning of Mr. Nixon's resignation may not be discerned for another generation or two. Those living through it could be too close to see it clearly in all its elements. One aspect generally overlooked has been what the experience has done to the central figure — Richard Nixon. As skillfully as he was able, Mr. Frost extracted that information, visually as well as verbally.

For once, in close-up detail, Mr. Nixon the politician, the poser, the image-maker, became a mere mortal, capable, in the impertinent stare of camera lenses, to display his anguish, his disappointment, his self-doubt. He was no longer the candidate, the high office holder, assuring listeners of his insights, his vast knowledge, his rectitude and exalted decision-making abilities.

Although still not ready to identify for himself the ultimate reason for his downfall, Mr. Nixon could at last openly acknowledge the catastrophic nature of his errors. Unprepared to voluntarily concede impeachable offenses, the disgraced former President nonetheless confessed a series of personal uncertainties, inept calculations and irresponsible misjudgments. It was a Richard Nixon self-estimation the kind of which not generally associated with this man who for so many years dominated American politics.

In the future, no part of the interview may be as instructive in human terms as the full-face portrait of the obviously stunned Mr. Nixon, murmuring in halting cadence: "I let down my friends. I let down the country, I let down our system of government. I let the American people down, and I have to carry that burden with me for the rest of my life."

History will likely be harsh on Mr. Nixon and his mistakes. But with Wednesday night's interview, the record can include a more complete understanding of how "Watergate" influenced people as well as events.

THE ATLANTA CONSTITUTION
Atlanta, Ga., May 6, 1977

David Frost played Perry Mason with a British accent.

Richard Nixon played Richard Nixon with no changes whatsoever.

Those who believe there should have been a trial in either the Senate or a court to determine whether Nixon was guilty or not in the Watergate case may derive a measure of satisfaction from the now historic Frost-Nixon interview.

Nixon was like a defendant in the witness chair harassed by an aggressive, mercilessly probing and well-prepared prosecutor.

Frost, who had a reputation for being a gentle interviewer, proved he was capable of toughness when required.

The immediate result of the trial seems to be a hung jury. Those who admired and defended Nixon seem still inclined to do so. They buy his contention that while he made mistakes of judgment, "mistakes of the heart," he was acting out of basically humanitarian motives and not out of a desire to obstruct justice or protect himself.

Those who believed Nixon had deceived them with lies and had abused his office have even more reason to feel that way. The former president, a lawyer, was on the ropes and groggy as Frost, who is not a lawyer, pummeled him with expertise on the legal aspects of Watergate.

This first Nixon-Frost encounter (three more will follow this month) didn't really tell us anything new. Nixon went farther than before in admitting that he had erred, that he had let his friends and the country down, but he couldn't see where he had done anything legally wrong or even seriously wrong morally.

He came across as a man incapable of admitting to himself that he broke the law. But that was already known. Perhaps the closest he came to revealing inner uncertainty was when he said that he had "impeached" himself by resigning. There were poignant moments when the former president told of his extreme torment in having to fire his top aides. Referring to a remark by Prime Minister Gladstone, the 19th century statesman, who said that a leader must be something of a butcher, Nixon said he could not be a butcher, he could not easily cut off his aides.

Nixon's apologetic tone, his extended regrets about letting friends and country down, had a sincere ring. He sees the effort to extract an admission of guilt as an attempt to make him grovel—and to that the former president says, "No. Never."

While the interview did not introduce new elements, it was a highly dramatic hour and a half—one of the most interesting in the history of television. What made it interesting was the human encounter, not the rehash of Watergate. And while probably few people will change their opinions of Nixon, perhaps they have a deeper insight into a man who was the central figure of a national nightmare.

THE SAGINAW NEWS
Saginaw, Mich., May 5, 1977

The Nixon-Frost interview last night had all the elements of a bullfight.

The bull was there in the person of the former President. His fate was sealed by the public record of Watergate before the first question was asked. He would have moments when he was in command of the interview, defiant of his critics, flashing his old self-confidence. But eventually there was no hiding from the reality of his wrongdoing.

The matador was interviewer David Frost. He came prepared by a staff of researchers with enough ammunition to make 10 public figures look bad. He was determined to tear Mr. Nixon apart bit by bit, and finally to get him to break down and "grovel in the dust," as the former President accurately observed.

Drama certainly was not lacking. Where else could one witness the cross-examination of a former President as though he were a common criminal?

The audience was there. Some just curious, but others hoping to see blood.

The commercial element was part and parcel of the whole affair. Not only was it money that had enticed the former President to expose himself to the questions, but it was a carefully orchestrated promotional campaign that provided the background to the entire evening.

The result was a "good show" in the sense of entertainment for those with a streak of sadism. Certainly it was memorable television that historians 200 years from now will watch and not believe their eyes and ears.

As far as contributing to our knowledge of Watergate and related affairs, the program did nothing except provide a pathetic glimpse into a guilt-ridden psyche. No one who followed Watergate closely three years ago — and maintained an open mind — could have reached any conclusion other than that the President was guilty of an impeachable offense. It was ludicrous to hear Mr. Nixon still weakly denying that.

The nation did not need this revival of bitter, tragic memories. Now that this painful episode is over, however, perhaps we can leave Mr. Nixon in peace, to live out the rest of his days in well-deserved disgrace.

THE EMPORIA GAZETTE
Emporia, Kans., May 5, 1977

ONE segment, actually less than one, serves every purpose, answers any doubt.

Surely virtually no one questions any longer that Richard Nixon knew immediately afterward, if not before, about the Watergate burglary, that he tried to cover it up, that he lied about that, that he continues to say whatever suits his purposes. Any lingering doubt about the man's integrity is immediately laid to rest by a glimpse of the televised interview with David Frost, which debuted Wednesday night with commercials about automobiles and dog food.

One segment is enough. Give him the money. Put him back out of sight. A former president of the United States is an embarrassment to the nation.

The man's manner and his past make it difficult to believe anything he says. The dissembling, the darting glances, perhaps were not as prevalent as usual. But still they were there.

The eyes lit up only once, toward the end, when, in speaking about the Watergate cover-up and the fact that it failed, Richard Nixon seemed to seize upon a triumphant point and said "I could have done it. You know how I could have done it?" By offering clemency to everyone, that's how. A fine idea. Clemency for all. Nationwide. Broad enough presumably to cover everyone who voted in 1968 and 1972. — J.N.

THE ARIZONA REPUBLIC
Phoenix, Ariz., May 6, 1977

RICHARD NIXON didn't do what David Frost obviously wanted him to do in the 90-minute taped interview shown to television viewers Wednesday evening.

The former President didn't admit he had committed a crime. He didn't crawl on his knees to please Frost, or grovel in the dirt of Watergate, to please his enemies.

Nixon did say, for all the world to hear, that he had lied to the American people. That was crime enough.

The President of the United States occasionally fudges. He stands by his subordinates, as Harry Truman and Dwight Eisenhower did. He ducks a question by telling a reporter to go stand in the corner, as Franklin Roosevelt did. But the President doesn't repeatedly, with malicious intent, lie about his part in a conspiracy to misinform the public.

It was the lie about the coverup that undid Nixon. As he put it, "I brought myself down. I let the country down. I let down our system of government." He also let his wife and his daughters down, and he shook an entire generation's confidence in the ability of honest people to serve in the government.

"My President lied to me," is the way one of the country's best political commentators, James J. Kilpatrick, ended a lifetime of support for Nixon. Whatever he says or does, however much he may have been victimized by his associates, Nixon has placed the blame for his fall where it belongs — on himself.

What will the next three Nixon interviews bring forth? Presumably some more pathos, such as Nixon's speech about how he cried when he realized that he had to let Haldeman and Ehrlichman go. As a matter of fact, he was stretching the truth when he claimed that was the first time he had cried since Eisenhower's death. Nixon didn't like Ike. And he resorted to tears on other occasions.

The remaining tapes, it is hoped, will also reflect the very substantial contributions President Nixon made in improving relations with Russia and China, in controlling nuclear proliferation, in allowing the nations of Africa to sort out their own problems.

The Nixon-Frost interviews have again demonstrated the marvelous theatrical possibilities in television. Frost, TV's original Nice Guy, became a relentless prosecuting attorney determined to destroy the man in the dock. Nixon, the scowling villain of the Oval office, alternately charmed and cajoled his interviewer.

And what of the American people? We doubt if very many viewers changed their minds about Nixon. Actually, the record remains as it was. No one has proved Nixon knew about the break-in of Watergate before it happened. Everyone knows he said he could raise a million dollars, if necessary, to put an end to the Watergate revelations.

Nixon cited, in the first interview, the fact that the bottom line was that he didn't raise the million dollars, he didn't give his associates clemency, he did "impeach himself by resigning" the presidency.

Few viewers were impressed by these claims. The man admitted he had lied once. Why believe him now?

It would be no great loss to the nation if a curtain could fall on the Watergate drama. But the major political story of our times isn't going to go away very soon. Particularly when the central figure in that story can get $2 million for writing his memoirs and perhaps as much as $1 million for allowing a British dude to engage him in oratorical combat.

Post-Tribune
Gary, Ind., May 9, 1977

We doubt if former President Richard M. Nixon made many converts in the first of his television interviews last week.

He came out again a "tragic" figure at the end of the interview as he did at the time of his resignation, yet throughout his interrogation on the Watergate aspects of his ill-fated second term, he seemed so "shifty" and evasive and occasionally combative that it was hardly a performance to elicit sympathy.

The ultra-cynical may hold the view that he cared more about the more than $500,000 the interviews will net him than about getting his side of the story over to the public, yet we seriously doubt that was anywhere near the full case.

His — and to a considerable extent the nation's — tragedy lay in his admission at the end that he had "let down my friends...the country...our system of government and the dreams of all those young people that ought to get into government, but think it is all too corrupt and the rest."

Yet while admitting that he had "impeached myself," the former President's quibbling over semantics and arguing over interpretations of the tapes on the basis of which he was questioned by David Frost served mainly to emphasize the views of most Americans that he was always deep in the cover-up of a governmental crime, but refused to admit it — possibly even to himself.

However, while Nixon's image may have been further tarnished, that of his interviewer, Frost, was greatly improved by his documented persistence.

Whatever one thinks, though, of Nixon's part in Watergate, we definitely recommend listening to the rest of the telecasts, the next of which is set for airing this Thursday.

Nixon was President, and only one who has been in that office can cite its problems, failures and triumphs. Not everything about his administrations was sordid, particularly in foreign policy, and listening to him may give us educational television at its best

The Standard-Times
New Bedford, Mass., May 5, 1977

The Frost-Nixon television presentation, aimed at offering the nation for the first time the former president's view of his Watergate role, has been described wryly by one of the defendants in that tragic situation as "checkbook journalism."

This evaluation is reasonable and so is the conclusion that the programs Messrs. Nixon and Frost have put together will change neither the course of history nor of public opinion.

Essentially, what Mr. Nixon has said is that he "let down" his friends, the American people, and our form of government by inhibiting the taking of testimony and the gathering of evidence in connection with the Watergate matter. But the former president argued that (a) he did this motivated, not by a desire to obstruct justice, but for reasons aimed at political containment, and (b) whatever he did in this direction, he did not do for very long.

There are two answers to these two arguments and both of them are effective. First, as James F. Neal, Watergate prosecutor, has pointed out, H.R. Haldeman, Nixon aide, relied in his defense upon the "political containment" motive. Both judge and jury rejected it, concluding that justice obstructed is justice obstructed, and that the degree of corruption in the motive is irrelevant. Haldeman was found guilty. What reason is there to assume, had Mr. Nixon stood trial, that the same defense would have stood him in better stead?

Second, as Mr. Neal pointed out in the aftermath of the first Nixon-Frost television program, the U.S. Supreme Court has concluded efforts to obstruct justice do not even have to be successful necessarily in order for judge or jury to return a finding of guilty and that the duration of the efforts is immaterial. As Mr. Neal noted, "Whether it was five minutes, five hours, or five days, makes no difference." As a lawyer, Mr. Nixon must surely be aware of this.

There may be some in the nation who enjoy the spectacle of a man brought down; most do not, and we are among those. Some moments in the Frost-Nixon presentation were, inevitably, Macbethian and so must necessarily have moved and excited compassion among thinking men and women. Nixon's observation that it was he who brought about his own downfall, the obvious suffering that accompanied his departure from public life under such unique and awful circumstances, and his conclusion that he cannot return to that life — these were real and sobering.

But, as Mr. Neal remarked, "When he came down to the facts, I didn't think he had much," and that is about the way it was.

The Dallas Morning News

Dallas, Tex., May 6, 1977

THE FIRST half hour or so of David Frost's Nixon interview chugged along in the slightly monotonous fashion that almost from the start has marked Watergate discourse. The reporter probing, Nixon parrying; the mind-numbing quibbles over place and time, the what-did-you-know, the when-did-you-know-it.

For a time, the fallen president peered down at Frost as though from a parapet. Then, suddenly, he opened the gate and walked forth, weaponless, with head bowed.

The more ferocious Nixon-baiters will complain that still the man is not contrite enough; that even now he has failed to acknowledge and bewail his manifold sins and wickedness.

Yet what the viewers of the Frost interview witnessed was, in its context, a very remarkable thing. Here was a proud man, saying as best he could say it, that he was sorry. Sorry for all the anguish and grief that unintentionally he had caused.

Sorry for Haldeman and Ehrlichman, friends as well as advisers, whom it took him two anguished weeks to fire. And sorry for his country, moreover.

"I let down my friends," said Richard Nixon. "I let down the country. I let down our system of government and the dreams of all those young people that ought to get into government but think it's all too corrupt and the rest.

"Most of all, I let down an opportunity that I would have had for 2½ more years to proceed on great projects and programs for building a lasting peace, which has been my dream . . . Yep, I let the American people down, and I have to carry that burden with me for the rest of my life."

Perhaps that is not the wail of repentance that Nixon's worst enemies would love to hear. But it is a considerable admission all the same. Almost a handsome one. And surely, for now, it suffices.

It suffices if only because the man who talked so candidly to Frost is so clearly a beaten man, a man without hope or future. "My political life is over," said Nixon. "I will never yet, and never again have an opportunity to serve in any official position." Yes, of course. Everyone knows this. But what an agonizing acknowledgment from a man who scaled the topmost pinnacle of the political heights and knows—how well he knows it!—that "I brought myself down."

To say that Nixon did wrong is to say the obvious. Still, the time has come to forgive; to cease, or rather leave for the historians, these endless wrangles about the night of March 21 and so on. It avails nothing to make Nixon the butt of sneers and wisecracks. They can be no more painful to him than is the knowledge of what he did to himself.

Pain is in fact the chief residue of this dreary, depressing affair. The pain etched on the face of a broken man, wedged between the syllables of each word. Pain, too, in the hearts of those who watch and listen, or even weep, as men will, at the spectacle of human tragedy. May not that spectacle at last be brought to a dignified close?

The Boston Herald American

Boston, Mass., May 6, 1977

Richard Nixon did not confess everything, as some would have liked. Neither did he cover up everything, as others had hoped. Furthermore, he was far from "shattered," as a spate of pre-program ballyhoo would have had America believe.

Thus, the former President's first of four interviews with David Frost left everyone dissatisfied to varying degrees. None of the unsettling events of Watergate were "settled," once and for all.

What did happen, however, was the fallen President's most direct admission of guilt since his resignation Aug. 8, 1974. He did wrong, and so proclaimed to the public for the first time. But the words "admission" and "guilt" and "wrong" must be used guardedly, as neither Frost nor Nixon was using the same dictionary Wednesday night. This caused some analysts to say Nixon confessed to lies, while others said he had insisted on his innocence.

The performance defied precise interpretations. For the first 60 minutes Mr. Nixon doggedly (if raggedly) defended his conduct, for the next 20 he talked of "mistakes," and for the final ten let his hair down by confessing he had let "the American people down."

It was a three-step sequence of self-defense, self-explanation and self-accusation, with the middle part producing the highest drama of the evening. When Nixon generalized about mistakes, Frost asked him to speak with more precision, to use more exact words. "What words would you suggest?" asked Nixon, and the Battle of the Semanticists was joined.

Frost asked his adversary to address himself directly to "wrongdoing, abuse of power, and the need to apologize, or", said he in uncharacteristic burst of emotion, "You'll regret it the rest of your life."

Again adhering to his own dictionary, Nixon avoided all three suggestions, instead admitting he may have exaggerated, or said something misleading or not true. All of which, he emphasized, were cause for regretting, but not groveling.

Despite the differences in the language spoken, the first Frost-Nixon exchange did have its rewards, however mixed or minimal. The American people have had the opportunity to see their only resigned president submit to a cross examination by one of the best examiners in the business. And a former president who had been unbelieved so often was given an opportunity to be believed when he confessed his sorrow at not living up fully to his oath of office. For the first time Mr. Nixon confessed to some of his sins of Watergate, and his choice of words could not obscure others he may have skipped over.

The Washington Post

Washington, D.C., May 6, 1977

THAT WAS GOOD television and bad history when David Frost and Richard Nixon grappled for 90 minutes on Channel 5 Wednesday night. Mr. Nixon has revised his interpretation of the Watergate events that caused him to leave office in August of 1974. He no longer explains his own errant actions as the behavior of a President seeking to limit the "national-security" damage to the nation and one who was abysmally ignorant of what had been going on. His emphasis now is on what he describes as an early attempt to limit the *political* damage of Watergate and on his own large-heartedness as a kind of tragic flaw. He could not help trying to act as a defense lawyer for Bob Haldeman and John Ehrlichman, he said. He had let his heart get the better of his head. He just did not have the instincts of a "butcher."

In a way this line of defense is more tawdry than what had gone before. It puts it all on Mr. Nixon's friends and associates whom he was allegedly trying to help, and it implies that had it not been for this excess of human decency Richard Nixon would not now be the lonely exile of San Clemente. That, of course, is exactly wrong. Mr. Nixon's efforts to save himself were what got him in trouble. His closest aides had been acting in his name and with his authority, presumably carrying out what they took to be his purposes. He tried to conceal his own involvement as well as theirs. He told a lot of lies. He finally got thrown out of office. That is what happened.

We do not mean to be too cut-and-dried about it. There were some very emotional moments in Wednesday night's interview—Mr. Nixon's account of the strain of firing Messrs. Haldeman and Ehrlichman and his recollection of his last evening in the White House, accompanied by the concession that he had "let the American people down." But these were pitiful moments, not ennobling ones. And perhaps the most pitiful moment of all was that in which the former President asserted that he would not "grovel," which he seemed to equate with admitting that he had knowingly done wrong. But Mr. Nixon has already "grovelled" in this sense—although he doesn't seem to recognize the fact—in accepting the pardon offered by Gerald Ford.

What the former President evidently does not understand is what people are asking of him now. As we perceive it, what is being asked is some acknowledgment on Mr. Nixon's part that he in fact understands what happened to him—and not incidentally to the country—in the two-year Watergate drama. This he either will not or cannot give. He still sees twisting swords and fifth columns and partisan excesses as the engines of his downfall. And this is so, even though Mr. Nixon now says he has only himself to blame—because what he is blaming is some extravagance of compassion he purportedly felt for the sinners around him.

We don't for a moment suppose that the impulses of all those demanding more from Richard Nixon are pure or that there isn't a large dose of sanctimony and even sadism on the part of some who keep insisting that he must "confess." But we do think that most people who are unsatisfied with the Nixon post-presidential performance so far are asking something reasonable: evidence that Richard Nixon will accept the *moral* responsibility for his actions, not just the political responsibility. This, as he made plain Wednesday night, he is still unwilling to do.

Reprinted by permission of the Chicago Tribune-New York News Syndicate

THE MILWAUKEE JOURNAL
Milwaukee, Wisc., May 1, 1977

The man was bitter. The press, he said, "has established itself as a reviewer of our secrets, no matter how destructive to the United States." The secret activities of the Central Intelligence Agency have "drawn most fire from the press and our Communist enemies." The TV exposure of Watergate he called a "television extravaganza to discredit our American way of life."

For this he got $2,000 — his standard lecture fee. The audience swarmed about him to get autographs.

The man is E. Howard Hunt Jr., who went to prison for planning the Watergate burglary. He is a convicted criminal. Most criminals are shunned. But many involved in Watergate and the Nixon scandals are on the lecture circuit, have gotten big contracts for books and movie rights, and are considered celebrities (to some, perhaps even heroes).

Ordinary curiosity partly explains the phenomenon. Yet, in some ways, what is happening is pitiful. These men, not the press or TV or some other handy scapegoat, discredited "our American way of life." They demeaned our political system and threatened our democracy. Now they reap huge monetary rewards and catch whiffs of popularity. Are we not treating our reprobates too well?

Newsday
Garden City, N.Y., May 3, 1977

A disgraced ex-president and a British talk show host certainly aren't the likeliest ingredients of a TV blockbuster. But thanks to skillful merchandising, Richard Nixon and David Frost may carry it off tomorrow night. After their circus parade through Mediaville this past weekend, Nixon was getting almost as many headlines 1,000 days out of the presidency as Jimmy Carter 100 days into it.

Somehow Frost had managed to lay his hands on some previously unpublished Watergate transcripts that showed once again Nixon's early involvement in the cover-up. Considering the meticulous security that surrounded the lengthy taping of the Nixon-Frost interviews, the simultaneous exposure on the covers of Time and Newsweek over the weekend certainly smacks of a deal.

Indeed, Time practically admitted as much, although its publisher took great pains to point out it hadn't practiced checkbook journalism to get the scoop. Re-alizing that "this first lengthy explanation by Richard Nixon to the American people would have considerable historical value," he said, the magazine "approached Frost last winter and arranged with him (though not for a fee) to have a Time correspondent cover Operation Nixon."

Together with the Newsweek cover, page-one treatment in The Washington Post and The New York Times, and a segment on CBS' "60 Minutes" Sunday night, the Time story is bound to hype the ratings for tomorrow night's show. The publicity also induced more independent television stations to carry the show.

All this means more money for Frost—and for Nixon, who reportedly gets 10 per cent of the profits in addition to his $600,000 fee for submitting to the interviews. That's not bad pay for 29 hours of answering questions. It's certainly a lot more than he would have received if he had been called on to answer the same questions in a court of law.

AKRON BEACON JOURNAL
Akron, Ohio, May 3, 1977

"COME ONE, come all, to the Greatest Show on Earth. Watch Richard Nixon squirm under the strenuous questioning of David Frost as the former President discusses Watergate publicly for the first time since his resignation Aug. 9, 1974. Share the excitement as the sweat trickles down his face when he's asked the ultimate question: Why didn't he destroy the tapes?"

If that circus-style promotion seems out of place in connection with the Nixon-Frost interviews which begin Wednesday night, it is only a slight exaggeration of the publicity hype the four shows have been receiving the last few days. It's enough to make P. T. Barnum envious. It also helps assure ratings so high that the few advertising spots still open will be sold, putting more money in Nixon's pocket.

First, we are treated to White House tape transcripts from the Watergate period never before made public. The transcripts were prepared for a 1974 Watergate coverup trial, but never introduced as evidence. The tapes have been sealed by court order until the Supreme Court decides whether they belong to Nixon or the government.

The transcripts, which contain little new information, are leaked strategically to the Washington Post and New York Times for Sunday publication not only in those newspapers, but scores of others which subscribe to Times and Post wire services. Most papers give the story front-page treatment.

Then Time, Newsweek and TV Guide carry major articles about the series, including details on the content. Time tells us that, at one point, "Nixon looks shaken." Newsweek adds that as Frost reads a list of self-incriminating remarks from a transcript of the President's March 21, 1973, conversation with counsel John W. Dean III, Nixon "seems on the verge of tears, a tragic figure."

And then we hear that all this 11th-hour publicity has virtually guaranteed that, after a slow start signing up stations for the special network and peddling advertising holes, the series will finish in the black. There are reports Nixon will pocket at least $600,000 for his participation, plus 10 percent of any profits.

Somehow or other, we can't escape the conclusion that we are being hustled in a fashion unheard of since Bobby Riggs and Billie Jean King did their bit on the tennis court.

We don't begrudge Nixon the opportunity to discuss his presidency and his role in Watergate. Indeed, for the benefit of history, he ought to be heard, even though what he says must be tempered by the realization that his interest is to rehabilitate the image of Richard Nixon — not bare his soul.

But we do find it hard to swallow the commercialization of his remarks. We can't forget that had it not been for that pardon from President Ford, Nixon might have had to answer the same questions (and probably tougher ones) served up in a court setting, where no one would have been spreading six-figure fees on the table.

THE ☼ SUN

Baltimore, Md., May 3, 1977

Tomorrow night Richard Nixon returns to American living rooms, trying to restore his reputation and providing historians the first raw material of his perspective on the most significant of his famous crises—Watergate.

The forum will be the first of a series of interviews conducted by David Frost, a sometime comedian, sometime journalist, sometime television "personality." This interview comes after one of the most remarkable—and successful—publicity blitzes in recent huckstering: cover stories in *Time, Newsweek* and the most wide-ly-circulated magazine of all, *TV Guide;* Page One stories in every major newspaper.

Mr. Nixon is going to make about a million dollars for the show. This blending of "checkbook journalism," honest investigative reporting, history, show business and public relations, is disturbing. But it has become so much a part of our age that it is probably useless to complain anymore.

Viewers should keep this in mind tomorrow night. They should keep in mind that Mr. Nixon would not answer these and similar Watergate questions under oath in courtrooms, or for reporters who could not pay him a fortune. They should keep in mind that he is even now trying to thwart a court order that would allow the Americans to hear the White House tapes used in the trial of his top aides. They should keep in mind that he is trying to thwart a law that would allow historians and journalists access to other tapes. They should keep in mind that Richard Nixon is untruthful.

And they should keep in mind that it will probably be a fascinating, valuable 90 minutes.

TULSA WORLD

Tulsa, Okla., May 3, 1977

LIKE A child watching an old horror movie again and again, Americans will be drawn to their television sets by the millions beginning Wednesday to hear former PRESIDENT NIXON interviewed by tv personality DAVID FROST.

Despite last minute publicity about previously unpublished information regarding NIXON's Watergate activities, there aren't likely to be many surprises.

We can expect the former PRESIDENT to stubbornly defend his actions in the face of what some news sources have described as a relentless interviewer in FROST.

There appears to be little for the nation to gain from a rerun of the national trauma that Watergate produced. The former PRESIDENT of course seeks the understanding of the nation as to why he did what he did, but that understanding, if ever granted, will be bestowed by some future generation, not this one.

History will judge NIXON in a perspective that has yet to emerge and cannot emerge in several hours of interviews on television.

Of far more immediate interest—particularly to those involved in the production of the programs—are whether they are going to be profitable.

One thing is for certain, they will be profitable for NIXON who is assured of a $600,000 fee and 10 per cent of the profits.

Advertising for the programs reportedly has been tough to sell as commercial firms are reluctant to allow their names to be used on the program despite the fact that the viewing audience ought to be a huge one.

Like so many political situations, the programs aren't likely to change many minds. The NIXON haters will see little to alter their minds; his partisans will see much to justify their own opinion of the man.

The programs will provide the former PRESIDENT with an invaluable chance to tell his side of the story for future historians. That in itself is a beneficial function of the program and one afforded few, if any, historical figures of the past.

Perhaps that is justification enough for airing the program if one is needed beyond the almost morbid interest that all of us will show when we tune in to watch.

The Boston Globe

Boston, Mass., May 3, 1977

There is a certain rough justice to Richard Nixon's appearance on television tomorrow night with performer David Frost. The commercial sordidness is distressing; so are the promotional hypes, the apparently orchestrated leaks from tapes that before now had been closely guarded. But the show — and it is at bottom an entertainment — does nudge Nixon closer to a moment of truth with an accuser than he is likely to be again, on this earth.

Whether, as Time magazine reports, Frost "humbles and shatters" Nixon is unimportant. Apparently few things in life have had that effect on Nixon, who seems protected by an impenetrable barrier of rationalization.

The important thing, in any event, is not the impact of Frost's questioning on Nixon but its impact on the nation, which is still left with unresolved questions about Watergate.

The Frost show is America's only way to confront the practical problems created by Ford's pardon of Nixon — a pardon which short-circuited the judicial process as it moved toward full disclosure of the truth.

It is by no means a satisfactory way. Frost is a showman, not a prosecutor. If Nixon is a defendant in the dock, he is a highly-paid one who can earn as much as $1 million by his participation in the production. He is under no compulsion to tell the TV viewers anything new, or provide any details that are not self-serving.

Under the circumstances the most the show is likely to contribute are those theatrical moments when the world can watch Nixon's face as he is confronted by evidence — some of it made public only in the last few days — that brought down his Presidency. Those dramatic moments when Nixon, as Newsweek puts it, is "on the verge of tears" when his "voice grows hoarse" or his "eyes dart and his face falls for an instant" could prove critical because they have a political component.

People who will look to the Frost encounter for graphic proof of Nixon's crime and punishment may be satisfied or further frustrated. Those unpersuaded by the evidence against Nixon may see in the former President's distress signs of his martyrdom. The rehabilitation of Nixon could be under way.

One day Nixon may accept his guilt and responsibility. It is doubtful that when and if that day arrives he will need a David Frost or a dog food company to help him get the message across.

Meanwhile, we must make do with what we have: an uncontrite Richard Nixon willing to venture out of his California retreat and address the facts of Watergate only in return for a lucrative contract.

We will know tomorrow night whether the Frost approach was an improvement on the silence from San Clemente.

DAILY ☼ NEWS

New York, N.Y., May 6, 1977

It may have been good television entertainment, but Richard Nixon's million-dollar performance with David Frost fell far short of shedding any new light on the former President's role in the Watergate scandal.

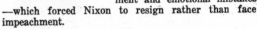

Richard Nixon

It was somewhat surprising to see the only chief executive to resign from office as contrite as he was at times.

But the real "letdown" was Nixon's same old technique of hanging tough—refusing to admit he did and said the specific things which are on tape and in official records.

It was the evidence of those precise words and deeds —not simply errors in judgment and emotional mistakes —which forced Nixon to resign rather than face impeachment.

The American people may have been entertained during the 90-minute program, but it isn't likely that many will be impressed with Nixon's emotional apologies as long as he tries to deny his willing participation in a conspiracy to obstruct justice.

ARKANSAS DEMOCRAT

Little Rock, Ark., May 4, 1977

Who listens to radio? Lots of people. For example: Anyone in Little Rock who's interested in hearing the four-part interview tonight of former President Nixon, conducted by David Frost. There's no other way, to receive it this side of the river except on KXLR.

Three local TV channels have stonewalled the ex-president's views of the Watergate scandal, which forced his resignation. We think that's unconscionable after the televising of innumerable hours of "news analysis" over a two-year period, from the time of the break-in until after the resignation. All the Dan Rathers had their full say, rehashing the Plumbers' activities, the controversy over the tapes, the tax-evasion charges, the indiscretions of the Committee to Re-elect, and all the rest.

After three years in virtual exile, the ex-president has a right to have his side heard in Little Rock.

The stations' excuses for denying that right are lame: "No new information," said one who had not yet viewed the series. "Little public response," said another. And a third said he had no desire further to enrich the ex-president.

Little Rock residents are beholden to Joe Dickey, station manager of radio station KXLR, who has proved open minded enough to broadcast Nixon's side of the controversy, beginning at 6:30 p.m. tonight. North Little Rock, Sherwood and Jacksonville viewers, of course, can watch the interviews on the TV cable from KTVT, Channel 11, Fort Worth.

We hope many thoughtful persons in the Little Rock "blackout zone" will tune their radio dials to 1150 tonight to hear Nixon's side of what happened.

Regulation: How Much and By Whom?

The Communications Act, passed by Congress over 40 years ago, created the television industry and has continued to regulate it ever since. The 1934 law established the seven-man Federal Communications Commission and endowed that group with the responsibility to ensure that broadcasters serve "the public interest, convenience, and necessity." That mandate was established at a time when few persons, if anyone, understood the potential impact the medium would have on the future. At the end of World War II, the FCC had six television stations to control. By the end of 1952, that number had reached 108. In 1970, this country had 872 television stations. At last count (1978) there were a total of 995 stations under FCC jurisdiction.

The current chairman of the House Subcommittee on Communications, Rep. Lionel Van Deerlin of California, has proposed a total rewrite of the 1934 act in order, he says, to make the law "conform to the times, to make it serve the interests of the consuming public and not just the varied industrial or business interests involved." The proposed new law would, among other things, abolish the FCC, replacing it with a less powerful communications regulatory commission, and would require broadcasters to pay an annual license fee for use of the airwaves. The bill would end federal regulation of cable television, turning over that responsibility to state and local officials. License renewals for commercial TV would be eliminated 10 years after the bill's enactment. The existing "fairness doctrine" would be whittled down to a new "equity principle" calling for "equitable" treatment of controversial issues when — and if — they were covered.

The measure, in its entirety, is aimed at increasing competition and technological innovation while cutting back government regulation. Van Deerlin says that "with cable TV and with the mix of cable and satellites, I cannot conceive that 10 years from now there are still going to be three networks dominating the entertainment scene in this country."

There have been other efforts made by the government to encourage competition in broadcasting, and the battles have been hard-fought. In

1978, the U.S. Supreme Court upheld a government rule preventing newspapers from acquiring radio or television outlets in their communities. A 1975 FCC order had permitted all but 16 of the nation's more than 140 media conglomerates to continue, but placed restrictions on the creation of future monopolies in the same geographic area. The media went to court to have the FCC regulation declared illegal. On the other hand, the U.S. Justice Department and the National Citizens' Committee for Broadcasting, a public-interest group, sought to have the policy extended to break up existing combinations. The Supreme Court's ruling reversed an appeals court ruling that would have required the abolition of existing cross-ownership. Justice Thurgood Marshall wrote that the ban on future media monopolies was "a reasonable means of promoting the public interest in diversified mass communications."

Few people expect congressional action on the deregulation bill in the near future. Legislators and Capitol Hill aides express the view that as long as television doesn't go up in price, there won't be much incentive to change its policy. They believe that with critical concerns, such as inflation, taxes, unemployment and energy, there is little public pressure to reform communications law. Nevertheless, the absence of pressure on law-makers should not be construed as indiference. It is more likely a reflection of public impatience with the bureaucratic process and a disenchantment with regulatory catch-phrases. For in the last five years, the number of private-interest groups exerting direct pressure on network programmers has steadily increased. In 1977, there were more than 250 active broadcast reform groups in the U.S. In 1975, the estimate was under 200. Targets of the groups' protests include indiscriminate and widespread violence, profane language, sexual innuendo, sterotypical portrayals of minorities and the quantity and quality of advertising.

In the vanguard of the "viewers' rebellion" is the National Parent-Teacher Association (PTA), a group that has undertaken a variety of studies indicating that the brutality depicted on television contributes to aggressive behavior among children. The PTA regularly surveys television fare and rates the programs in terms of violence, "offensiveness" and overall quality. The organization has threatened to challenge the license renewals of five network-owned stations if the networks continue to ignore pleas to improve the quality of programming based on PTA standards.

Another private-interest group that monitors the quality of television is Action for Children's Television (ACT). Peggy Charren, president of the Boston-based group, is critical of the PTA's rating methods. Charren believes that much of the PTA's preferred programming is "very simplistically sweet." She notes that "someone else's most offensive program might be my favorite," which raises the inherent problem in any attempt to regulate a mass medium.

Although the viewer reform groups have not always agreed on what constitutes suitable entertainment, they have all employed the boycott as an effective technique to bring about change. Since programmers are exclusively concerned with satisfying advertisers, who in turn are interested only in reaching the largest possible market, the PTA, ACT and other groups urge viewers not to purchase products manufactured by those advertisers who sponsor violent, or otherwise undesirable shows. In 1976, J. Walter Thompson, one of the nation's largest advertising agencies, warned its clients that the public was beginning to reject the violence portrayed on television and was consciously avoiding products that subsidized violent programs.

Sears Roebuck & Co., the country's sixth largest advertiser during prime television hours, announced in 1978 that it would withdraw its commercials from two top-rated shows. It acted under pressure from the National Federation for Decency, a company spokesman said. The federation, headed by Rev. Donald E. Wilmon of Mississippi, had picketed Sears' national headquarters in Chicago before the company decided not to sponsor any programs containing "excessive violence or anti-social behavior."

Constitutionally guaranteed freedoms, the laws of profit and variations in human perception make the regulation of television a highly sensitive issue in a democratic system, where the role of "watchdog" is a particularly ambiguous one. Yet, it is essential that responsibility be assigned somewhere, in order to see that television's immense power is not abused. It must be protected from manipulation and exploitation as much as from censorship. Both the medium and the viewer suffer the consequences of too much or too little control.

The Idaho STATESMAN

Boise, Idaho, June 16, 1978

Proposals to revamp and sharply curtail regulation of the broadcasting industry are long overdue. Thus, the bill introduced in the House of Representatives to accomplish these ends is welcome — more as a vehicle for debate perhaps than as an indication of what eventually will be accomplished.

The Federal Communications Commission and its regulations grew up in a different era. They were designed to deal with an industry that bears little resemblence to today's broadcasting enterprises. In the early days of radio, chaos reigned. Stations popped up and closed down hither and thither. They broadcast when and on whatever frequency suited their fancy. Often competitors would attempt to outblast each other on the same frequency. The infant medium appeared about ready to self-destruct. Enter the concept of public ownership of the airwaves and government regulation, applauded by most serious broadcasters of the day.

Broadcasting of 1978 is much different. While the industry is not yet mature, and perhaps never will be because of technological changes, at least we are dealing with economic units whose institutional characteristics are fairly well defined. Fred Silverman not withstanding, the wild days are gone, and regulation should be modified to fit that reality. To draw an analogy between the life of broadcasting and that of a human, one allows an adult more freedom and flexibility than a babe.

In some areas, regulators, no matter how good their intentions, have actually hindered the maturation of broadcasting. The Fairness Doctrine, by which persons are granted the right of reply, and the equal-time provision for political issues are the two most notable examples. The provisions are meant to insure that the powerful media of radio and television are not used to unfair advantage by one side on public debates.

Yet the result of these regulations has been an unquestionable retardation in the growth of serious public affairs programming. Many a small station refuses to examine certain issues or talk with candidates because they fear leaving themselves open to the equal-time or right-of-reply provisions. Obviously these two ill-conceived regulations should be scrapped by Congress.

It is interesting to note that Boise-area broadcasters, interviewed after the bill's contents were made known, oppose permanent licensing. To a person, they found some good to come from the renewal provision, but wished only that the licensing interval be extended from three years to from five to 10 years. We agree.

While Congress might well wish to ease up on the regulation of what broadcasters can and cannot do, the limited airwaves still belong to the public, and stations, particularly television stations, must be required to operate in the public convenience and necessity. Within the framework of less stringent regulations, there must be a method for evaluating periodically how well each stations carries out that charge.

One note of caution we would sound, however: In rewriting the statute governing broadcasting, consideration must be given to continuing restraints on consolidation of the broadcast media in the hands of a few owners at least for the foreseeable future. Economic consolidation appears the name of the game in the United States today, and broadcasting is a very lucrative business. Without safeguards, we can envision the day when a very few groups might effectively control television broadcasting in this nation. Perhaps the marketplace serves as sufficient restraint against abuse of consolidated power, but we are not certain, particularly so long as the number of channels available is so limited. Perhap this will not be such a problem when technology increases the availability of television channels or video technology makes the airwaves only one alternative.

Congress will undoubtably take its time in considering such a revolutionary overhaul of broadcast regulation, as well it should. The questions to be answered are complex and often metaphysical. But it is definitely time that attention be focused on the problem. In few other areas has regulation lagged so far behind the industry being regulated.

THE KANSAS CITY STAR

Kansas City, Mo., November 20, 1977

The House Communications Subcommittee held hearings early this month that were supposed to look into TV network sports programming and advertising and ask the question: Can the networks find true happiness in sports events as they traditionally have occurred or must they be presented in a framework of drama and hype that is unnatural and maybe even untrue?

It was suggested that boxing and tennis matches had been portrayed as dramatic "winner-take-all" contests when such was not the case — winners and losers all had guarantees of fees. The special counsel of the subcommittee said before the hearings that "the thrust . . . is, 'What control do networks have over sports?' " The subcommittee chairman went a bit further and said the people wanted to know whether we can trust "what we see and hear as being accurate."

Some of the witnesses and a few members of the committee thought that the hearings went far afield and degenerated into a general attack on television and specious judgments on programming. Lionel Van Deerlin, D-Calif., the chairman, said he thought the group surely could consider the possible disruption of sports events by TV without getting into First Amendment matters.

Television is young, but it is a giant of frightening power that increasingly will be held accountable for what others consider misdeeds. It will be given the short shrift reserved for the bearer of bad tidings that the print press long ago learned to accept no matter how unfair or frustrating that treatment may be. People do not welcome bad news and sometimes they take it out on the messenger. Of course nearly everybody is an expert on television because nearly everybody watches it. A lot of the concern is brought about because of the sheer magnetism and effectiveness of the medium. It is pervasive. It is a very important part of life for most persons in areas of entertainment and information.

The novelty that accompanied TV in the 1950s when entire neighborhoods would gather to watch a flickering screen the size of a cereal box is long gone. People can look at it or leave it alone. An entire generation has always known it. But the combination of motion, sound and color can be hypnotic and compelling. The very attractiveness of TV is at once its strength and its greatest weakness.

For example, the burning of a vacant building on the edge of the city can make spectacular pictures with the orange inferno and black smoke there before your eyes. You can hear the sirens and the shouts of scurrying firemen. Visual impact! But it is, after all, only an empty building burning up. It might rate a paragraph in the paper. The viewer has seen an exciting picture but he has not been informed of important news.

In the same way — still looking through a magnifying glass — the set can bring into your living room pictures of a riot or demonstration. It looks like the world is coming to an end or at least that the revolution has arrived. Alarums and excursions. Angry voices. Fearful faces. Violence and impending doom seem to fill the screen and you are ready to flee to Australia. But it can turn out that the scene was quite limited, that the people on the next street hardly knew anything was happening.

Thus the effect of TV can be to make a nothing into a something or a rather routine incident into momentous news. Print headlines can do the same, but not persistently, or the reader will lose faith and dismiss such exaggeration. On the screen viewers are seeing it with their own eyes. The incisive photography of TV can, in itself, be distorting.

And so there will continue to be clamor and concern. It has never yet been figured out just how the First Amendment guarantees of freedom of the press and government control of the limited channels of the public's air can be reconciled. But most such decisions ought to be on the side of free expression.

Politicians and economic interests will try to use TV as they have always tried to use newspapers and magazines. That is part of the game of politics and business and getting information out. Public relations people make a living trying to get free and favorable publicity. Editors make a living trying to decide what is news and what is deception or shameless puffery.

From the beginning entertainment has been a more pronounced part of radio and television than it was in early journals of news and opinion, and that is part of the problem. Balancing the news-entertainment ratio in print is not so hard because the reader is free to glance and discard. But *time* is the iron dictator of TV. There are only 24 hours of it for a single channel and only a few hours a day when many people will be looking. Time must be measured and cut up for news, entertainment, advertising and public service, and not even a Solomon could do it to the satisfaction of all.

In the future public TV may take over a greater share of cultural and public service activities. It will need much greater resources than it has now. It would be in poor shape today without British programs. In the meantime people will argue about the social contribution of presenting dramatizations of Harold Robbins novels, endless car chases and beauty contests. They will criticize news and documentaries just as they have criticized print journalism. They will damn and praise TV and give it more influence than it has and think it less important than it really is.

But in the long run the only reason for a free press is to make available accurate information and a variety of opinion so that the people under a form of representative government can make intelligent decisions at the polls and in the marketplace. Television is an increasingly important part of that process. To the extent that it polices itself and holds itself accountable, the excuse for government to intervene is reduced.

Oregon *Journal*

Portland, Ore., June 7, 1978

For the first time in many years Congress may make a thorough review of what the federal role should be in regulating radio and television stations.

The Federal Communications Act of 1934 has become a hodgepodge that probably goes much too far in controlling the affairs of broadcasters while failing to do much to assure quality.

There is genuine concern about what the governmental role should be. When one contemplates the pervasive influence television can have, especially on children, the prospect of controls over both programming and commercials has a certain amount of appeal.

But then consider the fairness doctrine and equal time provisions that, in effect, put bureaucracy in the editor's chair, and federal control does not sound like what the founding fathers had in mind.

Indeed, had they been able to imagine radio and television, they probably would have figured out a way to include broadcasting with the press in the First Amendment's protections.

The maze of regulations that have accumulated over the years are all based on the theory that the stations use the air waves and the air waves belong to the public. But that contention would indicate that the main — perhaps the only — governmental role would be that of traffic cop to assure that competing stations were not using the same wave at the same time.

While the concepts of fairness and of equal time are honorable, they have not served to promote thorough coverage of public affairs. Rather they have provided the escape hatch for mediocrity. Were the stations fully responsible for what they put on the air, they probably would be more conscientious about it.

Legislation finally is before the House to reform the communications act. It still would authorize a good deal of governmental meddling, but not nearly as much as is presently required. More importantly, however, it provides the vehicle for congressional focus on the Federal Communications Commission, where a complete review and overhaul are called for.

THE CHRISTIAN SCIENCE MONITOR

Boston, Mass., June 20, 1978

At a time government deregulation is very much in vogue, a House subcommittee after a year of study has introduced legislation that would drastically revise the U.S. communications industry, leaving radio and TV broadcasters and telephone companies virtually free of government controls. Writers of the bill, which would overhaul the 1934 Communications Act that has governed the communications industry from its infancy, boast that it would in effect replace the current government regulated industry with one answerable strictly to a free market. But in doing so, the bill leaves open the disturbing possibility of citizens being deprived of what might be called their basic right to ownership of the public airwaves.

Among other things, the proposed revisions would do away with the traditional concept that commercial broadcasters are trustees of the public airwaves and thus answerable to the public — via the Federal Communications Commission — for ensuring that radio and TV frequencies are used in the public interest. It would eliminate the current "fairness doctrine" which requires broadcasters to air all sides of a controversial issue and severely weaken the "equal-time" provision assuring

political opponents equal access to the airwaves. The new law would also give station owners indefinite use of licenses, exempting them from periodic public challenges as to their qualifications. In short, public accountability would almost be wiped out.

While good arguments can be made for trimming away needless government regulations in general, the broadcast industry nevertheless poses unique problems. By its very nature, the number of broadcasters using the airwaves must of necessity be limited. Many broadcasters already enjoy a virtual monopoly, in small towns in particular, and the House subcommittee proposal for granting licenses with indefinite terms would tend to perpetuate such monopolies.

Deleting the fairness and equal-time doctrines might further remove the public's voice in determining programming. Admittedly current licensing procedures seldom result in FCC rejection of a station's renewal application. But the mere fact that station owners are reminded periodically of their responsibility to operate in "the public interest, convenience, and necessity" encourages the airing of controversial topics and at least some public-affairs programming and community oriented

shows. Without such requirements, broadcasters would have little incentive to devote time to controversial public issues.

Restricting the equal-time requirement to major elections would also open up possibilities for abuse at a time when radio and television already hold too much sway in the political process.

Other provisions in the communications bill appear to have merit, however. Reliance on competition rather than regulation in the telephone industry, for instance, may help keep phone rates down. Allowing the giant AT&T Company to expand into other telecommunication fields, and the possible divestiture of its telephone equipment-making subsidiary Western Electric, might also foster competition and spur innovations in telecommunications.

The bill, which has stirred little support in the Senate, is not likely to make it through Congress in its present form. Nor should it, with its obvious inadequacies. But the bill does represent a welcome start of serious discussions about the complex problems of the nation's communications industry and the need to revise federal laws to accommodate the rapid changes taking place in the industry and the nation.

The Hartford Courant

Hartford, Conn., July 15, 1978

When the late Walter Winchell greeted his radio listeners with, "Good evening Mr. and Mrs. North and South America and all the ships at sea," he almost meant it. Radio and television are what the U.S. Supreme Court recently called a "uniquely pervasive presence in the lives of all Americans."

The uneasy federal regulation of the private electronic media has never been totally satisfactory. Now, pending legislation in Congress would dramatically lessen that regulation.

The bill would replace the Federal Communications Commission with a new agency, which would have much less power. It would virtually deregulate the radio industry, and greatly reduce the government influence on television.

The new legislation would weaken the most powerful regulatory threat to the electronic media — loss of license. License renewals, and the threat of outside challenges to renewal, would be eliminated in the radio industry, and television renewal would be required only once every five years. After an owner had a television station for 10 years, renewal would also be eliminated for that station.

While we have reservations about such a carte blanche for television stations, the basic thrust of the legislation is correct.

The Communications Act of 1934 created a regulatory structure with the basic purpose of controlling radio frequencies and avoiding electronic interference between competing stations.

The premise of the government regulation has been that the scarcity of available air space obligated radio and television to use that resource in the public's best interests. Determining the public interest has been a difficult task, and the scarcity of outlets has become an increasingly outdated

and irrelevant justification for government intrusion.

Continuing regulation of the radio industry is particularly difficult to justify. The number of stations in markets of reasonable size are generally sufficient, especially in an industry capable of overnight program changes in an effort to meet competitive challenges.

While a lessened government role in television is also reasonable, we would urge Congress to devote serious study to the proposed deregulation. Especially in markets like Hartford, with limited access to VHF stations with strong signals, audience access to competitive programming is quite limited.

With the rise of the public television networks, and the potential for almost unlimited cable television access, the commercial monopoly becomes less important.

The basic issue raised by the legislation is whether government regulation is worth the obvious First Amendment difficulties that arise when government seeks to control public access to information. The FCC's warning to a New York radio station for playing a comedy album segment with naughty words in it was supported this month by a 5-4 U.S. Supreme Court decision. The high court was clearly divided on whether the government has a mandate to censor when the pretext is so flimsy, and the new legislation should make it clear that the republic can suffer dirty words with less danger than is posed by government control of the airwaves.

The mood in Congress and the mood of the nation leans toward a reduction in federal government regulation that produces few tangible benefits. In the communications field, this new legislation offers worthwhile opportunity to study the federal impact, and carefully move toward a lessening of controls.

The Miami Herald

Miami, Fla., September 20, 1978

IRONIC: A landmark policy decision is due shortly concerning one of the nation's most powerful and highly visible industries, broadcasting. Yet there is very little public notice.

Van Deerlin

Maybe it's the setting that obscures the importance of what is going on. After all, the subcommittee on communications of the House Committee on Interstate and Foreign Commerce is hardly the center ring of the Capitol Hill circus.

Or perhaps it's the low-key personality of the subcommittee's chairman, Rep. Lionel Van Deerlin of California. The former television newsman is not a frequent item in *People* magazine's pages.

But surely the lack of public notice is not a sign that the hearings lack significance, for what Congressman Van Deerlin's subcommittee does could shape the future of radio and television in this country.

Mr. Van Deerlin and his colleagues are working on the Communications Act of 1978 (HR 13015), a sweeping bill that would substantially alter the Federal Government's relationship with broadcasting.

HR 13015 would replace the Federal Communications Act of 1934, which has become obsolete because of changes in the economics and the technology of broadcasting in the 44 years since it was enacted.

The general thrust of the Van Deerlin proposal is toward less regulation. That is a goal we applaud in any competitive industry. For broadcasting, deregulation has the further attraction of reducing the potential for Government infringement of First Amendment rights.

The deregulatory features of HR 13015 include limiting the applicability of the "fairness" or "equal time" doctrine; liberalizing the license-renewal process for stations; and curtailing the powers of the Federal Communications Commission, which would be altered and renamed the Communications Regulatory Commission.

We believe these steps are desirable. But we also believe the public interest would be served better if the legislation mandated a more competitive structure for commercial televison, where past regulation has resulted in a powerful oligopoly.

Broadcasters and their lobbyists are on hand for the hearings on the communications act. So are lobbyists for the self-appointed media watchdogs, many of them demanding more, not less, Government regulation of broadcasting's content.

Unfortunately, the general public is under-represented and largely uninformed of the issues at stake here. Too bad, because the outcome is too important to entrust to a melange of competing special interests.

We happen to believe that Mr. Van Deerlin's proposed legislation is, for the most part, a good thing. A fortuitous combination of circumstances has brought forth this omnibus rewrite of the 1934 act at a time when deregulation is somewhat the fashion and when the key congressional committtee is chaired by a thoughtful man sensitive to the First Amendment issues raised by Government regulation of broadcasting.

We further believe that some kind of rewrite of the 1934 act is inevitable because conditions have changed since the days when listeners were fretting over crystal sets, trying to pick up Pittsburgh's KDKA. Nowadays, comunications satellites enable people to watch history being made halfway 'round the world.

But one thing has not changed much since 1934. There is still a belief that the "air waves" belong to the general public. It is fitting for the public to have a say about the future use of this precious public asset.

As the hearings on the Van Deerlin proposal go forward, then, the occasion might well be used as the forum for a full-fledged national debate on the future direction of broadcasting in this country.

The Birmingham News

Birmingham, Ala., June 14, 1978

The notion that government which governs too much governs poorly has led to worthwhile reviews of confusing and excessive federal regulation in the transportation and energy fields. But it does not follow that all controls should be lifted from radio and television stations so they can broadcast whatever they wish.

To a large extent the airwaves are already filled with the programmers' idea of what tunes in the viewers and listeners. The networks play follow-the-leader in telecasting sex, violence, cops and robbers, for the benefit of the 1,000 TV stations, while the same pop tunes are relentlessly played over and over again in the formats of many of the nation's 9,000 radio outlets.

Yet a proposed rewrite of the 1934 Federal Communications Act would remove what barriers remain to safeguard taste and decency, fairness, equal time and public affairs. The legislation offered by the members and staff of a House subcommittee would let the marketplace decide what the airwaves should carry.

It may be that broadcasters feel themselves put upon by irksome and contradictory interpretations served up by the Federal Communications Commission. Yet it would be hard to show that the FCC has blocked innovation and creativity.

"As ineffective as the FCC has been," says Nicholas Johnson, a former FCC commissioner, "it has at least maintained...a floor beneath which no one can sink." Enacting the revised FCC law would let the bottom drop out, says Johnson.

Congress has moved to examine burdensome regulations by federal agencies in setting natural gas prices, airline ticket costs, and interstate trucking routes. Such over-regulation can discourage competition, stifle new ideas, and cost the consumer more. The same evidence has not been offered in the case of the FCC law. As the legislation works its way through Congress during the next year, the lawmakers will hopefully consider ways to modernize the communications code without discarding the still valid belief that the airwaves belong to the public, not those licensed to operate on them.

THE BLADE

Toleado, Ohio, June 26, 1978

SINCE 1934 the Federal Communications Commission has attempted to regulate broadcasting in the public interest. This is a vague mandate, hard to define, and the FCC has been forced to operate and make ad hoc policy decisions under a law which predates the electronic revolution that has taken place since World War II.

The first major effort in many years to overhaul the Federal Communications Act is now before the U.S. House of Representatives — the result of 20 months of hearings, panel discussions, and staff study of the telecommunications industry. Basically, the proposal, the authors of which are Rep. Louis Frey of Florida and Rep. Lionel Van Deerlin of California, is designed to reduce the amount of federal regulation and permit marketplace competition to act as a self-regulatory mechanism.

Among other things, the bill would deregulate radio broadcasting except for technical matters, lead to similar deregulation of television in a 10-year period, eliminate the controversial "fairness doctrine" and "equal time" provision which some broadcasters have contended are an abridgment of the First Amendment, eliminate federal regulation of cable television, and require users of broadcast frequencies to pay fees based on the value of that portion of the electromagnetic spectrum they use. Part of the fees would be used to support public broadcasting, to provide loans to promote minority ownership of broadcasting stations, and to promote rural broadcasting development.

The legislation has been described as a series of trade-offs in which FCC-regulated industries would stand to gain some things and to lose others. Such a monumental change in national telecommunications policy is not to be viewed lightly, and it is likely that the bill will require many months to reach a decision stage, if ever, in Congress.

But the bill could have the effect of breaking a regulatory stalemate. Few broadcasters or, for that matter, other interested parties are totally satisfied with the FCC's operation. The commission has been sluggish in responding to either public or industry needs, and the criticism has been made that it, like most such regulatory bodies, has been too cozy with the industry it regulates. At the same time, efforts to force broadcasters to be more "responsible" often have led to simply more blandness in programming.

An enlightened regulatory process in this area would take into consideration the historical context in which the ownership configuration of American broadcasting has been determined. The recent Supreme Court decision upholding the FCC decision to allow present newspaper-broadcasting combinations in the same market to continue (but banning future such combinations) seems to be recognition of this fact.

The FCC's hand at the regulatory helm has been for the most part a dead hand. The Van Deerlin-Frey proposal at least will give Congress and the country a useful vehicle for the exploration of alternatives to present forms of regulation — alternatives that would take into consideration technological changes in the U.S. communications system.

The Miami Herald

Miami, Fla., June 15, 1978

A S *The Herald* urged more than 14 months ago, the U.S. Supreme Court has reversed a lower-court ruling on the cross-ownership of broadcast properties by newspapers.

The decision will allow the Federal Communications Commission to proceed with its orderly plans to foster competition and diversity of ownership — but without creating havoc or causing serious economic losses, as the lower court's approach would have done.

The High Court's ruling is not only correct, but timely as well. It ends a long period of uncertainty during which owners of broadcasting stations did not know what the ground rules were going to be.

The ruling also comes at a time when the Senate and House are both considering extensive revision or replacement of the Communications Act of 1934, which defines the authority of the FCC.

Cognizant of the Supreme Court's ruling on cross-ownership, Congress and the FCC itself can now look to ways other than forced divestiture by which to encourage diversity and competition in broadcasting.

The San Diego Union

San Diego, Calif.,
June 14, 1978

The Supreme Court's decision to allow newspaper-broadcast operations to continue in most cities appears, at first blush, to be a victory for publishers. Take another look: the real winner is the Federal Communications Commission.

The issue was whether joint ownership of print and broadcast media in the same market area is in the public interest. The FCC said in 1975 that it is not, and banned future combinations. At the same time, however, it allowed existing cross-ownerships in 44 states to continue operations except for 16 "small-market" cities. In those cities, newspapers would be forced to divest themselves of broadcast operations. The FCC argued that for a monopoly newspaper in a given market also to control the airwaves was unhealthy, if not dangerous; that decision we would not quarrel with.

The FCC also said that most cross-ownerships are in areas where there is more than a single newspaper and numerous radio and television stations — in other words, there is no monopoly of news — and that forcing divestiture everywhere would disrupt the industry, cause individual hardship and possibly harm the public interest.

An appeals court had overturned that part of the FCC ruling, saying that everybody has to play by the same rules; it ordered divestiture in 150 cities in 44 states — and sent shock waves throughout the industry.

It was the appeals court order that the Supreme Court overturned on Monday. It was not imparting its blessing to cross-ownership, however welcome its decision was in all but 16 cities. What the Court said was that the FCC has the authority to make the rules, when it comes to the nation's airways.

The court has enhanced the authority of an already powerful commission. That is bound to temper whatever joy and relief its divestiture ruling brought to the conference rooms of the nation's broadcasters.

The Washington Star
and Daily News

Washington, D.C., June 16, 1978

The Supreme Court dealt this week with an issue that is of more than casual interest to this newspaper: the 1975 "cross-ownership" regulations of the Federal Communications Commission.

These rules, which the Court upheld *in toto*, are aimed, so the FCC says, at "promoting competition among the mass media . . . and maximizing diversification of . . . sources and viewpoints." The rules forbid newspaper owners to acquire television or radio stations in the same market; but except for 16 "egregious" monopolies, mostly in smaller cities, they allow existing combines to stand so long as they meet other FCC standards of public service.

The Court, in other words, allowed the "grandfather clause" to stand, thus confining the breakup of media concentrations to the future; and in that respect overruled the U.S. Court of Appeals for the District of Columbia whose more searching opinion on the media-monopoly issue last year disallowed it.

We mentioned at the outset this newspaper's special interest in the cross-ownership rules, not because it is ours but because *The Star's* case illustrates the ironies of FCC policy and the gap between regulatory aim and regulatory effect.

When this paper and affiliated Washington TV and radio stations were sold to a new owner three years ago, the combination became subject to the FCC cross-ownership ban. The ultimate result was that *The Star* itself is now owned by Time, Inc.; the radio station by ABC News; and WJLA-TV (as it now is) by *The Star's* former publisher, Joe L. Allbritton.

You could say that "diversification" of *ownership* was achieved. But in view of the size and the extensive holdings of all three new owners, it remains to be seen how much "competition" was also promoted. Some, no doubt, in Washington; little, it may well appear to independent observers, in the net.

The ironies of the *Star* case demonstrate the fallacy of automatically associating "diversification of viewpoints" with mere changes in ownership and structure. The FCC, as Justice Thurgood Marshall notes in his opinion, found "no pattern of specific abuses by existing cross-owners" during the customary five-year period when the proposed rules were under discussion.

That came as no surprise to those in the news business, though it possibly did to others, since the owners of large concentrations of "media," print and electronic, usually strain to promote diversity among their properties. This, of course, from a mixture of motives, both principled and self-interested. In the last resort, the First Amendment is more dependent on a consciousness of civic obligation than on anti-trust rulings by government commissions.

The Court's opinion in the FCC case is sound enough but utterly unadventurous. It is unadventurous in accepting the primitive assumptions about electronic technology on which the licensing authority of the FCC rests. Justice Marshall refers without so much as a quibble to "the physical scarcity of broadcast frequencies" and believes that the "physical limitations of the broadcast spectrum are well known."

In fact, as the more penetrating Court of Appeals opinion noted, it may now be technically possible to expand the "broadcast spectrum" for television to an extent that is, for practical purposes, unlimited. Neither the FCC nor the broadcast industry has begun to come to terms with this expansion, whose implications are deeply unsettling for both. The all but unmentionable fact is that for television, at least, if not for radio, the rationale of close regulation has now been undermined; and the case for far more extensive competition among channels brought into dim view on the horizon.

Whether, and when, this fact will be boldly faced we cannot imagine. Certain deregulation initiatives elsewhere (e.g., in the airlines industry) have shown that a cozy and mutually supportive alliance often exists between government regulators and the businesses they regulate. The FCC, the three giant television networks and their affiliates all share a vested interest in pretending that "the physical limitations of the broadcast spectrum" make the FCC, this aging and rather clumsy electronics nanny, necessary, when in fact those "physical limitations" vanished when the coaxial cable arrived.

Given the potential limned by modern electronics, it is probably fair to say that the FCC suppresses as much competition as it promotes — as indeed the U.S. Court of Appeals found in its recent ruling on pay television. Solemn protestations of interest in "promoting competition among the mass media" and "maximizing diversification" belong much more to the realm of decorative sloganeering than vital principle.

It will be a sign that the FCC's zeal for competition is genuine when it follows the Civil Aeronautics Board in calling upon Congress to strip it of regulatory powers that are, in fact, both needlessly meddlesome and in their net effect anti-competitive.

But don't hold your breath until it does so.

The Chattanooga Times

Chattanooga, Tenn., June 23, 1978

It was an interesting coincidence that last week produced a major Supreme Court decision on the question of joint ownership of newspapers and television and radio stations, and the release of a far-reaching bill that would rewrite the Communications Act of 1934. In an age of vast media influence over our daily lives, Congress would do well to take the former into account when it debates the latter.

* * *

Essentially, the Court's ruling will prevent newspapers from acquiring a radio or TV station (and vice versa) in its own community. The joint ownerships which now exist will be allowed to continue except in 16 cities (now reduced to 13) where the same corporation operates the only newspaper and the only radio or television station diversitutres there are required by 1980. The same requirement will be made in other markets if there is a change in ownership of the combinations.

The Court's decision may not be all that the broadcasters had hoped for but at least it overturned a lower court ruling that had ordered the Federal Communications Commission to order general divestiture immediately. That court used a sort of "one remedy for all" approach that could have wreaked havoc in the broadcasting industry as "cross-owners" sought to divest themselves of print or broadcast properties out of a primary consideration of an arbitrary deadline, not the public interest.

One disturbing aspect of the decision was pointed up by Broadcasting Magazine, which noted that the Court relied on its 1969 Red Lion (Pa.) case to restate the proposition that broadcasters are not automatically entitled to the First Amendment guarantee of press freedom. It did that by asserting once again "the fundamental proposition that there is no 'unabridgeable First Amendment right to broadcast comparable to the right of every individual to speak, write or publish.'" That kind of attitude can only be changed by congressional action.

THE MILWAUKEE JOURNAL

Milwaukee, Wisc., June 24, 1978

Should a newspaper be allowed to own a radio or TV station in the same community where it publishes? The US Supreme Court grappled with that question the other day when it upheld present Federal Communications Commission (FCC) policy.

The high court rendered two judgments: First, it ruled that an appeals court decision requiring the divestiture of *all* local newspaper-radio-TV combinations was too drastic a way to promote diversity in broadcasting. Second, the court found the FCC's policy of allowing most existing combinations to continue while banning such future amalgamations was a reasonable approach to the problem.

The Journal Co., which owns two newspapers and a radio and TV station in this community, has a vested interest in these findings. However, granting that, we would like to offer a few comments on the outcome.

In rejecting the extreme view of the appeals court, the Supreme Court fairly took into account the historical growth of radio and TV broadcasting. Many newspapers were pioneers in radio and TV (The Journal Co. included) and were granted licenses by the FCC on the basis of their expertise in communications. As the high court pointed out, the FCC "specifically noted that the existing newspaper-broadcast cross-owners as a group had a 'long record of service' in the public interest . . . and had established and continued 'traditions of service' from the outset."

To undo all this indiscriminately, to attempt to turn back the clock as though the last 40 years did not exist, as the appeals court wanted to do, would amount to drastically changing the rules in midgame. That would be not only unfair but also unnecessarily disruptive. The FCC stated, and the Supreme Court agreed in overturning the appeals court, that requiring widespread divestiture could cause more damage to broadcasting — and the public interest — than it would cure.

One of the major adverse effects of sweeping divestiture would be a lessening of local ownership of broadcast stations. As the Supreme Court noted, roughly 75% of the existing newspaper-broadcast combinations are locally owned; and "these owners' knowledge of their local communities and concern for local affairs, built over a period of years, would be lost if they were replaced with outside interests."

All of which brings us to the policy on cross-ownership that the FCC is now free to apply. Actually, the number of newspaper-broadcast combinations has been declining in recent years. For example, the share of TV channels controlled by newspapers has dropped from 40% in 1950 to 10% in 1975. Nonetheless, the FCC will require the breaking up of 16 newspaper-broadcast combinations — each distinguishable by the fact that the only newspaper in town owns the only TV or radio station. For the other existing combinations (all of which face broadcast competition), there is no jeopardy as long as the public interest is properly served.

Although we are not among the imperiled 16, we find their fate troubling. They, too, can cite records of service. They, too, can plead the virtues of local ownership. As long as they continue to serve their communities well, it seems inequitable and shortsighted to order divestiture.

The opportunity to prove any abuse is available when stations periodically come up for license renewal before the FCC. This procedure amply permits any truly harmful effects of media concentration to be curbed without unduly penalizing those newspaper-broadcast combinations that are doing good jobs.

Sentinel Star

Orlando, Fla., March 8, 1977

THAT THERE is a place in the scheme of things for both newspapers and television is amply demonstrated by America's acceptance of both — the newspaper as a medium to inform and incidentally to entertain, and television as a medium to entertain and incidentally to inform.

Nor is the public necessarily badly served if a newspaper owns a television station, or vice versa.

If a combination restrains trade by cutting the quality of coverage or setting exorbitant ad rates in a monopoly market, there are existing public recourses. One of them is the present Federal Communications Commission authority to review TV station licenses and fail to renew the ones that are deemed not to serve the public adequately.

That's why we disagree with a decision by a three-judge federal panel in Washington voiding the FCC rule that allows newspapers to own broadcasting stations in the same city where they publish.

Under the court ruling, such combinations could exist only on submission of proof to the FCC that "cross ownership is (clearly) in the public interest."

In our judgment this puts the horse on the wrong end of the cart. The way it is, and the way it should remain, the FCC allows cross ownership unless proof is submitted showing that it is contrary to public interest.

The newspaper in a number of localities has become an endangered species since emergence of the Cinderella medium of television. Yet the printed page is important and should be preserved even if a certain amount of subsidy is required from a companion TV station.

Those who are adversely affected by this court ruling should take their case to the U.S. Supreme Court where, it is hoped, the FCC will be upheld.

The Courier-Journal

Louisville, Ky., June 15, 1978

BY COMING DOWN on the side of most of those who own newspapers and broadcast stations in the same American communities, the Supreme Court doubtless prompted celebrations in many boardrooms this week. That was certainly true in those controlled by the Bingham family, which owns *The Courier-Journal and Louisville Times* and WHAS, Inc., as separate corporations. But the decision also raises several troubling questions about the future of newspapers and the First Amendment in this country.

Under the ruling, some 150 newspapers, 65 television stations and 130 radio stations will continue under local joint ownerships. But formation of similar arrangements by others in the future is forbidden, except where the properties are in different communities. If a present combination is sold, the newspaper and broadcast holdings cannot go to the same buyer.

Admittedly, in no communities did the Federal Communications Commission, the Justice Department or the lower court find a "pattern of specific abuses by existing cross-owners." But the Supreme Court, hearing the case on appeal, echoed the general philosophy it had accepted in a 1953 case. This is that "It is unrealistic to expect true diversity from a commonly owned station-newspaper combination. The divergency of their viewpoints cannot be expected to be the same as if they were antagonistically run."

Even so, the Court "grandfathered in" most of the existing joint ownerships, with the exception of 16 cities in which the only newspaper also owns the only broadcast station. One or the other will have to be sold, which makes many of these ownerships victims of a true Catch 22.

The Anniston, Alabama, *Star* is a good example. The paper's owners have been involved in radio broadcasting since the 1930s and television since the 1960s. They are now among those to be divested because the FCC and Supreme Court find insufficient diversity of media voices in the community. But the FCC allocated only one television frequency to Anniston, and granted it to the newspaper publisher. Where a federal agency fails to create the opportunity for diversity, should the victims of its short-sightedness be penalized?

The Court agrees with the FCC that about 75 percent of the nation's cross-owned properties are presently in local hands, and sees some loss if they are sold to absentees with less interest in the communities involved. Yet its divestiture of joint ownerships in 16 smaller communities will bring more absentee ownership — a questionable benefit in either the broadcasting or publishing businesses.

Through this double standard, the Supreme Court has established a special class of newspaper and broadcast station owners. In a philosophical sense this is a worrisome problem. The court and the FCC recognize the "long record of service" of many of these co-owned properties, and agree that "forced dissolution of all existing co-located combinations, though fostering diversity, would disrupt the industry and cause individual hardship and would or might harm the public interest in several respects."

Also, in singling out 16 cases for divestiture, the Court repeatedly quotes from an earlier decision that there is no "unabridgable First Amendment right to broadcast comparable to the right of every individual to speak, write, or publish." But in practice this decision does impose a strong limitation of First Amendment rights. For instance, a broadcaster may not now start or acquire a newspaper in his own hometown. Thus broadcasters as a class (except where "grandfathered" by this decision) have been limited in their First Amendment rights to publish.

Finally, one of our gravest concerns involves the future of America's newspapers. The escalating cost of newspaper production and delivery is rapidly forcing them to consider alternative means of delivery. This almost certainly will mean that one day you'll have the option of having your daily paper electronically delivered to your home.

But the Supreme Court decision precludes a newspaper from owning a radio or television channel over which words and pictures could be thus transmitted. The FCC also has forbidden the joint ownership of newspapers and cable TV systems. For future generations and the continued health of a free press in this country, this exclusion from the "electronic alternative" may be the most devastating impact of the decision.

Concern for the future

So the Supreme Court's ruling is a mixed blessing. It protects a special class of jointly owned broadcast and publishing groups because they got into broadcasting in the early days and aren't monopolies in their towns. That seems a dubious justification for a long-term policy. Other co-owners will be divested, and no new cross-ownerships may be formed, despite the absence of any claimed "abuse" of those joint relationships. That must, at least, raise some questions of fairness.

We think this decision will have a negative effect, in years to come, on exercise of the First Amendment and thus on the public interest. So any rejoicing in the boardrooms must be tempered with genuine concern for the long-term future of communications in the fields of publishing and broadcasting.

Rocky Mountain News

A Scripps-Howard Newspaper   Reg. U.S. Pat. Off.   Colorado's First Newspaper—Founded in 1859

Denver, Colo., October 20, 1977

THE U.S. SUPREME Court makes as much law by the cases it chooses not to hear as by those on which it hands down decisions.

Early this month, the court declined to review a ruling made last March by the U.S. Court of Appeals for the District of Columbia in the matter of the Federal Communication Commission versus Home Box Office. The action – or non-action – could have far-reaching effects on the kind of television programming available to Americans in years to come.

The decision by the Court of Appeals was the culmination of a long-running battle between commercial television broadcasters and the cable television industry, between so-called free TV and pay TV, with the FCC in the middle.

At issue were the FCC's regulations limiting movies and sports events which could be shown on cable television, the system under which subscribers pay a monthly fee to have special programs piped into their homes. Cablecasters were prohibited, for example, from showing any film between three and 10 years old, as well as many major sports events, even those not broadcast by commercial television.

The three-judge appeals panel found unanimously that there was no evidence that cable television would adversely affect either the public interest or over-the-air television; that the FCC had no statutory authority to regulate pay cable TV; and that its restrictions violated the medium's First Amendment right of free speech.

Thus released from FCC regulation, will pay TV now proceed to "siphon off" events like the World Series or the Super Bowl which Americans now watch for free, as the commercial broadcasters have warned from the beginning?

In testimony before a Senate subcommittee this summer, spokesman for the cable television industry said they had no intention of doing so.

In any event, nothing is going to change very much very quickly. For one thing, although some 3,000 cable TV systems currently serve nearly 12 million homes around the country, the industry is still up against commercial TV's enormous bidding power and what the cablecasters charge is the networks' "contractual lock" on new movies.

And should the adverse effects the Court of Appeals saw no sign of begin to materialize, there is nothing to prevent Congress from enacting legislation to protect free TV.

What the decision has done is to lift a cloud of uncertainty that has hovered over the future of cable TV and to give promise not of less but of greater program diversity for the television watching public.

The Washington Star

and Daily News

Washington, D.C., April 3, 1977

If the nation's commercial television establishment suffers any pinch of the pocketbook nerve from last week's U.S. Court of Appeals decision on cable television, the pain will be largely self-inflicted.

The "over-the-air" television industry has for years battled to obstruct the development of cable television and the Federal Communications Commission ultimately adopted rules for cable TV reflecting its point of view. (For example, cable companies could buy and show first-run movies only within three years, or after 10 years, of their release.)

The Court of Appeals here in Washington found this and other rules defective and directed the FCC to fashion new ones. The new rules will surely be less restrictive, less biased in favor of "over-the-air" television, and more closely attuned to competitive and free-speech principles.

The broadcasters' war against the coaxial cable — which greatly expands the potential number of television channels — was a study in overreaching.

The commercial broadcasters had argued — and the FCC substantially adopted the view — that cable TV (whose subscribers get the service in return for a monthly fee ranging from $6 to $10) ought to be "ancillary" or "supplemental" to broadcast programming. They had argued that unrestricted bidding by cable-TV companies for special features (e.g., sports events and first-run movies) would "siphon" away the best programming. Cable TV, they suggested, would then become an elite service for those who could afford it while stripping all the good stuff from "free" commercial television — all to the hurt of the poor and rural areas where the per capita cost of cable development might be prohibitive.

As the court found, these arguments are less than overpowering; and the FCC rules based on them raise First Amendment and anti-trust problems.

The argument that conventional commercial television is a "free" service (in contrast to the fee-based cable) is unpersuasive. Advertising fees that sustain "free" commercial television are, of course, passed to the consumer. A Florida television critic even submitted the following ingenious calculation: "If we figure our time is worth the minimum wage, then watching what we don't want to see (i.e., the commercials) for a typical 18½-hour 'free' television day can cost us a phantom total of $9.09 per day."

Since the FCC rules also deny cable television the right to carry advertising, and thus lower fees for the convenience of those too straitened to afford it, the Court of Appeals concluded: ". .

. If the Commission is serious about helping the poor, its regulations are arbitrary; but if it is serious about its rules, it cannot really be relying on harm to the poor."

The further contention that pay cable television, unthrottled, would "siphon off" the best features the Court of Appeals simply found to be unsupported by the record. The court noted that average profitability at the networks — more than twice that of American industry as a whole — hardly leaves them without resources to bid for the best features against the cable impresarios.

The fundamental miscalculation of the commercial broadcasters, however, was their failure to reckon on the anti-regulatory mood of the country — especially when regulation seems to play favorites. When the cable rules of the FCC came under judicial scrutiny, cable had in its corner not only the Justice Department's anti-trust division and the House communications subcommittee but a number of independent observers such as the Committee for Economic Development.

In throwing out the present restrictive rules the other day, the court did *not* say that cable television is a candidate for wholesale deregulation. It did insist that the FCC write rules consistent with the First Amendment and with fair competitive ideals. And it insisted that if any restrictions are to be based on the "siphoning" scare, they must stem from demonstrable need rather than speculation.

We are confident that the FCC, taking the Court of Appeals decision in *Home Box Office v. FCC* as its guide, can frame rules that free cable television to compete on an equal footing with over-the-air television. We are not, that is, among those who view the court's decision as a pretext for Congress to replace the FCC as the writer of regulations.

Indeed, in scolding the FCC for permitting undisclosed "ex-parte" influence in its rule-making procedure, the Court footnoted an interesting revelation by a network senior vice president. In 1974, when the FCC was considering a modification of pay-cable rules, "we (that is, the commercial network) took the leadership in opposing these proposals with the result that key members of Congress made it known in no uncertain terms that they did not expect the Commission to act on such a far-reaching policy matter without guidance. The Commission got the message . . ."

If that is how "key members of Congress" deal with weighty issues of television regulation, we fail to see why the rule-making process should be shifted from the FCC and the courts into their hands.

The Washington Post

Washington, D.C., May 8, 1978

THE COMMUNICATIONS business should be governed more by the marketplace and less by the FCC. That is what Charles D. Ferris, chairman of the Federal Communications Commission, has been emphasizing in his first major policy speeches. He "will rely on competition instead of rules whenever that is promising or possible," Mr. Ferris told the National Association of Broadcasters last month. In particular, he wants to "encourage new technology and services." Broadcasters, he said, will have to sustain their profits, and their place in American homes, by offering more diverse programing, more community services and new means of channeling information through television sets.

In blunter terms, Mr. Ferris told the National Cable Television Association last week that if cable does not fulfill its promises of innovation, "it may be bypassed in the marketplace by those who do." That must have jarred his audience a bit. As Mr. Ferris noted, the cable industry was constrained for years by regulatory policies that often favored broadcasters and telephone companies. Now, fresh from major victories in Congress and the courts, the cable operators had been looking forward to a better reception at the FCC. Instead, the chairman wants to encourage a new generation of competitors.

Mr. Ferris, a newcomer to communications fields, has evidently not been captured by the established interests there. If anything, he is captivated by technology and the potentiality of satellites, computers, two-way cables, home video systems and the like. There is good reason to be bullish on electronics these days. Home video recorders are growing less expensive and more popular. Home computers are approaching the mass marketplace. In Columbus, Ohio, Warner Cable is trying out a two-way cable system called Qube; in Great Britain, advanced networks for transmitting data are already in use.

In general, national communications policies have lagged behind this hurtling technology. As in the case of cable, each new entrant has had to battle for a fair place in regulatory schemes set up when broadcasting, telephones and other older-line industries were young. One central question now, therefore, is whether regulation should be modernized to take in new technologies, or eased substantially. This is the point on which we find Mr. Ferris's views most interesting and encouraging. He does not want the FCC to dictate future communications systems and services. Instead, he thinks the "public interest" should be defined, to a greater extent, by what the public is actually interested in buying and subscribing to—in short, by competition in the marketplace.

Of course, stating that view is easier than spelling it out in regulatory decisions—or selling it to the consumer groups, as well as industries, who have come to rely so heavily on the FCC. We hope, though, that Mr. Ferris will persevere. In our view, he has set out on a creative course.

The Kansas City Times

Kansas City, Mo., February 18, 1978

Discussion before the Mayor's Committee on Cable Television has been confined, for the most part, to complaints from so called "free" stations. It is clear that the City Council does not want to do anything that would interfere with the business of TV. But the council does have a responsibility to the taxpayers for the granting of a proper franchise and to viewers who want more freedom of choice.

TV series, sporting events and movies are the focal points of cable TV for the time being, and those matters dominate the talk. Because of the nearly obstacle-free viewing area, there has been no dire need for the installation of a cable system in Kansas City. The area has three commercial network outlets, an independent UHF commercial station, a public broadcast station and will have a religious TV station. The UHF stations, for technical reasons relating to TV receivers, have the most reception difficulties. Otherwise, an overwhelming majority of the viewers are able to get commercial broadcasts paid for by advertising through the air. Thus the push for alternatives to pre-empted programs becomes the battleground for wiring the city.

When the council committee took up the issue of cable TV a few years ago it was decided that the area did not need such a system. Now that cable companies are wiring the suburbs, Kansas City is caught in the midst of a drive for cable again.

Instead of examining the use of cable TV solely as an alternative to local programs, the committee should take a broader approach. Television still is in its infancy. Certainly technological advances have enabled TV to cut its baby teeth, but the future indicates clearly that cable TV is going to mean more to communities than dozens of channels of reruns and assorted game shows.

Proponents of the cable are quick to point out its potential in education and never fail to grasp that as a security blanket in making presentations. Education, or the use of cable systems by school districts, merely scratches the surface. The prospects for cable communications system rival science fiction, and it is with that vision that the committee should approach the entire question.

The committee is supposed to provide a blueprint. If that blueprint offers no more foresight than approval of an arrangement which could be worthless in terms of public interest by the end of the century, then the citizens will suffer a great disservice. The committee should think of Kansas City's needs far into the future. Testimony from persons in communications research, who do not have an immediate interest in whether the city adopts cable TV, would be of significant benefit. Reports of the full range of educational and other services which could be given the community would be valuable in making the decision. Also, public income from the franchise is a basic question.

We mean no criticism of the hard work put in by the committee. That voluntary group ought to receive a thank you from the rest of us. When we think of cable TV for the entire city, however, we become infinitely more concerned with the future of communications and the interests of the taxpayers than in whether "Star Trek" reruns could be supplemented by similar choices. An ordinance governing the installation and operation of cable TV in Kansas City ought to be responsive to the needs of the people, and not just serve as a mere point of mediation between cable and existing commercial TV companies. The issues go far beyond that.

The Birmingham News

Birmingham, Ala., August 14, 1978

In increasing numbers Americans are talking back to their television sets, warning of station licensing battles, viewer boycotts and campaigns against indifferent advertisers. The long-standing battle over the good (of which many say there is not enough), the bad, and the ugly content of programming is beginning to take on the fervor of the anti-tax rebellion.

The National PTA is set to dispute license renewals of network-owned stations in several major cities. The big three—ABC, CBS and NBC—may be particularly vulnerable to this tactic, since these stations unlike affiliates are wholly-owned by the networks. PTA officials say they will continue monitoring programs this fall and if the networks, which are in charge of dispensing shows seen across the land, don't clean up their act the station licenses will be challenged.

Holding a license over a station's head has not, since television began, proved very effective. But the din raised by the PTA, which rated the 10 best and worst shows of last season, will find support from such groups as the Tupelo, Miss., National Federation for Decency. It wants viewers to boycott ABC in November when ratings which relate to advertising rates are done.

The trend, say the anti-programming groups, has been somewhat away from violence of the cops-and-robbers sort, and more towards sex, profanity and general poor taste. And if shows produced for television aren't bad enough, they contend, the crop of recent motion pictures now turning up on the tube are little improvement.

Government regulation is supposedly supplied through the Federal Communications Commission, by virtue of assigning broadcast frequencies which are held to be public property. But not since Newton Minnow, FCC chairman of the early 1960s, talked about a "wasteland," has the agency taken a constructively critical posture. While no one is suggesting that the government directly censor programs, or approve the scripts, there is need for a formula which sets some reasonable standards.

For example, programming blocks might win acceptance. The evening could begin with child and family type shows, move on to light comedy, music and variety shows, then documentaries and drama, with the detective, heavy romance and presumed more mature material coming up later, say 10 p.m. This would tend to keep the most questionable programming from the eyes of the young, and offer the advantage of like programs competing against each other.

The above approach is rather similar to the format of the Public Broadcasting Service whose level of programming has not been criticized by those seeking to cleanse the commercial networks. Perhaps the biggest complaint is that viewers are compelled to accept whatever the networks serve up for the bulk of the evening, against which switching the dial no longer offers much defense.

ARKANSAS DEMOCRAT

Little Rock, Ark., August 26, 1977

The producers of three cops-and-robbers series, with the producer of "Roots", have complained to a panel of *TV Guide* editors at Radnor, Pa., that the campaigns of indirect censorship of "violence" being waged against the networks, who are always running scared, may mean the effective end of TV programming, "as we have known it."

This might not be too bad an idea at that, since commercial TV in our own judgment had already begun its season-by-season decline roughly at about the time the cable got to Little Rock (natch!), except for one thing: A fresh start would mean nothing, since the industry has long since lost any vestige of the inventiveness that introduced the new medium, for good or ill.

While the crime show producers have a vested interest in the matter of how much TV violence, their complaints against the organized pressure groups and the timorous nets are not invalidated merely by that.

It seems to us that both propositions are almost equally valid. Yes, there *is* "too much violence" on TV, but, yes, there also is too much farina already, with even implied censorship likely to reduce all of it to pap, and more-or-less identical pap at that.

The root problem of these two irreconcilables is the notion that everyone should watch everything on TV full-time, the right, nay, duty, of personal decision as to what to watch and what not to watch defaulted to the nets, which naturally want us to watch everything, or at least everything that a particular net has going for it at a particular time; defaulted to the nets and defaulted to the self-appointed guardians of our personal taste and even elemental sense of discrimination.

Since the two *are*, for all practical purposes, irreconcilables, we have no idea how to resolve them, except to say that censorship is not the answer. Already we have wall-to-wall "family" shows all over the tube, but if anybody thinks the policers ought to be satisfied with what they've got, he is simply unfamiliar with the mind of the policer.

Serious though the subject is, there were a couple of unconscious funnies in the producers' lament to *TV Guide*.

For example, there was David Gerber of "Police Story", who said that "our worry now is that we have lost the battle of violence, next will be sex." We thought that sex had been first, but experts are for listening to, as we know. Then Aaron Spelling of Spelling-Goldberg Productions tells us that if things go on as they've been going lately, *we are going to be faced with plastic television that's going to breed a plastic society.*" We sure don't want *that* to happen, do we?

The News and Courier

Charleston, N.C., May 14, 1977

A psychiatrist's testimony this week before a Senate subcommittee that violence on television poses a "health hazard" for children corroborates what other medical experts and many lay people have been saying for some time. It also tends to support the intent of a bill being offered by Sen. Strom Thurmond to give the Federal Communications Commission authority to ban sex-and-violence programs from the air. Like a lot of other parents of young, impressionable children, the senator advocates more responsible programming. He thinks broadcasters should be required by law to meet their responsibilities if they won't meet them voluntarily.

The TV fare these days gives Sen. Thurmond and those who share his views ample reason to argue for governmental control over program content. The more broadcasters fill the home screens with death and destruction, the more appealing becomes the proposition to have the FCC say, "Stop, enough".

Yet attractive as the idea is to give government that kind of power to promote child health, caution must be exercised. The intent may be good, but in that direction lies infringement on constitutional right. In that direction is censorship, plain and simple.

Concerned parents and others who care would do better to complain to sponsors and network chiefs, and to take upon themselves the responsibility for monitoring what their children watch on television. In the health area, there is a parental obligation to guard against adverse psychological impact, just as there is obligation to guard against the dangers posed by riding tricycles in the middle of the street.

The TENNESSEAN
Nashville, Tenn., May 1, 1977

VIOLENCE in television programming has become the subject of numerous sociological studies and the object of growing public criticism.

Citizen groups are pressing networks to reduce or eliminate much of the TV violence. Some church leaders are urging people to tune out violent programs. Others are calling for boycotts of products of sponsors who pay for programs that feature excessive violence.

Some television industry executives may see these citizen groups as enemies of their industry. Actually the groups who call for citizen action to bring the networks to voluntarily cut down on shows with violence may turn out to be the best friends of the industry.

When the public gets aroused about a societal problem the tendency has been to turn to the federal government to solve it. Already there are rumblings that the national Parent-Teachers Association is thinking of asking the Federal Communications Commission to revoke TV licenses of telecasters who continue to program violence.

When government enters the picture the threat to First Amendment rights are real. The FCC has flirted with broadcast rights for years and at times has overstepped constitutional bounds. But should the industry remain intractable in the present controversy, then the issue of TV violence may become so emotion-packed as to encourage the FCC, or even Congress, to get into the dangerous business of censorship.

The question of whether violence in programming has a causal effect on viewers is one about which every social scientist has an answer, based upon some study. Research over several years has found, for instance, that in Saturday morning programs, commonly known as "the children's hour" there were acts of violence every three and a half minutes. Other researchers have estimated that by the time a child reaches 15 years of age he or she may have viewed 13,000 acts of killing — and 18,000 by the time of high school graduation.

Still another study, sponsored by the ABC network, found that 22 out of 100 juvenile law violators interviewed said they copied their criminal activity after methods observed on television.

At the same time, ratings surveys over the years consistently have shown that the American public is fascinated by violence on TV and faithfully views programs which are built around crime and bloodshed. Thus the networks may argue, with some evidence, that the industry has given the public what it wanted.

Still, there is substantial sentiment growing in favor of cutting down on violent programming. The networks should not ignore that. If they do, the result will be a growing clamor for the government to require different programming. That, of course, is the first big step toward censorship.

Some such demands are already being made. In the April issue of the *Columbia Journalism Review* there is an article by Mr. Franz J. Ingelfinger, editor of the *New England Journal of Medicine,* who gives a scathing critical review of an NBC special on violence in America. The program, telecast last January, was a weak apology for TV violence, according to Mr. Ingelfinger, who concludes that "society is entitled to impose limits" upon the amount of violence that can be broadcast on TV. He makes no bones about it: "Society" in this context means "government." He acknowledges that efforts to create such limits "are opposed as interfering with rights of free speech..."

But he brushes aside First Amendment concerns and favors government regulation of programming.

Thus, the industry should look with a spirit of cooperation on suggestions that it voluntarily reduce the amount of violence on television.

Those who want to reduce television violence should continue to impress their point of view upon the industry. But they should understand that if they urge government intervention they will be encouraging nothing less than federal censorship and control of what they may and may not see on the tube.

The best and only legitimate censor ought to be the individuals who simply turn off the set or switch channels in order to avoid violence in programming — and who let the stations, networks and sponsors know why they did it. Faced with the threat of government regulation of programming the industry will respond and may even come to appreciate those who now criticize shows dedicated to violence.

The Evening Bulletin
Philadelphia, Pa., May 18, 1977

A singularly bad idea surfaced a few days ago at a Senate subcommittee hearing on the state of the television industry.

During a discussion of sex and violence on television, Sen. Strom Thurmond, D-S.C., made it known that he favors government regulation of the content of TV programs. He and Sen. James Eastland, D-Miss., have introduced a bill to prohibit scenes of nudity, obscenity, or "gross physical violence."

The Thurmond-Eastland bill probably doesn't have a prayer of passing in Congress. The idea of banning sex and violence on television may initially play well with the folks at home, but in the long run the idea of free speech plays better. Surely there are enough congressmen determined to protect First Amendment rights to squelch any move toward government censorship of television programming.

All of which is not to say that unbridled mayhem on the tube is a good idea. For several years debates have raged about the effects of television violence on children and others in our society. Although different studies draw different conclusions, the weight of the evidence indicates that broadcast violence does have some dire effects.

Television violence may desensitize people to violent behavior, it may frighten or disturb children, or it may actually inspire twisted minds to commit crimes, some researchers have said. National organizations, including the Parent-Teacher Association and the American Medical Association, have joined the battle against television violence. Special interest groups like Action for Children's Television have pressed the issue before the Federal Communications Commission and the National Association of Broadcasters. Pressure has been brought against advertisers, some of whom have refused to sponsor violent shows.

It is unclear whether all this activity has changed what is seen on the home screen.

Quite apart from how many shootings or punches-in-the-nose occur nightly on television, it is obvious to even the casual viewer that there is a lot of gratuitous violence on the screen. A serious question remains as to what can be done about it and by whom.

Government censorship like that proposed in the Thurmond-Eastland bill clearly is not the answer.

A better approach might be for interest groups to continue to publicize the names of the most objectionable shows and exert more pressure on advertisers. The National Association of Broadcasters, a voluntary association of networks and stations, can provide moral leadership, though its only sanction is to deny an offender the use of its seal of approval.

Probably the most effective weapon against tasteless television is already available to most of us. It involves a couple of steps across the floor and a flick of the wrist.

DAYTON DAILY NEWS
Dayton, Ohio, May 14, 1977

Poor Congress. Ever the hare in races with innumerable tortoises. Frantic legislative running-around, only to show up late at the finish line.

So Sen. Strom Thurmond (R-S.C.) is pressing legislation that would allow — practically force — the Federal Communications Commission to crack down on TV violence. But the networks have just published next fall's schedules, the least violent in many seasons.

Aside from the matter of whether the nation wants its TV morals brooded over by Strom Thurmond, a famous racist of questionable reconstruction, there is additionally, always, the problem of censorship.

First, there's vigorous argument among anti-violence groups about what is violent. Is it even the cartoon cat chasing the cartoon mouse with cartoon mayhem in mind? And second, do we really want some panel of federal appointees to decide? Could it be counted on to keep the revolvers out of view without also banning the last act of *Hamlet*, in the unlikely event *Hamlet* ever should bump Charlie's angels?

Happily, it begins to appear that we can trust ourselves without the the risks of empaneling formal inquisitors. As a psychiatrist testified in supporting federal action, TV violence is a public health hazard. It tends to incite like behavior in many watchers. TV's oddly casual violence makes real-life resorts to violence not laudable but expected and thus sort of okay.

But thanks initially to consciousness- and Hell-raising by some do-gooder groups and thanks finally to TV advertisers, disturbed by the bloodbaths for the self-interested reason that the excitement takes the zing out of their commercials, the networks have whitewashed their planned programming. Gone will be nearly all the cop shows, which were major sources and ironic ones: Real cops rarely shoot anyone; they spend more time talking drunks out of doing something stupid, and talking very creatively at that.

Enter, next fall, lots of singing and dancing, sitcoms imitating sitcoms, pop dramas. I begin to seem that, at least long-run, over-all, the public can look out of its own sensed interests and spare itself official disapprovers. Even with the inevitable lapses and backsliding, that would be best.

THE SAGINAW NEWS
Saginaw, Mich., April 8, 1977

It's probably true that whatever is perceived as violence these days on commercial network television is in the eye of the beholder.

It's also undeniably true that there are growing numbers of beholders whose eyes see much too much violence. And they have started a reform movement that has considerably shaken three major industries — television, advertising and entertainment

In the forefront is the National Citizens Committee for Broadcasting. And running right up there with NCCB is the national organization of Parents and Teachers.

The resulting pressures brought to bear as the result of numerous public hearings In Washington, D.C. and elsewhere, is causing a general upheaval across the TV spectrum. This is now documented by the Wall Street Journal.

Advertisers, particularly major ones, are becoming more chary about what programs they'll associate with in sponsored advertising. The major networks are getting more cautious about total programming — particularly in the cops and robbers categories. And producers and script writers are taking extra pains to write out anything that appears to be what is now defined as "excessive" or "gratuitous" violence in numbers of scenes. For example, a police arrest is one thing. Pistol whipping is being eliminated.

Fundamentally, we're not against this reform so long as we can perceive it to be aimed in its current direction. And that is to lower the over-all effect of some programs that tend to establish extreme violence as a nominal way of life.

So long as it sticks to this course, we think it not a bad thing. If it reaches the point of censorship of the news or total censorship of everything we view then we back away.

The principal contention of the reformers just now is not extreme. It is that any medium of expression or communication that pours into millions of homes for millions of viewing hours daily carries a powerful impact. And one like TV that can saturate the airwaves with portrayals of violence can have a de-sensitizing effect on everybody — and particularly young viewers.

Studies have indicated that this is true. Acting becomes the role model. Young sensibilities can be dulled. Violence can become the acceptable, expectable norm of every day life. Nothing shocks. There is little room left for affection, true love, compassion.

It is this fear of the medium becoming the message, the overriding one in an already violent society, that is propelling the reformers — even, if sometimes, to stated extremes. They're demanding a little less action in the "action" series, more programs over-all that show the decent, nominal side of life. And there is also that.

At any rate, television and its attendant industries are being forced to take notice. Not everybody associated with the art-business form likes it. There are some discomfitures just now over advertisers pulling out of sponsorship. And a lot of money is being spent making adjustments.

But a move is on to sensitize TV a bit more to the anti-social impact of rampant violence in the world of make believe on the home screen. Some of that won't hurt. Even if it gets rid of those absurd and patently overdone squealing-tire car chases which we have often resented most of all as a bad influence on teen-age drivers.

The Hartford Courant
Hartford, Conn., February 20, 1977

Spokesmen for major television networks told Parent-Teacher Association President Carol Kimmel in 1975 that they believe programming rules are being obeyed and PTA protests against TV violence won't change anything. Last year, the national unit of 6.6 million members decided to conduct eight regional marathon hearings hoping that publicizing the views of behavioral experts, pollsters and others involved with children will raise parental awareness to the electronic baby-sitter's negative influence on their youngsters. PTA hopes an aroused public will pressure TV to clean up.

Probably the most revealing information coming from the hearings — the most recent one just ended in Hartford — is the vast amount of time American young people spend watching TV. By the time a youngster is 14 he has witnessed 11,000 murders plus countless nonfatal muggings, robberies, rapes and shootings. What they see more often than not suggests that violence pays, goals attained that way in more than half of all plots. The kids can't avoid the deluge, since they spend 50 per cent more time in front of the tube than in school, and slightly less than they spend sleeping. Teachers say they can tell what kinds of shows their pupils saw the night before by the amount of pushing and punching that goes on.

Although a recent Gallup Poll showed that the majority of people want violent shows to be aired after 10 p.m., a study in East Lyme revealed that 25 per cent of kids through Grade 2 watch until 11, and many are still watching at midnight. A young man said recently that he learned about sex, not from his father, but from late TV talk shows, for instance. At the same time, a juvenile court judge attests that young offenders these days are "so desensitized" that they "don't cry much in court any more." Connecticut Education Commissioner Mark Shedd told the Hartford gathering that TV has changed childhood more than any other invention in history.

Saturday morning, the traditional children's program time, was monitored by a Massachusetts research project, revealing that 71 per cent of the fare includes at least one violent incident. One every two minutes is not unusual.

Do parents know or care about all this? Gallup also revealed that although 70 per cent of parents of children through age 17 believe there is a relationship between TV violence and the rising crime rate, nearly half put no restrictions on the types of programs the kids can watch and only 36 per cent restrict the numbers of viewing hours.

During this 90th anniversary year of PTA, the unit may score its greatest victory on behalf of children who are its main concern. If anyone can get parents together, it is the one to do it, with its close ties with the schools. It plans local TV monitoring, boycotts of offensive programs and sponsor's products, letter-writing campaigns, and visits to studios. It may question Federal Communications Commission licenses when a station appears not to be working in the public interest.

None of these will work, however, without cooperation in the homes by parents who understand what is going on, who care and do something about it where it counts—affecting the ratings. And in all proceedings, there must be no recourse to censorship lest the public lose more than it gains.

RAPID CITY JOURNAL—

Rapid City, S.D., December 13, 1977

The new chairman of the Federal Communications Commission, Charles Ferris, says the public, rather than the federal government, should take the responsibility for curbing violence on television.

We concur.

While a reduction in television violence is a desirable end, government involvement is not the proper means to attain it. Such involvement implies government censorship in violation of First Amendment rights.

Actions such as those taken by the Parent Teachers Association, the American Medical Association, National Citizens Committee for Broadcasting, religious and other public groups which have expressed their concerns about specific programs is a more viable method of improving programming than government intervention.

Protesting television violence to local stations, networks and advertisers is a proper exercise of the public's First Amendment rights without infringing on the First Amendment rights of the broadcasting industry.

Ratings are the name of the game in television and when the public tunes out violent programs they no longer will be profitable and will go off the air.

But the decision as to what goes and what stays should be made by the public and not the federal government.

THE CHRISTIAN SCIENCE MONITOR

Boston, Mass., August 31, 1977

Americans concerned about excessive violence and sex on television will have at least one reason to cheer this fall. Network shows for the new season promise to be far less violent than those of previous years, and much of the credit for this turn-around in network programming can go to citizen groups such as Action for Children's Television (ACT) and the national Parent-Teachers Association which are keeping close tabs on TV fare and successfully pressuring sponsors to eliminate violence for violence's sake.

Most encouraging in this welcome downtrend in violence is the indication that Americans appear to be gaining a greater say in determining what type of programming the three commercial networks beam into their living rooms every evening. More public participation in influencing the quality and types of programs is essential if the medium is ever to abandon its pandering to the lowest common denominator of interests for the admittedly more difficult goal of elevating the aspirations and desires of the viewing public to more lasting and redeeming values. After all, the airways do belong to the public. In light of current projections that new uses for television will make it an even bigger and more influential part of people's lives in decades to come, the public has an increasing stake in deciding how its airways are to be used.

Some television producers understandably are concerned that "sanitizing" violence out of TV dramas threatens to deter artistic creativity, present an unrealistic view of society, and lead to "plastic television" and a "plastic society," as one producer remarked. Totally eliminating violence from the screen is not the answer. The key factor is how violence is handled. As an incidental part of a series such as "Roots," for instance, which necessarily portrayed some of the horrors inherent in slavery, a certain amount of violence should be tolerated by a mature audience. But gratuitous gore introduced solely for sensationalism is inexcusable.

Unfortunately sexual innuendos will mark the so-called "mature" shows this season, and network executives should expect to be bombarded with complaints from religious and other groups rightly concerned about such tastelessness.

However, "vigilantism" by special interest groups seeking to impose their own opinions on the viewing public needs to be kept in check. Excessive restrictions however well intentioned will not serve the public nor the medium.

Obviously, setting national standards for television remains a difficult and complex task, one in which the voice — or voices — of the public should be predominant. It is encouraging that the networks apparently are starting to listen.

Press Herald

Portland, Me., August 14, 1978

The National PTA has a glorious opportunity to contribute to the improvement of our society but it has no business attempting to dictate the programming by television networks.

The highly controversial status of public education right now, and for the last several years, has invited the attention of some organizations such as the PTA.

That organization might very well direct its influence and energies toward reversing the decline in parental responsibility. But in many localities the PTA has become a withering organization.

The National PTA has selected what it considers to be the best and the worst network TV shows. If the networks don't respond to the organization's wishes it threatens to contest the license renewal applications of five network owned and operated stations.

The right of any organization to contest a license application is not challenged. But we certainly hope the Federal Communications Commission will never deny a station a license because it shows "Kojak," singled out by the PTA as one of the worst shows.

Just what qualifies the PTA to pass judgment on the "program quality" of a television presentation? Since when has a "positive contribution to the quality of life" been a requisite for any medium of entertainment?

There is one infallible method of swaying the judgment of network moguls. That is the ratings. If people don't watch, the program doesn't last.

But the PTA cannot achieve its goal through that route. It's already been made evident that many parents cannot control what their offspring watch on the tube. Other parents don't even attempt to exercise that responsibility. And we suspect that there is within the PTA membership a goodly number of people who want something more from TV than a diet of the Osmonds, Lawrence Welk and "Sixty Minutes."

What the nation doesn't need is a group of self-appointed censors telling us all what we may or may not watch on television.

TULSA WORLD

Tulsa, Okla., June 21, 1976

CHICAGO'S Mayor RICHARD DALEY, as the "people's champion," threw a protective blanket over the community's youth by executive fiat.

The pliant Chicago City Council on May 26, at the request of the Mayor, approved an ordinance that prohibits the showing of excessively violent films to persons under 18 years old. The affected films were defined as those "devoted primarily or substantially to such acts as assaults, cuttings, stabbings, shootings, beatings, eye-gougings, brutal kickings, burnings, dismemberments and other reprehensible conduct."

If the ordinance were enforceable, which is doubtful, its effect would be completely negated by the tens of thousands of television sets available for viewing by youths 18 years and under. Portrayals of violence are a staple of night-time television. Thus, the troubling question arises:

How to keep impressionable, or otherwise, young people from getting their daily menu of mayhem which one cynic has described "as American as cherry pie."

Many psychologists believe that prolonged exposure to violence on the house screen is more likely to lead to aggressive behavior than is the viewing of an occasional violent movie. This belief is shared by the National Parent-Teacher Association. Its president CAROL KIMMEL, said: "The children aren't talking to their families; they are almost in a state of sleep. And some school people believe that violence and vandalism in the schools always follows a pattern of what the kids have seen on tv the week before."

Unless Chicago's City Council can find a way to keep impressionable youth from being constantly exposed to the glut of tv turbulence, we see Mayor DALEY'S campaign as nothing more than a grand gesture.

Chicago Tribune

Chicago, Ill., May 28, 1976

There is a certain irony in seeing Mayor Daley's stooges in the Chicago City Council rise, one after the other, to proclaim the importance of protecting our young from evil influences. But this time their cause was a desirable one, namely to protect children from the sort of glorified violence that is being offered in many of today's movies.

By a vote of 43 to 2, the council approved Mr. Daley's ordinance prohibiting the admission of anyone under 18 to movies that are obscene or that show "cuttings, stabbings, floggings, eye gouging, brutal kicking, and dismemberment."

The hazards of such legislation are obvious. It is bound to be challenged in court, first as an infringement of the 1st Amendment's guarantee of free speech and second because of the manifest difficulty of defining intolerable violence—a difficulty made all the more apparent by the council's own effort to define it.

But the evil at which the ordinance is directed is too clear to be ignored any longer. There is abundant and increasing evidence that exposure to filmed violence does influence children and can affect their behavior throughout life.

The 1st Amendment does not require that we allow our children to be subjected to this influence. It is well established in law that the freedoms guaranteed to us as mature citizens do not always extend to the young. We have minimum age laws for drinking and driving and for voting.

Nor does the 1st Amendment grant total freedom even to adults. There are laws against libel and incitements to violence [which, come to think of it, might apply to some of these movies]; and the Supreme Court has repeatedly held that the 1st Amendment does not protect obscenity — though it has had a good deal of trouble deciding just what is obscene.

If society can protect itself against intolerable obscenity, whatever that is, then it would be reasonable for it to have a similar right of protection against the display of intolerable violence.

The problem of definition is probably a stickier one. Can a line be drawn in plain words between the accepted violence of war films and stories like "Treasure Island," on the one hand, and the unacceptable sadism of exploited violence on the other? As a Chicago assistant corporation counsel says, "There isn't much legal history in the violence area."

But the motion picture industry has managed to do better than the Supreme Court in defining obscenity. It has done this by devising a system of grading films which generally seems to have won the approval of the public. The industry should likewise be able to do better than ordinances or courts in defining intolerable violence, and ordinances like Chicago's should prompt it to try.

Industry action has several advantages over legislative action. First, it allows for the reason and flexibility that is hard to achieve in legislation [and thus can prevent the resurrection of those old-fashioned police censorship boards that were often manned, or rather womanned, by widows of deserving politicians]. Second, it would give us national protection instead of a patchwork of city ordinances which might vary and would never extend beyond the city limits. And third, it would give us something to fall back on if the ordinances should be found unconstitutional.

The important things are to protect children from a diet of violence; to demonstrate a public consensus that some of these movies have gone too far; and, by mobilizing public opinion, to exert a restraining influence on movie makers, television programmers, and others who may be tempted to exploit violence. Either course, if properly followed, could achieve these goals.

The Providence Journal

Providence, R.I., May 12, 1976

Chicago's Mayor Richard J. Daley thinks he has the answer to excessive violence in films and its effect on the young. He would bar anyone under 18 from viewing what one writer described as "films glutted with scenes of gratuitous mayhem."

We wholeheartedly support the mayor in one respect — the commercialization of brutality and physical suffering is reprehensible. It markets for an immature clientele the lurid and sensational without regard for potential consequences. If sexual obscenity has lost some of its appeal through an overabundance of X-rated films, violence is being parlayed as the latest drawing card. Along with Mayor Daley, we deplore it.

Unlike the mayor, however, we cannot subscribe to a "cure" of censorship. Short of banning all violence in films, how much is too much? By what standard would a violent act be judged necessary to the total film entity or merely a gratuitous spectacle designed to arouse emotion in the viewer? And if censorship of violent films were sanctioned, by what logic could television and the stage escape official purification?

The First Amendment does not admit such mischief by official bodies without a system of rigid safeguards that no one yet has successfully devised. The film industry's voluntary ratings which have helped to guide parents in the supervision of their youngsters are perfectly acceptable. But Mayor Daley would take a giant step beyond, and in doing so he goes too far.

The Boston Globe

Boston, Mass., May 11, 1976

"Entertainment" is so violent these days that the typical 10-year-old has witnessed more beatings, stabbings, shootings and burnings that the most battle-hardened man saw during World War II. No one can prove a link between our brutal amusements and our increasingly vicious society, but we know violent crime has soared, especially among the young, in the decades since television turned to gore.

Every teleplay or film of bizarre violence seems to inspire imitators. A recent study suggests, moreover, that aggression is only part of the outcome — others in the audience, perhaps a majority, come to see themselves as inevitably passive victims.

And surely the repeated scenes of streetcorner justice, with police or vigilantes acting as judge and jury, contribute to our disregard for courts and their measured, orderly administration of justice.

Even the TV networks and filmmakers acknowledge the problem, and talk about voluntary restraint. But despite the new "family hour" rules the nightly TV schedule is statistically as brutal as ever, and the rating system for films has identified only the cruelest excesses.

Pressure is building for laws to ban the production and distribution of violent entertainment, or at least to keep the brutality out of view of impressionable children and imitative adolescents.

The mayor of Chicago, Richard J. Daley, best known to the nation for his defense of a 1968 police riot, is seeking a censorship law in Chicago to ban admission to violent films for everyone under 18.

The American Civil Liberties Union has raised some valid questions about Daley's political intentions — he said he wanted to ban "raw propaganda" — and about the procedure for review, which would give initial power to the four elderly women on the Chicago Police Department's film review board.

As the civil libertarians argue, the dangers are enormous in any infringement on the first amendment right of free speech and expression. And the ACLU is right when it says parental control must be the ultimate basis for building peaceful attitudes among children.

But we share Mayor Daley's belief that the availability of violent films can undo parental caution in some cases, and reinforce parental neglect in many others. We believe, moreover, that the time has come for a uniform agreement among the TV networks to cut back on police and crime shows and to eliminate violence entirely or at least until a very late hour.

The legal route is cumbersome and real voluntary restraint is vastly preferable. But violent movies and TV programs need not be made, imported or shown, and it is time the entertainment industry committed itself to portraying the kind of just society we must be and not the hellhole we could become.

Richmond Times-Dispatch

Richmond, Va., February 19, 1977

Television, through its excessive display of violence, has been adversely affecting the minds of children for at least two decades, but only now is society beginning to rise up and demand curtailment of the mayhem that fills the screen.

For years, studies have shown that exposure to TV's steady diet of violence day after day, year after year, has had a devastating effect on many youngsters. Defenders of violence have scoffed at these findings, contending (if they concede anything) that the only children affected are those who are emotionally unstable to begin with.

But society in general has had enough of blood and brutality on the living room screen. A clamor is being heard for reform. And the clamor is so loud, and is coming from so many sources, that one may take heart that reform is on the way.

The American Medical Association has announced that it has asked 10 major corporations to reconsider their policies concerning the sponsorship of programs featuring violence.

The national Parent-Teacher Association, with 6.6 million members, has launched a campaign to arouse the public to the grave danger from television's gore.

Reflecting this new concern over TV's preoccupation with vicious criminality, *Newsweek* magazine devotes its cover story this week to "What TV Does to Kids."

"The overwhelming body of evidence — drawn from more than 2,300 studies and reports — is decidedly negative," the magazine declares. "Most showed that viewing violence tends to produce aggressive behavior among the young."

That children and teen-agers — and, indeed, some adults — get ideas for criminal acts from television is no longer mere supposition. *Newsweek* cites studies which have revealed that juvenile offenders have copied actions they have seen on the TV screen. Furthermore, the magazine adds, there is evidence that "the tide of TV carnage increases children's tolerance of violent behavior in others."

Writing in the American Medical Association's *American Medical News*, Dr. (Ph.D.) George Gerbner, dean of the Annenberg School of Communications at the University of Pennsylvania, says that "violence on television is unlike that in movies or books, because television is a very different medium."

"It is accessible from cradle to grave; you don't have to go anywhere to see it, and you don't even need to know how to read. It comes home to all classes and groups everywhere in the industrialized world. And it is used nonselectively. . .The TV clock is on over six hours a day in the average U.S. household.

"Television violence . . . generates fear of victimization and a sense of insecurity, as well as the inclination by some to take advantage of the fears of others. Children growing up with television learn its lessons and rehearse its roles."

New York City "stands practically paralyzed in the face of rampant criminality on the streets, in subways and in schools," declared Rabbi Judah Cahn, president of the New York Board of Rabbis, at the annual meeting of that organization Wednesday. And the "major cause" of that deplorable situation, Rabbi Cahn said, is television. Young TV viewers, he said, are being brought up on a "diet of raw violence . . . knifings, shootings, rapes and strangulations day in and day out."

Defenders of the violence like to respond to criticism by saying that any adults who don't want their children to see it need only switch the set off. But this does not solve the problem. If John's parents prevent him from seeing and being influenced by television violence it does nothing whatever toward protecting them from criminal behavior that may be triggered in the mind of the boy next door whose parents allow him to sit for hours in mesmerized attention watching *Starsky & Hutch, Baretta, Hawaii Five-O* and other blood-filled shows.

If the relationship between the nation's present high crime rate and the enormous exposure of society to television violence could be accurately measured, the findings might be so shocking as to arouse public indignation to the point of demanding immediate corrective action on the part of those responsible for what is seen on the tube. The full relationship, the extent of the effect of TV violence on young minds, will never be ascertainable. But studies that have been made, plus common sense, provide enough reason for society to seek reform — not through governmental action but through action by those involved in the whole process of providing television entertainment.

The Washington Star
and Daily News

Washington, D.C., June 12, 1976

The Desensitization of America is the title of a film produced by the J. Walter Thompson advertising agency, and now being shown to ad groups around the country. The film was produced by the heavyweight advertising agency for reasons both social and commercial, according to the firm's executive vice president, Arnold Grisman:

The sex-violence vernacular of the media, particularly television, is creating a syndrome of fear in America; and advertisers who hawk their products on programs built around sexuality and violence are risking consumer reaction.

Mr. Grisman brought the presentation here to the American Advertising Federation's annual convention. The film portrays Americans, as *The Star's* Bailey Morris put it, "as a people who have moved from a state of innocence and folksiness in the early TV years to a society that nothing shocks yet many things terrify."

The generalization has a dismal quotient of accuracy. The J. Walter Thompson firm deserves appreciation for yelping where it may do some good.

It is, of course, unclear yet just how profoundly the pervasive tube has influenced our habits and customs and manner of regarding ourselves and others. That television is dramatically influential is denied by few; the quality or lack of quality in its influence is the argument.

Our inclination is to believe that too much television programming is at best mindless and at worst corrupting — the emphasis on violence, by word and by deed, permeates much of prime time, network denials notwithstanding; sexuality often is violent in context.

Whose responsibility is this? A portion belongs to the viewer — i.e., sets are equipped with on-off switches. And as Mr. Grisman points out, the sample the ad firm has taken of viewer reaction shows that 10 per cent of its adult sample actively reacts against products sandwiched between sawed-off shotgun blasts and pistol-whippings and the majority of them express their distaste in purchasing.

That answer does beg the wider question which perhaps at base is one of taste. At any rate, came the semi-rebuttal to the Thompson film by Tom Swafford, vice president for programming of CBS-TV: "Are we condemning society or the media that reflect that society?" he asked.

Now there's a tricky assumption in his statement, one embraced repeatedly by network vice presidents feeling defensive — "that reflect" society? That is a concession we are not willing to make.

We also quarrel with Arthur Kretchmer, the editorial director of *Playboy* magazine, who after viewing the J. Walter Thompson film allowed as how he felt "conned." Mr. Kretchmer said, "I wouldn't trade 1976 for the neurotic '50s" — this to buttress his argument that the ad firm's film suggested that "America was once a better place than it is now." The facile either-or is not very intelligent; we suspect Mr. Kretchmer has spent most of his reading time on the content of his own magazine.

Were the 1950s really "neurotic"? Compared to what? Who is suggesting a return to the past? — an absurdity in any event. And finally Mr. Kretchmer wraps himself in egalitarianism and complains that the thrust of the film showed an intent to "lead the *common man* (emphasis ours) to a better place and a better level of taste." Aside from his presumptuousness, it is amusing to hear an executive of a publication catering to "playboy" tastes come galloping to the defense of the "common man."

The subject of nihilistic violence and titillating sex is too important for that sort of shrillness. The merit of the J. Walter Thompson approach is that it may push advertisers to induce television Pooh-Bahs to recognize how puerile and destructive much of their programming is — and to re-think the smug assumption that commercial television "reflects" society. If there ever was a shaping medium, it is television.

Chicago Tribune
Chicago, Ill., February 9, 1977

Sears Roebuck & Co. has set what deserves to become a trend by announcing that it "will not knowingly place commercials in any programming that contains excessive violence or sanctions antisocial behavior." Its action should increase the moral and commercial pressure on other big advertisers to do the same.

The announcement from Sears was triggered by a plea from the American Medical Association to 10 major corporations to reconsider their practice of buying commercials on violent TV shows. The nine others have not yet responded.

Voluntary action of this nature to discourage televised violence is a far more satisfactory way to handle the problem than government intervention. If the big corporations that swing so much power in our society fail to do what so clearly needs to be done, then they invite government interference, censorship, and other encroachments on our basic liberty.

The AMA is right in declaring war on excessive TV violence. Innumerable studies have proved that watching violence on television leads to an increase in aggression, violence, and antisocial behavior in real life; and that the effect is a lasting one, not just a passing one. The relationship is especially alarming when you realize that children today spend more time watching television than they do in school and that the average youngster probably sees more than 15,000 violent deaths on TV before reaching the age of 18.

Advertisers can't deny the pervasive influence of TV; they invest billions of dollars every year in commercials based on their own — and network — studies showing how effectively television can influence behavior.

Sears' response to the AMA's move is an example of how a free society should work, how a powerful business should understand that it cannot divorce its own interests from those of society as a whole. And all of us who value a peaceful and law-abiding existence can do our part by using the marketplace to reward companies that stop sponsoring violent programs and others — like 10 identified by the AMA — which already sponsor programs that offer us fine alternatives to violence.

The Evening Gazette
Worcester, Mass., November 25, 1977

There's little doubt that television programs affect how Americans think and act — and sometimes not for the best.

So it is no surprise that churches and other groups that want people to think and act as much as possible for the best are trying everything from newsletters to economic boycott to blast "bad" programs off the air.

The latest organization to weigh in on the side of electronic right is the Church of God, which has a million members. Its approach is ambitious. It has surveyed its members and come up with a list of the shows they consider "most offensive" in portrayal of violence, sex, use of alcohol, drugs, profanity and degradation of family life. The church wants its members and other evangelical Christians to boycott both the shows and their sponsors' products.

Surprisingly, "Maude" nosed out "Soap" for the position of dishonor at the top of the "10 worst" list. "All in the Family" placed second, followed by "Three's Company," "Baretta," "M-A-S-H," "Charlie's Angels," "The Jeffersons," "Kojak" and the performer, Redd Foxx.

Not to be thought merely negative, the church has also gotten up a list of the programs its members consider "most acceptable." That list is headed by "Little House on the Prairie," "The Waltons" and "Wonderful World of Disney."

Three of the other shows on the list — "Young Dan'l Boone," "The Fitzpatricks" and "Oregon Trail" — have been canceled by their networks since the survey was taken because of low ratings. That says something about the relationship of "acceptability" to popular taste. The other "most acceptable" shows are "Grizzly Adams," "Happy Days," "Eight Is Enough" and "Family."

These lists demonstrate a difficulty that organizers of any TV or product boycott face. We venture that most readers — including many evangelical Christians — are far from agreement that all the "bad" shows listed are objectionable or that the "good" shows list is sufficiently inclusive.

Do we all agree that "All in the Family" does America a disservice by showing Archie's and Edith's limitations even while portraying them as largely sympathetic characters? And

what on earth is the evil influence of those comic yet dedicated combat surgeons of "M-A-S-H"?

Is it the blandness of the many family shows listed as "acceptable" that makes them so? Every one of them but the show that bears the name "Family" is aimed primarily at youthful audiences. Aren't adults supposed to watch TV too? Why aren't "60 Minutes," "Columbo," "Rafferty" or "Lou Grant" on the list?

Moral judgments about TV shows commonly overlook artistic considerations. Some wholesome shows are boring. And, perhaps unfortunately, some raunchy shows are highly entertaining and, for most viewers, harmless.

If members of the Church of God are serious about influencing TV for the public good, they should write letters to the networks about specific episodes of series that they find distasteful — and why. We doubt that the church will gain widespread support for its buckshot approach of an economic boycott against 10 whole series of shows condemned, for reasons not specified, on the basis of a few episodes.

CASPER STAR-TRIBUNE
Casper, Wyo., February 28, 1977

There may have been a few raised eyebrows, and undoubtedly resentment in the television industry, of the step taken by the American Medical Association in thrusting itself into the problem of excessive TV violence and portrayal of generally anti-social attitudes.

The AMA requested ten large national advertisers to withdraw their support from programs on prime time TV which were characteristically violent. At the same time that it was making the request to withhold advertising support from these large corporations it also complimented and praised another group of large TV advertisers which support shows that are non-violent.

There is good reason why the medical association should inject itself into the controversy and

condemnation of violence on TV.

The doctors are the first ones other than ambulance attendents to see and treat the victims of violence. The see those who have been shot and stabbed, those who have been raped or mugged or beaten by violent criminals, who are often teenagers.

There have been numerous instances of youngsters perpetrating crimes within a few days after the commission of such a crime was shown on TV.

There is the case of one prison where the inmates watch TV shows and make notes of the ways in which crimes are committed for future use after they have been released. Humane and sympathetic doctors must often be appalled at the human wreckage which they have to treat as the result of gang and individual violence.

One doctor recently wrote in the Los Angeles Times of the night shift in the emergency room at his hospital and told the tragic story of a young girl brought in as the result of being shot in the head while reading on a couch in her living room. In what was probably a gang incident a car had driven by and sprayed the home with bullets, one of which struck her in the head. The girl died of severe brain damage. To the newspaper reader, who saw the news item after her death, it was just another crime. But to the doctor who treated her, and knew from the first that she was going to die, it was a tragic waste of human life brought on by unthinking violence.

It is perfectly understandable why the AMA has intervened to try to get the TV industry to tone down the violence which has been

the cause of such concern to many people.

The courts overthrew the concept of "family viewing time" which would have provided that scenes of violence, among other things, could not be shown at hours when young and impressionable people would ordinarily be viewing. It considered it a violation of freedom of speech.

The AMA has, however, already had some results from its campaign. Sears has agreed to review its policies towards supporting shows which are violent. AMA President Dr. Richard Palmer has been informed that the giant retailer will not knowingly place commercials on any program which contains excessive violence or sanctions anti-social behaviour.

That's closing the purse string which pay for the shows in the first place.

The Birmingham News

Birmingham, Ala., June 22, 1976

Eventually the television industry will get the message—right in the billfold—that people don't want excessive violence portrayed in TV programs.

There has been, all this time, the greatest invention to control what children or adults watch on television, right on the front of the set. But, for some strange reason chronic viewers won't turn the knob.

But they are now beginning to tell advertisers, who hold the real key to programming, that they are "turned off" by TV violence and will refuse to buy a product advertised on an exceptionally violent program.

A survey recently by J. Walter Thompson, the nation's largest advertising agency, found that viewers are rejecting violent TV programs so strongly that they are also rejecting products advertised on the programs.

They actively consider not buying products because they are advertised on programs they consider excessively violent.

This may be the answer to the problem, for no advertiser wants to spend money plugging a product for a program which is going to cause sales to go down.

Opponents of TV violence have been writing letters of protest and some have boycotted products—which is an indicator that public hostility to violent TV programming is growing.

Recently the Federal Communications Commission issued a statement that it is not authorized to censor or interfere with the content of individual programs. FCC intervention had been sought by groups opposing sex and violence on television.

The ad agency, by conducting the survey, may have hit on a simple answer to a complex problem—if viewers don't like the programming, they won't pay for the product which finances that particular show or series.

The American public learned during the Vietnam War that continual viewing of newscasts hich showed suffering and dying tends to desensitize even stable adults. They become indifferent.

Also, recent incidents have been reported where unstable adults have modeled crimes on television dramas. Social research has established that if children are constantly given models of violent behavior, their behavior will probably turn violent.

Whether "turning off" to products supporting violent programs is an indicator that people are getting smarter about the power they hold over the television set is debatable. But if that is the catalyst to bring about more sensible television programming then it may be the most important discovery since TV was invented.

The Charlotte Observer

Charlotte, N.C., June 21, 1976

Five national advertisers recently withdrew their commercials from the Saturday and Sunday afternoon horror movies on a Los Angeles TV station in response to viewer protest against violence during the hours TV is most accessible to youngsters. A citizens group had warned advertisers that it planned to publicize "the obvious fact that the programs could not exist" without the companies' sponsorship.

The station's general manager, Richard Frank, was upset by the action. "What we have is one pressure group trying to make a programming decision by coercing our advertisers," he said. "What's going to stop another pressure group from telling NBC next week they want the news changed?"

An interesting question, but hardly a new one. Pressure groups are always telling newspapers and TV stations to make changes. Sometimes the pressure groups are right, sometimes not. Sometimes they succeed and the result is disgraceful, as when CBS dropped John Henry Faulk after anti-Communist zealots with no visible regard for the truth smeared him. Other times it isn't, as when protesting fans of "Apartment 3-G" persuaded The Observer to bring back that comic strip after dropping it.

It is more difficult to pressure newspapers than TV by appealing to advertisers. In newspapers, advertisers lack control over what stories are printed next to their ads.

TV is different. Advertisers often buy commercial time during specific programs. That opportunity to choose makes advertiser identification with program content much stronger in television than in newspapers. That's one reason many print journalists disapproved of Xerox's underwriting a long article by Harrison Salisbury in Esquire magazine: Making an advertiser the sponsor of a specific article could lead to pressure on an editor to please the sponsor.

What's to stop a pressure group from telling a network to change the news? Nothing. It happens all the time. Newspapers and TV stations must draw a line between their legitimate desire to give their audience what it wants and their professional obligation to cover the news. CBS, for instance, telecast "The Guns of Autumn," a flawed documentary about the horrors of hunting, despite the withdrawal under pressure of all but one advertiser. The New York Times kept David Halberstam in Vietnam even when President Kennedy urged his transfer.

Engineers, lawyers, fire inspectors, policemen, auditors — every group with professional standards must sometimes choose between popularity and integrity. What's new about that?

DAYTON DAILY NEWS

Dayton, Ohio, September 2, 1977

Means do matter. For instance, the means that are being used to harass the televison networks.

"Concerned viewers," generally liberals, used several methods to pester the networks into cutting violence in their programming this year. One of the most effective was putting heat on sponsors supporting the cop shows that left the streets of Los Angeles more littered with bodies than the streets of frontier Dodge City ever were.

The advertisers panicked and the nets panicked with them. The ends were inarguably good. Research has pretty well established that watching a lot if violence promotes real-life violence in many persons and misleads many more into thinking crime is much commoner than it really is, a mistake that has distorted our politics.

Inevitably, however, others have picked up the knack and are now using it to ward off, they hope, the reported next TV trend, sex. The networks are said to be using that ancient hustle to compensate for their spiked guns, and although most of the sort-of-risque shows have not yet appeared, already the forces of chastity have come to the defense of TV's virginity.

If two shows that have appeared — *Love Boat* and *Three's Company* — are typical, however, this is much ado about next to nothing. For sexual incitement, the comedies rank with dime-store cologne. There is no skin; there are only entendres that aren't even quite double, more like 1.5 entendres, and like a piece of music built on one note, these sitcoms, built on one joke, quickly bore.

But let that go. What matters more is the repressive technique and the increasing resort to it. Ford Motors, for example, was scared off from sponsoring what turned out to be a splendid life of Jesus last spring because fundamentalists got it in their heads, from what source if any was never clear, that the program was going to be a sacrilege.

American life is stand-off of pressure groups organized to take offense. If TV is to become the machine on which each builds its muscles, mere inoffensivenss will become the only goal of programming. There is a basic decision coming up: Either we allow the medium, to some reasonable degree, to reflect and serve a variety of interests or we beat it into a pulp that, offending no one, suits no one.

Arguments about whether TV is going too far this way or that can be healthy, and are inevitable anyway. But sponsor blackmail, begun for a good deed, is a dangerous device. If fundamentalists cause Ford to renounce Jesus, couldn't Christian liberals menace local sponsors on stations that, as many do, occasionally give over three long hours to syndicated hard-sell evangelism?

TV is one of the arenas into which a lot of social fights are spilling over. Okay. But in the process, we will have to learn that the manner is crucial. As a diverse and contentious people, shouldn't we be combining into an irresistible constituency for diversity instead of squaring off to deny one another room? And isn't TV, though the current ground, the least of places that should apply?

THE ARIZONA REPUBLIC
Phoenix, Ariz., May 23, 1978

IF all goes the way Morality in Media hopes, thousands of television sets will remain black tonight in homes across the nation.

The group, which claims 200,000 members, hopes that a massive tune-out of television will force network executives to rethink their decision to program more shows next fall that emphasize sex.

"It's the only language television understands," commented Rabbi Julius Neumann, chairman of the group, referring to ratings.

Morality in Media's use of organized TV blackouts is but one manifestation of growing public criticism of television program content.

Sears Roebuck and Co., the nation's largest retail chain, announced it will withdraw its sponsorship of two high-rated ABC television shows — *Charlie's Angels* and *Three's Company* — because of episodes which are "sexually suggestive."

And last year, the Phoenix-based Greyhound Corp. announced it would not schedule commercials on any TV show that goes out of its way to use violence and sex to attract viewers.

The withdrawal of Sears or Greyhound or other advertisers from certain shows is no real immediate economic threat to the multibillion dollar TV industry.

But the public debate, and public criticism, of TV's program content cannot be shrugged off in the executive planning suites of the network's New York offices.

The longer such criticism persists, and as more groups rally to the strategy of blackouts and advertiser boycotts, television inevitably must respond.

If ratings suffer from organized tuneouts, networks will have some explaining to do to advertisers who are promised certain audiences.

And if advertisers on controversial shows become the targets of consumer boycotts, they're bound to reconsider where advertising dollars are placed.

Few would argue with television's right to accurately portray and reasonably reflect the seedy characteristics of life around us. But programs which have become virtually pointless, except to glamorize gore and sex, are a reflection on TV's rush to flood American living rooms with cultural garbage unfit for consumption.

The crisis facing TV now is whether it can defend its program judgment against this expanded onslaught of viewer criticism. Or, will it take seriously its enormous responsibility to provide the American home with shows more reflective of a sane and mannerly society.

OKLAHOMA CITY TIMES
Oklahoma City, Okla., June 27, 1977

TELEVISION viewing control begins at home. "If you don't want your kids watching some show, you can always turn the set off," is the usual comment when someone criticizes sex, violence and obscenity on TV.

Of course, that's not the final answer. It's impossible for any parent to sit at home and decide show by show whether to turn the set off. One person, a Methodist minister in Mississippi, decided it would be more practical to crusade for morally cleaner TV shows, and (correctly) he decided that would have to be done through the sponsors who finance the shows.

Details of his efforts appeared in a story in The Sunday Oklahoman's TV News last week.

One of the minister's ideas was a "Turn Off the TV Week" which does not seem to be the correct approach. But his idea of viewers telling sponsors which shows they believe are bad **and good** is meeting with success.

The minister is not alone in his concern about declining morality on television. One other concerned group is the most significant of all ... the boards of the giant corporations which sponsor a majority of national TV network programs. Sears, Procter & Gamble and Colgate-Palmolive (all big TV sponsors) are now evaluating the programs they sponsor.

The minister's small group (with the big-sounding name "National Federation for Decency") succeeded in convincing Sears to drop commercials from four programs the group felt bad for television.

Much can be said for "let the viewer decide" and "no one is forced to watch TV", but television is a bit different from the freedom to buy porno magazines in a neighborhood store. Television comes into the home; it needs a bit of temperance.

Maybe a rating system like the movies' G, PG, R and X is the answer. Maybe moving the questionable shows out of prime time is the answer.

Whatever the answer, one must admire the Methodist minister whose convictions are strong enough for him to take on the networks ... and, certainly, it is good news to know that the big sponsors are also concerned.

The best idea of all to come from the minister's National Federation of Decency is "Write the sponsor; let him know if you like or dislike the 'decency quotient' of the shows he sponsors."

St. Louis Review
St. Louis, Mo., May 19, 1978

Morality in Media Inc. is a small but growing interdenominational organization set up to counter the trend to increased sex and violence in the programming of the communications industry.

Rabbi Dr. Julius G. Neumann, chairman of the board of directors of Morality in Media has announced that MM's board of directors has called for a national blackout of the TV set on Tuesday, May 23, 1978. The reason for selecting this date is that MM regards Tuesday as one of the most offensive nights for current television programming.

There is very much in the aims of Morality in Media which our bishops and religious leaders generally can support. We are dismayed by the obvious trend toward more sex and violence in television shows. We are well aware that this trend can only be reversed by massive public pressure.

Why, then, did the U.S. Catholic Conference announce that it will not support TV Blackout Day? The answer given by Jesuit Father Patrick Sullivan of the U.S. Catholic Conference Office for Film and Broadcasting is that it was not asked to do so.

We applaud the efforts of Morality in Media to upgrade TV programming and the tactic they have chosen can be very effective. At the same time, MM must realize that our Church leaders can only make decisions after studying an issue carefully, and weighing the merits of a particular plan of action. MM did not invite the U.S. Catholic bishops or any other group of religious leaders to participate in the decision-making about TV Blackout Day. Their board of directors decided on a plan and then, on March 28, 1978, sent letters to leading churchmen inviting them to endorse the program. Nothing which could be described as serious documentation accompanied this request.

A small board of directors like that of MM can arrive at a decision and make an announcement very quickly. Organizing the response of the Catholic Church and communicating an intelligent and intelligible proposal to all of the Catholic Churches in the country is a more complex process.

Apart from this, responsible leadership would require that the bishops participate in the decision-making. Is it really clear that TV programming on Tuesday is the most offensive in the week? On what was this judgment based?

We understand that part of MM's growing pains will involve learning how to interrelate with churches and church leaders and other groups to secure their effective collaboration. In the meantime we sincerely hope that their initial effort at a TV blackout makes a significant impression on TV's moguls.

— Msgr. Joseph W. Baker

THE ATLANTA CONSTITUTION
Atlanta, Ga., February 18, 1977

There's enough violence in real life to satisfy even the most bloodthirsty. Why, then, must we be bombarded with pretend-violence on so many television programs?

A lot of people are wondering the same thing. One of the obvious answers is that it sells. It sells air time and it sells T-shirts and little dolls that look like the leading characters in the violent shows. It sells children and adults on the products that sponsor the programs.

But a few groups and an increasing number of individuals are not sold. They are doing everything they can to wipe violence off the tube. The best way to go, some are convinced, is to turn off the set. This conclusion comes no doubt after years of trying to persuade programmers to clean up their acts.

One of the groups is the PTA. And one of the individuals is a man from Mississippi, Rev. Donald Wildmon. The PTA has launched a sophisticated fight against television violence, citing studies that show how much harm it does to the minds of children. And the group is showing communities how to challenge licenses on the basis of inferior (violent) programming.

Rev. Wildmon has led one television boycott and is gearing up for another,

scheduled for July 24-30. Wildmon calls his protest "Turn the Television Off Week." Here's what he says about the movement: "It is time that the networks got the message that we are fed up with the sick minds responsible for their programs. Loss of viewers means loss of advertising. That means loss of money. That seems to be the only language they understand."

If that is the only language they understand, then the situation is sad indeed. For television is a medium with fantastic potential. It could be great, with the ability to entertain, to instruct, to help in times of emergency. Instead it satisfies itself with too many meaningless programs, laced with violence, that at best do no good and according to countless reports actually do harm.

Wildmon and people like him have reached a point of frustration and feel there is nothing left to do but turn off. He claims that 20,000 organizations and churches in 20 cities are with him on his second boycott. There is no way to tell how many television sets actually will be turned off in protest. But the potential for a mass turn-off certainly is there. Before the movement grows we hope television powers will curb the violence and move the medium toward the greatness of which it is capable.

The Evening Gazette
Worcester, Mass., June 5, 1978

The nationwide television "blackout" to combat excessive cheesecake on TV apparently bombed.

Morality in Media, a New York-based group, urged viewers to unplug television sets last Tuesday to protest the rash of programs featuring scantily clad females.

The Nielsen ratings for Tuesday show that television viewing went up during prime time. Apparently, Tuesday's programming was too much to resist.

Evelyn Dukovic, MIM's executive director, said she couldn't explain the Nielsen rating but "we estimate that about 6 million viewers turned off their sets." She based the estimates on the volume of mail MIM received in favor of the blackout.

Even if 6 million viewers didn't turn off their sets, MIM's blackout wasn't without effect.

Parents and organizations that banned together to protest too much violence on TV are shifting their attention to the industry's newest preoccupation — "sexploitation."

They are sending their protest letters not just to TV executives but to the advertisers: They are coupling

their complaints with threats of product boycotts.

The result is growing concern in corporate boardrooms.

Although network officials scoff at the idea, The New York Times reports that sources close to the television advertising industry say major sponsors are seriously considering putting pressure on the networks to adopt a rating system. It would be similar to the "G" through "X" code used in motion pictures.

If the networks insist on exploiting sexual themes and innuendo, a rating system might make a difference. Some corporate offices concede that the public has a right to know what programs contain. We agree. A brief announcement at show time calling attention to objectionable material is not sufficient.

At the same time, however, a double standard prevails. While some viewers state their ire at sexploitation, shows such as "Three's Company," and "Charlie's Angels" are consistently at or near the top of the ratings. One person's sexploitation is another's favorite entertainment.

That's the problem; people are so darn contradictory.

The Washington Star
Washington, D.C., March 12, 1977

Last week, you may have noticed, was billed as "turn off TV" week. The campaign spoke in a small voice. A Mississippi clergyman issued the call on behalf, he said, of several thousand church groups and other organizations annoyed by tubish mayhem and claptrap.

During the week, a respected columnist who works at a newspaper on L Street NW recalled his experience in banishing the television from household life. The contraption, said Colman McCarthy, was junked because he considered it a form of "child abuse," usurping the glorious jumble of young imaginations.

We thought, very briefly, about joining the "turn off." But had we consented to the crusade, we would have missed "The Pallisers" on Monday — the brilliant BBC/PBS serial. Tuesday would have not been a particular loss, except for the MacNeil-Lehrer half hour which is a must throughout the week and an example of the quality to which television news can aspire. Wednesday's CBS special, "Minstrel Man" was decent TV drama, we are told (though it was not watched in our home, it was available).

To turn off the television that Thursday was unthinkable: The Atlantic Coast Conference basketball tournament began, a sports highlight of the year (Lefty apparently forgot to remind his Terrapins that rebounding is an integral part of basketball). The ACC tournament, of course, continued through the week, and there was the usual Saturday night hour that is worth the price of a set — Mary Tyler Moore and Bob Newhart.

So, sorry, we just couldn't join the well-intentioned "turn off" week. That is not the solution to execrable commercial programming. Columnist McCarthy is closer: He noted his tubeless family recently has been babysitting for a friend's TV. There is a more worthy exercise of man's faculty to choose, Mr. McCarthy suggested — "to be able to live with or without it." Amen.

A good thing, by the way, the blackout campaign wasn't this week. The local public television stations have been engaged in their annual fund raising. Washington's Channel 26 has a slogan that addresses this whole question nicely: "For a breath of fresh air."

The Providence Journal

Providence, R.I.,
September 6, 1977

Soap, from all accounts, is anything but 99 and 44 one-hundredths percent pure, a fact that seems to have gotten many well-meaning folk in a lather.

Across the country, various church groups have risen to the bait of advance publicity put out by American Broadcasting Corp. Taking ABC at its word, that *Soap* would wash the scales from the eyes of the public and regale TV audiences with all the delectable evils of the Garden of Eden, Sodom, Gomorrah and declining Rome, some well-intended men of the cloth have condemned *Soap,* sight unseen. By inveighing against its release, they have guaranteed ABC a full house when its new fall offering slithers across the tube.

To their credit, the clergy of Rhode Island have not jumped aboard the censorship bandwagon with blindfolds on. Bishop Gelineau requested a sneak preview, which WPRI-TV agreed to unwrap for him. After sleeping on it, the Bishop issued a moderately worded assessment of ABC's new fall offering. While he found *Soap* to be "superficial...often offensive," and at best "a poor use of mass communication's resources," Bishop Gelineau wisely made no attempt to coerce a ban on its showing. "The ultimate decision regarding the presentation of *Soap* in this area," he said, "is solely that of WPRI-TV."

Reportedly the Bishop is considering writing a pastoral letter for the guidance of his flock, in regard to *Soap;* as spiritual leader of the diocese, that is his prerogative, and is confined to his special area of ecclesiastical responsibility. Other community and religious leaders have been granted previews of the program; reportedly they generally shared the Bishop's less-than-enthusiastic view of the program's lapses in taste and sensitivity to widely shared moral values. But again, unlike some zealous groups elsewhere, whatever impurities the Rhode Island clergy found in *Soap,* they made no ill-advised attempt to ban the bar.

If any conclusion is to be drawn from this rather minor stirring on the surface of electronic pop culture, it is that a deeper reservoir of common sense, moderation and perspective undergirds the gauzier aspects of this society than may always be apparent. Both the state's clergy and the management of WPRI-TV — which has decided to show *Soap* — have been respectful of each others' particular mandates.

As for *Soap,* one suspects that like many of the mildly sex-exploitive soap operas it sets out to spoof, it will survive the tepid waters of public curiosity for but a season or two, before it dissolves and gurgles down the drain. Audiences will see and hear little that they have not already been exposed to, to the point of boredom. And there always remains the hope that some of the bored will be driven to taste the real delights and fresh wonders of such marvels as the *Masterpiece Theatre* series, available on Channels 2 and 36 at the twist of the dial.

The Boston Globe

Boston, Mass., September 4, 1977

The problem this year is sex. Not how to get it or how to get more of it. But how to keep it off the television airways.

As the new season gets under way with an unprecedented 22 new series, these efforts have intensified and are focused, for now, on a single program, ABC's controversial spoof, "Soap."

The Christian Life Commission of the Southern Baptist Convention, the United States Catholic Conference, smaller religious groups and some self-styled watchdogs of public morality have denounced the program as ridiculing "morals" and religion.

Producers and network officials have raised the specter of censorship as a result of these activities. Uncertain about the safest course, advertisers are shunning controversy and have instructed their agents to avoid buying time slots for "Soap."

But the issue goes beyond any one program or series to the general question of standards.

Should special-interest groups impose their standards on a national audience? Should any group be allowed to preempt the judgment of the television audience by suppressing shows before they are broadcast? How can television serve the broad interests of a diverse adult audience while catering to the demands of more parochial audiences?

Television programming and the creative themes that flow from it are regulated by a self-imposed broadcasters' code and by audience reaction.

The code reflects the give-and-take educational process of trying out a new idea on television and waiting, as at Sardi's, for the reviews to come in.

Audience reaction is part of the process. If the audience dislikes the show, it will switch channels or turn off the sets and ratings will fall. Because the American television audience is the most extensively polled and analyzed in the world, it is no secret what turns them — and their sets — off.

Among the progressive steps this process has led to are the reduction of gratuitously offensive racial and sexual stereotypes in television programming, a curb on "adult" material in the first hour of prime time (8 to 9 p.m. in the East) and the development of more "relevant" and more "sensitive" programs.

Special-interest groups, ironically, have helped this process succeed by presenting coordinated and focused critiques of network shows to local and national network officials, regulators and government.

But to submit to such groups by banning programs before the public gets its chance to decide would be to turn the process on its head.

Because there is a television in 97 percent of American households, television is a ubiquitous medium with unknown power of suggestion and persuasion. It is clearly not a medium for unrestricted access or broadcast.

But if television is ever going to transcend the bland and the insipid, restriction and controls must be broad enough — and broadminded enough — to provide for maximum creativity, originality and experimentation.

The Washington Post

Washington, D.C., September 4, 1977

A LOT OF PEOPLE are in a lather about "Soap," the forthcoming ABC-TV situation comedy that is said to be obsessed with sexual themes. Although the network has toned down the first two episodes, a few ABC affiliates—including WJZ-TV in Baltimore—have refused to air them. Now "Soap" is also under attack from religious groups concerned about the trend toward more sex-oriented television shows. Some of these groups, notably the Christian Life Commission of the Southern Baptist Convention, have been putting pressure on advertisers with barrages of letters and hints about boycotts of products sold on "Soap." The controversy has caused some major companies to shy away from the show.

Well, we haven't seen "Soap"—it won't go on the air until Sept. 13—and so we don't know if it's racy or funny, raunchy or worthwhile, or all of those things. But neither do a lot of the show's critics, who haven't seen it either but have set themselves up as authorities on the subject anyway. And that's just the point about a lot of these protests. Second-hand reports or published summaries may be the only guide viewers have for deciding whether to tune in. But these sketchy critiques are skimpy grounds for a judgment that the program should not be aired at all.

Nonetheless, more and more groups with fervent views of one kind or another have been launching preemptive assaults on programs they consider objectionable by putting pressure on television stations, networks and advertisers. Last year CBS-TV got a flood of mail against a documentary on hunting—months before the program was shown. Such attacks are disturbing, and not just because they come from groups with a special focus and a particular ax to grind. They also are a form of censorship of the airwaves that denies most viewers a chance to decide for themselves whether controversial programs are interesting, tasteful or fair. What's worrisome is that commercial television—which has been innovating gingerly—may buckle under this pressure and retreat still further into blandness and inanity, without giving most viewers a chance to be heard.

Some critics of "Soap" are taking a more reasonable approach. The National Council of Churches, the United Church of Christ, the United Methodist Church and the National Council of Catholic Bishops are urging their member congregations to watch the show's first episodes and *then* tell local stations if they think the show is inappropriate or should be shown later at night. Ironically, that may plump up the ratings for the first few weeks. Even more ironically, so may the publicity generated by the protests. We wonder whether those who are doing the loudest shouting—without benefit of a preview—have thought about that. In any case, it says something about their case against "Soap" that they are not prepared to allow the viewers' response to be the final test.

The Hartford Courant

Hartford, Conn., September 2, 1977

The self-appointed censors are at it again. Their latest target is ABC-TV's controversial new comedy, "Soap," scheduled to premiere in two weeks.

According to advance publicity, "Soap" will be more controversial than "Mary Hartman, Mary Hartman," and "Fernwood 2-Night," both of which have been criticized for making fun of almost everything, including religion, ethnic groups and sex.

Advertising agencies have recently reported that, because of letter-writing campaigns by several religious groups, potential sponsors are consciously avoiding "Soap", and ABC says some sponsors who signed up have now withdrawn.

Frederick Pierce, president of the network, touched the crucial issue when he commented, "It is a very unhealthy situation when special-inter-est groups, stimulated by hearsay before a program goes on the air, determine what is right, and what isn't, for the viewing public."

Does a special interest group have the right to determine what the general public should view on television, or hear on the radio or read?

In the history of American censorship of books, film and electronic media, the main thrust of pressure groups has been against obscenity. Four years ago, the U.S. Supreme Court refused to rule in favor of national standards of obscenity. In Miller vs. California, the court laid down its current test, which allows each community to determine its own standards for obscenity, and to take its own action to ban what it considers obscene from its own community.

The decision can logically be applied to the attempts of interest groups to, in effect, censor television programming. When they threaten sponsors with boycotts of their products, their obvious goal is to use economic leverage to control what America watches on the tube, to impose their own special-interest judgment.

The threat of a product boycott, or an actual boycott of a sponsor's products, is clearly the wrong approach to effecting changes in TV programming.

If the products are good, and fairly priced, then a boycott would be an unwarranted attack on the products, and only an indirect attack on network programming. Thus far, network officials say, the indirect attack on programming — through pressure groups' letter-writing campaigns — has created problems for sponsors, but has not caused any controversial network programs to be dropped.

The direct approach, for those groups concerned about certain network programs, is to express their disapproval by turning the programs off, and by encouraging others with similar views to do the same.

Programs depend on approval, measured through ratings. If enough people have decided not to watch a certain program, then they have — in a very real sense— voted against it, and in the ratings game the votes are counted. If a program is not popular, then it is taken off the air.

This is the public approach to programming decisions. It does not involve strong-arming sponsors, with threats of boycott. It is in the public interest because the public, in the final analysis, decides what will be on the public airwaves. It is consumerism. It is democracy.

Rocky Mountain News

Denver, Colo., September 10, 1977

IRONICALLY, the most controversy of the new TV season is over a show that hasn't been seen yet. It's an ABC offering called "Soap" that is said to go in for more sex than any show on the airwaves to date.

In advance of "Soap's" Sept. 13 debut, a number of religious bodies have protested and warned sponsors of boycotts. Some sponsors have withdrawn and a couple of ABC affiliates have refused to carry the show.

Predictably, TV programmers and Madison Avenue ad agencies are decrying "censorship" and claiming the religious protesters are stifling their creativity.

If "Soap" were a news program or a documentary, the criticism of the show and pressure on sponsors would be a cause for great concern.

The show, however, is a coldblooded commercial venture. Its producers think there is money in sex so that is what they are peddling. They and their sponsors would like the public to accept in silence whatever is broadcast, but they overlook one main point: They are using the public's airwaves.

In this case the public has a lot to say. If religious groups feel a show contains too much explicit sex, they have a right to say so – and to withdraw their patronage from sponsors of the objectionable program.

Similar protests and messages to sponsors last year resulted in a marked decline in gratuitous violence on TV, especially in programs watched by children. Who other than a few hucksters will say that this change is bad for the country?

What is disturbing in the anti-"Soap" campaign is that it is waged by people who act because of hearsay or reports by TV reporters who have had advance peeks. They ought to see for themselves first.

This is what a number of church groups, including the National Council of Churches, United Church of Christ and United Methodist Church, are doing. They've asked their members to tune in on "Soap" and then to let their local stations know what they think. Fair enough.

The Evening Bulletin

Philadelphia, Pa., September 13, 1977

"Soap" appears on the home screen tonight, and undoubtedly a lot of Americans will be riveted there to see what all the fuss has been about. If some reviewers are to be believed, they won't be riveted there very long because boredom will drive them elsewhere. But that's for people to decide individually and for Neilsen to analyze collectively. The pros and cons of the show's content aside for a moment, the hullabaloo that has accompanied the advent of "Soap" deserves some attention.

For refreshers: "Soap" has been touted as a better and more daring "Mary Hartman." Supposedly it is a comedy that deals with all the taboo themes—incest, homosexuality, impotence, infidelity, you name it. When the word was leaked that this was the stuff of which "Soap" was made, various individuals and organizations reacted with dismay. Letters and protests flew, potential sponsors of "Soap" backed off, some episodes were toned down, and some stations that had planned to air the show dropped it. Television executives and advertisers postured, shouting "censorship" and decrying the loss of artistic freedom.

A couple of points are worth making about all this. First, the people who wrote to the ABC network and to local stations to protest "Soap" had a perfect right to do so. True, most of them had not seen one episode of the show and many of them may have been reacting with knee-jerk horror to the idea of certain sexual themes being dealt with in prime time.

But commercial television is a marketplace medium subject to the vagaries of popular tastes. People make known their tastes by what they choose to watch. Another way is by writing letters or boycotting sponsors of shows they find offensive.

Broadcasting is protected under the First Amendment right of free speech. Although the Government uses its licensing authority to see the broadcasters meet a vague requirement to serve the "public interest," the Government may not censor program content. Regulation of content is done indirectly by members of the public, who can and should make their opinions known.

So, having defended the protesters' right to have their say, we add an important caveat: The more intelligent comments about "Soap" can only be made after people have seen it. Several national church organizations recognize this. They have urged their members to watch the first few episodes of "Soap" and then tell local stations what they think of it. If enough people are turned off by the show—and subsequently turn it off—you can bet it won't last long.

On the other hand, if enough people feel "Soap" represents a creative and entertaining break from the usual TV fare, it will last. Although producers and network executives have the last say, the public will, indirectly, decide whether this brand of "Soap" washes.

'FAMILY HOUR' ON TV RULED ILLEGAL; GOVERNMENT CENSORSHIP CHARGED

A district judge in Los Angeles ruled Nov. 3 that "family hour" on television violated the Constitution's guarantee of freedom of speech. Judge Warren J. Ferguson said that the television networks' decision to ban violence and sexual subject matter between 7 p.m. and 9 p.m. "may or may not be desirable," but "Censorship by government or privately created review boards cannot be tolerated" under the Constitution.

The networks had agreed upon the policy of not showing programs unsuitable "for general viewing" in September 1975. Judge Ferguson said in his 223-page decision that the decision was reached because of pressure from Richard E. Wiley, chairman of the Federal Communications Commission: "Based on the totality of the evidence accumulated in this case, the court finds that Chairman Wiley, acting on behalf of the commission and with the approval of the commissioners, in response to Congressional committee pressure, launched a campaign primarily designed to alter the concept of entertainment programming in the early evening hours.... Government activities involved amounted to virtually unprecedented orchestration of regulatory tools by the FCC."

Wiley told the *New York Times* that he did not use threats. "In expressing concern to the industry with the problem of violence and urging it to adopt voluntary reforms, I believe my colleagues and I were operating in a responsible and proper manner and in the best interest." He stressed, "At no time were any threats expressed or implied and I reject and suggest to the contrary."

The ruling was made on two lawsuits brought by the Writers Guild of America, the Directors Guild of America, the Screen Actors Guild and individuals and companies in the television industry. The FCC, the three major networks, and the National Association of Broadcasters were defendants.

The Topeka Daily Capital

Topeka, Kans., November 7, 1976

The "TV Family Hour" decision handed down by U.S. District Judge Warren Ferguson in Los Angeles may displease those who believe TV stations should limit violence and sex in programs shown when children watch TV.

But Judge Ferguson made an important point which, if upheld, will protect the First Amendment right of freedom of speech — as applied to the electronic media.

The Family Hour concept was adopted by TV networks and the National Association of Broadcasters early in 1975. It was hoped it would clean up programs aired from 7 p.m. to 9 p.m. local time.

The Family Hour was attacked in a suit by guilds representing writers, producers, directors and actors, who named the Federal Communications Commission, the NAB and ABC, CBS and NBC as defendants.

Judge Ferguson ruled the concept violates the First Amendment guarantee of freedom of speech, but that his court cannot end it.

Note that he did not object to limiting the type of program broadcast in early evening hours but to the way he believes the ban was imposed.

It was unconstitutional, he said, because testimony showed the Federal Communications Commission, an arm of government, pressured networks and NAB into adopting a programming policy they did not want.

FCC argues with this interpretation and may appeal. CBS says it will continue the "Family Hour" voluntarily, but will appeal.

Ferguson says the networks are free to discontinue any variant of the policy, provided that their decisions are made independent of any concern for government reaction.

Neither the FCC nor NAB has the right to compromise the independent judgment of individual station owner licensees, the judge ruled.

This is a good ruling, because it denies the right of a government agency to influence what the people may hear or see on television.

That decision should be made carefully — but it should be made by the individual broadcasting stations with due regard for their audiences.

The Courier-Journal

Louisville, Ky., November 11, 1976

THE FACT THAT a federal court has struck down the networks' "family hour" policy doesn't necessarily mean that TV screens must now be filled with violence and sex during the early evening when children are likely to be watching. What it does mean is that viewers, not the government, must demand network adherence to this practice. So long as the First Amendment survives, that's the only way it should be.

The judge found that the Federal Communications Commission had hinted at governmental retaliation if the networks didn't adopt such a policy. The FCC denies this. But discussions did take place between the agency and the broadcasters, and an industry subject to government approval for license renewal may justifiably have considered even a hint to be as good as an order.

Because of the FCC role in regulating use of the nation's airwaves, First Amendment freedoms are much more vulnerable to governmental censorship in the broadcast media than they ever could be in the printed press. That's why the courts must be particularly vigilant against even the slightest hint of government intimidation in the formulation of programming policies.

This is not to deny that the content of television programming has, at times, caused concern, particularly among parents dismayed at the fare offered their children for after-supper viewing. The crusade against a surfeit of violence and sex began with the 1970-1972 Surgeon General's report which, though generally inconclusive, found the possibility of a causal relationship between violence on the screen and aggressive behavior by children.

During that period the television industry began to hear complaints from parents, and so did Congress, which in turn put pressure on the FCC. The result was the "family hour" — actually two hours, from 7 p.m. to 9 p.m. — agreed upon by the networks just two years ago.

Both CBS and ABC say they'll continue the family hour. (So far, NBC has made no comment.) The court said this was permissible so long as the action was truly independent, not in response to governmental pressure. But how long the networks can keep it up is another matter. The 7-9 p.m. slot is prime time, when the networks compete hardest for viewers and advertising dollars. The actors and writers whose lawsuit challenged the validity of the family hour doubtless will continue to speak out loudly when programming decisions are made.

Many viewers have challenged the family hour for another reason: that in their judgment it hasn't made all that much difference. The National Parent-Teacher Association, for example, earlier this year felt sufficient concern to start its own study of TV violence and its effect on children.

Part of the trouble is that the family hour was only a half an answer to the problem of cleaning up television for young viewers. Millions of them are watching at other times of day, when brutality, mayhem and adult themes are freely portrayed on the screen. Yet few would suggest that *all* television programs be limited to what is suitable for a 10-year-old child.

In the end, the issue surely comes down to parental responsibility. Network cooperation in showing police shows and torrid movies at later hours certainly would be welcome. But it's up to the viewers to complain to the networks — and to the advertisers — when programs seem objectionable. Most importantly, it's our duty as parents to monitor what our children see on the small screen just as carefully as we decide what movies they may attend. There's no such thing as a free baby-sitter.

THE DAILY HERALD

Biloxi, Miss., November 9, 1976

District Judge Warren J. Ferguson's ruling against the manner in which television's family hour policy has been handled strikes a blow for free speech. But we suspect it will also have a tendency to open wider the gates that allow violence and sexually explicit material to flood television screens, while hoping that that assessment is incorrect.

Judge Ferguson did not rule that there could not be a family viewing hour. The evidence on the tube indicates the family hour is essential to prevent the moral degradation of television to a level of X-rated movies. What the judge said was that the three major networks couldn't delegate authority for setting the policy to the National Association of Broadcasters.

The family hour has been successful in quieting public protest by keeping sex and violence from early-evening television, likely to be watched by children. It has also been responsible, we believe, for encouraging more explicit violence and sex in the programs that follow the family hour.

Consider for a moment the rapidity with which change in television content has been progressing. A year or so ago, such spicy scenes as those which proliferated the 12-hour showing of Rich Man, Poor Man, were taboo. But television exposed viewers to the successful series, which fea-tured at least one implicitly nude bedroom scene a week. Similar scenes are part and parcel of the current serial, Captains and Kings. Examples of violence abound in the shows seen locally after 8 p.m.

And there have been no loud outbursts of public clamor. It's as if the acceptance of the family viewing hour policy by the public somehow has become a justification for a lowering of standards of content during subsequent viewing hours.

Judge Ferguson's decision places the initial responsibility for determining program content squarely where it belongs, upon the individual networks for the shows which originate there. Another line of responsibility exists at the individual stations, and the judge's ruling does not prohibit the stations from joining together and agreeing upon a mutual code.

CBS has already stated its intention of voluntarily continuing to adhere to the family viewing concept. We applaud that network for its stance, and predict that it will not suffer a decline in viewers because of that decision.

We urge the other two major networks to follow the example of CBS.

Ultimately, the responsibility for what is seen in American homes falls upon the occupants of those homes and we trust that American viewers will not support a continued deterioration in program content, whatever the hours they are shown.

The Des Moines Register

Des Moines, Iowa, November 11, 1976

Attacked repeatedly by directors, script writers and others associated with television, the family hour took its sharpest blow last week from a federal judge who called it an unconstitutional infringement on free speech.

The first hour of prime time on evening television (7 to 8 in Iowa) was designated the family hour by the major broadcasters last year. Sex and violence were supposed to be minimized on programs scheduled for that hour. At other times broadcasters were to give occasional "advisories" to warn audiences when parts of a program might be objectionable to some viewers.

But programs with questionable dialogue, though not with sexual or violent scenes, began appearing in the family hour. Advisories were seldom included.

Judge Warren Ferguson directed his strongest criticism at Federal Communications Commission Chairman Richard Wiley, who was blamed for pressuring broadcast-ers into agreeing to voluntary restraints embodied in the family hour policy. Trial testimony indicated that Wiley threatened broadcasters with a denial of license renewals unless they reduced sex and violence on TV. The court found that Wiley acted on behalf of the federal agency and with its approval.

The judge said that nothing prevents the networks from continuing the family hour, provided they decide to do so without government pressure. The networks should take steps to curb sex and violence, but the government should keep its nose out of programming. Threatening the licenses of broadcasters because of too much violence is a short step to threatening them because of too much criticial comment about the administration in power.

The networks need the good taste to improve their programming — and the courage to resist whenever the government tries to play the part of censor.

THE INDIANAPOLIS NEWS

Indianapolis, Ind., November 15, 1976

A synonym for voluntary self-censorship might be "good taste." A synonym for coercion up until last week might have been the "family hour."

If the findings of Judge Warren Ferguson, who declared the television networks' family hour unconstitutional, are correct, then writers and producers did indeed face Federal censorship.

It was not the concept of a family hour with which Judge Ferguson found fault. Desirability of the plan which sees to restrict the hours of 7 to 9 p.m. to programing suitable for all members of the family was not the issue. Nor, stressed the judge, did he have the authority to declare an end to the practice.

What the judge rightly objected to was the element of Federal coercion which he found to have motivated the networks in their concern for viewers of a tender age.

The court found that Federal Communications Commission Chairman Richard Wiley, in the course of his campaign to institute a family hour, "threatened the industry with regulatory action if it did not adopt the essence of his scheduling programs." Added the judge, "The threat of regulatory action was not only a substantial factor leading to adoption but a crucial, necessary and indispensable cause."

In effect, the ruling exposes and denounces an agreement on the part of the three major networks, the FCC and the National Association of Broadcasters which set up the NAB television code review board as a national board of censors for American television. This, said the judge, violates the First Amendment. Networks should be making independent programing judgments.

"Judgment" is the key word, because if they so desire, networks are free to continue the family hour policy. The dictates of good taste offer excellent criteria for a self-censorship on the part of networks.

Federal muscle is not required to dictate programing content to a network. Viewers should speak more loudly than bureaucrats, and they are free to encourage a voluntary family hour policy — both with their letters and their patronage. And, should all else fail, it is an American right to reach out and turn off the boob tube.

The Boston Globe

Boston, Mass., November 6, 1976

Sometime in the distant past a "family hour" meant a part of the day when the family gathered together and talked. Now, courtesy of the Federal Communications Commission, it means the period from 7 to 9 p.m. when television is somewhat less violent and sexual than it is later in the evening — but not less violent than it is on the biff-bam-pow-sock Saturday morning cartoon shows, nor less sexual than on the after-school soap operas.

It probably came as a body blow to many Americans Thursday when Federal District Judge Warren Ferguson ruled the "family hour" was, as imposed by the FCC, a violation of the Constitution's First Amendment.

Yet the nation's leading opponent of degrading children's programming, Action for Children's Television, based in Newton, joined the writers, producers, and performers who filed suit against the "family hour."

They shared the artists' contention that the FCC should not be censoring television, using threats and pressure to deprive networks and their creative employees of free expression.

More important, ACT said, the "family hour concept (is) merely a public relations effort that would dissuade people from exerting meaningful efforts toward improvement of children's TV."

The networks and the FCC denied, ineffectually, that the "family hour" was involuntary. ABC, CBS, NBC and the National Assn. of Broadcasters have found by polls that the idea is popular and they plan to continue it.

Banning sex and violence is a sim-pleminded approach to the moral vacuum of much television. Few dramas are more wrenchingly violent than "King Lear," few agonies more troublingly sexual than Prince Hamlet's. But those Shakespearean stories are told in a context of moral values, of profound individual concern with right and wrong.

The trouble with the violence and sex on television is that they often are presented as sensational entertainment. In the familiar language of the Supreme Court decisions on obscenity, TV's programs are often without "redeeming social importance."

The writers, producers and performers who opposed the "family hour" are among the most vigorous supporters of better, tougher, more thoughtful television. Norman Lear's "All in the Family," "Maude," "The Jeffersons" and other shows are popular entertainment, topical and sometimes unsettling, but they are about the real world. And although they do little obeisance to the rituals of conventional morality, their underlying themes are honesty, decency, candor and brotherhood.

In any case, television should not be censored by the FCC. And a "family hour" rule is a clumsy, bureaucratic substitute for real self-regulation. The racism and sexism of much Saturday morning TV, as Action for Children's Television has argued, do far more damage than even some brutal police shows. The "family hour" accomplishes little, except to make television less controversial at the time when parents are most likely to see what their children are watching.

The Hartford Courant

Hartford, Conn., November 25, 1976

A federal judge in Los Angeles has ruled that television's "children's hour" violates the First Amendment right to free speech. He's right. But we are tempted to ask, what children's hour?

Since September 1975 the major TV networks and the National Association of Broadcasters have had in effect an agreement that programs aired before 9 p.m. be suitable for "family viewing." After that hour, producers are given more freedom to explore what are supposedly more "mature" subjects.

This was essentially a private agreement, but in the background was a threat of government intervention if it was not done. The judge properly recognized the covert government influence on free speech and ruled the children's hour unconstitutional.

Don't expect, though, that television will show any great sense of responsibility in using its new freedom. The children's hour, the prime time between 8 and 9 p.m., is already rife with suggestive material. The hour of 9 brings no appreciable change.

Occasionally a viewer can find drama, a documentary or even a comedy which treats human sexuality in artistic and sensitive fashion.

For the most part, though, script writers seem capable of producing no better drama than simulated violence, and no better comedy than an off-color joke strung out to 30-minute length.

If TV uses its talents and its freedom to present such material, that is its right. The Constitution grants equal protection of the law to good taste and bad.

Viewers, however, also have a right to demand a higher standard of artistic responsibility. They should make such demands both to broadcasters and to advertisers. Then, until their demands are met, they should use the "off" switch for its intended purpose.

The Chattanooga Times

Chattanooga, Tenn., November 8, 1976

It is ironic—though no less welcome—that a key decision regarding the importance of the First Amendment to television resulted from a lawsuit filed by the producers and writers of dramatic and "sitcom" programs carried by the networks. But it is disturbing that two networks — ABC and CBS — have announced plans to appeal the federal court ruling.

At issue was the "family viewing" policy adopted by the three commercial networks and the National Association of Broadcasters and which went into effect a year ago. Generally, it is a vague rule which says that programs deemed "inappropriate for viewing by a general family audience" may not be broadcast during the first prime-time hour of network programming or the hour immediately preceding it—usually from 7-9 p.m.

U.S. District Court Judge Warren J. Ferguson ruled that the commercial networks and the NAB violated the First Amendment in adopting the policy. The plaintiffs contended in their lawsuit that the policy amounted to a "prime time censorship rule" that violates the First Amendment rights of free speech and constitutes a chilling effect on creative expression.

CBS's response to the ruling illustrates not only the judge's wisdom but also the dangers—as yet unrealized—of the "family viewing" policy. CBS was the network that originated the attempt to make the policy a part of the NAB code. Yet a CBS spokesman said that Judge Ferguson's ruling for "unfairly singled out the broadcast industry" and "set a dangerous precedent that threatens the American tradition of voluntary self-regulation" by industry codes. The CBS protest dramatically overstates the situation.

It is absurd to complain that the ruling unfairly singles out the broadcasting industry when that industry—the networks, the NAB and the Federal Communications Commission—was the original defendant in the lawsuit. Who else could have been "singled out"?

Further, we could not disagree more that the ruling sets a dangerous precedent that threatens self-regulation. If a network chooses not to show programs containing excessive violence or "adult" themes during the 8-9 p.m. prime time hour, it need only purchase shows that fit that criterion. Besides, the networks have little or no control over the fare offered by local stations in the 7-8 p.m. slot. The result is that many shows—mostly old series now in syndication—give families almost as much violence as is available during prime time.

The key point lies in Judge Ferguson's suggestion that the FCC violated the First Amendment by threatening government action if the industry failed to adopt the family viewing rule. The FCC chairman has disputed this point but it seems clear that there was at least an implied threat, which in the long run can be just as destructive of constitutional guarantees.

The principle involved is much more important than whether a racy sitcom will ever be aired at the wrong hour. It is that the step from regulating the content or air time of dramatic production to that of regulating the content of television news program is a short one.

The Knickerbocker News
··· UNION-STAR ···
Albany, N.Y., November 8, 1976

A federal judge has ruled that the Federal Communications Commission was off its constitutional rocker when it pressured the three television networks to institute a so-called family hour.

We concur.

As desirable as it might be to have sanitized viewing—no violence, no very sexy sex—during that 7 p.m.-to-9 p.m. nightly period, the government should keep its freedom-encroaching hands off television content. When there is too much stabbing, shooting, raping, gouging, kicking, strangling and punching on the TV screen, there are a couple of solutions that don't require federal intervention. One is to turn the set off. Another is for local stations to exercise discretion about whether they're going to use network programming. For instance, WAST-TV in this area is refusing to show an ABC movie because the station management considers the flick to be excessively violent.

Of course, the local stations are pretty well dominated by the monopoly held by ABC, NBC and CBS, and it's not that easy for them to go their own way. Here is a place where the federal government could play a role.

On the grounds that the networks are in violation of at least the spirit of the antitrust laws, the government could move to lessen their control over affiliated stations in a variety of ways that might lead to more competition and more diversity over the airwaves. The problem, after all, isn't just too much violence. Many of the non-violent shows do violence to the sensibilities of anyone who wasn't raised by apes in the jungle. What is needed is television programming as intelligent as the people watching it. The government shouldn't dictate what we watch or don't watch, but it can restructure the system in such a way as to make better programming more likely.

The Providence Journal
Providence, R.I., November 9, 1976

The American public in the last few years has made plain its outrage over a concentration of sex and violence on commercial television during hours when children are most often watching. Parents and religious groups have lashed out at forms of "entertainment" that expose youngsters to the worst kinds of depravity — to amoral and immoral behavior, to criminal activity with emphasis on physical violence, prostitution, adultery and all the rest.

Under pressure from their constituents, Congress became deeply involved in an investigation of the problem. To what extent should that body legislate against offensive types of television programming? Were the public airwaves being used in a manner inimical to the public interest and if so should the Federal Communications Commission exercise its regulatory power to curb alleged abuses?

Enormous pressure was applied to the three major TV networks to practice restraint. If the public's insatiable appetite for "adult fare" was such that it forced broadcasters to air such stuff, for reasons of profit and competition, let it be at least after most children are in bed.

Fortunately, Congress and the FCC concluded, rightly, that free speech guarantees under the First Amendment to the Constitution preclude any kind of government action bordering on censorship. That position is unassailable in our view.

At the same time, public concern had reached a point where something had to be done. The networks could not be granted a free hand with a generation of young people for whom television was close to an addiction. Faced with a massive outpouring of viewer sentiment, not to mention obvious displeasure of Congress and the FCC, the industry responded. The networks in concert with the National Association of Broadcasters set aside the hours from 7 p.m. to 9 p.m. as hours for family viewing.

The action was widely acclaimed. If the results were not perfect, at least they indicated a willingness among broadcasters to police themselves. If TV was not purged of the lurid and sensational, at least the juvenile prime time zone had been cleansed to a degree.

In a decision of major significance handed down last week, however, a federal district court in Los Angeles set the stage for undoing any good that has been done. Judge Warren J. Ferguson held (1) that by agreeing to ban programs containing violence and sexual subject matter, the networks had violated the First Amendment; and (2) that "government activities involved amounted to virtually unprecedented orchestration of regulatory tools by the FCC."

If allowed to stand on appeal, this ruling has the potential of ending self-policing in the broadcast industry. Judge Ferguson said the networks and NAB were liable for financial damages. That finding alone could topple this house of cards. Should one network back away from the "family hour" commitment, competition for the TV audience and the advertising dollar would surely do the rest.

It should be emphasized that these newspapers are unalterably opposed to all forms of censorship. Government guidelines for approved TV programming would be totally unacceptable. But we are greatly troubled by a court ruling that appears to place industry self-regulation in conflict with freedom of speech.

If the courts persist in cracking down on cooperative restraint, the only alternative evident at this point is a television industry free to fill the screen with virtually anything that appeals to the lowest common denominator. For parents of small children in particular, that prospect is a pill that will go down hard.

The San Diego Union
San Diego, Calif., November 9, 1976

The free speech guarantees of the First Amendment have been reaffirmed in Federal Judge Warren J. Ferguson's ruling against the controversial "family hour" on television. We applaud his decision, but at the same time we hope it does not spell the end of the policy which has tried to keep shows exploiting sex and violence off the television screen between 7 and 9 p.m.

That may sound paradoxical, but this important case did not turn on whether the family viewing policy is good or not. It dealt with the relationship between the Federal Communications Commission and the broadcasting industry. This has become, and remains, a difficult area for application of the First Amendment — reconciling the long-accepted need for federal regulation of broadcasting with the Bill of Rights guarantee that Congress shall make no law abridging freedom of speech or of the press.

Judge Ferguson found that the FCC had by-passed administrative procedures established by law when it pressured the television industry into adopting the family viewing policy. Evidence was submitted that broadcasters were led to believe they might lose their licenses if they did not comply. This kind of behind-the-scenes activity should not substitute for the formal procedures which provide for public hearings on regulatory policies.

It would hardly be more satisfying if the FCC did follow legal procedures in an effort to impose the family viewing policy. It has already extended its authority into programming with its fairness doctrine, which can inhibit discussion of controversial issues on radio and television and creates recurring problems at election time.

The "family hour" probably has been welcomed by parents who are worried about exposure of their children to lurid depiction of violence and sexually suggestive situations and dialogue, both in movie theaters and on television. The movie rating system has been of some value in protecting children from unsuitable entertainment, and it is regrettable that a similar problem should now be represented by television sets in American homes. The rating system, for all its imperfections, is an effort by the movie industry to meet a public problem by policing itself.

Television producers who took the family viewing policy into court had a good case on constitutional grounds. It is another matter whether they could argue as well against the principle of following some guidelines of taste and morality in programs aired before the bedtime of small children. Although Judge Ferguson has given the FCC a dressing down for the way it tried to impose such guidelines, the need for them still exists. If broadcasters are sensitive to their responsibility to the public, they will not abandon the principle of the "family hour" just because a judge has told them they can. They are still subject to the judgment of viewers.

THE ROANOKE TIMES
Roanoke, Va., November 9, 1976

The federal court ruling against the required "family viewing time" on television is disturbing. It blocks out one more area in which society is forbidden to govern itself. It makes no difference what the people, Congress or the Federal Communications Commission think, the court ruled in effect. Those who want to bring violence to the television screen, when young people are most likely to be looking at it, can do so and nothing can be done about it.

The basis for the ruling is the First or "free speech" amendment to the Constitution. Certainly a conflict between this amendment and television could be imagined. The FCC might rule that criticism of the government was not permissible on television until after midnight. The networks might combine to freeze out unpopular views and the FCC might wink at their conspiracy. But is a simple rule to restrict violence in the living room, during family viewing hours, what George Mason, James Madison, Thomas Jefferson, et als, had in mind when they insisted upon a First Amendment?

Mason, Madison, Jefferson and the early Americans who adopted the First Amendment didn't know about television, or radio, either. A modern court necessarily has to deduce what they would have thought and what the words should mean today. We agree that a Constitution should not be frozen into its first environment. But the Constitution is not made of elastic or rubber, either.

The decision should be appealed and the Supreme Court should take a very hard look. Using the "free speech" amendment and using even more the provisions on "equality" (a concept that can be stretched to infinity) the courts are taking over the powers of government at all levels. If the courts are to become the government, it may be time to elect the judges and abolish tenure.

The Evening Gazette

Worcester, Mass., November 6, 1976

Now that a federal judge has struck down television's "family hour" as a violation of the First Amendment, one wonders what protection the American family has against the sort of visual rotgut that the networks have been contemplating.

As the situation comedies get raunchier and raunchier, as the language of even "children's" programs gets rougher and rougher, as the ratio of homosexuals, prostitutes, pimps and sadists get thicker and thicker, many parents are wondering whether it might be better to chuck the tube, once and for all.

Not that Judge Warren Ferguson didn't have a point. If the Federal Communications Commission actually did put pressure on the networks to adopt the "family hour" then that is contrary to the First Amendment protections against free speech. But if the networks more or less voluntarily agreed to the notion, it hardly seems much of a blow against the Constitution.

The problem, as we see it, goes deeper and we do not know what the answer is. As long as the networks are competing for the life blood of Neilsen ratings above all, they seem willing to turn up the shock value of their shows as far as necessary. Imaginative acts of violence on ABC have to be topped by even more imaginative episodes on CBS and NBC, and the race for the gutter never stops.

The programmers have what they think is the ultimate answer to any objections. They say that they are giving the public what it wants and unfortunately there is a good deal of truth in that. But must society idly stand by and watch its young people steadily debauched in the name of the First Amendment? Do we have to accept titillating sex, followed by soft core sex, followed by hard core sex and nauseating violence every step of the way? Are there no protections at all?

The only thing preventing that from happening is the fear by the networks that Congress might be roused to take some sort of action. That would be unfortunate, for then censorship might be a fact. But does it have to come to that? Are there no standards of taste and self restraint left in the broadcasting industry? We would hate to think that there is no hope in that direction.

The Arizona Republic

Phoenix, Ariz., November 7, 1976

Last year the three major television networks agreed to set aside the time between 7 and 9 each evening for "family viewing."

On the theory that these were the hours when the largest number of impressionable children would be watching television, the networks agreed to omit programs that stressed sex and violence.

The action wasn't exactly voluntary. It was urged on the networks by the Federal Communications Commission. But it seemed like a fine thing to allow children to watch the Big Eye without being instructed in the fine arts of mayhem, rape and robbery.

Now a federal judge in Los Angeles has ruled that the establishment of "family viewing" was a violation of the First Amendment. The judge did admit that he couldn't ban the custom, but he said it violated the free speech rights of producers, directors and writers who brought suit.

The U. S. Supreme Court will have to decide the issue, since the networks are going to appeal the district court's ruling. We trust it will reverse the lower court.

We don't see how anyone's right to free speech can be violated by broadcasters who decide to elevate the standards of television for a couple of hours a day.

The FCC is clearly mandated to prescribe the conditions under which the nation's airwaves are used. In fact, there is considerable doubt as to whether the First Amendment applies to the owners of television and radio stations. Since there is a limited number of wave lengths, the electronic media must be regulated. There is no such limitation on the number of presses that can be manufactured.

But if the First Amendment does apply to radio and television, that doesn't mean broadcasters can't air programs free from sex and violence if they wish to do so. To the contrary, to tell them they must broadcast such questionable material would be to violate their First Amendment freedoms.

Some printed publications have plumbed the absolute depths of salacious pornography. If the television networks want to set higher standards than some magazines, the courts shouldn't question their right to do so.

The Cincinnati Enquirer

Cincinnati, Ohio, November 14, 1976

ONE FIFTH-GRADE GIRL of our acquaintance loves television's "family hour." She seems grateful the networks care enough to delay the sex, violence and obscenity programs until after she heads for bed.

Our guess is that millions upon millions of children, and certainly their parents, would hate to give up the family hour. Many families, perhaps, would like to see it expanded. For excessive violence and barnyard antics at any hour may offend viewers of any age.

But now comes a federal district court ruling in Los Angeles that the family hour is unconstitutional. Judge Warren Ferguson feels it constitutes censorship, violating the First Amendment. What he held, in effect, was that writers and producers are free to pour what filth and violence they prefer into the country any hour of the day or night. He did say local stations have the right to show or not show any programs telecast by the networks.

One shudders at the potential of the Ferguson decision, if upheld. Commendably, the Columbia Broadcasting System (CBS) and American Broadcasting Co. (ABC) announced immediate plans to carry the ruling to the U. S. Circuit Court of Appeals—and, presumably, to the Supreme Court, if necessary.

The suit against the family hour was brought by producer Norman Lear and others, including the Directors, Writers and Screen Actors Guilds. They charged the Federal Communications Commission (FCC) and the three major networks with violating their First Amendment rights.

Significantly, two Cincinnatians, Walter E. Bartlett and Robert D. Gordon, played important roles in the family hour establishment as top officers in 1975 of the National Association of Broadcasters' (NAB) television board—Mr. Bartlett, WLW-T general manager, as chairman and Mr. Gordon, WCPO-TV general manager, as vice chairman. Both were strongly in favor of family hour viewing. Mr. Gordon even tried to get the NAB television board to fight for round-the-clock family programming. But his motion to that effect failed.

Given the Ferguson ruling, Mr. Gordon's remarks to our Steve Hoffman in an interview published May 4, 1975, may be all the more relevant: "My motion said in effect that we should place things in their proper perspective. I felt the public was critical of television sex and violence, not just because children were exposed, but that thoughtful, intelligent adults are offended by certain aspects of television." His position also was that many children, certainly, were up later than 9 p.m., and could be subjected to worse "adult material" than they had been getting with a 9 p.m. cutoff of the family hour.

One fact which had impressed Mr. Gordon, apparently, was the jump in viewer complaints to the FCC from around 2500 in 1972 to about 33,000 in 1973—a 1500% increase. Viewers had had enough unbridled obscenity and violence at all hours. The family hour was all that saved TV, perhaps, from a viewer revolution that would have rocked the halls of Congress.

Certainly the airwaves belong to the public. The FCC was created with that understanding. Station licenses are a privilege. So it does seem there should be some public input into what is seen and heard via television. We would therefore hope the Ferguson ruling does not become the law of the land. One can only imagine the rising tide of public protest that would—and should—develop if it does.

Arkansas Gazette.
Little Rock, Ark., March 26, 1976

Robert B. Beusse, communications secretary of the United States Catholic Conference, has demanded of the FCC what he calls the "right" of both religious and secular news services to see an advance screening of all network TV programming planned for showing at *any* hour, lest a child stumble before a home receiver at, say, 3:30 a.m.

Mr. Beusse's basic pre-screening demand is as unsurprising as is the corollary proposition that, this privilege, if conceded, would amount to a form of censorship, as was proved by the long record of the Breen Office with regard to motion picture releases.

What *was* surprising, pleasantly surprising because of its honesty, was Beusse's follow-up statement on the matter of children's supposed proper viewing hours, and his almost angry refusal to be put off by the "family hour" sop thrown out by the nets in a vain attempt to placate people like Beusee, who, underneath, do not want anything they disapprove of shown to anybody of any age at any hour. The difference between the national Catholic communications director, is that he unlike most of the others, will admit it.

Thus, if the networks did not already know it before—and apparently they didn't—they now have been told directly to their face that there is no placating the implacable. It is all rather like those people in the information business—which is to say, the news business—who think they can buy some sort of effective immunity from even the most red-fanged critics of the press by devoting as much time to "self-policing" (read that "voluntary censorship") as in reporting the news.

In saying that some child somewhere may be watching TV at any hour, Mr. Beusse was not just spinning it off the top of his head, but quoting from a Nielsen rating service study showing that children watch TV "in numbers so significant that it can be said family viewing is any time a program is on the air." Up to 18,000,000 "tots" are still gazing fixedly into the tube after 9 p.m., an hour proclaimed for their being arbitrarily ordered to their room by the network executives, if not by the supposedly responsible parents involved, for whom Mr. Beusse now would provide a barrage of anti-propaganda against this or that new network show so that they might live up to their responsibilities as parents.

Almost nothing is so pleasing as to have one of your own hunches—nay, near certainties—confirmed in such authoritative fashion as it has been here by Mr. Beusse and his supportive audience figures taken from the Nielsen folks. We have long had this mental image of a toddler in a little nightshirt yawning around in the living room as in the old Fisk tire ads of the '20s and '30s ("Time to re-tire, get a Fisk"), on his way to the set at the aforementioned 3:30 a.m. to turn the set back on to the rilly, rilly, late show—a hot one—while the folks continue to snoozle away.

It does not ever seem to occur to those people who want every single TV show to be fit for supposedly innocent juvenile eyes that the larger problem might not be so much what children watch as that they watch . . . and watch . . . and watch.

THE SACRAMENTO BEE
Sacramento, Calif., December 12, 1975

The brouhaha over television's new "family hour" is growing louder. Not since Monday night football first lumbered onto the television playing field and punted family dinner from the kitchen table to the TV tray, has television programming been such a contentious issue. But this time, more is at stake than the logistics of TV dining. The proper role of censorship in a free society is in question.

Ostensibly, the national networks adopted the "family hour" last September in an effort to limit the numbing violence and gratuitous sexual references which blighted early-evening TV screens. Congress and the FCC had been prodding the television industry for some time to assume greater self-regulation. But it was not until this year that it finally responded with the rather modest and benign policy of setting aside the first hour of network programming each evening for programs with general family appeal.

Predictably, this has unleashed cries of censorship and foul play. In fact, the three Brahmins of prime-time TV—Alan Alda, Mary Tyler Moore and Carroll O'Connor—have filed federal suit against both the FCC and the major networks, charging "self-regulatory censorship which restrains free speech and ideas in violation of the First Amendment." Hollywood's three biggest unions have backed them up by calling for an injunction against the "family hour because its repressive atmosphere has had a chilling effect on the creative community."

While such outrage is no doubt sincere, it is unfounded and misses the point.

Censorship is not the issue here. Lizzie Borden can still wield her ax after 9 p.m. and the S.W.A.T. team can still lay siege to Los Angeles. The networks have merely instituted a sensible zoning ordinance for television — separating those types of programs which are most appropriate for early time slots from those which are not.

As for the charge the "family hour" has had a chilling effect on the creative community, this is less an indictment of the "family hour" than an admission of television's cerebral paralysis which was evident long before September. In fact, by liberating the TV industry from its worn-out equation of mayhem and verbal abuse — if only for an hour — the opportunities for creativity and innovation have actually expanded. This is not to say the way in which the "family hour" is being applied is without flaw. Distinguishing between what is — and is not — for family audiences is bound to be somewhat arbitrary. And perhaps suitability is too often sought negatively, through excluding what is thought to be objectionable, rather than positively — through programming of the excellence that would really be for the whole family.

A recent national poll found 82 per cent of the television viewing public favors the "family hour" programming code. The responsibility for responding to this public concern has been placed on the shoulders of the FCC and the television and broadcasting industries where it belongs.

But the public interest will only be served if they are given a fair chance. The drive against media exploitation of sex and violence, with a double emphasis on the latter, should continue — and not only for the children's sake.

BUFFALO EVENING NEWS
Buffalo, N.Y., January 23, 1979

Two Buffalo-area mothers are doing parents of young children a favor with their efforts to encourage local TV stations to dump such risque fare as "The $1.98 Beauty Show," "The Newlywed Game" and "The Dating Game" from their early-evening time slots.

This particular rating game, a project headed by Mrs. Bette Jo Brown and sponsored by the local chapter of the American Association of University Women, is, in a word, flunking what television calls the "family hour."

"This programming has been a constant irritation," says the other mother, Mrs. Lorri Duquin, of similar shows aired between 7 and 8 p.m. "It is adult humor that doesn't belong on the air when children are watching."

Describing it as "adult humor" may stretch a point. Even "The $1.98 Beauty Show" looks over-priced. Surely, though, there are better times to broadcast these commercially attractive syndicated packages, designed as much for tasteless titillation as anything else, than in the early evening when children would normally form a significant portion of the audience. The two women are not advocating censorship ("We don't care if they carry shows at later hours"), says Mrs. Duquin). They merely ask, reasonably enough, for more appropriate programs for children, preferably originating here in Buffalo, during the early evening.

Responding to the mounting criticism sparked by the two women, Channel 2 has mercifully decided to junk the beauty show. Other local stations ought to take a similar cue.

The Seattle Times

Seattle, Wash., November 8, 1976

LOOKING beyond the high-flown rhetoric about free-speech rights and a "victory having been won for Americans everywhere" (Producer Norman Lear's phrase), the flap over television's "family hour" viewing policy largely is a sham battle.

The "victory" won by Lear and assorted TV writers, actors and directors was last week's ruling by a federal judge in Los Angeles against arbitrary, across-the-board imposition of the policy on programmers.

United States District Judge Warren Ferguson held that the policy had been adopted by the networks under improper pressure from the Federal Communications Commission chairman, Richard Wiley, himself getting heat from Congress and the public to do something about sex and violence on TV screens.

Theoretically, the policy bans the showing of programs with sexual or violent material between 7 p.m. and 9 p.m.

Its adoption produced two inevitable results:

Programs in the "family viewing" period for the most part became even more sophomoric and insipid.

And the sex and violence in hours immediately preceding and following the "family hour" only got worse, including Lear's often tasteless Mary Hartman, Mary Hartman, shown in this region at 5 p.m.

Reports from industry sources indicate that the "family" policy probably will be shelved, regardless of the outcome of an appeal from Judge Ferguson's decision.

The policy never amounted to much more than a public-relations gimmick in the first place.

All of which amounts to a sad commentary on an industry that — despite occasional flashes of brilliance (Olympic Games and political-convention coverage, etc.) — too often is willing to settle in its 25th-anniversary year for the likes of The Bionic Woman, Hawaii Five-O and Kojak.

Oregon Journal

Portland, Ore., November 9, 1976

Censorship — the idea of controlling what an individual may see, read, hear, think or say — has, over the years in this country, become a "bad" word.

Usually, censorship has been applied against something which some consider to be immoral, unpatriotic or subversive.

This is what makes the recent ruling of a federal judge unusual.

The judge ruled, in effect, that imposition by the TV networks of a "family hour" policy, designed to improve the family viewing, is censorship and therefore unconstitutional.

He said individual program makers and station managements must be free to make such decisions on their own, "independent of concern for government reaction," or industry agreements.

U.S. District Court Judge Warren J. Ferguson said the "desirability or undesirability of family viewing is not the issue.

"The question is who should have the right to decide what shall and shall not be broadcast and how and on what basis these decisions are made."

The network chiefs insisted that they adopted the rules on their own, not because of government pressure, but the judge ruled that Federal Communications Commission pressure "in this case was persistent, pronounced and unmistakable."

There were several plaintiffs in the case and one of them was Norman Lear, producer of "All in the Family" and other topical humor series, who claimed damages because his show was shifted out of its audience pulling slot at 8 p.m. on Saturday nights.

The ruling of the judge does not preclude family hour programming. Individual program makers and station managements are free, under the ruling, to make this decision on their own.

However, probably it is too much to expect the individual network or station to schedule a family hour in prime viewing time if there is the chance that a rival will schedule a sex and violence program and draw a larger audience.

The Washington Post

Washington, D.C., November 13, 1976

FEDERAL DISTRICT JUDGE Warren J. Ferguson of Los Angeles did not cancel television's "family hour" last week, but he certainly left its future (and related questions) up in the air. The judge expressed no view about the *merits* of restricting early-evening entertainment to programs suitable for children, even though he did uphold challenges to that policy by television producers, writers and others. What Judge Ferguson found objectionable was the way in which the family-viewing plan had been adopted by the National Association of Broadcasters' code board under pressure from Federal Communications Commission Chairman Richard E. Wiley—who had in turn been pushed by Congress to do something about excessive violence and sex on the living-room screen.

Unfortunately, Judge Ferguson did not confine himself to a narrow ruling on this one case of informal official influence on programming. He went on to declare that any "censorship" by "privately created review boards" would be unconstitutional even if no governmental intervention were involved. While key parts of the 223-page opinion are quite opaque, some of the language suggests that he would object to almost any industry-wide code of standards, no matter how voluntary, as an improper restraint on individual broadcasters.

That concept puts enormous burdens on each network's or station's capacity for self-discipline. Unless some general understandings can be reached, the best intentions of individual broadcasters are usually too frail to withstand the competitive pressures for rating points. The producers, writers and actors who brought the suits are quite aware of this. While they have argued largely in First Amendment terms, they are also trying to expand the commercial markets for their work. Producer Norman Lear has sued for damages on the ground that the "family hour" has arbitrarily curtailed his access to the early-evening marketplace. A verdict for Mr. Lear would bring on a blizzard of such suits and further discourage broadcasters from taking any initiatives in areas of timeliness and taste.

Purists will argue that programming ought to be diverse, controlled primarily by viewers through their power to change channels or turn off the set. This approach has its hazards, though, especially in the perennially controversial area of televised violence and sex. Viewers concerned about gory, graphic or "adult" programming and its impact on children may be a minority, but they do not confine their protests to twisting the dials. They also complain to Congress and the FCC. Thus, a lessening of self-restraints by the industry could lead to formal regulation of a sort far more restrictive and intrusive than any voluntary codes.

In that context, the "family hour" has been an experiment in network self-protection and self-defense. The plan is hardly perfect. Its timetable is obviously arbitrary and affects various time zones differently. It has also produced too much pap and inanity before 9 p.m. and too much gore and sensationalism starting at 9:01. For all of that, the concept is commendable. We hope the networks will manage to adhere to it, even as the legal battles go on. The producers and writers, too, could show their own professional maturity by tempering their demands for "freedom" and accepting the creative challenge to come up with more programs that are entertaining without being unduly shocking or provocative.

THE ATLANTA CONSTITUTION

Atlanta, Ga., November 8, 1976

Freedom of speech is one of those concepts that are absolutely fundamental in a democratic society and yet are extremely difficult to define.

Our courts are frequently involved in trying to figure out what this constitutional guarantee really means. Generally it is agreed that "speech" is not just the right of an individual to stand up and sound off—it involves other methods of expressing opinion, of criticizing, of proposing or opposing. It involves access to the press and to the broadcaster's airwaves, for instance. Attempts to censor or control the press or the airwaves can be a form of interference with free speech. Such attempts are constantly being made—and unmade. Recently a judge barred the press from reporting a public trial. It was ruled by a higher court that he shouldn't have done that —the ruling coming after the trial.

There are those who believe in an absolute right of free speech, but they are in a minority. Justice Oliver Wendell Holmes offered a workable rule of thumb when he said free speech did not include the right to stand up in a crowded theater and yell "fire!" when there was no fire. This utilitarian approach is much more common, but critics argue that it only defends free speech so long as it isn't deemed dangerous.

Last week there was a court decision by a federal judge in Los Angeles that held television's "family hour," an effort to restrict sex and violence while the children were likely to be watching, was unconstitutional. The networks had adopted this policy in 1975, but plaintiffs argued that they were pressured to do so by the Federal Communications Commission. Judge Warren Ferguson said the problem was not the desirability of a family hour but who had the right to decide what should and should not be broadcast. He held the government did not have that right.

This latest effort to define free speech took up 223 pages. But it is safe to say that the definition of free speech is still not settled.

THE INDIANAPOLIS STAR
Indianapolis, Ind., November 16, 1976

After 10 days or so of looking at it, a Federal judge's ruling on network television's "family hour" seems as murky as a cloud of ink from a squid.

At issue is an agreement that the period from 7 p.m. to 9 p.m., local time, should be set aside for shows with a minimum of sex and violence.

In Los Angeles on Nov. 4 United States District Court Judge Warren Ferguson found three networks (ABC, CBS, NBC), the National Association of Broadcasters (NAB) and the Federal Communications Commission (FCC) all in violation of the free speech clause of the First Amendment to the Constitution for creating the "family hour."

Now that is a strange ruling, considering that what the First Amendment says about free speech is that Congress shall make no law abridging it.

That prohibition is logically construed to apply, by extension, to actions of creatures of Congress such as the FCC. But how can it be construed to apply to private enterprises which are not creatures of Congress?

The gist of Judge Ferguson's ruling, as reported by United Press International, is that the "family hour" was forced on the networks, against their wishes, by the FCC and the NAB.

If the FCC commanded the networks to do its bidding with respect to program content, that decidedly was in violation of the First Amendment. No governmental body has the right to abridge freedom of speech.

But the NAB is a private, voluntary association. What it and its network members were dealing with was their own freedom of speech. As for the networks, spokesmen have said they will appeal this decision.

Ferguson's decision came in a suit brought by guilds representing writers, producers, directors and actors. He wrote that the desirability or undesirability of the family viewing policy was not the issue.

He appeared uncertain at times whether the First Amendment applied to television or not. He seemed to conclude that if the First Amendment does apply to television, it may be circumvented by Congress and bureaucrats if it is circumvented in the proper formal, legislatively mandated manner.

Censorship by government, it is generally agreed, is prohibited by the First Amendment. Censorship, so-called, by privately created boards could in many cases be simply a matter of freedom of choice by members of a group to reject and to refuse to deal in material they find repugnant.

Certainly it is questionable whether their freedom to reject repugnant matter should yield, under government power of any kind, to the pressure of merchandisers of repugnant matter.

Ferguson's decision has opened a barrel of confusion. Perhaps an appeals court can clear up the muddle.

ARKANSAS DEMOCRAT
Little Rock, Ark., November 8, 1976

A California federal judge says the Federal Communications Commission overstepped its bounds in pressuring the National Association of Broadcasters and major networks to police up the sex and violence on prime-time television.

The judge is right, insofar as the letter of constitutional law is concerned. The informal encouragement from the FCC probably amounted to a prior restraint on the constitutionally-guaranteed freedoms of speech and expression.

The decision puts the responsibility for screening objectionable network programming squarely where it should be: upon the private networks themselves. A local television executive has said the private sector is willing and able to consider the public need for acceptable programs without the artificiality of a "family hour" restriction.

We hope so. Certainly, those in the forefront of the "family hour" challenge have a point. Why should Sonny Bono be able to say "hell" at 9:05 p. m. but not 10 minutes earlier? Why should Norman Lear productions be barred from prime time?

Of course, the "sanctity of the living room" argument has unquestioned merit. Parents have the right to expect that impressionable children will not be exposed to televised acts of violence or immorality in their own living rooms.

But the responsibility for such safeguards rests primarily with the network itself, secondarily with parent supervision the child's viewing habits and, only as a last resort, with the government. When that final recourse is invoked, it should not be through secret negotiation between government and private enterprise nor should it involve prior restraints.

Networks now advise whenever programming may be objectionable. They should not only continue to do so, but should encourage feedback from the viewers as to what their objections are to such programs.

Television in this country is a private enterprise and, as such, it functions best when regulated less by the government and more by the marketplace.

It remains for the networks now to demonstrate how capably they can police themselves and provide acceptable programming for their audience. We hope they'll do a creditable job of it.

Chicago Tribune
Chicago, Ill., November 7, 1976

In his ruling in the "family hour" case, Judge Warren J. Ferguson in Los Angeles has held that "neither the Federal Communications Commission nor the National Association of Broadcasters has the right to compromise the independent judgments of individual station owner licensees. If the family hour continues, it should continue because broadcasters, in their independent judgment, decide that it is a desirable policy, not because of government pressures or NAB regulations." The suit was brought by writers, directors, and actors who contended that "the family hour" impaired their freedom—and their profits.

Judicial reaffirmation of the controlling authority of the 1st Amendment is always welcome. But is the 13-month-old "family hour" policy of the TV networks a product of intolerable "censorship by government or privately created review board," as Judge Ferguson contends?

Richard E. Wiley, chairman of the FCC, says it is not. He said the FCC had not gone beyond "expressing concern to the industry with the problem of violence and urging it to adopt voluntary reforms." John A. Schneider, president of the Columbia Broadcasting System, said Judge Ferguson's ruling "threatens the American tradition of voluntary self-regulation."

The public interest calls both for maximum freedom from censorship and for relief from a preoccupation with violence and sex that has overtaken mass media entertainment to a disconcerting extent. The 1st Amendment bulwark against censorship was intended primarily to defend uninhibited political expression, not uninhibited pornography and antisocial exhibitions of cruelty. To accept political censorship would mean death to freedom in both government and the arts. But law and society have never succeeded in disentangling two kinds of censorship, political and moralistic, from each other, and perhaps never will.

The "voluntary self-regulation" of which Mr. Schneider speaks is clearly different from government censorship. [But of course if the National Association of Broadcasters is keeping some stations and writers from doing what they want to do, the regulation is not wholly voluntary.] Mr. Schneider says, "Voluntary industry standards of quality, content, and ethics . . . have long been in effect all across the range of professional and business activities in this country." If Judge Ferguson contends that business and the professions should have no power to define and enforce standards, he clearly has gone too far. Freedom does not mean that everyone is invited to do his own thing, no matter how antisocial his conduct may be.

Of course the ideal control over mass media programming would be that of a market that rewards excellence and punishes sleaziness by ignoring it, thus denying it financial support. A public that overwhelmingly preferred quality programming to a steady diet of murder and mayhem could be more beneficial than resort to anything that anyone could call censorship. Unfortunately, though, either many people want shoddy programming or they do not dislike it enough to turn it off.

Government censorship, voluntary standards, and public taste—none of these is likely to provide a good solution to the really severe problem of TV programming that warps the characters and values of innumerable Americans, especially children. Can anything short of government censorship solve it? If not, those who watch TV [and that means the American people] should blame no one more than themselves.

RAPID CITY JOURNAL—

Rapid City, S.D., November 16, 1976

A federal judge in California has ruled that broadcasters are free to continue or discontinue television's "family hour" standards.

The ruling came in a suit brought by some producers of television programs who contended the collective policy of "family hour" censorship violated the constitutional guarantee of free speech.

The court found that the National Association of Broadcasters had adopted the policy under pressure from the Federal Communications Commission and therefore the industry agreement was, in fact, a violation of the free speech guarantee.

At the time the broadcasters got together on the "family hour" policy of laundered programs during early evening hours, there was speculation that they were acting on their own against exploitation of sex and violence to forestall government intervention.

On the basis of the court's ruling, it appears that what seemed to be self-discipline was actually government-imposed regulation.

But for whatever reason it was instituted, the "family hour" has received favorable comment from the public in polls even though some of the content still seems questionable.

Now that broadcasters are free to continue or discontinue "family hour" standards on the basis of their own judgment, we hope they will see fit to continue them. If they don't, they could well subject themselves to something more drastic than government regulation — the ire of an aroused public.

The News and Courier

Charleston, S.C., November 9, 1976

A judge's ruling that the television business is out of line in prescribing a "family viewing" policy intended to give relief from bad taste and violence in programming leaves us with mixed emotions.

On one hand there is concern that ugly aspects of the TV screen put temporarily at bay will return in full force. On the other hand, there is a feeling of relief due to the prospect of escape from the wasteland of dullness which is the only territory open to viewers at that hour.

When the "family hour" first hit the screen, hope was high that television could somehow find a way to produce interesting programs without resorting to the flashy, noisy, sexy, repetitiveness which dominates evening hours. The hope has not been realized. Even in the "family hour", TV continues to cater to the least intellectual, least perspective, least discriminating members of its audience.

On balance, however, we guess we would prefer the "family hour" to what may replace it if the judge's ruling holds up. It is true it holds nothing much for adult viewers. At least it affords an interlude of predictable character. Parents can let the kids watch TV at that time without having to worry unduly about exposure to the worst vulgarity and the crassest of commercialism, which is a break from the usual.

WINSTON-SALEM JOURNAL

Winston-Salem, N.C., November 9, 1976

At first blush, a federal judge's ruling on the TV "family hour" sounded like a victory for First Amendment freedom. That's the way Norman Lear, TV's hottest and most controversial producer, chose to characterize it. Lear and several groups of TV writers had sued the three networks, the National Association of Broadcasters and the Federal Communications Commission over the rule.

The victory may be illusory. Judge Warren Ferguson of Los Angeles did not throw out the "family hour" idea, by which "adult" themes are kept off the air between 7 and 9 p.m. Rather, he said that the rule could not be forced on the networks by the FCC or the NAB; the networks are free to continue it on their own, and evidently they will. The FCC has insisted all along that there was no pressure. Judge Ferguson concluded that there was.

To Lear and his allies, "family hour" translates into censorship. In Lear's case, it could also be translated into dollars and cents, for the profitability of his assorted "adult" situation comedies apparently depends on their being sold for re-runs in higher - priced prime time. For the general public, the rule may mean being denied access to important ideas and viewpoints by those who monopolize the limited number of TV channels.

Resolving such problems by resorting to the Bill of Rights has never been easy and rarely satisfactory. Recognizing that a government - created monopoly is involved, the Supreme Court has consistently rejected broadcasters' claims of unfettered control over use of the air-waves. The FCC's efforts to enhance access to the air have been upheld. Here, however, a rule tended to deny access, at least to the larger prime-time audiences. On the other side of the balance is the commendable effort to make programming seen by children more wholesome.

This conflict of values might be easier to resolve if the "family hour" had clearly accomplished what it set out to do. Our impression is that, in its first year, it has not. It has succeeded in pushing into odd hours some of TV's best offerings, including several Lear productions, while filling the vacuum thus created with more and more pap. The criteria applied have been vague and more prissy than constructive. Gratuitous violence may indeed have been purged from the 7-to-9 period, but so has stimulation of any kind.

The constitutional problem of access to broadcasting will not be solved in this case, particularly if, as seems likely, the initial decision is reversed by the Supreme Court. Past experience suggests that the Court would find a time-of-day rule, even if openly decreed by the FCC, constitutionally permissible. The real issue in the case, it seems to us, is one of economic rather than constitutional freedom. If the three companies that between them monopolize network broadcasting jointly agreed to boycott certain producers or programming, then they may have restrained trade in violation of the antitrust laws, at least in spirit. That's another kind of problem. First impressions aside, "family hour" fare does not seem likely to be determined by reference to the First Amendment.

CIVIL RIGHTS PANEL REPORTS BIAS IN TV EMPLOYMENT, PROGRAMMING

The television industry was guilty of job discrimination and of perpetuating racial and sexual stereotypes in programming, according to a study released Aug. 15 by the U.S. Commission on Civil Rights. The report, entitled *Window Dressing on the Set: Women and Minorities in Television,* was based on employment data obtained from 40 commercial and public television stations, programs broadcast between 1969 and 1974 and on news shows broadcast between March 1974 and February 1975.

Local stations, the report said, had "misrepresented" their employment practices to the Federal Communications Commission, the agency charged with overseeing the industry. These stations were accused of placing women and minorities "in highly visible positions on the air," while leaving them "without comparable representation in decision-making positions."

The study called the current FCC policy of letting the industry regulate itself as much as possible a "failure." It suggested that the agency adopt "a variety of regulatory alternatives" to correct the alleged program bias. Commenting on the report, FCC Chairman Richard E. Wiley Aug. 15 said it was "difficult to conceive" how his agency could "deal with stereotyping without becoming inevitably drawn into the role of a censor."

White males, according to the study, dominated both entertainment programs and news shows. In the former, white males were said to have appeared in 65.3% of all major and minor roles, compared to the 23.8% of all roles played by white females. The report claimed that, while men were portrayed as older, serious, independent and the holders of prestige jobs, women were portrayed as younger, "family bound," usually unemployed and were more often found in comic roles. Those women portrayed as employed, the commission said, "were in stereotyped and sometimes subservient occupations." The study asserted that only 10.9% of all roles were played by members of minority groups (8.6% by nonwhite males, 2.3% by nonwhite females). Minority actors were said to appear primarily in ethnic settings or as tokens in all-white shows.

Amsterdam News
New York, N.Y., August 20, 1977

During the year 1973, the popular television series Hawaii Five-O used Blacks in major roles on nine different occasions. The roles chosen for the Black actors and actresses were: five as pimps, two as prostitutes, two as students.

This is only one of many examples in a report just released by the United States Commission on Civil Rights titled: "Window Dressing: Women and Minorities in Television."

Window Dressing indeed!

The racism and tokenism on American television is a national disgrace. It warms the minds of our young people; it limits the vision of our adults; it places our fine actors and actresses in the position of having no choice but too play play parts that they know are gross stereotypes.

The Civil Service Commission has called on the Federal Communications Commission to step in to regulate employment practices among the TV networks and to force the networks to change their racist practices.

The FCC, so far, has declined.

Perhaps it's time that Blacks began to boycott certain shows, certain series, certain producers and certain advertisers. We are major consumers of television in the major cities in the country. We can make or break a TV show or series. We have the power to force change. But do we have the leadership and the will?

Los Angeles Times
Los Angeles, Calif., August 21, 1977

The U.S. Civil Rights Commission is on firm ground in its insistence that television place more emphasis on equal employment and on promotion opportunities for minorities and women. Discriminatory practices are deeply rooted, and yield only to continuous efforts.

But our concern goes to the commission's proposed remedies, which, through the Federal Communications Commission, would involve the government directly in both the employment and the programming practices of the television industry.

Such a drastic intrusion by government, as the FCC chairman commented, would create a "regulatory nightmare." More than that, it would raise fundamental First Amendment issues.

The FCC in 1969 established guidelines for television to comply with national standards on the hiring of minorities. Women were added as a group in 1971. In its review of the record over the past eight years, the Civil Rights Commission report was almost entirely negative. It found that white males dominated the decision-making process in television, and, while granting that women and minorities had made progress in the industry, dismissed this as relatively insignificant.

Entitled "Window Dressing on the Set," the report came to these conclusions:

—Minorities and women, particularly minority women, continue to be underrepresented in dramatic programs and on the news, and their portrayals continue to be stereotyped. These stereotypes "are perpetrated by the networks in their pursuit of higher ratings and profits."

—Women and minorities are used increasingly in "visible positions as on-the-air talent," but the commission dismissed these gains as mere "window dressing."

Such judgments are highly subjective, and discount the wide variety of elements that go into programming decisions. Evidence to support such conclusions approached the ludicrous. For example, the report emphasized that, on All in the Family, Edith Bunker "scoots into the kitchen to fetch Archie a beer and rarely fails to have dinner on the table by 6 p.m." All this indicates is the failure of the humorless authors of the report to understand the artistic content of the program. Prejudice and stereotyping, rather than being promoted on All in the Family, are the targets of ridicule.

Television news, the report says, suggests that issues pertinent to minorities and women are not important. The reverse is true. The access of civil-rights groups and women to television has made television a significant instrument in breaking down the barriers of prejudice.

The report ignores the significance of TV license-renewal procedures, which require stations to justify in elaborate detail their public-service function and their employment practices. A vital part of this procedure is the introduction of evidence from community groups seeking to bar a station's license renewal or to influence its programs. These procedures probably have made television more sensitive to discriminatory practices than any other industry.

To end the discrimination that it charges is pervasive in television, the Civil Rights Commission urges Congress to give the FCC power to regulate employment practices of the industry, and urges the FCC to institute regulations to eliminate "stereotyping" of minorities and women on TV programs. The first would put the government in charge of industry hiring, and the second would impose government censorship on TV programs. This is a classic case of the cure being worse than the disease.

𝕻𝖎𝖙𝖙𝖘𝖇𝖚𝖗𝖌𝖍 𝕻𝖔𝖘𝖙-𝕲𝖆𝖟𝖊𝖙𝖙𝖊

Pittsburgh, Pa., September 24, 1977

THE U.S. Civil Rights Commission deserves and is getting criticism for a report it issued last week entitled "Window Dressing on the Set: Women and Minorities in Television." The report indicts commercial television programming for "stereotyping" women and minority-group members, and buttresses that indictment with some literal-minded citations from situation comedies like "The Mary Tyler Moore Show," "The Jeffersons," and "All in the Family" (a program which seems to bear the burden of a lot of wrong-headed sociologizing).

What is most immediately shocking about the report is its authors' lack of sophistication about what happen to be some of television's subtler attempts to combine comedy and social comment. The report finds chauvinist fault in the fact that the character played by Mary Tyler Moore called her boss of long standing "Mr. Grant" instead of "Lou," a commentary regular viewers would find incredible. *They* know that Mary's inability to shift to a first-name familiarity

with her employer was a calculated illustration of a very individual character's inhibitions.

Likewise, the authors of the civil rights report found cause to cluck in the fact that Edith Bunker, Archie's dingbat spouse on "All in the Family" always obeys her husband's order to fetch him a beer. In fact, the Edith character has been the instrument of some amusing exploration of the effects of feminism on a middle-class housewife.

The report's failure to appreciate the nuances of the programs it singled out for analysis is disturbing. But more disturbing is the recommendation the report bases on such dubious exegesis: that the Federal Communications Commission "undertake an inquiry and proposed rulemaking regarding the portrayals of minorities and women on network television." The chairman of the Federal Communications Commission rightly foreswore any such mission for his commission, recognizing the danger of censoring an already too-inhibited medium.

Unfortunately, the misguided worldview of the authors of "Window Dressing" is not confined to the U.S. Civil Rights Commission and ranges over a field wider than television prime-time. Under the banner of doing away with sexual "stereotypes," some feminists have mounted an assault on elementary-school curriculums and reading lists. Not surprisingly, many classics do not adequately visualize the brave new world in which activities like playing with dolls or even sailing down the Mississippi on a raft are not "sex-linked." The result, by whatever name it is called, is censorship of the actual in the name of the desirable.

Serious literature — or television — can be visionary or realistic or an artful combination of the two. What are called "stereotypes" partake as much of reality as of prejudice. Hard-and-fast rules to differentiate one from another are unlikely to be successful, especially in hands as clumsy as those which put together "Window Dressing on the Set."

The Washington Star
and Daily News

Washington, D.C., August 18, 1977

𝕿𝖍𝖊 🌳 𝕾𝖙𝖆𝖙𝖊

Columbia, S.C., August 21, 1977

FEDERAL Communications Commission Chairman Richard E. Wiley was right in rejecting a recent suggestion by the U.S. Civil Rights Commission to halt stereotyping of minorities and women on television.

Whether such alleged stereotyping is more imagined than real, we don't know. But we observe that Americans seem to have lost the great capacity we once had to laugh at ourselves. That is another way of saying we take ourselves too seriously.

And that, we think, is what the Civil Rights Commission is doing. As a purgative, we propose that the commissioners spend some time watching "All In The Family" and that stereotype of a northern redneck, Archie Bunker, and his "dingaling" wife, Edith.

That done, the Civil Rights Commission should then propose a pure script for that show, air it and see if that's what Americans want.

There is no way short of government imposed censorship to enforce an ideal which can become, as the FCC commissioner said, "highly subjective."

The U.S. Commission on Civil Rights has challenged the television industry and the Federal Communications Commission on two fronts — the portrayal of minorities and women in drama and news programs, and the alleged underrepresentation of the same groups on industry payrolls.

It would be tempting to sit back and enjoy the mayhem while the combatants fight it out with those deadly weapons of righteousness, stale statistics and legalisms. We will refrain, in any case, from getting deeply into the employment discussion, rather than be forced to decide, for instance, what proportion of black writers should be hired to write a series about women deepsea divers. Television employers are under the same anti-discriminatory laws as everyone else, the observance of which should assure that women and minorities have equal opportunity in bidding for TV jobs.

The Civil Rights Commission proposes a stronger FCC role enforcing a form of job quota, to bring the underrepresented groups up to "80 per cent of parity with their representation in the labor force of the station's service area." This has the drawback of all such quota plans — the potentiality of discriminating against qualified applicants who don't happen to meet the needs of the numbers game at a given moment. The bureaucracy already applies such pressure through rules for companies with federal contracts; the broadcasters are reachable for this treatment by being a regulated industry.

In an area of more startling precedent, the Civil Rights Commission suggests a new federal role in policing the content of dramatic programs on both commercial and public television. The FCC, according to the report, "should conduct an inquiry and proposed rulemaking on the portrayal of minorities and women. . ." And to get more favorable coverage of women and minorities on news programs, the report suggests putting more representatives of these groups in decision-making news jobs.

The Civil Rights Commission denies that it es-

pouses censorship, or wishes the FCC to "oversee day-to-day content of entertainment programs, preview scripts, select news stories. . ." But if the FCC were to attempt to lay down and enforce rules about program content, it could be called nothing but censorship. A nightmarish new area of government regulation this would be; we feel safe in predicting it will not happen.

Television does stereotype women and minorities, even as the Civil Rights Commission claims, and a boring percentage of the leading characters are white males. But the report uses outdated examples and statistics (1969 through 1974 for drama, and 1974 and 1975 for a news sampling), which do not take recent changes into account.

Women and blacks are turning up in more and more unaccustomed places on the tube, a trend that presumably will continue in accord with corresponding developments in American society generally. But television drama tends to stereotype *everyone*, white males included. The reasons are many, and include the commercial need to find broad national audiences for advertisers, the urge to imitate successful program formulas and the scarcity of writing talent. The real complaint about most TV drama, serious (violent) or sitcomic, is that it is of abominable quality.

As for the critique of how women and minorities are treated in the news, or their particular political causes ignored, that is mostly a comment on the world at large. (The emphases in TV news are not that different from those in the newspaper headlines.) The people calling the shots in the day's newsworthy happenings are mostly men, and in the Western World they are mostly white men. If the white male features of Jimmy Carter seem to be getting a disproportionate amount of newsplay, that is a function of his job rather than his race and gender. It does not seem to change the day's outpouring from the White House if the anchorperson is female, black or both.

Rocky Mountain News
Denver, Colo., August 27, 1977

OVER THE YEARS the U.S. Civil Rights Commission has performed valuable service in the struggle against discrimination and deserves good marks from the public.

However, the commission now wishes to change the way women and minorities are portrayed in television dramas, and this could violate one of the nation's most cherished rights: Freedom from censorship.

In a 181-page report the agency claims that the television industry is perpetuating racial and sexual stereotypes and it calls on the Federal Communications Commission (FCC) to do something about it.

For example, the commission complains that on "All in the Family," Edith Bunker "scoots into the kitchen to fetch Archie a beer and rarely fails to have dinner on the table by 6 p.m."

Now maybe there is something wrong in showing Edith Bunker as a submissive wife, but the "cure" implied by the commission is far worse. It would have the FCC order Edith portrayed in a positive light (as an atomic scientist perhaps).

After that, how long would it be before the FCC moved on from TV drama and started telling Walter Cronkite what to feature on the evening news?

FCC Chairman Richard E. Wiley made a brief but cogent response to the civil rights group's report: "It seems difficult to conceive of how a federal agency would deal with stereotyping without becoming inevitably drawn into a role of a censor."

The commission was upset because the television shows it monitored showed men as more independent and more likely to hold prestigious jobs. Women were often unemployed and more "family bound."

This really is an unwitting compliment to TV for showing life more or less as it is, not as the commission would like it to be. Because of the social history of the country and the advantages males had, they hold most of the higher-ranking jobs.

The current situation is not necessarily fair nor does it have to last. It can be changed by training more women for so-called men's jobs, opening up opportunities for them and treating them fairly at promotion time.

But the answer is not to skew the content of television shows to show women in roles they rarely fill but where the commission would have them. That is not programming, it's propaganda, and we shouldn't accept it, even if it comes labeled as civil rights.

The Seattle Times
Seattle, Wash., August 18, 1977

WHETHER network-television presentations regularly portray women and minorities as stereotypes — the United States Civil Rights Commission says they do — is a question most viewers can answer for themselves.

But there can be no argument about the commission's proposed remedy for sexual and racial stereotyping. It is dead wrong.

Complaining that white males dominate television drama, appearing "more frequently in serious roles and portraying older, more independent characters having diverse and prestigious occupations," the commission wants Congress to intervene in the writing of TV shows.

Congress, the civil-rights group says, should give the Federal Communications Commission power to draft rules to end TV's stereotyping, such as having "minorities appear primarily in ethnic settings" or females as often "comic characters . . . younger, underemployed, and tied to the family."

Since the granting of such power in effect would have the government dictating the style and content of television dramas, commercials and so on, the civil-rights body is proposing one of the worst civil-rights abuses of all: Censorship.

To make matters worse, if that's possible, the rulemaking would be left to the F.C.C., which already holds considerable power over broadcasting through its licensing function.

Wisconsin State Journal
Madison, Wisc., August 19, 1977

The U. S. Civil Rights Commission studied television programing and found that it perpetuates racial and sexual stereotypes.

It probably does. Most television fare is empty-headed garbage. It's stock in trade is stereotypes and formula writing.

The commission is appalled at this but its proposed solution is all wrong. It wants Congress to give the Federal Communications Commission (FCC) power to write rules to end sexual and racial stereotyping in commercials and dramatic programs.

In other words, put government in charge of television programing to satisfy the taste of the U. S. Civil Rights Commission. It won't work. And it shouldn't.

Richard E. Wiley, FCC chairman, said:

"It seems difficult to conceive of how a federal agency would deal with stereotyping without becoming inevitably drawn into the role of censor."

Arthur Fleming, chairman of the Civil Rights Commission, quickly denied any inclination toward censorship.

He said the commission is proposing a "genuine commitment" to civil rights, not censorship.

"What we desperately need in this industry is leaders...who have a commitment to enforcement of the Constitution. Our generalization is that people do not have that commitment."

He said that FCC regulations to eliminate stereotyping of minorities and women on TV shows could stop "well short of program censorship."

"I do not see any correlation between censorship and enforcement of the Constitution," he said.

We would be interested in having Fleming point out where the Constitution prohibits stereotyping any group of people in any dramatic or literary production.

If the U.S. Constitution has any meaning at all, it is to safeguard the right of individuals and groups to express themselves freely, regardless of the merit of their expression or whether it hurts the feelings of others.

Aside from the practical impossibility of defining stereotypes and monitoring television programs to police some vague regulation against them, to have the government dictate program content would be the first step toward government control of every facet of communications — a necessary step on the road to totalitarianism.

The Civil Rights Commission is right in deploring the quality of television dramatic fare. It is dead wrong in trying to stop it through censorship — or whatever Fleming chooses to call censorship.

THE COMMERCIAL APPEAL
Memphis, Tenn., September 6, 1977

THE U.S. Civil Rights Commission has done many good works, but in its recent review of the television medium it has set a standard for unreasonableness that few of the public and private agencies and institutions it's investigated over the years would have dared to follow.

The commission's lengthy report focuses primarily on two issues: Employment practices by the networks and by broadcasting stations and the portrayal of women and minorities on television shows.

On the employment issue, the commission not surprisingly found ample statistics to bear out the contention that women and minorities have been discriminated against. The commission's recommended solution was to be expected: Hire more women and minority members, from camerapersons to writers to station managers, and set up training programs if necessary. Quotas, of course, would be helpful. Maybe even conscription?

The commission has said the same thing so many times that we wonder why it bothered to conduct a study. Unfortunately, the commission's acerbic, pontifical tone tends to interfere, like snow on the tube, with a clear picture of legitimate grievances and realistic progress toward eliminating them.

BUT IT WAS the second issue that set the commission off on an astounding venture into the possibilities of a managed society.

Starting with the premise that "television should accurately reflect the ethnic and gender diversity of the nation," the commission concluded that "corrective action" should be taken "that will place all Americans in true perspective on television . . ." (Are there to be casting quotas, too?)

The report's list of television's sins is impressive, as an achievement in nitpicking if for no other reason. Julia lacked any "redeeming social value" (which made it obscene in a clean-cut way). I Love Lucy "demeaned" American womanhood. Mary Tyler Moore's independence was compromised because she had to call Mr. Grant "Mr. Grant" when everyone else could call him "Lou." White Americans have gotten a distorted idea of what Asians are really like because of reruns of Charlie Chan and Fu Manchu movies. (And of the British, too, because of Sherlock Holmes reruns?) White males made up 65.3 per cent of the characters on TV shows.

The commission, however, didn't have to gather all its pages of documentation to prove that the quality of television programming is, on the whole, pretty low or that the medium panders to the lowest common denominator of public taste. The commission hasn't bathed American social thought with any new insight by observing that the commercialism of the industry has led it sheepishly down the path of trite formulas, spinoffs and stereotypes (of white males as well as everyone else, it must be noted).

Television is show business, entertainment, escapism. It holds a mirror up to the fancies of the viewers, if not up to nature. It fights for ratings because that's where the money is to pay exorbitant production costs and return a profit.

This isn't to say television is blameless. It can be improved — greatly. One day it may even fulfill the educational role envisioned for it in its infancy, which wasn't very long ago. But the issue is how should this come about — by the process that has been marked by such outstanding programming as "The Autobiography of Miss Jane Pittman" and "Roots" or by government intervention?

The commission says it doesn't want censorship, only "rules." Rules, we assume, that will assure a "true perspective." Who's "true perspective"? Rules, the commission says, that will help shape in a predetermined and acceptable way "viewers' beliefs, attitudes and behavior" concerning "issues of critical importance." In the context of the classroom or the pulpit, that may be considered "education." In the context of government control over a pervasive and hypnotic medium, it sounds much more like indoctrination.

THIS KIND OF excess in the commission's recommendations may have the counterproductive effect of deadening the ears of both the government and the public to whatever merit and useful information the report contains. It leads us to wonder if the commission shouldn't re-evalute its role as a gadfly and reformer.

Of course there should be equal employment opportunities for minorities and women. Of course the television industry should take a long look at the quality of its products. Of course every effort should be made to provide the viewers with programs that inform and stimulate as well as entertain. But not the commission's way. Not under the gun of government edict or the declamations of federal appointees in shining armor.

The commmission, for instance, didn't take into account the youth of the television industry or the fact that neither American journalism nor entertainment had any significant tradition of employment for minorities and women until fairly recent years. Television can be blamed for not opening up employment opportunities right away, but that isn't going to solve the problem of a shortage of trained job applicants. Perhaps that's the sort of issue the commission could do a worthwhile study of. It would be a welcome change from the perfervid demands for quotas and more government controls.

HERALD EXAMINER
Los Angeles, Calif.,
August 24, 1977

As an idiotic exercise in mischief-making and wholly irresponsible behavior, the television study just issued by the United States Civil Rights Commission would be hard to beat. It not only suggests government censorship of the electronic free press; it does so with such obvious bias and crusade axe-grinding as to make itself ridiculous.

In its 181-page report, entitled "Window Dressing on the Set: Women and Minorities in Television," the independent and supposedly non-partisan fact-finding agency documented what it found wrong on the tube during the six-year period from 1969-1975. Mostly, according to the commission, what it found was appalling.

White males, if you watch the TV programs blasted by the report, seem to have most of the power and professional authority in this country. Loving wives like Edith Bunker trot to fetch them beer. Non-white characters in general are given less important and stereotyped roles. And female news correspondents seldom take over in reporting crucial national stories.

All this is a terrible situation, according to the report. It's not the way matters should be, see, and the Federal Communications Commission better do something drastic about it. The report, in effect, demands that women and minorities be portrayed with the authority their activists seek. No more beer-trotting Edith Bunkers. And if you want to show a bank president, make sure he is black.

It is obvious what would happen if the FCC moved to implement this mush-headed report. Whatever reality is left on the TV screen would be replaced by a screwball dream world compounded of all sorts of unrealistic nonsense. And pretty soon nobody would tune in.

Unless, of course, they were compelled to do so by a government with authority to decide what they should or should not see.

The Evening Bulletin
Philadelphia, Pa., August 24, 1977

If you've been repulsed by what you watch on television, you might be cheered by word that your Federal Government is worried about you, and wants to help.

Be careful, though. The trouble is that Uncle Sam isn't worried about inane plots, idiotic commercials or senseless violence. No, what your Uncle Sam - through your Civil Rights Commission - is worried about is that the dramas and situation comedies aren't realistic in their portrayal of women and minorities.

Well, the Civil Rights Commission has offered recommendations and criticism in the past that made sense. But in trying to become chief scriptwriter and editor for the networks we think the commission makes no sense at all. The agency's big gripe is that women and minorities don't get roles that show them in a very positive, inspirational way.

Still with us? What upsets the Civil Rights Commission is that Mary Richards is the only one in that TV newsroom who calls Lou Grant "Mister." And how about Edith Bunker? Why can't Archie get up out of his chair, waddle into the kitchen and get his own beer? Then there's Louise Jefferson. Why won't husband George let her have a career job?

Well, we don't like racial or sexual stereotypes and we're happy that most have disappeared. But we can't get upset because Mary says "Mister Grant." Somehow, we see Edith Bunker as the warmly intelligent member of that couple - with or without a can of beer in her hand. A dingbat she's not.

The Federal Communications Commission noted very properly that this nonsense could turn the Federal Government into "censoring of all free speech." So Edith and Archie and Mary and Lou need not worry.

We do keep wondering, though, why the Civil Rights Commission didn't spend just a second or so checking why the heroes in those action-packed dramas are always young and tall — with full heads of hair. That doesn't sound like realism to us. Why couldn't a little guy who is thick in the middle and thin on top get the girl — just once?

Arkansas Gazette.
Little Rock, September 19, 1977

The United States Civil Rights Commission performs some valuable — yea, indispensable — duties of advice and instruction to the government, and to the public at large, but it went far afield in one recent recommendation. A report from the commission urged action against alleged discrimination in hiring by the television networks, which is the sort of proposal it makes quite frequently. But it went much farther this time, calling for use of federal regulatory power to influence the content of TV programs so that minorities and women would not be portrayed in stereotyped or unfavorable roles.

To be sure, there is a good deal of crudity in much that goes on The Tube as mass entertainment. Some people are placed in ethnic molds for purposes of comedy in sloppy ways, and in some other molds as well (even Archie Bunker is a stereotype), and some racial "humor" with very little taste comes into our living rooms. The commission is particularly piqued by the ethnic situation comedies and the undeniable fact that women appear as subordinate to men on many shows (not to speak of many commercials). But the question is, if a line were to be drawn, who's to say where it would be? Some black citizens probably would consider that portions of the great drama "Roots" presented black people in demeaning stereotypes. Some Americans of Italian descent might consider that the inimitable detective Colombo offers altogether too slovenly an image from their point of view. On and on it would go, and the arbiter of it would have an impossible task, and one which, if attempted, would be bound to have a repressive and dulling effect, in the long run, on all forms of dramatic expression.

It is nothing, in other words, for a free society to be undertaking, and we marvel that the commission displayed so little judgment as even to mention such an idea, involving such an obvious collision with constitutional rights. In any case, Chairman Richard Wiley of the Federal Communications Commission was quite right in making short work of the proposition, which he said was "perilously close" to a call for his agency to censor entertainment. "While the Commission on Civil Rights does not advocate censorship as such," he said, "it is clear to me that the FCC inevitably would be drawn into such a role if it were to begin down the road suggested by the commission." And the result would be "a regulatory nightmare."

Indeed it would be much worse than that: an invasion of expressive freedom which would be impossible to contain to the more offensive programs. The commission should realize that in the necessary task of protecting people's rights under the 14th Amendment and the civil rights laws, it is neither necessary or proper to propose a reduction of freedoms guaranteed by the First Amendment. Almost all of our expressions are offensive to *someone*, and, as the founders knew so well, tolerance is the glue that holds liberty in place.

THE PLAIN DEALER
Cleveland, Ohio, August 27, 1977

Television is a daily companion that transcends race and sex for millions of Americans. And yet the medium to which many turn for escape from life's realities is another example of the much-maligned, white-male-dominated world.

"Window Dressing on the Set," the 181-page report presented to the President and Congress last week by the U.S. Civil Rights Commission, revealed some of the equal employment shortcomings of the television industry.

The report accuses the Federal Communications Commission (FCC) of collaborating with licensees to circumvent equal employment practices. For instance, FCC regulations require stations to report recruiting and training efforts, but make no provisions for reporting actual hiring.

The rights panel further says the industry places minorities and women "in a few highly visible positions" instead of in decision-making jobs.

Stations' frequently "misclassify" jobs to make it appear that more women and minorities are in professional and managerial positions, the report said. Arthur S. Flemming, rights commission chairman, said some have "supervisors of word processing" and "administrators in charge of computer printouts."

In other words, the stations have used outright deceit to avoid fair employment practices. The civil rights panel maintains that "women and men of each racial group should be employed at each station in reasonable proportion to their availability in the local labor force."

If that yardstick were applied here, we would certainly find local stations lacking. Unlike some sections of the country, Cleveland has a widely diverse labor force.

Congress in rewriting the Communications Act of 1934 should explore, then remedy the areas in which television is failing to fulfill fair employment goals if the FCC cannot or will not adequately function as a regulatory agent.

As it is, the FCC is being criticized by another governmental agency for its inadequacies. Until now, such scathing reports, license challenges and unfavorable studies emerged from citizen's groups like the National Citizens Committee, which is headed by a former FCC member; the National Black Media Coalition and the National Organization for Women.

Unfortunately, the prevailing view from the television side has been too much like a recent statement from CBS President Robert Wussler: "Television should not be a leader of society. It should always be a half or three-quarters of a step behind society." We think it should catch

Chicago Defender
Chicago, Ill., December 27, 1977

Anyone who watches television cannot help but notice the serious and frequent inclusion of black personnel in the singing commercials, even in the entertainment patterns.

To look at television and see the steadiness of this representation one might well get the impression that the utopia of integration has arrived.

It is all to the good that this presence, the black child gobbling a new cereal, the pretty black woman wearing some smart new dress, the black worker-mechanic endorsing the virtues in some new model automobile - is there. All to the good.

Now, if that pace of inclusion characterised other less visible areas of the national economy we'd be really going places - forward.

In the academy it is all very controversail at the moment.

In jobs for our youth the record is abysmal when it isn't plan rank and rotten.

The U.S. Government talks about creating jobs for about four million people. They better get to it very soon. When we hear that blacks are bringing home a bit of bacon - from jobs and earned income - then that representation we have on the boob tube will seem more even, more appropriate, more just.

In the meantime we hope TV keeps employing blacks - even if the angle is to get the black market.

WORCESTER TELEGRAM
Worcester, Mass., September 3, 1977

Almost every week we read of some new study showing that television does not reflect life as it really is.

The findings of George Gerbner, dean of the Annenberg School of Communications at the University of Pennsylvania, are typical.

He says men outnumber women four to one in TV drama and that married people, especially men, are relatively rare. He adds that half the men and 26 per cent of the women become involved in violence. And he notes that for every young woman shown in a TV role with some power over her life, two are portrayed as victims.

Such studies make a valid point — that the world of make-believe is not the same as the real world. It never has been, of course, in books, on stage or in the movies. But the implication of the TV studies is that this one medium has so much influence over such a broad audience that it should be required to reflect real life accurately.

Perhaps so, though real life can be pretty dull, and it is television's business to entertain. If life as it really is were all that entertaining, we suppose nobody would bother to watch TV.

The implication of such studies is at least preferable to the urgings of various groups that TV should go out of its way to distort its portrayal of life in order to jolly viewers into thinking life is rosier than it is.

A federally funded project called "Getting On," for instance, is concerned over how the elderly are depicted on TV. It recently told network executives they should make a point of showing oldsters in "productive" situations. This despite the same organization's complaint that lack of productiveness is a real-life frustration that plagues most retired people.

We gather the idea is that viewers should be propagandized into thinking most elderly people are happily productive when in fact they aren't. It is felt that this will somehow bring about a desired change for the elderly.

Groups supporting other commendable goals — true equality for blacks and for women, for instance — seem to be making the same sort of pitch to TV: Show life as it ought to be and reality will grow to resemble its image on the tube.

One of these days Americans are going to have to make up their minds what they really want of television. Should it precisely reflect humdrum reality? Should it be used as a medium of wishful thinking in hopes that we'll learn to live life as we view it?

Or should we all relax a bit, impose only reasonable standards as regard violence, fairness and propriety, and let TV concentrate on entertaining us. Viewers do have the final veto on programming. They can switch to another channel — or turn the set off.

NEW YORK POST

New York, N.Y., August 20, 1977

The U. S. Civil Rights Commission has lost its grip on reality. It wants to impose racial and sexual quotas on the hiring of people who don't exist—the characters on TV's sitcoms and crime shows.

The commission was right on target in a recent report when it criticized hiring and promotion practices in the TV industry and warned scriptwriters and casting directors against racial or sexual stereotyping.

But the commission proposal that the remedy lies in FCC guidelines for the depiction of minorities and women on the TV drama shows is way out of focus. We are happy to see the FCC commissioners blow a tube at the prospect.

The idea amounts to turning our TV entertainment, by government fiat, into a form of agitprop pushing the image of what our society ought to be—but isn't.

It comes uncomfortably close to the unacceptable view that the media are outlets for a social policy determined by the state.

The Charlotte Observer

Charlotte, N.C., August 29, 1977

After the U.S. Civil Rights Commission last week chastised the major TV networks' treatment of women and minorities, the responses were pretty much what you'd expect. NBC complained of "broad-brush charges;" ABC talked about the "significant progress" it has made; Washington Post columnist Tom Shales called the report "extremism in the pursuit of fairness."

The networks have made progress in both programming and employment practices — the two areas the report dealt with. But the CRC's charges were not outlandish.

Both program characters and news people on TV are role models. If women and minorities are poorly represented or stereotyped, the implicit message is that they "may not matter," the report said. And there's no denying the fact that white males still dominate in both news and entertainment.

The broadcast industry points out that the CRC data was several years old; a lot has changed, they say. That's true, but one night of prime time TV is enough to show how far the networks have to go.

Despite a proliferation of shows about blacks, there's still a tendency to portray them as empty-headed jive-talkers. Women don't fare much better, often being restricted to earth mother or sexy cop roles.

Mr. Shales argues that too much concern over stereotyping is "a recipe for a boring universe of faultless ciphers." He's wrong. It's the recipe for a universe of real human beings. That's the group — regardless of sex, age or race — that's still the most underrepresented on television.

Richmond Times-Dispatch

Richmond, Va., August 21, 1977

Freedom of expression is one of the most sacred of all the rights American citizens enjoy, but it is not too sacred for civil rights fanatics to threaten. To them, it seems, egalitarianism is more important than freedom; and they do not mind mangling the Constitution to achieve their objectives.

This is evident from a report released this week by the United States Civil Rights Commission. Entitled "Window Dressing on the Set," the report, in effect, advocates federal censorship to force television networks to give minorities and women more numerous and more prominent roles in news and entertainment programs.

The commission complains that white males dominate the television screen. They appear in 65 per cent of all major and minor roles, they appear more frequently in serious roles and they fill most of the roles that call for characters of independence and distinction. White women, on the other hand, have about 23 per cent of all roles; and many of the characters they portray are comic, young, unemployed and extremely domestic. Minorities tend to appear in ethnic settings or in token roles, says the commission.

Minority and female news correspondents are rarely permitted to report crucial national stories, the commission says, and network television tends to give only "minimal coverage" to civil and women's rights topics. All this indicates to the commission that

women and minorities "may not matter" to television.

The report concludes, incredibly, that the Federal Communications Commission should be empowered to regulate network practices to alter these conditions. The Civil Rights Commission believes, in other words, that the federal government should forget constitutional guarantees of freedom of expression and review the script of every television show to make certain that women and blacks are acceptably cast in an acceptable number of roles. It believes, the First Amendment to the contrary notwithstanding, that the federal government should regulate the presentation and content of television news programs. For the sake of achieving racial and sexual balance on the screen, the commission would resort to the tactics of Hitler, Stalin and other tyrants who have tried to control the minds of men.

It is difficult to believe that such a tyrannical approach to the civil rights issue could be seriously proposed by a supposedly responsible group. The recommendation should be too preposterous for Congress even to consider; but it has done some strange things in the name of civil rights in recent years, and its reaction to this suggestion cannot be taken for granted. That some members of Congress might attempt to promote the commission's plan would be shocking, but it is not at all unthinkable.

THE ARIZONA REPUBLIC

Phoenix, Ariz., August 17, 1977

HARDLY anyone likes television except the 200 million Americans, give or take a handful, who spend countless hours watching it.

The intellectuals, the pundits, the bureaucrats are unanimous. Television, they agree, is responsible for every ailment that afflicts the nation, from juvenile delinquency to overweight and crimes of violence, from the fact that Johnny can't read to his sister Sally's cavities

Just name it. They can trace it back to TV.

And they all have the same remedy: Stricter control over television programming by the Federal Communications Commission.

We have now the Civil Rights Commission charging the networks with fostering sexual and racial stereotypes. In TV drama, laments the commission, white males dominate the screen, appearing in 65.3 per cent of all major and minor roles.

What appalls the commission even more is that white males appear more frequently in serious roles and portray older, more independent characters having diverse and prestigious occupations.

Naturally, the Civil Rights Commission wants the FCC to force the networks to rectify this situation.

We have news for the commissioners. White males dominate the TV screen because they dominate the nation. They have more diverse and more prestigious occupations on the screen because they have more diverse and more prestigious occupations in real life.

This may be unfortunate, it may be deplorable, but it's a fact.

If television depicted men and women and minorities in any other way, it would become even more divorced from reality than it already is.

Just imagine Kojack as a black woman, which apparently is what the Human Rights Commission wants.

True, the role of women and minorities in our society has been changing in recent years, but no one can accuse television of failing to reflect this. Maude is hardly the stereotype of a suburban housewife, whatever else she may be. Nor is Mrs. Romano in "One Day at a Time." She is a divorcee, bringing up two daughters by herself, and the job she holds is a reasonably prestigious one — advertising copywriter.

And if ever there was a liberated woman, it's Charley in "All's Fair." Incidentally, her middle-aged boy friend's assistant Al is a black, not precisely a stereotype either.

The Human Rights Commission seems to believe there should be more Maudes and more Mrs. Romanos and more Charleys on the air. If that is what the public wants, there will be more without the intervention of the FCC.

The networks are fiercely competitive. They are in a constant battle for ratings because a one point rise in the ratings can be worth a million dollars.

If the Human Rights Commission doesn't like their programming, that's just too bad. The public does. The commission and the FCC should leave the networks alone.

SUPREME COURT RULINGS:

Ban on "Dirty Words" Broadcasting Upheld

The Supreme Court ruled, 5-4, July 3 that the Federal Communications Commission could prohibit the broadcasting of language that was not legally obscene. The case was *FCC v. Pacifica Foundation.*

The case involved a portion of a record album by comedian George Carlin broadcast over the radio in 1973 by WBAI-FM, the New York City station of the Pacifica Foundation. In the 12-minute monologue, entitled "Filthy Words," Carlin discussed seven words "you couldn't say on the public airwaves . . . shit, piss, fuck, cunt, cocksucker, motherfucker and tits. Those are the ones that will curve your spine, grow hair on your hands and maybe bring us, God help us, peace without honor."

A motorist subsequently complained to the FCC that his young son had heard the broadcast, which had played at 2 p.m. The FCC reprimanded WBAI, though the agency indicated that the broadcast might have been permissible late at night, when children were less likely to be listening.

Pacifica challenged the reprimand in court, arguing that the FCC's action violated the First Amendment. The foundation claimed that the monologue was not legally obscene under constitutional interpretations. (The current legal doctrine said that material was obscene if it offended community standards and lacked "serious literary, artistic, political or scientific value.")

The station won its case in the U.S. Court of Appeals for the District of Columbia. The Supreme Court reversed the appeals court. Writing for the majority, Justice John Paul Stevens held that "patently offensive, indecent material presented over the airwaves confronts the citizen, not only in public, but also in the privacy of the home, where the individual's right to be let alone plainly outweighs the First Amendment rights of the intruder."

Stevens noted that the FCC was empowered by Congress to curb the broadcast of "obscene, indecent or profane language." The FCC, he said, was free to conclude that language was "indecent," even though it lacked "prurient appeal. . . . We hold simply that when the commission finds that a pig has entered the parlor, the exercise of its regulatory power doesn't depend on proof that the pig is obscene."

Stevens stressed that the majority was taking a narrow stand on the issue. He suggested that "an occasional expletive" broadcast over the airwaves would not justify FCC sanctions.

In dissent, Justice Potter Stewart backed the Pacifica argument that the Carlin monologue was not "obscene" in the legal sense of the word. Stewart was joined by Justices William J. Brennan Jr., Byron R. White and Thurgood Marshall."

Brennan and Marshall issued a separate dissent objecting to the majority's stand that broadcasts had only limited First Amendment protection because they went into the home. Brennan said that the stand permitted "majoritarian tastes" to dictate the content of broadcasts.

THE MILWAUKEE JOURNAL
Milwaukee, Wisc., July 7, 1978

The Supreme Court's 5 to 4 ruling in the George Carlin "dirty words" case ventured uncomfortably close to infringement on freedom of speech. The outcome of this case doesn't particularly bother us, but some of the court's reasoning does.

The issue arose when the Federal Communications Commission reprimanded a radio station for broadcasting a recording of comedian Carlin's controversial monolog that includes seven dirty words. A listener who had heard the afternoon broadcast while driving in his car with his son complained to the FCC.

The high court upheld FCC authority to prohibit the broadcast of obscene and indecent material. But it was not just that the seven words were indecent, Justice Stevens wrote for the court's majority. The crucial point was that they were broadcast at a time when children could reasonably be expected to be listening. The decision indicated that late night broadcast of the material would not have warranted FCC action.

"We have not decided that an occasional expletive . . . would justify any sanction . . ." Stevens said. "A nuisance may be merely a right thing in the wrong place — like a pig in the parlor instead of the barnyard."

Broadcasters long have been aware that they can get in trouble for airing obscene or indecent material. What the court has now done is to define "indecent," at least to the extent of these seven words.

But it also based its decision partly on the intrusiveness of radio, or what Stevens termed the "uniquely pervasive presence" of the broadcast media. Equating an offensive broadcast with an indecent phone call, Stevens also said: "Patently offensive, indecent material presented over the airwaves confronts the citizen, not only in public, but also in the privacy of the home, where the individual's right to be let alone plainly outweighs the First Amendment rights of an intruder."

There is a certain similarity between this ruling and state laws that reasonably prohibit outdoor theaters from showing sexually explicit films unless the movie screen is shielded from the theater's neighbors and passersby. We don't think government has any business regulating the content of films in closed theaters, where adults can freely choose to attend or stay away. But the outdoor sex film can intrude on unsuspecting and unwilling eyes unless it is shielded. Similarly, anybody who happens to tune into a radio or TV station is immediately bombarded with whatever a station is broadcasting.

But if there is an element of sense in this intrusiveness doctrine, there also is potential peril to free speech in its application to broadcast media. If the high court can use radio or television intrusiveness as justification for banning "indecent" language in the afternoon when children would likely be listening, where will it stop in some future case — at 6 p.m., midnight or when? And what other kinds of speech might the court someday find it permissible to curb because of the intrusiveness of broadcasting?

We are pleased that Stevens was so cautious in outlining the limits of the Carlin decision. But we are uneasy at the prospect of some future court using the intrusiveness theory to justify abhorrent forms of direct or indirect broadcast censorship.

The Seattle Times

Seattle, Wash., July 7, 1978

EVEN as Congress begins deliberating proposed deregulation of the broadcasting industry, the United States Supreme Court has handed down a 5-to-4 decision that reasserts government control over radio and television.

This week's ruling was in the context of a single episode — a New York radio station's broadcast of a George Carlin "comedy" album containing some indecent language — but its meaning appears to be much broader.

The court majority said the Federal Communications Commission, which holds licensing powers over radio and TV stations, has the authority to punish a station for airing offensive language.

The ruling was based, the opinion said, on broadcasting's "unique" characteristics, society's need to insulate children from "inappropriate speech," and the right of citizens of all ages to be protected from hearing offensive language against their will.

Within the narrow confines of the Carlin case, the court's reasoning doubtless was well received by many Americans concerned over the tastelessness of much broadcast fare these days.

But the decision has deeper implications for the government's role in regulating broadcast licensees. Until now, the rationale for licensing rested largely on technological grounds — that since the availability of radio and TV frequencies is not infinite, the public interest requires not only an equitable sharing of the airwaves, but their use in the "public interest, convenience and necessity."

Although government has no power to dictate program content, it has exercised control in other important ways, such as the "fairness doctrine" applying to the broadcast of controversial viewpoints. The result has been the oft-cited distinction between virtually unlimited free-speech guarantees to the printed press and the qualified freedom granted broadcasters.

On Capitol Hill, a bill introduced recently by California Representative Lionel Van Deerlin takes the position that new technology has rendered the old argument about the scarcity of airwaves obsolete; that licensees should be given almost unlimited tenure to their broadcast channels, and that there should be far fewer regulations, not more.

But this week's high-court decision has cast a cloud on the legislation by suggesting that there are other than technological reasons for perpetuating the limitations on broadcasters' free-speech rights. Thus, the prospect is for maintaining the status quo.

That is not a particularly happy prospect. The existing regulatory setup has inhibited the handling of legitimate news and public-affairs broadcasts, all the while seeming to promote lowest-common-denominator program offerings during most hours of the broadcast day.

The Washington Post

Washington, D.C., July 7, 1978

ALL HECK HAS BROKEN loose in the radio and television world this week as a result of the Supreme Court's decision Monday in the case involving seven naughty words. The outcome was unexpected. The court, according to many experts, had been regarded as almost certain to hold unconstitutional the warning the Federal Communications Commission had given a radio station for broadcasting a 12-minute-long monologue in which those bad words were used over and over again. But the justices didn't go according to form; they upheld the warning by a vote of 5 to 4. We are glad they did.

This is one of those cases that never should have reached either the Supreme Court or the FCC. The monologue—recorded in a California theater by comedian George Carlin—may be regarded as funny by some; the transcript indicates he was interrupted 83 times by laughter or applause. But its prime appeal is its shock value. (Mr. Carlin used, on the average, one of his self-styled "filthy words" every 10 seconds during those 12 minutes.) Even as part of a program about society's attitude toward language—which is the way the station owner, Pacifica Foundation, described its use—the monologue did not belong on the air, as a matter of policy, in mid-afternoon.

As the court handled the case, the issue is quite narrow. It does not involve the power of the FCC to control the content of radio and television programs. Nor does it involve the power of that agency to censor scripts or prohibit the use at any time of certain words. All it involves is the right of the FCC to warn a broadcaster that it may have trouble getting its license renewed if it deliberately broadcasts a "patently offensive" program at 2 p.m. The time is important. The court made clear that it was not ruling on a broadcast of the same program at 2 a.m., when children, presumably, would not be a potential part of the audience.

Broadcasters had hoped to win in this case a ruling that their First Amendment rights are identical to those of the print media and of public speakers and entertainers. In other words, they sought the right to put on the air at any time any words or pictures that are not obscene. The court rejected that view, noting that broadcasting has "the most limited First Amendment protection" of all the forms of communication. Of the reasons for that distinction, it set out two as relevant to this case: the easy accessibility of children to radio and television programs, and the pervasive presence of those programs in homes where the audience tunes in and out and may be entitled to protection against indecent as well as obscene material.

The immediate reaction of some broadcasting officials and critics is that this decision opens the way for substantial censorship by the FCC and gives station managers an excuse for suppressing realistic news and dramas that pull no punches in their substance or language. The tone of the opinions of Justices John Paul Stevens and Lewis F. Powell seem to suggest just the opposite. Neither suggests that the FCC should require that the occasional dirty word be bleeped out or that programming should always be aimed only at family audiences. Implicit in both opinions is the suggestion that if broadcasters target their audiences (late evenings or, in cable systems, special channels), the permissible range of words and pictures may be much broader than that presented on most stations today. Justice Stevens, in treating the Carlin monologue in part as a nuisance, noted that the court once defined a nuisance as something that "may be merely a right thing in the wrong place."

AKRON BEACON JOURNAL
Akron, Ohio, July 8, 1978

THE SUPREME Court's ruling that the government has the power to bar broadcasting of "patently offensive" words opens again the whole perplexing question of what makes sense when law undertakes to deal with questions of taste or morality.

The court upheld the power of the Federal Communications Commission to reprimand New York radio station WBAI-FM for broadcasting "patently offensive reference to excretory and sexual organs and activities" and to prohibit any repetition of this.

But defining "patently offensive" in some objective way that could be disputed by none is an impossibility.

What is regarded as patently offensive by everybody at one house may be judged normal and acceptable by everybody at another.

There is also a "generation problem": Much once regarded as unprintable in a family newspaper, for example, now commonly appears in this and many other newspapers.

Consider the candor with which incest, homosexuality and venereal disease, for instance, are now discussed in print; all were once taboo in papers of general circulation.

What is controlling here is a judgment as to what the abstract "average reader" views as acceptable at a given time; the sanction is possible loss of readers. The sanction in broadcasting has sharper teeth: The broadcaster who misjudges what the FCC will tolerate risks loss of his license.

Broadcasters learned this much from the decision: It's an error, at least at hours when children are likely to be listening, to air seven words not listed in the news reports on the ruling. They were recited in the George Carlin album WBAI was censured for playing.

The album called them words "that will curve your spine, grow hair on your hands and maybe even bring us, God help us, peace without honor." Few broadcasters will have much trouble identifying the words.

But in a dissent, Justice William Brennan put his finger on the central and unsolvable problem in this and every other case of its kind.

"In our land of cultural pluralism," he wrote, "there are many who think, act and talk differently from members of this Court, and who do not share their fragile sensibilities."

The majority reasoning, he said, could justify banning works by Shakespeare and Chaucer, or parts of the Bible or the Watergate tapes.

Granting that gross deviation from "usual" standards can be an embarrassing and irritating nuisance to most of us, the uneasy feeling continues that the law would do better to get out of this area altogether and let the public control such behavior in commerce by acceptance or rejection.

Oregon Journal

Portland, Ore., July 6, 1978

The U.S. Supreme Court contains five justices who ignore the fact this nation is made up of many tastes and cultures. Out of that ignorance the court has upheld federal authority to censor broadcast media in the United States.

The court ruled 5-4 this week that the Federal Communications may ban certain "filthy" words from the airwaves at certain times during the day in order to protect children from exposure.

Implicit in the banning authority the FCC carries is the ability of the agency to fine a station or revoke its license for violating its ban on words it deems "indecent."

That general society claims to avoid these words in everyday talk ignores the fact that certain taboo words are current in the vocabularies of millions of people, young and old, of varying strata of society.

The broadcast media in this country, luckily for us, are becoming increasingly responsive to the divergent tastes of the public. In Portland, for example, one can tune into a diet of the sort of music one hears in elevators and supermarkets, or to stations which prefer the avant-garde in music, poetry and political discussions.

There is no one rule that can be or should be imposed to try to control language. Words are powerful, but their energy varies according to the way they are used — and they way they are received.

This newspaper's editors, for example, would not in most cases consider printing any of the seven words the Supreme Court discussed in its broadcast ruling. The idea of discussing words and their impact but not referring to them directly may be absurd, but such is the societal taboo that surrounds them.

The point is, the high court has upheld the right of a government agency to listen to the broadcasters, issue condemnations, fines and other roadblocks which amount to harassment of free expression, all in the name of government-ordered good taste.

That sort of activity in itself is distasteful.

THE BLADE

Toledo, Ohio, July 14, 1978

THERE seems to be quite a run on the First Amendment this summer, the latest incident arising over the efforts of the Federal Communications Commission to oversee the interests of children who might be offended by profane words broadcast during prime time.

The Supreme Court has said it would be proper for the FCC to warn a New York radio station that use of vulgar words familiar to most adults — to say nothing of their children — during periods of time when the youngsters might be listening could affect its license at renewal time.

The station had broadcast a 12-minute monologue by comedian George Carlin at 2 o'clock in the afternoon which made repeated use of seven "filthy words," presumably in an effort to ridicule Americans' sensitivities about the public use of them. As a night club act, of course, the monologue might be quite acceptable; one does not go to such establishments to hear a sermon on the Golden Rule.

Broadcasting is something else again. It comes into American living rooms as an invited or tolerated guest, and ordinarily behaves as polite guests do. The same is true, although perhaps to a lesser degree, of a general-circulation newspaper or magazine. (And, of course, there is no FCC which regulates print media.) But the communicator in either print or broadcasting is conscious of the diverse audience served, and makes judgments about taste accordingly.

The Supreme Court held in its decision — a narrow one which attempted to avoid First Amendment complications — that the FCC was not going beyond the scope of its authority by warning the station about the use of the seven dirty words. But Justice Stevens suggested that some profanity in, say, a literary context was permissible, and that even the more open use of vulgar or profane expressions might be used at an hour when children are not listening — if, he might have added, there is such an hour. The high court agreed with a lower court opinion that a flat ban by the FCC on the use of such expressions was unconstitutional.

Our view is that the FCC ought not to be a censor, that matters of taste are best decided by the broadcasting station involved, that at certain times and under certain circumstances stations ought to be able to cater to more adult tastes, and that in any case the listener is free to change stations or turn the blamed thing off.

But so far as we know, few, if any, of the newspapers which expressed doubt over the FCC's jurisdiction in such matters saw fit to repeat the seven dirty expressions, even though editors know that most of their readers know them and many even use them on occasion. This is, in itself, a commentary on the case. Moreover, the situation just does not seem to call for reprinting these terms, unlike the incident involving former Agriculture Secretary Earl Butz. In that case, his vulgar joke resulted in his departure from high office and had ramifications for the presidential election campaign then in progress. The Blade and some other newspapers published Mr. Butz's comment.

There is no free-speech issue really involved in this case; the words used by Mr. Carlin are readily available in other forms, and they contribute nothing to public dialogue. Nor does it seem that the First Amendment right of freedom of speech or of the press will be harmed if a radio station exercises some discretion about when, if ever, it broadcasts profanity in whatever context it might be used. Many people who use profanity on occasion do not care to be surrounded by it, any more than a farmer, inured to the smell of the stable, cares to have a reminder of it in his living room.

Richmond Times-Dispatch

Richmond, Va., July 10, 1978

The line against vulgar and indecent material on the airways must be drawn somewhere, and the U.S. Supreme Court properly drew it in an opinion last Monday.

Comedian George Carlin delivered a 12-minute monologue entitled "Filthy Words" before an audience in a California theater. Subsequently, at 2 o'clock in the afternoon one day, a New York radio station broadcast a recording of the monologue. A "filthy word" was heard on the average of once every 10 seconds, the repetition obviously being intended for shock value.

The Federal Communications Commission issued a warning to the station against what it termed a "patently offensive" broadcast. In later statements, the FCC explained that it never intended to place an absolute prohibition on the kind of language at issue "but rather sought to channel it to times of day when children most likely would not be exposed to it."

A federal appeals court rejected as invalid the FCC's action in the case; but last Monday, by a 5-to-4 vote, the Supreme Court upheld the agency. The majority opinion pointed out that laws make distinctions between print and broadcast media as far as First Amendment free speech and free press rights are concerned, explaining:

"Patently offensive, indecent material presented over the airwaves confronts the citizen, not only in public, but also in the privacy of the home, where the individual's right to be let alone plainly outweighs the First Amendment rights of an intruder. Because the broadcast audience is constantly tuning in and out, prior warnings cannot completely protect the listener or viewer from unexpected program content. To say that one may avoid further offense by turning off the radio when he hears indecent language is like saying that the remedy for an assault is to run away after the first blow. . . . Broadcasting is uniquely accessible to children, even those too young to read."

The Supreme Court's two most liberal members, Justices William J. Brennan Jr. and Thurgood Marshall, complained in a dissenting opinion that the court's decision "really is another of the dominant culture's inevitable efforts to force those groups who do not share its mores to conform to its way of thinking, acting and speaking." Most Americans, we believe, disagree with that view and look upon the decision as representing a reasonable approach to the problem of keeping highly offensive material off the air during periods when many children may be exposed to it.

Chicago Tribune

Chicago, Ill., July 10, 1978

The "Filthy Words" case [Federal Communications Commission vs. Pacifica Foundation et al.] was and will remain a close call. Close—and we believe, wrong.

A father, driving with his young son, tuned in to an afternoon radio broadcast that moved him to complain to the FCC. The FCC investigated, sided with the complainant, and put notice of that fact in the station's file, to be considered with other material at license renewal time. By a 2 to 1 vote, a Court of Appeals reversed the FCC. Now, by a 5 to 4 vote, the Supreme Court has reversed the Appellate Court. Close.

Justice John Paul Stevens, writing for the majority, began by saying, "This case requires that we decide whether the FCC has any power to regulate a radio broadcast that is indecent but not obscene." All the justices agree that the broadcast in question lacked the appeal to prurient interest essential to obscenity. The "satiric humorist" in question, George Carlin, had a respectable point—that prevailing attitudes towards "filthy words" are silly. But in making his point he repeatedly used words that are generally taboo.

Of the four different opinions written on this difficult case, that in dissent by Justice William J. Brennan Jr. is the one we find most convincing. He wrote, "I would place the responsibility and right to weed worthless and offensive communications from the public airways where it belongs and where, until today, it resided: in a public free to choose those communications worthy of its attention from a marketplace unsullied by the censor's hand. . . . It is only an acute ethnocentric myopia that enables the court to approve the censorship of communications solely because of the words they contain."

The majority would disclaim "censorship." They carefully point out the difference between prior censorship and penalties imposed after the event. They contend that government may discipline "the public broadcast of indecent language," and that it appropriately exercised its power in the present instance.

We have said in these columns that obscenity is not covered by the protections of the First Amendment. But for the government to go beyond obscenity and to penalize what the court calls merely "indecent language" is to threaten freedom of speech.

A transcript of the "Filthy Words" broadcast accompanies the majority opinion. The Tribune agrees with the FCC and the Supreme Court majority in finding the broadcast offensive, unworthy of the applause and laughter it elicited from the live audience present at its recording. We also agree that it lacks prurient appeal. As has been said before, the effect is more emetic than erotic.

But there are other and better ways to chide poor taste on the part of a radio station's management than for the FCC to take disciplinary action. The marketplace of speech and thought should feel the heavy hand of government as little as possible. Invasion of domestic privacy by vulgar language can be minimized by turning a knob on the radio. The best way to minimize the exposure of unsupervised children to inappropriate broadcasting is to supervise the children. Neither defense can be total, but some slippage on both counts is less dangerous and damaging than chipping away at the First Amendment.

WORCESTER TELEGRAM.

Worcester, Mass., July 8, 1978

The U.S. Supreme Court's 5-to-4 ruling on the "seven dirty words" looks like more trouble down the line for freedom of speech in this country.

The case involved a program broadcast in 1973 by New York City radio station WBAI featuring the seven dirty words as part of a series on "societal attitudes toward language." When a listener objected, the Federal Communications Commission told the owner of the station that it "could have been the subject of administrative sanctions." Although the FCC did not impose any sanctions, the threat was obvious. The station took the case to court. It eventually wound up before the Supreme Court which decided that the FCC had not exceeded its constitutional authority.

In speaking for the majority, Justice John Paul Stevens went to great lengths to point out the narrow grounds on which the ruling was based. It "rested entirely on the nuisance rationale in which context is all-important," he said. He took into account "a host of variables," including the time of day when the words were broadcast (2 p.m.), and the composition of the audience.

Stevens quoted the late Justice George Sutherland, who wrote that a "nuisance may be merely a right thing in the wrong place — like a pig in a parlor instead of a barnyard." Stevens indicated that the seven dirty words, at other times and in other contexts, would be beyond the FCC's jurisdiction.

Nonetheless, the decision is worrisome. The National Association of Broadcasters calls it "a harsh blow to the freedom of expression of every person in this country." The three television networks and the Motion Picture Association of America were aligned in opposition.

Writing in The Washington Post, Tom Shales says the First Amendment "is being trampled." He says that "the Supreme Court has given managements and owners of TV and radio stations terrific new ammunition to use against reporters, news directors, producers and writers who want to put potentially explosive or controversial material on the air."

Shales may be exaggerating. It is clear from the Stevens decision that the Supreme Court did not intend to endorse Grundyism.

The use of dirty words for no purpose is offensive to most people. However, it is better to let them use their freedom to switch to another channel than it is to give a bunch of political appointees even implied censorship rights over TV and radio programming.

The important thing to keep in mind is the narrowness of the decision's application, as stated by Justice Stevens. Perhaps the damage can be contained short of the First Amendment.

ST. LOUIS POST-DISPATCH

St. Louis, Mo., July 6, 1978

Thank heavens — or at least the U.S. Supreme Court. It's about time some radio and television personalities had their filthy mouths washed.

That's exactly what a majority of the justices did in ruling that constitutional guarantees could not be stretched and twisted to protect four-letter words blaring out of radio and TV speakers.

The issue revolved around the warped sense of humor of comedian George Carlin, who delivered a monologue, "Filthy Words," on a New York radio station. The top court upheld a ruling of the Federal Communications Commission condemning the station for the broadcast.

The decision restores a degree of sanctity to the home — at least in the daylight hours because the court insisted on limiting its ruling to the specific broadcast, which was transmitted in the afternoon.

The majority held government may constitutionally bar use of certain words because radio broadcasts are "uniquely accessible to children" and intrude into the privacy of people's homes.

A dirty-mouthed personality is unwelcome in decent households. He has no more legal right to barge in and intrude with his vulgarity than a law enforcement officer has to break down a door to examine the premises without a search warrant. Unfortunately, the court didn't go far enough. It should have jammed such filthy performances by banning them both day and night.

Arkansas Gazette.

Little Rock, Ark., July 6, 1978

Justice John Paul Stevens's ruling on George Carlin's "seven dirty words" not only was erosive of the First Amendment guarantee of freedom of expression and, therefore, wrong in our judgment, it contained one built-in "analogy" that was enough to reduce the adjective, "analogous," to utter meaninglessness if not outright gibberish.

Justice Stevens wrote and apparently really believes that hearing a "patently offensive" word on a radio broadcast that you have deliberately exposed yourself to is no different from receiving an unsolicited dirty telephone call from a talker (though not, one would gather, from a mere "breather.") Four other members of the Court joined in the majority opinion in the Carlin Case.

To extend his supposed analogy into the farther realms of ludicrousness, Justice Stevens wrote that the "patently offensive, indecent, material presented over the airwaves confronts the citizen, not only in public, but also in the privacy of the home, where the individual's *right to be let alone* (our italics) plainly outweighs the First Amendment rights of an intruder."

The right to be let alone in the privacy of the home rests in self-control of the off-and-on switch. There it rests and there alone, since there are, so far as we know, no break-in artists who specialize in going into the home to tune in to material that potentially may be "offensive" to householders thus held captive against their will.

Justice Stevens's opinion thus makes as good law as it does logic, and vice-versa.

George Carlin is one of those comedians who feel psychologically naked when they are deprived of their blue material, and says he was using the seven words in question with intent to shock, all right, but also with the intent of trying to show that words in themselves are *not* all or any one of the things that the Supreme Court was to rule later that they were.

We rather hate to say it, but we fear that Mr. Carlin's reiterated rationale after the fact of the Court's ruling made a great deal more sense than the rationale of Justice Stevens's majority opinion.

"Should these words have this power over us?," he asked rhetorically. "I feel the words themselves are not harmful. They're not immoral, they're not indecent." This, in a way, was a kind of restatement in radio-TV terms of Mayor Jimmie Walker's classic observation that he had never known a woman who had been raped by a book.

But if Carlin's post-mortem made more sense than Justice Stevens's justification for his far-reaching assault on the First Amendment, it did not make any more sense than the opinion of Justice William J. Brennan, in dissent, which amounted to a kind of classic re-enunciation of what the First Amendment is all about, offering as it did the case for freedom of thought and of speech. The Court majority, he said, had shown "a depressing inability to appreciate that in our land of cultural pluralism, there are many who think, act and talk differently from members of this Court and who do not share their fragile sensibilities."

Then on to the obvious argument that the same test laid down by the majority on the Court in this case could be used to justify the banning from the radio of works by Shakespeare and Chaucer, as well as of portions of the Bible or the Watergate tapes. (Now, there's an item that's *really* dirty, the Watergate Tapes, cut by you know whom.) Could be used, and no doubt will be, if not by the volunteer censors who are everywhere, then by nervous broadcasters made even more nervous by the Carlin ruling.

Justice Stevens's opinion was such a dandy that it also included a passage extending the "daylight hours" tabu imposed by the FCC at first instance on material that may fall upon the ears of babes into the "late night hours," when the airing of the Carlin broadcast might be permissible. This is familiar ground, indeed, though not usually in a Supreme Court ruling, and we suppose some future Court will finally have to pick an exact cut-on hour for the adults (here we would get into the problem of clear-channel stations cutting across differing time zones); that is, if the present Court doesn't get around to *that*, too, once it really gets warmed up.

Finally, one further note on the language used in the majority opinion. Justice Stevens also wrote that an "occasional" expletive might be permissible, presumably at any broadcasting hour. Just *how* occasional? We mean, at what intervals of time? We need some more specific guidelines in these matters.

The Detroit News

Detroit, Mich., July 9, 1978

Concerned as we are with the right of free speech, we fail to detect any serious threat to the First Amendment from the U.S. Supreme Court's ruling in the case of the seven dirty words. Nothing in the Constitution protects the indiscriminate broadcasting of filth for filth's sake.

The case in question stemmed from a New York City radio station's afternoon airing of a George Carlin comedy routine, "Filthy Words," which deliberately exploited the shock value of offensive slang words that describe sexual and excretory organs and activities.

A father, disturbed because his young son heard the broadcast, complained to the FCC, which properly reprimanded the station and told it to quit broadcasting foul language — specifically, those seven words — at times of day when children listen. The Supreme Court upheld the order. Hysteria ensued.

Dissenting, Justice William J. Brennan said the ruling could justify banning Shakespeare, Chaucer and the Bible from radio. Vincent T. Wasilewski, president of the National Association of Broadcasters, called the ruling "a harsh blow to the freedom of expression of everybody in this country." Nonsense.

In the first place, expletives were incidental to the dramatic and literary purposes of Shakespeare, Chaucer and the Bible. Sensibly, the Supreme Court distinguished between occasional expletives and a massive assault such as Carlin's upon the sensibilities. In his majority opinion, Justice John Paul Stevens observed: "This case does not involve two-way radio conversation between a cab driver and a dispatcher, or a telecast of an Elizabethan comedy."

Naturally, the child's mind must not serve as the denominator for radio and TV programing. (If it did, George Carlin's routines, minus the seven filthy words, might dominate the media.) Nor does the court's decision establish such a standard. Justice Stevens confined his opinion to the narrow issue of Carlin's broadcast and even suggested that such a broadcast might be acceptable at night rather than in the afternoon.

However, he made it clear that the broadcast media, because of their "uniquely pervasive presence in the lives of all Americans," must observe certain restraints. The restraint imposed in this case seems neither harsh nor unreasonable. In the court's words, the FCC found that a pig had entered the parlor. Extending the figure of speech, we observe that the integrity of the First Amendment does not hinge on making the pig comfortable on the sofa.

The Philadelphia Inquirer

Philadelphia, Pa., July 13, 1978

On a Tuesday afternoon, five years ago, a New York man and his son were driving in a car listening to the radio when on to the air came a record entitled "Filthy Words" by satirist George Carlin. The gist of Mr. Carlin's monolgue was that there are seven words that are not said on the radio. Then, of course, he said them — again and again.

Whether the father immediately turned off the radio at the sound of the first word or whether he listened to the entire 12-minute monologue is unknown. What is known is that he thought the broadcast was inappropriate and told the Federal Communications Commission as much. Pacifica Foundation, which owns the radio station and whose forte is unconventional but serious programing, considered the Carlin routine a commentary on society's attitude toward language. The FCC thought otherwise and warned Pacifica that it might lose its license if it persisted in broadcasting what the FCC considered offensive programs during the afternoon hours.

With one thing leading to another, Mr. Carlin's filthy words finally reached the ears of the justices of the U.S. Supreme Court. Most knowledgeable observers expected the court to remind the FCC about the First Amendment and, perhaps, remind the father that he can always turn to another station. Instead, a divided court handed down a 22-page opinion last week that poses far greater dangers than Mr. Carlin's seven filthy words.

Although the court admitted that Mr. Carlin's dialogue did not fall under the definition of obscenity, which has been held to be subject to government control, the majority,

nonetheless, said the FCC had the power to regulate a broadcast that is indecent, though not obscene. Justice John Paul Stevens, who wrote the majority decision, said the court simply was trying to protect children and went to great pains to emphasize the narrowness of the ruling by noting that the broadcast was at a time when children would most likely hear it and, secondly, that Mr. Carlin's routine was intended for shock value.

With the Supreme Court having failed miserably in its attempt to navigate the muddy waters of obscenity, it's a wonder that it ventured into a new quagmire. If a broadcast is inappropriate in the afternoon at 2 o'clock, or what about in the early evening, say, at 7? Or what about 10 p.m.? Or is the clock moved back in the summer when children stay up later? Or on weekends? And at what age are children no longer considered children — 15, 16, 18? And if Mr. Carlin's "Filthy Words" are indecent, how about Richard Nixon's Watergate tapes, which contain the same words — and then some — and has a message far more offensive to America's ideals?

With family programs as endangered as the snail darter and with each generation seeming to lose its innocence earlier than the previous one, many parents might welcome having a governmental bureacracy — the FCC — protect everyone's sensibilities. However, for the sake of personal freedom, it would be far better if the government kept its hands off the selection knob and parents exercised their responsibility to decide what is proper for their children to see, hear or read.

As Justice William Brennan said in

a blistering dissent, not everyone blushes at the same words as might the court's majority or the FCC. "Yet there runs throughout the opinions . . . another vein which I find equally disturbing: a depressing inability to appreciate that in our land of cultural pluralism, there are many who think, act, and talk differently from the Members of this Court, and who do not share their fragile sensibilities. . . . In this context," Justice Brennan continued, "the Court's decision may be seen for what, in the broader perspective, it really is: another of the dominant culture's inevitable efforts to force those groups who do not share its mores to conform to its way of thinking, acting and speaking."

Indeed, the most pressing problem in broadcasting today is not the occasional George Carlin-type routines that are aired at inappropriate times, but the timidity of broadcasters to present a diversity of provocative and stimulating programs. Ironically, only a few days before the court's decision Philadelphia viewers were denied an opportunity to see a powerful documentary on juvenile delinquency. Although the program, which was produced by the American Broadcasting Company and shown elsewhere, received rave reviews and was scheduled for 10 p.m., WPVI-TV (Channel 6), the local affiliate, refused to air it, contending that it contained language that might be offensive.

As that incident indicates, broadcasters need no legal prodding from the Supreme Court to avoid controversy. That practice comes quite naturally to them already and, frankly, is more offensive than George Carlin's seven naughty words.

THE CHRISTIAN SCIENCE MONITOR

Boston, Mass., July 7, 1978

A father was riding with his son one afternoon when they heard on the car radio some words Dad considered unfit for the child's ears. It is hard to wash out the mouth of an FM station with soap. Instead, the man complained to the FCC (Federal Communications Commission). Now the Supreme Court has upheld the FCC's ensuing reprimand to the station and affirmed that the government may ban certain words from the air in certain contexts.

Whatever the legal questions raised by the decision, here is an example of the effect one aroused citizen can have. If American listeners and viewers want to keep themselves from being subjected to what the offending program itself called "filthy words," they must let broadcasters know they care.

One way is through selective dialing. But there is the practical problem of not always knowing in advance what should have been tuned out. The court majority seemed to recognize such matters by describing the broadcast media's "uniquely pervasive presence in the lives of all Americans."

Unless one is to deny that this presence has any potential constructive effects, its potential destructive effects cannot be denied either. And contributing to the debasement of language through unchecked vulgarity is a sad alternative to broadcasting's possibilities for enhancing language and the thought it expresses.

However, the responsibility for maintaining standards should not be left to the government in the case of the broadcast media any more than it should in the case of books or the printed press. It is broadcasters, publishers, and editors who should not be let off the hook by the public.

Legal doubts about the decision are indicated by the unusual circumstance that the Justice Department did not support the FCC before the Supreme Court but came down on the side that the FCC order in question violated the First Amendment. The court majority stressed the narrowness of its ruling in favor of the FCC. But dissenters rightly warned of the possible unintended inhibiting effects on airing political speech, for example, or classic drama.

Government control of what words broadcasters permit on the air is not the answer. Self-control is — helped along by individuals willing to talk back.

Roanoke Times & World-News

Roanoke, Va., July 2, 1978

The U.S. Supreme Court, which has tied itself in knots trying to determine the permissible bounds of obscenity, had almost as much trouble the other day with a question of indecency. The court split 5-4, but the majority agreed that — First Amendment notwithstanding — the government can prohibit radio broadcasting of "patently offensive" words.

Just about everybody, especially in these times, knows what those words are. They refer mainly to sexual and excretory functions. Comedian George Carlin narrowed the list of the most offensive terms to seven, which he incorporated into a comedy routine (with, it should be noted, a serious message). His recorded act was played during daytime hours in 1973 over WBAI-FM in New York City, which prompted a rebuke from the Federal Communications Commission (FCC) — and led to the court case at hand.

There is no question that, in law, the government has control over radio (and television) that it does not have over printed media. To prevent the chaos of stations sending out signals on the same frequencies in the same cities, Uncle Sam assigns broadcasting rights.

Wisely, government regulators have not tried to dictate program content. But from the beginning, they have set standards — of public service as well as decency — that station operators must meet or risk loss of license. The airwaves, it is reasoned, belong to the public, and — in contrast to the quantity of printing presses that could be set up — there are limits to the number of stations that can use the air.

As a practical matter, though, economics dictates more limits than does

physics. Use of higher frequencies, both in radio and TV, has made the broadcasting spectrum wide enough to take all comers. It is much less expensive, in most cases, to open a station than to start up a newspaper.

So regulation no longer turns upon the issue of plentiful printing presses vs. scarce airwaves. Ruling on the "Seven Dirty Words" case, the Supreme Court rested instead on what Associate Justice John Paul Stevens called the broadcast's "uniquely pervasive presence in the lives of all Americans." In effect, it invades the home and individual privacy in a way that printed publications do not; therefore, the citizen has a right to be protected from "patently offensive, indecent material" that might be projected through the walls of his house, into the lap of his family.

Well, it is a narrow call; as close as the 5-4 vote of the high court. This newspaper will not attempt to sermonize. Things are printed on its pages nowadays that offend people who used to depend upon certain protections from a family newspaper. And the idea of censorship, or retaliation, bothers us.

Still, we think the FCC probably was within bounds in rebuking WBAI-FM. Spoken, the four-letter word carries more emotion and more potential for offense. Broadcast, it bursts into the home unbidden, almost in the manner of the obscene telephone call (which no one has said should have First Amendment rights). The citizen ought to have a few more protections against that kind of intrusion than taking out his telephone — or doing without a radio or TV set.

Denver, Colo., July 9, 1978

IN A RULING with which we strongly agree, the Supreme Court has upheld the Federal Communications Commission's right to limit radio broadcasting of indecent words that fall short of being legally obscene.

The 5-4 decision came in what has become known as the "seven dirty words case." The words were gingerly described by the high court as "patently offensive reference to excretory and sexual organs and activities."

Their repeated use formed the basis for a record by comedian George Carlin, which was broadcast by a New York City station in 1973. A man who heard the broadcast on a car radio with his young son complained to the FCC.

After investigation, the commission reprimanded the station for playing the record at 2 p.m. It quite reasonably issued an order against broadcasting indecent language at times of the day when children are in the audience.

Justice John Paul Stevens, writing for the majority, rejected claims that the FCC had violated the First Amendment right of free speech. He aptly compared the offensive broadcast with an obscene phone call, which is not legal.

"Patently offensive, indecent material presented over the airwaves," Stevens wrote, "confronts the citizen . . . in the privacy of the home, where the individual's right to be let alone plainly outweighs the First Amendment rights of an intruder."

The court carefully stressed that it was not ruling out "an occasional expletive" on the airwaves. In addition, it suggested that the Carlin recording might be acceptable if broadcast late at night rather than in midafternoon.

Nevertheless, the National Association of Broadcasters decried the decision as "a harsh blow to the freedom of expression of every person in this country." It claimed to fear that the FCC "will not stop with the seven dirty words."

The NAB is misguided. The commission has no desire to censor program content. But if broadcasters are permitted complete license, some will seek audiences with obscenity, as they have with sex and violence.

AND UNRESTRAINED FILTH on the air will bring irresistible public demands for government censorship. The broadcasters apparently don't know when they are well-off.

Justice Stevens correctly described the Carlin broadcast as a nuisance in the context in which it took place. He recalled that Justice George Sutherland had written in 1926 that "a nuisance may be merely a right thing in the wrong place — like a pig in the parlor instead of the barnyard."

"We simply hold," Stevens wrote, "that when the (FCC) finds that a pig has entered the parlor, the exercise of its regulatory power does not depend on proof that the pig is obscene."

Exactly. Let us keep pigs out of people's parlors and preserve broadcasting for a nobler role than instantly providing children with a gutter vocabulary.

ALBUQUERQUE JOURNAL

Albuquerque, N.M., July 7, 1978

Millions of American parents will be gratified by the U.S. Supreme Court's ruling that the Federal Communications Commission has a valid authority to ban the broadcast of "filthy words" during hours when children are likely to be listening.

And the nation's editors and civil rights advocates will find some consolation that two overlapping opinions went to great length to resolve the issue on grounds not to be confused with the constitutional guarantee of free speech. One of the two concurring opinions emphasized, instead, society's right to protect children from "inappropriate" speech and the interest of unwilling adults in "not being assaulted" with offensive speech in their homes.

Justice John Paul Stevens, to guard against broad applications of his opinion to situations not involving children or unwilling adults, emphasized that the court was not considering "a two-way radio conversation between a cab driver and a dispatcher, or a telecast of an Elizabethan comedy."

"We have not decided that an occasional expletive in either setting would justify any sanctions or, indeed that this broadcast (a recording of comedian George Carlin's "Seven Filthy Words") would justify a criminal prosecution," Justice Stevens emphasized.

DAYTON DAILY NEWS

Dayton, Ohio, July 6, 1978

With its decision that the Federal Communications Commission can scold radio stations that talk dirty, the Supreme Court confirmed the point of the recorded comic routine whose broadcast set off this case: That certain words — seven, in the routine — exert irrational power over us.

But the court's ruling does not, as the author/comedian George Carlin said, diminish the First Amendment. It leaves the amendment just as bothered as ever, but no more bothered than before, with the issue of broadcast "obscenity."

In this instance, no claim can be made that the "obscenity" would incite dangerous sexual behavior (the case often made, though contrary to the evidence, against pornography). The charge against the broadcast was simply that the words are still so offensive to many persons that the imposing powers of federal regulation and Supreme Court case law can be commanded to silence them, even when they are used to make a legitimate point.

This leaves broadcasting uniquely picked on under the First Amendment. Newspapers might cut their own circulation throats by reprinting Carlin's routine, but there would never be any serious argument that they could be forbidden by law from doing so.

How, then, is a society in which broadcast words and images play increasing informational and aesthetic roles ever to win anything like the freedoms for its electronic media that it traditionally has asserted for its printed word?

There is probably a way, if the bluenoses and the blue-minded will compromise. Utterance freely available from the atmosphere can be regulated, without serious menace to liberty, to a more civil standard than other broadcasts. That would free closed-circuit programs and special channels in cable TV and radio systems. Those require the recipient to make personal effort for the message, by subscribing to cable or plunking down money for pay-TV programs.

This is less than perfect freedom, but in updated form it would reflect the familiar distinction between the family parlor — or night club — and the public park.

The Kansas City Times

Kansas City, Mo., July 15, 1978

The licensing power of the Federal Communications Commission, established only in 1934, will continue to collide with the First Amendment guaranteeing freedom of speech and of the press as channels of communication proliferate with technological advances. The regulatory power of the FCC is based on the concept of the "public air" and the obvious need for order to prevent overlapping and blurred broadcasts. Along with the concept, however, has come a standard of "public interest," a necessarily subjective concern for the commission.

Now the Supreme Court has said that the FCC may restrict the use of "indecent" language over the air. The court stuck to the traditional view that prior restraint (censorship) is not permissible, but that the use of "dirty words" (seven of them referring to sexual and excretory matters) could bring subsequent punishment.

This is one of the most difficult areas into which the court ever ventures and satisfactory definitions never have been determined, let alone categories of obscenity for which there is general agreement. The court gets lost in rambling discussions of "dominant prurient interest," "community standards," "redeeming social value" and "pandering to prurient

ence." Obviously, all these terms are variously defined by the multitudes. What is obscene to one person is mildly amusing to another. Standards change. Once the court was all torn up over D.H. Lawrence and "Lady Chatterley's Lover," and James Joyce's "Ulysses." Mark Twain, Boccaccio and Flaubert have been banned in various communities. Movies once were removed from theaters because the soundtrack contained such words as "pregnant" or talked of birth control. Other films were suppressed by boards who considered them sacrilegeous. The world never lacks for people who want the power to decide what everybody else may see or read or say.

Ideally there should be no restrictions on the freedom of speech outside the usual prohibitions against libel, slander, incitement to violence and the like, and even these often involve difficult borderline cases. Yet who wants an unbridled outpouring of expletives from a television or radio speaker, turning the air blue in the presence of children and family gatherings? Practically, there must be restraints. The question always is how and where, and there probably will never be a universal rule. Whether the power to punish ought to be turned over to the FCC is debatable. It is an easy but not very satisfactory way out.

ST. LOUIS POST-DISPATCH

St. Louis, Mo., July 6, 1978

In a case involving seven words, the Supreme Court has split government censorship in two—still in favor of censorship. With a 5-4 ruling, the court has held that the Federal Communications Commission cannot censor broadcasts in advance, but can punish broadcasters after they use "dirty words" on the air, even to the extent of considering the matter in broadcast license renewals.

The FCC had said seven words used in a broadcast by comedian George Carlin on a New York station were indecent—its definition of indecency being "variable obscenity." Even the high court itself has never accepted so vague a definition, but it is willing to allow the FCC to use it. The decision overturns an appeals court holding that the FCC's total ban on the words was so broad as to violate freedom of speech.

Where censorship is concerned, advance censorship may be more threatening than censorship after the fact, but the latter is censorship all the same. We doubt if the Supreme Court would have allowed it had not the obscenity issue been involved. Who, after all, likes dirty words? Most broadcasters who value their audience ratings will not use them. But who also has not heard such words? The answer for displeased individuals is to turn off the set. Government censorship of the airwaves is about as unnecessary as it is undesirable in a land of free speech.

Behavior: Does TV Shape or Reflect?

Extensive research has been conducted, and is continuing, to determine how, and to what extent, watching television influences human behavior. It is a matter that concerns social psychologists as much as media theorists, educators and clergymen alike. It is a cause adopted by those seeking an explanation for social ills, such as illiteracy, delinquency and addiction, that are afflicting ever increasing numbers of young people.

The youth audience (pre-school through high school-age) is television's most avid and impressionable audience. According to recent studies, the generation of Americans now aged 18 has spent 15,000 hours watching television compared with 11,000 hours spent in the classroom. Television, experts estimate, commands the attention of 3-to-4-year-olds for 20 percent of their waking hours.

Critics of excessive TV-viewing fault both form and content. Some say that the act of watching *per se* fosters a passive attitude and sense of spectatorship in the young. Teachers complain that students have shorter attention spans because they are accustomed to being interrupted for a "station break" every five or ten minutes. Some teachers feel that television's slick production techniques and gimmickry make it impossible for them to compete for the students' interest. There is also evidence that television's "instant" diversion has limited children's use of their imaginations and their interaction with other children.

Television, because it is a visual rather than a verbal medium, is frequently cited as a reason for the recent drop in students' reading skills. The networks are now encouraging teachers to make use of television scripts, supplied by the networks, to induce elementary and secondary school students to read. The project hopes to exploit the existing enthusiasm for television to motivate interest in language and creative writing.

Commericals, some authorities believe, exert a particularly strong influence on children. The 2-to-8-year-old generally cannot distinguish between a commerical message and a program's content. Very young children lack the experience to understand that the inherent purpose of an ad is to persuade. Citizen's groups, led by Action for Children's

103

Television (ACT), claim that frequent, enticing commercials for sugar-coated breakfast cereals and candy constitute a health hazard, since sugar is a proven cause of tooth decay. Toys, according to ACT president Peggy Charren, "are now designed to make a good commerical instead of a good plaything. That's why the dolls walk, talk, blow bubbles, burp and write their names. A rag doll, by comparison, looks dead on television."

ACT is responsible for a current proposal under consideration by the Federal Trade Commission (FTC) recommending a ban on all television advertising directed at children under 8 years of age. The new regulations would also require that ads for sugared foods be balanced by nutritional messages. Michael Pertschuk, chairman of the FTC, told an ACT conference that "Children trust television because it is part of their world — it is everywhere."

While the Federal Communications Commission and the FTC were holding hearings on children and television advertising, the American Broadcasting Company announced in January 1979 that it would reduce the advertising time on children's weekend shows by more than 20 percent over two years, beginning in 1980. An ABC spokesman indicated that the "free time" resulting from the cutback in commericals would be used for "special messages on nutrition, health, public service announcements" and "children's news briefs."

Values, motivation and social responsibility are at the heart of the debate over televised violence. Dr. George Gerbner, dean of the University of Pennsylvania's Annenberg School of Communication, believes that "Television has profoundly affected the way in which members of the human race learn to become human beings." In 1972, the results of an intensive government study were released in a report to the U.S. Surgeon General. The study found "some evidence of a causal relationship between TV violence and later aggressive behavior on the part of children."

A more recent 530-page report completed in 1978, found that the more violence a boy sees on television, the more likely he is to be violent himself. The six-year study of television's effect on British youth aged 12 to 17 was financed by the Columbia Broadcasting System (CBS). Dr. Bill Belson, author of the report, states that the most harmful programs are those that allow the viewer to identify with the aggressor, glorifying violence by presenting it as a successful method of coping with conflict.

Television producers and executives answer such findings by pointing to all the violence that actually exists in our daily lives and claiming that to "water down" reality would make television an untruthful medium. Action and conflict are considered the essence of drama, particularly of American popular drama as typified by the gunplay in Hollywood Westerns. It is arguable that the public enjoys watching violence, and perhaps even gets vicarious satisfaction out of one TV character's assaults on another. TV violence may be a practical outlet for aggressive feelings, a means of diffusing anxiety or a harmless release from pressure.

The electronic age has introduced a stimulus into our lives that is in no way comparable to any other. As television has taken over as the dominant institution in our society, its ceaseless input fundamentally contributes to our collective thinking, and to some extent, our collective motivation. If televised violence does, in fact, have a brutalizing effect on viewers, can we differentiate between the gratuitous murders portrayed on "action dramas" and the actual slayings reported on the evening news? Does watching a video tape of real bloodshed in a war-torn village impose reality on us or desensitize us to it? Until a definite cause-effect relationship can be established, might not laying our troubles on television's doorstep be a classic case of blaming the messenger for the message? The inconclusiveness of so much study is testimony to how little we understand the factors that detemine behavior, and how eagerly we seek a controlling force to take responsibility for it.

Roanoke Times & World-News

Roanoke, Va., September 27, 1977

For 14 consecutive years, *Newsweek* magazine tells us, scores on Scholastic Aptitude Tests (SAT) had been dropping sharply, and the College Entrance Examination Board named a study commission to find out why.

The panel came up with a number of causes, but gave greatest emphasis to a decline in scholastic standards. The judgment already has been confirmed by a host of employers, college teachers and administrators, and many others in position to judge high school graduates.

Two professors at Washington and Lee—who made their observations independently of each other—commented recently on what one called a national crisis, the other a national scandal. Hampden M. Smith, who teaches journalism, said this in an article for W&L's alumni magazine:

The sad fact is that the vast majority of the young people pouring into the nation's colleges today are, in the most generous critical sense, nearly illiterate . . . . In this increasingly complex world, an inability to understand or be understood is a crippling burden. It is not that today's college students, or high school juniors, or third graders, are dullards. The fact is that they have not been taught.

Sidney M. B. Coulling said the following to the Richmond chapter of W&L alumni:

Even with highly selective admissions policies and careful screening, some students are admitted . . . who are not fully prepared for college work, particularly in English and mathematics. The difficulty they encounter breeds discouragement; discouragement breeds frustration; and frustration often breeds a sense of defeat.

At least partly because of this, the characteristic malaise among students in recent years has been the simple inability to do a job, to complete an assignment, to write a required paper. It has replaced sex and religion, the university chaplain tells me, as the students' number one problem.

Lack of fundamental training isn't the only reason students aren't doing as well on Scholastic Aptitude Tests. There's too much television viewing and not enough reading. The study panel also remarked upon changes in American home life that have had negative impact on children. For whatever reasons, students seem less motivated nowadays to learn.

In all this, one thing appears fairly certain. Most students will perform only as well as they are expected to. Young people can't be expected to raise the schools' academic standards on their own. It's up to teachers, administrators and parents to enforce higher educational goals and to insist on proper discipline in class and at home. Our schools do students no favors in letting them get by with less and less, when life in the late 20th century demands more and more.

THE KANSAS CITY STAR

Kansas City, Mo., May 3, 1978

High-brow semantic arguments against obvious social flaws are getting to be annoying. Lending institutions swear they do not practice redlining — prohibiting loans in certain geographical areas of the city — but there is vivid evidence of the effects of strangling communities of mortgage money.

Now there are those who say there is no hard data that proves TV is dulling the intellect.

No hard data indeed.

When children learn the entire dialogue of a 30-second commercial months before they can construct the alphabet, there is little doubt that TV has the power to overcome constructive learning. It becomes of little consequence whether data can quantify the loss of learning time or whether correlations between time in front of the tube and ability to learn can be put together.

Television — the visual medium — is not going to fade. We do hope that programming such as viewed on public TV will become more of the rule in support of education; not the raging cacophony of commercial TV that can present an exceptional deterrent.

Richmond Times-Dispatch

Richmond, Va., November 1, 1977

The pervasiveness of television in American family life is indicated by the latest A.C. Nielsen survey.

At least one television set can be found in 98 percent of American households. A color set is present in more than three out of four TV-owning households. In almost 50 percent of the TV households there are two or more TV sets.

Many critics fret about the effect of TV viewing on the nation's young. Previous Neilsen surveys have shown that children watch TV 23 hours and 16 minutes a week, on the average, while teen-agers tune in 19 hours and 49 minutes. This is more time than some will spend in the classroom, and easily more than most will spend reading books. Additionally, there is the concern that many of the shows depict acts of violence or a distorted attitude toward sex that could influence children to engage in anti-social behavior.

Confronted with these charges and asked whether children wouldn't be better off outside throwing a ball as opposed to being "glued to the tube," a network executive gave a rather surprising answer at a Washington Journalism Center seminar recently.

"I agree," said Lester Strong, ABC's East Coast manager of children's television. "Television is addictive. Kids, especially kids 2 to 5, need to be out in the sunshine, skipping rope, playing, involving themselves in creative activities."

Mr. Strong said that parents need to monitor and limit their children's television viewing. Toward that objective, ABC has begun airing a warning to parents that too much watching of the tube may be harmful to their children.

The warning is one of the small victories that have been achieved by a private group called Action for Children's television (ACT), which formed in the Newton, Mass., living room of Mrs. Peggy Charren in 1968. ACT proposed the TV-hazard message in the style of the cigarette warnings. And the citizens' group, which now has members in every state, also claims credit for reducing the air time of commercials on Saturday morning kiddie shows by 40 percent (from 16 minutes an hour to 9½), eliminating advertising of children's vitamins on children's TV programs, and stopping the hosts of kiddie shows from doubling as hawkers of various commercial products.

Mrs. Charren, who remains the dynamic president of ACT, says that efforts are continuing to improve the content of children's programming. The pitching of ads for candy and other nutritionally dubious foods to immature minds is one of her major concerns. But she doesn't go as far as Marie Winn, author of *The Plug-in Drug*, who argues that children are harmed by the very process of passively watching TV.

The problem, in Mrs. Charren's view, is that children watch so much TV, and with such lack of discrimination as to quality. Children can benefit from some "constructive viewing"—there are actually some worthwhile shows for children — but parents need to exert discipline over the tube's use. She tells her own daughter that she may watch as much TV as she reads: If she reads for a half-hour, she may watch TV for a half-hour.

With all the assailing of TV for what ails us, ranging from declining literary skill to soaring crime, two points are well worth keeping in mind. The parent has the ability to sit down with the child and discuss critically what comes on TV. And the parent has the authority to cut off the set at any time.

The Afro-American

Baltimore, Md., August 30, 1977

The annual Back-to-School season is an opportune time to take stock of what our children are learning—especially following the past week's revelation that television is doing severe damage to American education.

If the alarm is a flash for society at large, then blacks should take special notice. For, it is our schools—and our youths—that generally get the worst of everything. And what does the worst of garbage add up to?

At a time when we want to consolidate gains of the past decade and build our communities in every way, in making certain the "dream" that Dr. Martin Luther King Jr. spoke of 14 years ago become a reality as soon as possible, we'd better be taking a close look at our children's learning.

It is as true today as it was when the Biblical author wrote it: A tree grows as the twig is bent.

First of all, what does your child see on TV? He sees an overabundance of violence. He sees fictional situations that often are hard to distinguish from reality.

On the morning of Christmas 1976 — it fell on a Saturday last year—as your children opened their holiday gifts, the cartoon shows advertised still more toys.

Black-oriented TV still depicts very little of the variety and distorts what it does show. There still is too little "roots" and too much "Dy-No-Mite" and "Huggy Bear."

And then, your child sits there for hours on end and gets spoon-fed. With so many images dancing before their weary eyes and polluting what cannot help but become lazy minds, some don't even read comic books. Educational shows cannot do it all. They can only augment good education.

The Detroit News
Detroit, Mich., July 23, 1977

The latest horror story about American illiteracy tells of the sailor who caused $250,000 damage to an engine because he couldn't read instructions.

That sounds apocryphal in view of the Navy's entrance requirements. However, it wouldn't surprise delegates to the annual meeting of the American Library Association.

The librarians, who recently held their national conference in Detroit, hardly need proof of the disgraceful illiteracy rate, estimated at one in seven.

But the librarians did hear many useful suggestions for the fight against illiteracy.

One of the best suggestions was simply said but not easily done: turn off the television set.

Watching TV has become so engrained a habit — and so marvelous a babysitter for harassed parents — that one professor said his students had logged 18,000 hours of television time.

Some American families have been leaving their TV sets off for a week and happily discovering the joys of reading, talking and playing chess and other games.

Prof. Daniel Fader of the University of Michigan had a good idea for parents: "Have a library, however small, in your home. Get your children used to seeing books, seeing you reading books."

Fader also told ALA delegates something that should be engraved over the entrance to every school and university in the land: all teachers — not just English teachers — must teach English.

A University of Syracuse professor suggested that parents encourage the child to keep a diary — an exercise that teaches one to write, to observe and to think. Literacy, by the way, doesn't achieve much in the absence of thought.

HOUSTON CHRONICLE
Houston, Tex., August 25, 1977

Scholastic aptitude test scores have been dropping since 1963, and that has been a cause for some concern.

A new report on why those test scores dropped is a cause for real worry.

The report found that the declining scores are probably the result of a multitude of reasons. Taken together, those reasons point to a trend that may be very difficult to erase.

It would have been much nicer, much neater, if the committee appointed by the testing services had been able to put a finger on specifics, such as the need for an extra hour of English instruction in the fifth grade and more math in the seventh grade.

But, as is typical with most matters involving education, the reasons for the drop in scores are much more complex.

The committee, headed by Willard Wirtz, who was labor secretary under President Lyndon Johnson, conducted 38 research projects. The panel was established because, since 1963, the average score in the Scholastic Aptitude Test (SAT) verbal section has dropped 49 points from 478 to 429. The average mathematics score declined from 502 to 470. Many colleges judge applicants on the basis of these tests.

The committee concluded that the decline can be attributed to a great variety of factors, including the Vietnam War, the Watergate scandal, too much television watching, the addition of electives at the expense of required courses in high schools, changes in family life and the increasing number of minority and poor students taking the test. There has been a marked drop in the motivation of young people to learn, the committee reported.

A combination of negative educational and social factors are involved, then. Perhaps the decline in scores reflects basic cultural changes, a different emphasis on certain values.

Committee chairman Willard Wirtz said that the drop in scores parallels a drop in national self-esteem. "We've wondered sometimes during the course of our inquiry why the score declines haven't been larger," he said.

Even though the conclusions of the report are disturbing, the committee has performed a real service. It held up a mirror, and the reflection is not a bright one.

THE SAGINAW NEWS
Saginaw, Mich., August 31, 1977

The many screens of television, which we have long thought of as bubble gum for the optic nerves, are evident in a series of releases from differing sources in the past few days.

Something of an indictment is channeled television's way by a panel, headed by former Secretary of Labor Willard Wirtz, which alleged TV — and relaxed teaching standards — were to blame for a 14-year decline in Scholastic Aptitude Tests.

Then a survey commissioned by the Corporation for Public Broadcasting, which is careful not to credit its sponsors as sponsors, points out that viewers are more satisfied with public TV programming than with television as a whole.

Viewers interviewed cited a lack of nature and science programs and gave lowest priorities to classical and contemporary music, programs of interest to minorities, situation comedy and dramatic plays.

All of which leaves Army training films, Lawrence Welk and, as the commercial goes, "apple pie and Chevrolet."

But then comes a television special which NBC offered Tuesday evening pointing out that most children with learning disabilities can overcome their handicap if the condition is diagnosed and treated at an early age. The program reported on puzzling neurological disorders which can prevent otherwise bright children from learning.

It was sponsored by Northwestern Mutual Life Insurance Co. which is to be commended for its interest.

Children are the nation's most valuable asset.

Los Angeles Times
Los Angeles, Calif., November 11, 1976

Daniel J. Boorstin, the librarian of Congress and graceful historian of American civilization, was commenting on these pages the other day about the relationship between television and reading, and suggesting that the two means of entertainment and communication, rather than being in conflict as many suppose, could in fact prove to be mutually supporting. Particularly, as Boorstin sees it, might television be used to stimulate greater reading.

Some evidence of recent years happily supports that view.

One of the hottest things in TV right now, for example, is the production of "miniseries" based on best-selling novels. Readers of a book often will tune in to see the dramatization of a story they liked. More significantly, though, as the publishers report, many who watch a series often are prompted to go out and buy—and presumably read—the book on which it is based.

An even more interesting development has been the publication of books that originated as TV programs. Alistair Cooke's "America," Sir Kenneth Clark's "Civilization," Jacob Bronowski's "The Ascent of Man" have all been purchased in remarkable numbers. Each book emerged from a series first shown on public television. Similarly, public TV's showing of "The Forsyte Saga" led to a new readership for the John Galsworthy novels.

It is easy, of course, to make too much of a link between television and reading. For one thing, people who watch a lot of television—and the average household does have a TV set on for a good part of the waking hours—are not likely to have either the time or the inclination to do much reading. Acknowledging that, though, it seems to us that Boorstin's point is still well taken. Television does have a very considerable and largely unexploited potential for referring people to the written word. Realizing that potential seems to us to be very much in the public interest.

In his interview with Times Associate Editor Robert J. Donovan, Boorstin had a specific suggestion. "Every TV program of substance," as he put it —documentaries, historical dramas, productions of major works of literature and the like—ought to carry at the end a list of books that the interested viewer could consult, either to pursue further information or to obtain a permanent record. We think that proposal makes a great deal of sense.

Television does a lot of good things. But with its inherent limitations there is no way that it can completely satisfy the public's need and desire for information and clarification of complex issues, for serious entertainment and background on important contemporary and historical events. That is one reason why providing aid and encouragement to its viewers in consulting published sources would be so helpful.

We like Boorstin's idea very much. We hope the TV industry will, too.

WORCESTER TELEGRAM.

Worcester, Mass., March 20, 1976

If what Ted K. Kilty says is true, then the inability of most Americans to read well is an even more serious handicap than many of us supposed.

Kilty is an associate professor of education at Western Michigan University. He has carried a step further the study published last year by the U.S. Office of Education indicating that 22 per cent of adult Americans are illiterate and another 32 per cent are only marginally literate.

He has correlated this finding with a readability study of written materials that the average American encounters on a day-to-day basis. His results suggest that a majority of adult Americans are not only unable to read legal papers, insurance policies and news magazines, they are also befuddled by the instructions on a package of gelatin, a frozen TV dinner or a bottle of buffered aspirin.

Kilty used a readability formula developed at Ohio State University. It links the difficulty of words with the average number of words in a sentence.

According to this formula, the gelatin instructions could be understood only by someone of at least seventh grade reading level; the TV dinner directions, eighth grade, and the aspirin, 10th grade.

A person of marginal literacy is defined as one who reads at only sixth grade level. So Kilty concludes that 54 per cent of adult Americans are unable to comprehend directions for preparing simple meals or taking common medicines.

That is a dramatically more serious comment on the effect of television and the failure of the schools than people realized when the U.S. literacy study was first made public.

Lincoln Journal

Lincoln, Neb., August 24, 1977

After two years of study and 38 research projects, a prestigious 21-member committee has issued a 75-page report on why college entrance test scores are declining. The gist of it is: we're not sure, but there are probably several causes.

One might have hoped for a more definitive finding. Yet the report is valuable for two reasons. First, it tends to explode the tempting myth that there is, behind this educational phenomenon, a single villain which might be readily routed. Second, it reinforces the common-sense perceptions that some remedial measures are available.

In short, the committee, commissioned by the College Board and Educational Testing Service, arrives at conclusions which most thoughtful Americans had probably already reached.

What the committee stated is pretty much the conventional wisdom: The quality of elementary and secondary education is down. More students come from homes with only one parent. They have lived in traumatic times — Vietnam and Watergate. Television is a pervasive influence. And a broader range of students, as opposed to only the brightest, are going on to college — the fruits of our drive for expanded educational opportunity. Why shouldn't scores be down?

Some still are not convinced there is a serious problem. Test scores are, after all, only one measure of past or probable intellectual achievement. But if our nation believes a problem exists, the committee study reaffirms that there are steps which can be taken.

Schools, for example, can be upgraded to provide more for — and demand more from — students. This means, in the terms of the report, more emphasis on basic skills and knowledge and fewer elective "easy" courses. It means more homework and less automatic promotion from grade to grade.

Another example: the place of television in our lives has to be reduced. Or at least altered. Clearly, as the committee says, the 10,000 to 15,000 hours of TV a typical child watches before age 16 detracts from homework and competes with schooling.

But just as clearly TV is not likely to be displaced as a major cultural force. As the panel puts it, television gives "the future of learning its largest promise." But the promise will be realized only if TV offers less pap and more intellectual nourishment, less entertainment and more education in the broadest sense.

Such measures are no less difficult for being obvious. They require both individual and collective action. Schools cannot toughen their standards without support from parents. Teachers cannot demand more homework if parents are hostile to it.

TV's pernicious effect will not be overcome — or superseded by a salutary effect — until parents assert firm control over children's viewing habits and insist on different network habits. This is a challenging task, but perhaps not impossible, judging from the current PTA campaign against TV violence.

All of this, of course, ultimately goes back to the values by which a society and its members live — the importance they attach to education, and what they expect of schools and of their children.

What the committee study suggests is that we already know some ways in which education might be improved, or at least education as reflected by college tests. What it doesn't and can't answer is whether we really care enough to do these things.

The Washington Star

Washington, D.C., December 14, 1978

The problem with the wonderfully pragmatic philosophy of "if you can't beat 'em, join 'em," is that it can, ever so easily, lead to amnesia about what it was you were trying to beat in the first place. For that reason, we note with some concern the joining up — apparently in sizable number — of teachers with prime-time television: The intent is to stimulate literacy among the young. The vehicle is called "scripting."

"The new teaching device is beginning to have a major impact," *The New York Times* reports. What happens is this: Two or three weeks before a selected program is to be shown, the script is provided to students. They read it and discuss it in class. After the show, the students discuss it again, and this may involve dipping into literature, history, economics and so forth, according to the theory.

"The key word among script-reading advocates is 'motivation,' " *The Times'* continues. "Access to advance scripts suddenly makes youngsters insiders — would-be writers, producers, critics." This exercise, it is hoped, may combat the passivity of television addiction that can deaden imaginative exuberance, a quality which is one of the few advantages of being young.

However, the "scripting" idea unfortunately suggests more of the effort to make learning "fun," a queer concept that can be delusory: Intellectual accomplishment at any level requires a degree of application that is strewn with chunks of tedium and shards of drudgery. To try to peddle the learning process as an unrelieved delight is to create some very skeptical customers.

The "scripting" idea may also mistake the acquisition of literacy as an end in itself: There is, it seems to us, a question being rather severely begged here. We note, for instance, that thousands of students spent time recently with an advance script of a "Waltons" program — "Day of Infamy" broadcast on Dec. 7.

"The Waltons" is a popular show. The Pearl Harbor show may have been evocative and interesting. But we are not comfortable with the thought of students being introduced to a dominant chapter of modern history by so cozy and simplistic a vehicle. This point was raised on a television network feature on "scripting" and the "Waltons." The reporter wondered whether there might be some problems with the historical precision of the Dec. 7 show; a man identified as an educator bluntly retorted that the concern was "irrelevant."

Well, we envy the educator's certitude as much as we worry about his perspective. But the problem of non-reading and inability to read has become so critical among the young that one should not be dismissive of any initiative. Henry Adams once noted that the habit of expression will lead finally to something worth expressing. Perhaps the same might hold for "scripting."

St. Louis Globe-Democrat

St. Louis, Mo., April 13, 1978

Homework and television don't mix, according to a study of 17-year-olds.

The more homework the teen-agers did and the less television they watched, the better they fared, according to the National Assessment of Educational Progress.

Perhaps the boob tube deserves more blame than it receives for the sad state of affairs in the U.S. education system. More than 60 percent of the 10,000 students participating in the test reported they spend fewer than five hours a week on homework, and most of them admitted devoting as much or more time in front of the television on school nights, the study found.

How far the situation has gone in the wrong direction can be deduced from estimates of federal officials who say the average child has watched 3,000 to 4,000 hours of television prior to becoming a first-grader. By age 16 the total climbs to 15,000 hours — or more time than is spent in the classroom.

Students taking part in the study scored higher in a math test if they had newspapers, encyclopedias and magazines in their homes. This finding further proves that when it comes to education, the television set is completely out of focus.

WORCESTER TELEGRAM.

Worcester, Mass., November 21, 1976

The best way for parents to get a child interested in reading is for them to set an example and let the child see them reading for enjoyment. But a lot of parents don't set that example, so maybe adults at school should start doing so.

That is the reasoning behind a novel experimemt conducted in all five Shrewsbury elementary schools the other day. For 15 minutes, all other activity stopped as teachers, administrators, cooks and janitors sat down with 2,300 students for a period of silent reading of novels, magazines and textbooks.

A second grade teacher at Spring Street School found the idea in a teachers' magazine and suggested it at a "brainstorming" session on ways to improve school reading programs. All the town's elementary schools decided the try the idea in hopes of a carryover into the youngsters' homes.

Shrewsbury's "Stop to Read" program is an interesting idea. Scheduled regularly, it might indeed help youngsters to understand that reading is not just work to be done for school, that it is a means of fun and enlightenment enjoyed regularly by millions of adults. It might help convince the children that reading is a prince among pastimes, that it can be engaged in almost anywhere, in any spare time, at little or no expense.

Any school program that helps the written word in its present-day struggle with television for the attention of children is probably worthwhile. Yet along with merit there is the implication of warning in the "Stop to Read" program. The adults at school would not need to set the reading-for-pleasure example if the adults at home were already doing so.

MANCHESTER NEW HAMPSHIRE UNION LEADER

Manchester, N.H., September 8, 1977

We have little doubt about the accuracy of the report issued by a special panel headed by former Labor Secretary Willard Wirtz to the effect that television and relaxed teaching standards are responsible for the shocking drop in Scholastic Aptitude Test scores over the past 14 years. Indeed, it is to be hoped that all Americans will view seriously the recommendation the panel issued after two years of studying scores on the college entrance tests — namely, that "everybody interested in education," parents, teachers, school boards and taxpayers, should take a hand in helping to resolve the educational crisis.

However, we can see no real solution until there is a general awareness of what should be obvious —i. e., that "education" is not simply a process that occurs in the classrooms of the nation's schools. Unless and until it is understood that parents particularly have as much of a role to play in education as the teachers to whom they entrust their charges, the quality of education will continue to deteriorate.

Consider, for example, the use — or abuse — of the boob tube in the average American home. It should be apparent that it is not the television set that is responsible for the fact that Johnny can't read. In fact, the standard television fare, miserable as it is, must have some educational value — if only in that it makes Johnny more glib and thus better able to conceal his basic lack of knowledge.

The problem is that so many parents have allowed the boob tube to become the major source — and sometimes the sole source — of information and instruction for themselves as well as their children. If Johnny can't read, often as not the basic cause is the fact that his parents can but won't. Thus, as teachers, parents fail miserably to fulfill their proper role in the educational process. Why, then, should they be surprised that even conscientious professional teachers throw up their hands in despair when confronted with the motivation-less children coming from homes where the boob tube is both teacher and baby sitter?

There will be many formulas suggested, most of them so complicated as to be impractical, for resolving the crisis in education outlined by the Wirtz panel. The simple, obvious solutions will probably never come through to the average parent.

For example. This fall, with the beginning of the school year, try a new educational twist in the home. Twist the TV knob to "off." Then take the obvious additional step of having little Johnny begin to READ — the day's newspaper, magazines, books. Help him. Ask him questions about what he has read. Watch as, wonder of wonders, he begins to enjoy it, even to the point where, self-motivated, he becomes more discriminating in his use of the boob tube.

Who knows? He may then even be able to instruct his parents on the art of using television rather than allowing it to use them.

The Oregonian

Portland, Ore., August 26, 1977

A panel of experts has completed a two-year study into declining College Board scores, and has come up with a number of expectable but not very satisfactory reasons.

The Scholastic Aptitude Test is a 2½-hour examination given to about a million high school students each year and is used by many colleges and universities as a guide in assessing future students' potential. Basically, it is a two-level test covering verbal and mathematical skills as accumulated by students in their pre-college education.

The 21-member panel, headed by former Secretary of Labor Willard Wirtz, blames the decline on national "traumas" such as the Vietnam War, Watergate, political scandals, on lower education standards and the increasing number of minority, poor and inferior students taking the tests. The "decade of distraction," broken homes, automatic grade and high school promotion, less required homework and television have led to a "diminished seriousness of purpose," the panel concluded, and are the prime reasons for the 14-year decline in SAT scores.

All very well, and probably true. What the panel did not make clear is that the SAT is basically an intelligence test, a test to measure the capacity to assimilate and use information every child is exposed to. Scores do not necessarily reflect a student's grade pattern. A young person who has squeezed through school by the skin of his ears, whose grades are so poor that only a few years ago he would never have been allowed to graduate, can and often does, score much higher than straight-A students.

But that child, who didn't do his homework, dreamed through classes, paid as little attention to the teacher as he could get away with, may have been soaking up knowledge, and with it comprehension, at a greater rate than the class grind.

This "learning sponge" can be from any background, or any level of society or ethnic group. What sets him apart is curiosity. He is interested in the world around him and cannot help but take it in through his eyes, ears, pores, the soles of his feet. And whether he gets good grades in school really has no bearing on what he has actually learned.

SAT results are evaluated on a "bell curve" — a graph that starts on the left with the lowest scores, goes up to normal or average at the top, and curves symmetrically down again as scores rise. What worries educators is that the top of the bell is getting lower. Therefore, if one accepts the theory of the test at all, it means the average kid of today is dumber than the average kid of 10 or 14 or 20 years ago.

This seems hard to accept. Young people are exposed to so much more these days than they ever were in the past. What it probably means is that most of them are not paying attention to the important things. There is so much to divert a young mind from the necessarily regimented world of forced study, so many pleasures to hurry-up-and-enjoy, that he has no will to learn the hard things.

Television can probably take the blame for most of this — and yet, as the panel reports, television gives "the future of learning its greatest promise."

How to fulfill that promise; that's the problem.

The Cleveland Press

Cleveland, Ohio, June 16, 1977

Television frequently can be a magic carpet of sorts, sweeping young viewers swiftly to distant lands. But their view of the world can be surprisingly imprecise unless TV's visual images are reinforced by classroom study.

This is the upshot of a survey sponsored and recently issued by the U.S. Office of Education. Some 1800 public school students of various ages in 27 states were quizzed. The performance of the older ones was typical.

Nearly half the high school seniors thought Israel was an Arab nation. More than a quarter thought Golda Meir, the former Israeli prime minister, was president of Egypt. Asked which of four countries — China, India, Poland or Russia — is located in both Europe and Asia, only 54 per cent correctly answered Russia.

Schools, teachers and parents must be blamed for blind spots such as these. Either geography isn't taught widely enough or it isn't taught well — or both. Children who live in a global village should be reading maps and books as well as watching television.

THE INDIANAPOLIS NEWS

Indianapolis, Ind., December 16, 1977

Once upon a time the TV industry swore by the rating system.

When the validity of using 1,200 families to determine the television taste for 210 million people was questioned, the industry wiseacres pooh-poohed the question and proclaimed that the Nielsen system was infallible — an accurate indication of American television preferences.

Meantime, back at the living rooms of America, something has been happening that causes the industry to change its mind about Nielsen. National Nielson data for October and November showed an 8 percent drop in viewing levels during daytime and a 3 percent drop during prime time for last year. The Nielsen drop was corroborated by the Arbitron company, another ratings service, and, together, they agree that there has been a decline of about 1.2 million daytime viewing household and around 250,000 nighttime homes.

The network executives point to a serious error made by the Nielsen firm two years ago, when it did not allow for an increase in the number of childless families in the 1,200 homes of its sampling. They suggest that if Nielsen made a serious mistake in 1975, it could have made a similar mistake in 1977.

Nielsen executives have other explanations. They point out the size of the average television household has dropped from 3.23 persons per home in 1963 to 2.8 persons per home in 1977, and that larger families watch proportionally more television. There is also declining interest in television among 18-to-34-year-olds, the only age group increasing in number. Another reason is that the number of women in the work force is on the rise, and working women watch less television than nonworking women.

Throughout the analysis no one has mentioned the most evident reason of all: Parents may have finally awakened to the fact that their children are being shortchanged by television viewing and that it is not a substitute for reading and conversation. Across the land test scores in English reveal an appalling decline in writing and speaking abilities.

Passive television viewing may have some benefits in expanding mental horizons, but it accomplishes little in building essential reading and writing skills. It's possible that not only parents, but also the children themselves, have concluded that the written and spoken word, not the picture, is the basis of communication.

The Burlington Free Press

Burlington, Vt., September 12, 1977

IN THIS television age, parents all across the nation are having difficulties in controlling youngsters who become addicted to watching "the tube" many hours a day.

Psychiatrists treating children who develop unhealthy reactions from too much TV-watching are issuing warnings that parents need to establish clearly-understood rules for their youngsters with regard to how much time they are allowed to watch TV and what programs they may watch.

An interview with Dr. Robert L. Stubblefield, child psychiatrist and medical director, Silver Hill Foundation, New Canaan, Conn., in the current issue of U.S. News & World Report, outlines the dangers to children from too much TV watching and makes suggestions for establishing controls.

Dr. Stubblefield says it is being recognized by family doctors that excessive TV watching by children is a growing health problem, especially among those who watch more than 25 hours a week, which is the national average. There is evidence, he notes, that such youngsters have more difficulty in school than those who spend less time with TV.

Asked what symptoms to watch for in children's reactions to TV, he cited "hyperactive behavior, loss of appetite, difficulty in sleeping, bad dreams, or refusal to play with children their own age."

That applies to younger children. As they grow older, "heavy watchers are more likely to dwell in excessive fantasies, keeping themselves out of the new world of boy-girl relationships and social activities. They drift and become indecisive."

In reply to a question about methods of controlling television watching by children, Dr. Stubblefield said that in serious cases it might be necessary to deny use of the TV set completely, "particularly if it interferes with activities that are essential for his personal development."

But he suggested that, except in serious cases, parents might better "limit the child's viewing to a certain number of hours per week" and provide guidance as to the programs to be watched.

"Be firm — but accompany it with an explanation. Tell them the plain truth that television is somehow interfering with their opportunities to learn more about themselves and about what other children are feeling and doing.

"Remember that a child preoccupied with television is likely to be functioning at six to 18 months below his or her age level, so use simple words with no sign of vaccilation."

Dr. Stubblefield noted that children "model most of their behavior after their parents — so you have to be prepared to turn the set off and pick up a book yourself" in order to get children to do their homework instead of watching TV.

Children who have learned to cooperate in wise use of TV can be allowed more choice in programs they will watch as they grow older.

Parents who are concerned about the progress of their children in school will check with teachers to determine whether television watching may be a problem needing attention.

Parents' organizations have prepared documents suggesting codes of television watching to be adopted through cooperation of parents and children. In many cases these codes are circulated in schools.

When there are good relationships between parents and children, these problems can be solved.

Richmond Times-Dispatch

Richmond, Va., April 20, 1978

That the lure of "Charlie's Angels" and other weeknight television programming gets in the way of school homework will not come as news to most parents of teen-age children. Perhaps the biggest surprise in a study made by the National Assessment of Educational Progress was that nearly half of the responding 17-year-olds said they watch either no television or less than one hour of TV on "school nights"—Sunday through Thursday.

But with the other half, some heavy TV-watching goes on: one to three hours nightly for 35 percent, three to five hours for 12 percent, and five or more hours for 5 percent. And with both halves, there is the possibility that the youngsters underestimated their TV time.

In any event, the study showed that those students who reported doing the most homework and the least TV-watching also tended to score highest on the National Assessment's tests of educational achievement.

The highest-achieving group — the students answering an average of 80 percent of the questions correctly — watched less than an hour of TV a night and did more than 10 hours of homework a week.

Those 17-year-olds who reported doing between 5 and 10 hours of homework a week and watching less than an hour of TV nightly answered 73 percent of the questions correctly. But, interesingly and maybe significantly, those who said they likewise did between 5 and 10 hours of homework a week while still managing, somehow, to watch five or more hours of TV a night, answered only 57 percent of the questions correctly.

Apart from the possible impact of TV, the study gives ammunition to homework-assigning teachers who want to respond to any critics. The study found that the performance level of pupils who reported that they aren't given any homework assignments was low regardless of how much or how little TV they said they watched. Those pupils answered only 50 to 55 percent of the questions correctly no matter whether they watched an hour or five hours of TV nightly.

Additionally, the study provides an ego boost for those who work in the print media. Scoring consistently higher were those pupils who have access to reading materials in the home. The average was 8 percentage points higher for those with newspapers, 10 points higher for those with encyclopedias or other reference books, and 13 points higher for those with magazines.

The study may not prove a definite cause-and-effect relationship between television and low educational achievement. It is possible that low achievers would just find another way to "goof off" if there were no TV in the house.

But we're sure, even though the study didn't cover this point, that such a causal relationship must exist when one tries to do the homework and TV viewing *at the same time.* On the basis of experience in occasionally trying to do office "homework" sprawled before the tube, we solemnly testify that Cheryl Ladd or the antics of "The Fonz" can be terribly distracting.

Democrat and Chronicle

Rochester, N.Y., August 14, 1976

Educators have complained for years that they cannot and must not be asked to compensate for failures in the home.

In an interview in The National Observer, outgoing U.S. Commissioner of Education Terrence H. Bell agrees with that assessment, but he also applies the converse rule. The home, he says cannot make up for the failure of the schools. And neither can operate well in an unhealthy society.

Like many educators, Bell reports that today's life styles are having bad effects on children. High divorce rates and the tendency of families to pack up and move frequently disorients children emotionally and hurts their education, he feels. He describes teenage drug and alcohol use at "almost epidemic proportions."

And he notes that television, which should be a great teaching tool, is failing to upgrade and uplift. Competing with the home and school influences, it offers children a diet of "trivia and violence" which constantly refuels the sicker sides of our society.

Bell tells it as it is. The young mirror the influences to which they are exposed. Is it the young who are going wrong, or are they only reflecting the conditioning our society provides?

DAILY NEWS

New York, N.Y., October 31, 1977

American children spend an average of 5,000 hours watching television before they set foot in school. They sit and stare at the tube for more hours than they spend doing anything else—except sleeping.

The results are no secret. Reading and writing skills have fallen sharply. Television has become the surrogate parent and convenient baby sitter. The effect of soaking up years of mindless, inane, often violent programing has a devastating effect on the development of many children.

But it doesn't have to be that way. A responsible group called Action for Children's Television has developed some guidelines for parents which we are happy to pass along.

Children should be limited to an hour or an hour and a half of television a day. Programs should be carefully chosen by parents with their children. Studies show the ill effect of television, and especially commercials aimed at children, are offset if parents watch with their children and talk with them about what they see.

It may not be easy to curb the addiction, but less television—and more reading and other varied interests—can make a lifetime's difference in a child's development.

The Hartford Courant

Hartford, Conn., September 27, 1978

Senator Ribicoff was on safe ground in addressing the Connecticut Book Publishers Association in Middletown. He deplored the decline in reading skills among American children and placed much of the blame on television which "presents an image of people who are paid a great deal just to talk. It does not glamorize writing skills."

Across the Atlantic, a different but no less severe attack on television has been made by West Germany's Chancellor Helmut Schmidt who accused the medium of giving people a false picture of real life by portraying violence as a normal occurrence. He proposed that his countrymen have one television-free day each week, allowing them more time to discuss important problems relating to the family.

Television deserves being criticized for too much violence and mediocrity. But it shouldn't be blamed for all of society's ills. Mr. Ribicoff noted that the average American child watches two to four hours of television a day. Stricter parent and teacher supervision could divert some of that time to reading. Public officials could help by expanding the budgets of libraries which have little money to promote their facilities, much less buy new books.

Chancellor Schmidt's idea of a TV-less day has merit if only for the relief it would provide to deafened ears.

As for mediocrity, Aram Bakshian Jr., a communications officer at Union Carbide, has described its prevalence as "inherent in any mass entertainment form. Television, like the gladiatorial games, music halls, medicine shows, midway carnies, pulp paperbacks and comic books, must by its nature contain liberal amounts of syrup, suet and gore. People like it, and in a democracy people are supposed to get what they want."

Hartford, Conn., April 5, 1977

The television habit has been blamed for the decline in reading scores and other school work among students at all grade levels.

Some critics of education say, however, that television has gotten too much of the blame from educators who have been preoccupied with developing innovative programs — rather than in student performance in necessary skills like reading, writing and arithmetic.

There is no doubt that the television habit must get some of the blame for the decline in student performance, if only for the fact that students, as well as almost everyone else, spend hours watching television each week.

One class, the sixth grade students at Enfield Street School, Enfield have decided to do something about their television habit. Led by their teacher, Mrs. Mary Cashman, the students have cut down drastically on television viewing since Feb. 22 when they began their program to break the TV habit. The sixth grade has carried its campaign to the rest of the school.

Students in the sixth grade class had averaged more than two hours a night before their campaign, but many have cut back to as little as 10 minutes a night.

And the students who have kicked the TV habit have discovered their grades have improved, because they have allowed themselves more time for homework, and they have read more, and have gotten more involved in sports, and games with their families. Mrs. Cashman has gone so far as to say that some students show "drastic improvement" in their school work.

Some students found they had some trouble cutting down on their TV time at first, but then it came easily.

In testimony before Congressional committees studying the effects of television on youth, network executives have said that parents should supervise their children's TV watching, and reduce the amount of time they spend watching television, particularly those shows depicting violence, a major focus of many television series.

Mrs. Cashman's students, however, are putting the blame, where it belongs, on themselves, and they are taking the responsibility to do something about it. That's the adult way for youth—self-discipline, not waiting for adults to set up rules and penalties.

The Providence Journal

Providence, R.I., May 7, 1977

The position enjoyed by books in America's so-called culture is going through something of a disturbing paradox. More books than ever are being published and sold (and perhaps even read). Yet in many high schools and colleges, the ability of students to read, write and comprehend seems to be slipping.

Librarians still tell young readers that "books are your friends," but somehow something is missing. We are drifting away from the time when books, words, language and written-down ideas were the keystones of civilization and its transmittal from one generation to the next. We are, as Sen.

Pell thoughtfully put it in a recent speech, in serious danger of turning into a nation of "intellectual illiterates."

The book sold these days, as likely as not, is in paperback and not hard cover, and thus is not permanent. It is likely to be either a potboiler, a "how-to" guide or an overspecialized work of interest to few. Reading as an active pursuit, whether for enjoyment, information or enlightenment, is a fading skill because we have settled into a passive time: we have become a nation of spectators — sports events, canned music, television — and the active perusal of worthwhile books is declining.

Senator Pell, who as the prime force behind creation of the National Endowment on the Arts and the Humanities has done a great deal to stir the nation's awareness of its cultural needs, has made a serious and timely warning. He supports more federal money for educational books, university presses, small independent publishing houses and libraries. These moves would encourage production of books, and thus are worthwhile. But an even greater need may be for the nations' schools and teachers to tighten standards for reading and writing. All the books in the world are useless if we've forgotten what they're for.

The Virginian-Pilot

Norfolk, Va., September 20, 1978

The book publishing industry has paid a considerable sum to learn the painful, unprofitable truth we all suspected: nearly half the American people never read a book. Not even a paperback.

The typical book reader has polished off eight books in the past six months at a cost of $18. Considering the shortage of hardcover books these days selling for less than $10, that statistic reveals that paperback sales heavily dominate the trade.

The most susceptible book buyer, the survey indicated, is a well-educated, affluent, white woman under 50.

Only one of five book buyers is a member of a book club. One of every

four is a student, who buys used as well as new volumes.

Book sales don't necessarily translate into reading. Two of five buyers confessed that they often buy books and then put them aside to read later.

Self-help books are not the most popular non-fiction numbers, or at least that's what most of the 1,450 persons over 16 told the interviewers. Biographies and autobiographies are tops, followed by cookbooks, history, religion, instruction, current events, sports, and psychology.

Fiction lovers rated action adventure stories highest. Historical novels, mysteries, short stories, modern dramatic novels, and romances followed.

This is one of those cases where an

optimist and a pessimist disagree on whether the glass is half full or half empty.

The book industry takes a positive view of a nation of half non-readers of books. That statistic explodes the myth that television has wiped out a generation of readers, insisted one publishing spokesman.

The survey showed that only 6 percent read nothing at all. The rest of the folks read something, but 39 percent read only newspapers or magazines. The remaining 55 percent read books as well as papers and periodicals.

That should comfort anyone with an anxiety that we are destined to become a nation of tube boobs.

The Morning Union

Springfield, Mass., May 31, 1977

Little wonder that the reading proficiency of American high school students has tended to drop in recent years. Symptomatic of that trend — or perhaps causal — is the unwillingness of young people to read the great American and English classics.

According to a survey by The New York Times, educators around the nation are bemoaning the decline of interest in great literature in our public schools. Apparently, dime store novels mean more to many students than the works of Dickens, Bronte, Chaucer and even Fitzgerald.

What's worse is that in this free - spirited era, high school students are not required to read the classics. And in cases where there are literature requirements, many students get by on superficial plot summaries.

College preparatory students who do not subject themselves to the disciplines of the classics are only putting off the inevitable, since they are asking for trouble when

they get to college. But educators are more disturbed by what they see as a slipping intellectual grasp that could have serious consequences when young people reach adulthood.

The issue here is more than enriching the minds of our young people in our literary heritage. Bad habits acquired during youth tend to perpetuate themselves in adulthood. We are developing a society of television watchers rather than thoughtful readers — and that is truly unfortunate.

A vicious cycle has formed that must be broken. Perhaps because students are not reading great literature, their reading proficiency has slipped. And with a decline in reading proficiency comes an inability to comprehend the classics. This is a dilemma which must concern American educators. And perhaps the only solution is an aggressive marketing effort to convince young people of the delights of "Jane Eyre," "Bleak House" and "Lord Jim."

Oregon Journal

Portland, Ore., June 19, 1975

Teachers and parents alike complain that children no longer like to read or be read to as a form of entertainment.

The reason, of course, is that they find television more exciting. The old Mother Goose stories and fairy tales no longer have much zip for the space-age child.

Perhaps the answer is to bring our children's literature up to date.

So, we offer a couple of examples of what might be done.

The first is from "The Space Child's Mother Goose" by Frederick Winsor, published by Simon and Schuster.

Little Miss Muffet
Sits on her tuffet
In a nonchalant sort of way.
With her force field around her
The spider, the bounder,
Is not in the picture today.

And then, there is "Little Willie," published by Doubleday.

Little Willie, full of glee,
Put radium in Grandma's tea.
Now he thinks it quite a lark
To see her shining in the dark.
There now, maybe that will make the little rascals sit up and beg for more.

BUFFALO EVENING NEWS

Buffalo, N.Y., September 12, 1975

Those Scholastic Aptitude Tests which well over a million high school juniors and seniors sweat out annually as a measure of their college potential may not be an altogether reliable indication of academic potential. But there is no better available measure of nationwide achievement patterns, a n d when the scores in both the basic math and verbal areas show the sharpest drop in over 20 years, as they have this year, it is plainly time for the educators and school-testing experts to do some self-examining.

Actually, the latest drop, as the College Entrance Examination Board reports, continues a steady decline that dates from the 1963 peak in average S.A.T. scores. But a consistent downward pattern only sharpens the puzzlement and sense of dismay among test administrators in their groping for rational explanations.

How to account for it? Is it the 14,000 or so hours an average pupil has spent before the TV tube by the time he or she enters high school? Or is it a reflection of the shortcomings in teaching approaches

and a softening of the "Three R" fiber attributed by some critics to classroom practices in the early learning years? Or is this across-the-board slippage more a measure of the changing mix in college-going population, including an enlarged representation of slum-bred youngsters whose rearing put them at a disadvantage when measured by customary yardsticks of verbal or mathematical sophistication?

Probably the explanation does not lie in any single factor, and our own guess coincides with that of the admissions experts in suspecting a combination of explanations, including perhaps some more subtle factors having to do with personal motivation and with belief in the values of intellectual attainment. Yet the coinciding of this steadily depressing pattern with the impact of passive TV-watching — the hours, in short, spent as a mind-numbed spectator without the imaginative input required of reading adventures — is something that cannot be discounted, and this is a cause for concern for all of us in the world of print as well as in the nation's classrooms.

THE CHRISTIAN SCIENCE MONITOR

Boston, Mass., December 26, 1978

The old question was: "In the four quarters of the globe, who reads an American book?" (Sydney Smith, 1820).

The new question is: "In the four quarters of the United States, who reads any book?" (US reading survey, 1978).

Are there at least a few American readers left like the Britons of whom we have such a cozy image from a recent discussion of why British novels tend to be shorter than American ones? "A contributory factor is the library user's requirement to have a novel, six of which can be read in a fortnight by a somnolent borrower who customarily spends half an hour or so at the exercise in bed before going to sleep."

The quotation is from J. A. Sutherland's new University of London volume, "Fiction and the Fiction Industry," which also contains an answer to Sydney Smith's old question in a period when American books have penetrated to all corners of the globe: "In the nineteenth century, according to the famous insult, there was no American literature – only English literature published in America. Soon [as of the 1960s] it seemed there might be no English literature, only American literature published in England."

This has not happened yet, thank goodness. The world is not ready to do without English literature, or at least we're not.

But what about that other question? Of making many books there is no end, but who in America reads them?

Not much more than half the adult (over-16) population, alas, according to a survey made for a book industry group this year. We say "alas," because the 45 percent who deprive themselves of reading books are like people who reject the wheel. They fail to take advantage of humanity's most efficient tool for individuals to travel beyond their own experience to horizons of thought and feeling as far and wide as they choose.

The good news is that the Americans who do read books seem to be reading as much as or more than before the competition of television for leisure time. A survey of three decades

ago, in the early days of TV, estimated that at least a book a month was read by at least a quarter of the public. This year a quarter read at least 10 books in six months, with 10 percent reading more than 25. Readers who spent 15 hours a week on TV still spent 14 hours on books. A sponsor of the survey hailed its countering of such "myths" as that "people who watch TV are inhibited from reading" and that "leisure time for other activities is so overwhelming that people have no time left over for books when the fact is that the busiest people do read."

Then, too, almost 40 percent of those surveyed read magazines and newspapers if not books. They can't be all bad, from a newspaper's point of view.

Indeed, being bound in book form is no guarantee of quality. The important thing is for individuals to retain the inquiring mind, the open mind, the capacity for wonder and delight which are served by the best books but not by books alone.

Are American adults doing enough to encourage the coming generation along these lines? Parents who never pick up a book can hardly be surprised if their children follow suit. Communities that cut support for free public libraries give young people an object lesson in how much their elders value books. Schools that make reading drudgery instead of an enjoyable skill risk turning books into enemies rather than lifelong friends.

And how about the authors? The big-figure contracts for lurid best sellers get the headlines. But to do their bit for the survival of books, writers ought to consider whether they are nourishing the reservoir of the written word or merely tainting it.

"If they aren't readers when they leave high school, they aren't going to become readers," said a survey executive, placing a burden on all of us in a position to help or hinder the process. It is a warning to be heeded. Yet our own view, bolstered by episodes in the burgeoning field of continuing education, is that it is never too late to begin a new life-enhancing venture, including the savoring of books.

The Star-Ledger

Newark, N.J., May 13, 1978

A study of the adverse impact of television watching on the performance of students provided some insightful aspects beyond this predictable basic finding:

As expected, the study by the National Assessment of Educational Progress, showed that the 10,-000 teen-agers in the research group who did more homework and watched less television fared better than their counterparts who did the reverse.

Thirty per cent of the 17-year-olds said they did five to 10 hours of homework a week, and six per cent spent more than 10 hours. Slightly more than half reported doing less than five hours, while another seven per cent said they didn't do assigned homework and six per cent said none was assigned.

The higher scorers in the math test (80 per cent or higher) watched television less than an hour a night and did 10 hours homework a week. Those who were addicted to television fared poorly. Mixing a fair amount of homework with a lot of television evidently didn't help grades.

The highly negative inroads television has made on learning is evident in the extensive early exposure of youngsters to the medium. U.S. education officials estimate that the average child has watched 3,000 to 4,000 hours of TV before entering the first grade. By age 16 — a span covering a crucial aspect of education — the average soars to 15,000 hours. This is more TV watching than the time spent in classrooms.

It is apparent that these ingrained, distracting habits constitute a root cause for learning deficiencies — a deflection from fundamental educational commitments for which parents must assume the major blame.

The Seattle Times

Seattle, Wash., May 7, 1978

IT WOULD be difficult to find a more controversial issue than the latest one the Federal Trade Commission has taken on: the regulation of television advertising directed at children.

Arguments already have been heard on First Amendment freedoms, tooth decay, parental control, nutrition, commercialism, and corporate responsibility, to mention just a few of the elements involved. And the F.T.C. stepped into the fray only a few weeks ago.

A 340-page commission staff report is at the heart of what is expected to be a two-year process of hearings on possible governmental regulations.

The report has recommended a ban of all television advertising directed at children under the age of 8; a ban of TV ads for sugared products likely to cause tooth decay for children under 12, and a requirement that TV ads aimed at children under 12 for other sugared products be balanced by separate dental and nutritional messages.

The debate over the staff report was joined early on by Peggy Charren, president of Action for Children's Television — one of the groups demanding the regulations. She said the report was "not as strong as we'd like it."

The National Association of Broadcasters, on the other hand, condemned the report two weeks before it was issued formally, saying the industry could police itself and "we believe that if a product is harmful, it should be dealt with in the marketplace."

The idea of regulating the advertising of candy and other sugared products, particularly presweetened cereals, has been supported by the U.S. surgeon general and the commissioner of food and drugs. The Cereal Institute, however, has defended the nutritional value of presweetened cereals, contending that many children would skip breakfast entirely if they did not eat them.

Messages extolling the benefits of regular dental care and a balanced diet already are aired during the times children are believed to be the predominant television audience. But critics note that these "spots," prepared by the Department of Agriculture, are a poor second when compared with the polished, slick-sell commercials produced by the ad agencies.

There also is the question of whether regulations confined to the Saturday-morning commercial fare, as is proposed, are adequate when children are exposed to similar ads during afternoon and prime-time TV as well.

And there is the very basic issue of how far the government can intrude into what many see as the proper role of the parent in determining children's eating and television-viewing habits.

Meanwhile, we can expect noticeable changes in commercials on children's programs as advertisers and broadcasters back away from the initial heat. How far they will back away and how long they will stay there will be determined by the tone of the testimony and the direction the F.T.C. appears to take with possible regulations.

Richmond Times-Dispatch

Richmond, Va., March 11, 1978

The Federal Trade Commission has embarked on another mission to reinforce its image as the Mary Poppins of us all. It is not an instance which many parents will consider supercalifragilisticexpialidocious, however.

The FTC has bowed to the wishes of a few busy-body groups upset by televised advertisements aimed at children. During the coming weeks, the FTC wants to survey public response to a demand that it ban this advertising from television. Such a step would "protect" children from ads promoting snacks and other products that might cause tooth decay.

The reasoning goes thus: Children spend many hours watching television. Their programs are sponsored by companies selling candy, soft-drinks, and sugar-coated cereals. These items are low in nutrition and high in sugar, but young viewers don't know that. They pester their parents to buy the advertised products, and the result is, "Look, Mom, 21 per cent more cavities." So a proposed "solution" is to ban the ads.

That is the prevalent trend, and it is the wrong one. Presumably, most young television viewers are not orphans. They have parents who have the authority (a) to say "no," and (b) to turn off the tube. Nor does anyone force these parents to buy snack products or sweets. If in fact they indulge their children, who consequently develop cavities, the first few dental bills will be enough to establish a cause-and-effect factor in an adult's mind — and perhaps even in a child's mind.

But Big Government does not suppose that parents will be wise enough to control their offspring's dietary or viewing habits. The bureaucratic response is to intervene by banning the offending ads. Of course, if the FTC can impose a broad ban on this category of advertising, it can ban any other form of advertising that someone finds offensive. Hand-in-hand with the Consumer Product Safety Commission and the Food and Drug Administration, the FTC could forbid television advertising for any product that might be suspected of causing hives, heart attacks, cancer, gout, diabetes, influenza, and the common cold. And a spoonful of sugar won't help *that* medicine go down.

Arkansas Gazette.

Little Rock, Ark., April 11, 1978

Elton G. Rule, president of ABC-TV, to us was on the firmest of ground in a statement last week in opposition to one of the FCC's latest nifties, which would place restrictions on advertisements shown on children's programming.

The FTC proposal is yet another concession to the fire-breathing lobby that in one breath says it is against censorship, but . . . and in the next tries to make children's shows out of *all* TV programming; or, rather, to make all programming "fit" for children's eyes, which amounts to the same thing.

It is a shame, to be sure, some of the children's TV ads that the kids are exposed to today, but it also is a shame that they ever have to grow up to be exposed to the really, really, hard-core adult TV advertising, which alone is enough to keep the old blinking eye turned off and shuttered for at least 90 per cent of the time in some sometime viewers' home.

Projecting special advertisements toward kids as kids is a particularly offensive part of the American way, and the *theory* of restricting such is all right; it would be the practicing of the theory where we are in trouble. The ad people want to nail their victims early and indoctrinate them, then, but here as in all other forms of commercial broadcasting, it is the sponsors who pick up the tab and keep the old tube humming. It is the American Way.

This is something that too many people lose sight of when they want to impose censorship on the nets while claiming that they only want more "quality" programs. You don't impose quality on the nets or on individual sponsors. What you ought to be is grateful that once in a great while you actually get quality, such as in Texaco's TV broadcasts of live opera from the Met this year, as a companion to its long-standing airing of operas on the radio.

There is one more point about children's TV advertising. Do we want the tads to be thrown naked into the world of adult TV advertising, once the day comes when there would be no choice. Of course we don't, do we?

Summing up on the proposed new FCC rule, here is ABC's Mr. Rule again saying that the advertising limitations broached actually would amount to "an insult to parents," adding that the government in effect would supplant the parents with "national nannies" in supervising children's television viewing. That's the size of it, and in our judgment the *exact* size of it.

EVENING JOURNAL
Wilmington, Del., March 14, 1978

Recently, the Federal Trade Commission banned an advertisement that showed a child washing a doll's hair and then using an electric hair dryer right next to a sink filled with water. That ad, the FTC said, depicted a dangerous situation without warning the child-viewer of the danger of electric shock if the dryer were to come in contact with the water. The FTC, in our view, was justified in ordering that ad to be stopped.

But this does not mean that it would be acceptable for the FTC to become committed to a broad ban against any advertising aimed at "very young" children or advertising of most "sugared products" for children under age 12. Yet a staff committee of the FTC has recommended consideration of just that kind of far-flung restriction on child-geared advertising. And there are a couple of well-meaning citizens groups seriously advocating this kind of restriction.

The ban proponents say that children are unfair targets for sophisticated advertising techniques. These ads can make the youngsters want things that are not good for them, the argument goes, and puts the parents in the awkward position of having to deny their children items that television praised to the sky. The result can be a parent-child confrontation over an advertised product, or a parent giving in to avoid conflict and thus leading the child on the path of tooth decay and-or obesity with sugared products or spoiling the child with acquisitions way beyond the child's needs.

While there is no denying the effectiveness of television advertising or the mind-boggling statistic that the average child spends three hours a day watching television, to place the onus for anything that goes wrong in the child-parent relationship on the evils of advertising is a simplistic exaggeration. Even the child who sits in front of the television set for three hours a day must spend the rest of his or her waking hours doing some other things such as going to a neighbor's house, attending school, going to a store, playing in the yard. And while doing any of these things, the child is exposed to temptation — the neighbor's toys, the cookies on the store shelf, the blocks in the play corner in school, and son. Surely, these temptations are as real as the untouchable television ads. And yet who would say that the child must be kept in isolation so that he does not know what is available beyond his own home

Adults have to make choices every day between what they can and cannot afford, between what is good for them and not. As these adults raise children, they try to instill in them the skill to make those choices too. It is part of the growing up process to have wants that cannot be fulfilled.

Surely, the FTC's staff committee is not telling us that parents are cop-outs and cannot be trusted with teaching their children to distinguish right from wrong, healthful from harmful, worthwhile from worthless. Yet the ban they propose on child-directed advertising would mean just that.

THE MILWAUKEE JOURNAL
Milwaukee, Wisc., May 31, 1978

Should government place bans on television advertisements aimed at children? That's the question before the Federal Trade Commission.

We can understand why parents sometimes find the ads objectionable, but we believe that any ban would be a harmful, ham-handed response.

First, some background: A recent report by the FTC staff recommended a ban on all TV ads directed at children under age 8, and a ban on ads for highly sugared foods (such as pre-sweetened cereals) on programs seen by large numbers of children between ages 8 and 12. The report also recommends that the FTC require advertisers to pay for public service nutritional messages.

The report cites studies indicating young children (1) often cannot distinguish between a television program and a commercial, and (2) cannot perceive exaggeration in a commercial message, thereby accepting it at face value. In short, the FTC staff contends that TV ads aimed at children violate their right to protection from adult exploitation.

The staff has a point. TV ads probably have helped turn many children into what one ad man terms "highly successful little naggers." Little children may not be able to buy products, but anyone who has ever observed tots in a supermarket knows they often can wheedle a harried parent into questionable purchases. If children did not exert substantial influence on their parents' buying habits, advertisers would not spend $600 million a year trying to influence them.

However, to slap wholesale bans on ads would be overkill. There are other ways to address the problem short of government obliterating an advertiser's right to advertise legal products. Such abridgement would set a fearsome precedent for all forms of expression.

It's highly debatable whether commercials per se harm children. Take high-sugar food. The chief problem comes when parents allow themselves to be pressured into buying too many unhealthful goodies. Parental common sense and fortitude remain the best protection for children.

Parents can limit a child's TV watching, and many do. They can also say no at the supermarket and toy store. Many have been saying no for years.

The burden on all parents can be eased, however, by the TV industry and advertisers themselves. Stations should run public service messages for children on the importance of eating right and the danger of too much sugar. The public messages can be as catchy as commercials and reinforce parents' efforts to discourage bad eating habits.

Networks and advertisers also should review the frequency and content of children's commercials. In that regard, growing parental concern and the threat of government intervention may already be having a corrective effect.

In summary, a full or partial ban on advertising would not transform weak parents into good ones, but it would represent encroachment on the First Amendment. And after bans on children's ads, what next? Already one consumer group wants the FTC to ban advertisements for high-fat foods, such as hamburgers and ice cream.

When government begins to censor the air waves in this manner, divining which messages are good and which are harmful, there is no logical limit to potential intervention. We find that scarier than any box of sugar coated flakes.

The Cleveland Press
Cleveland, Ohio, March 6, 1978

In its desire to stop children from eating too much sugar and harming their teeth, the Federal Trade Commission is considering a worrisome set of restrictions on television advertising.

Urged on by its activist staff, the FTC has called for public comment on proposed rules that would:

Ban advertising on programs aimed at children under 8 years old; bar ads for sugar-coated products likely to cause tooth decay from programs for youngsters under 12; force advertisers of other sugary products on under-12 programs to pay for "nutritional and health" messages — in effect discouraging use of their own wares.

The FTC's concern is understandable. Kids are easily tempted by products touted on TV and pester their parents to buy them. But is it the duty of the FTC or of parents to decide what children watch on TV and what they eat?

The answer is easy. If the drift to ever-increasing government intrusion in people's lives is to be stopped, parents will have to learn to say to their children, "No, you can't have everything you see on TV" and "No, Sugar Gloppies aren't good for you and you can't have them for breakfast."

Of course the FTC can cite the ban on TV cigarette commercials as precedent for what it wants to do. But there is a big difference between the hazards of lung cancer and toothache. Logically the next step would be to attack products that the regulators think cause hangnail.

If the FTC gains the power to censor commercials, how long will it be before other agencies seek to influence the contents of the programs themselves? It doesn't take much imagination to foresee the Civil Rights Commission wanting to indoctrinate children in "correct" racial attitudes, the Internal Revenue Service teaching that taxpaying is a pleasure and the Pentagon huckstering kiddie support for one of its pet wars.

And if the FTC finally gets its way and bumps from the airwaves products it thinks causes tooth decay, what good will it do? The same brand-name products will be artfully displayed and available on supermarket shelves. And they will be bought.

In addition, a host of rarely advertised "generic" candies such as lollipops, gumdrops and jellybeans will continue to fill the candy stores. All loaded with sugar and presumably capable of causing caries.

What then? Well, if the FTC runs true to form it will want to station an FBI agent in every candy store in the country. Ideally the agent will be a big tough fellow, like Kojak and when a sugar-crazed delinquent comes in seeking a lollipop fix, the G-man will threaten to break both his legs.

After all, as long as we're moving toward big brotherism, why not do it right?

THE SACRAMENTO BEE
Sacramento, Cal., April 20, 1978

For the first time in its history, the Federal Trade Commission is considering a ban not just on one series of television commercials but on all advertising directed to young children. In a report to the commission, the FTC staff concluded that there is inherent unfairness in TV ads arising out of the "striking imbalance of sophistication and power between well-financed adult advertisers...and children, many of whom are too young to appreciate what advertising is." The proposal strikes directly at an issue that concerns thousands of parents who have become increasingly angry at the commercials for toys, candy and junk food pushed on youngsters during children's programs.

All members of the commission agree that there is enough unfairness and deception in current advertising to require some kind of regulation, particularly with respect to commercials for candy and high-sugar cereals, but the majority appears to favor something short of outright prohibition. We share those reservations, particularly in light of the uncertain effects of an outright ban.

Although the FTC staff estimates that the average child sees 20,000 commercials a year, among them 7,000 for sugared cereals, we feel parents share the responsibility for what children see and believe on television, and that alternatives to an outright ban should be considered. Among those being contemplated by the FTC are requirements that advertisers include nutritional information in their ads, restrictions on the techniques used, and limits on the number of commercials that can be aired in any given period.

The FTC is now soliciting comments from individuals and interested groups and will conduct hearings in San Francisco and Washington this summer. A final decision is due sometime next year. We think a rule is needed but we hope it will, at least initially, consist of something short of outright prohibition. If the FTC can find one broad category of commercials as inherently unfair and deceptive, it can make the same finding for others. There is no safe way that the government can completely protect parents from the Pied Piper or from the children whom he leads astray.

The Wichita Eagle
Wichita, Kans., January 23, 1979

Almost everyone, from time to time, complains about television advertising. There are too many ads, they insult your intelligence, they are repeated too often — these are the usual gripes.

But there is a big segment of television watchers who seldom complain. They are the children of America, who watch an average of 20,000 commercials a year while stationed in front of the tube. That figures out to 55 advertisements each and every day.

Rightfully, the Federal Communications Commission has gotten involved in examining the effects that kind of exposure to mass merchandising may be having on kids. Hearings began earlier this week on proposals that either would ban altogether or severely limit television ads aimed at children.

Probably the worst offenders are the dozens of commercials promoting the myriad of pre-sweetened breakfast cereals and the "action" toys that so appeal to youngsters. Saturday morning cartoon shows, although stripped of much of the violence of a few years ago, still are thoroughly shot through by endless advertisements exhorting the young viewers to buy this or that product.

The cereal and toy companies argue they have the right to promote their products, and that banning children's television ads would infringe on their right to do business and their freedom of speech.

But do they have the right to convince children that heavily-sugared cereals that may cause tooth decay are the best thing for them? Or to lead them to believe that a toy will perform as flawlessly for them as for the child

in a commercial? There is a question of simple honesty involved.

The main fear, of course, is that children are being preyed on before they have the ability to evaluate and make reasonable choices on the products being pushed. It must be extremely confusing for a child to see every cereal and every toy touted as "the best." The long-term effects of being treated as a consumer from the time a person is a toddler have yet to be examined, but surely such treatment must dull that person's ability to evaluate the quality of products.

The American Academy of Pediatrics is concerned enough that its membership of 15,000 children's doctors has gone on record favoring an end to "the commercial exploitation of children through excessive and inappropriate television advertising." While calling for a ban on aimed-for-children ads, the academy also, however, urges its members to "remind parents that the ultimate responsibility for monitoring television's effect on children rests with the family."

That makes sense because even the most convincing commercial usually must have a willing or permissive adult's consent to be effective when it comes time to make a purchase. There aren't many children who have the opportunity to go out and buy a box of sweetened cereal or a new toy strictly on their own.

Whether limits on children's TV advertising, an all-out ban, or offsetting educational ads are in order, the time has come for adults on both sides to accept their responsibilities. All parents must try to help children make the right decisions for the right reasons, as part of the growing-up process.

THE WALL STREET JOURNAL
New York, N.Y., August 29, 1978

It makes us sleep better at night to know that the staff of the Federal Trade Commission never slackens in its pursuit of the evils of television advertising. We've recently learned, for instance, that our regulators are no longer content just to watch over the words that advertisers put on the tube; now they want to go after the pictures as well.

By now the commission has made it very dangerous for an advertiser to use any words on TV that might be construed as misleading to consumers. But FTC staffers are disturbed by the way the admen have responded to their new constraints. Instead of starting to produce commercials full of wholesome information, the Madison Avenue types—clever devils that they are—have begun to rely more heavily on pictures of evocative scenery and beautiful people to put their message across. "The media," one FTC official summed it up, "have left the written word behind in a cloud of dust."

But where the TV commercial goes, the FTC will follow; so the FTC staff is now thinking about how to deal with the advertising impact that visual images make. Granted, they're going to run into new kinds of problems in expanding their efforts: It's "difficult to agree on the meaning or message communicated by a photograph," said one man in the Bureau of Consumer Protection, "and thus difficult to agree whether a theme or message in a picture is legally deceptive." So now they're concocting ways to get around that.

They may set up a panel of consumers to see whether people agree on what TV ad pictures mean. Or, because "the average person wouldn't know what's going on," they may hire a media expert to do the judging instead. They might even seek access to company or ad agency studies of consumer reactions to particular commercials. Of course the commission might have trouble with this new enterprise in the courts: Judges and lawyers, you see, have an unfortunate tendency to be narrowly word-oriented. But the regulators will persevere. Otherwise, "we'll be nitpicking over words while the media are ahead of us."

The FTC staff says it's doing just what its authorizing legislation tells it to do: The commission is supposed to stop deceptive trade practices, and if it leaves out the picture part of advertising "we won't be carrying out our mandate." But when a regulatory agency starts going after an "offense" that has just about no standing in legal doctrine or public opinion, it's clearly not fulfilling a mandate but creating one. The FTC says it doesn't want advertisers to deceive. But a search like the one it's engaged in now shows that what it really doesn't like is that advertising might have the power to persuade.

So the commission finds advertising practices deceptive, advertisers develop new methods to cope with the new rules, the commission says the new methods also deceive, and the game continues. It's a pretty dispiriting performance by regulators without the courage of their convictions to attack free enterprise frontally, and by advertisers who are all too often afraid to defend it.

THE COMMERCIAL APPEAL

Memphis, Tenn., March 8, 1978

IF THE FEDERAL Trade Commission goes off on the latest tangent it's thought up, all of us might as well quit thinking for ourselves.

A few of us have been naive enough to think it's still the prerogative of parents (with help from grandparents, uncles, aunts and perhaps school teachers) to advise their children on what to eat and not to eat. It was generally conceded — or so we thought — that if Mom and Pop wanted to treat the kids to chocolate bars, taffy, ice cream and cake, corn on the cob, pizza pie, or grape jelly and peanut butter, that was their business.

Apparently the FTC differs. At least it does in the field of sugary products advertised on television.

Ah, television, that regulated wasteland of popular taste which represents on the one hand the mass desire to avoid making the brain cells grind against each other at work and on the other the federal bureaucracy's belief that it can think better for all of us than the TV industry or its commercial sponsors.

Poor television, which tries to please the majority and to sell whatever the majority wants most to buy. Of course, one of the pastimes of TV viewers is cursing the commercials, which makes one won-

der why the FTC feels the need to get into the act.

TV is fair game for anybody who wants to deplore anything on the screen. Everybody can be a critic. Even TV personality Steve Allen says, **"Much of television is what I call junk food for the mind."** But Allen adds, **"You have this problem of popular taste."**

YOU HAVE THAT problem in life, too. People have to learn to make choices about what's good for them and what's bad. Individuals have to learn how to avoid sickness, and tooth cavities, and overdosing, and flabbiness, and over-exertion, and so on. They learn as kids, from parents mostly. And if they grow up ignorant of what sugar-coated wheat can do to teeth and gums, it won't be because the FTC does or does not do.

If it's junk, call it that. But spare us the censor.

The Pittsburgh Press

Pittsburgh, Pa., January 28, 1979

The Federal Trade Comission has seen fit to inquire into the insidious threat posed by children's television advertising but so far its hearings have generated little useful information.

At the opening of testimony in San Francisco — there were two weeks of hearings there and there will be five more in Washington — a psychologist warned that 'kidvid' ads could create "inexcusable conflict" between parent and child when the parent says, no, that sugar-coated cereal isn't good for you or no, you can't have that superduper rocket racer (batteries not included).

Next day, an advertising executive suggested that kids have to learn to make marketplace judgments eventually, so the younger they are when they're deceived the sooner they will develop a healthy skepticism.

It would be best to entertain a healthy skepticism about both assumptions.

It's obvious, of course, that the sellers of certain products believe that the shortest route to a parent's pocketbook is through his children. Last year, sponsors spent half-a-billion dollars on television advertising specifically aimed at children.

But is this the government's problem, if it is a problem at all?

Consider that the FTC not only wants to ban all advertising from programs for children under 8 and ban ads for products likely to cause tooth decay from programs for children under 12. It would also require advertisers to pay for FTC-approved "messages" promoting good nutrition and health habits.

If the FTC gets away with this, how long will it be before it — and other agencies — seek to control the actual content of children's programming? And after that, all television programming?

Unfortunately, ABC has already panicked and announced that it will cut back its advertising directed at children by 20 percent beginning next January.

At this rate, bureaucrats will have the broadcasters well under their thumbs by the time the FTC hearings are concluded.

DESERET NEWS

Salt Lake City, Utah, November 20, 1976

Authorities long have agreed that violence too frequently depicted on television harms the emotions, attitude and behavior of children.

Now comes the charge from Action for Children's Television (ACT) that television commercials often have an adverse effect on the minds and bodies of young viewers. ACT is a Boston-based group of parents and educators working since 1968 to upgrade children's TV programming.

The subject will be discussed at the Sixth National Symposium on Children's Television, which opens Sunday at Harvard University. The symposium will examine such things as children's perceptions of advertising messages, television as a tool in consumer education, and regulations to protect children.

The statistics on television's attraction to children are staggering. The National PTA says that by the time the average child graduates from high school, he or she will have spent more time sitting in front of a television set

than studying in the classroom. Other studies indicate the average American child watches more than 25,000 television commercials a year.

ACT has been effective in its efforts to prompt reform in children's programming. Pressured by ACT, the National Association of Broadcasters has lowered advertising time aimed at children on weekends from 16 minutes to nine and one-half minutes per hour.

Parents could help in two ways. They could limit the time children are permitted to watch television and they could protest any commercial or program they believe to be potentially harmful.

There's no doubting television's great potential as an educational tool. Instead of allowing itself to become a tool for mis-teaching children, television ought to find a way — on purpose — to teach children to improve their attitudes, habits and tastes. If such an objective is not soon sought and realized, it may have to be achieved by government regulation.

The Washington Star

Washington, D.C., December 6, 1976

Those who cuddle with the notion that government must save us from ourselves sustain the idea by positing demons to demonstrate the impotence of the populace. We are indebted to Ellen Goodman, of the *Boston Globe*, whose column appears locally in the O.P., for an example of this mentality, as banal as it is poignant.

The subject was "kidvid" advertising. There was convened recently something called the Action for Children's Television Workshop and the subject was "Children as Consumers."

". . . The three-day conference in Cambridge finally got down to wrestling with the most basic truth about advertising — that its morality rests on the product," she wrote. It appears that this group has recognized a distinction between false ads and "true" ads that have a harmful potential.

In other words, an advertisement on the tube may be "true" to the qualities of the product, yet insidious in its effect on the impressionable young minds mesmerized in front of the TV. The organization, under the acronym of "ACT," has a suit pending against Milky Way candy bars which, Ms. Goodman asserts, "clearly did overdo it with an ad urging, 'At home, at work, at play, all day . . . Milky Way.' "

Obviously, only a pet rock would not react indignantly to that sort of manipulation by cynical corporations.

Ms. Goodman brought front and center Dr. Joan Gussow, head of the nutrition department at Columbia University — remember the name; if she ends up in the federal bureaucracy, we'll see some gorgeous "mandates." Dr. Gussow asks, rhetorically, we presume, "Is it moral — or even sensible — to allow them (the children) to be assaulted with a barrage of food products that add up to audio-visual diabetes?" She

noted, in the columnist's words, that "we permit a handful of companies to induce bad habits in children that lead to disease and add to the problems and expenses of an entire society."

Have we sunk into such vegetative passivity that the television is an *inducer* of bad habits among the young? Have parents become so spineless that they are helpless before the child's command to buy the sugar-loaded breakfast cereal or whatever? How does a six-year-old react to a Milky Way ad on the tube? Well, unless the child has an independent income, he or she has to get the dime (or whatever it costs now) for the candy bar somewhere. Do we face the prospect of a guerrilla war from tricycle riders whose parents have been so repressive as to say, "No"?

It is easy enough to dismiss crusaders of the sort gathered at Cambridge as merely silly. But their agony over kidvid advertising reveals a dolorous, and dubious, view of the American people — a mindless and Pavlovian folk, prisoners of tube and tots.

The good soldiers of "ACT" are apparently unaware of a basic fact about products: Corporations are timid; the larger they are, the more timid. A breakfast cereal that is 50 per cent sugar will remain on the shelves only so long as parents — not children — purchase it. Ads do not induce bad habits. Those who believe that government regulation is an appropriate mechanism for reforming national bad habits should attend more than a Cambridge workshop.

The "ACT" people are indeed correct that there is a good deal of junk flogged on TV. But the trouble is that they have the problem by the tail — and think they can strangle it from that end of the animal.

The Salt Lake Tribune

Salt Lake City, Utah, August 6, 1976

There's no use debating the point: Television has become an immensely powerful influence in American life. So much so that few people really know how to handle the issues this development raises.

Recently, the U.S. House communications subcommittee concluded hearings undecided what to do about commercials that may have an undesirable affect on children. Outspoken subcommittee members were convinced the affect occurs, but weren't sure how the federal government can help. And for several reasons.

Basically, regulating commercials — when they should appear, what they can be allowed to say — risks serious tampering with the country's freedom of speech guarantees. Once you start censoring commercials, it's a shorter jump to regulating program content. Then, why limit these restrictions to television only? How about objectionable material in magazines, newspapers, on radio or in theaters? Give comstockery some rein and it will soon be off at a full gallop.

The subcommittee proceedings illustrated what is often so pernicious about the censorship impulse. Congressmen discovered very little research has been done on what possible harm youngsters might suffer from viewing particular TV commercials. No one has successfully isolated this affect from all other influences a child encounters on a daily basis.

To a large extent, then, it's merely suspected that the problem is serious enough to justify federal interference. And while much legislation may pass on those grounds, they aren't sufficient when a right as fundamental as free speech is at stake.

Advertising can be seen prospecting a community's outer limits of good taste and propriety. It is, in that sense, a dynamic communications form, both anticipating and reflecting changes in public standards. By and large, however, the process has been responsible, avoiding obviously objectionable or harmful methods and altering content when the unexpected or unintended occurs. After all, the advertiser depends on the public's good will, not its anger and resentment.

Continued emphasis on self-regulation may be appropriate, principally because it always is. But no case for increasing the insidious imposition of federal control on TV or other advertising has been made.

HERALD EXAMINER

Los Angeles, Cal., February 1, 1979

It was Justice Louis Brandeis who warned that we should "be most on our guard when the government's purposes are beneficent." Brandeis' point was that one man's conscience is always another's favorite comedian. This is a relatively harmless dynamic ordinarily but it can become a cruel joke when government gets into the business of regulating conscience.

Which is precisely what the Federal Trade Commission (FTC) is up to these days. The FTC has been holding hearings on proposed rules which would limit or ban certain kinds of television advertising aimed at children. The goal of the "kid-vid" rules, as they are called, is to cut down on the amount of sugar our children eat.

Think about it:

If someone you knew had

a problem with alcohol . . .

That is a laudatory aim no one can really dispute. However, studies show that Americans have been eating the amount of sugar they eat now since the turn of the century — in other words, before television, since television, and in spite of television. So what is being disputed, by cereal manufacturers and others, is not the purpose of the ban, but rather the way the FTC has chosen to pursue its goal of behavior modification.

Think about it: If someone you knew had a problem with alcohol, would you send them to Alcoholics Anonymous, or seek a ban on alcohol advertising? Would you try to stop them from drinking alcohol, or would you rail at those who sell them the stuff?

Well, you say, that misses the point. The point is that alcohol is bad for you and shouldn't be available on the market.

Without arguing the pros and cons of that issue, we would simply say: fine. Have the government fund an exhaustive study of the subject, and if the product is determined harmful, then remove it from the market.

But, you say, the alcohol lobby is too strong. The product will never be banned. The best we can do is to ban the advertising of alcohol.

In other words, since we are unable to remove the object of temptation from the market, we will eliminate all incentives to that temptation. This is the same reason we are now considering full public financing of elections; but we're not sure that what works for politicians will necessarily work for kids.

For one, this represents an extraordinarily generous assessment of the influence of advertising on rug rats. We remember when we were children, when we regularly bolted from the TV during commercials to raid the refrigerator. Upon opening that refrigerator, however, we found no Cap'n Crunch. There were no Sugar Loops or Fruit Freakies or Choco-Pops or Clark bars. There wasn't so much as a cookie. There was nothing but that dull, tedious fare children know to be "good for them," and resent, for the same reason they resent going to school.

Why was the cupboard bare of teeth-rotting, evilly-sugared goodies? Very simply because the Chancellor of the Exchequer wouldn't have that garbage in the house. And frankly, her word was law.

Which brings us back to the "law" the FTC is currently considering. It is motivated, we believe, not by a pressing need to reduce the sugar consumption of our children. Instead, it is an attempt — a rather misguided and clumsy attempt — to address fundamental changes in our society.

The telling phrase is in the FTC staff report which prompted the proposed rules. It is a bit of gratuitous psycho-babble which alleges that kiddie advertising increases the incidence of parent-child "conflict." Increases, in other words, the potential for guilt in the single parent, who works all week in order to keep Junior in Choco-Pops thereby allowing Junior's regular baby sitter to be the television. So that when Mom or Dad has to "pay" the sitter — when Mom or Dad has to rip the Choco Pops out of Junior's hands at the supermarket — Mom or Dad, already mightily guilty, feels even worse.

But we doubt that banning children's advertising will solve that problem. Increased government funding for day care centers might help; more generous tax credits for children, and for single parents with children, might do even more. And a shot in the arm to PBS which would result in competitive, interesting programming might obviate the mess altogether.

The point is, if Mom and Dad can't stop Junior from buying something at the market, then why will an absence of TV advertising change things? If the logic of the ad ban is truly "out of sight, out of mind," then the only efficacious solution is to leave Junior in front of the tube when

. . . would you send him to

AA, or seek a ban on

alcohol advertising?

they go shopping. Because — ads or no ads — Choco Pops will still be there at the store, waiting to work their ineffable magic on the kids.

There is another issue which the FTC proposals raise, and it is an ugly one. This is the issue of whether we are going to hold advertisers responsible for every motivational-behavior pattern we perceive as a problem.

If we are going to do so, is it fair to presume that we will also ban the ad which advises us to "Join the people who've joined the Army"? After all, this ad clearly fails to advise us that military service may be harmful to our health.

We doubt it. In the situation of the Army, as in the situation of the "kid-vid" rule, the consumer best represents his own self-interest. If parents don't like sugared goods, let them boycott those goods. If the goods are really harmful to our health, let the government take them off the market. But if we just think they pose a clear and present danger to our peace of mind on Saturday morning when we do the shopping — that's another story. And it's not a story the government should be plotting for us.

The Miami Herald

Miami, Fla., March 4, 1978

TELEVISION affects children who watch it — there's not much doubt about that. Research confirms the subjective impression formed by many parents who've observed their own offspring sitting transfixed before the tube on Saturday mornings, intent upon whatever the networks dish out.

What commercial television dishes out for children these days is a a steady diet of pap programming interspersed with hard-sell advertising designed to motivate youngsters to buy products or to induce their parents to do so.

Critics point out that many of the products are worse than useless. These range from sugar-coated cereals that rot the teeth to toys and games that promote mayhem among playmates.

Trouble is, having identified a problem, some of the critics have come up with the wrong solution: Government intervention to ban advertising from children's television.

The Federal Trade Commission has begun hearings on whether or not such advertising ought to be banned. Do-gooders are turning out in force to lobby for such a rule.

It is part of a disquieting trend that began with the banning of cigaret advertising from television. Waiting in the wings are bans on other types of advertising.

These proposed bans run counter to recent decisions of the U.S. Supreme Court. Increasingly it has held that "paid speech" is entitled to First Amendment protection against Governmental restraint.

We trust, therefore, that any move to extend ad bans will be vigorously opposed in the courts by advertisers and the television industry. But that would take time and money — for both industry and the Government.

Moreover, the overburdened court system often has shown a reluctance of late to tread on territory belonging to "the fourth branch of Government," regulatory agencies such as the FTC. So there is no assurance that the industry would get its day in court.

Even if it does, the case could drag on for years before a final ruling emerges. In the meantime, if a ban were allowed to remain in force pending a court decision, the industries involved would be unfairly deprived of substantial sums of money — sums far exceeding the amounts of fines the Government has levied for corporate wrongdoing.

It seems to us that there must be better approaches to the problems arising from the powerful effects of television on children — approaches that are fairer to all concerned and that do not raise First Amendment issues.

Indeed, it is encouraging to note that the FTC, in its opening session on the matter, appeared to be looking for alternatives to a ban.

Better parental supervision of what children watch is one way. Better education about nutrition — to counter the sugar-coated appeals that seem to be at the heart of the present controversy — is another.

Counter-propaganda, it seems to us, would be much more in line with the American concept of a free marketplace of ideas than would be a ban on advertising. Such bans open the door to ever-broader censorship. That is why we hope the FTC will reject such a solution for children's television.

Newsday

Gardin City, N.Y., August 21, 1978

Are cavities bad for you?

Are fat children unhappier and unhealthier than other children?

Is peddling sugar to kids a bad idea?

For a lot of people the answer to those questions is yes, and for some it follows that the government ought to do something about it. As a result, the television industry has another problem just as it was celebrating a California judge's ruling that it couldn't be held liable for the effects of violence on the tube unless incitement was proved.

The issue now is TV commercials aimed at children, a $500-million-a-year business. Of that, a goodly portion goes toward persuading kiddies to get their mommies to buy candy and sugar-laden breakfast cereals. Unfortunately, a lot of mommies do.

Now two federal agencies are looking into the situation despite strenuous opposition from advertisers and broadcasters, who argue that nutrition is a matter of parental discretion. That's easy to say until you've tried to drag a screaming 5-year-old away from the TV-touted Honeyhops and Loonifruits on the supermarket cereal shelf.

In the forefront of the controversy is the Federal Trade Commission, which intends to hold extensive hearings beginning in November. The Federal Communications Commission plans to look into the broader question of children's programing and advertising later this year.

The FTC staff has prepared a number of options, such as requiring counter-commercials to promote good nutrition, restricting commercials aimed at the very youngest viewers and imposing an outright ban on TV ads aimed at children.

With one exception, the cereal and candy industries have opposed the FTC inquiry unanimously. The lone dissenting voice belongs to Kenneth Mason, president of the Quaker Oats Co., which last year spent $57.7 million on TV commercials. He thinks there's a need for fundamental change in the way commercial television is used to entertain and enlighten the very young.

Senator Lowell Weicker (R-Conn.) is trying to stop the inquiry by refusing funds to conduct it. But at the very least it's worth trying to find out just how kids are affected and what, if anything, can be done to improve the spiritual nourishment they receive via the tube along with the bodily nourishment it promotes. Then, we hope, the issues can be debated on their merits.

The Boston Globe

Boston, Mass., October 6, 1977

As we all know, some people will do anything for a buck. But a recent report that television advertising researchers are using American children as guinea pigs in secret studies to determine their hidden needs is reprehensible and should be promptly stopped. Out of the mouths of babes, indeed.

According to TV Guide magazine, the research findings are used "to develop television commercials calculated to make children grab for supermarket-impulse items or nag parents for sponsor brands." As if they weren't doing that already.

Today there are more than 50 million American children under the age of 13. It is estimated that they watch an average of at least 22,000 commercials a year. Firms making a sales pitch to young audiences spend some $76 million a year in the process. That's not hay.

It has long been the contention of concerned parents that the average child is no match for the hard-sell challenge. He hasn't the perspective his parents have developed with years of practice on humbug. By watching, the child is enticed to long for things his family cannot always afford or for things he should not necessarily have and which, when they are in hand, do not add up to the promises of what he expected.

Advertising aimed at children is unfair. It pits a four or five-year-old against million-dollar industries. A child glued to the set may be in far greater need of consumer protection than his parents.

This has long been the contention of Newton-based Action for Children's Television, a nonprofit, foundation-supported organization that has been waging a lengthy and highly popular campaign to remove, or at least substantially improve, advertising on children's television programs. It deserves support.

ARKANSAS DEMOCRAT
Little Rock, Ark., April 12, 1977

Action for Children's Television, the consumer group that nobly aspires to make TV viewing fit for impressionable young minds, has asked the Federal Trade Commission to ban candy advertising from the tube. And unfortunately, it wouldn't be out of character for the FTC to try to perpetrate such a farce.

ACT contends that TV candy butchers prey on kids' gullibility, so ACT has set out to protect young minds from cruel distortions of fact, and to protect young mouths from the consequent ravages of tooth decay. Ironically, ACT could care less about protecting the First Amendment's guarantee of free commerical speech.

The anti-candy ad group shows no interest in protecting the advertiser's right to free speech and free access to the marketplace of goods, services and ideas; nor does ACT seem interested in protecting consumers — child and adult — in their unquestioned right to obtain whatever information about a product its advertising may impart.

Obviously, much advertising aimed at youngsters is poorly-conceived, frivolous and some of it may even be deceptive. But that's true of ads aimed at adult target markets, too. What ACT must realize is that, in our free-enterprise economic system, nothing can happen until someone sells something. Advertising is one means of promoting those sales, and television — an effective means of advertising, and the only medium to combine simultaneous visual and verbal images — must remain available to every advertiser.

Children may be naive consumers, but no more naive about their purchasing than are many adults; and the earlier in life that youngsters realize that ads can be misleading as well as informative the better prepared they will be, if guided by their parents in buying decisions, to grow into adults who are better able to function within the free-enterprise system.

THE SUN
Baltimore, Md., March 3, 1978

The cereal industry's arguments against a ban on sugared breakfast cereal television ads aimed at children are only superficially plausible. The industry insists there is nutritional value in the cereals and no doubt there is. But—as Federal Trade Commission staffers point out in their proposal to ban the ads—not all that much. Moreover the sugar, which can be a third of the total content of the cereal, represents "empty calories." That is, it is without nutritional value. So if a child's diet is otherwise nutritionally balanced, the sugar may add enough useless calories to promote obesity. Or, conversely, if a child relies on these empty calories for too much of his total diet, he can become malnourished.

The ban on sugared cereal ads is one of a sweeping set of FTC staff proposals. Included also is a proposal to end TV advertising specifically aimed at "very young" children. Another proposal would require TV advertisers of various non-cereal sugared products to pay for countervailing nutritional messages on TV. Advertisers and broadcasters no doubt will insist the proposals would violate the First Amendment's free speech guarantees.

It is unclear now just how much First Amendment protection commercials enjoy. Until 1974, commercials were regarded as being without such protection, but in that year the U.S. Supreme Court ruled, in effect, that a government agency wishing to restrict commercials would have to demonstrate a compelling interest in doing so. Given the tendency of the courts to go out of their way to protect children, it may not be difficult for the FTC to establish that a compelling interest exists. Commercials aimed at very young children are a sort of brainwashing. Children cannot normally be expected to make wise nutritional choices and ought to be protected against skillful pleas for unwise ones.

Although we find the FTC staffers' ultimate goals laudable, we are not fully convinced that advertising bans are the answer. It might be more effective to allow the commercials to continue, but to insist that they be balanced by educational messages pointing out the ads' flawed reasoning and distortion of the facts. Reportedly the tobacco industry tacitly acquiesced in the banning of cigarette advertising on TV because anti-cigarette messages were removed at the same time. This is a strong endorsement for the efficacy of the educational messages.

The Evening Gazette
Worcester, Mass., September 9, 1978

A big issue these days involves television commercials and children. The thinking is that gullible youngsters are prey to the sharp selling techniques for everything from sugar-coated cereal to toy models of the "Million Dollar Man."

But a hotter issue lately involves the question of who should rescue the children from television hype.

Some advocate the easy way out. They urge a government ban on commercials beamed at children. Another school of thought that surfaced the other day at the American Psychological Association's annual meeting holds that youngsters should be "immunized" against persuasive TV ads. The "vaccine" would be television films that tell the "truth" about the products and counter the persuasiveness of the commercials.

We doubt either group has the answer.

Federal intervention would simply amount to censorship. An insulated bureaucrat in Washington would decide what we should watch on television. The ramifications of that are obvious. Beyond that, there is the government's dismal record in attempting to regulate anything at all. Government meddling usually means further restraints on free enterprise, restraints on personal freedom, and pouring millions of dollars down the drain in the effort to do it.

Are more people being persuaded not to smoke because the government has banned cigarette ads on television? We doubt it. Has illiteracy been wiped out because the government spent millions upon millions in the last decade to teach people how to read? An exhaustive recent study concluded that the program was for the most part a huge waste of time and dollars.

The "immunization" technique doesn't seem much more hopeful. Under that system, presumably the networks would have to air "equal time" slots about tooth decay every time a cereal maker aired a pitch for its sugary breakfast flakes. The danger again is the government interfering with the people's right to develop their own critical choices in life.

The best and perhaps the only real answer to the problem lies in the home. What children watch and eat should be regulated by their parents. Let's leave it up to the family to educate children to develop a healthy skepticism toward life's commercial and other appeals.

RENO EVENING GAZETTE
Reno, Nev., March 1, 1978

The Federal Trade Commission (FTC) is widening the war against, sugar-coated cerals by studying ways to slow down the steady, unending flow of television commercials. Children see 20,000 commercials a year and sweets are the most touted product.

Anyone who has sampled the likes of "Booberry" or "Count Chocula" and who has watched some of the slapdash, two-frames-a-second cartoons that hold the cereal ads apart on Saturday morning TV, has got to seriously question his children's taste in both food and television fare.

The FTC shares your concern that sugar-coated cereals are probably not the most wholesome things kids can eat and that they very likely contribute to tooth decay. It is also a probability that eight hours a day of TV-watching (16 on Saturday) can contribute to mental decay.

Placing the FTC's well-meaning intentions aside for a moment, after agreeing that their concerns for physical and mental health are quite genuine, the job of policing the situation rests finally and irrevocably with the parent.

The parent is the one who should have enough gumption to say "It's time to turn off the TV, clean up your rooms and go outside and play," when the kids would rather sit like a row of little bumps on a log for the rest of the day

The second challenge comes in the grocery store. Parents should be willing to say "no" when youngsters begin the inevitable clamor for the latest innovation in the science of breakfast foods.

We agree that it is a shallow industry that takes pride in the ability to con several million preschoolers into pestering their mothers for a particular brand of cereal. And we have little patience with a TV cartoon industry that cranks out plotless, humorless and amateurish products that make Mickey Mouse, Bugs Bunny and Roadrunner aficionados hoot and scoff.

However, we draw the line at presuming that it is the FTC's job to dictate good judgment to the television consumer. The most efficient quality control device is still the on-off switch.

This year, for the first time since television became commercially feasible, audiences have declined instead of increasing. Baffled experts have blamed everything from the advent of video games to the energy crisis. We suggest that people are learning to switch off mediocrity and the industry is so stunned and pre-conditioned, they haven't yet grasped the significance of the situation.

But in the final analysis, regularly tuning out enervating cartoons and steadfastly declining to buy the latest sugar-coated fad, would kill them quicker and more effectively than the FTC could every hope to do with a whole new book of regulations.

FORT WORTH STAR-TELEGRAM

Fort Worth, Texas, January 23, 1978

Those vendors of sugary treats, toys and advertising time who are screaming that the Federal Trade Commission should not intrude its regulatory nose in the area of television commercials directed toward children may be correct.

Perhaps the Environmental Protection Agency should be looking into the matter instead. It could be argued that what is being debated in the FTC hearings in San Francisco is a pollution matter.

Of course, the EPA has not yet promulgated any regulations aimed at abating child pollution; therefore the FTC appears to be stuck with trying to use its machinery to force the Good Ship Lollipop to clean up its effluent.

At the center of the debate are recommendations from the FTC staff to the effect that:

—All television advertising beamed toward children less than eight should be banned. The assumption underlying that recommendation is that children so young cannot understand that they are being tempted to buy something.

—Television advertising of such highly-sugared products as pre-sweetened cereals, snacks and soft drinks aimed at children less than 12 should be banned.

—Commercials shown in conjunction with childrens television shows for other kinds of sweets should be accompanied by mandatory, counter-balancing health and nutritional spots.

Those are very strong prescriptions. The resistance of the vendors of children's fare and television advertising to taking them is understandable. They envision revenue losses mounting into the hundreds of millions of dollars collectively, if those rules go into effect.

They suggest that their advertising does not promote dental or other kinds of health damage either physical nor psychological

—Parents, they argue further, can solve any problem they perceive relative to the commercials by merely limiting the television viewing of their children.

They are joined in their defensive stance by editorialists with several major publications and other concerned civil libertarians who see a threat to freedom of speech if the FTC gets this kind of regulatory authority.

The position of some "experts" to the effect that no harm is being done by that kind of advertising flies in the face of common sense and experience.

Any non-expert with television-viewing small children knows what those commercials are like and how they affect their children and their relationships with them.

To say that parents can solve the problem is to beg the question. And the perveyors of children's fare know that the overwhelming majority of parents will not ban Saturday morning television viewing for their small children.

They wouldn't suggest that if they believed it would happen because they would lose as much money from a parental boycott as they fear they would from an FTC ban.

The FTC is considering those proposed regulations because they have been urged to do so by many parents, dentists, pediatricians and other concerned citizens.

The suggestion of a threat to freedom of speech presents a painful dilemma. Regulation that threatens to impinge upon this cherished right should be resisted.

But regulation is all too often born out of abuse. And many merchandisers of children's fare appear to have abused their accessibility to tender, impressionable minds.

Even some representatives of the cereal industry, which dispenses sugar-coated munchies, have implied that.

The president of Quaker Oats Co., Kenneth Mason recently criticized "the frequency, blatancy, and often the sheer idiocy of some of the commercials."

Perhaps this whole debate could be abated and the need for strong FTC restrictions obviated, if the kiddy polluters would decide now to clean up their acts.

If the Good Ship Lollipop can't steer a better course, someone will just have to take it in tow.

The San Diego Union

San Diego, Cal., January 21, 1979

There may be no clearer example of empire building by government regulators than the Federal Trade Commission's current crusade to dictate the content of television advertising aimed at children.

To save America from the menace of pre-sugared cereals, candy bars, and toys that fail to meet a bureaucrat's arbitrary standard of suitability, the FTC is considering:

— Banning all television advertising directed at children under eight years of age.

— Prohibiting commercials for sugared products that might contribute to tooth decay in children under 12 years of age.

— Requiring advertisers to pay for "nutrition" and "health" ads whose content would be determined by the commission.

In short, the Federal Trade Commission proposes to become, in the words of the Washington Post, a great national nanny.

The legitimate role of parents gets short shrift from the commission. Overlooked is the simple fact that children too young to understand that television commercials are sales pitches rarely do the family shopping. Mom and Dad buy the food. And Mom and Dad are perfectly capable of saying no to a child whose vision of dinner is a dozen candy bars or a box of Fruit Loops.

Has it occurred to the commission that even children who have never watched an hour of television in their lives might still favor a breakfast of ice cream and lollipops?

Admittedly, the FTC staff report on which these proposals are based does mention parents. The report suggests that parental disapproval of a child's television-induced gastronomical fantasies fosters "alienation" and "child-parent conflict." Bunk. Any responsible parent finds it necessary to say no to a child a dozen times a day, and does so without producing neurosis.

As for tooth decay, even the FTC doesn't pretend that there is a direct correlation between watching television commercials and the incidence of dental cavities.

Another real puzzler is how the commission would square its compulsory health and nutrition advertising with its own staff report's conclusion that "the representation that one food is more healthful than another . . . is false and deceptive." But should the proposal be adopted, it would cost food marketers and consumers tens of millions of dollars to find out.

As if all this were not enough to bury the FTC proposals under an avalanche of ridicule, consider the First Amendment implications of these potential regulations. If the commission, acting on the basis of bogus or nonexistent scientific evidence, can ban or restrict ads for cereal, candy and toys, what form of commercial speech is safe from the Washington censors?

Will asparagus marketers have to include a 30-second homily on the need for a balanced diet as the price for getting their ad on the air? What about potatoes? An undiluted diet of spuds surely must contain its own special threat to health. Are teenagers sufficiently cognizant of these dangers to resist a pitch for french fries?

And how is the commission to decide which commercials are beamed solely at seven year olds and thus subject to outright prohibition?

There simply is no end to the mischief that might be wrought under the precedents inherent in these proposed regulations.

All this is not to say that the FTC should relax its enforcement of existing law against false and misleading advertising. But we do think the agency should give parents a modicum of credit for common sense in raising their own offspring.

This year, it will cost American taxpayers $66.4 million to maintain the Federal Trade Commission in the style to which it has become accustomed. For that kind of money, we are entitled to something more constructive than a holy war on chocolate bars and breakfast cereal.

St. Petersburg Times

St. Petersburg, Fla., March 10, 1976

Some people say just watching TV is enough to drive them to drink, but they don't really mean it. Now comes a Senate subcommittee, however, which is exploring this question for real.

It wants to know whether frequent televised portrayals of social or on-the-job drinking contribute to an unhealthy attitude toward liquor and an increase in alcoholism.

Don Newcombe, the ex-Brooklyn Dodger who drank himself off the diamond, testified he first hit the bottle at age 8 because other family members were drinking. But he said since his recovery, and in his subsequent educational campaign against excessive drinking, he has concluded that TV helps build a false success myth around liquor.

"SEVERAL TIMES a night, hundreds of times a week, thousands of times a year, the message that comes across is that alcohol is an important and necessary part of life," Newcombe said.

CBS Vice President Thomas J. Swafford, also a recovered alcoholic, denied this contention. He said the fact is that drinking is a part of life, and that TV can't pretend that it isn't.

Of course, that also was TV's answer, for years, when studies were suggesting a correlation between televised violence and increases in crime. Finally, under popular pressure, the industry has taken steps at least to limit violence in shows during an evening "family viewing" hour.

The idea here was to shield impressionable youth. Unfortunately, youth doesn't always confine its viewing to this particular time. Millions of children still spend many hours every week glued to the tube, absorbing the tough talk, fist fights and shootings.

According to Newcombe, they also are being needlessly immersed in the message that drinking is one of the keys to success. Although it no doubt can be shown there are other and more significant causes of alcoholism, there has to be some merit in Newcombe's contention.

And we have no doubt that, without any offensive effort at censorship, the industry could reduce materially the extent to which the social drink is regularly used as a crutch for lazy scriptwriters.

SWAFFORD SAYS the industry is aware of the problem and already is acting to delete misleading and superfluous references to drinking both from its programs and its advertising.

That is good news. Thoughtful parents will be watching to see how it works out. In the end, though, final responsibility no doubt will continue to rest with the parents to exercise discretion about what their children are watching.

Reprinted by permission

The Hartford Courant

Hartford, Conn., July 10, 1975

Does television mold attitudes of viewers or merely reflect their lifestyle? Does watching a tv hero or heroine have a scotch on the rocks "normalize" that activity or is its purpose to put "realism" into the action? Whatever the case plenty of liquor flows on prime time on the three major networks.

The Christian Science Monitor surveyed 249 shows in 250 hours of viewing over a two-month period. It found that although commercial advertising of hard alcoholic spirits is prohibited and the tv code says liquor use should be "de-emphasized" both good guys and bad guys pour themselves a drink with unrelenting regularity.

Champion elbow-benders are Gunsmoke and MASH, both of CBS, where liquor was poured once every eight minutes. CBS broadcast five of the ten top baddies. Altogether, 83 per cent of CBS programs included use of or reference to an alcoholic beverage. Of those, 62 per cent mentioned hard booze

NBC led that category with use of hard stuff on 66 per cent of its shows while ABC matched CBS with 62 per cent. Of the 249 shows, 201 made reference to or used alcoholic drinks while 159 poured nonalcoholic refreshment ranging from a total of 95 cups of coffee to one glass of lemonade.

A tv spokesman explains that a bar is a "logical gathering place . . . a way of bringing people together . . . to get something done in terms of plot and characterization." Police often are in a bar "quite normal for cops, when they go off duty," an NBC vice president said. But just as they have a beer to relax, so do leading characters when facing a stressful confrontation or decision, contrary to the code.

It would be bad enough if tippling was limited to the 8 p.m. to 11 p.m. time slot. But daytime shows also use alcohol, plus some reruns of old night-time programs. A serial included "an awful lot" of bourbon until it was learned that representatives of the bourbon industry had "kind of hit upon some of these people sending them letters and so forth" as a TV executive said. A stop was put to that.

Meanwhile, pressure from the public to end tv drinking is almost nonexistent even though mail is watched carefully by programmers. It could be that the nation's 9 million alcoholics or alcohol abusers would be the last to protest or other millions of moderate users fail to feel threatened. However, steady picturing of drinking gives it a sense of normality that cannot help but contribute to the statistics that show an estimated 1.13 million children aged 12 to 17 get drunk at least once a week. Whether on prime time or not millions of youngsters are among the audience.

Sweden formally complained in June about heavy drinking on tv as a danger to society and there is a move in Great Britain to put a stop to the practice there. American tv devotees would do well to be more analytical and more verbal if they don't like what they see. The address of the National Association of Broadcasters is 1771 N St., N.W., Washington, D.C. 20036. NBC, CBS and ABC all are based in New York City. That's all the address needed to put a cork on this subliminal promotion of alcohol, intended or not.

MANCHESTER NEW HAMPSHIRE UNION LEADER

Manchester, N.H., September 5, 1977

The ABC television series, "Soap," has no business appearing on U. S. television or any other television screen.

It is, in the opinion of this newspaper, a filthy, degenerate work which has no reason for being—except to appeal to certain elements of our society who want to be shocked by immorality.

It is not realism; it is just a series of dirty episodes for the purpose of sensationalism.

The series concerns two families who are related by marriage. In one family the father commits adultery with everyone he can get his hands on. His wife does the same with her tennis instructor and he, in turn, does the same with her daughter. The other family is mixed up with equally unpleasant and nasty incidents, including one homosexual. Then, there is an unfortunate racial aspect to it. There is a black butler who is insulted by a deranged grandfather.

The whole thing is so revolting and so unhealthy and unnatural that it has no place on the American TV screen.

It is also an insult to the American people. They are not a bunch of pornographic-minded dolts, as apparently ABC thinks they are. The American Broadcasting Company should give the public a little credit for being interested in a few more instructive and moral aspects of life than are depicted in the filthy "Soap."

If ABC DOESN'T think that way, then someone should go down to the home office in New York and wash out a few mouths with some good old-fashioned laundry soap.

Honolulu Star-Bulletin

Honolulu, Hawaii, July 4, 1977

Network television is heeding public protest and swinging away from violence, we're told. Its substitute in the ratings battle will be sex.

Given a choice between the two, sex is better.

Serious and competent research suggests that the most violent societies in the world are those where there is the most repression of physical pleasure.

So the TV people may be closer to the right track now than before. But apparently not very close.

At least one proposed ABC comedy serial called "Soap" already is churning up suds because its story-line is seen by one viewer as "one long dirty joke".

Its characters include a homosexual desirous of a sex-change operation, a puritanical young girl who is termed "a latent nun", a youth obsessed with pornography, a mother and daughter having separate affairs with the same tennis pro, and a husband being blackmailed by his secretary, who is also his mistress of a dozen years.

"Soap" appears to out-sex and out-deviate "Mary Hartman, Mary Hartman" and do so even more controversially because it is headed for prime evening time rather than the late evening hours when "Mary Hartman" has been shown.

Assorted sources predict "Soap" will be a hit, and they may be right, but the TV industry seems to be swinging from one extreme to the other with such program choices.

Instead of warped sex, it might try some good old fashioned love and affection and see how that sells at the box office.

Pretty well, we'd say, looking at how well the birds and the bees have made out down over the centuries.

The Boston Herald American

Boston, Mass., November 5, 1977

John Chancellor, the respected television news commentator, found himself apologizing with obvious embarrassment one evening recently for a filmed report from Los Angeles that was about to be shown on the National Broadcasting Company's nightly news program. He warned the coast-to-coast audience that the report might seem to many adults offensive and unsuitable for children to see because it showed teenaged boys as prostitutes soliciting male customers on the Los Angeles streets. Chancellor suggested that many families viewing the news broadcast might want to turn off their TV sets, or switch to another channel, before the report came on the air.

If the report had to be introduced with such a warning, why did NBC put it on the air? Certainly an early evening news broadcast, watched by a family audience, can achieve a code of decent good taste without reaching for a touch of the sexy sensationalism that is soiling so many of the later prime-time dramas, comedies and talk-shows on television this season.

The disregard for decency displayed by the television networks

in recent weeks as they compete frantically for bigger audiences would never have been permitted by those same networks a few years ago, or even last year. Families who turned on the usually funny "All in the Family" one Sunday evening found themselves watching poor Edith Bunker fighting off a rapist in her living room.

On that same Sunday night, NBC presented the opening lurid installment of a six-hour television dramatization of Harold Robbins' sex novel, "79 Park Avenue." That was a story about a young girl who becomes a prostitute after being raped by her stepfather, and then moves up in the world as the madam of a plush Park Avenue Bordello.

If this new trend in television becomes popular, maybe John Walton, the father of the Walton family, will soon be operating a network of call girls on Walton's Mountain.

Censorship is regarded as a bad word these days. But the Federal Communications Commission, which has the duty of regulating the broadcasting industry, should be taking firm measures to insure the quality of decency in television.

The Idaho STATESMAN

Boise, Idaho, October 20, 1977

Sex on television has become so unavoidable for children that normally calm, slow-to-anger parents are ready to put a foot through their tubes. And the real villain is not the shows themselves, but the promotional ads.

It is unquestionably the responsibility of parents to keep children away from the more adult fare on television if that is their desire. In no way can the television industry be required to assume parental authority in deciding what children see.

What angers parents, and rightly so, is that this type of fare cannot be avoided. The common response to criticisms of television is that one can simply turn off the set or change stations. This is not entirely true, however. Many families do excercise responsible selection of programs for their children but still see their kids bombarded by material that is beyond their years.

The reason: Graphic promotional ads for mature programs are sandwiched unpredictably into family fare. Often the most explosive scenes are spotlighted in the ads.

Compare this with motion pictures. Even the previews are rated, and attempts are made to suit the previews to the audience that has come to see the major attraction.

The issue of television sex has nothing to do with prudishness or avoidance of human sexuality. A child will unavoidably be exposed to sexuality in the real world, and a family must be prepared to deal with it. But the telescoped exposure children are receiving in the promotional ads on the tube is unhealthy. When a 4-year-old comes away from the set asking what a sex change operation is or why that man was wearing a wig and lipstick, a family's prerogatives for leading youngsters into a healthy understanding of sexuality have been violated.

Young adults may find the programs and ads of great interest. Older persons can mentally reject the ads and avoid the programs if that is their bent. But for families with children, the options are to turn the set off or keep it strictly on the educational channel. These are options that more and more people may begin excercising if the networks do not quit mixing family and adult fare in an indiscriminate manner.

THE DAILY OKLAHOMAN
Oklahoma City, Okla., April 3, 1978

CITY Councilman Merle McCollum's concern that cable television might bring X- and R-rated movies into Oklahoma City living rooms is commendable, but a bit late.

In light of prime-time television shows being offered this season, Councilman McCollum's fears seem to have already reached our homes.

When the three commercial networks were called down for too much violence in their shows, they turned to sex.

The current crop of shows may not be X-rated because of unclothed bodies, but they certainly are not for general audiences in a great many cases. And let's not overlook public television in the too-sexy area. That government- and donations-supported entity is as bad as the commercial networks in bringing sex into our homes (although PBS cloaks it as "art").

A few network shows have dealt with sex subjects objectively and in a discreet manner.

"Eight Is Enough," for example, has handled such problems in good taste. Generally, there has been a lesson to be learned from some such programs.

But far overshadowing the few good sex-subject shows on TV are the scores which handle it crudely. Even the teen-age-oriented shows — or maybe it should be especially the teen-age-oriented shows — seem to be the worst of all.

The discouraging part of the situation is that the general pub-lic doesn't seem to care anymore. No one gets disturbed enough about it to contact the station, the network or the sponsor.

Councilman McCollum also suggested a "parental-guidance key" with which the parents could lock out channels carrying R-rated movies. TV sets already have such a key — it's called the On-Off switch — but like a "parental-guidance key", it won't work without parental discipline.

OKLAHOMA CITY TIMES
Oklahoma City, Okla., January 24, 1978

TELEVISION is getting a big rap from its critics these days, and a good deal of it is probably deserved. The trouble is that TV plays such a major role in people's lives they can't see it as just another commercial enterprise out to make money.

For that matter, television has caused some sweeping changes in our culture, in our attitudes and even in our living styles. By its nature it has a pervasive influence over human endeavor — from high-powered international diplomacy to simple family activities.

One organization striking back is the National PTA, which has launched a campaign against excessive violence on television. It has set up a National PTA Television Action Center to serve as a clearinghouse of in-formation and is monitoring TV programs to try to force improvement in their quality.

The project is a worthy one, no doubt applauded by millions of parents. Unfortunately, it is silent on another kind of TV violence: the impact on viewer sensitivities of the expression of loose morality on certain programs. No one can deny that physical violence is overplayed on some police and western shows. But is violent expression in carrying forward a plot any worse than portraying immoral actions and principles as acceptable?

No one in his right mind wants the government to wield a heavier hand in TV regulation than it does at present. To its credit the PTA specifically shuns this "solution." The common-sense approach would be for the net-works themselves to curb the use of gratuitous violence (violence for its own sake) and sexual immorality themes.

Anita Bryant, the Oklahoma girl who has gained some national attention of late, also is carrying on a campaign to clean up TV. She says television should have more "wholesome family entertainment" to replace perverted sex and violence. She rightly fears the latter are undermining the family unit by presenting alternative life styles as natural and normal. It's clear she's talking about homosexuality, but there are other equally offensive kinds of immorality that crop up in TV programming.

Some viewers, of course, may prefer the risque and resent any effort to "censor" what they watch. But many people would welcome cleaner TV, not only for the sake of their own children but also because they don't want to see the nation abased. Television already has helped shape attitudes toward the home, church and family relationships that are repugnant to the more traditional-minded.

Some religious organizations have accepted homosexuals as ministers, and in San Francisco the council is considering a proposal to hire two high-level administrators to cater to that community's homosexual population.

Those who abhor sexual immorality and unnecessary violence on TV will have to do more than pay lip service to their convictions. They'll have to monitor their own family viewing habits and, beyond that, let the TV networks — and the sponsors — know how they feel.

BUFFALO EVENING NEWS
Buffalo, N.Y., March 2, 1978

Even before the programs now in the works for next fall take shape, the network television moguls are bracing themselves for an unprecedented protest wave — based on the strongly adverse reactions churned up by this season's more repulsively sex-oriented situation comedies.

In a recent cover story, Newsweek magazine cited the storm stirred among parent and church groups by themes morally offensive for their increasingly salacious exploitation of human sexuality.

Summing up the issues posed by the trend toward sexual themes in place of violence on the tube, Newsweek observed:

"Only incurable prudes would insist that a medium purporting to portray the human condition should draw a curtain over so integral a part of human activity. What is disturbing, however, is that so much of the sex on TV seems designed to pander to prurience in the most cheaply exploitative manner. With snigger and smirk, the new batch of sitcoms and mini-series flaunt their boldness like prepubescents mouthing dirty words."

It isn't just that TV screenwriters have taken a leaf from Hollywood's R-rated films in pushing the boundaries of imagery and innuendos in dramatic subject matter. It is, rather, that television has largely replaced books, magazines and the cinema as the most influential medium in molding attitudes and in setting moral tones.

Critics' accusations that an alarmingly steep rise in teen-age pregnancies is more than coincidentally related to the wave of sexually permissive programming are, of course, not easily susceptible to proof. Yet it is not necessary to establish such a linkage to deplore the uniquely intrusive qualities of risque programming insensitive to its impact on impressionable adolescents. The trouble with sophomoric handling of sexual themes, as one national religious leader says, is that it rarely deals with the consequences.

A mother of three teen-age daughters observes in a Rochester newspaper: "I'm sick to death of this total preoccupation we seem to have with sex as fun and games. It's no wonder our teenagers are falling into bed, and pregnancies, and venereal disease at epidemic rates. They are made to feel foolish if they don't play the game. Nowhere is the voice of commitment, respect and deep love heard. I'm sorry, but 'James at 15' or 'Joan at 16,' or any teen isn't ready for that kind of love."

The blue hue on the tube is defended by some rating-minded TV spokesmen as merely reflecting the evolution in sexual attitudes. But this smacks of hypocritical upside-down alibiing by an industry that has no peer in shaping moral values about life.

It is true enough that television, in dealing with all aspects of life, cannot please all viewers. But this can too easily become a cop-out excuse for the current infatuation with themes that, if not quite yet explicit, are sophomoric in their graffiti shock-effect treatment of a vital activity of life.

The evolution in what is acceptable among adult audiences does not give the networks any license to bombard the tube with a saturation of sexual smut treated with leering juvenilism. And while a disregard of sensibilities is not something that should or can be cured by any heavy-handed censorship, it is a trend that should warrant a searching appraisal in responsible network board rooms on what can properly be beamed into American homes and how a better line can be drawn between good taste and locker room "porn" in discussing serious themes.

Chicago Tribune

Chicago, Ill., September 13, 1978

Big time television, which has veered away from excessive violence only reluctantly under public pressure, is turning to adolescent leering as a cheap substitute. CBS and ABC, in particular, according to our critic, Gary Deeb, are counting on what are basically girlie peep shows to hype fall ratings. What the networks call "T-and-A shows" [referring to certain parts of female anatomy] are expected to stimulate sales curves and audience ratings.

It's easy to see how network moguls fell into the Charlie's Angels syndrome. Network decision makers have always considered TV audiences to have minimum mentality. Girlie magazines now sell 16 million copies a month. Sex-oriented business take in at least $4 billion dollars a year. If you have to cut down on violence, what better substitute for gore than girls?

This coffee-tea-or-me attitude toward women is a lame example male chauvinism. It is particularly disturbing to think that so powerful and pervasive a shaper of public attitudes as national television is reduced to showing women primarily as Barbie doll stereotypes. It's as if, in the midst of the struggle for black civil rights and racial equality, television began offering a dozen programs about Step-N-Fetchits who had rhythmn.

The T-and-A strategy may just backfire on the networks, however. Those supposedly smart TV moguls should take a look at some of the new marketing data showing how much women now earn and what a massive influence they have on the nation's consumer spending. New marketing strategies are now stressing that women should be treated seriously and as equals in advertising appeals because they are rapidly becoming equal in both business and family life. NBC has had second thoughts about its sexy-girl programs and has killed two of them and toned down a third.

If the women allow this kind of programming to proceed without an outcry of protest, our confidence in their spirit is badly misplaced.

THE EMPORIA GAZETTE

Emporia, Kans., November 5, 1977

OUR esteemed colleague down at Parsons, the honorable Clyde Reed, has come out against sex on television. (Has the toll of time cooled the passions of this thoroughbred war horse?)

In an editorial this week he asked this question: "Will the television networks turn from an excess of violence to an abundance of sex on television?"

"That's not a frivolous question," he added. "At least it isn't to some of the nation's biggest and most powerful advertisers. They see it as a potential threat now that the public reaction has forced the networks to reduce the violence content of their programs. The big advertisers met recently with networks at Hot Springs, Va., to express their concern. . . . The association recommended that advertisers set up their own standards on subjects 'which may be objectionable to an all-family mass audience.' That action again appears to mirror a fear that the worst may happen unless vigilance is exercised. One era has ended on the networks — a real nightmare — and another isn't needed."

We are somewhat astonished that the Parsons editor would throw in with a group of "big advertisers" who want to set up their own censorship board to monitor television programs.

We would have presumed that Mr. Reed might take the opposite stand and resist an attempt by advertisers to control the creative work of writers.

And what's wrong with sex? Properly presented, it is a wholesome, natural sort of thing.

Perhaps American audiences are not yet ready for pornography, but even that would be better than "Baretta" or "C.P.O. Sharkey." — R.C.

ARKANSAS DEMOCRAT

Little Rock, Ark., September 2, 1978

Poor CBS-TV, feeling the slings and arrows more usually associated with *ABC*-TV, barely had got onto the air with the premiere of a touted new series on airline stewardesses, than here, predictably, was the president of the Association of Flight Attendants complaining that the series puts too much emphasis on the sex of the girls and not enough on their efficiency, rigorously screened training, etc., etc.

We realize that any occupational group, any, feels that its calling is subjected to a distorted image whenever it is put on the stage or on camera. We certainly should know, since nothing has been more consistently misrepresented down through the years than has newspapering.

This circumstance is inescapable, however, since the duller, more routinized, side of any job that one takes on, for money *or* love, cannot expect to be shown to any audience other than one made up of people who actually like to be bored or are outright masochists. (Come to think of it, the two conditions may be synonymous in the context.)

Anyway, our own first impression of the series in question, "Flying High," was directly opposed to that of the flight attendants' association who was so quick to criticize it, Patricia Robertson. It was all introductory stuff, of course, but the initial offering gave us a great deal of what purported at least to be how it is in stewardess training programs, concern for passenger safety and all, plus, of course, a running plot that was no sillier than most plots in a TV series — with or without a stress on pretty girls — and less silly than a lot of them. Of course, neither we nor Miss Robertson know what the future holdeth if the series catches on, nor do we know any more than she whether we will even look at it again.

We do know that airline stewardesses, new ones, especially, have a fun side to their lives, too, as girls of their same age bracket, do anywhere, the difference being that their off-duty hours frequently are spent in more interesting locales than most girls have the opportunity to see until the settings, too, become routinized by repetition.

We realize that stewardesses, for obvious reasons, are in a situation where they are thought to be fair game for snatching and grabbing by their more meatheated passengers, some of them, we suppose, even equipped with hand buzzers and funny hats, but most male passengers who fly on any kind of regular basis, we think, treat the "stews" as they would expect to be treated by them—with courtesy. Ample defenses have been devised for dealing with the minority of wowsers.

Let us face it, however, Airlines are in competition with each other, and when one airline can contract with an Emilio Pucci to design an all-new inflight costume for its girls, as Braniff did several years ago now, and as other lines have done with other fashion designers, then clearly we are selling something more than frozen lunches and dinners in order to get the fares, else they could have the girls fitted out in Mother Hubbards, or possibly even in sackcloth and ashes.

Miss Robertson's complaint, which we are sure will soon be taken up by network purgers with no connection whatever with the stewardesses' profession, especially by women purgers who increasingly seem to be trying to create an impression that not only is it wrong to watch pretty girls on the screen, but wrong for the networks to *put them there*, to be looked at or not as the case may be. As always, the young kids are made the fall guys for these thinly veiled censorship attempts, the would-be purgers all the while denying that they are in any sense purgers, and we can only repeat what we have said before, which is that if we in this country were really as concerned for the kids' wellbeing in every other area as so many people profess to be in what the tykes of 17 or 18 and under see on their TV screens, at any hour apparently, why, then we would all be rolling in clover on the child care front. We will not go into the question of why so many women want to see to it that nobody better looking than they are themselves ever gets on camera, but will leave that one to the psychologists.

★　　★　　★

As it happens, James E. Duffy, president of the aforementioned pincushioned target net, ABC-TV, got into print more or less simultaneously with the stewardesses' association spokesman. Duffy fired a welcome counterblast at the disguised organizational censors, saying that they are not as concerned with the quality level of today's programming as they want the rest of us to take them to be, but in reality want to seize control of the networks from the people who own them and run them. If this is not the goal, unconscious or otherwise, it is one that would be realized anyway if the private censors and judges of that amorphous thing called "quality of programming" were to be allowed to have their way. You would think that these people would never forget that talking of "quality of programming" in terms of the mass audience that is attracted to TV entertainment shows is a resounding contradiction in terms, but you would, alas, be wrong.

The Charlotte Observer

Charlotte, N.C., November 20, 1978

The Flesh Peddlers...covers the whole dirty story, from the street hookers and the pimps that exploit them, to the shadowy world of escort services and massage parlors.
— from a WSOC Eyewitness News advertisement

This is Chris. She's nineteen. She makes $50,000 a year. She's a hooker!
— from a 36 (WRET) Action News advertisement

Why the sudden fascination with sex in Charlotte on two local TV news shows? Because if that's what viewers want to watch, these sexual circuses may mean bread for the stations.

Each November, the Neilsen organization does extensive surveys (called "sweeps") of some 200 TV markets, including Charlotte. The local data on how many viewers are watching what provide the basis for the price of national spot advertising.

That's why WRET came along with its five-part series, "Sex Peddlers," and WSOC followed with a five-part series, "The Sex Peddlers" ("Flesh 2," Observer TV Critic Ron Alridge called it). Sex is easy to sell, whether it's on Trade Street or television. Attracting more viewers means a higher price for commercial time. On the street or TV, you see, the motive is money.

Sexy news no doubt provides momentary titilation, and it's certainly zingier than reporting about land-use planning or consolidation. But does it have any longterm benefits — for viewers or the station?

That's up to viewers. It is interesting to note that WBTV, which over the years has produced Charlotte's best and most-watched TV news programs, hasn't gone into peeping-tomism in pursuit of ratings. And WBTV hasn't had to.

Minneapolis Tribune

Minneapolis, Minn., June 12, 1978

Television advertisers are in a bind because of the increasing number of television programs that emphasize sexual innuendo and exploit the female body. Sponsors receive complaints and even threats of boycotts. But advertisers who avoid such programs may miss reaching potential customers, since the aptly named "sexploitation" programs are popular.

Some major advertisers are shying away from such programs, as well as from those emphasizing violence. Some are doing so for economic reasons, but many see a responsibility for helping raise the level of taste on television. These companies hope that by sponsoring only shows that don't exploit sex and violence they will encourage networks to develop more such programs.

We hope that the effort succeeds, for two reasons. First, we'd like to see more choice on television — and fewer programs that give children a distorted idea of sexual relationships and the role of women. Second, and more important, we prefer the advertisers' approach to an increasingly mentioned alternative — some form of censorship. Censorship violates people's rights, and it is hard to implement: How could censorship rules ban tasteless sex and gratuitous violence without also banning serious dramatic works?

If advertisers perceive that a significant segment of the public wants something other than sexploitation, and that the way to reach that market is by sponsoring other kinds of programs, they will do so. The question is: What *does* the public want? If sexploitation continues to draw viewers, some advertisers will sponsor such programs. And if they do, they shouldn't be blamed for helping give people the programs they want. In the end, the public controls what it sees.

Los Angeles Times

Los Angeles, Cal., March 26, 1978

With a wink and a leer and a smirk and a giggle, network television is preparing to give its vast prime-time audiences what it perceives that those audiences want.

The violence that has been the backbone of so much TV programming for several seasons isn't exactly going to disappear, but it is going to be deemphasized. What gimmick will replace it? What else but sex! Or, in keeping with the maturity and subtlety with which that theme is apparently being packaged,

S E X ! ! !

And so here it comes, the experience that we've all been waiting for. A veritable gusher of new series and made-for-TV movies is in the works whose titles alone are calculated to set 10 million male pulses pounding and 20 million male lungs hyperventilating. In preparation for our viewing pleasure are, among others, "Centerfold," "The Cheerleaders," "Scandal Hall," "Wayward Girls," "California Girls," "The Beach Girls." Clearly, imaginativeness in programming knows no limits.

At least three of the new projects, we read, will feature women who wear no brassieres. In other words, we will all have the chance to stare to our hearts' content at *jiggling breasts!* Fantastic. Forget about innuendo, here's the *real thing!* Or at least as close to the real thing as TV will give us until it gives us, well, the real thing. And that's probably in the works for the following season.

We don't want to mislead or be misunderstood. We pride ourselves on our tolerance for good, clean sex. We recognize that there is even a place for good, dirty sex. Yes, sexuality is a part of the human experience. Yes, there is a place on TV for candor, directness, the erotic. Public broadcasting's "I, Claudius" is a recent example of how sex—presented more explicitly than the commercial networks have so far dared—can be tastefully and necessarily made integral to a story. Somehow, though, we doubt that programs with titles like "Legs" and "Girl on the Road" will quite reach these standards.

Some TV actresses have complained, and justifiably, about losing TV parts because of their objections to the demeaning sexual behavior that proffered roles have demanded. To no avail. For every actress who says no, a score apparently are eager to say yes. In the audition studios there is no shortage of talent, at least as it exists between the neck and the knees.

Coming TV hours, then, promise to provide us with acres of female flesh in motion. The calculated results will be fantasy time in homes across America, and happy time at the bank for TV networks and producers. Give 'em sex, and you hype the ratings; hype the ratings, and the cash registers ring.

The sex trend, say the gurus of programming, is a response to changing public values, a recognition of more sophisticated tastes. It is also, more to the point, a pretty sure-fire way to make a buck. And that, as they say in show biz, is the bottom line.

The Evening Gazette

Worcester, Mass., March 27, 1978

Hit television shows seem to reflect their own special brand of sex. It consists of sophomoric sexual situations, double meanings and sexual innuendo.

There is nothing novel about this one-dimensional view of human sexuality. Shakespeare occasionally used broad puns and slapstick sexual innuendo to keep the commoners interested in his plays.

But the networks' proposed fall schedules seem to suggest that television viewers are going to be watching "Three's Company," "Charlie's Angels," and similar exercises in smirksome taste until they expire of boredom. There is a limit to mediocrity.

Scheduled series will deal with problems of a living-together couple, with sexual adventures in a college dormitory, with sexual hijinks of airplane flight attendants.

The successful "Charlie's Angels" formula has spawned the derivative "Rollergirls," "California Girls" and "Wayward Girls."

The networks' argument is that moral standards of the public have changed and that which was once too sexually frank is now acceptable. A cynical response is that the television industry is less interested in moral standards than in cash rewards.

According to The New York Times, although network officials cite changing standards as the reason for increased emphasis on sex, they have done no public polling or other scientific survey to back up this assertion.

Television has never claimed to be an innovative medium. It tends to reflect rather than lead public opinion. Therefore, the claims that viewers want shows like "Three's Company" and "Charlie's Angels" are probably true.

But television whiz Fred Silverman, soon to be president at NBC and former programming chief of ABC and CBS, also espouses a theory that people will watch the "least objectionable" programs. That view would support the idea that viewers do not so much choose to watch a program as they choose not to watch something else.

Since most people watch television for relaxation, frothy escapist sit-coms do fulfill a legitimate need.

But a lot of Suzanne Sommers and Cheryl Ladd and little Laurence Olivier and Joanne Woodward tend to make for a dull television season.

The Cincinnati Post
TIMES ⭐ STAR

DAYTON DAILY NEWS
Dayton, Ohio, October 18, 1976

A comitted TV watcher the week of Oct. 9 saw the following (as quoted from *TV Datebook*:)

— "George is overjoyed when Louise accuses him of having an affair with another woman."

— A man tries to deal with his wife and his mistress, "who is tired of their furtive, sordid lunchtime sex sessions."

— Pepper Policewoman "is falsely accused of sexually molesting a female criminal suspect."

— Bumper policeman "stirs up trouble among the hoodlums and hookers on his beat."

—" Charlie's Angels," — softcore cheesecake.

— Alice is arrested as a prostitute.

— Fred Sanford is attracted to a person who turns out to be a transvestite.

— "Hutch falls in love with a call girl."

Somebody, apparently, has told the networks the facts of life. Does this mean there is hope that in a few years they will grow up?

Want a preview of the coming television season? Well, the small screen will be loaded with shows featuring very well-endowed young women in scanty attire getting into situations that show off their attributes.

In other words there's a wave of sexploitation in our TV-viewing future. As a columnist from Los Angeles puts it, the industry is readying "TV's Titillation Sweepstakes."

The reasons behind the sex shows are simple. Gore and violence used to be the TV producer's road to riches. But recently pressure from church and parent groups took some of the profit out of peddling violence.

At the same time the industry noticed the commercial success of shows like Charlie's Angels and Three's Company. And since TV programmers are nothing if not copycats, a call went out through Hollywood for actresses with 38-D chests and masses of blonde hair.

Fortunately, the public and especially parents do not have to put up meekly with anything the networks want to sell. They showed their clout in getting egregious violence toned down

and they can do the same if they find the sexploitation shows offensive.

In a recent article Margita White, a member of the Federal Communications Commission, warned against expecting the FCC to "do something." She accurately pointed out that censorship by the commission of program content is unlawful as well as undesirable.

However, Ms. White said, people can let their local stations know how they view the coming invasion of sex programs. The stations don't have to run network programs, and they won't if they understand that audiences will be tuning in competing shows.

"Unless I'm sadly mistaken," Ms. White wrote, "I do not believe that programming that television executives casually refer to in a phrase for female body parts will stand a chance if viewers let their stations know what they think, and oversee what their children watch."

Ms. White deals with the problem with such calm good sense that one wonders what she's doing in Washington.

St. Louis ⚓ Review
St. Louis, Mo., October 7, 1977

The so-called permissive society which has grown more permissive by leaps and bounds since the middle of the sixties is certainly being reflected in television programing so that at the present time there is hardly anything that is not considered suitable "adult" fare.

While this reflects current thinking in our society it is also influencing the thinking of millions who otherwise would not be affected by the current thinking. Even people who feel that they will not be influenced by any undesirable programs on TV do become

influenced gradually over a long period of time.

Children of course are most impressionable and yet many of them watch television constantly day and night. Only the very youngest are in any way affected by the family hours which are really a farce and only an empty gesture of the television industry which is somewhat worried about the growing criticism of its production.

No doubt the advertisers bear a major responsibility for what is being offered on TV today. As usual, true to their capitalistic principles, they feel

that making money is the prime objective of life and in order to achieve this the end justifies any means.

This season "Soap" has become the target for much opposition from indignant groups who are repelled by its blatant immorality. This is well and good. But this only scratches the surface. The whole approach to much of TV programing and advertising needs a thorough cleaning up despite some few examples of good and constructive programing which deserve our plaudits.

—Msgr. John T. Byrne

THE CHRISTIAN SCIENCE MONITOR
Boston, Mass., March 30, 1978

It is not only little old refugees from Victorian prudery who are or should be up in arms over what is happening to sex on American television. Writers who want to treat the subject responsibly lament the network demand for leering exploitation of it. A member of the Federal Communications Commission warns of a wave of new shows packaging women as sex playthings — just when the battle against stereotyping women in commercials and programming had been showing some results if not victory. Such voices ought to be listened to and joined by everyone with an ounce of regard for decency in sexual relations and for a national cultural environment pervaded by TV.

If the present trend continues, the spectrum of living color will have room for little but blue; blue, that is, in the dictionary sense of "indecent; risqué; suggestive." Even now, tuning in to a typical game show during the supposedly respectable early hours is to bring a virtually nonstop stream of innuendo into the home. The TV host, guests, and audience all grin and chortle as if, my, isn't this cute and aren't we having fun? A barrel of sniggers.

Next season, according to reports, the nighttime violence which public pressure has muted will be replaced by blue jokes and female flesh.

Is this what viewers want, as profit-minded network programmers must suppose? Even if they do want it, should a powerful user of the public airwaves pander to such tastes at the expense of the better programming of which it is capable? This week's TV tribute to itself by CBS recalls how many excellent shows in the past somehow managed to be moving, funny, dramatic, delightful without resorting to the predicted — or present — level of sexploitation.

Part of the problem is put succinctly by John Furia Jr., past chairman of the Writers' Guild of America, as quoted in the New York Times:

"The Writers' Guild has been very vocal in opposition to censorship, and we now find ourselves in a peculiar postion — we want the broadest possible expression on television, but the sex we have been forced to defend has not been healthy or constructive but leering and at the sophomoric level; instead of using sex in a good way, the networks have exploited it."

A part of the solution is suggested by FCC member Margita E. White:

"Unless I'm sadly mistaken, I do not believe that programming that television executives casually refer to in a phrase for female body parts will stand a chance if viewers let their stations know what they think, and oversee what their children watch."

By all means, viewers ought to take responsibility for what channels are switched to in their homes. By all means, if they want to change things, they should let stations and network heads know what they like and don't like in specific detail.

Yet finally they must ask themselves the question implied by some network excuses for sexploitation as simply reflecting the wants and attitudes of the society of which TV is a part. How much do Americans already reflect or tolerate in "real life" a degree of the demeaning attitude toward sexual relations that is being exploited on the small screen as it recently has been on the large screen of the movie theater? Only each individual can answer today's variation on Shakespeare: "Is the fault, dear Brutus, in our TV or in ourselves?"

TEXAS JUDGE AFFIRMS PRESS' RIGHT TO WITNESS EXECUTIONS IN STATE

A federal judge Jan. 3 ordered the Texas Department of Corrections to allow reporters to witness any future executions and to interview prisoners awaiting execution. The department's director, W. J. Estelle, had issued a directive in December stopping reporters' access to death row prisoners. Judge William Taylor Jr. called Estelle's ban unconstitutional, claiming that newsmen had a constitutional right to witness all executions held in Texas.

Judge Taylor's ruling was challenged by the attorney for Jerry Jurek, who was scheduled to die in the electric chair in Texas Jan. 19. Included in the petition for a postponement of the execution was a legal objection to its televised filming. Jurek's lawyer, Jay Topkis, said the order was not "consistent with evolving standards of decency." The suit against Estelle's ban had been filed by a Dallas television newsman and the American Civil Liberties Union.

FORT WORTH STAR-TELEGRAM
Fort Worth, Tex., January 10, 1977

Most people are reacting vociferously to a federal judge's ruling to allow television stations to film executions in the state prison at Huntsville.

That's understandable. Few subjects stir such volatile emotions as the death penalty—as death itself, for that matter.

And it's understandable that many people, including State Atty. Gen. John Hill, who says he is appealing the ruling, express revulsion at the idea of having the grisly scenes from the death chamber flashed electronically into their living rooms.

However, the primary concerns dealt with in Judge William Taylor's ruling had to be fact and law, not emotions or public preferences in the area of TV viewing.

The fact is that the State of Texas does have a capital punishment law.

Given that fact, certain other points follow in order, namely:

• The death penalty law is part of the criminal justice system in Texas—part of what the Constitution calls "due process."

• As such, an execution carried out under the law is an official action to which public access, under the Constitution, cannot be denied.

Thus, Dallas television newsman Tony Garrett acted properly in seeking the intervention of a federal court to assure his right of access, and that of other TV as well as print media representatives, to executions.

And Judge Taylor was correct in the ruling he issued, allowing representatives of the television medium to cover executions on the same basis as print media representatives have covered them in the past—that is, through "pool reporters" who share their reports with others.

This ruling was most important from the standpoint of the public's right to know, which is actually what the First Amendment freedom of the press guarantee is all about.

It should be the prerogative of the public, not the state, to decide who witnesses an execution.

The ruling staunchly reaffirms that point.

The right to witness an execution and the actual witnessing of one, however, are too entirely different questions. And on that point hangs the issue of whether or not executions will ever actually be shown on television or displayed pictorially in the print media.

If the public overwhelmingly opposes such display of the execution scenes, it is doubtful that many TV stations or newspapers will offer it.

Those who present it once might be so inundated with protests that they would never try a repeat performance.

Signs of public protest already are becoming evident. Although some TV newsmen seem to feel that executions would draw a huge audience, most stations, according to one poll, indicate that they would be reluctant to carry them.

Whatever the ultimate decisions on the showing of execution scenes, however, Judge Taylor's ruling left the switch in the hands of the people, and that's a development to applaud.

Where the power to make such decisions have been allowed to pass to the hands of the state, the people often have regretted it—and have usually been a long time getting it back.

ARKANSAS DEMOCRAT
Little Rock, Ark., January 8, 1977

A Texas state judge has ruled that electronic media (TV) may no more be excluded from filming an execution than the print media may be barred from reporting it — even if the filming means that an electrocution (one of which could occur Jan. 14) might be broadcast into homes soon after it occurs.

There's been no execution in the United States for almost a decade. During that time, the immediacy of TV newscasts has improved markedly. So the question of televising executions is a new one. And it has more than a little significance, since the Parent-Teacher Association, Action for Children's Television and like groups already are battling the TV violence that now exists.

Live violence on television is not unprecedented. Millions watched aghast when Jack Ruby fatally shot Lee Harvey Oswald in front of the cameras in 1963. And about that time networks began using satellites to beam back grisly filmed violence from Vietnam battlefields, all to be served up at suppertime on national newscasts.

Vivid, lurid accounts of men injured in combat, of civilians victimized by crossfire, were tremedously influential in molding public opinion and causing President Nixon to wind down the war. So the power of television with its graphic depiction and impact of immediacy, no longer may be denied as a powerful factor in pricking the social conscience of Americans.

It's difficult to imagine the impact on us all if, in effect, television returns us to the days of "public" executions, when throngs of curious persons flocked to witness well-orchestrated "events" — hangings, shootings, decapitations and quarterings.

Shocking as the Oswald slaying was to see, televised executions would be more so because TV viewers must know it is they who sanction the killing of the culprit by the state of which they are citizens. An executioner is but their agent, the one who detonates the gas pellet or pulls the switch on the behalf of society.

Perceptive viewers in the 1960s realized this about the Vietnam films, too — that the death and mutilation they were seeing from Vietnam was perpetrated in their names and that of their fellow Americans. Never before had a war been so realistically and instantaneously brought home to us — certainly not in the newsreels of the 1940s, or in the days-old film clips from Korea.

If the Texas judge's ruling holds, and if capital punishment is to resume in earnest, it seems we all may have the chance to witness the moment of truth, the ultimate in televised violence — an execution — from the comfort of our favorite easy chairs. Like the old public executions, the TV version may or may not deter crime.

What's more certain, television viewers will no longer be removed from the reality of imposed death. It will all be there on the 6 o'clock news. Rated "PG" for parental guidance.

ST. LOUIS POST-DISPATCH

St. Louis, Mo., January 10, 1977

There are two ways of viewing a ruling by U.S. District Judge William Taylor Jr. of Dallas to the effect that television reporters have a constitutional right to film executions and to broadcast the film to the public. One way is to consider the decision in the light of the public's right to be informed visually, as well as in print, of what is undeniably a public function. As Judge Taylor said, it would be "unthinkable to conduct an execution in private." Another way to look at the decision is to consider its result in terms of the revolting impact it may produce on viewers of home screens.

Although many Americans may recoil at the prospect of seeing a hanging or an electrocution on home television, is that a reason for government to step in to bar television cameras from an event being carried out by authority of the state as a part of its law enforcement function? Television should have the right to convey, and the public receive, visual reports of an execution under the same rationale that television may convey, and the public receive, visual reports of the sometimes abhorrent conditions inside prisons or the loathsome scenes of killing in war.

The question of the impact on home viewers is one to be considered by television editors and by individuals concerned. Editors can control the time of the broadcast, bearing in mind the potential viewing audience. And they can put viewers on notice of what is to come — as they do now with respect to scenes of carnage — so that prospective viewers may choose not to watch. But government should not seek to bar the public from viewing what is being done in its name.

THE SACRAMENTO BEE

Sacramento, Calif., January 7, 1977

A Texas television station that recently won a court decision permitting it to televise executions in the state's electric chair at Huntsville is now pondering whether or not to do it.

There is no question in our mind about this abhorrent prospect. It shouldn't be done.

The death of a human being at the hands of the state, no matter how reprehensible the crime for which the ultimate penalty is demanded, should be treated with gravity and common decency.

Turning it into a TV spectacular would create a carnival atmosphere. Inevitably, it would be exploited to pander to morbid curiosity. And we see no countervailing good purpose to be served by giving viewers the opportunity to watch a person die on camera.

The very idea of it runs against the grain of Americans' traditional sensibilities. Even during the years when capital punishment was commonplace in this country, public executions were prohibited largely because of the people's innate revulsion and a general sense that even the worst criminal deserves respect as a human being at the moment of death.

There are many things television and other news media have a legal right to present to the public but don't, largely as a matter of decency. Execution of a criminal by the state surely should be one of them.

The Philadelphia Inquirer

Philadelphia, Pa., January 12, 1977

The premise, however, is false. There is simply no evidence, none whatsoever, proving that the death penalty does deter. Indeed, as Dr. Samuel Johnson observed a couple of centuries ago, the best place to find pickpockets plying their trade in London was among the crowds assembled to watch pickpockets and other malefactors being hanged.

As representatives of what people sometimes call the print media, we want no advantages over the electronic media. But then we don't want ever to see another execution, because we hold, with Justice William Brennan, that "the punishment of death, like punishments on the rack, the screw and the wheel, is no longer morally tolerable in our civilized society."

If you have a taste for gallows humor, or, in this instance, electric-chair humor, consider the recent ruling of a federal judge in Dallas.

Judge William M. Taylor, in a suit filed by a television newsman, has ruled that Texas prison officials could not prohibit filming an execution in the Texas electric chair. The judge declared that such an execution is an "act of state" and that it is "inconceivable" as well as "unthinkable" to conduct it in secret.

Well, if you start on the premise that the death penalty is a deterrent, the judge's ruling makes a kind of macabre sense. Why not show executions on TV? Why not broadcast them on prime time and encourage the kiddies to watch as a human being is fried or gassed or shot or hanged?

BUFFALO EVENING NEWS

Buffalo, N.Y., January 5, 1977

Casting discreet restraint and human sensitivity to the winds, a federal judge in Texas has ruled that the television media have as much right as print reporters to record every last-gasp detail of a prison execution — not, mind you, just as reporters taking notes and reporting what they saw, but on film for broadcast into everyone's living-room.

"How," asked District Judge William Taylor Jr., "can you say we will let someone in with a pencil and notebook but not a camera or tape recorder?"

The answer, of course, is that the long-standing distinction between a reporter's account and camera coverage in the case of executions is as valid as the well-established and respected court tradition prohibiting the intrusion of cameras in public trials. For there is, after all, a vast difference between a reporter's description or artist's sketch of court proceedings, and the distracting hippodrome effect of opening these to massive multi-media coverage by camera and live TV.

Thus the issue, contrary to Judge Taylor's reasoning, is not whether all media should have the same right to be represented at executions. Rather, it is whether such events should be turned into media-event circuses or, as we believe, governed by coverage rules similar to those which protect the dignity and decorum of the courts.

Surely the television tube is saturated enough already with fictional mayhem without letting the revival of capital punishment become a signal for a luridly tasteless and dehumanizing exploitation of that ultimate penalty of criminal justice for its dramatic effect. The arousal of morbid fascination in such media-smotherage could mark a sad retrogression to Wild West lynch-mob days.

The Detroit News

Detroit, Mich., January 10, 1977

The ruling of a federal judge and the words of a prominent politician have recently turned back the pages of history to those bloody times when supposedly civilized countries staged hangings in public.

U.S. District Judge William M. Taylor Jr. ruled last week in Dallas, Tex., that television reporters should be permitted to film and later televise executions. This ruling followed close upon a remark by former Texas Gov. John Connally that if capital punishment returns, he favors televising executions as an "impressive deterrent" to crime. The ghouls are obviously on the loose once more.

During the Middle Ages and at certain later times, executions were treated in Great Britain as public holidays. A British clergymen of the early 19th century described the festive mood that surrounded the hanging of Josiah Misters in 1841:

"The town was converted for the day into a fair. The country people flocked in their holiday dresses, and the whole town was a scene of drunkenness and debauchery of every kind...A very large number of children were present: children and females constituted the larger proportion of the attendance."

While local citizens would flock in great numbers to see the corpses twisting on the gibbets, attendance from any great distance was naturally prevented by lack of speedy transportation. Today, however, millions of persons sitting in their own homes could attend the picnic — or at least a rerun of it — by merely turning on their TV sets. Perhaps in the case of multiple executions, the good judge could also provide for brass bands and baton twirlers to relieve the monotony of halftime.

However, we're glad to find that not everybody in Texas is mad. Remarking that "There are some things we just don't do," Texas Atty. Gen. John L. Hill last week announced he will appeal Judge Taylor's ruling. If allowed to stand, the ruling would open the way for the ultimate in violence on a medium already soaked in blood. And in this case, the blood would be not fictional but real.

THE MILWAUKEE JOURNAL
Milwaukee, Wisc., January 16, 1977

The impending revival of executions in the United States raises a nauseating question: Will the killing be televised? Already a federal judge in Texas has ruled that the frying of persons in the state's electric chair can be filmed and broadcast.

TV stations might shun the opportunity, concluding that the scene would be too offensive to beam into living rooms. However, a reasonable argument for televising can be made by both the supporters and foes of capital punishment.

A supporter, believing that the death penalty deters violent crime, could argue that the horror of televised executions would heighten deterrence. A foe of the death penalty, believing it cruel and unusual punishment, could contend that executions in dying color would drive home the barbarity of the practice and end it.

Of course, one could also argue that when hangings were public they did not seem to deter crime; it is said that the surest place to find pickpockets at work in 18th century London was in a crowd assembled to witness one of their own being hanged. Or one might speculate that televised executions could steadily desensitize, inuring the public to killing in cold blood.

Appalling argumentation? Sickening speculation? So it is with the capital punishment controversy; the stink in the nostrils simply gets stronger as death rows again fill and states move from abstract debate to grisly reality in the video age. The best option, still available in states reviving the death penalty, is to abandon the degrading policy of official killing before the first person is methodically roasted, gassed, hanged or shot — on cue and perhaps on camera.

THE ATLANTA CONSTITUTION
Atlanta, Ga., January 8, 1977

Televised executions? The idea has been seriously proposed and a federal judge in Texas has signed an order that would allow it.

With capital punishment now revived by the Supreme Court, and with execution dates definitely set for many, including Gary Gilmore on Jan. 17, the possibility of televised hangings, shootings, gassings or electrocutions is not mere talk.

You—and the children—may soon have the opportunity to view the ultimate in television violence as the states begin executing the several hundred prisoners now on death rows. Parental guidance is advised.

Since the purpose of executions supposedly is to deter, there is a grim but undeniable logic in this proposal. Watching another human being put to death should certainly convey a message to all but the most obtuse. Don't do what this person did—or, perhaps, don't get caught as he did.

Those who may favor capital punishment, but feel a little squeamish about featuring it on the 7 o'clock news, should consider the fact that we are all used to seeing people killed by the scores on television. Mostly, of course, it is just play acting; but sometimes it is for real. Jack Ruby killed Lee Harvey Oswald on camera. The Saigon police chief executed a Viet Cong prisoner on TV during the late war.

Probably most Americans favor capital punishment (over 60 per cent in some recent polls) but prefer that it be carried out discreetly removed from public view. We want it done but we don't care to watch it. The proposal to make a spectacle of executions has the merit of testing whether we really believe in capital punishment. Opposition to the Vietnam War intensified rapidly as the reality of that war was presented on our television screens. It could be that televised executions, instead of having a salutary effect, would disgust most people, brutalize others, and change quite a few minds.

There hasn't been an execution in this country in almost a decade. There hasn't been a *public* execution in 40 years, and these have been rare in our century. Rising crime and an intensified public reaction against it have brought us back around to this extreme form of punishment. But putting it on television—that will challenge our commitment to it.

AKRON BEACON JOURNAL
Akron, Ohio, January 12, 1977

WE FIND no fault in principle in the ruling of a judge in Texas that it is legally proper for television newscasters to film and broadcast an execution.

The television camera is a new and powerful instrument of journalism, and this seems a logical extension of long-established free press rights that had to come sometime.

Even so, it's hard to restrain a shudder.

Maybe a nice film sequence on finishing off a malefactor with a firing squad or a whiff in the gas chamber or a jolt or two in the electric chair is just what America needs to liven up the evening TV news.

You don't have to go back very far in the history of American newspapers to find essentially the same thing, in lurid pictures and stories, jazzing up the lead pages of tabloids and a lot of other papers.

And maybe it will be good for us to watch the real thing. Toughening us up, you might say, for a return to the good old days.

The good old days . . .

The Romans, after all, came in droves to watch the lions polish off the dirty Christians, the cheers filling the Colosseum like the "oles" saluting the matador as he slaughters the bull with style.

Crowds of the French watched happily, munching their lunches, as the guillotine of the Terror did its efficient work.

And in our own country the good, popular hanging was once a bigger crowd-pleaser than a Sunday church social.

How this new access will affect views on capital punishment is impossible to say. It will almost certainly increase discussion of it, but may do no more than reinforce already existing attitudes.

In any case, the thought of it makes us uneasy.

DAYTON DAILY NEWS
Dayton, Ohio, January 6, 1977

Now that a federal court has said a television stations can film an electric chair execution in Texas, Americans are faced with some peculiar questions.

For instance, should televised executions be encouraged in the hope that the repulsiveness would stop the killing, or should they be discouraged because they would burst the lid off the Nielsen ratings and heat up blood lust coast-to-coast?

There is something to be said for bringing Americans face to face with the violence they are accepting in capital punishment, just as the Vietnam war came to be resisted because it was occuring at 6:30 p.m. daily in our living rooms.

The media violence in America, though pervasive, also is sanitary: the routine killings on the westerns and cop shows are perhaps a bit bloody but rarely gory. Violence is portrayed as a clean, rather decisive solution, like the excision of a wart.

People who have witnessed car wrecks, shootings and stabbings know that death and pain are not usually so pretty. Even newspaper reports cannot convey the horror the way the visual media can; most newspapers forego most of the photo "opportunities" and descriptions available to them. It is a game society plays to keep some sense of its own tenuous civility.

But it seems marginally better for Americans to have illusions about the reality of their policies than to indulge the worst of them as prime time entertainment. Television should be free to get the news, but careful in what it presents.

Admittedly, it seems hypocritical to recommend good taste in presenting something that is inherently tasteless. And that, really, is what the issue boils down to: capital punishment itself. It is the killing that is wrong, whether it is some kid stabbing an old person in the Bronx or Texas pulling the switch after the pretty couple oozes through the Geritol commercial.

Should we, as a people, do anything as a public policy that we aren't proud to have our children watch us do?

THE ARIZONA REPUBLIC
Phoenix, Ariz., January 11, 1977

Federal Judge William Taylor Jr. ruled in Dallas the other day that the press could not be barred from a legal execution, if the death sentence is re-established.

Nor, said the judge, could the press be denied the right to interview prisoners on death row if the prisoners were willing to talk.

We think the judge is right.

There would be an instinctive public suspicion of an execution which was not witnessed by at least some members of the public and of the press. And certainly a condemned person should be allowed to tell the public what he thinks and feels.

But the judge went too far in holding that television reporters could take and broadcast pictures of the gassing or of the electrocution of a condemned criminal.

Judge Taylor compared a newspaper reporter's pencil and notebook to a television reporter's camera.

That's a bad comparison.

Print media people don't need to throw an intense light on the subject they are writing about. Frequently they don't even need a notebook. But the TV reporter has to lug 30 or 40 pounds of equipment around with him. He has to tell his subject when to start talking (or acting) and when to stop.

He and his camera have their place in the collection and dispersal of news. But that place is not inside an execution chamber in an American prison.

The Dallas Morning News
Dallas, Tex., January 5, 1977

FEDERAL JUDGE William Taylor's ruling to allow filming of executions in Huntsville was not a victory for the ghoulish as some might contend.

Judge Taylor simply said that an execution was an act of state, therefore it would be unthinkable for the media to be excluded. The state, he implied, does not have the right of prior restraint to determine what the news media may publish. And on this point, the judge is on sound constitutional ground.

Tony Garrett, a reporter for KERA-TV, challenged, with the assistance of the American Civil Liberties Union, new rules set down by W. J. Estelle Jr., director of the Texas Department of Corrections, prohibiting interviews with death-row inmates, prohibiting a news media representative from the execution chamber and banning cameras in the chamber.

Estelle, who has a commendable record in his relations with the news media, contended that the state's criminal procedures do not specifically allow interviews with the condemned and do not specifically name media representatives among the persons required or allowed to be present in the execution chamber.

If Taylor's ruling is upheld, the decision on whether the execution should appear on television or whether still photographs of it should appear in newspapers properly will rest on the shoulders of the news directors and editors of these institutions, as it should in a free society.

And the question of taste, no doubt, will be a subject of heated debates across the nation.

There is ample precedent for showing mortal violence on television. How many times, for example, have Americans seen the assassination of John F. Kennedy? Or Lee Harvey Oswald's death? And the Vietnam War, including executions of citizens, has been televised repeatedly.

If the death penalty is to be a deterrent to would-be criminals—and The News believes it is—a strong argument can be made for publicizing the actual execution through all media.

Prison officials have expressed concern that filming of the execution could make the act a circus. And it shouldn't. But that responsibility rests, too, with the media to approach an execution with professionalism and good taste.

The U.S. Constitution assures this nation not a responsible press but a free one. The media must provide the responsibility themselves, and they can be controlled through public attitudes toward their actions.

So Judge Taylor came down firmly on the side of the free press. It is up to the media to exercise restraint in this reaffirmed freedom. Death is never a game, and in covering executions, the dignity of the victims of the criminals should be preserved by making society's retribution the solemn act it is intended to be.

Arkansas Gazette.
Little Rock, Ark., January 17, 1977

From our point of view the notion of televising executions is abhorrent, and if this comes to pass it will be one more sign of the descent of American society in matters of decency, which is to say, matters of civilization.

We're glad to note that this view seems to be shared by the CBS and NBC networks. Spokesmen for both of these have said their news organizations will cover executions of condemned criminals but will not show the death penalty being carried out, either live or on their national news programs. It's regrettable, however, that ABC remains indecisive, its news president saying "I would not rule out * * * pictures on a news broadcast." He seems preoccupied with the legalities: "If the print press has access to an execution, we believe we have the same rights * * *."

Hence the First Amendment is called into this morbid picture, and indeed a federal judge down in Texas has ruled that television does have an equal right to project official killings, the first of which in many years is tentatively scheduled in that state next Wednesday. Still, we expect that this is not the final word of law; higher judges eventually may or may not decide there is a legal difference between telling of an execution in print and bringing it into our living rooms with all its writhings and twitches. The licensed public-domain status of television may bear upon the outcome, as well as the plea that a person has a right to die with at least a minimum of dignity, without his final contortions being made a public spectacle.

These are sticky and unpleasant questions of law. No one likes to place restrictions on television news coverage. But there is news, and there is show business, and sometimes it's difficult to tell where one ends and the other begins on The Tube. Nor is the freedom to televise unrestricted even now under law—it's denied in most courtrooms of the nation. The question there is fair trial, while this proposition related to official killings raises mainly ethical and social questions, and the point that even a condemned person may have entitlement to at least a fragment of privacy in accord with civilized standards: Not to be made the authentic sideshow to all the violent drama on TV.

The official shooting to death of Gary Gilmore in Utah will be news, all right, but who can say it would not also be entertainment for a great many viewers, in the perverse definition of the term which has become all too largely a reality in our time? Who can say it would not be one more factor in desensitizing us to violence? According to one expert estimate, the average American child upon reaching age 14 has seen 11,000 murders on TV. If these do not reflect the real thing, in many cases it's not for lack of trying by the producers. Some observers say that to bring the real thing to us, undiluted, might be a shock which would instill more regard for human life and less regard for capital punishment. But the possibility also exists that it might only cheapen human life a bit more.

This isn't to say that executions for entertainment are anything new. The Romans popularized this, and the great lawyer and psychologist Clarence Darrow clearly defined its troubling import for modern society. Years past, in Arkansas, people sometimes traveled 50 miles by wagon to see a public execution, assembling in crowds of hundreds and having dinners on the grounds. But there is something even more obscene about the thought of all of us seeing them idly in our recliners in the evenings while sipping refreshment. Is it possible that someday we may have commercial sponsors clamoring to get their spots on the Execution of the Month?

Maybe not, but we think the judge in Texas went somewhat too far, too fast, in considering this, and that Utah has gone too far the other way in prohibiting any of the press from even witnessing Gary Gilmore's execution, so as to relay back to the public even the bare news that he actually was shot.

Extremism in either direction often makes for the emergence of bad law and poor policy in the end. We must hope, finally, that the television industry exercises decent discretion—that ABC will not be a hold-out for giving us "living" death, which might make the other networks decide their present admirable policy is untenable from the standpoint of competition. The competition in televised violence already has exceeded civilized limits.

THE DALLAS TIMES HERALD

Dallas, Texas, June 17, 1976

MOST AMERICANS probably agree with the point argued by Texas Atty. Gen. John Hill before a three-judge panel in federal court the other day: Executions have no place on television.

But that point is secondary to the central question in the case, which is: Who should decide whether or not executions should be shown on television newscasts, the government or the TV stations?

In other words, is television protected by the First Amendment or not?

U.S. Dist. Judge William Taylor Jr. of Dallas has ruled that television is, indeed, part of the press and is therefore entitled to the same freedom enjoyed by the writers, editors and publishers of newspapers, books and magazines.

He ruled that Tony Garrett, who was a reporter for Channel 13 in Dallas when the suit was filed, could not be barred by the warden of the Texas penitentiary from filming an execution, and that the state has no right to prohibit the airing of such a film by a television station or network. Whether or not an execution — or any other news event — is to be filmed and aired is, he ruled, a decision to be made by television news directors, just as they are made by the editors of the print media.

Atty. Gen. Hill's main argument is that "executions should not be made public spectacles." He has asked, "Can anyone say what possible good it could do to watch some poor, unfortunate person go to sleep?" His plea is based on decency and good taste. But it is a dangerous argument which, if successful, could be expanded to include all kinds of news that government officials might consider offensive.

The case is an important one for the future of television as a news medium. Unlike the printing presses of the print media, the air waves are owned by the public and are regulated by the federal government. And broadcasters are only too aware that they are subject to governmental intimidation. Fear of reprisal by an angered Federal Communications Commission has often been cited as the reason — or the excuse — for television's retarded development as a strong arm of the free press.

Both sides in the Garrett case say that the status of television under the First Amendment should be enunciated by the Supreme Court, and we agree.

Whatever the decision of the three-judge panel on the attorney general's appeal, we hope that the case will work its way to that tribunal and that the justices will affirm Judge Taylor's ruling that television newsmen have the right to film and broadcast an execution.

Then we hope that the TV stations, exercising their own sense of decency and good taste, won't do it.

THE ATLANTA CONSTITUTION

Atlanta, Ga., January 31, 1977

The folks at NBC television believe violence has had it.

"We're saying 'Enough of that'," said Robert T. Howard, president of the network. "We're going to try new avenues."

The effect of vicarious violence, especially on children, has been a matter of spirited (if not violent) debate since long before television. You can find some pretty rough stuff going on in the fairy tales of the Brothers Grimm and Hans Christian Andersen. Take Injun Joe and the graveyard scene out of *Tom Sawyer* and you'll lose a lot of young readers of Mark Twain's classic. Even Walt Disney's films—*Pinnochio*, *Bambi*, *Dumbo*, *Snow White*, *Fantasia*, and others—have moments when violence figures in the plot.

Violence has been a common theme in all literature, good and bad, from Homer to James Bond. How many people are killed off in the last act of *Hamlet*? Practically every important personage in the play.

But television, of course, is considered more "real" than other arts—and therefore presumably has a more devastating impact on the young mind. So it is not surprising that the Parent Teachers Association, the American Medical Association, the National Citizens Committee for Broadcasting and other groups and individuals are concerned about the gory stuff on TV. They are convinced not only that violence breeds violence, which few would dispute, but also that the *representation* of violence breeds violence—which some might dispute.

No doubt about it, there are sickies in the entertainment industry and the arts who go too far—there always are. The people who brought you *The Texas Chain Saw Massacre* or the rumored pornographic "snuff flicks" where people allegedly were actually killed for the amusement of the viewing audience would certainly qualify.

But the fact remains that all popular art is based on lots of action, and that is the key ingredient in the popular police melodramas on TV—*Kojak*, *Columbo*, *Charlie's Angels*, *Baretta*—which are among the programs frequently cited for excessive violence. Action provides the vicarious thrills the audience, safe in its armchairs, demands. Action can take various forms, however: an automobile chase, a mountain climbing expedition or the gunfight at the OK corral. The kind of action protested is where people are shown getting killed or hurt—and the protests become more intense as the degree of realism in the TV program or the movie increases. Yet is it less "real" for Hamlet to stab Polonius through the curtain than for Kojak to kill off the killer at the end of that popular TV drama?

"People have said they want another direction and that's what we are going to give them," the NBC exec said in announcing the cutback on violence. Fine. But we have a feeling that it is not what *people* say, but what the *ratings* say that determine what will be shown. The ratings reflect what people actually watch, not what they say they would like to watch. Human nature being what it is, the two are not always the same.

Please. We are not pleading for more violence on TV. We would prefer less. We certainly believe in a sense of responsibility, in restraint. But we do have the strong feeling that programs like *Kojak* are here to stay. After all, they've been around ever since human beings started trying to understand themselves better through drama, literature and art.

Herald News

Fall River, Mass., April 10, 1977

An article in the New England Journal of Medicine calls the violence on so many television programs a menace to the health of the nation's youth. The article convincingly contends that the impulse to initiate the violence shown on tv screens leads to an increasing number of injuries and deaths each year, mostly among young people.

The number of murders committed by young people has soared dramatically. So has the number of youthful crimes, including crimes of violence. "Violence has become a major health problem," the article says. "For an alarming number it has become a way of life."

For years specialists in juvenile behavior, to say nothing of clerics of all denominations, have been saying the same thing. Perhaps now that the spread of youthful violence has been called a health problem, attention will be paid to it. The only authorities these days are medical, and for that reason it is probably a good thing that what is, strictly speaking, a social or moral problem should be taken over by physicians.

Television programming doubtless does exploit the appetite for violence among the young, but is must be said that if violence is to be kept off the home screens, programs of international news will have to be strictly censored. In this most warlike of centuries, what can prevent young people from feeling and acting on the same violent impulses which obviously inspire their elders?

Perhaps it is not television that needs to change so much as the 20th century life style, and while tv is certainly not guiltless, especially of bad taste, it is also being made the scapegoat for forces and impulses that are both more widespread and more profound.

Oregon Journal

Portland, Ore., December 7, 1976

Former Texas Gov. John Connally is a canny politician who possibly could be the next GOP presidential candidate or chairman of the Republican National Committee.

However, when it comes to criminal psychology, Connally's views become a bit fuzzy.

The former governor recently expressed the view that televised executions of prisoners "would be an even more impressive deterrent to crime."

He said that in some Arab countries, at one time, the penalty for thievery was the cutting off of a hand. Connally claims there is no thievery in those countries today.

Perhaps he forgets that, at one time, in Merry Old England, the penalty for picking pockets was a public hanging.

While the thrill-seeking people were totally absorbed in the executions, the remaining pickpockets had a field day.

"Death is a horrible thing to contemplate," Connally said. "If it was televised, everyone could see the real horror of it. It would be an even more impressive deterrent."

Perhaps Gov. Connally doesn't watch television very much.

On any given night the public can watch one or more "bad guys" being executed, usually by gunfire, by law enforcement officers (the good guys.)

And the crime rate goes up and up and up.

HERALD EXAMINER

Los Angeles, Cal., June 29, 1977

Violence, unfortunately, has been around since the beginning of history. In addition to wars, there is violence in homes and on the streets, and one is inclined to accept it as a part of daily life. That, we believe, is a mistake. Television, like the movie, dotes on violence, a handsome money-maker. The American Medical Assn., recently meeting in San Francisco, brought the nation up to date on the impact of TV on the population.

Dr. George Gerbner, dean of the Annenberg School of Communications of the University of Pennsylvania, says TV, the new "industrial-corporate religion," has a stranglehold on American society, influencing every facet of life, creating an unreal world.

What is TV doing to children? Some parents complain that their children can't read or add and subtract after six years in school. After spending their formative years glued to the tube, watching police and gangster shootouts, children face a confused, uncertain adulthood. Dr. Robert Stubblefield, a child psychologist, warned the AMA convention that TV may have more effect on children's behavior than schools and, in some cases, more than parents.

TV certainly can't be blamed for all the nation's ills. Without the "box," life would be dull, indeed.

Violence in this world probably never will be eradicated, but it can be controlled through tighter parental and school discipline and increased police vigilance.

The AMA psychiatrists have suggested a way for TV to do its part. Along with others, it can help bring down the illiteracy and crime rates by cooling it on brute force and murders.

The Charleston Gazette

Charleston, W.Va., June 19, 1976

It was inevitable that a criminal defense would be built upon the illusions created by television, and a jury's rejection of a plea that "Kojak" prompted a slaying does not mean that there will be no more such pleas.

We do not believe television sends killers into the street, but there is no question that television exerts an enormous influence on the daily lives of Americans, a fact heavily counted on by advertisers and politicians. The changes in buying habits and political life wrought by TV are spectacularly visible.

Television also has turned millions of active people into passive human beings. In his book, "Telegarbage," Gregg Lewis observes that "habits, attitudes, values — things which traditionally have been taught by parents, by the church, or by religious leaders — are now being taught by television."

An Orwellian scene is unfolding. Daily, millions of Americans turn to the tube for their fix, their tranquilizer, their dose of illusion, and moral instruction given, perhaps, by a fat, balding, middle aged private detective who beats hell out of muscular young fellows.

The distortion of reality is television's strong suit even when it turns its cameras to happenings such as political events and uses sex to sell shaving cream. And in standard television drama, not even a bow toward reality is made. Physicians never ask payment for their services. Hospitals admit the impecunious without question. Newspapermen are either buffoons who hinder police investigations or godlike creatures purifying the nation's soul. Nobody gets hurt in furious gun battles often fought, for reasons we have never comprehended, in warehouses. Everybody finds parking space.

What happens to young people reared on such illusions? How do viewers manipulated by skilled actors respond to real persons and everyday situations? The "Kojak defense" was rebuffed, perhaps, because every viewer knows television shootings are too commonplace to be serious. Anyway, everybody knows the Good Guy never gets hurt. But the teachings of television aren't limited to orientation in violence.

Dr. George Gerbner, dean of the University of Pennsylvania's Annenberg School of Communications, placed under clinical observation a large group of 12-year-olds. He discovered that nearly half of them watch six or more hours of television every day. It seems to us that too many American parents have surrendered a teaching reponsibility to television. We suggest that they regain control of family life before a generation of zombies is hatched.

Has television no shame?

The assassinated mayor and supervisor of San Francisco were hardly in their graves before the ABC network was making sport of the tragedy. On the popular "Saturday Night Live" show last weekend, one sketch showed films of a mass gathering of Chinese in a parody of the San Francisco mourning scene while a woman's voice narrated what purported to be a news account of the double shooting, with heavy emphasis on the homosexuality of the slain supervisor. The sound of studio audience laughter cackled unaccountably in the background.

Comedian Walter Matthau, star of the show, and his writers were evidently so insensitive as to believe that, in the name of humor, anything goes. More alarming than the bad judgment of the network was the sheep-like response of members of the audience. Laughter dominated the few boos of protest.

"Saturday Night Live" is an all-time favorite show, a poll in The Daily Break reveals, but this parody and other sexually suggestive sketches plumbed new depths of tastelessness— a "Hustler" turning its own pages.

Ironically, many viewers who followed Matthau and Company into this dismal swamp of the mind probably were dismayed at news of the mindless mass suicides in Guyana. One need not join an obscure cult, however, to follow misguided leaders.

While social scientists may ponder the influence that the Reverend Jim Jones possessed over his flock, a more fertile field perhaps would be to analyze the hypnotic effect of TV over millions of its addicts. Which came first, the boob or the tube?

Columnist Georgie Anne Geyer, convinced of a direct tie between the violence of our times and the violent behavior portrayed on TV, calls it a psychic contagion. Impulses, temptations, visceral urges, common to all of us, may be contained in a wholesome environment but unleashed into violent behavior by suggestive influences. Is TV such a dangerous influence?

The Federal Trade Commission is alarmed about cavities in children's teeth, possibly induced by commercials for sugary cereals on kiddies' programs. Should we not consider the cavities of the mind that daily are filled with gunfire, heroically dramatized, entertainingly sanitized?

Government suppression of tasteless programming smacks of censorship. Better to be our own censors. If the networks lack the good judgment to provide entirely wholesome entertainment, we all have an effective remedy: the off switch or channel selector.

TV, no longer in its infancy, is still trying to grow up. But it needs guidance. It is capable of, and occasionally comes through with, outstanding performances, such as "Upstairs, Downstairs," unmatched in visual scope and impact. Such memorable moments make its gross behavior all the harder to take.

The violence in our society, if Columnist Geyer is right, should be a warning. We have only ourselves to blame if we become a nation that fears to venture out at night, huddled close to the tube for the latest series of hilarious fellows bumping off one another. If so, we will have come full cycle. The caveman returneth.

Instead of fearing wild animals, we hide in our elegant caves from wild people, the supposed crazies and cultists. But isn't it a bit crazy of us members of the TV cult to hole up in our caves, fearing violence outside, while inviting it into our midst as entertainment?

If the contagion reaches our cave, we may discover that we have met the crazies and they are us.

THE PLAIN DEALER

Cleveland, Ohio, December 24, 1977

The relationship, if indeed one exists, between television violence and real crime remains unproven, but widely suspected. What is less subject to doubt is the assertion that by presenting violence in a highly stylized and unrealistic manner, television sanitizes the subject.

A new study by the U.S. Conference of Mayors charges that most television violence is "antiseptic" and that most of its pretend victims die quietly or at least out of camera range.

Anyone who has witnessed real violence and its aftermath would agree that the mayhem on the boob tube is so pale by comparison as to be virtually unrelated. It must be particularly easy for children to grow up lacking an appreciation for the agonizing trauma of real-life violence.

Unfortunately, in this case, identifying the problem is much, much easier than devising an acceptable solution.

Transforming television's countless murders, assaults, rapes and miscellaneous slaughter into something approaching the horror of the real thing would drive millions of viewers, including children, into shock or worse. As a daily diet, it simply could not be permitted.

Banning all violence on television, stylized or otherwise, is unacceptable on constitutional grounds at the very least.

Preservation of the status quo, in which scores, if not hundreds, of television performers die with little fuss each week only to reappear happily on some other show, is less than desirable.

What emerges then as the only practical solution is some sort of self-regulating restraint by stations and networks matched by even greater restraint and discretion on the part of parents monitoring their children's viewing habits.

But while we all wait for this self-regulation to take effect, a good deal more discussion and study on the problem is certainly in order.

St. Louis Globe-Democrat

St. Louis, Mo., February 2, 1977

One of the anomalies of American society is that while a great many citizens have been crusading against violence the three major television networks have been promoting it.

In the face of mounting attacks on television violence from the Parent-Teachers Association, the American Medical Association and many other citizen groups, the National Broadcasting Company announced it would de-emphasize violence in the season that begins in the fall.

That's a good start. But CBS and ABC should be asked to follow NBC's example. One network can't do the whole job. It will take all three to clear the airwaves of the mind-polluting violence that pervades so many tv shows.

By now there are reams of studies linking tv violence to violent, criminal and callous behavior by those who watch it.

Convicted murderer Michael Edward Drabing of Lincoln, Ill., testified at his trial in December that he drew his inspiration for the hideous hunting knife slaying of three members of the Lloyd Schneider family of rural Lincoln from watching the first television broadcast of "Helter Skelter," in March of 1976. This is the film depicting the gruesome murders committed by the Charles Manson sect.

Drabing testified that "they (the Manson family) killed all those rich people, and I saw if you killed them that erases the problem. It was the final piece of the puzzle."

After seeing this program Drabing said he bought the book and read it at least four times. Then in August Drabing invaded the home of Schneider, a wealthy hog farmer, and stabbed the three family members more than 100 times.

Apparently believing the public needed more of such bloody fare, CBS re-broadcast Helter Skelter in December. But not all CBS local stations shared the network's fondness of this gory film. A Peoria, Ill., station decided not to air the movie after viewers complained and because of its own concern over five stabbing deaths in its viewing area.

At the recent national PTA hearings on tv violence, Dr. Keith Reisinger, professor of pediatrics and psychiatry at the University of Pittsburgh, said that "the message shown (on tv) is that violence pays. Television continuously instructs us that we can easily resolve problems by use of force."

Allegheny County Judge Patrick Tamillia testified that he had seen evidence that many children in juvenile court believe that violence pays.

"Kids don't cry anymore . . . the hardness of heart is just incomprehensible," Judge Tamillia said. "They are looking at all that violence on tv where there is really no remorse shown. . . . So when they do something wrong and hurt somebody else, they don't feel they've done it to a human being."

Speaking for the American Medical Association, Dr. Frank J. Jirka said the AMA had concluded that tv violence is "an environmental hazard that threatens the life of America." He said "the weight of scientific evidence indicates there is a relationship between violence and aggressive behavior among some youthful offenders."

Along with this heavy fare of violence, viewers have complained about the introduction of explicit sex and themes that attack traditional family moral values. Some consider this trend just as bad or worse than the violence.

Spokesmen for the networks point out they have reduced the amount of violence in some of their shows. But judging from the rising chorus of complaints the volume of violence is still much too great.

If the United States ever is to become a law-abiding nation it must have the cooperation of the amusement industry, including television. To portray violence for entertainment and profit denotes sickness — a sickness which must be cured.

The Detroit News

Detroit, Mich., August 29, 1977

Complaining about pressures brought to bear on the TV industry to eliminate violence from programs, producer Aaron Spelling told a panel of TV Guide editors the other day:

"I tell you, the industry is slowing down the violence to a degree that is dangerous."

Although his way of putting it was hardly felicitous, the man did have a point, expressed more persuasively by another producer, David Wolper of "Roots" fame.

Observing that he could not have made "Roots" under the standards now imposed on the industry, Wolper said: "In 'Roots' I kept saying the slaves have to be hit with whips, because that's really what happened. And the more violence there is and the more repulsive it is, the more these people will feel the horror of what it was really like."

He is right. Like explicit sex and other raw realities of life, violence may be suitable in a dramatic production if it illustrates an essential point of the story — if it exists for a valid dramatic purpose and not merely for its own sake.

Unfortunately, few of the TV cops-and-robbers shows which are criticized for their violence offer any redeeming dramatic qualities. Indeed, the plots, such as they are, exist as flimsy vehicles for bloodshed, mayhem, demolition and terror.

These are the programs that ignited the crusade to eliminate TV violence, a crusade that could, if it went too far, fulfill one producer's fear that TV will become a "plastic" medium that will breed a "plastic society."

Actually, with or without violence, TV has gone a long way toward that fate because of its sad lack of imagination, its reluctance to experiment, its devotion to the familiar, its fear of excellence. Mindless violence is but one of the ropes with which TV, as a medium for worthwhile dramatic production, has been strangling itself.

AKRON BEACON JOURNAL

Akron, Ohio, July 27, 1976

POW!

If you have a television set, it hits you in the face like a karate chop on Police Woman, a pie in the face from the Three Stooges, a shotgun blast from the late movie or an anvil smashing into the head of that poor coyote on the Saturday morning cartoon show.

It is violence, the stuff that is often packaged by the networks as filler between the toothpaste and car wax commercials, and it rat-a-tat-tats into living rooms like World War III.

Almost as frequently as the kicks and punches come warnings that violence on television makes children more aggressive. Here is another.

Dr. Robert M. Liebert, professor of psychology and psychiatry at the State University of New York, Stony Brook campus, says there is a definite connection between a youngster's aggressive tendencies and the amount of violence he or she watches on the tube.

"The single best prediction of how aggressive a young man will be at age 19 is the amount of television violence he was exposed to," said Dr. Liebert, who is involved in research for the United States surgeon general.

Dozens of studies have shown "a positive relationship" between the number of violent actions seen on television and the child's use of aggression in dealing with problems, he said.

The average child watches at least two to three hours of television a day and spends more time in front of the TV than in the classroom by graduation time.

Youngsters are affected by example, Dr. Liebert told a conference sponsored by the American Association of School Librarians and the Action for Children's Television group. The young viewers learn from "exposure to violence (committed) by heroes as well as villains (that) violence is a way to resolve conflict," he said.

Among the worst offenders: the Saturday morning cartoons, where somebody is getting thumped, pummeled or smashed about every two minutes.

Certainly, Captain Kangaroo and Sesame Street offer better examples for coping with problems than Baretta or some spinach-popping sailor with a penchant for pounding opponents senseless. And certainly, parents should exercise some guidance on what their children watch — or, for that matter, whether they should watch so much TV instead of reading books or playing outside.

But hold on. Let's not punch CBS in its eye or kick ABC and NBC for all the aggressive action of today's youngsters. The networks are in business. They want to attract viewers so they can charge advertisers lots of money. So they try to offer programming they think will lure men, women and children in front of the set.

And there is the question: Are violence-packed television programs shaping society or are they reflecting the prevailing attitude? Which is cause and which is effect?

There is little doubt that the programming on television is often terrible. There is too much violence inside the TV set, just as there is too much on the street. But it would be an oversimplification to blame the television industry for all of it. If society demanded that television violence be toned down, the networks would listen, because they want to draw big audiences.

Television has a tremendous role in shaping society's values, make no mistake. And violence should have less play, particularly on shows aimed at juvenile audiences. But don't place all the blame on the network moguls; there is plenty of blame to go around.

The State

Columbia, S.C., March 5, 1977

AN OFFICIAL of the National Humanities Center recently commented that American children are getting their heroes from television, "an unreliable source for anything so important."

Dr. William J. Bennett, executive officer of the center, cited a newspaper survey of 368 eighth graders. Seven of their top 10 heroes were TV actors: Henry "The Fonz" Winkler, Farrah Fawcett, Lee Majors, John Travolta, Paul Michael Glaser, David Soul, and Lynda Carter.

Dr. Bennett's view is that the youngsters are responding to a "set of packaged TV personalities in contrived roles and situations." He concluded that teachers and parents don't advance to the children "real-life heroes, models of real human excellence."

The thought is provocative, and one which parents and teachers should seriously consider. They might begin by listing their own set of heroes. And that may prove more difficult than one might imagine.

Thus, it opens the question of just who are authentic living American heroes today. And if they are hard to name, why is that so? For our part, we suggest that the trouble lies in a national climate of cynicism — too many idols have turned up with clay feet, and we have come to expect the worst of men, not the best.

But, perhaps we look too far away for the "real-life heroes, models of real human excellence." Should they not also be found in the homes and classrooms of this country?

THE MILWAUKEE JOURNAL

Milwaukee, Wisc., February 15, 1977

Many fathers have long suspected that the talking box they bought for a few hundred dollars has snookered them out of a key role in raising their children. But confirmation of it hardly is welcome. An expert on educational development testified at a recent hearing on TV violence that TV ranks second only to mothers in influencing a child's attitudes, ideas and values. It is more important than fathers, family income and ethnic background.

Given the time a child spends taking in TV's message, that seems inevitable. Through the growing years, a child spends 15,000 hours watching murder, burglary and other crime, with abysmally small tokens of love and tenderness. In contrast, a study of fathers with infants a year old found that intimate interaction between father and child averaged 38 seconds a day. Other studies show decreasing parent-child interaction across the board.

The developing mind has not learned to discriminate and judge what it takes in. It absorbs whatever is offered. Television management, to its credit, has a growing sense of responsibility about the quality of programming. But the best answer lies in parents' reclaiming the right to determine how their children grow. They may not have 15,000 hours. But they can't do it in 38 seconds a day.

THE SUN

Baltimore, Md., March 4, 1977

A research group sponsored by the National Institute of Mental Health reports that violence within the American family is widespread and severe. Researchers reported that annually some 1.5 million American children between the ages of 3 and 17 are attacked by their parents in ways that could cause severe bodily harm or death. Spouses frequently attack each other physically, to the extent, for example, that prevention of wife-beating has become a major purpose of many feminist organizations.

The next project of the NIMH researchers is to attempt to define the reasons for the family violence. While this may be far more difficult than merely documenting the problem, earlier research may point out some directions. According to earlier studies, for instance, people exposed to a regular diet of televised violence not only became more callous toward the victims of violence but at the same time tended to see violence more often as an option for dealing with their own problems.

Pinpointing the causes of family violence could reveal at least one relatively easy cure. If televised violence indeed is a major cause of much real-life family violence, as is increasingly suspected, clearing it from the screen would not be all that difficult. In fact, removing violence from the tube might be the single most effective action against family violence that can be accomplished with relative ease. The pressure on the networks to reduce violence is growing, and it may grow yet more when the NIMH researchers release their findings.

The Burlington Free Press

Burlington, Vt., March 10, 1977

ALTHOUGH CHILDREN in the United States are assumed to have superior advantages and prospects for achieving "the good things of life," a high percentage of American children (ages 7 to 11) live with fears which influence their lives, according to the results of a nationwide study.

Robert W. Merry, writing in National Observer, says in reporting on the results of this study:

"Two-thirds of America's children harbor fears that 'somebody bad' will get into their homes. And that fear, says a new study, is so widespread — cutting across residential, economic and ethnic groups — that television's contribution to it is unmistakable.

"In fact, the study indicates that nearly a quarter of American kids actually fear certain television programs, and heavy TV watchers — four hours or more a day — are twice as likely as other children to say they become frightened often.

"These perceptions about children's fears were among the conclusions of a national survey of children's thoughts and feelings. The survey was sponsored by the New York-based Foundation for Child Development and conducted by Temple University's Institute for Survey Research. More than 2,200 children ... were interviewed about their lives, home and school experiences, their neighborhoods and their views. According to Foundation officials, the kids interviewed were scientifically selected to represent a cross section of America's 17.7 million grammar-school-age children."

Many of the children interviewed said they were allowed to watch any television programs they chose and it was evident that they had seen those intended for adults as well as the ones intended primarily for children. This raises questions about the responsibility of parents for selectivity in what children are allowed to see.

But the fears that children have are not entirely due to what they see on television, the results of the study indicate. Nearly a third of the children interviewed said they were afraid of specific persons who had either hurt them or threatened them with bodily injury.

More than 40 per cent said they had been bothered by older kids who threatened to injure them, and 13 per cent said they had been bothered by adults. Specific cases were not listed, but there was evidence that some of the 13 per cent had been physically beaten.

More than a fourth of the children interviewed did not live with their actual fathers, indicating that they had been born out of wedlock or their parents had separated.

Commenting on these facts, Nicholas Zill, project director of the study, is quoted as saying: "We are becoming a nation of absentee and part-time fathers."

But the study showed also that the fears of children more often grew out of living in an environment of marital discord than from troubles resulting from separation of parents.

It was learned by interviewing mothers that about one child in seven was the result of an unwanted pregnancy, and such children were found to be frequently filled with fears because they came to feel unwanted. They tended to have poorer health and have more problems in school.

Director Zill commented that one recommendation coming out of the survey was more education to control reproduction. He indicated his belief that children had a right to be born into homes where they were wanted and prepared to give them good care.

It was recommended in the report that unless TV networks take action soon to reduce violence, the federal government step in to do the clean-up job. Undoubtedly there will be other suggestions.

St. Petersburg Times
St. Petersburg, Fla., March 17, 1977

The hostages were barely released in Washington last week when second-guessing began about the role played in this near-disaster by the press and broadcasters. A "media event," it was called by some people. If the papers and the TV and radio stations weren't exactly to blame for it, they still were said to have a lot of explaining to do.

THE IDEA seemed to be that excessive publicity about this 40-hour reign of terror in the heart of the nation's capital tended to incite future violence by promising a media payoff to other frustrated and deranged persons or groups.

Andrew Young, the U.S. ambassador to the United Nations, called for a law "to restrict publication of information about violent crime." He suggested that the Supreme Court "clarify" the First Amendment to accommodate this. The White House, when asked about Young's remarks, said President Carter "has no desire to seek legislation or to otherwise impose a solution," but that he recognized that a problem exists.

Sure there's a problem. Nobody recognizes that fact more than the press. Unbalanced persons in some cases undoubtedly have fed on publicity about violent crime to nurture their own twisted dreams of national fame. Newsmen and their editors regularly sweat out tough judgments on this.

BUT THAT ISN'T the problem we mean. The problem is that in emotional response to one of these outrageous acts, somebody can always be found to suggest that those who keep the public informed about crime somehow must share the blame for the fact it exists, and to say there ought to be a law to prevent it.

In this case, of all unlikely people, that somebody was Ambassador Young.

"I think we create a lot of these phenomena for ourselves, for we have so glorified and publicized events," Young told reporters. "In a sense we're advertising to neurotic people that when you want a lot of attention, do something suicidal and ridiculous."

AS FOR the First Amendment, which bars restraints on free speech and the press, Young said he wasn't sure it was meant to protect the right to destroy freedom itself. And he said when the Bill of Rights was composed, there was no instant transmission of news; the people in California wouldn't even have known about violence in Washington then.

We knew Young had come a long way from Selma, the march on Montgomery, the police dogs, the fire hoses, the other confrontations of the civil rights struggle. But we didn't think he could have forgotten. The charge by press critics then was that all the TV footage and news copy on boat-rockers like Young were just spreading dissent and inviting more trouble.

FORTUNATELY, our faith now has been restored in Young's sense of proportion, and we like his readiness to admit he was wrong.

Interviewed on the CBS morning news show about his earlier comments, what he did was take 'em all back. He said he, like many other folks, was concerned about society's "glamorization" of crime. And he thinks TV, particularly, ought to consider its impact in this.

But as for court tests, or legal restrictions, or anything else smacking of censorship, Young said he, especially with his background, certainly isn't for that. In explanation of his earlier shots from the hip, Young grinned and allowed that in his new role he'll have to start saying "no comment" sometimes to the press.

MEANTIME, we were impressed with comments on this subject, here, by Carl Rowan, another eminent black and former diplomat, now a nationally syndicated columnist. He told Eckerd College students the freed Washington hostages actually may owe their lives to the press.

"It was the press, particularly television, that allowed (the terrorist leader) to get what he wanted to say off his chest," Rowan said. "Because he did have a release, he backed off."

Sure, in this unprecedented case there were failures in media reaction. Maybe there was an excess of dramatics. But when large chunks of downtown within blocks of the White House, were cordoned off by police, workers and area residents didn't have to be told that parts of the city were under virtual siege.

AND THINK of the rumors if they hadn't been told. Also consider how much faith they (and you) could have in the press if word got around that for legal or some other reason, serious crimes were taking place about which the public was being kept in the dark.

Democrat and Chronicle
Rochester, N.Y., March 21, 1977

THE MEDIA have become, curiously, a scapegoat for events which people dislike. The "wrong" person got elected? Blame the media by saying they didn't give the opponents enough coverage. A bill gets defeated in Congress? Blame the media which gave certain special interest groups too much space. Too many people drinking too much? Why, they would all put the corks back in the bottles if the media wouldn't carry liquor ads.

Now add to the list the notion that the media are responsible for terrorist activities including hijackings, bombings, and kidnappings. This comes from no one other than our brand-new U.N. ambassador, Andrew Young, who wants to shackle the press so it won't report violence.

Recently, in Sacramento, Young offered the myopic panacea of media restraint to discourage terrorist outbursts like the Hanafi Moslem take-over in Washington, D.C. Young said that in-depth coverage of such violence "is advertising to neurotic people." "We're creating a climate of violence for ourselves," he said.

Since when do the media create the news? People commit terrible crimes and wondrous deeds. The media report what happens. Are the media to remain silent when 134 people are held hostage? Are they to ignore other acts of violence including war? How will people know whether or not loved ones are caught in a net of public violence?

Yes, terrorists do want their grievances publicized. But Young overlooks the media's main function: to keep people informed and to eliminate rumor. Terrorism won't be stopped by ignoring the perpetrators, for they are frustrated walking time-bombs. The best way is to address the reasons for their desperation, not to handcuff the press.

THE MILWAUKEE JOURNAL
Milwaukee, Wisc., March 24, 1977

There is no doubt that the surge of terrorism in America presents painful dilemmas for the mass media.

Citizens, for example, need to know what is happening so they can take defensive steps, as individuals and as a society. Yet there is reason to fear that publicizing the plague can help spread it.

One answer may be a more subdued form of coverage, making terrorism less spectacular and perhaps less alluring to the demented. Yet, sometimes, massive publicity may be a crucial safety valve, giving the terrorist an outlet for murderous rage that might otherwise be directed at helpless hostages.

Plainly, there are no quick, all-purpose answers. Yet some observers are impelled to propose them. A dismaying example is Andrew Young, our fast talking UN ambassador. He thinks coverage of terrorism should be restricted by law, noting that "the First Amendment has got to be clarified by the Supreme Court in the light of the power of the mass media."

From the constitutional standpoint, such a proposal is outlandish. Yet it apparently makes some practical sense to Young — even though as a famed civil rights leader he should be among the last to suggest curbing the press. Not many years ago, when local police were siccing dogs on demonstrating blacks, breaking up protest meetings and brutalizing those who wanted freedom, the press carried the story to the nation day after day. And public opinion forced action to insure civil rights.

Where would Young be now had a free press not reported the plight of blacks?

Young might retort that terrorism is a special problem. However, he is still flirting with censorship. And, quite aside from enormous constitutional defects, such an approach is riddled with appalling practical flaws.

For example, censorship would not stop accounts of terrorism from circulating in some form, if only word of mouth. That means condemning a terrorized community or nation to a diet of rumor. Uncertainty, confusion, distrust would gnaw at the citizenry — which, all the while, would be denied reliable information needed to debate and develop constructive responses (such as assembling expert teams to outwit terrorists).

Even more vexing are these questions: Who would play censor? Who would decide when a disturbance should be hushed up: maybe an attorney general like John Mitchell? Once censorship is used to deal with terrorists, would its extension to coverage of other "troublemakers" — maybe even civil rights leaders — be very difficult?

Editors and broadcasters should continuously review terrorism coverage, guarding against excess and explaining inherent dilemmas to fellow citizens. While disagreement over approaches is inevitable, there should be clear public consensus on one point: Control of basic information to citizens can never be placed in governmental hands without running ghastly risks.

■■■

Crime and Courts:

FLORIDA JURY REJECTS DEFENSE PLEA OF 'TV INTOXICATION' IN ZAMORA CASE

Despite his plea of television-induced insanity, Ronald Zamora was convicted Oct. 6 of first degree murder. The jury in Miami debated less than two hours, rejecting the defense plea that the 15-year-old had shot his neighbor during a robbery because of his "prolonged, involuntary subliminal intoxication with television." Jury foreman John Kateb said, "This TV thing—that's ridiculous."

Zamora was also convicted of armed robbery, burglary, and possession of a firearm in the commission of a felony. He had shot Elinor Haggart, 82, when she surprised him and another boy as they were robbing her Miami Beach home in June. The defense had contended that the youth had watched television constantly since he arrived in the United States 10 years ago, learning to speak English and to kill in emulation of the violence portrayed. The defense had entered a plea of temporary insanity at the time of the murder, claiming Zamora was unable to distinguish between his actions and a television drama. Circuit Judge Paul Baker agreed to a defense request for a presentence investigation of Zamora's background and set sentencing for Nov. 7. The trial was televised under a year-long experiment by the Florida Supreme Court.

The Charlotte Observer

Charlotte, N.C., October 3, 1977

How does television affect our society? A trial underway in Miami won't answer that question. But it may provoke further debate on two troublesome issues: whether TV violence makes children aggressive, and whether televising trials distorts the judicial process.

Fifteen-year-old Ronnie Zamora is on trial for murder. His lawyer contends the boy was rendered insane by overexposure to TV violence, left unable "to appreciate the criminality of his conduct."

That may be hard to prove. But it is an unsettling possibility when you consider that children watch an average six hours of TV daily.

That's not the only unsettling thing about the case. "Highlights" of the trial are being shown on Miami television — competing, in some cases, with the same violent fare being examined.

Florida is allowing cameras in courtrooms in a one-year experiment. That is still a rarity, however.

The U.S. Supreme Court held in 1965 that Billy Sol Estes was denied due process because his trial was televised. The court said TV creates a "circus" atmosphere, distorting the trial and the public's understanding of it. "A defendant on trial ... is entitled to his day in court, not in a stadium, or a city or nationwide area," the justices wrote.

It's true that TV equipment is less intrusive than it once was. And we doubt that lawyers will ham it more with cameras than without them. But the Constitution guarantees both a public trial and due process. Trials are already public. And it is possible that cameras might infringe on the right to a fair trial.

Opponents argue that televised trials could make witnesses more reluctant to testify, subject highly visible jurors to undue pressure, and mislead the public by showing only the most dramatic moments in the most controversial trials.

These contentions — like the those on the effects of TV violence — may be hard to prove. But they deserve serious consideration. The publicity now being given to the Miami trial may, whatever the verdict, help bring the issues into better focus.

THE CHRISTIAN SCIENCE MONITOR
Boston, Mass., October 7, 1977

If good TV programs are to be granted the possibility of affecting viewers, it can hardly be said that bad programs have no such possibility. The defense attorney for a 15-year-old confessed killer has gone so far as to argue that his client acted "under the influence of television violence" in a state of "involuntary subliminal television intoxication" to the point of insanity. The trial of this youth, Ronald Zamora, began in Florida not long after a six-year study of British adolescent boys found that those who watched a lot of television violence were almost 50 percent more likely to indulge in some sort of violence than those who do not.

The study's cause-and-effect linking of TV violence and actual violence has been challenged by a British governmental paper – even as the Zamora "television intoxication" defense has been challenged in court. As in previous instances of concern about the impact of fictionalized violence – in the movies, in comic books – it may be impossible to isolate the influence of TV violence sufficiently to prove that it was the controlling factor in an individual's conduct. Much less could any such case be the basis for an assumption that young viewers in general cannot overcome being manipulated by what they have seen on the tube. Nor should TV or any other possible influence become an easy scapegoat to avoid personal moral responsibility.

But surely there is no reason for youngsters to continue gorging on what has even the possibility of causing the effect described by William Belson, the author of the study of British boys: "It looks as if television has reduced or broken down the inhibitions against being violent that had been built up in the child by parents and other socializing influences." And surely, in this light, parents cannot abdicate responsibility for guiding their children's TV watching by precept and example.

The Zamora defense attorney outlines the kind of approach to TV in the home that should be avoided even if no connection with violence should ever be proved. He says young Ronny had been plopped in front of the TV set for many hours a day since the age of four. TV was his babysitter. "The tube took the place of the home, the school, and the church," according to the attorney.

Outsiders cannot presume to judge a family situation in which there have been various problems. The resort to TV may be a sad symptom as much as a cause of difficulty. But it does not take any specter of leading to violence to expose the error of endless hours before the set. Consider the emptiness and artificiality in this way of growing up. Manufactured fantasies substitute for the natural imagination of the child. TV in excess becomes a diversion from participating in the world instead of the enhancement to such participation which TV at its best and in its proper role can be.

And what of the networks presenting the kind of violent shows Ronald Zamora watched and Dr. Belson found so egregiously influential? Can America's CBS, for example, which financed the Belson study, read it without questioning every gratuitous act of violence in its programs, every instance of violence purporting to be in a good cause? These kinds were reportedly found by Dr. Belson to have particular impact in increasing violent activity by the viewer.

It is too easy to blame the public alone for giving violent programs high ratings. Indeed, a countercurrent of public outrage over violence is credited with some reduction in violence in the new American TV season. What must continue to be combated is such a high level of taken-for-granted violence that a generation of viewers becomes too callous to be outraged by it on the screen or off – even if they never throw a punch or, as Ronald Zamora did, slay the 82-year-old widow next door.

The Evening Bulletin

Philadelphia, Pa., October 10, 1977

Spending as much as six hours a day glued to the television tube was hardly beneficial for Ronnie Zamora, no more than it would be for any growing youngster — or even most adults.

Young Zamora certainly could have used all of those hours to do a whole world of constructive and creative things — the kind of activities that might have contributed to his own normal development and perhaps helped others, too.

Most television shows don't contribute to this kind of effort, but it does seem that the one saving grace of any TV cop "shoot 'em up" show is its simple, and often childlike, distinction between right and wrong. Couldn't Ronny Zamora have managed somehow to absorb at least that?

So it seems that 15-year-old Ronny Zamora really wasn't being true to his so-called "television addiction" when he walked next-door to rob and fatally shoot Elinor Haggart in their Miami neighborhood. Television couldn't have blurred his values to the point where an act that wasn't justified on-screen could somehow be justified in the off-screen world. It took a jury less than two hours to decide that last week.

For that jury to have accepted that young man's insanity plea would have given television far too much credit, in terms of its power to make impressionable minds consider unlawful acts — and too little credit for at least putting white hats on the good guys and dark hats on the villains.

The television defense was simply a cop-out for Ronny Zamora.

The Providence Journal

Providence, R.I., October 8, 1977

For a murder defense, it was extraordinary. The youth, 15, charged with the fatal shooting of an elderly Florida woman, had pleaded innocent by reason of insanity due to his long exposure to violence on television.

The boy, Ronny Zamora, was convicted Thursday night. The verdict, at least insofar as it represents the jury's rejection of the "TV insanity" defense, is sound. The defense lawyer for the boy had argued that years of watching violent TV programs had eroded his ability to distinguish between right and wrong, so that, when he committed the crime, he acted in a state of "voluntary subliminal television intoxication." This argument, while novel, stretches the imputed impact of violent TV programming on viewers' minds to and illogical and untenable degree.

Yet by reaching for an unusual defense argument, the lawyer has focused fresh attention on a most serious issue: to what extent *does* prolonged exposure to TV violence affect the behavior of impressionable TV-watchers?

The Zamora jury found it impossible to isolate the boy's TV-soaked childhood as a controlling element in his behavior, and properly rejected any idea that televised violence should be admitted as a scapegoat to excuse personal violence. Beyond this, though, there is a growing body of opinion that TV violence, by deadening sensibilities and eroding inhibitions, can adversely affect a viewer's outlook. Mindless, gratuitous TV violence needs to be fought, and the Zamora defense, while extreme, ought to prompt parents to exercise much closer control over what programs their children watch.

ST. LOUIS POST-DISPATCH

St. Louis, Mo., October 1, 1977

Television is confronting television in a Miami murder trial, and at this stage no one can say which side, if either, will win. Defense attorneys for 15-year-old Ronald Zamora, accused of killing an elderly woman, are contending that the defendant was temporarily insane because of "intoxication with television violence." "Kojak" is said to have been his favorite television show; and the murder is said by the defense to have closely paralleled a Kojak show.

As the trial goes on, a television camera sweeps the courtroom, as part of a one-year experiment in which cameras are allowed in Florida courts. Public station WPBT plans to show extended segments of two to three hours of the trial each evening. So television will be on trial outside the courtroom as well as inside.

Who can tell where this confusing scenario will end? If the televising of trials wins a vote of confidence, the decision will be that a televised murder drama in the courtroom is okay — which would mean more violence on the home screen. Yet such scenes from the courtroom could be instructive on our system of justice. The public thus might lose if televised trials lose.

If the television insanity defense wins, the public might lose — if the defendant eventually goes free. And worse still, we might conclude that, if television violence continues, we will wind up a nation of mad people. If the television insanity plea loses, the programmers may decide violence can't hurt us and proceed to give us a bigger dose of it.

The possible variations of these scenarios are so limitless that they should give broadcasters and lawyers enough material to argue about for a long time.

The Morning News

Wilmington, Del., October 4, 1977

Highlights of Miami's celebrated "Kojak" murder trial are being shown on public television, and that's appropriate.

Attorneys for one of the defendants, a 15-year-old boy, claim he was insane at the time the murder was committed, a victim of "involuntary television intoxication."

While a murder trial, particularly one involving such a novel defense, may have its share of excitement, it's likely most viewers would prefer watching "Kojak" to the cross examination of Telly Savalas.

There's nothing wrong with the concept of trials on television. If nothing else, the exposure would give Americans a better view of the legal system than they ever got from "Perry Mason."

But the courtroom usually makes for bad theater.

Regular observers will admit that many days in court are boring. For example, while the Wilmington desegregation case may be of broad public interest, regular members of the courtroom audience have found much of the testimony repetitive and dreadfully dull.

It's hard to imagine a significant case that would have less viewer interest than the federal antitrust suit against IBM, now playing in a New York courtroom. The trial is a real yawner, but, by the time the appeals process is through, the case could have a run as long as "I Love Lucy."

Most trials don't steadily rise to a television-like dramatic peak, with some real-life Raymond Burr magically producing a last-minute mystery witness to get the defendant off the hook while the real criminal gasps from the courtroom's back bench.

The televised Miami trial has already created some interesting developments, like viewers telling attorneys to watch out for particular jurors.

If the television test succeeds, the networks might even get interested, and the possibilities are intriguing.

Will lawyers and witnesses need makeup to appear more telegenic?

Will the judges sacrifice their traditional black robes for more colorful garb?

Will the hallowed five-minute recess be traded for a series of 60-second commercial breaks?

And, if there's a really good trial, will some network suggest a prime time showing, forcing the judges and lawyers to work at night?

The courtroom could compete with "Kojak" for Nielsen points. Telly Savalas would win.

The Star-Ledger

Newark, N.J., October 11, 1977

A jury was not persuaded by a unique defense in a murder trial — the contention that a 15-year-old defendant was driven to murdering an elderly woman by "involuntary television intoxication."

The defense attorney maintained that it was constant viewing of violence on television programs that motivated the homicidal action.

While the television industry certainly is not blameless on the disturbing issue of excessive violence, it would have been a grave distortion of justice if this novel defense had been sustained in court.

But the unfortunate experience of this youngster should serve as a grim reminder to indulgent parents who permit their children to be exposed to a constant barrage of television violence of potential lethal anti-social implications. Their time could be better spent on school work than nightly distractions of unending television watching; the disruptive effects being painfully evident in the learning deficiencies among millions of young Americans.

Press Herald

Portland, Me., October 3, 1977

The Zamora trial by television may very well become Exhibit A in the case against allowing electronic news coverage of courtroom proceedings.

It is ironic that this case should be the first major test of a one-year experiment in permitting the camera in the courtroom. The test was ordered by the Florida Supreme Court.

Ronny Zamora is 15 years old. He and Darrell Agrella 14, are charged with the murder of Zamora's 83-year-old neighbor, Elinor Haggart. Defended by a flamboyant lawyer, Ellis Rubin, Zamora's defense is predicated on the argument that he was insane "because of involuntary television intoxication."

His counsel argues that Zamora killed in the course of a robbery because he was conditioned by seeing so much violence on television.

The first day of the trial appeared to confirm the most dire predictions of those who have opposed admitting electronic journalism to courtrooms.

People were calling Zamora's attorney with all sorts of suggestions. Even other lawyers called to offer advice. People, including the lawyers, were advising on the selection of jurors.

Is it consistent, we wonder, to televise a murder trial? Is it consistent with complaining about all the violence on TV? If, as the defense claims, television can be so mind penetrating as to cause someone to commit murder, what sort of thinking is the murder trial going to induce?

And there is all the predicted confusion with technicians and cameramen crowding hallways and creating the distraction expected wherever shooting live television occurs. Courtroom reaction is little different from football stadium reaction, apparently.

The experiment is worthwhile. But it was a most unfortunate choice of cases with which to begin it.

The Miami Herald

Miami, Fla., October 8, 1977

THERE can not be comfort for anyone in the murder conviction of 15-year-old Ronny Zamora; there can be renewed confidence and respect for the integrity and dedication of citizen-jurors.

For hundreds of thousands of people in South Florida and elsewhere, a better understanding, and respect, for what goes on in court has been gained because the Zamora trial was televised. Just as the gimmicky "TV intoxication" defense was found to be baseless by jurors and viewers alike, so was educational TV's coverage of the trial found not to be obtrusive or disruptive. Instead it was educational, and it was real to the vast majority who have never attended a criminal trial.

Because it was the first major trial to be shown under Florida's experimental program allowing cameras in the courtroom, it was unavoidable that greater attention than was perhaps necessary was given this case. Still, decorum ruled, and Judge Paul Baker made it clear that no other standard of behavior would be permitted.

It was, in fact, a simple trial. Prosecutor Thomas Headley proved his case beyond doubt. Defense counsel did nothing to enhance the image of the law profession with his inept, if novel, claim that watching television can be blamed for murder by pistol shot. In summation, Prosecutor Headley termed this line of defense "utter nonsense."

The jury agreed. Not that it matters, but so do we.

The Philadelphia Inquirer

Philadelphia, Pa., October 13, 1977

A Miami jury quickly dismissed the "TV intoxication defense" raised last week by the defense attorney of 15-year-old Ronny Zamora, accused of killing an 82-year-old neighbor.

Zamora's lawyer insisted that his client, an avid television fan, was simply reacting to the violence portrayed on television. The jury ruled otherwise. It deliberated for only two hours before convicting Zamora of murder and acquitting television — indirectly, at least — of being an accessory.

Television acquitted itself in another sense as well. The Zamora trial was televised from start to finish with thousands of viewers watching each day. It was the first major test of an experiment instituted by the Florida Supreme Court last July that permits television coverage of any trial without prior approval of the judge, the prosecutor or the defendant.

By the trial's conclusion, there were few, if any, complaints. And, by all accounts, the Florida experiment is a huge success so far.

Florida is one of five states that permit cameras in courtrooms. With the Zamora case receiving nationwide publicity, the Florida experiment is causing renewed examination of the courtroom blackout that exists virtually everywhere else.

Television and still cameras have been barred from courtrooms for decades. Not until 1964, however, was the ban justified on constitutional grounds. In a 5-4 decision, the U. S. Supreme Court ruled that Billy Sol Estes, a wheeler-dealer Texas businessman, had been denied a fair trial because his trial was televised.

Since then, the judiciary and legal profession have relied on the Estes case as a convenient shield to cast aside requests for television coverage.

Importantly, however, the U. S. Supreme Court stressed that its ruling applied to the state of technology that existed in 1964. "When the advances in those arts permit reporting by . . . television without their present hazards to a fair trial we will have another case," Justice Tom Clark wrote for the majority.

And, in a concurring opinion, Justice John Harlan added another qualification. "The day may come when television will have become so commonplace an affair in the daily life of the average person as to dissipate all reasonable likelihood that its use in the courtrooms may disparage the judicial process."

Thirteen years later that day may well be at hand. Large, bulky television cameras have been replaced with mini-cams. Still cameras rely on existing light, not popping flashbulbs. And television is so commonplace that men are seen walking on the moon, and congressional hearings, even quasi-judicial ones, such as the Nixon impeachment proceedings, are televised nightly.

Nevertheless, the courtroom doors in all but five jurisdictions remain closed. Why? It is argued that lawyers, judges, witnesses and jurors will play to the camera. Perhaps. But many already do that for print reporters or wait to play to the cameras outside the courtroom. Being in the public spotlight, moreover, is not necessarily bad. It can bring out the best in people, motivate them to be prepared.

If nothing is lost, what then is gained? As the Zamora case demonstrates, it permits thousands of persons to watch an important trial. Imagine how many people would have watched the Watergate trials. Or how interesting and educational it would have been if the Supreme Court permitted the oral arguments in the Bakke case to be televised.

The judiciary is a co-equal branch of government. Yet, few Americans have the opportunity to observe it first-hand. For many people, their only perception of a trial comes from Perry Mason. And that has as much resemblance to reality as "Welcome Back, Kotter" does to a city classroom.

Television coverage, to be sure, is no panacea. Nor is it free from risks. Nevertheless, the state of television technology is such that there are fewer and fewer reasons to justify an ironclad ban.

With residents of five states observing court proceedings on television, it is imperative that the judiciary and legal profession nationwide closely monitor those experiments with an eye toward lifting the ban elsewhere.

The Birmingham News

Birmingham, Ala., October 8, 1977

When a Florida jury recently convicted a 15-year-old of armed robbery and murder of an elderly neighbor, it also acquitted television of being a direct and lethal influence on youth.

A survey has shown that Americans will have watched 18,000 TV murders by the age of 18. While there is little in the way of social uplift in televised mass murder, there is no scientific proof to date of "television insanity."

Television influences everyone that tunes in to some extent. But so do newspapers, magazines, parents, educators, peer groups and other elements of a complex society.

Ronnie Zamora, who now may face a minimim of 25 years in prison, was no doubt a troubled youth. Two years before the murder-robbery incident he witnessed the drowning of a close friend.

It is doubtful, however, that he was trying to emulate TV's Kojak by killing an 82-year-old woman. If it was TV that turned Ronnie toward a life of crime, he quickly reverted to more traditional teenage behavior after the murder by taking four friends in the victim's car for a weekend of fun at Disney World.

It is a tragedy when an old woman's life is callously snuffed out just as it is a tragedy to have to send a 15-year-old to prison for the crime. But television should not be made a scapegoat for society's complex ills.

The Idaho STATESMAN

Boise, Idaho, September 30, 1977

Like a camera between two mirrors, photographing itself ad infinitum, a strange drama involving television unfolds in Florida. In the murder trial of a 15-year-old Miami youngster, television is on trial and the trial is on television.

Ronny Zamora stands accused of first-degree murder in the death of 83-year-old Elinor Haggart. His lawyer has announced plans to base Zamora's defense on "television intoxication," claiming that Zamora was led to commit the crime by watching too many crime shows.

By a strange twist, the trial will be televised in an experiment to determine if television and a fair trial are compatible. Thus, an experiment to determine television's social value on a high plane will involve discussion of television at its worst — the violent crime shows.

Two aspects of this drama deserve comment: The unusual defense and the potential for television in our judicial system.

The defense is tricky to evaluate. The pivotal point is the youngster's sanity as he watched those crime shows. If he was insane by normally accepted standards, or near the brink, then the defense may be right in arguing that television must share a great part of the blame for the crime. If he was sane, then no matter what the young man watched on television, he should be held responsible for his actions.

The worrisome aspect to the defense is that it will not be applied with this precision - it will degenerate into an attempt to substitute psychological excuses for personal responsibility in far too large a sense. Television may indeed be a large influence on the behavior of us all, and as such is a legitimate area for scientific study. But it is but only one among countless influences. It is one thing to say television has an effect, but quite another to suggest that man is but a hapless pawn before the tube.

As for television itself, the medium should be concerned more with subjects such as the murder trial of Ronny Zamora and less with Kojak, Baretta and the like. The State of Florida judiciary is to be congratulated for allowing television cameras into the courtroom in what hopefully will be a successful experiment.

If television can handle tastefully such subject matter as a murder trial, who knows, the need for Kojak and Baretta may become moot. Viewers might actually get turned on to real-life drama, which really is much more interesting, complex and varied than a stilted plot from a Kojak episode.

OKLAHOMA CITY TIMES

Oklahoma City, Okla., October 6, 1977

THE relationship between television watching and juvenile crime may be as hard to prove as that between smoking and cancer. The evidence thus far has been largely circumstantial, as in the case of cigarettes. But the search for a link continues.

In Miami a 15-year-old is on trial for murder in the shooting of an 83-year-old woman. His innocent-by-reason-of-insanity plea is based on what his attorney calls "television intoxication" suffered from imbibing too freely of tube-portrayed crime shows.

Meanwhile, the Carnegie Council on Children reports, following a five-year probe into "what American society is doing to and for children," that by the time he is 16 the average child has watched television for 12,000 to 15,000 hours. That is more time than he has spent in school . . . or with his parents.

Advent of the paste-on label: "WARNING: Excessive use of this instrument may be hazardous" could be just around the corner.

The Hartford Courant

Hartford, Conn., October 10, 1977

The Miami, Florida jury that convicted 15-year-old Ronny Zamora of murder last week rejected the defense contention that television violence blurred the young man's perceptions of right and wrong.

The pervasive influence of television on American lives, whether young or old, is clear. Whether general acts of violence can be attributed to particular crimes is not.

What was much more clear was the fact that young Zamora robbed and shot an 82-year-old neighbor. The defense was inspired, but not convincing.

If television can be blamed for crime, can it also be credited for good works? Even on the most violent of police shows, the criminal, in the end, is caught. It is perhaps as easy to suggest that television teaches children that crime doesn't pay as it is to argue that television inspires children to shoot down elderly women.

The violence and sexuality and banality of television is discouraging. Whether the screen is more encouraging of violence than a cockfight, a re-enactment of a Civil War battle, or a bloody battle in the hockey rink at the Hartford Civic Center is open to question.

The scholarly opinions are conflicting and unclear. There is certainly not enough convincing evidence to free a Ronny Zamora from responsibility for murder.

THE ARIZONA REPUBLIC

Phoenix, Ariz., October 5, 1977

IT was Yolanda Zamora's turn in the witness chair this week in a Miami, Fla. courtroom. It was her chance to help prove that her son, Ronny, 15, murdered an 83-year-old woman because television had hypnotized him.

What she told judge and jury followed the defense right down the line.

Her son, she said, watched TV for hours every day, especially shows filled with violence. He would watch TV into the night when he should have been asleep.

He became so infatuated with the television character Kojak that he wanted to shave his young head.

Parents everywhere can appreciate the bleak and helpless torment Mrs. Zamora is going through, and her frantic desire to save her son from his violent ways.

But she is starting too late.

The natural question is, where was she when her son became, as she claims, an emotional and psychological captive of The Tube?

Where was she when he spent his afternoons, his evenings and even some of his sleeptime hours sopping in fantasy, instead of reaching out into the real world?

Had Mrs. Zamora, mother of Ronny, simply abandoned him to his own wishes, his own vices, his own sense of teenage reward?

Indeed, Ronny Zamora should be pitied. Not for the murder he committed. But for the mother he didn't have.

THE LINCOLN STAR
Lincoln, Neb., October 8, 1977

The trial of Ronny Zamora, convicted Thursday of first-degree murder in Miami, Florida, was interesting in more ways than one.

First, the trial was an experiment in taking justice to the people — the trial was televised live. An assessment of how that experiment worked could have startling and long-lasting implications.

Second, and more immediately newsworthy if not as important, Zamora's defense of insanity — disbelieved by the jury — was based on the claim that the 15-year-old's mind was intoxicated by television violence. Too much "Kojak," too much "Baretta," too much violence on television, said the defense. Little wonder that Ronny, having been addicted to the tube since age 5, shot and killed his 83-year-old neighbor when she caught him and a friend ransacking her house. His experience was punctuated with violent responses seen on television, the defense said, and he had no other choice but to kill.

The defense argument raised points embraced by legions of American parents who fret about the content of programs flashed to the multitudes: too much violence, too much sex, too much of what is considered anti-family. Those who express concern about violence in the mass media are usually talking abstractly in terms of a causal relationship between a diet of violence on the tube and aberrant and criminal behavior on the part of those who watch it — especially the young. It is easy to draw the parallel: a kid sees violence night after night on television, so he goes out and gets violent; he sees sex night after night on the tube so he goes out and commits sex.

But what happens when a lawyer tries to make the connection in a court of law with a real case?

The judge won't let him fully examine the issue and the jury won't believe him — at least the jury in Miami didn't buy the point.

We're not saying the jury was wrong. The jurors are probably like most people who complain about television violence as an abstract argument, but who would, when presented with it as a defense against conviction for a violent crime, would probably say: "the punk was just plain mean and knew exactly what he was doing when he shot the old lady. Guilty as charged."

In other words, television aside, he should have known better. Society still puts great emphasis on individual responsibility.

The argument against violence and sex on television probably boils down to a matter of taste, not a deeply held conviction that television compels people to do things against their will.

SAN JOSE NEWS
San Jose, Calif., October 5, 1977

Violent programming on television is a legitimate concern of the American public, but to use TV violence as an excuse for murder is the ultimate dodge of personal responsibility.

Nevertheless, here is Ellis Rubin, an ingenious Florida lawyer with an uncanny sixth sense for publicity, defending an accused teenage murderer on the grounds that "TV intoxication" made him do it. Years of TV addiction, it is said, made it impossible for him to distinguish between the fantasy of television violence and the reality of his actions as he slayed an elderly neighbor.

This new twist on the old foil — defendant as victim of society — deserves speedy assignment to the legal scrap heap.

Virtually every element of modern society has been tried at one time or another for a defendant's alleged crimes. This says as much for the declining reality of American law as the ingenuity of trial lawyers.

Americans will have greater faith in their criminal justice system the moment the defendant rather than society is asked to answer for crime.

Meanwhile, if the TV set was guilty of murder, it obviously had an accomplice. (Lock them both up and throw the dial away?)

The Cleveland Press
Cleveland, Ohio, October 8, 1977

The debate over the effects of television watching on behavior will probably still be going on long after the case of Ronny Zamora is relegated to the dusty law books.

The 15-year-old Zamora had been charged with the shooting death of an 82-year-old neighbor when she discovered him and another boy burglarizing her apartment in Miami, Fla. At his trial, Zamora pleaded innocent, arguing that "prolonged, involuntary subliminal intoxication with television" had made him insane at the time of the murder.

The fact that it took the jury less than 2 hours to reach a verdict of guilty indicates that it was not at all impressed with this novel defense and was not about to set a precedent which, as the prosecuting attorney warned, would give everyone a virtual license to do anything he wanted to do.

This is not to claim that a lifetime of saturation with television, as was young Zamora's history, and the witnessing of thousands of acts of simulated violence, could not have an influence on a person's character.

The whole idea of education is grounded in the belief that character can be molded, and if "good" influences — books, films, television or whatever — can teach moral behavior, it follows that "bad" influences can teach the opposite, at least to some degree.

It is interesting to note however, that Zamora's favorite television program was "Kojak." He even wanted to shave his head to look like his hero. But Kojak is not a criminal, he is a fighter against criminals. He does not murder elderly widows.

If Ronny Zamora was subjected to evil influences, he was also subjected to ennobling ones, as are all of us every day of our lives.

We believe his jury was correct in finding that he knew right from wrong and knew what he was doing when he committed his crime, and thus must be held responsible for it.

The Virginian-Pilot
Norfolk, Va.
October 10, 1977

The Ronnie Zamora Show ran for more than a week, beating "Roots" and "Washington Behind Closed Doors" combined for length. Watching it was a privilege denied the dozen most interested potential viewers. That may be just as well: real-life courtroom drama tends to be slow, sporadic, tedious, and unrelieved by commercials.

Anyway, the 12 had work to do. They had to decide if young Zamora, a Miami schoolboy of 15, was to be punished for shooting to death the 82-year-old neighbor who caught him and a pal ransacking her home. The verdict went against the boy, and he may spend years in prison.

The crime, ordinary enough if wretched, was promoted to international celebrity through the ingenuity of the defense lawyer. He conceived a defense of innocence by reason of temporary insanity owing to a lifelong immersion in television and its heavy ration of violence. Ronnie Zamora was weaned and nourished on television; it babysat him as a moppet, and a steady diet turned him into a television junkie. The boy, it was argued, was trained like Pavlov's dog to respond to a stimulus—the threat of exposure. Only he reacted not by salivating but by killing.

Intriguing as that proposition may be, the trial judge kept reminding the defense that Zamora, not television, was the defendant, and excluded evidence critical to the defense theory. He also forbade the jurors to watch reruns of trial episodes filmed by public television as part of a year-long experiment in television trial coverage. There is irony to sink a barge: a televised trial of television on trial.

If young Zamora had absorbed the moral of those violent plays his lawyer said motivated him, right triumphant and evil punished, his hand logically would have been stayed. The point didn't elude the jurors, even if the show did; the trial/show came to a pat and predictable ending. All that is wanting is a sequel, a documentary telling how a gun came into the hand of a murderous boy.

The Washington Star
and Daily News
Washington, D.C., October 7, 1977

Perhaps it was to be expected. If the Wirtz panel on educational testing could arraign television (with some justice, in our view) as a party to the decline of literacy among the young, the Miami defense attorneys of a 15 year-old named Zamora could — and would — offer the bizarre theory that he suffered from "involuntary television intoxication" when he shot and killed an elderly woman while robbing her apartment.

There are, to be sure, worlds of difference between the two attempts to make a culprit of television. The trial judge in Miami has sensibly disallowed a full-blown "television defense." But he is admitting psychiatric testimony on the influence of television and at least one "expert" witness tried the other day to connect the Zamora youth's inordinate fascination with televised crime and violence to the standard plea of "insanity." Florida law recognizes the older of two standard theories of criminal insanity, turning on the ability to draw moral distinctions rather than rational control over the impulses at the time of the criminal act.

The attempt to link crime with saturation in cops-and-robbers television shows is a novelty only in that it is television, not books or movies or plays, that is in a sense on trial. Otherwise, the trial picks up on an old debate over the effects of representational forms on human behavior — a debate that has, over the years, generated more passions than conclusions.

The most interesting treatment of the problem was by Mrs. Pamela Hansford Johnson (Lady Snow) in her book On Iniquity, about a decade ago. She took up the issue when the "moors" murderers, accused of torturing and killing children, were found to possess an extensive paperback library of sadistic and pornographic literature. Lady Snow insisted that if this obsessive reading taste possibly caused the murder or torture of children that would constitute a case for its control or suppression: as indeed it would.

The difficulty invariably lies in demonstrating a causal relationship, as to either sadistic books or violent television programs. Obviously, millions of people watch "Kojak," the program frequently cited at the Zamora trial, and others like it, and at least thousands familiarize themselves with the diseased imagination of the Marquis de Sade and his imitators, without experiencing a rush of murderous or cruel impulses, let alone acting on them.

Is it more plausible to suppose that a morbid fascination with sadistic literature or violent trash-drama is a parallel symptom of some mental or spiritual disorder of which another symptom is insensitivity to suffering or death? No one knows; this hypothesized relationship, however stated, is one of the great imponderables.

What is less uncertain, in our view, is a modern proneness to try to account for savage behavior by facile reference to some kind of conditioning, social or literary or theatrical. If it is not hunger or poverty or poor housing that is blamed, it is the sinister influence of books or television plays or movies.

Again, it is clear that for most of us no such conditioning "causes" hostile or cruel acts. Significantly, Lady Snow, at the risk of seeming utterly out of date, turned to the old-fashioned term "iniquity": evil. Indeed, the missing element in our busy search for explanations of anti-social acts and attitudes is the hypothesis of evil, of proneness to what long ago was called sin. But we have become as prudish about diseases of the spirit as the Victorians were about diseases of the body and it is embarrassing to an enlightened age to speak or even think of such primitive matters. Secularism thus levies a heavy tribute upon our understanding; and the cost is that we thrash about for novel accounts of what to an earlier age was perfectly intelligible.

It was once commonly assumed that people not only lacked moral perfection but lacked even the capacity for it. That assumption is unfashionable today. "The devil is dead and what a pity," as Gerald Johnson once put it. So in a courtroom in Miami we soberly entertain the trendy argument that a youth can be driven to the terrible crime of shooting an elderly woman because he has seen too many episodes of "Kojak." Madness takes many forms. Our modern madness may be the unreflective dismissal of the inescapable — and natural — need for moral judgment.

THE DALLAS TIMES HERALD

Dallas, Tex., October 11, 1977

MUCH PUBLIC attention was given the murder trial of the Florida youth whose defense in a killing was temporary insanity caused by intoxication from watching television programs depicting violence.

The Florida jury which convicted the 15-year-old of first-degree murder rejected the intoxication theory.

The jury's decision, however, does not dispel the validity of the concern expressed by a growing number of parents and social scientists who say increased levels of television violence have an ill effect upon our society.

The ill effect may be limited to only a small percentage of the persons in our society whose disposition towards violence is shaped by other factors. A broken home, a home without love, and violence within a home are far more substantiated influences on children's behavior.

But our society also seems to have an insatiable appetite for violence, both real and imagined. That should be appalling. We teach our children to use weapons and to glorify war, conflict and violent sport.

There are those who contend that until we abhor violence even in fictional form, we cannot end the real killing and maiming.

National Broadcasting Company's satirical and comical program, "Saturday Night," this past weekend put the debate over TV violence in the chicken-and-egg perspective. A skit had the line, "Real life causes violence on TV."

Some critics of television programming may accept that viewpoint, but counter that violence on TV is more controllable than in real life.

It is ironic that the case of the Florida youth was the first one with national television coverage of a trial in progress.

Such courtroom broadcasting is itself a controversial issue in our society. It raises the question of how to inform society about the criminal justice system and at the same time to protect the rights of the accused.

On that issue the Florida case may have made some progress towards reaching an acceptable balance. But on the issue of TV's programming of fictional violence, the Florida case only heightened the controversy.

THE ATLANTA CONSTITUTION

Altanta, Ga., May 25, 1978

Last fall in Miami a teen-ager named Ronnie Zamora was charged with murdering an elderly neighbor while burglarizing her home. The trial was televised in its entirety as an experiment in opening courtrooms to television coverage. The other night on PBS (Channel 8) a two-hour program presented highlights of the trial —and raised a series of provocative questions. One such question was suggested in the title, "TV on Trial."

Zamora's attorney based the defense on the contention that the youth had killed in a state of temporary insanity brought on by exposure to excessive violence on television. It was the first time such a defense had been tried in a court of law. Since television has been blamed for many of the ills of modern life, it was inevitable that some lawyer sooner or later would blame it for the behavior of his client. But it didn't work. The tv camera exposed the ludicrously shallow thinking behind the defense. The judge, with eminent common sense and the solid backing of law, pointed out that Zamora was on trial, not television. He restricted the testimony about television's effect on susceptible viewers. The jury, too, concluded that Zamora had committed murder and there was no way that "Kojak," "Baretta" or "Police Woman" could be held responsible. Zamora was convicted and sentenced to life in prison.

The defense lawyer in this case was not in a league with Clarence Darrow. But even if he had been, the trial convincingly demonstrated that juries won't buy the idea that television violence relieves a criminal of responsibility for his crimes.

The Zamora trial raised other interesting questions, some old, some new. The testimony of psychologists and psychiatrists was again shown to be more confusing than helpful in cases since psychiatric opinion varies widely and both sides in a court case can mobilize the opinion they require. The old rule of law, in which a defendant is sane if he knew what he was doing and knew the consequences, is more reliable.

But a key question is whether it is a good idea to televise criminal trials at all. The judge in the Zamora case thought that the experiment was a success. Several courts in Georgia will allow such coverage. It has been tried in other states, and may become common. That troubles some people who fear television will inevitably change the system of justice and not necessarily for the better. Witnesses, juries, lawyers and judges—aware of the camera eye—may react in ways they wouldn't otherwise. The choice by television of which trials to cover and which to ignore could also have an adverse effect.

Televising the processes of justice, or the making of laws in the legislature, may be the coming thing. But it needs careful thought.

THE SACRAMENTO BEE

Sacramento, Calif., October 14, 1977

A jury in Miami, Fla., has rejected an unprecedented defense in a murder case — that the 15-year-old defendant was not accountable for his act because of "intoxication" from prolonged watching of television violence.

It is fortunate that the facts in the particular case did not, in the jurors' minds, support this novel defense.

It would be most troublesome to accept as a defense against murder that one has become unhinged by exposure to any of a number of influences in our society. Television is but one of these, even though a powerful one. But what about a person obsessed by certain literature, the movies, or pornography? Such stimuli abound, and it would be impossible to insulate everyone from their influence. The logical consequence would be to say that an individual is not responsible for his or her actions if under the sway of an obsession. How could anyone measure the grip of an obsession? There is a difference, admittedly difficult to define, between an obsession and criminal insanity.

Having said that, however, it must be acknowledged that the Miami case, which drew nationwide attention, does invite concern about the level of unnecessary violence in television.

Does the wanton depiction of violence tend to blunt human sensibilities and distort perceptions of life? Does it, as some studies suggest, tend to reinforce violent attitudes, especially among the young? These are questions the Miami case raises for television producers. Violence cannot be totally eliminated from TV, of course. It exists in the real world and is natural in drama. What is questionable is the depiction of violence for the sake of shock or titillation.

It seems undeniable that this can have some degree of influence on some minds, even if not to the extent of excusing murder or other violent acts. And to say that it does not excuse such acts is not to say it has no bearing upon them whatever.

Common sense would indicate that excessive violence in television is a pernicious influence that we can forgo without sacrificing artistic realism or freedom of expression.

THE DAILY HERALD

Biloxi, Miss., November 15, 1977

Everyone agrees that television is the most pervasive medium in the history of civilization, but there is scant agreement on the effects television exerts on society. Two recently released studies illustrate some agreement and some nuances that can stem from scientific observations of the influences of viewing TV violence.

In New Mexico, Dr. Joe Flippo, a university psychologist, completed a three-year study and announced that TV may teach children how to be violent. But children won't incorporate what they see into their behavior patterns unless they are reinforced, he said.

Another psychologist, Dr. Ronald Drabman of the University of Mississippi Medical Center's Department of Psychiatry and Human Behavior, came to different conclusions after his study of TV violence.

Dr. Drabman says TV violence can prompt aggressive behavior in children. Additionally, he found that TV violence dulls a child's response to real violence.

Both psychologists agree that television is a means of learning aggressive behavior. Dr. Flippo then says the problem comes when a child is urged to behave aggressively or is rewarded when he does.

Dr. Drabman is more concerned with television violence's ability to dull a child's response to real violence. He calls his findings "frightening." "Adults are shocked when they hear of people standing by while an innocent person is mugged and stabbed," he says. "The question is, will our children be?" And his answer is no, not if they are exposed to nightly television mayhem from infancy to adulthood.

The message from both psychologists is that parents cannot continue to consider TV viewing by their children as innocuous. Parents must monitor what their children watch.

More than 70 million American homes have at least one television set; more than 30 million have two or more sets; and television saturation of American homes is above 97 percent.

The attorney for Ronny Zamora, the 15-year-old Florida boy who was convicted of murder, lost his plea that his client was driven insane and committed the crime because of the influence of television.

Most of us would probably agree that the plea was a bit far-fetched, at least for the present.

But Dr. Flippo's and Dr. Drabman's studies tell us that children do learn aggressive behavior from watching television violence and their response to real violence is dulled by what they see on the tube.

They seem to indicate that the day may eventually come when a defense such as Zamora's may be successful. How much TV violence do your children watch?

THE COMMERCIAL APPEAL

Memphis, Tenn., October 10, 1977

THE COURTROOM defense of "innocent by reason of insanity" reached a preposterous peak in the case of Ronny Zamora, a 15-year-old Miamian charged with the first-degree murder of an elderly neighbor during an armed robbery.

Zamora's lawyer argued that the youth felt he was playing out a television drama at the moment he shot 82-year-old Elinor Haggart. His sense of right and wrong, the lawyer said, had been hopelessly confused by "prolonged, involuntary, subliminal intoxication with television."

Dr. Milton Gilbert, the psychiatrist who testified for the defense, pictured Zamora as an illegitimate, mentally unstable boy in a home ruled by a stern stepfather. Programs of violence on television, the psychiatrist said, had conditioned him to kill without understanding the consequences.

Fortunately, the jury had more common sense than to let itself be intoxicated by this fanciful rationalization. The judge also helped bring the argument back to earth when he reminded the jury that "even an accidental killing during the commission of a felony is first-degree murder." Premeditation, the judge added, need "exist only a few moments."

We don't discount the doctrine of innocent by reason of insanity or the contributions that the profession of psychiatry has made to understanding and treating mental disorders. But we recognize, as the jury did in the Zamora case, that these are highly subjective matters. The scientific bases for psychiatric findings don't alter the fact that both sides in a criminal trial usually are able to produce psychiatric testimony supporting different views of a defendant's mental state.

It's certainly not medieval to say that the standards and common sense of a jury are more reliable than the kind of overblown arguments that were made on behalf of Ronny Zamora.

DEFENSES BASED on insanity seem to have become more popular — or, at least, more popularized, perhaps because of two recent, spectacular cases. Patty Hearst was supposed to be brainwashed when she raked a street with gunfire and eluded a massive nationwide manhunt for a year. David Berkowitz, who is charged with the Son of Sam murders in New York City, is the subject of a continuing legal and psychiatric dispute about criminal responsibility.

BUT ALL THE finely crafted arguments ignore what the American public doesn't ignore — the direct relationship between a crime and the person or persons who commit it. That fact, once established beyond a reasonable doubt, calls out for direct legal action. Mitigating circumstances, if they exist, should be considered as part of the determination of sentence, not guilt or innocence.

The attempt to blame television in the Zamora case — to make it an accessory, as the prosecutor said — is an example of how far a defense can reach given the opportunity.

THE STATES-ITEM

New Orleans, La., November 10, 1977

Television violence has outraged a substantial segment of the American viewing public. Apparently attorney Ellis Rubin sought to capitalize on the current discontent when he based his defense of 15-year-old Ronny Zamora, charged with murdering an 83-year-old neighbor, on a claim that television violence had rendered the boy legally insane. It was a shaky, though novel and sensational, legal defense. Fortunately the jury in Miami could not accept it.

Television violence has many people upset. Protest movements by church groups and others are solid evidence that many parents are satisfied that there is some connection between the excess of unreal violence on television and acts of violence in the real world. Network managers have taken notice, and TV violence appears to be declining. This is a welcome development apart from any broad sociological ramifications. Television programming could benefit from a great deal more variety.

Whether there is, in fact, any substantial connection between television violence and real violence is the kind of generalized question that almost invariably defies conclusive proof. Experts with theories can be found on either side.

Occasionally individuals who have committed a crime profess to have been influenced by something they saw on television. It is plausible that the unstable or criminally inclined might be "set off" by something they see on TV. But they might also be provoked by something read in a book, a newspaper, a magazine, seen in a movie or heard from another individual.

The Zamora defense did not isolate on a single incidence of television violence but sought to hold the networks accountable for "addicting" the young defendant to violence. Blaming the networks is akin to blaming "society" for the weaknesses and failures of individuals. There are all sorts of addicts. Should the whiskey makers be held accountable for alcoholics?

Blaming the networks, like blaming society, transfers responsibility from the individual to a vast, amorphous entity. To blame society or the networks is to blame *no one*. What a field day the criminally inclined could have with such a scapegoat.

THE INDIANAPOLIS STAR
Indianapolis, Ind., October 11, 1977

For the sake of just about everyone in the Republic, it will be a good thing if sane Americans shoot down the notion that television violence is likely to make a youngster a killer.

The concept that it can was the gist of the defense of a teen-age youth on trial last week in Miami, Fla., for the slaying of an 82-year-old neighbor during a robbery.

The trial at Miami attracted nationwide attention largely because the boy's attorney said the defendant was brainwashed by TV violence, or in his words was "under the influence of involuntary subliminal television intoxication" and insane at the time of the crime.

That is a sort of concept that is apt to win a lot of followers in certain circles. It is akin to the notion, propagated widely a few years back, that "society is to blame" for crime. If enough people can be persuaded to swallow such nonsense, and enough of the people who do believe it can be seated on juries, murderers and other criminals will go free.

Likewise, if enough people can be convinced that watching TV violence makes the viewer go crazy so that if he murders someone he is not to blame and should not pay the penalty, then a whole new crop of killers with ready-made excuses will start preying on our long-suffering society.

But we think most Americans have too much sense to buy such tomfoolery. If a diet of TV violence turns kids into crazed killers why haven't the other 50 million school-age youngsters in America robbed and murdered their neighbors? The Miami trial jury apparently agreed. It found the youth guilty.

THE LOUISVILLE TIMES
Louisville, Ky., October 11, 1977

APPLAUSE for their good sense is due those Miami jurors who refused last week to accept the argument that a 15-year-old boy should be acquitted of a murder charge because he had been raised in front of a TV screen full of violence. The defense of "not guilty because of television insanity" has no validity in either our system of justice or our code of ethics.

That's not to minimize the need for concern about the killings and maimings to which children — and adults — are exposed day after day on the living room screen. Obviously this has an impact, if only by blunting the viewer's sensitivity to violence. One's sense of outrage and horror at the brutalities of life is bound to be dimmed after a steady diet of such entertainment.

But much of life sets bad examples. After all, many children grew up in destructive environments, even before the advent of television. Sociologists have long known that a child whose parents fight all the time, for instance, or both of whose parents regularly beat him, is quite likely to become aggressive. Others, raised in the anarchy of the streets, too often are virtually forced into lives of crime. But though we may understand why children, or even adults, behave the way they do, that doesn't release them from the consequences of their behavior.

The Miami case was, admittedly, extreme. The defendant is a youngster who, at age four was first left with the TV set as a baby-sitter. In the intervening years he had become so addicted to the tube that, according to his lawyer, he virtually lived in a "fantasy world of Kojak, Baretta and Police Woman." And, as the defense attorney further observed, companies wouldn't spend millions of dollars on television advertising if they didn't believe that their 30 seconds of exposure would have an impact on viewers.

But if we are not to be trapped in this fantasy world, too, we must draw a clear line between right and wrong. If the Miami case encourages viewers, and especially parents, to be more critical of what is offered on television, that's all to the good. But we can't allow our concept of individual responsibility or our system of justice to be undermined by allowing people with a distorted sense of right and wrong to use television as a crutch for their inadequacies.

Newsday
Garden City, N.Y., October 11, 1977

A Florida jury found a 15-year-old boy guilty of murder last week, rejecting his claim that he was a victim of television. But the jury did not find television innocent.

The case attracted widespread attention because the defense argued that the boy was addicted to television, and that it led to the violence he and a 14-year-old friend perpetrated on an 83-year-old woman living next door.

The jury held Ronny Zamora responsible for the murder on the grounds that he could tell right from wrong, but that doesn't mean television wasn't an accessory. The boy had been exposed to six to eight hours of television a day since he was 5 years old. Millions of American boys and girls are growing up on the same diet.

Television sells. If it didn't, companies wouldn't spend millions of dollars a year advertising their products on the tube. It sells ideas as well, or contenders for political office wouldn't spend a major portion of their campaign funds on TV "messages." The defense argued that the thousands of make-believe murders Zamora had witnessed on commercial television made his violent reaction to an old woman's threat to call the police seem natural and logical—to him.

It wasn't, of course, and the judge refused to admit evidence from some defense witnesses on the grounds that they could not cite specific cases establishing links between television violence and violent acts. Television was not on trial, he said; Zamora was. True enough, but unless someone holds television accountable, these types of senseless acts are bound to become more and more frequent.

Ironically, while the Florida trial drew attention to the bad side of television, it also demonstrated what television does best. Florida allows TV coverage of court proceedings, so viewers could get a glimpse of the real world of Ronny Zamora on the evening news. Unfortunately, it was followed by the unreal one he and other American children meet every night in their living rooms.

HERALD ⚓ EXAMINER
Los Angeles, Calif., October 10, 1977

An actor, even an actor with the clout of a super star, can only read the lines written by a writer and produced by a producer.

In a Florida murder case, a teenage defendant pleaded temporary insanity, allegedly caused by TV violence. The youth has been convicted, but an appeal is pending.

During the first trial, Telly Savalas, who plays the character of "Kojak" on the CBS series of that name, was considered as a defense witness.

It is understandable that a defense attorney, seeking to develop a sympathetic, even impassioned atmosphere for his client, would not be above dragging an actor through the headlines.

However, if TV violence is ever to be placed on trial, the proper witnesses would not be the actors but the writers (in "Kojak's" case quite a few including a string of free lancers) and the producers (Matthew Raps, executive producer, and James McAdams, supervising producer).

Indeed, the proper place to put TV violence on trial is in the living room. The jury is the audience. If the audience finds violence objectionable, it can turn the knob. No audience. No sponsors. No show.

WORCESTER TELEGRAM.

Worcester, Mass., April 5, 1979

Violence on television may or may not cause viewers to act more violently, but it does seem to cause them to be more afraid.

That was one of the conclusions in a continuing study cosponsored by the American Medical Association and the National Institute of Mental Health.

Violent programs, according to the study, tend to trigger an "exaggerated sense of danger and mistrust in heavy viewers compared to similar groups of light viewers."

People who watch a lot of crime and police shows, for example, are more likely to buy locks, dogs or guns to protect themselves, the study found. The heavy viewers are more likely to be afraid to walk alone in a city at night. In general, these viewers express a more pessimistic and alienated view of life.

Researchers found that, while the overall rate of television violence has dropped, more than two-thirds of all prime-time shows have violence. Violence is highest of all on weekend morning programming for children. In programming last fall, nine out of 10 children's shows had violent episodes.

Despite many studies, no definitive link has yet been made between television violence and violent behavior. Last year television was described as an "accessory" in the highly-publicized murder trial of 15-year-old Ronney Zamora. Zamora's lawyer claimed that television violence had rendered the youth incapable of distinguishing right from wrong when he murdered an elderly woman. But this unique defense for Zamora failed and he was given a life sentence.

Some argue that violence on television permits viewers to work out the hostile feelings inherent in us all. They point to Japanese television, which has plenty of violence, although the crime rate in Japan is notably low.

But if violent television shows encourage distrust, that is one reason for networks to take another look at their productions.

If violent shows encourage people to expect the worst from each other, that is another reason. Television continues to have an enormous impact on modern society.

The Evening Bulletin

Philadelphia, Pa., September 27, 1979

Does violence on television cause children to behave violently?

That question has been bandied about by so many people and answered in so many contradictory ways that it almost seems pointless to raise it again. But with the start of every new television season, the arguments on both sides are dragged out for renewed debate.

Now a new study with some very blunt conclusions is drawing attention. Sponsored by CBS, the study has been conducted over the past six years on some 1,565 London boys. It concludes, rather dramatically, that those who watch TV violence for long periods of time commit 50 percent more violent acts than those whose viewing is limited.

Researchers in this study conducted extended interviews with two groups of boys. The group that watched more-violent programs more often were found to have committed an average of 7.48 acts of serious violence in the past six months while those who had watched less-violent programs less often had committed an average of 5.02 such acts. Some examples of the kinds of violence the boys had committed are throwing bricks at a girl, kicking a boy in the crotch, burning a boy's chest with a cigaret, bashing a boy's head against a wall, and attempting rape.

Now, of course a number of criticisms

could be leveled against this study. For one thing, the researchers did not distinguish between violent Westerns or police stories and classics like Hamlet, which contain all sorts of murders and suicides. Also, a question has been raised as to whether more-violent people watch more violent television programs. If that is the case, then the violent behavior perhaps should not be blamed on violent television.

Nonetheless, the conclusion of this research doesn't differ from the weight of the evidence in from most previous research — namely, that broadcast violence does have some adverse affects on behavior, particularly of the young.

For some time, a number of respected national organizations like the American Medical Association and the Parent-Teacher Association have been battling television violence. Many believe pressure on networks and advertisers has succeeded in reducing the level of screen mayhem at least in the early evening hours.

This CBS-sponsored study may prompt more people to join the battle against screen violence. It also might inspire more individuals to take matters into their own hands right away— by greeting a violent TV program with a twist of the dial to another station or even to the "off" position.

Lincoln Journal

Lincoln, Neb., September 15, 1979

What effect televised violence has on viewers remains in dispute in this country, though enough studies have suggested a connection between violence on screen and off to raise some warning flags which the networks apparently would just as soon ignore.

A recently released British study may provide the kind of data some in this country have been waiting for. Dr. William Belson, a psychology researcher, concluded that young boys who watched violent TV programs were significantly more aggressive in their subsequent behavior than those who did not.

Significantly, a number of programs covered by the survey included U.S. imports.

Because it is one of the most thorough and carefully conducted undertakings of its kind to date, the study is receiving serious attention in Britain. Dr. Belson, a respected researcher, was supported by a skilled team from the London School of Economics, and the study looked at the viewing habits and behavior of 1,565 boys aged 13 through 16 over a 13-year period.

As a result of Belson's findings, both BBC and London's main weekday commercial channel, Thames Television, are reviewing their current and future schedules.

Contrast that to this country, where the networks have only very reluctantly reduced their diet of gore and mayhem. And where programmers tend to deride those who object to TV violence as busybodies, do-gooders and would-be censors.

FORT WORTH STAR-TELEGRAM

Fort Worth, Tex., January 15, 1979

A study released recently by the Yale University Family Television Research and Consultation Center says that too much television viewing by children, ages 3 and 4, will cause a significant amount of aggression. Any type of programming — from police thrillers to game shows — makes preschoolers more aggressive even in nursery school playtime.

The study showed that each child watched television an average of 23 hours each week. That translates into approximately 25 percent of a preschooler's waking hours each week.

Dr. Jerome Singer of Yale University said that the relationship of television and aggression remains the same even when taking into accout differences in IQ scores, social class, ethnic background and other variables.

"Detective-action shows seem to be the most implicated," he said. "The second type of programming strongly implicated, especially among girls, are the situation comedies and game shows where there's all that yelling and jumping around."

And if that revelation were not bad enough, the study also indicated that the reason for the television-aggression relationship was due to laxness of control over the television set.

Dr. Singer said that the kids who were the most aggressive came from homes where the parents didn't care about monitoring television viewing. And, we think the parents attitude is terrible.

Of course, we don't advocate eliminating television. Both teachers and parents can learn to use television in a constructive way by discussing with children the social issues and questions raised by some of the programming. The experts say, and we agree, that the question is how can parents, teachers, children, or anyone, for that matter, make the content of the program work constructively.

Perhaps this study will aid writers and producers who put the programs on the television as well as parents and teachers who decide what programs are suitable for children.

SUPREME COURT RULINGS:

Jury To Decide Network Liability in Rape Case

An $11 million negligence suit filed against the National Broadcasting Company (NBC) and its San Francisco affiliate station would be tried before a jury, according to a Supreme Court ruling April 24. The Court refused to review a California appellate court decision in the case *NBC v. Niemi,* in which Valeria Niemi claimed that the network was responsible for a sexual assault on her nine-year-old daughter in 1974.

The victim was raped by three girls and a boy, ranging in age from 10 to 15 years old, using a beverage bottle. The attack occurred three days after the broadcast of a made-for-television movie *Born Innocent*—about life in a reformatory for teenage girls—that depicted a group of inmates using the wooden handle of a "plumber's helper" to sexually abuse the fifteen-year-old heroine of the story. A San Francisco police investigator reported that at least one of the assailants said she had seen *Born Innocent* and had been inspired by it to imitate the violent rape scene.

The suit against NBC and the Chronicle Publishing Co., owners of KRON-TV, charged them with "negligent and reckless conduct" for showing the film at an hour (7:30 p.m. in some areas, 8 p.m. in others) when the broadcasters knew juveniles would be watching.

The suit was dismissed by a California Superior Court judge without impanelling a jury or hearing expert testimony on the case. However, the state Court of Appeals ruled on appeal that "despite [the] First Amendment protections" accorded broadcasters, under the California constitution a jury trial was an "inviolate right."

Various television and motion picture organizations had filed friend-of-the-court briefs in an effort to have the Supreme Court review the ruling and reverse the appellate court. CBS warned that the principle of media liability could be extended to press coverage of violent news, such as hijackings and murders. On the other hand, the California Medical Association, which supported the suit, called television "a school for violence and a college for crime." As evidence, the association cited a study commissioned by ABC in which 22 of 100 juvenile offenders confessed to having borrowed criminal techniques from television.

The Washington Star

Washington, D.C., April 29, 1978

Not many weeks ago lawyers for a 15-year-old Floridian, Ronny Zamora, sought to persuade a jury (unsuccessfully, in the end) that "involuntary intoxication" by television violence had impelled him to murder a close friend.

Now, in San Francisco, Mrs. Olivia Niemi is suing *NBC* and its local affiliate for $11 million in damages. She claims that the cruel rape of her nine-year-old daughter on a beach four years ago was inspired by a scene from a network drama, "Born Innocent," depicting a similar violation in a girl's reformatory.

The Niemi case, like the Zamora case before it, raises a host of old questions about the connection between dramatic representation and life itself. There are those who argue, sometimes persuasively, for censorship on grounds that art is either persuasive or nothing. Mr. Irving Kristol, if we recall, once argued for the judicious suppression of pornography because it debases the sensibilities, even as good art presumably elevates and instructs them.

But the theory can't be applied to ordinary visual representation (whether on stage, screen or television) without the most troublesome implications. Suppose, for the sake of argument, that the rape in California was in some sense the consequence of a scene from a television drama. Would the risk, if that were so, justify the bowdlerization of drama?

Consider Shakespeare. An impressionable viewer of *Othello* might conceivably come away with an overpowering urge to smother someone with a pillow, as the viewer of *Hamlet* might ache to pour poison in a sleeping brother's ear, or the viewer of *Titus Andronicus* might be swept up in sick fascination with mayhem and cannibalism. Yet these representations of cruelty, violence and lust are essential to the dramas they haunt.

The chairman of *NBC*, Mr. Julian Goodman, suggests a distinction between violence that "is an acceptable part of the dramatic action . . . not likely to be a model for violence (and) . . . a gratuitous act that makes violence attractive and has been inserted because the writer can't think of any other way to keep the attention of the viewer." The distinction is unhelpful, however, since it demands an aesthetic judgment, necessarily subjective, as to what is "gratuitous."

We know of no durable standard of moral responsibility, in fact, that absolves the perpetrators of cruel acts on any grounds — including the feeble argument that their wills were sapped by the dramatic representation of violence and cruelty. The indisputable fact is that millions of us watch unpleasant acts on stage and screen, and, when the drama is good, experience that "pity and terror" of which Aristotle spoke — not the unspeakable urge to go and do likewise.

The fault, we must consequently insist, usually lies in the viewer rather than the viewing. Certainly that is the only tolerable assumption in a society unprepared to surrender all its art, the good with the bad.

EVENING EXPRESS
Portland, Me., April 27, 1978

The U. S. Supreme Court has opened a particularly squirmy can of constitutional worms through a singular piece of judicial standoffishness.

The court refused appeals by NBC and a California television station to block a civil suit in behalf of a nine-year-old girl who was sexually assaulted by some older girls following the showing of a similar incident in a TV drama.

Attorneys for the youngster contend that the defendants were negligent and reckless in screening the film "Born Innocent" at a time of day when young people would likely be watching. Their client, they say, was the victim of the broadcasters' negligence, and they are asking $11 million in damages.

The case involves more than big money and a challenge to TV violence. It tests the whole concept of freedom of expression and the constitutional protections afforded by the First Amendment.

If telecasters can be sued for causing real life violence by showing violent dramas, can they also be sued for airing a news account of a violent act — an assassination attempt, say, or a skyjacking — which could inspire someone in the audience to imitate it?

Could a publisher of mystery novels be sued for distributing a book outlining a bizarre crime later imitated in real life by a reader?

These are questions of genuine concern to the National Association of Broadcasters, for one, which calls the lawsuit a threat to "virtually the entire range of creative expression."

And they are of concern to the American Library Association, which says if the distributor of a creative work, even one by Shakespeare, can be held liable because a person may use it as a model for a criminal act, "then libraries must close down and education must cease."

And they should be of concern to all citizens concerned with the erosion of First Amendment rights in the name of a worthy end.

We are disturbed by the ubiquity of television violence and its possible effects on viewers, particularly the young. And none can help but sympathize with the plight of a young victim of violence possibly inspired by a TV drama.

But the lifting of First Amendment protections to accommodate a lawsuit aimed at pinning liability for criminal acts upon the creative arts is a development of truly chilling dimensions.

Richmond Times-Dispatch
Richmond, Va., April 27, 1978

A nine-year-old California girl was the victim of a bizarre, unnatural sexual attack by four teenage girls who used a method which they told police they copied from what they had seen in a television drama. The victim's mother brought suit against the network and the local TV station for $11 million in damages on grounds that they were responsible.

A lower California court judge held that the First Amendment's free speech-free press guarantees protected the network and station from suit, but the state's court of appeals reversed that ruling and held that the victim had a right to try to persuade a jury that she had a valid claim for damages. On Monday of this week, the U.S. Supreme Court agreed with the court of appeals by refusing to review the case.

In initial reaction to the decision, the television industry — and the print media as well — could easily become greatly alarmed. It might seem that the court was saying that if anyone commits a crime in emulation of something he has seen or read, the victim of the crime may collect damages from the television network and station or the newspaper, magazine, book or other publication which produced the material that served as a model for the crime.

If that was what the court was saying, obviously the potential effects could be enormous. Any television drama or newscast, or any printed story or news report, that dealt with criminal behavior might be seized upon as causing an individual to commit an unlawful act. Such a situation would be disastrous for the media and for the public.

But what the high court said, in effect, was that there is no *automatic* First Amendment protection for *everything* that may be broadcast or printed about crime.

Of course, it would be reassuring to the media, from the legal standpoint, if the court had thrown a blanket of protection over everything broadcast or printed. But the justices apparently felt that they could not do that, for the same reason that the court has held that the guarantee of free speech does not protect a person who falsely yells "Fire!" in a crowded theater or who uses words that incite to riot.

Thus, the court sent the case back for trial so that the full story can be developed and can serve as the basis for a possible future consideration — if the plaintiff should win the case in the lower court — of the basic constitutional question involved. Obviously, no one can predict what the Supreme Court would do in such a situation, but we would think that on the basis of previous First Amendment decisions, the justices would hold that the television network and station were not responsible unless they displayed a wanton and reckless disregard for the public safety and welfare in the presentation of the drama in question.

But entirely apart from the television network's legal responsibility for what it broadcasts, the networks and stations have a deep moral responsibility to avoid presenting potentially harmful material, particularly at times and under conditions that are conducive to viewing by youngsters. The print media have a similar responsibility, but there's no denying that a vivid presentation depicting a crime and seen on the screen in the home can have far more effect on impressionable children and youth than words on paper can have.

The California Medical Association, which intervened in the rape case on behalf of the plaintiff, declared that "the health and welfare of our society demands that broadcasters be accountable for their programming." The doctors said they were "concerned about the impact which violent television programs have on the mental and physical health of the young." Various studies of the effect of TV on young minds suggest that the doctors' concern is justified.

The San Diego Union
San Diego, Calif., April 28, 1978

The other day, the U.S. Supreme Court let stand a decision by the California Court of Appeals that Niemi v. National Broadcasting Company may, after all, come to trial. The case is not yet familiar to American households. But soon it may be, and in a most direct way. For if Olivia Niemi can prove that NBC was negligent in showing the movie "Born Innocent," then doubtless the programming of the U.S. networks for television audiences will be substantially affected.

At 8 p.m. one evening in September, 1974, the NBC affiliate in San Francisco showed "Born Innocent." During the first fifteen minutes of the film, a young girl was sexually attacked in a shower by four other girls. Three days later, what had been seen on film became sordid reality as four girls and a boy similarly attacked a nine-year-old girl.

A trial judge turned aside the injured girl's lawsuit, which, he said, was prohibited by the First Amendment guarantee of freedom of speech. On appeal, however, it was decided that Niemi was entitled to a jury trial. And so now, with the Supreme Court's concurrence, she will try to prove her case in court.

Thus, the Supreme Court is opening to debate whether, as some civil libertarians are wont to say, free speech is indivisible. The libertarian formula is that there are no clear, safe distinctions, not only between such familiar pairings as speech and "symbolic" speech and persuasion and provocation, but also between such newly developed pairings as the words in a book and the dramatization of those words through the medium of television.

Certainly the issues are not simple, and if distinctions can be drawn, they probably are very fine ones. The exercise of free speech, if that's what the showing of films like "Born Innocent" truly is, may turn on whether a broadcaster airs the film at 8 p.m., when juveniles are apt to look on, or later in the evening, when the audience is presumed to be adult.

In any event, it is good that the Supreme Court has precipitated this debate. And, interesting to note, had the court ruled otherwise, agreeing with the lower court that the First Amendment insulated NBC from litigation, it would have censored the debate in the first place. We await with keen interest what comes from Niemi vs. NBC.

DAILY ☒ NEWS

New York, N.Y., April 26, 1978

Justice Brennan

Almost casually, the Supreme Court has cleared the way for trial of a damage action based on a crime-victim's claim that a television show inspired an assault on her.

Only Justice William Brennan appeared to perceive that the serious First Amendment questions raised by the case ought to be resolved quickly by the highest court.

Allowing the suit to proceed does not commit the Supreme Court to a position on those issues. As a practical matter, however, the tribunal's refusal to hear the appeal now can have serious consequences.

It will be months, even years, before the California courts plow through the necessary legal rituals. Meanwhile, newspapers, television networks, documentary producers, movie companies and book publishers will face a flood of similar multimillion-dollar negligence claims.

The mere fear of a costly judgment, and the expense of fighting the suits, may drastically curtail legitimate reporting of crime news.

We in no way condone the excessive brutality and violence depicted in numerous television dramas.

The answer to such abuses lies in the force of enlightened public opinion—not in creating a legal weapon so broad in scope that it could be used with devastating effect to curtail freedom of the press.

SAN JOSE NEWS

San Jose, Calif., April 26, 1978

There is widespread and legitimate concern about violence on television. Organizations from the National Parent-Teacher Association to the American Medical Association and the National Council of Churches have mobilized campaigns to limit such programs. There is a danger, however, that such campaigns can go too far, intruding on First Amendment rights, jeopardizing the free examination and expression of ideas.

A warning must be sounded when the controversy shifts from a public debate over "influence" to a courtroom battle over "liability" — as it has with the U.S. Supreme Court's refusal to halt a damage suit against the National Broadcasting Co. for the 1974 showing of the NBC film "Born Innocent" in which a teen-aged female delinquent was sexually assaulted with a blunt instrument by female reformatory inmates. Four days later, a 9-year-old San Francisco girl was attacked on a beach by three girls and a boy who sexually abused her with a bottle.

A suit in the girl's behalf, seeking $1 million in compensatory damages and $10 million in punitive damages from NBC and KRON-TV, was filed after the San Francisco juveniles told police their assault had been inspired by the movie.

It is possible to take exception to the film's assault scene and the time of its showing, during early evening viewing time, without permitting a group of juveniles to use simulated violence on TV as an excuse for real-life violence. Millions of youth saw the episode. Only four claim to have been inspired to violence.

There is too much violence and mindlessness on television, but this is no excuse to make TV the latest scapegoat for mankind's irresponsible acts. It is necessary to reaffirm the principle that an individual — not society, not poor housing, not books, not comics, not TV — is responsible for what he or she does.

Last year, the attorney for Ronnie Zamora, a Miama Beach, Fla., youth accused of shooting an 82-year-old neighbor woman, claimed he had been "intoxicated with television" violence. The jury rejected the defense, with the jury foreman concluding, "This TV thing—that's ridiculous."

The jury foreman's comments seem appropriate here. If television executives are forced to choose between defending themselves against a flood of costly liability suits or "censoring" all programs that may give offense — and remember films of civil rights protests and marches, along with combat film from Vietnam, were accused in the past of promoting violence — the losses may outweigh the supposed gains.

DESERET NEWS
Salt Lake City, Utah, April 26, 1978

Can and should broadcasters be held legally responsible when fictional violence is imitated in real life?

This week the U.S. Supreme Court cleared the way for a test of this pivotal question before a state court in San Francisco.

The case at hand seeks $11 million from NBC and station KRON-TV. The suit was filed on behalf of a nine-year-old girl who was sexually brutalized four days after a nationally-televised movie portrayed a similar crime.

It is hard to over-estimate the importance of this suit not only because of its potential impact on TV, but also because of the effect it could have on movies, magazines, newspapers, and books.

Though the trial is unprecedented, the remarkable thing is that such a suit was not filed before. Certainly there have been plenty of opportunities.

Three years ago, a number of skid row derelicts in Los Angeles were killed in a series of slayings that bore a close resemblance to an episode on the "Police Story" TV show.

In Utah, witnesses testified that two of the defendants in Ogden's Hi Fi Shop torture-killings had several times seen a movie in which one victim was forced to drink a caustic substance. The same thing was done to victims at the Hi Fi Shop.

Only last month, two teen-age boys were charged with killing a dealer in the numbers racket. The boys allegedly were hired by a rival gambler. Only a few days before this killing, the TV series "Kojak" aired an episode in which professional criminals hired juveniles as "hit men."

This disturbing pattern ought to give pause to those mass media moguls who insist that mindless violence is the key to higher ratings. So should a study a few years ago by the National Commission on the Causes and Prevention of Violence, which found:

— Violence on TV programs was initiated just as often by characters identified as the "good guys" as by the "bad guys."

— Nearly half of the characters on TV who kill someone and more than half of those performing other acts of violence achieved a happy ending on the programs.

— Arrest and trial followed violence in only two out of 10 TV programs.

Instead, how about portraying violence as illegal and socially unacceptable? How about showing that violence creates problems instead of solving them? In other words, how about getting realistic with violence instead of glamorizing it?

In fact, if TV wants to be starkly realistic, how about bringing back, say, "Perry Mason" or "The Defenders" with an episode showing some broadcasters whose bank accounts are drained by the high court costs of defending one of their more brutal programs even if they end up winning the case?

THE ATLANTA CONSTITUTION
Atlanta, Ga., April 26, 1978

A young California girl brought suit against the NBC TV network and a San Francisco station for $11 million in damages because they exhibited a program graphically depicting a sexual assault. She contends that a sexual attack against her by other children, all girls, was the result of that program. The U.S. Supreme Court has now ruled she has a case.

That is a ruling of potentially far-reaching implication. The basic question at issue is this: can a television network, a station—or, by extension, writers and publishers of newspaper stories or books or articles—be held responsible if they are blamed for the criminal acts of others?

The Supreme Court, with one dissenting vote, seems to be saying yes.

Lawyers for the defendant network and station argued that an attempt to say beforehand what programs may or may not be shown is "prior restraint," which is simply a form of censorship.

There are other questions—deeply disturbing ones. No responsible and concerned parent in America is happy about the violence that is almost standard fare on television—and, indeed, has always been standard fare in literary and dramatic works since ancient times. They fear it may *cause* viewers to imitate what they see. The contention in this suit is that a fictional drama, "Born Innocent," about a teen-aged unwanted child who is sexually attacked by other girls at a reformatory, *caused* four girls to "rape" the plaintiff, a 9-year-old. The immediate reaction of most people, no doubt, is to be horrified and to conclude that the rape must have been caused by the TV drama. But is this true? Can it be contended, for instance, that newspaper stories about the Colum-

bus stranglings cause more stranglings? Can it be contended that the murders in a novel or a play cause some twisted mind to go out and do the same? And if this reasoning is accepted, does it mean that the depiction or description of violence is in effect ruled out of drama and literature because it might trigger an insane or disturbed personality to act?

Assume that it does mean precisely that. Then what about a program such as the widely heralded and vividly graphic NBC series on the "Holocaust," in which mass murder on a terrible scale was shown on television. The intention of this program was not to encourage that happening again but to make sure that it does not happen again. Most people would probably agree that only an abnormal person would act out the violence he or she reads about or sees on a television program. If television and the rest of the media and the arts are to be held responsible for the actions of abnormal personalities—held responsible in courts of law—then programs like "Holocaust" and even old Sherlock Holmes movies might run the risk of lawsuits. Chief Justice Warren Burger has long contended that the courts are already overburdened with unnecessary and frivolous litigation. The opportunities offered by this decision for an enormous leap in that litigation are clear enough.

The issue of violence on television and in comic books and professional sports and almost across the entire spectrum of human activity has been argued long and heatedly. Compromises have been suggested—and adopted. The aim is not to protect adults from the vicarious violence of "Kojak" or "The Wild Bunch" or "Hamlet." It is to protect children, who are

deemed susceptible. And to avoid goading madmen. For television it has been suggested that the running of violent shows at a time when children are likely to be viewers should be voluntarily avoided. That may be done to some small degree, but even if fully carried out it would be an imperfect solution. *Gratuitous* violence—that unnecessary to the dramatic or documentary or informative point—is discouraged, too—again, an imperfect solution. The obvious and simple solution—turning off the set or restricting family reading—is often lost sight of in the controversy. But it may be the only practical one.

The plaintiff's lawyers argued that it was not the drama itself but the time that it was shown that was the real problem in this case. But is there any way in a nation of millions of people to insure that a television program will not be seen by a disturbed individual, child or adult? Common sense says there is not.

The truth is that there is *no* realistic solution to the problem of violence in the real world—not in the present state of human nature. Certainly bringing suit against television stations or writers or publishers is no solution. To be sure, the court is not saying that. The plaintiff's case has yet to be decided by a jury. But in saying that such cases may be brought, the court is certainly entering a vast and uncharted and very perilous territory.

If the effect of this decision is to encourage renewed soul-searching and more restraint by the media, perhaps that is all to the good. But if the effect is to open all creative or instructive or journalistic effort to the threat of anyone who can argue that a story or a play *caused* a crime—that is an insidious and ultimately dangerous form of censorship.

The Philadelphia Inquirer

Philadelphia, Pa., April 27, 1978

"The State of California is not about to begin using negligence as a vehicle to freeze the creative arts," Judge John A. Ertola said in dismissing a lawsuit against National Broadcasting Company and its San Francisco affiliate, KRON-TV. That's what he thinks.

The U.S. Supreme Court overturned Judge Ertola's ruling Monday and reinstated a lawsuit brought by the family of an eight-year-old girl who was sexually assaulted in a manner which closely resembled a fictional episode on an NBC program. In seeking $11 million in damages, the family's lawyers are arguing that the broadcasters were negligent in portraying the violence precisely because it would encourage real-life imitation.

Whether the family ultimately can prove a causal connection and overcome other legal obstacles remains to be seen. But the very fact that the U.S. Supreme Court is providing the opportunity does violence to constitutional guarantees of freedom of speech.

That is not to give a Good Housekeeping seal of approval to television programing. But the quality of television is not at issue. The U.S. Constitution is. If NBC can be held legally accountable for what occurs in the nation's streets because of what it shows in the nation's homes, then the sacred Constitutional principle of freedom of expression is not going to be worth much.

After NBC's entertainment department is held responsible for society's ills, then it will be the news department's turn to cough up millions of dollars for broadcasting some violent, if not gruesome, news event. Or as some film producers asked in a friend of court brief, "Is the writer of a future 'Crime and Punishment'. . . or the television adapter and producer of Dostoevski's classic to be liable to the victims and survivors of ax murders?"

The list of dire possibilities is virtually endless. One also would like to believe they are unthinkable; unfortunately, they are not, given the court's failure to dismiss the San Francisco lawsuit. The court wrote no opinion to explain why it decided not to hear the case, so its motivation is unclear. It may be that the court wanted to wait until the trial jury ruled before ruling on the constitutional implications.

Regardless, by paving the way for trial, the nation's top court is giving some credence to the concept that communications media can be held responsible for subsequent and independent acts of others, which is simply another way of killing the messenger because you do not like the message. That is one message the court should have nipped in the bud.

St. Petersburg Times

St. Petersburg, Fla., April 29, 1978

Should a television show be held financially responsible for causing a crime? That's the tough question a San Francisco jury will take up, thanks to recent action by the U.S. Supreme Court.

The court let stand a lower court decision that guarantees of freedom of speech do not automatically protect a television network and station from a lawsuit. So the mother of a 9-year-old girl, charging her daughter was sexually assaulted with a bottle in a re-enactment of a television crime, will be able to press a claim for $11-million in damages.

The TV movie, *Born Innocent*, was an NBC drama about what happens to a first offender sent to a big city detention center for young girls. It showed the public a forgotten side of juvenile justice, a place where youngsters who tell of drug use and sexual abuse by fellow inmates are seldom heard.

The drama showed several girls apparently raping the main character, portrayed by Linda Blair, with a wooden rod. Three days later four teen-age girls did the same thing to a child with a bottle. They told police they had seen the show.

ASSUMING THE movie really did trigger this awful crime, should NBC and the San Francisco television station which carried the movie therefore share responsibility for the assault?

We always thought individuals had to be held accountable for their own behavior. Sadly enough, girls have been raped with objects since before the invention of television. And millions who saw the show did not run out and assault a child. Can the drama itself be held guilty because of those who did?

The four teen-agers who assaulted the girl were convicted and sentenced to probation. In civil cases where minors cause damage, their parents are usually held responsible, and have to pay for it. Shouldn't that standard apply here? Doesn't the blame for this crime fall on the shoulders of those who committed it? And the financial liability on their parents?

NO AMOUNT of money can really compensate the victim, of course, and part of her mother's reason for pressing the case is to punish NBC and KRON-TV. Yet the drama raised important questions about the treatment of young girls who break the law. It may have influenced the way officials run juvenile detention centers. Perhaps it prevented one or more real life rapes. Should these questions have been squelched because some girls might be prompted to act out the dramatization?

We wonder if NBC could have handled the rape scene differently, and if that would have made any difference. Perhaps that is a possibility all three networks have been exploring since 1974, when the suit forced NBC to begin paying hefty legal fees. The networks do take some care in presenting violence. It wouldn't hurt to take more.

But should a jury force them to do it? The issue of free speech is at stake here, and not necessarily just for the creators of television drama. Fact can be just as provocative as fiction. What if a kidnap victim in Indianapolis can show that he probably was taken hostage because a local looney saw Walter Cronkite describe a kidnaping in Washington?

If CBS had to pay several million dollars as a result, news of kidnapings would probably dwindle. Is that good? Isn't secret crime scarier than known crime? Rumor and fear could easily replace fact, especially if magazines and newspapers became liable to the same damage suits.

In a sense newspapers are instant history, often more dramatic and fresher than the history books. But if the printed word were found liable for crime, the publishers of history books would also have to think twice.

Does the knowledge of Lincoln's assassination prompt some nut to take a shot at a new president? It was certainly a spectacular crime, and the books keep it alive. How do we know Lee Harvey Oswald or Squeaky Fromme hadn't just finished reading about John Wilkes Booth?

WHAT WE HAVE outlined is obviously a domino effect, but it is not necessarily a far-fetched one. And it must be taken into account in considering the question of *Born Innocent*, because the $11-million damage suit could tip the first domino.

We feel much sympathy for the little girl who was the victim of rape, and we can see how the mother would think her daughter would never have been attacked if the teen-aged girls hadn't seen it on TV. People do imitate violence, including suicide.

But to hold NBC and KRON-TV responsible for the imitation puts the blame in the wrong place. And the consequences of attaching a legal and enormous financial price tag to that mistake could harm us all.

CASPER STAR-TRIBUNE
Casper. Wyo., August 17, 1978

It was probably inevitable under the First Amendment that the plaintiffs in the "Born Innocent" suit would receive an adverse ruling. As it was the case was dismissed because of the judge's ruling that the lawyer for the plaintiff would have to show actual intent to incite by NBC television.

The case arose when San Francisco NBC affiliate KRON showed a movie at eight o'clock in the evening in which a fourteen year old girl in a home for wayward girls was artificially raped in a shower by four other girls.

Three days later a nine-year-old girl was raped in a similar manner to the scene in the movie. The suit was brought on the basis that NBC and the San Francisco station were negligent in showing the movie at a time when youngsters might be watching.

When the judge ruled that the attorney for the youngster would have to show intent by NBC to incite the action he declined to take the case before a jury under the bounds created by the judge. Hence the dismissal.

It has been our observation that there are few homes in which a child might not be looking at television at almost any time of the day or night.

And the fact that a crime or violent action is taking place on the picture tube does not incite others to emulate the action later.

There is no doubt that there has been far too much violence and sex stimulation on TV, but the remedy for that lies with the parents and children themselves whose moral standards have been created to find such actions repugnant.

The TV set, itself, contains the remedy for parents who do not want their children watching that type of scene. It is the little button that turns the set off.

It is an unfortunate aspect of life that all the world is not one of "Pollyanna". And literature throughout the ages has reflected this fact.

From the Bible to Shakespeare to Edgar Allen Poe to Columbo on TV crime and violence have been depicted. A verdict of guilty in the San Francisco case would have placed every library, even comic strips, in jeopardy.

The remedy lies, of course, in good taste being exercised and violent scenes being turned off. That is the hardest blow of all in TV because it would result in low ratings and the shows cancellation. More parental vigilance could rid the tube of these objectionable movies.

DESERET NEWS
Salt Lake City, Utah, August 10, 1978

If hard cases make bad law, some really outrageous law was made with this week's ruling by a San Francisco judge in an $11 million negligence suit against NBC.

Nor was the difficult situation helped by the self-serving claims of the network that this verdict is a victory for freedom of speech.

We're referring, of course, to the suit that grew out of NBC's 1974 showing of "Born Innocent," the televised movie in which a young girl was shown being raped by other youngsters with the handle of a plumber's plunger.

Four days after the film was shown in prime time, a similar attack was made on a California girl, whose parents subsequently sued the network for negligence.

This week Superior Court Judge Robert Dossee dismissed the suit after having ruled previously that the plaintiff would have to prove NBC intended to incite such crimes.

What an impossible requirement. Indeed, what an outrageous precedent.

Is Detroit to be immune from negligence suits when it can't be proven that the car makers intended to produce defective autos?

Is the motorist who parks on a hill without setting the brakes to be shielded from a negligence suit when it can't be demonstrated that he intended to let the vehicle roll away and into a house at the bottom?

What about the clothing manufacturer who produces sleepwear that turns out to be highly inflammable? What about

Well, you draw up your own list. It goes on and on. So do the absurdities that result if Judge Dossee's line of thinking is followed to its logical — or, rather, illogical — conclusion.

Instead, there's another kind of list that should be made.

It would include the boy who laced the family dinner with ground glass after observing the tactic on a TV crime show . . . the two New York teenagers charged with killing a numbers dealer after a "Kojak" episode on TV involving the use of juveniles as "hit men" . . . the skid row derelicts murdered in Los Angeles three years ago in a pattern like an episode on the "Police Story" TV show.

This is not to absolve individual wrong-doers, even young and impressionable ones, of responsibility. But isn't it a shared responsibility?

Isn't a communications medium able to sell millions of cars and kitchen appliances also selling something else when it shows the typical American youngster 11,000 killings by the time he becomes 15 years old?

"Born Innocent" could have been given an R or X rating and shown in movie houses all over the country to adult audiences. Or it could have been shown on TV at some time other than when millions of children were watching. So much, then, for the notion that the network must be absolved if freedom of speech and of artistic expression are to flourish.

This isn't the last that will be heard of this case. This week's ruling in California will be appealed — hopefully, all the way to the U.S. Supreme Court, if that's what it takes.

It's hard to believe that a high court which recently reprimanded TV for airing dirty words won't be tough on the prime-time airing of deeds that can be even more dirty and damaging.

The Wichita Beacon
Wichita, Kans., August 7, 1978

An $11 million damage suit against the NBC television network now under way in San Francisco hinges on the premise that youngsters exposed to explicit violence on TV may very well imitate the destructive behavior in real life. The case being tried involves the rape by four teenagers of a 9-year-old girl within a few days of a television showing of the movie "Born Innocent."

The attorney representing the victim's parents in the suit contends the crime would not have occurred without the stimulus of the TV program. What is not being pointed out, though, is that for four children to rape a child with a bottle, something much deeper than their recent television fare is to blame.

Such a violent act does not simply rise up from nowhere. Perhaps the TV program did play a role in the attack, in that it put into visual terms what must have been going on in the minds of the young rapists for some time. But to blame a single fictional depiction solely for the tragedy is to ignore the deeper seated problems that brought the attackers to the point of inflicting violence on a helpless child.

A similar tragic set of circumstances occurred recently when an 11-year-old boy was seriously burned as he tried to imitate the rock group Kiss' onstage fire-breathing act. While few adults see much merit in such antics by Kiss, there are few folks who don't "ooh" and "ah" when the same act is performed by a circus entertainer.

Just as neither Kiss nor circus fire breathers should be held accountable for the injuries suffered by an obviously impressionable youngster, neither should a TV program be held liable for a single gross, aberrant sexual assault. Perhaps both situations were triggered by a final visual impact, but the dangerous situation inside those who played out the imagery was loaded to the limit over a period of months or years.

These were neither normal acts nor normal children. To find and treat such bizzare behavior, we will have to look further than just to our television sets.

The Detroit News

Detroit, Mich., May 4, 1978

Agreed, TV is often needlessly violent as well as insultingly shallow. But how far should society go in penalizing television networks for bad judgment and bad taste? At some point the cure may prove more harmful than the evil attributed to bad TV programing.

In San Francisco, an $11-million damage suit has been filed against a television station and NBC because a 9-year-old girl was sexually assaulted four days after the depiction of a similar crime in a TV drama.

In Miami, a teen-ager convicted of murdering an 83-year-old woman has filed a $25-million suit against the three major TV networks, claiming that violent programs showed him how to kill. According to the suit, "The shooting and killing . . . was a foreseeable response to the stimulus of the offending programs."

We wait in fascination to see how the lawyers attempt to prove cause and effect. Can the attorney for the young murderer prove the existence of "involuntary television intoxication," as he calls it, and then prove that it contributed directly to criminal acts by the "intoxicated" youth? Objective evidence supporting such a claim must be very difficult, indeed, to obtain.

That issue aside, however, the big question is whether the courts are prepared to approve economic punishment for dramatic expression. If they do approve such a penalty in the case of TV, what will they say when someone comes to court claiming to have been steered into a life of crime by "theater intoxication" induced by violent stage plays? Or by "newspaper intoxication" or "magazine intoxication"?

There was a time when lawsuits such as those described above would have been dismissed out of hand. Why do plaintiffs believe they may now succeed? Wm. B. Spann Jr., president of the American Bar Association, recently said something which bears on this point.

Spann observed in a Law Day speech that citizens have become invested with "rights" never imagined by the Founding Fathers:

". . .It is a growing tendency on the part of the individual to demand compensation from someone for almost any kind of misfortune that befalls him. One social researcher calls it the psychology of entitlement. For example, one man lost a finger operating his power lawnmower and sued the manufacturer. It didn't matter to him — and it apparently didn't matter to the jury, either — that his injury occurred when he was using the lawnmower to cut a hedge. He was entitled to compensation. . . ."

As the result of large judgments handed down for such questionable claims, the public pays higher prices for the products and services of companies that suffer the heavy losses. In addition, courts become clogged with frivolous lawsuits, making it more difficult for the judicial system to provide timely justice for all.

Inevitably, today's indiscriminate and all-embracing definition of civil and consumer "rights" has led to a far more serious issue than whether the reckless operator of a lawnmower deserves compensation for a lost finger. The courts now seriously entertain the question whether a criminal, posing as a damaged consumer, can transfer the blame for his crime to the producer of a TV program. This question brings into doubt the principle of personal responsibility and, more important, the validity of the First Amendment.

If the courts rule against free expression under these incredible circumstances, we hate to imagine where the preoccupation — intoxication may be a better word — with consumer "rights" will take us next.

The Washington Post

Washington, D.C., August 10, 1978

IT IS UNLIKELY that 13-year-old Olivia Niemi will win her $13-million suit against NBC, but one can sympathize with her and with her family nevertheless. Miss Niemi was assaulted four years ago by teenagers on a San Francisco beach. The method of assault was almost an exact reenactment of a scene in a television drama, "Born Innocent," shown by NBC four days earlier—in which a young girl was assaulted with a plunger by inmates of a reformatory. Miss Niemi and her attorney contend that she never would have been assaulted had that scene not been shown. That may be so. At the moment there is some question whether the case will ever come to trial; but if it does, and if the trial proves that Miss Niemi's attackers did in fact watch "Born Innocent"—something yet to be proved—it is perfectly reasonable to assume that the fictional presentation served as the basis for the real-life crime. Therefore, it is also reasonable to share some of Miss Niemi's frustration.

To say that, however, is not to say that Miss Niemi ought to win her case. Judge Robert Dossee has ruled that the trial must be limited to the question of whether or not "Born Innocent" actually "incited" Miss Niemi's attackers. He has interpreted incitement to mean advocacy, as the Supreme Court has said it should be interpreted. Therefore, one would have to believe that NBC advocated the commission of the crime—a situation as unlikely as it would be impossible to prove.

Yet even if Judge Dossee's interpretation of incitement had come closer to negligence or recklessness, Miss Niemi's attorney has contended all along, Miss Niemi could not, and should not, prevail. If NBC were to be found culpable for indirectly inciting a crime through a dramatic presentation, in the future no scenes involving violence would ever be shown on television—in a play, or on the news, for that matter—for fear of prosecution. And television alone would not be affected. A violent scene in a book, or in an anecdote, would be equally liable.

At issue in this case is the influence of an idea: how far it goes and how it takes shape. There can be no doubt that the intention in showing the rape scene in "Born Innocent" was to cause revulsion and condemnation—the opposite of the effect it allegedly had on Miss Niemi's attackers. NBC would be pleased to take credit for the condemnation, but denies responsibility for the rape. In fact, it has responsibility for neither reaction, since it cannot account, nor be held to account, for the ways "Born Innocent" was received, much less acted upon.

Yet one still feels a sense of dissatisfaction here, as the true justice of Miss Niemi's case seems to hang somewhere between her suffering and the rightness and necessity of the First Amendment. In deciding to put on a serious work like "Born Innocent," NBC took a step up in TV programming, but there is no question that the network showed terrible judgment in scheduling the play at 8 p.m. As in the Ronney Zamora murder case a year ago, the first, and rather easy, thing we do in such matters is to assert that responsibilities for crimes reside with individuals. But no one who watched that rape scene would deny that it was capable of creating a disturbing impression. "Born Innocent" should have been shown much later in the evening, and with plenty of cautions to the viewer.

NBC will probably win the case eventually, but it and the other networks will win little else if they merely whoop it up and do not take warning from this experience. If in the future commercial television wishes to shed its customary insipidity and to start showing more programs that deal with life seriously, and brutally, then it must also show common sense as to when and how such programs are put on. This idea of individual responsibility for one's actions cuts several ways.

THE BLADE

Toledo, Ohio, August 19, 1978

THE freedom of expression guaranteed by the First Amendment has survived a serious, if sidelong, challenge in San Francisco. A trial judge there dismissed an $11 million damage suit against NBC-TV which had been brought on the novel theory that a television network should be held legally responsible if its programs "inspire" anti-social behavior.

The suit was brought as a negligence action by parents of a 9-year-old girl who was sexually assaulted by three other girls. Lawyers for the girl argued that the assault was inspired by a similar rape portrayed in an NBC drama.

That this suit even reached the trial stage is distressing. A lawyer who attempted to blame a novel or Broadway play — perhaps a revival of the violence-filled "Macbeth" — for real-life crimes would have been laughed out of court from the outset. But because of the widespread notion that television is a second-class medium with circumscribed constitutional rights, the San Francisco suit attracted widespread sympathy. And, most disturbing of all, the U.S. Supreme Court in April refused to rule in advance of the trial that holding fictional television programs responsible for their effect on unstable or deranged or merely malevolent minds was a violation of the First Amendment.

Fortunately, the trial judge in the case, Superior Court Judge Robert Dossee, proved to be more sensitive to the freedom implications of the TV-made-me-do-it theory. First the judge ruled that lawyers for the plaintiff had to prove that NBC had deliberately attempted to incite real-life assaults by presenting a serious drama in which an assault was simulated. That test was a difficult one, but the First Amendment contemplates that exceptions to free speech be subjected to the most rigorous tests possible.

When a lawyer for the plaintiff insisted on taking a negligence rather than an incitement theory to the jury, Judge Dossee threw the case out. That outcome will undoubtedly be disappointing to the plaintiff's family — and to those who believe that NBC's "deep pocket" is as good a source of financial comfort to the girl as any. But no other result would have preserved both free speech and the principle that criminal responsibility attaches to those who commit crimes — not to authors, playwrights, or television actors.

The alternative would be to discourage television producers — and by implication dramatists, novelists, and poets — from portraying or commenting upon real life and the violence which often marks it. In that event the First Amendment would be a dead letter.

The Ottawa Citizen

Ottawa Ont., August 8, 1978

Can a television network be held responsible in any way for the criminal acts its viewers might commit after-watching particular shows?

The plaintiffs in three fascinating law suits in the United States say "Yes." Fortunately, the courts so far haven't shared that opinion.

The first case to enjoy widespread publicity concerned 15-year-old Ronald Zamora from Miami. The defence argued that he was under the influence of "involuntary television intoxication" from watching crime shows when he robbed and murdered an 83-year-old neighbor.

Years of watching make-believe violence made him unable to tell killing was wrong, so the argument went. In other words, "viewer insanity." But is that Zamora's problem or the networks'?

Zamora was convicted. His parents then launched a $25-million suit against the major American networks — ABC, CBS and NBC — claiming their programming "showed the impressionable teen-ager how to kill."

From the age of five, said the suit, Zamora had watched 40,000 to 50,000 "violent destructions of fellow humans." Just where were his parents during those 10 years of chronic, indiscriminate viewing?

In another case, Richard Kane, a 46-year-old New Yorker wounded during a restaurant robbery in which his wife and two other people were fatally shot, launched a $10-million suit against NBC and the Federal Communications Commission claiming that the killer got his idea from an episode of *Police Story*.

He sued on principle: "I think this is the only way to do something in regard to all violence on television. When a jerk runs around and rubs out three people and says he got the idea from a television show, something is wrong." Indeed there is. With the murderer, at any rate.

NBC was sued again, this time for $11 million in San Francisco by a woman and her nine-year-old daughter after the daughter was raped with a bottle by three girls. The incident occurred four days after a film depicting a similar crime was aired.

During the trial, the plaintiff's lawyer argued that showing the film was "negligent, irresponsible and reckless."

The judge ruled that the plaintiff needed to prove that the network was trying to incite rape with this film, and dismissed the case when the lawyer refused to argue that line.

These cases underscore the growing belief that we are not responsible for our own actions; that we have no control over the brainwashing emanating from the boob tube.

The fact is that the viewer has ultimate control. It's called the on-off switch. Even one of the inventors of television refers to it as the best part of the machine.

All too often television becomes the scapegoat of irresponsible parents who fail to guide their children's viewing. Censoring the media, or burning books or banning movies, is not the cure for this failure.

Arkansas Gazette.

Little Rock, Ark., August 12, 1978

A new legal round has gone to NBC-TV in its defense against a suit for $11 million in compensatory and punitive damages brought at San Francisco by the mother of a nine-year-old girl who was raped with a mechanical device by three older girls only four days after the network's showing of a film, "Born Innocent", that had a similar scene within a women's reformatory as a kind of centerpiece for its plot.

The new court ruling came from Judge Robert Dessee of San Francisco Superior Court, who held that for the asked damages to be assessed against NBC and its local affiliate, KRON-TV, counsel for the plaintiffs would have had to prove that the network executives who put "Born Innocent" on the air in the first place did so with the intent to incite an actual rape.

This the plaintiff has so far failed to do — for reasons that the judge in the middle and plaintiff's counsel agreed, each from his differing angle — was the most obvious reason, which was that no such proof of any intent, primarily or even secondarily, *could be* adduced.

Attorney Marvin Lewis, who filed and pleaded the damages suit, said in fact that he was not even trying to prove any such intent, and so characterized Judge Dessee's argument on this point as "ridiculous," as a holding that would place "an impossible burden of proof" on his, Lewis's, attempts to prove mere *negligence* on the network's part (and, inferentially, on the

local station's part, since affiliates always retain the right to cull a show if they think it is too strong for them or for their viewers.)

We are inclined to think, *contra* Mr. Lewis, that the suit *itself* was rather ridiculous, venturing as it does into whole new unexplored and essentially unexplorable areas of law, though we can understand the indignation out of which the suit arose. We had said earlier of this same case that it is no kind of anti-feminist feeling that makes us say that, in our opinion, a violent rape of this kind, especially in light of the age of the victim, is one of the most truly heinous of all crimes. But that is not the point here, or even close to the point.

With all due allowance to whatever "creative" imagination was involved in the conceiving and producing of "Born Innocent", we will venture that the category of the crime came closer to the originating of the story idea than the other way around.

* * *

The show in question was not a documentary, but something that is supposed to pass for entertainment these days, but it cannot be stressed too much that girls were being raped by girls in and out of women's penitentiaries in actuality many years before "Born Innocent" surfaced, aberrant age differentials included.

Ditto, men's penitentiaries. Does

anybody remember when John W. Dean III, desperate, was pleading not to be sent to a federal correctional institution in consequence of the Watergate affair because he feared his boyish aspect might invite such an assault. Nothing of the sort happened, because Dean was one of the Watergate types who drew pretty much of a "country club" prison assignment, as they were called then, mainly, we suppose, because of the forthcoming and unshakeable quality of his federal court testimony.

Actually, to suggest that the American TV industry is inventive enough to confect any kind of new crime, one sexually oriented abnormally, normally, or one without sexual content at all, is to suggest entirely too much. The American TV industry is almost totally bereft of imagination, and the formula seems to work with most audiences.

The legal tangle precipitated by the "Born Innocent" suit, we gather still is not finally resolved. The Supreme Court of the United States has not yet ruled on the merits of the case, as such, only that an earlier California State court ruling throwing the case out of court summarily could not be upheld. The appellate channels will be reopened again, counsel for plaintiff has promised, so the High Court may and probably will get its chance to rule on the merits. It is a decision that we all ought to await with some trepidation, considering the possible precedent involved in a straight-out ruling on the merits.

THE ARIZONA REPUBLIC

Phoenix, Ariz., August 11, 1978

DISMISSAL of the suit against the National Broadcasting Co. for showing a film, *Born Innocent*, which depicted a brutal sexual assault on a girl, was victory for freedom of the press.

It would have become dangerous for any California newspaper or radio or TV station to report an unusual crime, however circumspectly, if state Superior Court Judge Robert Dossee had ruled other than he did.

The facts in the case were these:

In 1974, shortly after the showing of the film, Olivia Niemi, then 9, was sexually assaulted with a bottle by three girls on a San Francisco beach.

Her mother, Mrs. Valeria Niemi, sued NBC for $1 million on her own and the girl's behalf, saying the attack was inspired by the film.

There is reason to believe it was. However, Dossee ruled that Mrs. Niemi's lawyer would have to prove that, in showing the film, NBC intended to incite the attack.

This the lawyer could not do, and Dossee threw out the suit.

No one can help but sympathize with Valeria and Olivia Niemi, but it's an unfortunate fact of life that sick minds all but too often are inspired to imitate crimes they read about, or hear or see.

After Lee Harvey Oswald killed President Kennedy, there was a spate of assassinations and attempted assassinations, including the murder of his brother.

This is the reason Sen. Edward M. Kennedy's family has so opposed his running for the presidency. The family is afraid that some nut, attempting to emulate Oswald and Sirhan Sirhan, will shoot him, too.

There's no question but that reports in the media of successful skyjackings were in part responsible for the rash of skyjackings that plagued the nation for awhile. In fact, while the skyjackings were going on, some psychologists urged the media to stop reporting them. By giving the skyjackers publicity, they argued, the media were giving them exactly what they, in their sickness, sought.

That could be true, but the media can no more ignore a crime like skyjacking than it can the assassination of a president.

What goes for the media goes for the authors of novels and the producers of film. They cannot be expected to depict the world as other than it really is, and it's not all sweetness and light.

EDMONTON JOURNAL

Edmonton, Alta., August 17, 1978

The San Francisco judge who threw out an $11-million negligence suit against NBC has taken a crucial step in the protection of freedom of speech.

A rape victim and her mother are trying to sue the television network for "negligence and recklessness" in running *Born Innocent*, a movie which showed the rape of a young girl. Four days after the show was aired, Olivia Niemi, then nine years old, was raped in a similar fashion by three girls. Her mother contends the attack was prompted by the movie.

Judge Robert Dossee ruled that NBC was protected by constitutional guarantees of freedom of speech and dismissed the case before it started. In order to proceed, said the judge, the Niemi's lawyer would have to set out to prove the network was advocating or inciting a crime. The lawyer said he couldn't possibly make that charge and he plans to appeal.

Obviously it is against the law to incite violence but the media cannot be responsible for the actions of those unbalanced people who may well be prompted to commit crimes because of something they see on television. If that link is directly granted, newspapers should refrain from printing stories about crime, television newscasts should ignore coverage of wars and other violent news events, movies should be pared to the bone and public libraries will have to remove all books which contain references to violent acts. It may be argued that television is a special case because it invades the home, but no one is required to have a TV or watch it and every set comes with an off-button.

Certainly television violence is a legitimate area of concern and worry — the average teen-ager will watch 18,000 murders on TV by the time he is an adult. Psychologists differ over how television violence actually affects viewers and some studies even indicate it may make children less aggressive. But that's a matter for society to debate and for society to change through the regular channels of consumer pressure and consumer demand.

State censorship is not the answer and that's what a ruling against NBC would have been — a violation of the freedom of speech.

TULSA WORLD

Tulsa, Okla., August 10, 1978

A CALIFORNIA Judge has thrown out a lawsuit against NBC-TV, alleging that a network crime drama inspired a brutal sex attack on a 9-year-old girl.

The dismissal was not based directly on the merits of the case, but it should discourage future attempts to blame television or other societal and cultural influences for specific crimes.

Because television does bombard the public with a lot of violent trash, it is tempting to say that the broadcasters should be punished for the admittedly evil influence of their product. But the cure proposed in the San Francisco trial would cause much more grief than the disease. It would set a precedent for strict censorship, not only of television but of every public expression or utterance that might conceivably incite someone to commit a criminal act. And that covers a lot of ground, indeed.

In England a few years ago, a self-styled "vampire" admitted a brutal murder. He said he got his idea for the crime from a Church communion service in which participants drank the symbolic blood of Christ.

We simply cannot and must not allow television and, presumably, other forms of public expression to be tailored exclusively for sick minds. And even if we tried, there is no way of knowing for sure what might affect a deranged personality and what might not.

Any reasonable attempt to censor provocative violence from the airwaves would have to include Shakespeare along with Policewoman and Kojak. By some standards, the modern crime shows are pretty tame compared with some of Shakespeare's plays.

Another worrisome thing about the attempt to blame tv for criminal acts is that it suggests the criminal himself is not responsible. Nonsense.

Providing he is sane and able to distinguish right from wrong, an individual who commits a crime should be held personally responsible. Any law that tries to switch that responsibility to outside influences or to "society" can hardly be expected to discourage crime.

This does not mean, of course, that people have to patronize the advertisers who sponsor violent tv trash or that pressure cannot be brought to bear on broadcasters to clean up their act.

But legal censorship aimed at sick minds is not the answer.

The Knickerbocker News

Albany, N.Y., August 16, 1978

Although a California judge has dismissed an $11 million damage suit brought against NBC-TV by the parents of a 13-year-old girl who charged she was sexually assaulted in imitation of a rape scene from the TV film "Born Innocent," the TV networks have no reason to congratulate themselves.

NBC's abysmal judgment in showing the tasteless film on prime time was not on trial. Neither was the effect that such programs have on the suggestible young. The case was dismissed on the grounds that the girl's attorney failed to prove NBC intended to invite violence and that the program was protected by the First Amendment. For the judge to have ruled otherwise would have been to have invited program-by-program censorship.

Some may argue that this was a poor case on which to base a First Amendment defense, but it should be remembered that the guarantees of free speech and free press must protect the worst as well as the best if they are to have any meaning. If this were the best of all possible worlds, we might not need guarantees of the Constitution.

Even so, for NBC to contend, in defense of its decision to show "Born Innocent" during family viewing hours, that the artistic future of TV was at stake in this case was as silly as it was irresponsible.

Recent surveys indicate that progressively more Americans aren't buying the TV networks' offerings on any basis and are tuning out the tube. If any further reason were needed, one could look no further than the National Parent-Teacher Association's ranking of the 10 best and 10 worst TV programs. As one commentator observed after studying the list, "It's hard to say which are the most offensive, the worst or the best." If the 10 worst fall on the side of sex and violence, the 10 so-called best — with the exception of CBS' "60 Minutes" — are so syrupy and far from reality that they should be condemned for their excessive sugar content.

If "Donnie and Marie," which heads the national PTA's "10 best" list, is the very best that American commercial TV can offer, we're in deeper trouble than we thought.

ALBUQUERQUE JOURNAL

Albuquerque, N.M., August 16, 1978

The decision by a judge in San Francisco to throw out an $11 million negligence suit against NBC is a welcome victory for the First Amendment in a year marked by restraints on freedom of the press and freedom of expression.

NBC in its film "Born Innocent" depicted the sexual assault of a young girl by her fellow inmates in a juvenile detention home. Not long after the program aired a group of girls committed a similar assault on a 9-year-old girl on a California beach. By suing NBC the girl's mother hoped to prove that the attackers had no responsibility for the attack as individuals and that if the network had not portrayed the undeniable seamy facts of life the attackers could have lived lives of unblemished virtue. Naturally, such a suit ignores the responsibility of parents to teach good behavior and monitor childrens' viewing habits.

Suppose the court had found for the mother. Any murderer could have seriously argued he would not have murdered had he not read of murder in a newspaper or seen Kojak. The freedom of artists would have been lost as they pondered not the merits of their creations, but the risks of putting them on display.

The Honolulu Advertiser

Honolulu, Hawaii, August 13, 1978

The $11 million negligence suit against NBC filed in a California Superior Court bore implications for all the media, and in turn for what kind of information and entertainment and art are available to the American public.

Our view is that Judge Robert Dossee ruled properly in dismissing the claim, and that the appellate courts should uphold the verdict.

THE SUIT stemmed from a sexual assault by three girls against a younger girl. The victim's mother claimed the attack was prompted by NBC's showing on prime time four days earlier of the movie "Born Innocent," in which a similar incident took place.

The plaintiffs asked $1 million in compensatory damages and $10 million in punitive damages against the network and its San Francisco affiliate.

Judge Dossee indicated what his decision would be when he ruled near the outset that the case could proceed only if the plaintiffs argued that NBC intended to incite a crime with its film.

Based on a 1969 U.S. Supreme Court decision, Dossee maintained that otherwise NBC was protected by the First Amendment guarantee of free speech.

The attorney for the plaintiffs responded that it would be ridiculous for him to attempt to prove such intent. He then proceeded to argue that NBC was negligent and reckless, prompting the judge's decision to dismiss.

THE ATTORNEY says he will appeal on grounds the judge exercised "excessive authority" in narrowing the trial. But it seems to us that any favorable verdict for the plaintiffs would be unwarranted, not only because of First Amendment guarantees but also because the substance of the plaintiffs' arguments is highly questionable.

Research is unclear on the impact of television showings. As one communications professor concluded, there could have been positive as well as negative effects of the scene at issue. The film could have caused some people, for example, to avoid situations where rape might take place.

If the network, or any media, is held responsible by law for what an individual does after viewing or reading something, or after hearing second-hand about what is presented by the media, only the most sterile material then could be offered.

That principle would not necessarily stop at banning violence from television drama. Carried further, could it keep the news media from reporting on real-life violence — on the false hope that public ignorance would improve public safety?

THIS IS NOT to say that the media is absolved of all responsibility, or that viewers or readers have no recourse.

Such consumers can influence what is presented as entertainment by making known what standards they want observed. This potential has already been demonstrated by the reduced violence on television shows generally, and the scheduling for late evening hours of shows with violence.

Such decisions, however, must not be made by the courts if the First Amendment is to retain meaning.

Roanoke Times & World-News

Roanoke, Va.,
May 30, 1978

On May 11 in this space, we examined the issue raised by a California court case in which a young girl sued a TV network. When she was 9 years old, Olivia Niemi was sexually assaulted by four other girls, who said that the technique they used was copied from a televised drama they had recently seen — and that the show had stimulated them to act.

Many difficult questions are raised by this suit. Central is the issue of accountability. Even if a person is influenced by something on TV, in the movies or in print, isn't his evil-doing his own? If Olivia Niemi can convince a court that she became a victim of crime because of a TV drama, couldn't her assailants also claim that the network, and not they, were to blame for what they did?

Inasmuch as those four girls ultimately were released on probation, maybe that kind of claim figured in disposition of their case. Legal standards for juveniles are often different and usually should be. But it's interesting that a Florida youth convicted of murder — whose lawyer unsuccessfully tried to blame his act on "involuntary television intoxication" — recently sued the three major networks for $25 million. Ronny Zamora and his parents contend that violent TV programs "showed the impressionable teen-ager . . . how to kill."

The claim that society and its institutions bear most of the blame for crime, poverty, etc., has grown threadbare. If nobody's ultimately responsible for his own acts, we are all robots and nothing's either right or wrong. But there's another side to the coin. We're not all free agents either, in complete control of our destinies, impervious to external influences. The person who makes that kind of claim about other people is shrugging off his own responsibility. The task is to find an enlightened, compassionate approach that will guide us between those extremes.

BUFFALO EVENING NEWS
Buffalo, N.Y., August 14, 1978

A potential threat to expression in both the entertainment and news media has been dissipated, at least temporarily, by the dismissal of an $11 million lawsuit against NBC for showing a television drama that allegedly led to the rape of a 9-year-old girl.

The suit sought to argue that NBC had been negligent in showing the film. But a California state judge blocked that line of argument by ruling that the program fell under the constitutional protection of the First Amendment, and that the plaintiff would therefore have to prove that NBC had intended to incite rape in broadcasting it.

The plaintiff is appealing the judge's decision, so the last word on this case is yet to be written. But the present ruling gives satisfying recognition to the primacy of the constitutional guarantees of free speech. For almost any drama, documentary, book or even news report might conceivably lead to imitative acts, and there could be no end of lawsuits if broadcasters, publishers and others were to be vulnerable to resulting negligence claims. According to an NBC attorney, the American Library Association was concerned that it would be impossible to determine what books in libraries might not lead to imitative acts.

This is certainly not to excuse the TV networks for excessive and cynical preoccupation with sex and violence. Nor is it to contend that broadcasting the program involved in the suit during the early evening hours demonstrated good judgment. In fact, the ill-timed showing of this very film helped bring about the present rule designating the hours from 7 to 9 p.m. as "family viewing" time on television.

But the precedent of exposing television and other media to endless litigation in these circumstances would surely have a chilling effect in restricting freedom of expression in this country, to the undoubted detriment of viewers and readers. For now, at least, that specter has been removed.

The Virginian-Pilot
Norfolk, Va., August 14, 1978

Olivia Niemi's $11 million damage suit against the National Broadcasting Company has run up against the First Amendment and is foundering. The suit charges that NBC executives were reckless and negligent in telecasting a show at 8 p.m. that contained evocative scenes of sexual assault on a little girl. The show, "Born Innocent," according to Miss Niemi's lawyer, directly inspired a similar attack four days later on the plaintiff, who was nine years old.

Outside influences have been at issue before in sex assault cases, as when a Wisconsin judge found that, because of contemporary clothes and mores, a young rapist was not culpable for his crime. The judge in the Niemi case has a different view. He has ruled that, though the program may have inspired the attackers, the television network is protected by the First Amendment unless its purpose in scheduling Born Innocent was to incite crime.

The Niemi lawyer is not willing to go that far in his charges, especially since the network claims a noble purpose: Born Innocent sought to expose deplorable conditions in reformatories.

NBC has strong grounds for a dismissal. While the merits of the case are far from clear, if it succeeded, an essential freedom, that of speech, would be compromised. Any story, news item, play, book, show, or song containing unsavory conduct would become open to lawsuit.

Nonetheless, the Niemis were justified in bringing the action. The child was harmed and, whether or not legally culpable, NBC's executives deserve to be made to look at the consequences of their actions. It has been well documented that children are impressionable and that some will imitate the violence they see on television. For all its avowed moral purpose, NBC ran titillating previews for Born Innocent and its rape scene was such as might inspire sadistic do-it-yourselfers like those who attacked Olivia Niemi.

It has been suggested that the simple answer is for TV violence to be confined to late hours, as though children all go to bed early. But the answer is not so simple.

The value of a case such as this one, fortunately, does not rest on its success or on the simplicities it evokes, but on its mere existence. It reminds the networks that people are watching out here, and reminds all of us that, if prodigalized, even free speech can exact a high price.

Programming: To Inform, Entertain or Sell Time?

Success is a seven-letter word, spelled r-a-t-i-n-g-s in the world of commercial television. Ratings indicate the size of the viewing audience, the audience being the only real product the television industry has to offer. The consumer for television's product (the audience) is the advertiser seeking the mass market. Programs that attract the largest number of viewers get the best ratings and thus command the highest fees from sponsors. The upshot of this strategy is that what we see on television is decided exclusively on the basis of dollar profit to the networks. Numbers, (not quality) and corporate (not public) interest determine which programs survive in the battle for ratings.

Fred Silverman, the recently appointed president of the National Broadcasting Co. (NBC), catapulted the American Broadcasting Company (ABC) from third place to first in the three-way race for network supremacy. (CBS had been the highest rated network for twenty years.) Under Silverman's leadership, ABC added 22 new affiliate stations between 1976-78. Silverman is candid about the broadcasting bureaucracy: "Television critics and pasteboard programmers have all the answers (on paper) though they fail to realize that network television is basically a business with profit and loss columns, stockholders' meetings and annual reports."

Ratings are based on a recording and reporting system devised by the A. C. Nielsen Company. An audimeter, commonly referred to as the "little black box," is attached to television sets in 1,200 American households. The audimeter shows when the TV is on and which channel is being watched. Another 2,300 families keep diaries detailing what program is being watched, and who in the family is watching it. The nation's 727 commerical local stations conduct "sweeps" four times a year — during November, February, May and three weeks in July — to comprehensively measure audience size and accordingly adjust the cost of each commerical minute.

According to H. L. Mencken, "No one ever went broke underestimating the taste of the American public." Margita White, a former Federal Communications Commissioner who advocates the development of measuring devices to rate program quality, recently said, "the [present] rating system — by encouraging imitation rather than innovation....by encouraging bland programming to the lowest common denominator — may be the single major obstacle to better quality programming.''

In keeping with the economics of the television industry, everything that appears on the screen must have entertainment value, the ability to attract viewers and boost ratings. In the area of newscasting, anchormen/women and reporters have taken on the role of television ''personalities.'' Because of the ratings game, the electronic press has sometimes subordinated journalistic professionalalism to show business antics and Hollywood gloss.

When news is presented as entertainment, the problem arises of entertainment being construed as news. The advent of the genre known as documentary drama perfectly illustrates the ambiguity of fact and fiction on television. Can actual events be dramatized without violating the ''truth?'' The tendency to sensationalize seduces the viewer and betrays the networks' presumptions to authenticity. Commercial television is inclined (and broadcasters would say entitled) to insinuate, glamorize and speculate, all in the name of entertainment.

The Topeka Daily Capital

Topeka, Kans., December 6, 1978

Last week's Nielsen ratings, with "60 Minutes" at the top, were encouraging.

For several months, top ratings have gone to frothy, often risque comedies about live-in boy friends and girl friends — nothing unusual in this day and age, but hardly worth first place.

Second place last week went to "All in the Family," the once-controversial comedy of domestic life; and third to "Alice," a light comedy which includes less objectionable material than many other shows.

The "60 Minutes" show presents three segments of news or feature interest, plus a conservative-liberal debate and letters from viewers. It is a magazine of the air, often exploring cases of government graft, quackery or shady operations by fly-by-nights on the business fringe.

It attracts those interested in the unusual and in good reporting.

Its success has spurred competition from other networks — shows like "Weekend," which premiered Saturday, and "20-20."

Popularity of such shows proves what newspapers and magazines have known for a long time — that people are interested in real events and indepth reporting.

One of the best shows of this kind is the nightly "McNeill-Lehrer Report" on the public network. It explores a current event through interviews with persons on both sides of the issue.

When TV undertakes serious news coverage with experienced reporters and good camera work, it can be extremely effective.

The Washington Star
and Daily News

Washington, D.C., December 2, 1977

The American love-hate affair with commercial television runs to extremes, critical or uncritical — and usually the latter.

At one extreme — an extreme we happen to value — you have the guarded but significant indictment of television by the Wirtz panel, which recently examined the declining test scores of college applicants and concluded that television (consuming, on average, some 10,000 to 16,000 of our children's waking hours through age 16) is at best "a thief of time" and at worst a sort of drug that could "alter the neural mechanisms of the mind."

At the other extreme, you have a complacency that uncritically accepts the governing rules and values of commercial programming — the rule that the Nielsen ratings are sovereign, that advertisers may veto programs, that the lowest common denominator of quality must be served first.

In this complacency, every sign of audience restlessness is treated as an aberration, to be cured by more of the same old stuff.

This has certainly been the network reaction to the recent finding of the Nielsen Company that television's audience is shrinking. Primetime evening viewing is down 3 percent and daytime viewing down 8 percent from last year. The networks have hired consultants, *not* to consider what the Nielsen figures might tell us about the quality of programming but to find the flaw — there must be some mistake! — in the way ratings are assembled and computed.

We would regard it as good news indeed if television viewers were beginning to be revolted by the revolting — by the pandering to ever-lower levels of taste and imagination. It would be encouraging to believe that more and more of us are darkening our screens in disgust or boredom, and seeking better uses of our lives than to function for dozens of hours every week as "passive receivers of canned experience," in the words of Dr. Robert L. Stubblefield, an authority on juvenile TV viewing.

Even if that were the situation, the message apparently would take a long time to impress the impresarios who plan our evenings. Some weeks ago, *Time Magazine*, in a cover story distinguished by uncritical acceptance of the values it described, profiled Mr. Fred Silverman of ABC: the man whose genius for popular tastes is credited with putting his network so far ahead in the cannibalistic fight for prime-time audiences.

Mr. Silverman is probably only symptomatic, and we mean nothing personal. He is doing the job he was trained to do, and doing it very well. You can hardly expect him to pull a pistol on the goose that lays golden eggs.

What interested us about *Time's* story on Mr. Silverman, however, was the depressing observation that "he was born with perfect pitch for American pop TV taste." He is "the man with the golden gut," as one of his colleagues put it, apparently with unmixed admiration for golden guts. Mr. Silverman is not insulted, it would seem, by such characterizations; on the contrary, he relishes them. Mr. Silverman, we are told, is brought to tears by "Soap," and sees that series as exemplifying "the sanctity of the family unit." He will not be likely to lead a counter-revolution in television taste.

The characterizations somehow say it all: No more flattering words can be said about today's genius in television programming, the arbiter of taste for tens of millions, than that he has a "perfect" sense of gut appetites.

But suppose, to suppose the wildly improbable, that the networks really began to worry that people are turning off their sets because they want more imagination, more challenge, more stimulation in commercial television. A good beginning, which the Carter administration has endorsed, is putting more money into public television. Even in its financially straitened state, public television is often a yardstick embarrassing to the commercial networks: a reminder of what commercial television, with far greater financial resources, might be if it dared expand its horizons. The commercial networks are not indifferent to the influence of good example. The commercial imitations, usually feeble, of the excellent imported dramas we see on PBS programs like "Masterpiece Theater" tell us so.

A more revolutionary result, but far more improbable, would occur if the networks broke the chains they have forged for themselves over a generation of enslavement to the ratings and to the notion that their mission is to deliver the maximum number of bodies, whatever extremes of vulgarity and titillation the mission demands, and regardless, in fact, of the quality or attentiveness of the bodies.

This is what might be done, but probably won't be done unless one of the networks suddenly gains the courage to defy the rules of the rat-race and try something unorthodox.

We are well aware, of course, that all this is thoroughly heretical. To remind television of a higher responsibility to the public is to risk being accused of a sort of cultural fascism. Only a "cultural Hitler," a former FCC commissioner once told us, presumes to second-guess what popular audiences demand, as measured by the ratings.

Commercial television today seems fatally unconcerned with the possible distinction between programs that attract big audiences and programs that might inspire or instruct. Anyone who toys with the notion that there might be a difference or that television ought to act on it has his work cut out. But that work needs doing.

THE CHRISTIAN SCIENCE MONITOR

Boston, Mass., January 8, 1979

Anybody who has ever been dismayed to see a quality TV program or series vanish from the screen because it lost out in the TV "numbers" game – i.e., it had a low Nielsen rating – must have shared our longing for a better gauge to determine which shows will and will not be broadcast. And for that reason it is encouraging to see reports that government officials, a few influential people within the broadcast industry, and citizens groups are seriously discussing ways to supplement the Nielsen "headcounts" with a system that would take into account the quality of the programs along with the number of households tuned in to them.

The idea would be to sample audience reactions to programs through some yet-to-be-devised method. Reliance on telephone interviews, electronic recording devices, or viewer diaries are among the approaches being talked about. The advantages of tapping audience response ought to be obvious. The simple fact that a home TV set is tuned to a particular program does not automatically signal the viewers' appreciation, or lack of it, for the program. Too frequently the choices available for viewing at any particular time are so narrow — entertainment on all channels so bland or shallow — that the person determined to watch TV during that time slot has to settle for programs that he might not enjoy and would certainly not rate highly if given the chance.

Audience reaction should also benefit broadcasters by providing them with an additional factor to take into consideration when weighing the fate of a program with a good, but not outstanding, Nielsen rating. This might have helped CBS, say, in its final determination to keep "The Paper Chase" on the air. The program, praised by critics and others, nevertheless did not score among the top programs in the Nielsens, and for a time it looked as if it would not survive. A public outcry by critics and viewers helped convince CBS to keep the program.

Most importantly, qualitative ratings should encourage more innovative and imaginative programming, although network officials ought not to look upon any electronic audience-rating system as relieving them of the ultimate responsibility for cultivating better writing and acting on TV.

In the face of such positive prospects for qualitative ratings, it is disappointing that the networks and advertising agencies, those with the biggest say in programming, have expressed only lukewarm support, and in some cases actively oppose the concept. It certainly seems worth a try.

Pittsburgh Post-Gazette

Pittsburgh, Pa., September 19, 1978

With mind-numbing repetitiveness, the three major television networks have been bombarding viewers with catch-phrases designed to sell their new "seasons." As in past years, their slogans are a reliable index to the inventiveness and originality of the programs themselves. CBS tells viewers to "Turn Us On—We'll Turn You On." ABC's pitch is: "We're the One to Turn To." And NBC, which a few years ago spent close to a million dollars on a trademark identical to one developed for $100 by an obscure educational network, paid someone for "NB-See Us."

The new programs themselves continue a major-network tradition of self-parody. No successful programming formula has been left uncloned. The success of smirking "jiggle" comedies has spawned a new series about the lives and loves of stewardesses. Hubba hubba. And simpleminded "relevant" humor will be provided by a series pitting a with-it nun against a conservative priest.

Why is American commercial television so bad? The orthodox, and resigned, explanation is that the tyranny of mass-audience ratings guarantees that programming will be geared to the slowest common denominator. But the supposedly computerlike precision of the ratings system may amount

to less than meets the eye. Even if the ratings figures themselves are accurate, the network programmers who are paid handsomely to read such statistical entrails continue to produce "sure-fire" programs that do astonishingly poorly in those same ratings. Thus the inevitable "second season."

Amid the contrived hoopla surrounding the new television season, there are signs that network executives are beginning to question the conventional wisdom that mediocrity and imitation are prerequisites for success. TV Guide this week quotes executives from all three major networks on the need for television to be more innovative and experimental. NBC's president Fred Silverman, the godfather of "jiggle" comedy, is quoted as propounding the following bit of heresy: "In entertainment, we just must strike out in new directions."

Brave words, though judging from the new season they must have been accompanied by a *sotto voce* codicil of "Wait till next year." Still, the wait will be worth it if the network executives' born-again promises of innovation even begin to bear fruit. We can only hope that by "new directions," Mr. Silverman doesn't mean a musical version of "Gilligan's Island."

Des Moines Tribune

Des Moines, Iowa, May 5, 1976

The American Broadcasting Company's jump from distant third to challenging second for TV network ratings has been the story of the year in the broadcasting industry.

ABC compiled a stunning string of weekly "firsts" with help from its popular coverage of the Winter Olympics. The Olympics are over but ABC is hanging near the top with run-of-the-mill situation comedies ("Laverne and Shirley"), police dramas ("Baretta"), variety shows ("Donnie and Marie") and movies (last week it was "Jenny" and "Gold").

ABC aired 10 of the Top 20 shows, according to Nielsen ratings for the week that ended Apr. 25. Quite a change from those years when ABC was lucky to make the Top 20.

The rise of an underdog would elicit more cheers from us if it involved something other than a knack for generating popular mass entertainment.

CBS is still represented in the Top 20 by shows which broke through cliches to set new standards in characterization, realism and social commentary ("All in the Family," "M*A*S*H," "Maude"). NBC was represented among the Top 20 for the week in question with "Judge Horton and the Scottsboro Boys," a dramatization of the human toll behind the headlines of that celebrated case.

ABC has no such jewels in its ratings crown. Occasional glints of freshness and insight are quickly buried under formula farce in "Welcome Back, Kotter." The equality message in "Wonder Woman" is hard to take seriously when it results in episodes which treat the principal failing of the Nazis as male chauvinism.

It is too bad that ABC made its great leap forward in ratings by taking a great fall backward in programming.

Newsday

Garden City, N.Y., December 3, 1978

The top-rated television show in the nation last week was "60 Minutes"—practically the only program among the 61 shown in prime time that isn't based on what passes for fantasy in TV land.

More than 22 million homes tuned in the provocative CBS newsmagazine last Sunday night and, given television's propensity for imitating its successes, we were hoping its number-one rating would trigger a rash of other shows like it.

Alas, when the networks last week cancelled such trash as "Grandpa Goes to Washington," "Who's Watching the Kids?" and "UFO," they replaced it with sitcoms and "dramas" that weren't good enough to make the screen at the start of this year's television season.

The substitutes include "Sweepstakes," which is described as "a comedy-drama focusing on the finalists in a million-dollar lottery"; "Mrs. Columbo,"

which is—you guessed it—a spinoff from "Columbo," the detective series, and a sitcom about a presumably funny train. Oh, yes, there are also *two* takeoffs on the fraternity house movie that's the year's surprise hit.

Why couldn't the programers stick with their usual practice of trying to clone TV's successes? It sounds to us as if they're about to flood the tube with imitations of its failures.

The Evening Bulletin

Philadelphia, Pa., September 17, 1978

Seventeen years have elapsed since Newton Minow, then Federal Communications Commission chairman, described television programing as a "vast wasteland." Unhappily, his characterization today seems, if anything, even more accurate. "The Beverly Hillbillies" and "The Untouchables" have gone. Long live "Three's Company" and "Starsky and Hutch."

As this fall's series debut in a burst of hoopla, imitation continues to be the watchword. This season's biggest star is touted to be "Battlestar Galactica" — a super son of the movie "Star Wars" that uses the same plot, robots and even villains' helmets. In fact, the "new" science fiction shows feature such novel characters as Buck Rogers and Flash Gordon.

We're assured there will be less violence this season. "Kojak" is finally rele-

gated to reruns. Increasingly violent shows first drew protests from church and civic groups. The past season saw networks involved in cases alleging that their shows had caused child viewers to commit a gang rape and a murder. The the charges were dismissed, but the questions continue and the networks suffered from damaging publicity.

The preferred TV substitute for violence seems to be sex and slapstick comedy. Shows like "Charlie's Angels" fill the new "family hour." Their success spawned many imitators featuring nubile stewardesses, roommates and dancers. The new season also offers the unwary an assortment of "Gong Show" type programs. The idea seems to be to mix talent shows, beauty contests and pie throwing matches. The format is old, very old. It is credited with killing vaudeville.

Documentaries get barely a mention in the network promotion for the new viewer season. In fact, Bill Moyers, the best thing that happened to network documentaries since Edward R. Murrow, has returned to public television.

But even pure entertainment holds far broader possibilities. In its early days, television produced shows like "Playhouse 90," stressing original and challenging dramas that addressed serious subjects. Where are they now? Only occasionally on public broadcasting.

The programers rationalize their idolizing of ratings by maintaining that they are only giving the viewers what they want. Perhaps, but we think they are also dictating tastes. For a change, couldn't they set their sights higher instead of lower?

The Idaho STATESMAN

Boise, Idaho, September II, 1977

The ABC television network news organization has stooped to a new low in the selling of news. If continued, such practices will seriously jeopardize the integrity of television journalism.

The incident involved a Barbara Walters interview with Watergate conspirator G. Gordon Liddy broadcast Thursday evening.

Late in the evening, ABC cut in on programming with an ABC News special program, complete with logo, theme music, the works. A network correspondent introduced Walters, and viewers saw a one- or two-minute edited version of the Liddy interview.

The correspondent then announced that the full interview with Liddy would not be broadcast then — it would be upcoming in one-half hour, so stay tuned. The camera cut to the logo and theme, and we were back to regularly scheduled programming.

This two- or three-minute show was not a special news program as billed. It was pure hype, and that is sad, because American viewers have come to recognize the network news special logos as a signal that something important is about to come across the tube. Their attention captured, the network in this case proceeded to plug a show coming later.

All the networks promote their news programs; there is nothing wrong with that. But the ads normally are clearly identifiable as such. ABC could have done that with its Liddy promo. But to deliberately mislead the viewers to think they are going to get news and give them an ad is unconscionable. True, the boundary between show biz and news is tenuous at best in television, but it is there. Seldom has it been so grossly violated as in the Liddy episode.

Walters' interview with Liddy was intriguing. It was excellent journalism. Unfortunately, the network detracted from the interview itself in its rush to make a sales pitch.

THE PLAIN DEALER

Cleveland, Ohio, March 23, 1976

Plain Dealer television editor William Hickey suggested in a recent column that viewers are saturated with television news and documentaries.

A national study reported that the amount of such programming and the amount of money budgeted for network news operations have declined. The study placed the beginning of the downtrend at a point in time shortly after the resignation of Richard Nixon in August 1974.

If the trend is accurately reported, it is not a surprising development since the volume of news produced by Watergate and its aftermath was a once-in-a-lifetime phenomenon.

It should also be remembered, as Hickey pointed out in writing about the resignation last month of Av Westin, ABC News vice president, that at least some of the cutbacks, according to network officials, were temporary in order to free funds to be spent on coverage of this year's presidential primaries and the November election.

There is no particular reason to insist, or even to expect, that television journalism, which includes regular news programs, special reports and documentaries, should be an ever-expanding portion of total television programming. It is more reasonable to anticipate that broadcast journalism, having established a plateau in terms of

viewer response, will be somewhat variable in volume, according to the demands of events and issues, which also affect the public appetite for news programming.

The commercial television networks in the United States, after all, are private enterprises, though indirectly subject to federal regulation through licensing of channels. It would be foolish to insist that the profits from their entertainment shows be plowed back into unprofitable and unwatched news operations.

Sander Vanocur in several Plain Dealer columns has described enthusiastically the workings of the Japanese Broadcasting Corp., which operates two channels, general and educational, in competition with four commercial networks. The government broadcasting organization is funded through license fees paid by users of television sets, but it is set up as a private corporation and is free from government interference.

Vanocur's high opinion notwithstanding, such a system probably would not be popular in the United States for, as Vanocur notes, its programming is conservative.

The U.S. system of independent local public television stations, cooperating through a national umbrella organization, funded by a combination of private and public contributions, is far more suited to the many diversities of this country.

The Charleston Gazette

Charleston, W.Va., October 26, 1977

In the infancy of television news, commentators wore simple, deadpan faces when they reported the events of the day.

A new technique was developed. News, weather, and sports reporters began to talk to each other about trivial matters and viewers were subjected to much contrived banter.

The popularity of David Brinkley then sent news announcers to their mirrors where, presumably, they practiced the "wry" appearance and mannerisms for which Brinkley was celebrated.

In the Charleston viewing area, we have a plethora of banter among news reporters, who sometimes seem to be practicing a vaudeville act, and the inside jokes are becoming a bore.

We can also do without what we can only describe as wry-run-wild. We're talking about the fellow who greets us and bids us adieu with a practiced wink.

It's embarrassing. Will somebody ask him to stop?

Why can't we have another go at simple, deadpan reporting of the news? Walter Cronkite, the acknowledged master, doesn't wink at us.

THE MILWAUKEE JOURNAL

Milwaukee, Wisc., December 27, 1976

Walter Cronkite, America's favorite father figure, was right when he complained in a recent speech about broadcasters tending to "hypercompress the news." And one of Cronkite's remedies is worth exploring — one hour network newscasts to permit greater depth in reporting.

However, Cronkite's plea is weakened by how networks use time already available. As Tom Griffith, the media critic for Time magazine, fairly notes: "Their newscasts regularly sag, at about the two-thirds mark, into some forgettable feature."

Griffith blames that on the networks' "obsession with pace, variety and the eye appeal of film."

All of which brings to mind the MacNeil/Lehrer Report — public television's interesting experiment each weeknight with a half hour devoted to one major story. It is a supplement rather than a replacement for the brief network reports, and thus is not a wholly applicable model for reform. However, the program does illustrate how informative TV journalism can be when the folks in charge, as Griffith says, "have the courage to be serious."

Roanoke Times & World-News

Roanoke, Va., November II, 1977

People complain sometimes that they are inundated with information, but indications are that most Americans prefer to remain plugged in to what's going on. On any given day, the average person may get some news from listening to the radio, watching television or reading a newspaper—all three.

The big argument concerns where Mr. or Ms. Average gets most of his or her news. The Elmo Roper opinion survey has contended that two-thirds of the American public gets most of its news from TV.

This has lately been disputed by two different sources. Robert L. Stevenson, an assistant professor at the University of North Carolina School of Journalism, and Kathryn P. White, a graduate student, have written a report that indicates people get their news from a variety of sources. Only one-third of the public, they say, depends on TV, and less than one adult in four watches a televised evening news program. But nine of 10 read a newspaper.

Some of their findings may be criticized as dated, since one source was a 1969 government report. But an extensive survey taken in March of this year supports their conclusions.

The March survey involved 3,000

people at 200 sampling points across the country. It was conducted by the Newspaper Readership Council, an organization of 16 major national newspaper organizations. You may wish to take that fact into account in interpreting its findings. Essentially, these were that 69 percent of those interviewed read newspapers as a source of news on any given day—more than the number who got news from radio, TV or news magazines. Other statistics from the same survey put newspapers out front as a news source; 91 percent said they read newspapers at some time or other.

This is not to denigrate the role that radio and TV play in news coverage; radio has immediacy and TV dramatic impact. But no less a TV-radio personage than Walter Cronkite of CBS has said that if people depended on electronic media for all their news, they'd have a very inadequate picture of what's going on.

For variety and comprehensiveness, the printed page ranks first in conveying information—what the citizen must have to make intelligent decisions. The fact that Americans still read a good deal is welcome news not only to publishers but also to educators and anyone else concerned about the viability and vigor of our society.

The Chattanooga Times

Chattanooga, Tenn., June 30, 1976

There is widespread talk in the television industry, particularly among the three major networks, about increasing the length of the early-evening newscasts from 30 minutes to an hour each night.

Not surprisingly, the affiliate stations are opposed, because the extra half-hour would encroach on their profitable hour before prime time, when low-budget syndicated programs are broadcast and sponsored locally.

Now Donald H. McGannon, president and chairman of the Westinghouse Broadcasting Co., has a suggestion that the networks schedule a nightly program of news analysis and commentary at 9 o'clock, the peak of the prime time hours. Mr. McGannon, whose chain has two stations affiliated with NBC, two with CBS and one with ABC, told NBC affiliates and network representatives that "it is difficult to accept a schedule that is more than 50 per cent crime, violence and 'adult content' in the face of rising youth crime, venereal disease and alcoholism."

The reaction of his audience — he has made the same proposal to CBS and ABC — is not known. But given the enormous profit factor in network prime time programming, we expect to see such shows on a regular basis when the sun begins to rise in the west.

The Providence Journal

Providence, R.I., June 27, 1976

American network television, entered upon middle age and rather firmly set in its ways, continues to be the target for waves of would-be reformers. Two interesting proposals to alter networks' handling of program material emerged recently at the annual meeting of NBC's affiliate stations, and both deal with public affairs broadcasting.

One change, suggested by the Westinghouse Broadcasting Company president, asks the networks to schedule a regular program of news analysis and commentary nightly at 9 p.m., in the heart of the prime time period now largely given over to entertainment programs. This idea, which challenges the networks' pending plan to increase their early-evening news programs from 30 minutes to a full hour, has a strong initial appeal.

This plan would keep the networks from eating into local stations' news programming, or producing a 90-minute nightly news conglomeration that might prove almost undigestible. Moreover, a prime-time public affairs program would offer a healthy antidote to the bulk of routine evening programming which, as the Westinghouse official said, is "more than 50 percent crime, violence and 'adult content.'" Whether the networks would agree to such a drastic innovation remains doubtful, but the idea deserves examination.

The other proposal relates to advertising by political candidates. The president of NBC noted that this year's crop of presidential contenders had to scramble — often unsuccessfully — to place their five-minute or 30-minute programs. To remedy this, he suggests that networks set up a reserve pool of such time slots that candidates can buy well in advance.

The NBC president, Herbert S. Schlosser, said that such a system could avoid the confusion of the recent primary season, when networks found it difficult, impossible (or perhaps only inconvenient) to meet requests for paid air time. Some late requests would have to be dealt with as they arose, he said, but a pre-planned block of political slots available for purchase by candidates, and shared equally by all three major networks, could eliminate most of the problem.

This idea, too, seems worth close examination. The primary system is chaotic enough without candidates having to deal with networks on an emergency basis. For better or worse, political advertising on TV is with us to stay, and the networks might try to accommodate future candidates in ways that provide fair and equal access in an organized fashion.

St. Louis Review

St. Louis, Mo., November 18, 1976

Writing in the Columbia Journalism Review, Richard Townley, news director of WCMH-TV in Columbus, Ohio, makes a very interesting suggestion.

Mr. Townley suggests that the network newscast has become a relic whose prime time has passed. Networks have assumed a control over the news impossible to any printed news organ because the whole package of the network news is sent to the local station to be used in toto, with no possibility of local editing, despite the fact that under FCC rules it is the local station, not the network, that has ultimate responsibility for the material presented to the public. Mr. Townley suggests that the network should provide individual segments of news reports that the local station would assemble for broadcast, much like metropolitan newspapers are provided with national and international news by news agencies to be used or not used at the discretion of the individual paper.

We think the idea has merit, and we go even further. Affiliation with a network should not bind a local station to use that network's news. Rather the networks would become news producers like the Associated Press and United Press International and compete to sell their product to participating stations.

The value of this suggestion is that the monopoly on news exercised by a few people at the network level would effectively be broken. The local news editor would be free to choose among competing reports of the same events, much as a newspaper editor does. The local station would thereby be able to use the news reports best suited for its own market, and very quickly patterns of usage of material would give the viewer real power over the content of daily news reports.

New news gathering agencies could also be expected to enter the field, with better media access for the less-well-organized people and movements. After all, it was a small, independent news service that broke the My Lai story.

Networks might be expected to fight tooth and nail against any attempt to touch the mighty revenue-producing power of network news, and so any change in this direction would have to be mandated by the FCC. Recent Supreme Court decisions opposing monopolistic practices in news dissemination show that the courts might look favorably on such a proposal.

Too much news — especially television news — is smoothly packaged pap. The difficulty with television's dealing with hard news or, even more importantly, with backgrounders and explanatory pieces has been frequently commented upon. By opening up the source of news and giving choice to the local news director, the content of news programs could show marked improvement. And if it didn't, the viewer would have the right to complain to local people, not to a far-away and unresponsive multi-million dollar conglomerate.

—Msgr. Edward J. O'Donnell

The Hartford Courant

Hartford, Conn., March 9, 1976

ST. LOUIS POST-DISPATCH

St. Louis, Mo., March 22, 1976

After weathering the Watergate trauma, during which then President Nixon accused them of "outrageous, vicious, distorted" reporting, the television networks emerged with a brighter public image. A feared public backlash, perhaps engendered by Mr. Nixon's attacks, did not materialize. Basking in their medium's enhanced aura, network presidents and local broadcasters pledged to increase their commitment to news coverage and especially to investigative reporting.

A report by the Alfred I. duPont-Columbia University Survey of Broadcast Journalism has just concluded, however, that, instead of increasing their commitment to news, the networks have actually slacked off. All three commercial networks, and the Public Broadcasting Network as well, have, according to the survey, cut back in one way or another on their efforts in public affairs broadcasting.

One news director summed up the situation succinctly when he told the survey: "The amount of talent currently available for journalism is staggering, and the amount of serious journalism resulting from the time and money spent is appalling." Mr. Nixon, although no longer in office, seems to have gotten what he wanted from television—reduced or bland coverage of public affairs.

According to a just published survey of television news coverage none of the three major networks nor public TV has made an "increased commitment to serious news and public affairs" despite Watergate's proof of the privilege and power possessed by broadcast journalism. The current issue of Columbia Journalism Review summarizes the joint Alfred I. duPont-Columbia University study of more than 350 news directors and duPont-Columbia correspondents canvassed between the summer of 1974 and the fall of 1975. The failure of the broadcasters to follow through the initially excellent coverage of Watergate is the public's loss.

The current lack of in-depth news could have been predicted long ago. For even while Watergate was a timely and yet unfinished matter, the commercial networks rotated live coverage, which soon dwindled and disappeared from sight. Only public TV maintained continuous programming both of the Senate and House Watergate Committees.

The report said Watergate served to remind networks and stations of their duty to arouse the public and to move government. But they did nothing "with this prodigious privilege and power", the findings note. Instead, in some cases news staffs were increased during the study period for the purpose of "popularizing the news rather than improving coverage." Money went for small, portable cameras and other equipment to provide remote broadcasts. A broadcaster was quoted as wondering if such expenditures are not only a promotional excuse "to cover the superficial", since nothing is spent for investigative reporters.

Some of the viewing public may have guessed the true state of affairs without being told by a survey that too many news programs these days lean more heavily on an entertaining team, usually an "anchor newsman," sportscaster and a weatherman, than on good news coverage. Drama often seems to be the criterion for a story's inclusion rather than the importance of an event's effects on the public in general.

The minicamera can pick and choose and therefore slant what is happening while molding viewers' opinions of the occurrence by juxtaposing one incident upon another. In fairness, that may be a peculiar problem of the medium. But careful editing by a well-trained journalist could bring the portrayal of truth rather than fiction to the film. At the same time, commentary could explain what the picture cannot show. Instead, valuable minutes are wasted on jovial banter among team members.

What is most disconcerting is that the public remained firmly in favor of solid news even when a backlash against newscasters was feared after so much programming had been used for Watergate coverage. The survey shows that while prime time TV shows sagged six per cent, news shows maintained their ratings.

Unless broadcasters decide to get serious about the news, viewers will have to live with "30-second stories on extremely complex situations," among other trivialities as a Springfield newscaster complained to the surveyers. So much talent, time and money is going to waste that it is "staggering" and "appalling," he said. Too bad that TV has an important role to play but prefers instead to play around.

Arkansas Gazette.

Little Rock, Ark., September 27, 1978

We are of rather mixed feelings about a speech addressed to the annual meeting of the Radio and Television News Directors at Atlanta last week by Richard Salant, president of CBS News, in which Salant said that the news media should provide news on the basis of what its editors think is important rather than thinking first in terms of likely audience appeal.

"Our strong and distinct tilt must be toward that which is important rather than toward what people want, what they find interesting, what will attract the greatest possible numbers of them," he said, adding that "with the tide at the moment flowing against us and our freedoms, we must be worried about how the people and government — including the courts — perceive us." No argument there, not, certainly as an ideal, and even as more of a practicably realizable ideal than too many people in the news business sometimes realize.

And, "if they perceive us as concerned only with numbers — numbers of people and numbers of dollars — only as a business satisfying the vagrant wants and interests of an audience, we shall remain in trouble."

All true, too. But we would add the proviso here that one of the principal times the press generally is in the most

trouble with the public and the courts, especially, is when it is trying its hardest to *be* important, as in the jailing of investigative reporters, for example, and the fairly astonishing degree of expressed public support for the jailing of all reporters, or at least any who report something disagreeable to them.

Part of the problem here is in the catch-all term "news media", though, since Salant was addressing the broadcasters from a position within the industry, we probably can safely assume that he had TV and radio news uppermost in mind.

The print medium and the broadcasting medium have the First Amendment guarantees in common, and if either regards the other's rights of freedom to publish (air) as being of no moment, then in the end the two will most assuredly hang separately; which is to say, both will hang but with one going before the other.

Richard Salant has been one of the foremost tigers of his industry in opposing any encroachment upon the rights of either news form, and has been right up there in the forefront in the fight against censorship of TV entertainment shows as well as of news shows, especially, since TV, after all, is his medium.

But the two media *are* different, and

not only because radio-TV is under regulation by the Federal Communications Commission. In many ways TV has a larger built-in problem in meeting the CBS executive's standards than do the newspapers, since so much of TV broadcasting — the great majority of it, in fact — *is* entertainment, most of it entertainment that could and should be cast in far more serious or "important" terms than it is, but that, if it were, would be entertainment still.

There is a more-or-less natural lapover into news broadcasts, then, a handicap that the best of the network and local newscasters are aware of and do everything in their power to resist and draw the viewing public's attention to. Walter Cronkite, for example, has said many times that about the best the TV news can do is give the "headlines", with the body of the news still being supplied by the print medium. One trouble is that too many people do not recognize the limitations of TV news or care very much. For some of these, it possibly is enough to ask them to try to realize when the entertainment is supposed to stop for awhile and the news begin. Worse, many announcers in local situations seem to be confused about this themselves, which is, of course, one of the things that Mr. Salant was driving at in his Atlanta speech.

The News  American

Baltimore, Md., April 21, 1977

A BLAST at the nation's information media, including his own — television — was delivered this week at Johns Hopkins University by NBC's John Chancellor.

Mr. Chancellor, the NBC Nightly News co-anchor man, delivering the 11th annual Frank R. Kent memorial lecture in Shriver Hall, said that the papers "and television especially," seem to be concerned increasingly with "more people and gossip, more easy stories — because that's what the public wants."

Mr. Chancellor continued by quoting Walter Lippmann that news "must give a man a picture of the world upon which he can act. By presenting editorial junk food because it's popular, we're abdicating our presentation of significant news, and we're in danger of losing a precious, indispensible responsibility. It's our job to know what's important, not to drift into a new compact with the reader about what he wants."

This criticism is harsh indeed, and somewhat off the target. Many if not most newspapers, including this one, do present daily serious analytical articles and editorials on complex but vital subjects.

Hard news, indeed, is important, as Mr. Chancellor says. However, many readers — particularly younger readers — also enjoy light material, features, gossip columns, and the like. A newspaper must serve those readers too.

BUFFALO EVENING NEWS

Buffalo, N.Y., April 19, 1977

A survey in last week's U. S. News & World Report contains a fascinating study of power—of "Who Runs America." It is fascinating because it reflects the view of the very people who, you might think, themselves run America— some 1200 "key decision makers in politics, business and the professions."

Their list is headed, of course, by the President—now as always. But whereas last year's No. 2 was Secretary of State Kissinger, the new No. 2 is not a Carter appointee at all, but the holdover, much-respected and hard-to-push-around head of the Federal Reserve, Arthur F. Burns. Then, before any more Carter appointees show up, three more names appear: Chief Justice Burger, as an "ultimate decider"; George Meany for his "intimidating . . . muscle and clout," and Thomas P. O'Neill, "seasoned, effective" House speaker.

Among the top Carter people themselves, the only three in the top 10 are Bert Lance, Cyrus Vance and Michael Blumenthal. Eleven more show up in the next 20, starting with Vice President

Mondale and ending with HEW Secretary Califano. The latter's relatively low ranking is itself interesting, for in another section of the survey, where those polled name the most influential people in their own fields, Califano ranks No. 1 in health and No. 2 in education.

In the top-10 group, the only non-governmental figure besides George Meany is even more of a household name: Walter Cronkite. For a newsman whose only pretensions to power are his fatherly nighttime way of telling you "that's the way it is," such a sense of power must be humbling indeed, if only to his NBC and ABC rivals and his CBS bosses.

Overall, you may be reassured to know, the feeling of a clear majority of those surveyed was that the general caliber of the people who run America today—in government, business and the professions—is "somewhat better" than it was a year ago. Let us hope that will still be the prevailing opinion after the main actors here—the people who are just getting started at running the government—have been at it a little longer.

THE INDIANAPOLIS STAR

Indianapolis, Ind., November 9, 1976

The CBS television network made a shrewd response to a pro-strong-defense organization's charge that the network had virtually blacked out majority viewpoints on basic national security issues.

The American Security Council Education Foundation (ASCEF) filed a Fairness Doctrine complaint before the Federal Communications Commission charging the network with failure to inform the public adequately of Soviet military superiority.

In a reply that rang of "The Star-Spangled Banner" and the scratching of the Founding Fathers' pens on the newly written Constitution, CBS declared:

"This latest attempt to invoke the coercive powers of government to force a special interest group's views on the American people will be resisted fully and completely."

It is probable that there is not an editor or publisher or radio or television news executive or commentator in the nation who would not agree with the justness and correctness of the CBS stand as stated.

In that stand CBS is right.

But in our opinion CBS is, at the same time, falling down on its job of informing its viewers if it is deliberately soft-pedaling the facts about the relative military strengths of the United States and the Soviet Union, or the North Atlantic Treaty Organization and the Warsaw Pact nations.

For better or worse, millions of Americans get all of their "news" from network television, according to various experts on the mass media.

It seems to us that an essential part of the information that must go into the mind of an informed citizen is data, as accurate as the reporter is able to deliver, on the military strength of his country as related to that of its major potential adversaries.

If ASCEF's charge is accurate there are executives at CBS who do not agree. This being a free country, it is their right to disagree. In fact, it is their right to put out a diet of news and commentary that ignores national defense, relative military strength and related matters.

It is also the right of people who want to be well informed, or adequately informed, to turn away from network news shows that — whatever the reason — fail to report on the state of the national security that is the basis of survival and freedom.

THE DAILY OKLAHOMAN
Oklahoma City, Okla., September 9, 1976

THERE is more than meets the eye in the complaint filed with the Federal Communications Commission on Wednesday, charging that CBS News consistently handles national security news in a biased manner.

The complaint was filed by the American Security Council Educational Foundation, in Washington. This is a non-profit but hardly unbiased group of concerned Americans, who think omission of important news is a form of censorship which distorts the meaning of current events. The ASCEF follows the national security news closely. For several years, it has worked to document its feeling that not all the important news finds its way into the evening broadcasts.

In short, its complaint against CBS News, which it says might be applied to some degree against the other networks, is that important national security statements by responsible and prominent experts are consistently ignored, while every press release by a protest group, however minor, is featured as if it were earth-shaking in importance.

Two years ago, the same group published a study of the television treatment of security matters. The report had been compiled by a respected group of scholars, headed by Dr. Ernest Lefever, then of the Brookings Institution. After release of that report, critical of the television networks, Walter Cronkite was

interviewed by Betty Utterback of the Gannett News Service about its findings.

"There are always groups in Washington expressing views of alarm over the state of our defenses," he told her. "We don't carry these stories. The story is that there are those who want to cut defense spending." (The old man-bites-dog standard for what is news.)

In a nutshell, that is exactly what the ASCEF is now complaining about. Television news editors, the foundation charges, black out anything which does not support their own biased point of view on what the people ought to know. The TV cameras, as ASCEF sees it, use only one lens—the one pointed in the direction in which they want people to look. But there is often important news just out of camera range that is not covered.

The editorial decision as to what is news and what is not will never satisfy everyone. Every editor, whether putting out a daily newspaper or a newscast, makes dozens of such decisions daily. The decisions are very subjective.

But there is a fairness doctrine, and it applies not only to broadcasts but to all news coverage. Responsible editing requires that as much of the whole story be told as can be authenticated, and that includes presentation of opposing points of view.

The foundation has handed the FCC a hot potato.

THE COMMERCIAL APPEAL
Memphis, Tenn.,
April 25, 1976

BARBARA WALTERS, that thorny blossom of NBC's Today Show, has sold her chiffon presence to ABC for a reported million dollars a year.

She'll help Harry Reasoner with ABC's evening news. We thought Reasoner was one of the few television newsmen who could do the job without help. But then we don't claim to be experts in television news. You need a background in show business for that.

NBC got out of the bidding because of the "carnival atmosphere and demands unlike a journalist and more like a movie queen."

Miss Walters' success is a victory for Women's Lib, we guess. Maybe it's only a victory for NBC. It's surely not a victory for television news.

THE ATLANTA CONSTITUTION
Atlanta, Ga., April 24, 1976

For NBC's Barbara Walters it was *Today* today, gone tomorrow.

The hostess of the popular morning news and interview program, Miss Walters is moving over to ABC to share with Harry Reasoner the anchor role on the ABC Evening News. She's the first woman to hold such a position on the major network news staffs.

Miss Walters is a probing and sharp interviewer who is respected but not always liked. Her change to a new network and new responsibilities was accompanied by inter-network bickering, mostly about how much money and benefits were involved (*very* much, reports say), and a reported lack of wild enthusiasm on Reasoner's part. Reasoner now says any reservations he had are resolved. A woman as co-anchor, he said, "may well be an idea whose time has come, and, if it is, there is no better candidate." We agree with both sides of that statement.

Rocky Mountain News
Denver, Colo., April 26, 1976

IF THE Equal Rights Amendment finally is ratified, it will be an anticlimax for Barbara Walters. Maybe even a long step backward.

She's already more than merely equal.

The ABC television network is reported to have offered her a cool $1 million a year for five years to switch from NBC, where she is co-host of the morning "Today" show and where her annual income is now only half a million. At ABC, Miss Walter would co-anchor the Evening News with Harry Reasoner.

NBC is known to have counterattacked with an offer matching ABC's in money, but without a pledge to let her co-anchor the Nightly News with John Chancellor.

It seems Miss Walters yearns to make the evening scene as the only network female anchorperson, and she wants to get out of the early morning rat race.

But whichever way she decides to go, she'll be the financial queen bee of the news hive. By comparison, the likes of Reasoner, Chancellor, Walter Cronkite, Eric Sevareid and the rest of the teleprompter set are existing near the poverty level.

At a time when laborers in less glamorous vineyards have grown grudgingly accustomed to the enormous wages paid to Muhammed Ali, professional basketball players, TV private eyes and Hollywood stars of varying degrees of luminosity, Miss Walters' good fortune comes as a welcome change.

Who'd have thought that a no more than reasonably attractive middleaged woman, who speaks with a clattering Manhattan accent and neither sings nor dances, could match it dollar for dollar with Liberace?

We're all for it, and hope Miss Walters thoroughly enjoys the prestige of paying that extra income tax next year.

SAN JOSE NEWS
San Jose, Calif., April 26, 1976

Barbara Walters acceptance of a five-year, $1 million a year contract to join "The Evening News" at ABC exposes television news as the "entertainment" or show biz it frequently is, rather than dedicated news reporting.

No reader of a news teleprompter, male or female, seems worth a million dollars a year. But it creates an amusing possibility of Walter Cronkite, who makes an estimated $400,000 a year, pleading penury.

Oregon Journal
Portland, Ore., April 26, 1976

The decision by the ABC television network to hire Barbara Walters to "co-anchor" the evening news with Harry Reasoner was a victory for show business and a singular defeat for network journalism.

Miss Walters has been employed by NBC as an air "personality" on the Today show since 1963 after beginning as a writer in 1961. Her speciality has been in interviewing other personalities, an activity salted with pitches for pantyhose, dog food and children's toys. The show, which features a separate reading of the news, has been strong on entertainment and big name interviews. It offers a glorious opportunity for politicians, authors, actors and controversial figures who have something to peddle, whether a product or an idea, or as is usually the case, themselves.

ABC took Miss Walters away from NBC for a reported $1 million a year and various valuable fringe benefits. This is considerably more than Scott Mott, a new anchorman at a Florida TV station, is getting. But Mott is only six years old and undoubtedly the $300,000 reported offered the lad will keep him in marbles.

The question of why television does not spend this kind of money in improving its news coverage rarely gets asked. But it is a fair question.

THE INDIANAPOLIS NEWS
Indianapolis, Ind., April 29, 1976

Television's Barbara Walters has jumped ship from NBC to read the nightly news on ABC as the first female (network) co-anchor person.

The shock is still being felt all through TV land, not because of her defection or this feminine first, but because she was hired at a reported salary of $1 million a year. While to the general public such riches are inconceivable, to station managers it signals the start of a salary escalation and a checkbook war for TV talent.

ABC had several options to improve its new ratings and several choices on how to spend $1 million a year. The network could, for example, have hired more than 30 network reporters or about 20 network correspondents. It could have improved broadcast content or invested in new equipment, but it chose Barbara.

All of which supports the theory that in network journalism it's not what you say, it's the way that you say it. In its mad quest for Nielsen points, network news is trading more and more upon personality.

In which case, Barbara was a bargain. Johnny Carson is paid $3.2 million plus 15 weeks vacation yearly; Charles Bronson commands $2 million a movie and Liz Taylor asks for $1 million per picture.

Barbara's salary is also not so outrageous when one considers the profits. The calculations are that if she boosts the news rating by even one point on the Nielsen chart, that will translate into about $2 million in corporate profit. In light of such reasoning, Elizabeth Taylor might have been more worth the money.

The Dallas Morning News

Dallas, Tex., April 27, 1976

That arrangement which will bring anchorperson Barbara Walters from NBC to ABC is reportedly a million-dollar-a-year deal. And Miss Walter's salary contract is said to cover five years.

The network news chiefs were interviewed as to whether the stars of network news are really worth that kind of money. In essence, their answers boiled down to the conclusion that the value of the news' network celebrities is set by the market, period. In other words, a TV newsman is worth what the market will bear, what an employer is willing to pay.

That makes sense to conservatives. Indeed that sort of philosophy of a freely competitive market is at the core of conservatism.

The irony of it all is that no job field in America, with the possible exception of college teaching, is so dominated by advocates of the planned, controlled economy. Nor is any other sector of American society so effective in molding others' opinion to favor liberalism's solutions.

It is interesting that despite all we've been hearing from network commentators about the greed and callousness of business, the social injustice of windfall profits and so on, we've yet to hear a newscast or commentary that attempts to build public fervor for wage controls for television networks or salary ceilings for anchorpersons.

They may be for government-run economics for the rest of us, but so far as their own economics are concerned, it's laissez faire all the way—laissez faire, as you may remember, is French for "take the money and run."

THE MILWAUKEE JOURNAL

Milwaukee, Wisc., April 27, 1976

Barbara Walters has pulled off one of the great salary coups of the year — a $5 million contract with ABC to leave NBC and co-anchor ABC's evening news. That's a lot of moola to recite the highlights of the day's happenings, from whatever angle you view it.

What follows is going to sound like sour grapes. Maybe it is. There are a lot of people in the news industry who feel the equal of Barbara, even Harry Reasoner, but don't see that equality on payday. And who is going to fault Barbara if some chump corporation is willing to fork out that kind of cash for her professional reading talents? Isn't that what the free enterprise system is all about?

But there is something about the star system and its exorbitantly high remuneration that rankles, whether it is in TV, the movies, professional sports, or wherever. Can any one individual's talents really be worth that kind of dough? Don't pay scales of that magnitude distort values beyond reason? In the end, doesn't it all come out of the hide of the consumer who pays the freight by buying the product from the company that does the advertising on ABC that charges rates that bring a return high enough to cover costs — including Barbara — and make a profit?

While the public mulls over that one, we'll go home, sip our cocktail in front of the tube, watch Barb perform, and dream of the day when talent is universally recognized.

The Seattle Times

Seattle, Wash., May 6, 1976

CONSCIENTIOUS television journalists have fought a rear-guard action for years against the TV industry's rule of thumb that the number of people watching a program is far more significant than the program's content, even news and public-affairs offerings.

That battle's final encounter may have been fought — and lost — with the American Broadcasting Co.'s decision to pay a celebrity salary of $1 million a year, along with providing such amenities as a full-time hairdresser and a chauffeured limousine, to Barbara Walters, who built a substantial following as hostess of a morning news-and-interview program on the National Broadcasting Co. network.

No one is faulting Ms. Walters' credentials to become a principal news announcer on the A.B.C. evening news programs. But the size of the salary (predicated on the assumption that she will enlarge the networks' audience, and thereby raise its advertising revenues by millions of dollars) may set a precedent that the competition cannot ignore.

If the A.B.C. adventure succeeds financially, network news people of the future will be measured more by their potential as show-business personalities, capable of attracting millions of viewers, than on their skills as reporters and editors.

That trend already is evident at many local stations in the country, where economics-minded managers have hired consultants for advice less on how news is edited and reported, and more on how it is presented and by whom.

Thus, network news personnel have reason to be disturbed by the Walters affair. One veteran editor remarked that some network's advertising moguls now may try to add Cher to the evening news line-up.

Worse, he was only half kidding.

The Washington Star

Washington, D.C., April 25, 1976

ABC has a superstar. Barbara Walters will become not only the first woman to anchor a major network newscast but the highest paid performer in electronic journalism when she waves farewell to NBC.

The gender breakthrough will be viewed as significant by Ms. Walters's sisters who have had to scuffle to gain professional footholds, and we are pleased on that count.

There are elements of the transaction, however, that give one pause. As Bernie Harrison, reeling under news of the $1 million salary a year for five years and fringes, asked in *The Star*: "Is Barbara worth it? Is any news personality worth it?" Some of the guys, such as Ms. Walters's new partner, Harry Reasoner, draw paltry salaries, by some grotesque relativity; Mr. Reasoner has to get by on $400,000 per annum.

Consider the function for which such astronomical salaries are felt to be appropriate. We have seen various figures — 65 to 80 per cent — of the proportion of the population that relies primarily on television for its news. A significant part of the attraction seems to revolve around anchormen — make that anchorpersons. The Walter Cronkites and John Chancellors have become the household deities of a nation, this notion has it. A study done for ABC News showed that the three networks were about equal in newsgathering abilities — a major difference was the appeal of the personality anchoring the show.

There is a worrisome form-versus-substance question here. There are solid reporters on television and there are stories to which TV indisputably brings a unique dimension. But for much of the news — bread-and-butter coverage — the tube is sinfully superficial.

Ms. Walters, we gather, prefers to regard herself as a journalist. Which is fine — but why does news of a reporter changing jobs merit front-page stories in major newspapers and precious minutes of network time?

The "media celebrity" is still a rather fresh phenomenon, and it is both interesting and disturbing that the growth of the reporter as personality has coincided with increasing distrust of the news trade. Do you suppose there is a connection?

Even if there is, we trust Ms. Walters will enjoy her new job which reportedly comes with a personal hairdresser, public relations agent and limousine. That's the news biz — tubenewsbiz.

The Evening Bulletin

Philadelphia, Pa., May 5, 1976

The Barbara Walters flap continues, in the press, on the airwaves, in private conversations. Ms. Walters, at 43, with a background as an interviewer and writer on NBC's Today Show this fall will become not only the first woman to anchor the evening news, but also, at $1 million-a-year, the highest paid person in television news history.

Many of you have written that neither Ms. Walters nor any other person is worth $1 million-a-year. That's five times the salary of the President and some 80 times the salary of the average working American male. Others have written that you simply don't think Ms. Walters, with her aggressive interview style and her unusual voice, deserves either the money or the job. Still others suggest the controversy is a controversy only because Ms. Walters is not Mr. Walters.

We're interested in your reactions to this.

But we're also interested in what you think on related aspects of the question. Is salary, for instance, the real question? Is Ms. Walters the real issue? ABC television made the decisions, both to hire Ms. Walters and to pay her more dollars than any other newsman or woman in television. What do these decisions say about ABC? About all television networks?

Is ABC treating its evening news as a vital public service, or is it merely treating it as a vehicle for selling advertising? Is ABC interested in content and quality, or ratings and packaging?

Will ABC's decision affect the way you perceive network television news?

You, the public, own the airwaves over which television networks broadcast. In return for the use of the airwaves television interests are required to plow back some funds in public service programming. Should your watchdog, the Federal Communications Commission, have intervened in a decision such as this?

DAYTON DAILY NEWS

Dayton, Ohio, April 28, 1976

After show biz, news biz. Not only is Barbara Walters going to pocket, or enpurse, a million green ones a year. She is going to get these riches for doing a job that at last will let her sleep late.

Unless you've been bivouacked in your fallout shelter for the last two weeks, you know Miss Walters is defecting from NBC's *Today* show to become the co-anchorperson of ABC's evening news. She is thus instantly a higher paid journalist than even Woodstein, and without any of the hassle they went through.

Or pseudo-journalist. Television has created this promising new field. The other network anchorpersons have scratched their way to their positions story by story, as working journalists, but they are clearly a doomed breed.

Miss Walters comes aboard primarily as a TV personality, an intelligent and informed one to be sure but without the fire-engine-chasing and councilman-confronting background that holdout romantics in journalism still feel is somehow relevant to the job of presenting the news, in whatever medium.

A trend that began among their affiliates has bubbled up to the networks. Local stations originally relied on professional journalists who might communicate, if only by expression or tone of voice, some hint of the appalling implications of what they were reporting. But the stations long ago began to catch on that they were as well off, probably better off, having the news read by some beautiful smoothie whose handsome, caring presence takes the burrs and spikes off what he is saying.

Miss Walters is a pioneer all right, but not only because she will be the first female network anchorperson. Just as likely — although unwittingly — her example will be misused as the model for the first network news stewardess. Expect more, to make your brief flight through the real world, from sitcom to sitcom, as pleasant as possible.

WORCESTER TELEGRAM

Worcester, Mass., May 2, 1976

Even television viewers who find the "Today" show's Barbara Walters too haughty for their taste will have to concede that now she has something to be haughty about.

ABC has hired her away from NBC at a salary of $1 million a year to co-anchor the ABC evening news show. By some accounts, Harry Reasoner, who now anchors the show all by himself, earns only $400,000 a year. By other accounts he earns somewhat less, and his, Walter Cronkite's and John Chancellor's salaries all rolled together don't add up to $1 million.

Miss Walters will apparently be earning the biggest salary ever paid a journalist. Some have earned more in a year from salary plus book sales, movie rights and lecture fees, but Miss Walters will apparently receive her $1 million just by reading us half the news we can read for ourselves in greater detail in the morning newspaper.

For the record, The New York Times did a hasty survey the other day to find out who else in America gets paid $1 million a year. As might be expected, it turned up a number of movie stars like Robert Redford, James Caan and Jack Nicholson who are getting more than that for only a few weeks of work. TV's Johnny Carson is paid $3 million a year. And a few sports figures like pitcher Catfish Hunter and soccer star Pele get big salaries.

But, surprisingly, the Times could not find a single corporate executive in all of American industry who earns $1 million in salary, though many no doubt make much more through stock options, expense accounts, life insurance and other fringe benefits. And a few have made more in their first year in new jobs through up-front bonuses.

The highest straight corporate salary the Times was able to report was the $766,085 paid the chairman of International Telephone & Telegraph Corp. The chairman of Gulf & Western Industries, Inc., got second prize in the Times survey, a $588,560 salary. The top men at General Motors Corp. and at several other multinational industries are paid just over a half million.

Whether Miss Walters is really worth twice the pay of the chairman of General Motors is not really at issue. She is a public personality, a star, a "property," a drawing card — and he is not. Her $1 million salary is an indication of how the news business on TV has become also a form of show business.

We can hardly wait to find out what ABC will rechristen "The ABC News With Harry Reasoner." Perhaps "BARBARA WALTERS and the ABC News, with harry reasoner."

Oregon *Journal*

Portland, Ore., May 8, 1976

The public mind may have boggled at the salaries demanded and frequently paid to the superstars of the sports fields and arenas.

Now, there is a new and somewhat different mind-boggling event: The signing by American Broadcasting Co. of Barbara Walters as co-broadcaster with Harry Reasoner of the network's evening news show at $1 million a year for five years.

While the public may have been numbed by reports of the salaries paid to sports stars, this new block-buster has a different cast.

Professional sports stars have always been performers in what is strictly public entertainment or "show-biz."

Television networks have always attempted to attach at least the semblance of news reporting and commentary to their news telecasts.

Barbara Walters gained public popularity which won her the $1 million contract as co-host of National Broadcasting Co.'s "Today" show.

In this show, as in her other television endeavors, she won her fame primarily as an interviewer of celebrities, not as a reporter, news gatherer or writer.

While her interviews were good as well as entertaining, what she really sold was her personality and her television image.

To ask whether she is "worth it" is really beside the point. A single point increase in audience rating could mean as much as $2.7 million a year in advertising revenue for the network. Thus from the dollars and cents standpoint, she is at least worth the gamble.

The real question is whether, in opting for a celebrity rather than a seasoned reporter like Walter Cronkite or expansion of solid news coverage, ABC is leading a parade completely to transform television news reporting to "show-biz?"

One need look no farther than The Journal's newsroom for proof that women can be top-flight reporters and editors.

So, the question is neither Ms. Walter's sex nor her paycheck.

But with so many citizens getting their "news" via television, the public should be alert to determine whether it is getting news or show-biz.

THE ARIZONA REPUBLIC

Phoenix, Ariz., October 11, 1976

When ABC offered Barbara Walters $1 million a year on a five-year contract to become network television's first evening anchorwoman, the general reaction in news rooms across the nation was to consider it a personal affront.

How could anyone be worth that kind of money, especially someone whose job basically consists of reading what someone else has written?

ABC knew what it was doing; in fact, it now appears that Miss Walters may be worth even more than $1 million.

Until she joined Harry Reasoner on the ABC Evening News last week, the newscast's audience was trailing NBC's by 7 points and CBS's by 10 points in the Nielsen ratings.

That night, ABC had 31 per cent of the viewing audience in New York, compared to 16 per cent for CBS and 14 per cent for NBC.

In Chicago, Miss Walters' appearance gave ABC 36 per cent of the viewing audience to CBS's 8 per cent and NBC's 7 per cent.

In Los Angeles, ABC beat its rivals by more than 2 to 1.

Of course, most of those who switched to ABC from CBS and NBC did so out of curiosity and will soon return to CBS's Walter Cronkite and NBC's John Chancellor.

But some won't.

How many, no one can say, but if Miss Walter's can raise the Nielsen rating of the ABC Evening News by just one point, that will bring the network an extra $2 million in advertising revenue. Two points: $4 million. Three points: $6 million.

Miss Walters will more than earn her salary.

What those who thought paying Miss Walters $1 million forgot is that television news is designed as a form of entertainment. Says former ABC News vice president Av Westin: "Television is show business and thus TV news is part of show business."

Salaries in television, therefore, cannot properly be compared with salaries in the news business. The only valid comparison is with what Hollywood stars like Sofia Loren and Paul Newman make.

Unfortunately, while those who produce TV news programs realize it's part of show business, those who view them don't. They really believe that what they're getting is news, presented vividly and dramatically, but news.

They're suffering from a dangerous delusion.

The Virginian-Pilot

Norfolk, Va., April 25, 1976

"So far as I know," dramatist Moss Hart wrote in "Act One," his memoir of the theater, "anything worth hearing is not usually uttered at seven o'clock in the morning: and if it is, it will generally be repeated at a more reasonable hour for a larger and more wakeful audience."

Well, yes.

And so Barbara Walters is leaving NBC's "Today" show to become co-anchorperson with Harry Reasoner on the ABC evening newscast.

Miss Walters will be paid the princessly sum of $1 million per year for five years, according to network sources. That will make her the highest-paid newsperson on television. Even Walter Cronkite, the CBS father figure who's been making the world go round for years, isn't feeding on such hay.

Assuming Miss Walters appears on camera for 10 minutes each night, five nights per week, 50 weeks per year, she will be earning $400 each and every minute she is on the tube. Figuring it a second way, she will be getting a million bucks for the sum total of 41 2/3 hours of on-screen work. Only basketball players, movie stars, and rock singers are paid that kind of money.

"They made me an offer I couldn't refuse," said Miss Walters, who had been the mainstay of "Today" for 12 years. Reportedly she was making more than $500,000 per year at NBC. Commenting on her departure, Richard C. Wald, president of NBC News, said tongue-in-cheek, "I wish her all moderate success."

Hiring away Miss Walters is a competitive coup for ABC, which has been gaining in the ratings at the expense of NBC. And who knows? Maybe Miss Walters will bring us better news than we've been getting lately.

The Detroit News
Detroit, Mich., March 11, 1978

You will remember that not long ago Burt Lance, the President's friend who knew (and perhaps turned) Georgia banking inside out, did not brood for long after resigning under fire from his job as director of the Office of Management and Budget. He soon took a job as a television commentator in Atlanta.

And long before Lance brought his special talents to the tube, John Lindsay, the man many people credit with speeding New York City into insolvency during his time as mayor, became — and still is — an occasional television host.

Now, following in that great tradition, is Abraham Beame, another former New York mayor who, during his years as the city's chief accountant, managed the books in such a way that a lot of banks and private investors were long kept unaware that the city was prodigiously deep in hock. Beame has signed on as an urban-affairs consultant with a Manhattan TV station and will go on the air from time to time to comment on municipal problems.

Is this then where the future of television lies —

in regular appearances by failed public officials who will instruct the American people on matters great and small?

If so, forgive us a wince. We understand that TV stations have a lot of time to fill but, for ourselves, we would prefer that persons like Lance, Lindsay and Beame retire to the obscurity they have so thoroughly earned.

And if that leaves station managers scrambling around for old faces, well, we'll take a little more Bogey anytime.

DAYTON DAILY NEWS
Dayton, Ohio, February 10, 1977

The "star" sickness that infects national TV news has reached a new virulence with NBC's hiring of former President Gerald Ford to help develop what the network calls "programs that will be valuable to the American public."

It is hard to see how the arrangement will do that. It would be one thing to interview Mr. Ford, as a man with an intimate knowledge, supposedly, of the federal government and of the issues that arose while he was in office. That's been done before, and is usually interesting to watch even if it is self-serving for the former president being interviewed.

But Mr. Ford is not just to be interviewed; he is reportedly being paid millions of dollars to help NBC in some unspecified capacity. He has no special knowledge of journalism, no brightly-burning intellect, no unusual insights that anyone knows about. It is not

clear what he could contribute to NBC besides his prestige. Apparently that is what NBC is most interested in.

Columnist Sander Vanocur wonders rightfully what effect this funny arrangement might have on the objectivity of the NBC news department, or at least on the public's impression of NBC's objectivity.

There is also the question of whether NBC ought to be in the business of paying a politician millions of dollars and giving him priceless TV exposure when he may well decide to run for the presidency again, as Mr. Ford has said he may.

Apparently none of this bothers the NBC brass. Business is business. Ratings are ratings. Barbara Walters, Farrah Fawcett-Majors, Gerald Ford. Stars all.

The Evening Gazette
Worcester, Mass., February 11, 1978

Television has a new commentator with a household name and interesting background. He's Bert Lance: banker, politician, former director of the federal budget, White House insider and a friend of President Carter. Eric Sevareid had only a raspy voice and the friendly support of Edward R. Murrow when he started.

Lance made his debut the other night with an Atlanta television station, complete with messages from Carter, Jody Powell, Hamilton Jordan and others who still regard him as a hero unjustly maligned by the media.

It may be too early to assess his journalistic ability. But the station that employs Lance has a reputation for innovations in trying to boost its ratings. (One competitor suggested that the station should have hired Elizabeth Ray instead of Lance).

Lance's estimated annual salary of $60,000 — for three or five 90-second spots a week, depending on how well they go over — is only peanuts for a man whose debts are counted in the millions. There is speculation

that he took the job to enlarge his already sizable public profile and rejuvenate his political career.

Lance's venture into broadcasting is about as unusual as his other ventures. He is still under a federal grand jury investigation for possible banking irregularities. He works for a federally regulated company, owned by Combined Communications Co., while still maintaining close ties with the administration. His anchorman is a former kiddy-show host formerly known as "Mr. Pix", who showed cartoons and passed out jelly beans.

Still, Lance thinks he has much to offer. "I think I've gained rapport with the American people," he contends. "They seem to believe I have the couarge to speak out about what I believe and to articulate the issues that are of concern to them these days."

Bert Lance has maintained that most of his troubles have been caused by the unfriendly news media. It may just be that his venture into journalism is his ultimate revenge.

The Washington Star
Washington, D.C., February 20, 1977

Who, we wonder, has bitten off more than will be easily masticated — Henry Kissinger or the National Broadcasting Company? The former secretary of state and global philosopher of power has signed on with NBC for a five-year stint that will insure we not forget what Henry Kissinger looks like. It is not a network public-service initiative — the *New York Times* speculates that Mr. Kissinger's wages may be $1.5 million for the half-decade tour.

Money well spent, no doubt, from NBC's ratings-ragged perspective. You might have noticed as well that the people with the curious logo also signed up Gerald R. Ford for occasional appearances, and have laid out $100 million to the Russians for the privilege of telecasting long jumps and such during the 1980 Olympics.

Well, CBS and ABC didn't get to be the great institutions they are by sitting on their coups. It seems plausible the other two will begin desperately seeking a figure of power who has been toppled or fallen from the saddle to try to jiggle the Kissinger-NBC nexus. There just aren't that many ex-biggies out of work at the moment, however.

But back to Mr. Kissinger. NBC will probably turn him over to their body-and-fender shop to shape him up for the television matrix. "First thing, Hankbaby, we've got to get you down 40, maybe 50, pounds — that bulk will look like 100 extra pounds on camera. The hair and the glasses, of course, just will not do — nothing that can't be handled, a neat pair of aviator frames, a session with Mister Phyllis and you'll be ready to roar. The accent — well, you talk good, Hankbaby, real good, but that *auf Deutsch* is *too* far out — strictly late-movie-Battle-of-the-Bulge stuff. I mean, you could get away with that act in Foggy Bottom, but you're in the major leagues now. How would America react to, 'Und dot's der vay it vuz today'? It just won't go down, man . . ."

Perhaps the network won't fiddle over-much with the Kissinger persona. He is known as a man who likes to have his way and, being the expensive piece of merchandise he is, NBC may gamble that his avuncular physique and colorful accent are sufficiently acceptable.

Somehow, though, we can't avoid the suspicion that Mr. Kissinger is attracted to a puissant television network by more than six figures and the ego exposure. Would Henry Kissinger be content analyzing and providing background on foreign affairs after eight years as a shaper? The network may find itself frantically explaining shortly that last night's "Manifesto on the Third World, Detente and the Stratosphere" was in the nature of Kissinger commentary, not policy.

We doubt that this is one old soldier who will quietly fade away.

THE PLAIN DEALER

Cleveland, Ohio, January 16, 1978

The NBC television network is entitled to special praise for its production and airing of "Kissinger: on the Record" Friday evening.

For foreign policy buffs, and especially those interested in the rise of domestic Communist parties in Western Europe, the program and Henry Kissinger's commentary added up to a tour de force.

As secretary of state under former Presidents Richard Nixon and Gerald Ford, Kissinger's ability to speak frankly in public was naturally limited. Now he is under no such constraints, although it is clear that Kissinger is still very careful about what he says and how he says it.

But Kissinger left no room for doubt about his concern over the danger to the United States posed by Communist party gains in Italy and France.

NBC's own news staff should be credited with a superior job in presenting a country-by-country background briefing to set the stage for Kissinger's question-and-answer sessions with correspondent David Brinkley.

NBC is believed to have paid Kissinger about $1 million for a five-year contract that calls for him to act as a foreign affairs consultant to the network and to participate in at least one major news documentary each year. We will leave it up to NBC to decide at the conclusion of the contract whether the network received its money's worth. But judging by the first visible fruits of this remarkable arrangement, NBC's viewers will benefit handsomely from the network's bold experiment.

THE ARIZONA REPUBLIC

Phoenix, Ariz., January 30, 1978

HE may have been Super K as a diplomat, but on television he was Who Dat?

When former Secretary of State Henry A. Kissinger appeared on a special, highly-advertised NBC program with David Brinkley, he placed 94th — and last — in the Nielsen ratings.

Those who tuned Kissinger out didn't miss a thing. Except for a warning against Eurocommunism, his comments consisted for self-serving distortions of the policies he pursued in the State Department.

For example, he declared that democracy was saved in Portugal because Mario Soares was "determined to right the Communists" and had "united Western support."

Actually, Kissinger never lifted a finger to help Soares, and called him "a Kerensky" to his face.

HERALD ☰ EXAMINER

February 13, 1978
Los Angeles, Calif.,

Bert Lance, President Carter's old close buddy who was forced out of the budget director's job by his own money troubles, is still being investigated by a federal grand jury. In the meantime, Bert has gotten himself into a new line of work as a commentator on the nightly news at a television station in Atlanta.

What is Bert Lance talking about on the air? The two things he knows best — the government and money.

However, he can't talk right now about how he managed to get his own account at his own bank a few hundred thousand dollars overdrawn because that is a matter still being looked into by the grand jury.

Some observers are questioning the propriety of a former Carter Administration official, with close personal ties to the President, being employed, at a reported $50,000 a year, by a television station that is regulated, like all TV stations, by the federal government's communications commission.

The Virginian-Pilot

Norfolk, Va., February 21, 1977

"In television," NBC News President Dick Wald says, "the personality — the impact of one person on the viewer — is as important as style is to the written news."

And now NBC News has landed a major personality who'll bring a distinctive style to television. Former Secretary of State Henry A. Kissinger has signed an exclusive contract with NBC News for the next five years.

Mr. Kissinger is to do an annual documentary on international affairs, to appear on NBC's "Nightly News" to comment from time to time, to appear on other NBC programs, to act as a special consultant to the network, and to cooperate in a special that will be based on his memoirs.

The book is to be published in the fall of 1979 by Little, Brown & Company, a subsidiary of Time, Inc., that paid $2 million reportedly for the book rights. Now Mr. Kissinger is to appear in the book's serialization, so to speak, on prime-time television. As deals go nowadays, that's an agent's dream, exceeding even the Johnny Carson show.

What NBC is paying Dr. Kissinger is a secret. But industry insiders suggest that it is in excess of $1 million, and maybe nearer $1.5 million. It appears to be a bargain price.

For Mr. Kissinger is sure to upstage the other networks' superstars. Walter Cronkite, the anchorman at CBS, is the Gibraltar of newscasters. But Uncle Walter was never Secretary of State. Barbara Walters left NBC and the Today show to accept a million dollars as ABC's anchorwoman and a less-than-happy marriage on the air with Harry Reasoner. But Barbara never won any Nobel Peace Prizes.

"NBC is fortunate that this remarkable man has agreed to participate in NBC's effort to extend its coverage and analysis of foreign affairs," crowed the company's president, Herbert S. Schlosser. Certainly Mr. Kissinger is an authority on the subject. But the deal is tricky.

For the former Secretary of State has his own vested interest in particular policies, as well as a book that he is promoting. And what is the difference between buying the exclusive rights to Mr. Kissinger's memoirs and buying the exclusive rights to the astronauts' stories or Gary Mark Gilmore's story?

Yet Mr. Kissinger is doing nothing wrong. He is leaving public affairs to join the network team. Many others have left the media to accept government jobs, e.g., Ron Nessen, or to become candidates for office. Barry Goldwater and Ronald Reagan are syndicated. Mr. Kissinger is just the most prominent switchover. It's getting harder and harder to tell the players apart in the show-biz world of media/politics.

The Chattanooga Times

Chattanooga, Tenn., December 3, 1977

In Eric Sevareid's retirement from regularly scheduled broadcasting, television loses one of its keenest minds and most articulate commentators, and his audience one of its chief contributors to clearer understanding of complex issues.

Trained as a reporter with CBS News, his employer throughout his entire working career, he retained the newsman's devotion to factual accuracy while developing a base of knowledge from which he could give a broader perspective and a deeper meaning to events of the day.

In his final broadcast a few nights ago, he outlined what he called some self-imposed rules for airing his comments. Every journalist, and especially those with the responsibility for editorial expression, could well copy them: Never to underestimate the intelligence of the audience; to elucidate, when possible, more than to advocate; and "to retain the courage of one's doubts as well as one's convictions in this world of dangerously passionate certainties."

The last might be taken to heart by those who hear as well as those who speak. Unless we cling to the right to question because we simply refuse to take assured pronouncements at face value, we give away an unnecessary advantage to those who would mislead us for their own purpose.

The country, of course, has not heard the last from Eric Sevareid, whether through the electronic or the print media. For that we can be grateful.

THE CHRISTIAN SCIENCE MONITOR

Boston, Mass., November 29, 1977

CBS without Sevareid? It's enough to contradict the title of the long-time commentator's most celebrated book, "Not So Wild a Dream." If only it *were* a dream, and tomorrow night, when we wake up, there would be Eric Sevareid on the tube again, TV's answer to antiquity's oracle at Delphi.

Not that Sevareid has ever pretended to oracular powers or deific sources. It's just that his formidable gray presence on the screen gives his words the quality of being carved in stone, especially to younger viewers who never knew him any other way.

But to the generation that has followed Sevareid through the years, though a bit older or younger than the mandatory retirement age he has just reached, the Sevareid story is much more than the void to be left on the CBS evening news. It goes back at least to the call to the young newspaperman from one of the few to leave a comparable gap in broadcasting, Ed Murrow, to join that band of correspondents that adorned radio before World War II.

Always considering himself more of a writer than a performer, Sevareid is really an essayist who happens to have gone electronic. He has perfected his own literary form, blending fact and opinion in two minutes that somehow convey more depth than the law of space and time allows.

In recent years, the opinions have sometimes not seemed so clear-cut as in the Sevareid of memory. This impression probably reflects what he has said about the increasing complexity of events and issues since the World War II days when right and wrong seemed so much simpler.

What we have seen and been challenged to grow along with is a man trying to apply a consistent devotion to the truth to a time of enormous change and threat to the truth. A clear-cut opinion is not easy in the '70s. Needless to say, we want to see a post-CBS Sevareid continue in his quest, as he plans to do, along the lines of a recent speech:

"I have tried to remain objective, always aware, however, that objectivity and neutrality are not the same thing. Objectivity is a *way* of thinking *about* an issue, not the summation of the thought."

The Knickerbocker News

Albany, N.Y., December 30, 1977

One of the giants of American journalism leaves the air waves this week and we all will be the poorer for the departure.

After 50 years as a newsman, 38 of them with CBS, Eric Sevareid is retiring at 65. Henceforth, another voice will give the TV commentary on the *CBS Evening News with Walter Cronkite*.

In a medium in which too many of the practitioners seem cast from the same glutinous mold and appear more concerned over their profiles and hair styles than with their content, Eric Sevareid has stood apart and miles above the rest.

A master reporter and writer rather than a reader or speaker, Sevareid often conveys a dour mien and in recent years has been criticized for being what some critics have called pontifical, wishy-washy or both. These people don't know the real Eric Sevareid. What some have interpreted as gloominess reflects Sevareid's long-standing uncomfortableness on TV, with its emphasis on entertainment and personality rather than substance, and he doesn't care who knows it. And what has been seen as fence straddling actually is his conviction, born of long experience, that there simply are no pat solutions for today's incredibly complex problems. It takes more courage to admit this than to be glib and superficial.

In his superb biography, *Not So Wild a Dream*, Sevareid provides the clues to his sturdy character and lofty values. He is the product of a rugged Norwegian Lutheran family in Velva, N.D., and a child of the Great Depression. He worked his way through college, bummed around the country and after tough early training as a newspaper reporter, he became a member of the incomparable team of CBS radio newsmen organized by the late Ed Murrow.

During the war, Sevareid had several brushes with death, the closest during a flight "over the hump" of the Himalayas from India to China, when the Army Air Corps plane on which he was flying went down and he parachuted into a rugged area populated by fortunately friendly Naga tribesmen.

Because of such experiences, he never has been a cream-puff reporter and his commentaries, as well as his reports, always have conveyed the accurate impression that here was one newsman who really knew what he was talking or writing about.

And so it has been that despite his unease with the TV medium, he has been pre-eminent, if not virtually alone in his field as a TV commentator because his professionalism has shown through.

For these reasons, those of us in the news profession are proud to have had Eric Sevareid among us.

THE EMPORIA GAZETTE

Emporia, Kans., December 17, 1977

ERIC Sevareid, who retired this month as a commentator for CBS News, has some links with Emporia. For one thing, he gave a lecture in the Civic Auditorium on Feb. 22, 1961. While he was in town, Mr. Sevareid had dinner with several Emporians and after his talk he visited backstage with some of the people in the audience.

He also was a colleague of The Gazette's late editor, W.L. White. They covered the early part of World War II as radio correspondents and once Mr. White filled in for Mr. Sevareid who had to be with his wife as she was giving birth to their first child.

Thus Mr. Sevareid's retirement was of special interest to many Emporians.

—

Sad to say, Mr. Sevareid always seemed stern — even austere — in his nightly remarks for the Cronkite show. He revealed a much warmer personality this week in a televised conversation with Charles Kuralt. (Mr. Kuralt, by the way, has become perhaps the best, most human, of all the television network reporters.)

In the program, Mr. Sevareid gave the impression that he still prefers writing to broadcast journalism. He once compared the mechanics of television — the necessity for makeup and proper lighting — to "being nibbled to death by ducks."

He talked about some of the people he has worked with and admired, including Edward R. Murrow. He recalled that Mr. Murrow operated on combinations of coffee, whiskey, cigarettes and sleeping pills because he "couldn't pace himself."

In discussing the changes in the news business over the years he said journalists now are almost overwhelmed by the amount of information available to them. To control the flow, he jokingly suggested that reports be made only every other day: "No newspapers, no news broadcasts Monday, Wednesday and Friday."

—

Mr. Sevareid has a background and dignity that will be hard to replace on the CBS evening news. Viewers will miss his measured analysis of the news and his arguments in favor of reason and moderation. — R.C.

THE PLAIN DEALER

Cleveland, Ohio,
December 6, 1977

Over the course of a 40-year career, Eric Sevareid, became a giant in American journalism. When he retired Wednesday after 28 years at CBS News, a spate of news stories served as testimony that something akin to an era was at an end.

In the vernacular, he would be referred to as a "superstar," but Sevareid would surely eschew that label and so shall we. It was characteristic of the man and his work that he never came between his audience and the story.

As pompous as it might sound when used in reference to lesser journalists, it can truly be said that Sevareid's calling was to employ the tools of journalism in a search for truth and, ultimately, wisdom.

If he was less sure about the truth at the end of his career than at the beginning, that was nothing less than a measure of his wisdom and honesty.

Sevareid's impact on his profession came not as a result of his personality but because of the quality of his work and the fierce integrity he brought to the coverage and analysis of news.

Sevareid was, is, anything but flashy or flamboyant. Mostly, he seemed dour and pessimistic; a commentator who modestly recommended calm reason and moderation but did not necessarily expect these to prevail. For a journalist who covered his share of war, revolution and genocide, these were natural reactions.

Few men are truly indispensable. Sevareid's departure leaves legions of journalists with a sensitive nose for news and a finely tuned ear for truth hard at work reporting and interpreting the day's events. For the qualities he brought to their profession, all of them stand indebted to Eric Sevareid.

The Cleveland Press

Cleveland, Ohio, December 2, 1977

In his final commentary for the CBS Evening News, Eric Sevareid, retiring after a distinguished 38-year career with the network, offered good advice for his colleagues in the news business.

Sevareid did not label his advice as such, merely as "self-imposed" rules he had followed as a broadcast journalist, which included:

"Not to underestimate the intelligence of the audience and not to overestimate its information.

"To elucidate, when one can, more than to advocate.

"To retain the courage of one's doubts, as well as one's convictions, in this world of dangerously passionate certainties.

"To comfort oneself, in times of error, with the knowledge that the saving grace of the press — print or broadcast — is its self-correcting nature."

Everyone in the commenting field could do himself and his audience a favor by tacking Sevareid's rules on the wall, just above the typewriter.

The irony of Sevareid's success as a television commentator is that he never was really comfortable before the cameras. His career goes back to the early days of radio and a fond and distinguished partnership with Edward R. Murrow. The transition to TV was inevitable and brought him great fame, but his prose was meant for the ear, and the eye was a distraction rather than a help.

Perhaps the finest compliment paid him on his retirement came on the rival networks, ABC and NBC, rather than on CBS. It was there that a former colleague, Harry Reasoner, and John Chancellor, tossing all competitive restraints to the winds, bade him farewell in unabashedly sentimetal terms. Even portions of Sevareid's final commentary were shown on ABC.

That sort of magnanimity is not common in television. It is a mark of the high esteem Sevareid had earned as a newsman and essayist.

THE SAGINAW NEWS

Saginaw, Mich., December 2, 1977

Eric Sevareid's farewell to his national television audience was pure Sevareid.

The last broadcast on the threshhold of his retirement was as crisply delivered and devoid of wordiness as the thousands preceding it. His piercing eyes transmitted the usual effect of the man.

It was straight-from-the-shoulder stuff. He thanked everybody who, as he said, put up with him for a lot of years. Bowed to those whom he credited with "creating" him.

He gratefully acknowledged his viewers — critics particularly — as the most important part of his life, pictured himself now "a has been," and said good night.

Eric Sevareid was much too modest to the end.

He was not simply a crack commentator on the most startling news events of the past 35 years. He was a learned commentator, as much a scholar of history as a narrator of its passing events — a superb essayist of the century, as Walter Cronkite so aptly said of him.

Above all of this he was respected among his fellows for his total dedication to accuracy and fair-mindedness.

In a rival media trying to do the same kind of work, we're not often carried away by another's competency and integrity. Eric Sevareid's exceeded the usual and reached excellence consistently.

He was the total craftsman of journalism and a great image projector for all media. We'll miss him greatly, as will CBS.

The Burlington Free Press

Burlington, Vt., December 2, 1977

IF THERE was a hall of fame for newsmen, Eric Sevareid's name probably would be writ large on its walls along with other outstanding reporters whose significant contributions have made journalism what it is today.

He is clearly the elder statesman of a breed of newsmen whose careers began in the reportorial trenches at a time when good reporters were hard to come by.

Radio was his medium for reporting the events of World War II and his verbal accounts of the bombings and the battles often were just as vivid as the visual reports that are seen on television today. He risked life and limb to bring news to millions of listeners in this country.

Under Edward R. Murrow, Eric Sevareid grew in stature and experience during that war and emerged as a full-fledged, distinguished reporter. That, he probably would say, was his finest hour.

In 1964, he joined the CBS Evening News as a commentator, summoning his consummate wit and skill to present fair and balanced analyses of international and national events.

Few can disagree with his valedictory observation that he "passed the test" of fairness with the television public. He has indeed served that virtue well during his 39-year career with CBS News.

We join millions of other Americans in a sense of regret at the retirement of a man who came to be regarded as an old and valued friend during his tenure in broadcasting.

The Idaho STATESMAN

Boise, Idaho, November 14, 1978

Seldom does a commercial television show come along that merits editorial endorsement. And when they do, often they are destined for short lives.

The 1978 fall season offers another such quality show, and it too is in trouble. It deserves to succeed, and it will, we believe, if people will look in on it just once or twice.

The show is NBC's *Lifeline* on KTVB. It is not fiction; the people on the screen are not actors. Each episode chronicles the life of a different physician as he or she works to save the lives and restore the health of patients. All medical sequences are filmed as they happen, blood and all. Some of the scenes are not pretty, but they are gripping. They are infinitely more compelling than fiction. They are the drama of real life.

In the first show, a neurosurgeon struggled against the clock and unexpected complications to remove a blood system malformation from a young child's head. As time dragged on and the complexity of the situation unfolded, options became fewer. Difficult choices had to be made. The viewer was drawn painfully into these decisions with the family and medical staff. In the end, the physician was successful, but at a price: A very bright, outgoing verbal child was reduced to a speechless, withdrawn caricature, from which full recovery was not assured.

Patients on *Lifeline* are not the beautiful, composed people of fiction. They come in all shapes, sizes, colors. They react to pain and pressure the way real people react. They draw the viewer into their lives, and sometimes it hurts.

If one must find fault with *Lifeline*, it is the program's tendency to glorify the image of physicians in their day-to-day exercise of saving lives and mending bodies.

Lifeline apparently is in trouble. It has been running in the 9 p.m. Sunday time spot in Boise, 10 p.m. in the Eastern and Central time zones. Between Sept. 18 and Oct. 29, it ranked 54th in viewer preference. This week, in an apparent attempt to boost viewership, NBC is running the show as a two-part series at 7 p.m. on Tuesday and Thursday. The NBC ads argue that if you watch it once, you'll be hooked.

We agree. Give the show a try. It is one of the best demonstrations we've seen in years of what television is capable of. It would be a shame to lose it and to coincidentally send a message to the networks that such quality programming is not marketable.

NBC President Fred Silverman should be commended for his concern that this inspirational new concept in programming be given a chance to prove itself with viewers. *Lifeline* has been given temporary exemption to the rules which govern programs under television's almighty ratings game.

THE ARIZONA REPUBLIC

Phoenix, Ariz., October 25, 1978

TELEVISION'S fall program schedule has been characterized, both inside and outside the industry, as relying heavily on vapid shows which feature fleshy actresses.

Perhaps.

But NBC has fielded a fall entry that measures up to the real potential of television's visual power.

Lifeline is an hour-long documentary-type series which focuses on medical doctors and their patients in the stark world of hospital care and treatment.

With only minimum interference from a narrator, the physicians, their staffs, and the patients and their families are allowed to construct spellbinding stories as they actually happen.

The series is gripping, dramatic, spellbinding, often frightful. But it is modern medicine as few see it, or understand it.

The virtue of *Lifeline* is that it provides viewers with a keener appreciation of the complexities and costs of modern medicine, and of the men and women who devote skills and time to curing.

It is real, and not a contrived fantasy to fill the vacuum of boredom.

Unfortunately, *Lifeline* will not maintain the audience hold of, say, a shoot-'em-up crime show. It therefore faces a tenuous future on the air.

What will save *Lifeline*, if it is threatened with the programming ax, is the re-dedication of TV executives to provide diversification in the medium, and the resolve of commercial sponsors to stick with low-rated but mind-expanding creativity.

The Virginian-Pilot

Roanoke, Va., August 11, 1975

It was bound to happen; sooner or later, someone in the federal government would blame newspapers and television for helping bring on the malpractice crisis.

Dr. Roger O. Egeberg, special assistant to the Secretary of Health, Education and Welfare, was pretty fair about it. He did say that too much news is circulated about all the big malpractice judgments that patients win, and not enough about the cases that get thrown out. But in a speech to the annual meeting of the American Medical Association, he also laid blame on the entertainment media and on doctors. All of these, he said, had a part in creating "unrealistic expectations" among patients by painting misleading images of medical and surgical advances.

There is substance to Dr. Egeberg's remarks. The public does expect too much from medicine. Its expectations have been raised by gee-whiz stories in newspapers and periodicals about new drugs and medical techniques, stories that don't always tell enough about the fallibilities, limitations or costs involved. The "Marcus Welby syndrome," fostered by TV, overdramatizes medical matters and skims over inherent risks.

As for doctors, some of them enjoy the godlike status conferred on them by dramas and pseudo-scientific reporting. Not a few, it seems, have contributed to it. William A. Nolen, a Minnesota surgeon and author, wrote in a recent issue of an AMA magazine, *Prism:* "I've concluded from experience that where irresponsible medical reporting is concerned, neither the physicians nor the journalists are without sin. But if the scores are added up, most of the blame falls on the M.D.'s."

Our own conclusion is that there is blame enough to go around. Physicians and hospitals today have more skills and more methods than ever before to save lives and mend injuries. But they work precious few miracles, and the public hears as little about the patients doctors lose as about the malpractice cases doctors win. The public should be educated, by all involved, to share the same expectations as the physicians; as Dr. Egeberg put it, "A surgeon approaches many patients with the idea that, depending on the circumstances, he has an even or 80 per cent chance of improving or curing a condition." In real life, few achieve as high a batting average as Marcus Welby.

Richmond Times-Dispatch
Richmond, Va., September 19, 1977

Writing in the current issue of *Newsweek*, David Eisenhower expresses deep resentment over the way father-in-law Richard Nixon was portrayed on ABC's recent "docu-drama", *Washington. Behind Closed Doors.*

Mr. Eisenhower says the mini-series "carried entertainment's adulteration of history to fantastic lengths." He calls on "the best minds" of the nation to "begin resisting television's glib and cynical assumptions about politics and public figures, its slavish fascination with power and vanishing regard for the truth."

The former President's son-in-law cites an experience he recently had with ABC in connection with that network's plan to do a "docu-drama" on Dwight Eisenhower's war years. He says the network representatives insisted on highlighting what David Eisenhower termed his grandfather's "alleged affair" with a wartime secretary-driver. He says that although the "affair" has been "substantially refuted" by letters released by his family and others, the network "argued it was 'in the entertainment business'."

It is hard to see how any fair-minded person could deny that *Washington: Behind Closed Doors* gave a misleading picture of Mr. Nixon, his associates, the CIA, the FBI and other agencies of the government. Watergate was a low point in the history of the federal government, specifically of the people in the White House. But where the ABC series was misleading was in giving the impression that nothing was done during the Nixon administration except out of the crassest motives by the most venal people. One could almost draw the inference that the total concern of the CIA and FBI was with political shenanigans.

In staging a "docu-drama," the producers can use identifiable people ("Richard M. Monckton" was clearly Richard M. Nixon) and some recognizable incidents (a break-in clearly meant to resemble the Watergate entry) but then put those people and events in totally fictitious situations. The producers of such programs can say that they have no obligation to stick to the facts, since they are presenting drama. But the unfortunate result can be that since fact and fiction are all mixed up together, the average viewer may be totally confused as to what is real and what isn't. In the case of *Washington: Behind Closed Doors*, many viewers may have been led to believe that what they saw on their TV screens is typical of all that goes on in their government throughout the working day and, indeed, on into the night.

The series was well directed, well acted and dramatically absorbing. But we share David Eisenhower's concern that the distortion of facts, engrossing as it was, was unfair to many of those depicted and may have misled many viewers.

The Knickerbocker News
Albany, N.Y., September 13, 1977

When "Washington: Behind Closed Doors" ended Sunday night, viewers in millions of American households sat back, breathed a sigh of relief, and thanked the heavens Richard Nixon, the Great Brooder of San Clemente, as columnist Mike Royko calls him, isn't in the White House anymore.

Thanks to a brilliant rewrite of the so-so novel by ex-Nixon henchman John Erlichmann upon which the six-night miniseries was based and thanks to the excellent acting of Jason Robards, Robert Vaughn, Nicholas Pryor and others, the viciousness, vindictiveness and mad ambition of the Nixon years were exposed once more.

Obviously, not everything in the dramatization that used ficticious names but real characteristics and situations, was true. It was 100 per cent good theater, but only about 75 per cent reality.

Yet it had enough fact and impact to remind us once more, as if we needed it, that the Nixon reign was as close a brush with dictatorship as we have had in this century.

Nixon got off easy: resignation, the enmity of a nation, sure, but a hefty pension, taxpayer-financed home improvements that vastly increased his real estate values, millions of dollars from David Frost for semi-revealing his soul on TV, an IRS too cowardly to demand payment of his back taxes, and other goodies can make up for that.

It is his arrogance and domestic derring-do, his "My administration right or wrong" that live in the memories of Americans. And it is that arrogance and lack of sensitivity that so rankles us every time it rears its ugly head.

Jimmy Carter was one of Nixon's harshest critics and millions of voters cast their lots with Jimmy, sweeping him into the Oval Office on a wave of enthusiasm and longing for a breath of fresh air.

Now, with the Bert Lance affair, presidential arrogance again comes to the fore. Carter has seemed offended anyone would question the wisdom of keeping on a man who, in his financial wheeling and dealing before being appointed Carter's director of the Office of Management and Budget, showed his lack of judgement, even if it should be shown he is innocent of legal wrongdoing and guilty only of moral crimes.

The Lance affair has too many trappings of Nixonian logic, something we never dreamed we'd see from Jimmy Carter, the man who promised never to lie to us, always to treat us fairly and to respect us in the morning.

Well, Mr. Carter, we're sorry you're offended. Frankly, we're offended, too, perhaps more than you'll ever know. It makes us uncomfortable having a man like Bert Lance in a position of trust and judgement in our government.

Notice we said *our* government? That's the point Nixon constantly ignored. It's *our* government and merely because we voted you into office doesn't mean we have to agree with and bow to everything you decide. And if your decision is to stick with Bert Lance, you're going to have to have to suffer through having more and more of your decisions examined and questioned.

We won't lie to you, either. We want honest government, something we haven't experienced in decades. And we want it now, with no backsliding, no compromising, no doubletalk and no fancy sidestepping. Then we'll always treat you fairly, too.

THE PLAIN DEALER
Cleveland, Ohio, September 15, 1977

The American Broadcasting Co.'s "Washington: Behind Closed Doors" series has been praised as television at is best.

It also has been condemned for mixing fact with fiction indiscriminately.

The first observation is close to being correct, at least for viewers fascinated by the potential use and misuse of power. The "novel for television," a concept increasingly popular with television producers, certainly showed those potentials effectively. Performances on six consecutive nights last week by a first-rank corps of players were consistently excellent.

The second observation also is close to being correct. Fact was mixed with myth. But it was not done indiscriminately. Obviously, it had to be done purposely so that the series not be mistaken for a verbatim reconstruction of the presidential administration of Richard M. Nixon.

Just as obviously, the character of the fictionalized president, Richard M. Monckton, is based on Nixon. Nor is there any doubt as to the models for the other characters in the drama, from H. R. Haldeman (Frank Flaherty) through Richard Helms (William Martin) and Henry Kissinger (Karl Tessler) to the younger Nixon staff members who finally got tangled up in the Watergate scandal.

But while the characters are tied to real people, they are not meant to exactly duplicate those people. They are products of writers' imaginations, several times removed from the real personalities.

This is not history. It is tragedy written as a morality play. As such, it takes historical characters and events and embellishes, exaggerates, reduces them for the purposes of the play. Not to suggest more than a parallel in method, but Shakespeare did the same thing with English and other European rulers.

Anyone who followed the events that led to the downfall of Nixon and his cohort is aware of the fictionalization. It was perhaps a failing on ABC's part that a message disclaiming any attempt at faithful reconstruction of the Nixon years was not announced at various times during the presentation.

Any work of fiction is based on a writer's experience. The characters, the events, the places, all are people, places, things or composites that the writer has known or that have been made known to him.

In this case the drama was based on the novel "The Company," written by former Nixon counselor John D. Ehrlichman. And the novel — not meant to recite events verbatim — was reworked by two scriptwriters, removing it even further from what was real.

So the play, in this case, is not the real thing. The characters should be seen as just that — personalities based on real people but not supposed to be faithful representations. Some, in fact, could be recognized as combinations of at least two different White House aides.

The assumption is that ABC is not through with Monckton-Nixon. There are almost all the Watergate discoveries and subsequent action there to be picked over.

If the decision is made to go ahead, viewers are advised not to believe that everything they see and hear happened that way. And ABC should make it clear that what is being shown is not to be taken as historically accurate.

Then the drama can be judged in its proper context — as theater, not as politics.

MANCHESTER NEW HAMPSHIRE UNION LEADER
Manchester, N.H., September 11, 1977

The dangers of such a powerful vehicle of ideas as is American television are not limited to the biased presentation of news, such as the Panama Canal issue. They can be manifested also in the revising of history through thinly-veiled "docu-dramas."

ABC Television's soap opera saga "Washington Behind Closed Doors" is a case in point. This "fiction based on fact" can be extremely dangerous. Portions of it obviously are true, but others are not and the danger comes

in trying to separate the two.

It is an all but impossible task. We'd wager that even the Ehrlichmans, Haldemans, Hunts and Liddys — all of whom are President Nixon's men — would have a tough time of it. And, if the characters themselves can't keep things straight, how is the American viewer supposed to?

The much-ballyhooed, multi-night program has proved to be a distortion of a distortion. Originally to be based on former White House aide John Ehrlichman's supposed "real novel,"

the TV show was then "fleshed out" by Hollywood screen writers.

The network publicists, wary of libel suits, will insist it's all fiction, but they and their sponsors would be deeply hurt if the viewer didn't guess the real identity of the various characters and recognize the events portrayed.

This "Washington" program isn't the first television attempt to rewrite history and it won't be the last. Also set for this season are programs on Lee Harvey Oswald and Martin Luther King. They, too, may attempt to portray events as they should have been, rather than as they were. Truth rarely sells as well as fiction.

Newsday
Garden City, N.Y., September 8, 1977

This week's television mini-series "Washington" is an exercise in passing the buck by fictional President Richard Monckton and his cohorts. But on a different channel tonight, viewers will be treated to what may well be the ultimate in buckpassing: The real Richard Nixon seemingly blaming the whole Watergate mess on poor Martha Mitchell.

Nixon does tell interviewer David Frost that Watergate wasn't really her fault. But then he goes on to say: "If it hadn't been for Martha, there'd have been no Watergate, because John wasn't mindin' that store." As it turned out, she was entirely justified in her concern that Nixon would attempt to make her husband a scapegoat; he was the first one to be sacrificed as Haldeman and Ehrlichman pulled up the wagons around the White House.

It's only a coincidence that the last of the Frost interviews with Nixon is being aired during the week that ABC puts on its serial, which is loosely based on John Ehrlichman's book, "The Company," which is loosely based on the Watergate

affair. But both make the same point: Monckton and his men keep passing the buck and Richard Nixon still refuses to accept any responsibility for Watergate.

Those interested in comparing fact and fiction can tune in tonight at 7:30 on Channel 5 for a look at the real Nixon. Then switch to Channel 7 or 8 for the third installment of "Washington," in which campaign money is laundered, the CIA gets involved in politics and the Senate starts to get curious. Just remember, it's *not* a rerun; it only seems that way.

The Charlotte Observer
Charlotte, N.C., October 6, 1977

When ABC-TV began broadcasting "Washington: Behind Closed Doors" last month it labeled the six-part series, based on Nixon adviser John Ehrlichman's novel, as fiction. That distinction was lost on many people.

Several days ago we published a letter from a reader who had watched the series, and wrote, in part: "I feel that a maximum security prison with life sentences is not enough for Nixon, Ehrlichman, Haldeman, Mitchell, Dean, Liddy, Colson and all aides employed by the Tricky Dick administration for what they put over on the American people."

How many people do you suppose watched Robert Vaughn and Cliff Robertson play out Mr. Ehrlichman's cynical novel and thought what they were seeing was "real?" Many Americans are notoriously indifferent to history. If instead they feed on fiction they think is fact, what does that do to their ability to understand this society?

So-called docudramas did well last year. This year they're far longer on drama and shorter on documentation. If you liked television's "Truman At Potsdam" last year, where words the real President Truman never uttered were put into his mouth, then ABC's "The Trial Of Lee Harvey Oswald" last weekend was for you.

In it, Mr. Oswald, the man arrested for assassinating President Kennedy, stands trial for that assassination. The real Mr. Oswald died *on national television* when Jack Ruby shot him in the Dallas police station. In the docudrama, his real life death scene was reduced to a flashbulb popping and startling him.

ABC, with rich ratings and poor taste, has obliterated last season's blurry line between fact and fiction. That is irresponsible.

Television broadcasts primarily entertainment, but it also plays an important role in telling Americans about the real world. It should not confuse fact and fiction in order to entertain.

Novelist Herman Wouk is now converting his best-seller "The Winds Of War" into a television series. Daniel Schorr asked Mr. Wouk if he thought it was proper for actors playing Franklin Roosevelt, Winston Churchill and Joseph Stalin to say things the real men never uttered. "You have touched a very live nerve," replied Mr. Wouk. "I don't know if anyone has the answer."

The answer is that it is not proper.

Des Moines Tribune
Des Moines, Iowa, September 13, 1977

A cautionary word seems appropriate now that ABC-TV has aired a 12-hour piece of "fictionalized history" that evokes troubling questions about mixing fact and fantasy. Whatever the characters are called in "Washington: Behind Closed Doors," the story is obviously about the Nixon administration.

When President Richard Monckton, played by Jason Robards, puts on his hypocritical arm-waving act for the TV cameras, we recognize a character who fits what we have heard and read about Richard Nixon. The characterizations — and in some cases caricatures — in the TV series are less ambiguous than they are in John Ehrlichman's novel, "The Company," on which the Watergate-like TV scenario was loosely based.

As one critic put it, the drama "may bring home the grim reality of political corruption with more immediacy than any previous treatment of Watergate.... Never have TV viewers been offered such a concentrated and sustained prime-time dose of bad news about the American political system and the possibilities of abusing it."

This accomplishment fits the public mood of disenchantment with government and distrust of politicians. But that is one of the dangers of the ABC series. In order to appeal to the mass audience, has the network allowed dramatic liberties that magnify the fantasies and diminish the facts? If so, the result may be a public misperception of the federal government as a sordid mess with little prospect for reform.

Sexual entanglements add a soap-opera quality to several episodes, but even these leave the viewers wondering: Did a president, obviously meant to be Lyndon Johnson, actually bed down with the wife of a high government official?

For centuries, celebrated authors, playwrights and composers have drawn on historical events and figures to enrich their works. But there is a risk in doing so. That risk is magnified by television, where fact and fantasy appear side by side, sometimes in the same program. The results often are confusing to viewers, causing misconceptions that are detrimental to the public's understanding of important events and issues.

It is a risk the network executives had better not neglect during their hot pursuit of audience ratings. They do no public service by needlessly confusing viewers about the history of our times.

WORCESTER TELEGRAM.

Worcester, Mass., September 15, 1977

Truth is stranger than fiction, they say, and truth-fiction, an emerging television art form, is stranger than either.

A case in point is ABC-TV's recently concluded six-part semi-fictional soap opera, "Washington: Behind Closed Doors." Loosely based on John Ehrlichman's novel, "The Company," it was a thinly disguised look at the power politics behind the Watergate scandal from the inside.

It was a peculiar offering, one that disturbed some viewers, entertained or bored others and puzzled just about everybody else. While, in the words of Time magazine, "all the famous names have been changed to protect the guilty," it took very little imagination to identify the actors with some real-life characters. All the Watergate elements were there: a paranoid megalomaniac president, power-hungry White House staffers, wiretappings, illegal campaign funds, stonewalling, illegal intelligence gathering, FBI and CIA excesses, the works. A generous dose of bedroom scandal was laced in to hang on to those in the home audience not given to things political.

While many TV shows about politics have promised documentary and served up semi-fiction, this one advertised fiction but mixed make-believe with fact. The ethics of such an approach are questionable. Besides distorting recent history, it also splashes plenty of mud on individuals, still alive, who cannot defend themselves against fictionalized slander.

Not that this peculiar method is new in Washington. Back in 1880, Henry Adams anonymously published his novel, "Democracy," a tale of corruption and lost innocence on the Potomac. Gore Vidal gave the period of 1876 the half-fiction, half-history treatment in his recent trilogy. Allen Drury's "Advise and Consent," published in 1959, was a bestseller, not to mention such books as "Seven Days in May," and "Night of Camp David." A decade ago Norman Mailer puzzled his readers with his curious blend of daily journalism and personal introspect in "The Armies of the Night," an account of an anti-war demonstration in Washington.

But Watergate apparently pulled out all the stops. The paperback rights to former Nixon aide William Safire's novel, "Full Disclosure," went for $1.3 million, indicating that the airing of dirty political linen has hardly begun. Once the Nixon era is exhausted, we may see TV novels on some other recent presidents and their misadventures.

With fact being increasingly presented as fiction and fiction as fact, the distinction between the two becomes more blurred than ever. In this, as in all things, the viewer needs to retain a sense of perspective.

The Detroit News

Detroit, Mich., September 13, 1977

Fictionalizing history is not a new device but ABC carried it to new lengths — and depths — in its TV version of the novel, "The Company," by John D. Erlichman, chief adviser on domestic affairs during the Nixon administration.

Viewers reasonably familiar with the Watergate events were usually able to separate the facts from the fiction. But many others who saw the show thought they were viewing a documentary on the Nixon administration. In their minds, seeing is believing, even though on TV that isn't necessarily so.

Since they regarded the film as history, many viewers tried to find specific Nixon administration officials in the movie's cast. True, some of the characters were patterned after members of Nixon's staff. And in his speech and actions, Andy Griffith did bear some resemblance to President Johnson. Yet most of the characters were composites or caricatures.

The abrupt ending contributed to the impression that what ABC had portrayed in "Washington Behind Closed Doors" was history. The movie presumably closed as a prelude to the entire Watergate scandal, which, of course, it wasn't.

What Mr. Nixon and his political cohorts did to the presidency, the country and the people was bad enough. But ABC's version made their crimes even worse.

"Washington Behind Closed Doors" made it appear that the Watergate exceptions to honest government are now the rule and that everybody in Washington is on the make, financially, politically and morally. It tended to denigrate not only all politicians but the presidency, the CIA, the FBI and the other institutions of the federal government.

Already suspicious of government because of Watergate and the Vietnam war, the public is likely to get the impression that what happened in "Washington Behind Closed Doors" is an accurate reflection of the way Washington works. It isn't.

Nobody in the film spoke out on behalf of the public interest. Nobody ever explained the services the intelligence agencies perform for the nation. Everybody was selfishly looking out for his own interests. Almost everybody was breaking the law.

In short, it was a smear on politics and politicians. Even in the Nixon administration the great majority of federal officials and employes were honest people who were trying to do their jobs. Viewers never got that impression from "Washington Behind Closed Doors."

We're not suggesting that the series should not have been run or should have been censored. We do wish the producers had made it clear this was a fictionalized account loosely based on a novel by a man serving time in jail for his role in the Watergate scandals.

It was not a recreation of history. It was a blend of fact and fiction. The important distinction between the two never was drawn, presumably because that might have reduced the show's entertainment value and the size of ABC's audience.

BUFFALO EVENING NEWS

Buffalo, N.Y., September 17, 1977

Television's new fad of fictionalizing recent or even contemporary history has raised some very tricky questions — for producers, actors, viewers and, most of all, for living public figures being fictionally portrayed under transparent pseudonyms.

The problem has been with us for a long time in the form of fictionalized portrayals of real people like Marilyn Monroe, Howard Hughes or Harry Truman — usually after they are dead and cannot complain or sue — where history is twisted in quotes that were never uttered or love affairs invented to liven up the drama. But it took a more acute, and in some ways a more unsettling, form in this month's 12-hour ABC revisit of Watergate in "Washington: Behind Closed Doors."

The dilemma for those concerned with keeping some kind of line between truth and fiction is sharply defined by Thomas Griffith in his "Newswatch" column in Time magazine. The frontier between the two, he notes, is no longer the "well-lit border" it once was. "So many others are now romping in what used to be the press's own domain — contemporary history and the lives of current public figures — that it's hard to tell the truth without a score card, and no one is providing one."

The warmed-over-Watergate drama was a fine example in several dimensions. It was called fiction, which, as Mr. Griffith noted, "helps avoid libel suits," yet it stuck so close to recognizable traits and facts about most of its characters that there was no doubt at all who was supposed to be playing Nixon, Haldeman, Helms, Ziegler, Kissinger, etc., etc. But, in terms of distinguishing truth from fiction, the trouble was that only part of the show was loosely taken from John Ehrlichman's tell-all novel, "The Company." The rest was pure hoked-up network sex-interest stuff injected for spice. The result was a melange of both plausible and implausible characterization with viewers left to wonder which part of each portrayal of a recognizable public figure is supposed to be closer to the truth — that of his public life or his private life.

There is nothing new, of course, about the fictionalizing of history. The historical novel was a familiar device to readers and moviegoers long before television came on the scene. But television, as Mr. Griffith notes, is subject to a "special danger" when it mixes truth with fiction. Thus, when someone reads a book or goes to a movie, he expects to be entertained. But people who depend on the television screen for knowledge of real events "are bound to get mixed up" when networks mimic the actuality of those events.

We are reminded of British satirist Malcolm Muggeridge's description of television as "a world of fantasy in which we all live" — a fantasy of mingled sights and sounds; of "love found in a cigarette, beauty in a jar, peace in a capsule, joy in a brassiere and fulfillment in an automobile," and all of it mixed indistinguishably in with the news of wars, assassinations and other killings and with the entertainment show of make-believe wars, assassinations and other killings. Because of its pervasive impact on nearly every home, television surely has a special responsibility to be more careful than ever — rather than less and less so — to keep its truth and fiction correctly labeled.

TULSA WORLD
Tulsa, Okla., May 18, 1978

MAYBE there should be an Emmy for the most irresponsible abuse of truth and taste in television broadcasting. If there were, we would nominate NBC's "The Lincoln Conspiracy" for this year's honors. And the worst of it, the production was skillfully done and, in a perverse way, entertaining.

Briefly, the so-called "docudrama" presented a new version of Lincoln's assassination. John Wilkes Booth and his co-conspirators are no longer a group of misguided sickies acting on their own twisted motives. They are, according to the NBC version, the agents of a group of evil businessmen and politicians, including Secretary of War Edwin Stanton and Col. Lafayette Baker, founder of what was to later be called the Secret Service.

And Booth was not killed in a Virginia barn as history records. He escaped, according to NBC, and Baker, Stanton and dozens of other conspirators somehow managed to keep this fact secret — until now.

These twisted facts are based on rumors and legends that have kicked around since 1865 but have been discredited and laughed at by serious historians.

Admittedly, writers from Shakespeare down to the lowliest pulp magazine hack have always enjoyed a license to embellish and expand on historical facts. We all know that the words "Lend me your ears" are Shakespeare's, not Mark Antony's. But the NBC Lincoln docudrama goes much farther than this kind of artistic or poetic license. NBC rewrites — perverts is a better word — the central facts of history.

In fairness to NBC, the producers may have assumed that viewers would recognize "The Lincoln Conspiracy" as mostly fiction. But it wasn't all that clear. The facts and the hokum were all mixed together, giving millions of Americans a new and largely imaginary chapter of their country's history.

THE CHRISTIAN SCIENCE MONITOR
Boston, Mass., December 11, 1978

Taking verbal potshots at commercial television has become a favorite American pastime. But appropriate notice should be taken when, now and then, the networks show themselves capable of raising their standards.

Take this week's NBC presentation, "A Woman Called Moses." It follows in the vein of "Roots," "The Autobiography of Miss Jane Pittman," "King," and "Sounder," in offering viewers a poignant look at an often-neglected segment of American society.

Harriet Ross Tubman's heroic efforts to lead slaves to freedom in the North via the "underground railroad" is a bit of the past generally overlooked in American history classes. Mention of the contribution of blacks is most often limited to George Washington Carver and Booker T. Washington.

The NBC dramatization of Miss Tubman's life – her ordeal under slavery, her struggle to aid others to escape, her stint as a nurse in the Union Army, her service as a spy and government adviser – should help Americans of all races better understand and appreciate this courageous woman's part in history.

Such programs reveal television's great potential for educating and beneficially influencing society. All three networks, we are pleased to note, do have historical plays and documentaries and other examples of such programming on their schedules during the holiday season. This shows they could more often set their sights higher.

The Boston Globe
Boston, Mass., February 14, 1977

The television version of "Roots" and recent dramatizations of historical subjects ranging from the Adams Chronicles to "Tail Gunner Joe" about the late Sen. Joseph McCarthy have raised issues of accuracy and distortion for which the networks must ultimately take responsibility. Granted the allowable scope of artistic license in translating subjects into drama, productions that veer sharply from accepted (or even disputed) historical perceptions can have an extensive immediate impact that demands immediate perspective.

The images and information which the networks provide to a national audience are, for many people, the only images and information that stick. Competent television critics in the daily press and other periodicals alert the reading public to possible distortions, omissions, exaggerations or understatement but critics and their tools were essentially developed to analyze televised fictions, sitcoms and soap operas, not purportedly accurate history. In any event, print media critics are not likely to have the broad impact on perceptions implanted and reinforced by a powerful television program or series.

It makes no difference that the thrust of a particular historical program is positive, as in the case of "Roots." Nor does it matter that the dramatization may give the benefit of doubt to the villains of history. (Where in "Tail Gunner Joe," for example, was the vicious anti-Semitism and homophobia that characterized the McCarthy era?)

The point is that history requires perspective that dramatizations often do not provide.

Public television productions avoid this problem to some extent by employing commentators — Alistair Cooke being a notably effective example — to explain the context of a dramatization, even fictional ones such as "Upstairs Downstairs" that are heavily laced with social history.

Commercial television has a greater responsibility to provide a context if only because it reaches a much broader audience that is presumably less informed than the PBS audience.

Public education could have been enhanced, for instance, if the eight episodes of "Roots" had been preceded by an articulate, brief commentary on what was about to be broadcast, including mention of the varying opinions concerning the South before and after slavery. This is not to imply that "Roots" was inaccurate or distorted in any harmful way. In fact, the drama went far in revising and correcting common perceptions about black history in America.

But no one can claim that "Roots" was definitive, any more than anyone will claim that "Tail Gunner Joe" plumbed the depths of McCarthyism or that "Give 'em Hell, Harry" was an indisputably accurate portrayal of President Truman.

The historical record is sacred. Even disputed "facts" in the record are sacred because they give us a range of information for assessing history and what history has to tell us now. This perspective should be a necessary addition to any television dramatization that claims to be What Really Happened.

THE INDIANAPOLIS STAR
Indianapolis, Ind., April 16, 1977

One of the memorable scenes of NBC's Tail Gunner Joe "docu-drama" on the late Senator Joseph McCarthy showed the senator going wild in the hospital where he died.

NBC called its show "the incredible but true story of Senator Joseph McCarthy, the man who almost tore America apart."

A lot of people familiar with the facts of McCarthy's life wondered about the hospital episode. McCarthy's one-time aide, Roy Cohn, whose book on McCarthy is being re-issued in paperback, tells in the preface of asking the director of Tail Gunner Joe where the "wild man" information originated.

The director's answer, according to National Review: "Well . . . an unidentified hospital employe told it to an unidentified source."

Golly, isn't that what professional McCarthy-haters used to consider to be McCarthyism?

THE ARIZONA REPUBLIC
Phoenix, Ariz., December 2, 1978

PHOENIX thus far has been spared, but television viewers all over the country are being subjected to a barrage of blatant communist propaganda in the guise of a 20-part documentary on the conflict between Nazi Germany and Soviet Russia during World War II.

The film, entitled The Unknown War, lists Isaac Kleinerman, who made Victory at Sea, as executive producer. Actually, it was put together by a team of Soviet editors, working under the direction of Roman Karmen, a major figure in the Soviet cinema, who died shortly after completion of the project.

Kleinerman and his associates were free to make suggestions, some of which were adopted, but the final form of the series and its narration were decided in Moscow on a take-it-or-leave-it basis.

Neither in the credits or the narration by Burt Lancaster are these facts clearly stated.

The Unknown War is being distributed by Air Time International, which paid the Soviets $3.5 million for it.

According to Tom Buckley, television critic of The New York Times, who has viewed five episodes, although the film contains no outright falsehoods, "it distorts by commission, oversimplification and half truths."

Item: The Soviet invasion of Poland after the signing of the Hitler-Stalin pact is described as simply a case of the Soviets taking back territory wrested from them in 1921.

Item: The Soviet invasion of Finland is depicted as a border skirmish.

Item: The extent of the disaster that befell the Soviet army as a result of Stalin's refusal to believe allied intelligence reports that Hitler was preparing to attack is "grossly understated and without a word of blame for Stalin."

Buckley concludes: "The Unknown War is soft-core propaganda rather than an attempt to arrive at historical truth. Nothing makes this clearer than the fact that it is scheduled to be shown unaltered early next year on Soviet television."

We have to give the Soviets credit for canniness. No Yankee horse trader could match them.

Not only don't they have to spend a kopeck to blare their propaganda to millions of American television viewers, they've found a way to get a U. S. company to pay $3.5 million for the privilege of doing it for them.

In 1980, they'll be getting a reported $80 million from NBC for the privilege of broadcasting Soviet propaganda from the Moscow Olympiad.

If Khruschev's cry, "We will bury you," ever comes true, some U.S. television company probably will pay the Soviets tens of millions of dollars to cover the event.

DAILY ☰ NEWS
New York, N.Y., April 6, 1977

The first half of NBC-TV's "Jesus of Nazareth" overwhelmed the opposition's routine, shoot-'em-down shows, and the forecast for the second installment Sunday night is equally bright.

Taken together with the success of ABC-TV's "Roots," there is a clear message in this for the TV programmers and other hucksters who insist the way to corral big audiences is by appealing to the lowest common denominator.

Millions of Americans prefer to watch quality programs, including ones dealing with subjects as complex and sensitive as religion and race. They need decent choices. The networks should have the courage and faith to provide more of them.

BUFFALO EVENING NEWS
Buffalo, N.Y., April 9, 1977

Maybe it won't be remembered as the greatest version of the Greatest Story Ever Told, but if Sunday's second half of NBC's television film of "Jesus of Nazareth" is as well done as the first half was, it will provide a very moving and effective contribution to the religious celebration of the Easter season.

Certainly few dramatizations of the Gospels have won more general applause among leading spokesmen for the major Christian churches, and this one has likewise been praised by a spokesman for the American Jewish Committee for avoiding "negative images" of Judaism.

Much less inspiring than the production itself, however, were two discordant off-stage noises that preceded it. One was the mindlessly premature protest movement launched by the leader of one fundamentalist sect who admitted that he hadn't even seen the film—and who later withdrew his complaint, once he HAD seen it.

The other was the sudden panic this one group's outpouring of letters and phone calls caused in the august offices of General Motors, which had spent millions underwriting the production and had intended to sponsor the TV airing. GM, to put it bluntly, caved in completely to the fear that it might be sponsoring something controversial. Even while finding nothing objectionable in the show itself, it concluded lamely that its "commercial sponsorship could be regarded as inappropriate to the subject of the film."

While GM might be timid, however, it didn't get to be GM by being commercially dumb. It did have the wit reportedly to retain the rerun rights, just in case the controversy later subsided and "Jesus of Nazareth" turned out to be a smash hit. Meanwhile, NBC luckily found a willing substitue sponsor in Procter & Gamble.

So now whether the closing portion of this life of Jesus as portrayed by Franco Zeffirelli truly merits the applause so many churchmen have heaped upon it, or whether it deserves to be regarded as theologically and esthetically controversial after all, is a judgment which each adult televiewer who cares to spend Easter night watching it can make for himself or herself. Let those who like it and those who don't write and tell the sponsor; and while they're at it, they might also send a carbon of their views to the sponsor who chickened out.

WORCESTER TELEGRAM.
Worcester, Mass., April 6, 1977

Those who protested prematurely against Franco Zeffirelli's "Jesus of Nazareth" are being proved wrong by this remarkable six-hour television epic.

It is timely presentation at both the Jewish Passover and the most sacred of Christian holidays, Easter. It's a joy to watch and a spiritual experience to think about.

Most of the objection came from religious groups who thought — without even seeing his work — that Zeffirelli would strip Jesus of divinity and portray an ordinary man. The concern was prompted by the Italian director's rather cynical comments and his earlier portrayal of St. Francis of Assisi, an effort that, some thought, cast the recluse in the role of a hippie.

Such was the controversy that General Motors withdrew its sponsorship of the film. Procter & Gamble picked up financial support at the last minute. GM shrewdly retained rerun rights.

Zeffirelli's Jesus is both a fragile human being and clearly something much more. His story, perhaps for the first time in show business history, is warm, logical and totally in perspective. Both the script by Anthony Burgess and Zeffirelli's direction show a unique feeling for the period and the detail of life in Galilee 2,000 years ago.

While some of the scenes are straight out of the Renaissance school of painting, the film shies away from the loud tradition of Hollywood spectaculars. It's about the birth of Christianity but heavily emphasizes its roots, Judaism. That's why Christians and Jews alike can find satisfaction in it. An international cast of accomplished actors adds to the attraction.

The second part of the film will be shown on Easter Sunday, and those who have seen it say it's every bit as moving as the first three hours. It's ironic that television that can bring us such an enjoyment on rare occasions serves up endless mediocrity, or worse, most of the time.

Zeffirelli's work about Christ will be remembered. It will be remembered because it has brought the great mystery down to human level. And it proves how foolish it is to judge without the facts.

St. Louis 🐎 Review
St. Louis, Mo., April 8, 1977

Over the years we have become wary of attempts to translate Sacred Scripture to the motion picture medium. A large percentage of the biblical film epics tried a combination of spectacular production, a vague hint of a spiritual theme, and enough sex to titillate and to ensure box office success.

Attempts to present the life of Jesus on film have been spectacularly unsuccessful. Film makers have been so intent on being inoffensive that they have usually portrayed Jesus as brooding, humorless and thoroughly wooden.

The Franco Zeffirelli film, "Jesus of Nazareth," is a religious and film-making milestone. Near technical perfection, an excellent script and the combined talents of an extraordinarily gifted cast have been welded together to create for the viewer an artistic and religious experience.

This dramatization of the life of Our Lord can provide new spiritual insights for all of us. Priests and theologians could well profit from viewing this film. So often, we tend to intellectualize the Savior so much that we are unable to imagine Him as one who truly shared our humanity. Old and young will surely be assisted in their ability to relate to a Jesus of flesh and blood who once walked the dusty roads of Galilee.

Contrary to an unfortunate and groundless accusation, "Jesus of Nazareth" does not slight the divinity of Jesus Christ. The producer of this film quite evidently took seriously the recommendations of technical advisers provided by the Vatican and the Archbishop of Canterbury.

All too often, we find ourselves complaining about the deficiencies of the television and motion picture industry. Now, when they have combined to provide for us a unique and compelling and thoroughly reverent treatment of the life, suffering, death and resurrection of our Redeemer, we should be just as vocal in our praise. We would urge all who have had the opportunity to view the six-hour presentation of Jesus of Nazareth to write to KSD-TV, the network, and to the sponsors to express approval and gratitude.

—Msgr. Joseph W. Baker

The Honolulu Advertiser

Honolulu, Hawaii, February 17, 1978

The controversy over television docu-dramas has been revived with the recent showing of NBC's three-part series on Martin Luther King Jr.

Critics include several who worked closely with King and think the series didn't do him justice.

But King's widow, Coretta, disagrees. She also reminds critics that the series "is a drama and not a documentary."

SIMILAR DEBATES have erupted when television in the past has ventured into this twilight zone between history and fiction. The writer-director of the King series insists the characterizations are accurate, though specific incidents may not be.

What's unfortunate is that many viewers don't make the distinction, or at least aren't sure when to make the distinction. A viewer has to be fairly knowledgeable about the docu-drama's subject to really know whether a particular scene is fact or fiction.

Yet, as a recent survey among teen-agers by the federally funded National Assessment of Educational Progress indicates, political awareness in America has been declining in recent years. This is probably because none of today's issues arouse the intense feelings that civil rights, Vietnam and Watergate did.

WHATEVER the arguments over how accurately King's character was portrayed, the series at a minimum did well by reminding Americans of several instructive points.

One, King and others who worked to integrate America faced massive and often violent racism. Two, agencies of the government — including the FBI and local police organizations — in many instances subverted the civil rights movement. Three, King lost some of his support by criticizing the Vietnam war.

How could so much of the nation have responded so wrongly? One answer probably involves the public's political awareness.

MUCH OF THE public didn't know, or couldn't believe, that police agencies were abusing their power. Much of the public didn't know, or couldn't believe, that the government blundered badly on Vietnam.

Today's level of political awareness is not reassuring. The need for more people to pay thoughtful attention to public issues is strong.

The Philadelphia Inquirer

Philadelphia, Pa., February 16, 1978

It was advertised as "The most powerful drama ever made for television! 'KING' — The tragic and triumphant story of the Reverend Dr. Martin Luther King Jr." We watched as the special was shown in two-hour segments Sunday, Monday and Tuesday nights and were left troubled and asking ourselves what the hell the National Broadcasting Co. was trying to do?

The show was part-documentary and part pseudo-history. It ended up being neither. It was seen by millions of persons and presumably will be shown again. Many persons, particularly young people, who have no memory of the great movement which Dr. King led, were or will be given an inaccurate, distorted version of that very important segment of recent American history.

Take the ending which left the clear implication that the FBI and the Memphis police had a hand in Dr. King's assassination. Despite the late FBI Director J. Edgar Hoover's despicable, underhanded campaign against Dr. King, repeated investigation has not uncovered any hard evidence to support that implication and NBC did not present a shred of new evidence.

Or take the fact that almost every serious person who figured in the famous civil rights events of Dr. King's time was presented as one-dimensional — demeaned: Presidents John F. Kennedy and Lyndon Johnson; the Rev. Ralph Abernathy, who marched with Dr. King; Attorney General Robert Kennedy and yes, even Eugene "Bull" Connor, Birmingham's bigoted commissioner of public safety.

Dr. King deserved better. Perhaps the major problem in producing the show was to attempt to compress and dramatize all of Dr. King's life, instead of concentrating on the most significant events — the Montgomery bus strike, the Freedom Riders, the Birmingham demonstrations, the Selma to Montgomery march, the Chicago housing marches — and dealing with them in depth, perspective and accuracy. Certainly, the glorification of Dr. King, at the expense of all others who played significant roles in those events, was an unforgivable distortion.

Television is showing fewer and fewer documentaries and more and more pseudo-portrayals of prominent persons and great events — portrayals that show more of the writers' and producers' prejudices about what happened than about what really happened.

"King" carried the notation that it was a "dramatization," but hiding behind that disclaimer doesn't wash. Television with its enormous power over our minds and perceptions has a responsibility which it cannot lightly shed: to strive for accuracy and the truth in programs of this kind.

Dr. King's greatness was enhanced because he demonstrated repeatedly that he had unique courage to face the truth. NBC would have distinguished itself — and would have done better tribute to his memory — if it had followed his example.

The Washington Post

Washington, D.C., February 28, 1978

FOR SIX HOURS RECENTLY, television viewers had a chance to watch a production described as a "docu-drama." It purported to be the life story of the late Rev. Martin Luther King Jr. and, like some productions that preceded it, it was a curious mixture of reality and fantasy. That, we suppose, is what this new word was coined to describe. "King," as the program was called, was a drama to which documentary interludes were added to create a more powerful impact. Why anyone thought such tinkering with the story of Rev. King was needed is beyond us. Told as a straight documentary or, if you prefer, as a drama, that story is powerful enough. But in this version, film clips of actual events were interspersed with re-creations of the same events, the time sequence in which various incidents occurred was altered, and some conversations—in particular, those between John and Robert Kennedy—were figments of someone's imagination. Even people who were participants in or close observers of some of the events in Rev. King's life had difficulty separating truth from fiction as the hours rolled on.

To be fair about it, NBC did warn before each night's episode that "in some instances, dialogue, action and composite characters were created to advance the story." But even with such a warning, the program was on dangerous ground. This "docu-drama" merged two of the products television offers to the public—news and entertainment—in a way that made them indistinguishable from each other. By blurring the line, television undermines its greatest public service: letting people see and hear history in the making or in retrospect.

We are familiar with the argument that authors need a certain literary license to make dramas both realistic and interesting. But there is a difference between dramas based on current and past history; where a visual and oral record of history exists, the desirability of fabricating events, conversations and individuals diminishes drastically. There is also a difference between material written for television and that written for the stage or screen. People go to the theater or the movies for entertainment and even children quickly learn to take with a grain of salt the accuracy of historical events presented in such a setting. The same is not yet true of television, largely because of the efforts made by the producers of news programs and real documentaries to stick to the record. But it is likely to become true quickly if the spate of "docu-dramas" and similar productions continues.

"King," of course, is only the latest and most egregious offender. It was preceded by such programs as the one on Jack Ruby and Lee Harvey Oswald, in which at least an effort was made to distinguish between film clips and re-creations, and the one on Sen. Joe McCarthy. Somewhat similar, in a reverse kind of way, was "Washington Behind Closed Doors," in which every effort was made to make a piece of fiction appear to be a piece of history.

Television is much too powerful a medium of communication to be playing so loose with the line between fiction and fact. It is already hard enough to keep them separated. A "docu-drama" is as offensive to journalism and history as the word itself is to the English language.

The Charlotte Observer

Charlotte, N.C., February 18, 1978

As the movie "King" flickered across the television screen, my daughter Margaret, now 12 years old and in the seventh grade, watched intently. She couldn't believe some of what she saw.

When white men spat on Dr. King and threw him to the pavement, she asked, "Did people really act like that?" She hid her face when Bull Connor turned fire hoses on black children in Birmingham. She cried when nightriders killed Viola Liuzzo on the highway to Selma.

For her, and probably millions of young people like her, the six-hour movie was a shocking introduction to a South that seemed unreal because it no longer exists. A month before she was born, President Johnson signed the Voting Rights Act into law, clearing the way for blacks to shift their struggle from the streets to the ballot box. She was not quite three when Martin Luther King was killed.

This Time And Place

But for many other people, black and white, "King" brought back memories of a South — and a nation — that were too real. Perhaps that's why the movie didn't attract the audience its producers had anticipated. Many people apparently would prefer to let those old attitudes and feelings fade into the past.

But that is not likely to happen. The story of the civil rights revolution is too compelling for writers and dramatists to ignore. It will be revived again and again to shock and inspire generation after generation.

Real Drama Was Missing

The problem with "King" was that it was not dramatic enough. It failed to generate the power of the real events. Rather than capturing the magnetism of Martin Luther King, the movie underplayed him. The brooding, withdrawn man that actor Paul Winfield portrayed could not have led and sustained a revolution.

Three Charlotteans who knew Dr. King in real life say he was not the melancholy figure shown in the film. He was open, lively, witty — and committed. He had a brilliance, charisma and eloquence that inspired people and drew them to him.

'A Very Assured Person . . .'

The Rev. Jack Bullard, director of the Charlotte-Mecklenburg Community Relations Committee, roomed next door to Dr. King at Crozer Theological Seminary in Chester, Pa., in 1950-51. He remembers King as "a very assured person who knew exactly who he was and where he was going."

He said he thought the film was disjointed and "failed to portray Dr. King's deep religious conviction, and the direction and power that gave his ministry."

Maude Ballou, a teacher at J.T. Williams Jr. High, was Dr. King's secretary for six years in Montgomery and Atlanta and saw him lead the bus boycott and create the Southern Christian Leadership Conference. She said she watched the film "with dismay. They made Dr. King look like a coward. In all the time I was with him, I never saw him look like that."

She said knew Dr. King to be calm, humble and open, at ease with himself and able to put others at ease. He had a fine sense of humor and a quick wit, she said.

King

Dr. J. Randolph Taylor, pastor of Myers Park Presbyterian Church, was a minister in Washington, D.C., in the early '60s and met Dr. King during the Selma march and the march on Washington. He later moved to Atlanta and got to know the Kings even more closely there.

Watching the film had been "a moving experience," he said, because it reminded him again of the sequence of those epic events and of the courage of the people involved.

His Moral Courage Captured

He said he thought the movie oversimplified many issues but captured some of Dr. King's moral courage and his willingness to go up against powerful forces. But it missed the essence of the man himself. "There was a quickness in King's mood and expression, and a twinkle in his eye" that was not on the TV screen, he said.

Every good story awaits the right telling, but for Dr. King and the civil rights struggle, the movie "King" was not it. The movie cannot compete with the three-hour documentary, "From Montgomery to Memphis," which was put together from news film. It gives you Martin Luther King in all his eloquence and power. It shows the breadth of his understanding and the depth of his feeling.

First Speech Said It All

Further, it leaves no doubt about Dr. King's vision or commitment. He knew at the very outset what the civil rights movement was about and where it might lead. He spelled it out in the short but moving "If we are wrong, . . . God is wrong" speech that opened the Montgomery bus boycott. He was only 26 at the time, but almost everything he said later was an echo of themes from that speech.

As time passes and what was personal about Dr. King recedes into the past, his stature is certain to grow. One day he will be seen as a towering figure in American history, perhaps as a 20th century Lincoln. The reactions of young people like my daughter indicate how profoundly his life has changed ours.

— JACK CLAIBORNE
Associate Editor

The Wichita Beacon

Wichita, Kans., February 15, 1978

"King," NBC television's dramatized account of the life of Dr. Martin Luther King Jr., brought back a flood of memories. This bold and gentle preacher's son literally changed the face of the nation with his doctrine of non-violent protest, a doctrine that he adopted from the teachings of Jesus Christ and Mahatma Gandhi.

The three-part series that ended last night was more than a recitation of historical events. It was a reminder of how far we have to go yet to fulfill Dr. King's great dream of equal treatment for all Americans.

Not yet have we reached that blessed day when a black person's "little children will. . .live in a nation where they will not be judged by the color of their skin but by the content of their character."

Not yet are we at that point where "justice (is) a reality for all God's children."

But even though we have fallen short as a nation in fulfilling Dr. King's dream of equality, because of the sacrifices and the sufferings of him and his non-violent army, the United States is closer to that ideal now than at any time in its history.

As the television series so graphically portrayed, Dr. King and his followers exposed themselves to great personal danger time after time as they struggled to make his dream a reality.

Part of the dream was realized with passage of the Civil Rights Act of 1964, and another part with enactment of the Voting Rights Act of 1965. The latter well may have been responsible for the election in 1976 of the first president from the Deep South in more than a century.

And when the dream was almost snuffed out in rioting that swept Los Angeles, Newark and Detroit, Dr. King told a Kansas State University audience that the riots were "the language of the unheard, the angry explosion of bitterness over intolerable conditions."

Two of those cities now have black mayors; and across the nation there are thousands of black officeholders where once there were dozens.

It is possible that none of this would have happened if Martin Luther King Jr. had not once walked among us. But because he did, America is a better place, and for that we all owe him gratitude. We owe ourselves now the determination to see that the last vestiges of racism are stripped from the American fabric, and that all citizens of this country, in Dr. King's stirring words, are "free at last, free at last, thank God Almighty, (are) free at last!"

THE ATLANTA CONSTITUTION
Atlanta, Ga.,
February 10, 1978

Those who don't learn from history are condemned to repeat it.

The philosopher responsible for that insight failed to consider that maybe we like to repeat history—or at least to re-experience it. Writers have always known that. The Romans enjoyed reading Plutarch's *Lives*. The Elizabethans flocked to plays by Shakespeare and Marlowe, plays based on the lives of English kings and queens. Television isn't in that league, but it recognizes the hypnotic power of the dramatic events of the past.

The other night viewers were confronted with a three-hour re-enactment of the events and personalities surrounding the assassination of President Kennedy. *Ruby and Oswald*, which focused on those two personalities, is one more example of a trend that has been increasingly observed in recent years on the telly. Another three part drama is recreating the events in the life of Dr. Martin Luther King Jr.

Some call it docu-drama. In the past few years viewers have seen such recreations based on widely varied events—the Scottsboro case, the execution of of the Rosenbergs, the smearing of people during the McCarthy era, many others. And several different dramatizations of the events in Dallas in November, 1963. As dramatic presentations, some of these programs have been outstanding with viewers and with critics; some have been shoddy exploitations and distortions. Which raises a question. How are viewers to separate a reasonably balanced and accurate retelling from a biased one? If we are going to repeat history, shouldn't we make sure that we learn something from the repetition? And if so, what?

Ruby and Oswald was well acted, conscientiously directed and stuck close to the official version of events as reported by the Warren Commission and others. It added nothing to what we already know—or what we have been told. It steered clear of conspiracy theories. It presented—presumably—"the facts." Dramatized—but essentially accurate and without bias for or against institutions, like the Dallas police, or individuals like the two principals.

But another recent program based on the assassination was a far different story. It didn't pretend to present what happened, except up to a point, but what *might have happened*. Oswald is put on trial and the point of the drama was to see if the evidence was enough to convict him. This program caught a lot of criticism for distortions and for playing around with conspiracy theories.

Ruby and Oswald, while interesting enough as drama, didn't *say* anything. Viewers learn nothing about Oswald's motives, and nothing new about Ruby's. In short, it was history repeated with nothing to teach. *The Trial of Lee Harvey Oswald*, on the other hand, said far too much. It was history repeated and manhandled to fit theories or reflect prejudices. Those condemned to this repeat of history would have learned less than nothing.

The vividness of television, especially for young minds, worries thoughtful people. They are afraid that the recreation of an event will be virtually equated with the event itself and that this could lead to shallow or false conceptions of history. If history's teachings are useless, there is not much point in repeating it.

TULSA WORLD
Tulsa, Okla., October 3, 1977

FEW EVENTS in history have so completely fascinated the American public as the Kennedy Assassination.

Because of the bizarre sequence of events in Dallas in 1963, there has been a steady drumbeat of "evidence" in the form of "expert" testimony, "ignored witnesses," and "proof" of plots involving more than the lone gunman, Lee Harvey Oswald.

A movie proclaimed the theory that the President was the victim of a rightist plot; the bookstands still sprout the "real" stories of the assassination more than 14 years after the fact.

But now television has used the "what if" device in a program to put Lee Harvey Oswald on trial for the Kennedy killing. That allows all the old charges to be trotted out for review in a realistic manner.

It represents another step in the steady erosion of fact and its replacement with fantasy in the Kennedy case.

It feeds not only on the appetite of the American public for mystery and intrigue but on its refusal to believe that a lone loser like Oswald could actually kill the most important man in the world. It was a happening that defied belief.

The flood of misinformation, half-truths and wild conspiracy stories almost all were hatched to make money or fame out of the tragedy.

The television offering is in the same category. But many Americans will believe much of it to be "real truth" struggling to be told.

It becomes increasingly apparent that the Kennedy controversy will never die and the "what if" device is a big jump in the transition from fact to fantasy.

The Washington Star
Washington, D.C., October 8, 1977

There is hardly a modern institution, it may be argued, so slavish to faddish breezes as television. The ferocious imitation in programming is not as shameful as, say, stealing seeing-eye dogs, but neither is it admirable.

The latest trend is a formula called "docu-drama," which gives evidence of valuing the drama over the "docu." That television heavyweights have felt constrained to coin a label for this mutant form and its first cousin, the TV "dramatization," indicates a certain unease — and it should.

A documentary, in accepted understanding, is a reportorial presentation of a subject which, even if its conclusions are not universally accepted, is based on a verifiable body of information. It is a journalistic enterprise and answerable to journalistic standards. Drama, of course, is fictive and flys on imaginative wings; a "dramatization" answers to no standards but the producer's.

How congenial is the mating of these forms? Not very, based on early experiences. The dramatizations of Caryl Chessman, the rapist-murderer executed in California in the 1960s, for instance, was a polemic against capital punishment that did not linger on the crimes for which he was convicted.

Of particular note in this questionable trend was the recent two-part "docu-drama" by the American Broadcasting Company, "The Trial of Lee Harvey Oswald," purporting to portray the events of John F. Kennedy's assassination. ABC promoted the show as "based on historical fact, not speculation or rumor."

What the producers did, in the view of a critical *New York Times* editorial, was to present "a melange of fact and fabrication, permitting themselves 'inferences' which amount to as far-fetched a conspiracy theory as anyone yet devised. Without any new evidence they put the most sinister possible twists on what is known or half known, using dramatic techniques to plant suspicions that a shot was fired by some mysterious accomplice, that witnesses to the assassination were mysteriously murdered, that Oswald was connected with mysterious Americans, Russians and Cubans . . . Unless they are aware of more than the TV movie told, the audience can only have concluded that yes, he [Oswald] was guilty, and yes, he was part of a conspiracy that involved President Johnson, the Central Intelligence Agency, the Federal Bureau of Investigation, anti-Castro Cuban exiles, the Mafia and only ABC knows who else."

What can justify so slick a juxtaposition of unsubstantiated elements in a major television program about a national tragedy? One of the defenses we have read of the "docu-drama" is that, well, it is not history — it is entertainment. Entertainment! That is a shabby plea. It ignores the incredible power of television, a medium that tends to validate that which it presents as a special sort of reality. There's nothing very subtle about that — any reporter who has watched the effect of a television camera on those involved in a news event knows TV's extraordinary potency. A queer but undeniable credibility is inherent in the transmission of the image.

That is the danger in the facile — and intellectually suspect — blend of fact and fiction that seems the pernicious hallmark of "docu-drama."

One related example: *PBS's* "Masterpiece Theater" series, "Dickens of London." The television writer described his effort as a "speculative biography" of Charles Dickens, a bankrupt linking of terms. We feared the worst for Mr. Dickens, and our apprehension was not misplaced.

The worst distortion is the portrayal of young Charles taking the job in the blacking factory reluctantly — but voluntarily, because he is aware of his father's financial problems and wishes to help. That is the opposite of the truth.

Dickens' biographer Edgar Johnson points out that the boy knew nothing of the family's financial straits and believed he was being repudiated and abandoned by his parents. It was a descent into an abyss later recalled by Dickens as offering "no counsel, no assistance, no advice, no companionship — nothing, so help me God."

Most of the series changes are completely gratuitous and unnecessary — "the real thing was so much better," says Mr. Johnson.

What the television slicksters did to Dickens was sad. What they did to the Kennedy assassination was chilling. We can only hope that the "docu-dramas" very quickly run their course.

WEEK-LONG SCREENINGS OF 'ROOTS' VIEWED BY 80 MILLION AMERICANS

The opening segment of *Roots*, the televised adaptation of Alex Haley's best-selling novel, was seen by 61% of the audience, according to the Jan. 27 *New York Times*. ABC showed the 12-hour series Jan. 23–30, to an increasing nightly audience. Television experts estimate more than 80 million viewers for the eight-part series, with the concluding segment on Jan. 30 attracting the largest audience in television's history, 36 million households. A two-part showing of *Gone with the Wind* in November 1976 had held the record, with 33 million households watching each night.

The *Roots* success was a surprise to all the networks. The *Times* pointed out that ABC had presented *Roots* a week before the "sweep" period, one of the four weeks each year used to measure audience size. *Gone with the Wind* was presented by NBC during the last sweep week in November. Neither NBC nor CBS had planned special programs to compete with *Roots*.

Roots describes Haley's search for his family's history, beginning at the present and eventually reaching back to 1750 in Gambia, where Kunta Kinte, his ancestor, was born. Haley spent 12 years researching his family's origins, and *Roots* is in its 13th printing since publication last October. Haley Jan. 26 told the *Times* that he thought ABC has "preserved the integrity of the thing as best they could." He recounted his meeting with a viewer: "A black man saw me in the airport, and for a long time, didn't say anything. Finally, he turned to me and said, 'Look man, I just can't be cool. I've just got to say thank you.'"

Amsterdam News

New York, N.Y., January 29, 1977

The New York Amsterdam News is proud to salute the American Broadcasting Company, its staff and producers, for presenting to the American people the captivating serialization of Alex Haley's Roots in an eight-part network series during prime time.

Latest monitoring reports show that Roots has already captured 68 per cent of the nation's television audience and we are willing to wager that before the series is completed, the figure will go much closer to 100 per cent.

We proudly say that because from all reports available to us, the presentation of an idea of "Roots" is the presentation of an idea whose time has come.

"Roots" is a novel which had to be written, and Alex Haley has written it painstakingly and beautifully.

It was also a period in American history which deserved to be laid bare before the American people and now ABC has done that, beautifully and dramatically.

It is not a story of which white Americans can be proud. But white America can be proud that somebody at ABC had the guts to film it and other white Americans had the courage to sit down in their living rooms with their families and look at it.

So far as Blacks are concerned, they can be proud that "Roots" shows how deep their own roots really are and that it portrays the rage of a people to struggle toward manhood and dignity even in their darkest hour.

Hopefully, the depiction of that struggle so long ago, will enable many whites to better understand Blacks of today and the rocky roads they have travelled.

The struggle continues — but ABC has taken a giant step toward making the burden of Blacks a little lighter.

So far as we are concerned, ABC's presentation of "Roots" is television's first finest hours in America.

The Boston Globe

Boston, Mass., January 30, 1977

In a period when our sense of America's heritage has been rekindled with bicentennial zeal, the appearance of Alex Haley's book "Roots" and its popular televised dramatization adds a timely dimension to our national self-image. More than a drama of a single family's struggle, "Roots" is infant America's diary, peculiar but poignant, painful but satisfying, aggravating but, unexpectedly, a tonic. "Roots" is America's birthday story, warts and all.

Ours is a country of assimilating immigrants and children of immigrants. But the African experience in America has been marked from the beginning by such stark contradictions to national principles that comprehending it as an integrated part of the country's history—as part of every man's history—is all but impossible for most people.

As a result, the differences between the experiences of Africans and other ethnic groups have been obscured from the view of generations of Americans, overshadowed by the myth that barriers to black progress are no greater than those faced and scaled by the majority of European immigrants who came to the New World as free men and women.

Wrenched from their homes, transported under extreme cruelty, denied their language, religion, free associations, family lives and historical links, Africans bore a special burden of alienation that was unknown to Irish, Italian, Dutch and Scandinavian immigrants.

To assume that this American reality is a finished chapter before it has been absorbed into American hearts and minds is to perpetuate the misunderstandings that chain the children of former slaves and the children of former slaveholders and to delay the reconciliation of the races.

A particular value of the television broadcasts is that the unique nature of the Afro-American experience has been brought into millions of homes, not to inflame but to inform contemporary society of a history that has been shrouded in half-embarrassed, half-frightened pieties, myths and lies.

The broadcasts are destined to become the television ratings champion, attracting more than 80 million viewers a night. Ironically, the series will knock from first place last fall's airing of Gone With the Wind, a movie that has been criticized for idealizing the ante-bellum South and of distorting the image of Afro-Americans with unflattering stereotypes.

The fuller, unsanitized picture in "Roots" of America's "peculiar institution," as slavery came to be known, properly revises our historical understanding while reinforcing the South's singular achievement, symbolized by Jimmy Carter's inauguration, of rising from such troubled beginnings.

If the dramatization of "Roots" seemed romanticized or even sensationalized in parts, it might be forgiven in view of its over-all achievement of spearheading a new national perception of the Afro-American experience, humanizing it and elevating it to its proper place in the national consciousness.

To what ever degree there is a distinct American character, after all, it has its origins as much in Alex Haley's "Roots" as it does in any of our own.

THE ROANOKE TIMES

Roanoke, Va., February 13, 1977

Professional historians, who have been trained to verify and weigh the evidence, have been very slow to emerge from their cloisters and write about *Roots*, by Alex Haley. Why do people who have been studying this subject for years let a journalist sweep the field?

While they deliberated, a network made the story into a television movie which was a national event—which may make history by its impact on those who thought they were seeing history. Ernest Furgurson, writing in *The World-News* February 8, said (of the movie, not the book) that it was more one-sided than history, more cruel than life itself. Yet, he noted, especially for the young, poor and the black, television is "the real world and *Roots* the whole truth."

One of the few major league historians who has commented so far on the Haley book is David H. Donald, of Harvard (formerly, of Johns Hopkins) and he pays the book quite a few compliments. Reviewing for *Commentary* magazine, December issue, he said: "As the reconstruction of a genealogy, Haley's book is a tour de force. Like Herbert G. Gutman's recently published *The Black Family in Slavery and Freedom*, it reminds us how even in appallingly adverse circumstances blacks often maintained, through oral traditions, a full account of their lineage and a proper sense of their individual identities. Skillfully, Haley checked his oral history against surviving written documents and the family tree he has outlined seems not just plausible but authentic."

Having paid the Haley book the compliments due, Professor Donald details incident after incident recounted by Haley which were either impossible or improbable because of hard evidence to the contrary. Had he reviewed the movie, his comments would have been more cau_ic.

In contrast to the story of Haley's "legendary, almost mythical, African ancestors," Donald prefers the fully documented story of the Haley family, which migrated as a unit to Tennessee and established itself "so that members of the next generation could secure college educations." That story of triumph over adversity, Donald concludes, "would have been far more inspiring, as well as far more historically accurate, than any romanticized account of African ancestors."

Whether the television movie and the book, *Roots*, did any harm is problematical. The untutored and the unlearned, as well as the educated of all races, have their own common sense discounts which they apply to romantic mixtures of fact and fiction. Our main criticism of the book and movie is the same we would apply to the more careful and pretentious scholarship in black studies. If all they do is arouse self-pity among the blacks and guilt among the whites, they do no good and they contribute to a falsehood: that people today should be personally rewarded or penalized because of what reputed ancestors of like color experienced 200 years ago.

CHARLESTON EVENING POST

Charleston, S.C., February 1, 1977

Presented as an eight-part TV serial, "Roots" apparently achieved a tremendous audience for this version of slavery, based on a best-seller book by Alex Haley. Whether to describe it as history or allegory — or soap opera, as The Wall Street Journal labeled the production in a preview last week — we shall leave to local viewers to decide.

Some of them have told us that "Roots" is inflammatory, more likely to disturb race relations than to heal past grievances. We would like to hear from readers, especially black readers, on this subject.

Time Magazine took a dim view of the TV production of "Roots" It labeled the production "Middlebrow 'Mandingo' " The story concerns Kunta Kinte, a black African youth who was captured by slavers in his native country (now known as Gambia) and sold into bondage on a Virginia plantation before the American Revolution. Author Haley traced his own ancestry back to Africa by means of an account handed down by word of mouth through the generations.

Slavery is one of the somber chapters in the history of mankind. It has been practiced by people of many races and cultures, and is reported still to exist in some remote parts of the world. The American episode, of course, is peculiarly close to our people of both races, because in terms of history it is relatively recent.

Freed from legal slavery after the Civil War, black Americans still had a long way to go. Neither their problems nor the problems of their former masters were solved by the Emancipation Proclamation and the constitutional amendments that followed.

The TV version of "Roots" ended with migration of Kunta Kinte's progeny to Tennessee. The author himself briefly recapitulated on the screen what happened after that.

Whether "Roots" will establish a feeling of kinship with Africa and revive hostility to white Americans for past cruelties, or whether it will remind both races that slaves wrenched from their homeland became the ancestors of the luckiest blacks of their race anywhere in the world today, we cannot say.

The contrast of the transplanted blacks with the native red Indians who were all but exterminated is a lesson in survival that should not be overlooked. Indians could not endure slavery, and that was the reason why blacks were imported from Africa to provide the muscle for development of a continent. The blacks managed to adapt to conditions as they existed, including final achievement of the true freedom for which Kunta Kinte yearned in vain. We hope that readers may be moved to express their feelings in brief letters to the editor.

CASPER STAR-TRIBUNE

Casper, Wyo., January 29, 1977

Black Americans' search for identity as portrayed in ABC's "Novel for Television" leaves much to be desired in the way of electronic drama but we remain optimistic that some socially redeeming consequences can result from this week long marathon.

There are some of us who would prefer to give a boot to *Roots* for its many failings as a television production but having grown up with the medium we can only expect a romanticized and somewhat stereotyped version of history.

Lest you suffer from a fantasy that man's inhumanity to man is a thing of the past we suggest you pick up a copy of *Genocide in Paraguay* edited by Temple University law professor Richard Arens. It is not likely to be the next "Novel for Television."

Slavery continues in 1977 where the stone age tribe of the Ache Indians are being systematically exterminated in a most brutal fashion under the auspices of the Paraguay government.

"Ache are hunted down like animals and killed," Arens reports. "Women are sold as prostitutes. Children are sold into slavery for as little as 50 cents. Chiefs are tortured and publicly humiliated in order to break their authority. Indians are herded onto reservations where food and medical care are deliberately denied them so they die."

It is misleading to paint history in absolutes for the benefit of chastising a society for its past sins. Nothing is ever — excuse the expression — black or white.

Colonial slavetraders may have been ahead of their time as far as their livlihood is concerned but they certainly were not alone.

In *ROOTS* we see the white man as representative of all that is dastardly and Kunta Kinte, the noble savage, transported to America against his will to suffer incredible oppression. There is also a dash of frontal nudity, inexplicit sex and violence so that the production can be labeled "revolutionary" in the annals of television.

No attention is given to cause or effect. It's as if Americans have had a monopoly on subjugation of other races while Kunta Kinte and his descendants remain a composite of all that is good, witty and sly.

The criticism is not meant to take any praise away from author Alex Haley whose own story of the 12 years of reseach for *Roots* is, in some respects, more fascinating than the end product.

If nothing else, perhaps the estimated viewing audience of 90 million Americans tuned in to the seven night series will be able to gain an appreciation of relatively recent efforts on part of the Black community to establish solid, sustaining educational programs in public schools designed to create a pride in heritage among black children. In such a perspective *Roots* has a value other than its Walt Disney like approach to a dismal practice.

THE ARIZONA REPUBLIC
Phoenix, Ariz., February 3, 1977

Nothing in the world of television is quite like the 10-hour spectacular called "Roots." According to the rating services, it was seen by more people during its eight-day premier than any other theatrical event anywhere at any time.

"Roots" is the story of a black American's search for identity. Alex Haley did a superb detective job in tracing his ancestry back to the warrior who was captured in the African jungle, placed in chains on a slave ship, and brought to the United States.

The book ends with the slave's descendants achieving their independence after the Civil War and making their way from Virginia to Tennessee where they exercised the rights of citizenship.

This isn't the South of Stephen Foster or Rhett Butler. Historians have found errors in Haley's descriptions of the slave era in American history.

For instance, there could have been no substantial slave trade if black Africans hadn't sold their fellow tribesmen to the white men who sailed the ships from New England. Yet the film has white hunters going into the bush to capture the blacks.

At times the scenes move too slowly. But there is a glacial strength to the book and to its television version which rivals that of "Gone With the Wind."

Americans have engaged in five wars, including two global conflicts, since Lee surrendered to Grant at Appomattox.

But this nation has never suffered more nor paid a higher price to achieve, in part at least, the American dream. Which helps to explain the unparalleled attention given to two books that deal with the central theme of how the United States survived the traumatic experience of being half slave and half free.

Showing "Roots" on television has had some regrettable consequences. Black youths have rioted in Boston and elsewhere, aroused by brutal treatment of slaves in the picture.

But if "Roots" does nothing else, it shows how Americans, black and white, have gone farther than any nation to establish the validity of the proposition that all men are created equal.

THE DAILY OKLAHOMAN
Oklahoma City, Okla., January 31, 1977

BROADCAST of the longest television drama ever seen in this country, stretched over an eight-day period, has had a predictable effect on some viewers. Racial relations in some cities, especially among the young or immature, have worsened. "Roots" was a television dramatization of the novel by Alex Haley, and was based on his exploration of his own family history. It began with the capture of one of his ancestors in West Africa by slave traders.

The one thing which separates Americans of African origins from those who came from Europe and Asia, more than any other factor, is the fact of slavery. The whites came here by choice, to escape oppression. The blacks, for the most part, did not come by choice, and faced dominance they had not known before. Slavery continued, with humans owned as chattels, until the Emancipation Proclamation by President Lincoln during the Civil War. But by then many American blacks were free citizens, in the states where slavery had never existed.

Some of the facts of our history are being overlooked in the current interest in black history. One is that importation of slaves did not continue right up to the Civil War era, but stopped decades earlier. By Lincoln's day, most slaves had been born in this country, a fact abolitionists continued to contrast with the guarantees contained in the Constitution.

Another is that most slaves, by the 1850s, even though many were still unable to read and write (as were many whites), were far better educated and trained in technical skills than the natives of their ancestral homelands. While the difference between a free citizen, white or black, and a slave or newly freed black was great, the emancipated slaves had something of a head start toward their new freedom.

And overlooked in almost all black studies is the role of the white indentured immigrant from Europe, who was not a free citizen until his debt incurred for his passage had been paid. Unscrupulous masters could make this a long effort, sometimes lifelong. Men and women in this kind of bondage also paid a fearful price to become Americans.

Our roots are important to all of us. It is important to remember what our ancestors did to create this country. But generalizations are still inaccurate portrayals, and should be seen as such.

THE SAGINAW NEWS
Saginaw, Mich., January 31, 1977

Every so often television hits a peak of craftsmanship and professionalism. ABC has done so with its presentation of "Roots," a TV adaptation of the book by black author Alex Haley.

The network obviously took a gamble with its decision to program the narrative over eight consecutive nights beginning with two consecutive two-hour presentations. Considering the subject matter — a deeply probing insight into the origins of the black man in America via the dehumanizing route of slavery — it took an even bigger one at widespread public acceptance.

ABC and television in general has obviously won that gamble hands down. The adaptation of Haley's work based on a tracing of his own family roots, has held a goodly portion of the national TV audience spellbound for its entire eight-night run.

Not only in Saginaw but across the country "Roots" has been drawing rave notices. They are justly deserved — and we feel sorry for those who have been unable to accept it or cope. The mixed cast of black and white actors and actresses has performed brilliantly and with sensitivity.

But to suggest "Roots" is entertainment would totally miss the mark. It is a history lesson. It is more than that. The crafting of the production is incisively instructive of the modern black society in America, its priorities and differing value sets, and how they got that way. Some of it has been subtle, but not so subtle that it was easy to miss by anyone paying rapt attention and trying to understand.

That, to us, is the particular shading of brilliance in "Roots," — a brilliance that far overshadows the violence as Haley had to set it down. What we have seen is not nudity or sex or any other such subjects which some so easily seem to find objectionable.

What we have seen is a powerful portrayal of the best and worst of human instincts in a deeply moving narrative. It rates as "must" viewing for all Americans — particularly black and white-skinned. It has been television at its best and it will win awards as work of art, a work of truth.

The Afro American
Baltimore, Md., February 1, 1977

Author Alex Haley's "Roots," as dramatized in its exceedingly successful weeklong run run during prime time on the ABC-TV network, was a powerful recapitulation whose story told the lesson of from whence black Americans came, where they now stand and where they must go.

For some it was a learning; for others a re-learning.

It was designed to be a 12-hour story in which Alex Haley traced his family history back to 1750 when an ancestor, Kunta Kinte was born in The Gambia, West Africa. But it was much more.

For the average 80 million viewers who nightly followed the story of the best-selling novel, it was as significant a story as television has been privileged—or bold enough—to tell to the American people.

The timing, coming in the first month after the year-long celebration of the country's Bicentennial, could not have been better.

There are the critics who nit-pick about inaccuracies, who question the emphasis placed on certain events or attitudes, or, in some absurd instances, debate whether or not the show should have been televised at all.

We know of no book that has been completely accurate and able to cover all the cultural facets of any era; nor do we know of any television show or movie which has portrayed exactly the printed version on which it was based.

But the overall treatment of "Roots" by ABC-TV is a much more than adequate, positive representation of the epic story and sordid history it tells.

Only twice in history have television programs captured such fantastically large audiences and in neither case was the showing over as long a period.

Some people were shamed by "Roots." Some cried at the brutality of slavery. Not many people who watched it classified this masterpiece as just another show.

Some criticism of the show was based on ignorance of history; some out of a desire to ignore history.

But "Roots," as told in the book and on television, the Kunta Kintes and Fiddlers, the slave bosses and others; the impact such people and circumstances have on what America is today and what it will be in the immediate future, are historic challenges which no American dares ignore.

Newsday

Garden City, N.Y., January 26, 1977

It may be a bit melodramatic; it may paint the good guys as superheroes and the bad guys as supervillains; it may stray a bit from the strange and cruel saga of one family's encounter with America. But "Roots," on TV this week, is a powerful educational experience, and it's a pity the 12-part series has been scheduled too late for many youngsters.

"Roots" isn't fiction, of course. Kunta Kinte, author Alex Haley's ancestor, was born around 1750 in Gambia. His capture and his dreadful trip to the United States were repeated by thousands of African blacks. So were his experiences as a slave.

On television, "Roots" will chronicle the family's experiences until the Civil War and the freeing of the slaves. But Haley's book doesn't end there; it continues until contemporary times. ABC would perform a great service for all Americans, black as well as white, by presenting the rest of the story. The tribulations of America's blacks didn't end with the Civil War. In fact, they're not over yet.

The Providence Journal

Providence, R.I.,
February 2, 1977

The ABC-TV network detonated an explosion last week whose shock waves are likely to criss-cross this country for a long time to come.

It was no "bomb" in theatrical parlance. The eight-part serialization of Alex Haley's novel *Roots* was a dramatic and cultural triumph of extraordinary proportions. Rating experts believe some 80 million viewers tuned in each night, giving this saga of black slavery in America the largest cumulative audience of any television presentation.

The message that sends to the commercial television industry has to be instructive — if not revolutionary. If offered shows of high quality, in contrast to the milktoast mush that dominates much TV programming, the public will respond.

In fairness to the industry, *Roots* had everything going for it. It was aired while the book is still the No. 1 best-seller. The TV adaptation was superbly handled — writing, casting, acting, directing all were first-rate. Moreover, the content touched an exposed nerve in the American psyche as no other event has done since the civil rights marches of the 1960s. Slavery was not just a word in the history books; it was real, singeing the souls of its victims as the tip of the overseer's lash tore into their flesh.

Author Haley and ABC-TV deserve the highest commendation. As entertainment, *Roots* doubled as a significant educational event that ought to be repeated in a time zone suitable for every American youngster old enough to understand.

THE PLAIN DEALER

Cleveland, Ohio, February 1, 1977

"Roots," the story of one black family, going from freedom in Africa through slavery and back to freedom in America, was strong drama on ABC-TV. Millions of viewers felt the defeat, the pain, the terror and finally the joyous victory of it.

This was top-rank theater. It should rate with classics like Britain's "Forsyte Saga." It captured a much larger audience and it had as powerful emotional impact.

"Roots" is a fictionalized documentary, one family's story that tells the history of slavery in the South. It tells how Kunta Kinte, a proud young African, was captured and enslaved, and how his family nurtured its hidden hunger for freedom and finally won it.

Alex Haley, the descendant of Kunta Kinte, researched his beginnings and wrote them into a historical novel that rings true. It engulfs his listeners in slavery's brutish horrors — and in this family's invincible yearning to be free.

Every-actor, script writer, director, cameraman — everyone who contributed to this epic — deserves to share in some award. Their television drama gave a massive audience insights into the terrible slavery era and into the human spirit's unquenchable need for liberty.

The Philadelphia Inquirer

Philadelphia, Pa., February 2, 1977

In 1961, Newton Minow, then chairman of the Federal Communications Commission, challenged a group of television broadcasters to sit in front of their televisions without a book, magazine, newspaper or anything else to distract them. "I can assure you," Mr. Minow chided, "you will observe a vast wasteland."

In the 16 years since that speech, television programming has more often than not, proven Mr. Minow correct. And, consequently, when something unequivocally worthwhile does appear on television it gives us reason to cheer. And cheer we do.

For eight days, the American Broadcasting Company treated millions of Americans, a record number, in fact, to 12 hours of superb entertainment with its adaptation of Alex Haley's best selling novel, "Roots."

Just in case you are one of the few that has not seen, read or heard about it, "Roots" is an account by Mr. Haley, a black man, of his attempt to trace his origins back to an African village. The first episode started in 1750 with the birth of Kunta Kinte, an ancestor. Born free, Kunta Kinte is captured and brought to America as a slave. What follows in other episodes does not, in short, portray America at its best.

As one viewer was quoted as saying, "It has made the brutality of slavery more vivid for me than anything I've seen or read." Said another, "It's so powerful. It's so distressful. I just feel awful, but I'm glad my children are watching."

There were many other persons watching, as well — 80 million each night, according to one estimate. That even surprised ABC, which took a risk in presenting a program on eight consecutive nights in prime time. If the first episode had bombed, its ratings would have plunged for the entire week, a catastrophe in the competetive television industry.

But that did not occur, and ABC's risk paid off, making us all the richer.

THE SUN

Baltimore, Md., February 1, 1977

The American Broadcasting Company's dramatization of Alex Haley's novel, "Roots," deserves no awards for subtlety of characterization. But as a political *event* it deserves every medal television can bestow. In its depiction of good and evil, the TV version of "Roots" was, quite literally, a matter of black and white. There was very little shading. Not one major black character was shown in a really unfavorable light; not one member of the Southern white plantation class in a sympathetic way.

As history, the presentation suffered from its dismissal of the role of Arabs and coastal African tribes in enslaving inland peoples. As drama, it suffered from the common TV malady of turning much of life into soap opera, even when that is not intended. But "Roots" should not be viewed primarily as history, or as drama, but as a morality tale that goes to the heart of the American experience. Such outrages to humanity as genocide, slavery and caste cannot be confined to the bounds of history or drama. There is no way they can be treated in all their enormity except as experiences that sear the human conscience and offer instruction on the way man should treat man.

What "Roots" had to say was, of course, well known to literate Americans. The horrors of the slave trade have been laid out with more hair-raising precision than Mr. Haley attempted. The myth of darkies working contentedly for ole massah on de ole plantation was put to rest years ago. But because of the deficiences of our educational system and the mind-debilitating lure of the junk that TV offers, millions of Americans, especially young ones, do not adequately know and therefore do not adequately feel the forces that shaped our society.

Young blacks in scattered high schools have terrorized white classmates because they were emotionally aroused by "Roots." Some whites have fretted that the TV drama will exacerbate racial tensions because of the stark way in which the material was presented. But when the shock effect is over and the complaints of the drama critics are forgotten, we believe "Roots" will be remembered for what it was—a sermon on the sin of slavery and the heroic human spirit that emerged to fight it. Ours is a society blighted to this day by that sin but ennobled by the struggle to overcome it. That millions of Americans were taught or reminded of these elements of our history is enough to make "Roots" a profoundly political event.

The Detroit News

Detroit, Mich., February 1, 1977

A white youth in Texas told author Alex Haley that his father had always hated black people but after seeing "Roots," the boy said, "I watched my father cry for the first time in his life."

Such was the impact of "Roots," a television series that gripped the nation all last week.

The movie, an adaptation of Haley's book that traced the author's origins to an African village, contained nothing new to blacks or to anyone who has read histories such as John Hope Franklin's "From Slavery to Freedom."

Indeed, many blacks will tell you that the TV series only told half the truth about outrages done to blacks in American history.

But the "Roots" recitation of rape, mutilation, floggings, brutality, treachery, thievery, pillage, injustice and the other indignities of slavery had never before been brought home to so many people.

An estimated 80 million people viewed at least part of just one of the eight episodes. Those are fantastic numbers in the Nielsen ratings game.

But much more important than any ephemeral ratings: We feel the show helped immeasurably to impress on white Americans why blacks have such bitter feelings about whites.

The TV program, seeking greater dramatic impact, added characters and episodes not in the Haley book. But in general the film mirrored the book. It rang "true."

If at times the programs presented stereotyped, one-dimensional white villains, what else should white America expect? The film was presented from a black point of view. From any honest point of view the record of slavery has to be sordid and ugly.

The programs raised important questions, they troubled consciences and caused us all to think of American history — not in our usual rosy glow of myth — but as it really was.

That, too, is a triumph for television whose fare is seldom more nourishing than melodramas, situation comedies and gratuitous sex and violence.

The series ended Sunday with more upbeat and hopeful notes: The exultant cry of "freedom" after the Civil War ended; black field hands weeping over Lincoln's assassination; a white woman's tender admonition to a black boy, whose father had just been cruelly horsewhipped, to hate the deed but not whites, and the black man who had been so cruelly whipped passing up an opportunity to flog a "master" who deserved flogging — overcoming justified hatred in a Christ-like act.

It would be too much to expect that "Roots" will rout racism from America. That ignorant strain runs too deep.

But "Roots" should have seared indelibly in the consciences of all Americans what it has meant to be black in America.

Los Angeles Times

Los Angeles, Calif., February 1, 1977

A profound political event took place last week, not in Washington but on the television screens of millions of Americans.

What was there in "Roots" that drew that vast audience night after night, that made it the most watched, the most talked about program in the history of television?

It was not brilliant acting or subtle characterization, for, as some critics have pointed out, many of the characters were two-dimensional, and stereotypes abounded. The blacks were on the whole good to the point of nobility; nearly all the whites were at best weak, and most of them were despicable.

But the story is essentially true. It all happened: the capture in Africa, the unspeakable journey to these shores, the awful cruelty, the rending of families, the abuse of women, the generations of slavery followed by the cynical return to oppression after emancipation.

What drew us all to the set, what made Kunta Kinte a household name, is that for the first time we saw a central theme of the American story played out in fierce drama right before our eyes. Those of us who are black knew that story better; those of us who are not black knew it from the history books, but had not ever seen it so vividly presented to us.

We guess that for those of us who are black the reliving of the terrible story will be a source of awe and pride; for those of us who are not black, cause for deeper understanding and sober reflection, and for all of us together a vivid and wrenching reminder of how much there is yet for us to do.

Pittsburgh Post-Gazette

Pittsburgh, Pa., February 1, 1977

TO everyone's surprise the television show, "Roots," captured the attention of an incredibly high number of Americans in its unprecedentedly long eight-night presentation.

Not only were the ratings high from the first, but they kept going up. Obviously, word-of-mouth about this dramatization of the true story of an African captured by slavers and of his life and that of his descendants in slavery in Virginia persuaded many to tune in on later segments. The series, television at its best, thus became a cultural phenomenon with greater impact than even ABC network officials had dreamed.

What happened? In the first place, the basic story written by Alex Haley about his ancestors, starting with the captured Kinta Kunte, was fascinatingly handled, with multi-faceted black and white characters to hold attention. For blacks it had to touch the deepest roots of their being.

Second, for many whites it was a gripping and unusual look at the world through black eyes, and particularly through the eyes of a person deprived of his freedom and brutalized into slavery. It reminded people in a vivid way that the mind-set of the black brought in chains to this country was different, because he or she was deliberately cut off from the roots of the homeland and, moreover, forced to play the role of a child, rather than of a dignified adult.

Too many whites assume that the experiences that immigrants had in crossing the ocean and settling in the new land were alike, forgetting that the black experience was devastatingly different. Many of today's societal problems with poverty and crime and irresponsibility stem from slavery and its breaking of families and individual dignity on the wheel of bondage. The wonder is that so many black Americans after slavery became dependable, law-abiding, hard-working citizens despite the servile habits branded into them.

But "Roots" may have had wide appeal to Americans beyond the specific question of slavery. Many persons in crossing the ocean cut themselves off from homeland and even kin. Particularly was this true of the Anglo-Saxons who are the predominant population element in America (white ethnics were different in that respect). Just as the black heritage emphasis of the 1960s spurred a renewed interest in ethnic heritage, so will "Roots" tap the yearning in many people to know more about their ancestral background.

An appreciation of one's own heritage coupled with understanding the world as seen through the eyes of persons of other heritages is essential for making harmoniously workable our pluralistic society. The story of Kinta Kunte and his descendants was salutary in furthering that effort in American life.

The Washington Star

Washington, D.C., February 12, 1977

The Africa of "Roots," as TV viewers saw it, was Eden. Never mind what history has to say about black slave traders or tribal warfare unconstrained by the Geneva Convention. Never mind the position of women unconstrained by the ERA. The white slave traders, on the other hand, projected an integrity of evil unmatched since Charles Laughton played Captain Bligh.

Is this good or bad for the dignity of blacks and a multi-racial state's hopes of civic harmony? A little of each, probably.

On the plus side, there *is* a value in myth for rousing an awareness of identity. A clean-cut Us-and-Them situation reinforces loyalties and the pride of belonging, even when the power is with Them and a certain steadfastness in the victim's role is all that's possible for Us.

Yet, that warts-and-all truth conveys its own dignities. The complex blend of good and evil that reality presents when there isn't any sugaring is often a more powerful advocate than hyped perfection. "Roots" would have been more compelling still if it had presented slavery less as a simplistic story of what white people did to black people.

In fact, it's condescending to blacks to tell it that way. Like going along with the Goddess or Little Lady stereotypes of what women are like.

Nevertheless, the "Roots" phenomenon may herald a trend full of positive auguries. For example, the Newbery and Caldecott awards presented at the American Library Association meetings here last week gave evidence of a new awareness of the richness of black life as well as of its tragic dimension.

One of these top prizes for children's literature honored a novel about Mississippi blacks in the Depression. The other singled out a picture book delineating, in poetic line and color, customs of 26 African tribes. The novel is the work of a black writer, the picture book of a black artist collaborating with his wife, a white artist.

Idealizations both, both are artistically valid. Both project attractive, neglected aspects of human experience without melodramatic overkill.

Such cultural explorations enlarge reality as much for whites as for blacks. And vice versa. In the long run, the promise of our pluralism is that appreciating our separate identities can lead to appreciating what we have in common.

Minneapolis Tribune

Minneapolis, Minn., February 1, 1977

The "Roots" television experience is over for now, but talk about it goes on. Comments on the week-long adaptation of Alex Haley's saga of the route of his ancestors from West Africa to West Tennessee over two centuries are still coming in, and from all accounts those who saw it won't soon forget it. The agony of watching racial myths explode has been expressed in many ways.

A Minnesota grandmother who never saw a black person until she was 30: "After the second episode I had trouble eating. I couldn't get to sleep until the wee hours, and then I had nightmares the rest of the night."

The 18-year-old son in a middle-class New York City household: "Slavery was evil, and this shows how bad it was, stealing those people from their homes and carrying them far away and buying and selling them."

A black minister in the South: "It at least puts the moral question before them (the whites) in terms of whether they can allow the atrocity that was perpetrated on a people, whether we can allow the plight of those people to continue in 1977."

Gunnar Myrdal, the Swedish scholar who 35 years ago wrote a two-volume guidebook to the race problem in the United States, once said: "Most Americans saw clearly the inconsistency between American democracy and Negro slavery," yet, "the everyday American simply cannot commit himself to all the complex thinking required to sort out all the facts about the black race in America."

It takes no stretch of the imagination to see that "Roots" does the sorting in a manner to engage both the mind and the emotions. A case in point is how slavery brutalizes both the enslaver and the enslaved.

The size of the audience watching "Roots"—an estimated 75 million for each of the first two episodes—indicates that the timing for the series was just right. What was thought to be a risky enterprise by two of the three commercial networks became an unexpected success for the third. The reasons for such extraordinary reversals aren't always easy to explain. It seems, though, that the times and the mood of the country are such that people want to know where they are coming from.

Race has been a burdensome obsession in this country for more than 200 years. There was a time, not so long ago, when many believed that their entire existence depended on carefully nurtured myths. It was not unusual to hear someone say, in effect, "Don't bother me about my racial beliefs, even if they're wrong; destroy them and you destroy me." Somehow all that is changing. More and more people are yearning for the truth about almost everything—the FBI, sex, national heroes and race, among others—even if it hurts.

John Henrik Clarke, the black historian, has perhaps expressed it best about "Roots": "Over-all I think it has opened up a delicate situation that will cause some embarrassment on both the black and white side. But it has paved the way for a much-needed, long-overdue discussion."

The Idaho STATESMAN

Boise, Idaho, March 2, 1977

It isn't surprising that the post office in Henning, Tenn., is swamped with mail these days. The deluge is a tribute to "Roots," last month's television series that touched the lives of millions of Americans.

Since ABC aired the series, mail has been pouring into Henning addressed to Alex Haley, author of "Roots." Some of the letters ask Haley to help them find their ancestors, as Haley did in his 12-year search that traced his family from Henning back to a small African village.

A New York Times reviewer condemned "Roots," saying it was utterly lacking in artistic merit. To criticize a program like "Roots" for the sake of its artistry, good or bad, can be compared to criticizing the Oakland Raiders for not being pretty. "Roots" did not blaze artistic trails because that wasn't its intention. But its social value is perhaps greater than that of anything else that's been on television.

In the increasingly homogeneous and mobile society that is America, people are losing sight of who they are. Many never know in the first place. If a television program can make people appreciate their heritage, make them thankful for the realization that they didn't spring from a world of freeways and fast-food restaurants, it has accomplished something worth quite a lot.

But "Roots' " greatest contribution is increased understanding and empathy among the millions who saw it. It taught in a way no history book can. Not only did the program give many blacks a greater appreciation of their heritage, it made many modern-day whites understand that heritage, and the shameful role white people played in it, for the first time.

A comment made by a 14-year-old Boise black girl the day "Roots" ended sums it up as well as anything:

"A girl at school," she said, "never would talk to me and after this (Roots) came on, she told me she hated the way white folks used to treat us."

If a television program can do that, make people reach each other for the first time, it is an unqualified success.

We hear a lot of criticism these days, much of it justified, about television being superficial, excessively violent, even pernicious. "Roots," on the other hand, is definitive proof of the good television can accomplish.

Arkansas Gazette.

Little Rock, Ark., February 16, 1977

Roots appears to have been the most popular television show ever, on the record of audience ratings, and it has stirred a great outpouring of written commentary on the phenomenal public response to the specialized story. The show has been praised, analyzed, criticized, condemned. It is seen on the one hand as a powerful drama based on essential truth; it is also seen as a melodrama that neglects important distinctions and takes historical liberties. Some critics believe *Roots* will have enduring social impact, others believe it reveals more about the overpowering presence of television itself in our national life than it reveals about the institution of slavery, from which the story derives.

Certainly *Roots* is a moving story, masterfully told, and endowed with one of the greatest casts ever assembled for television. It is marvelous entertainment, at the least, and all of us will have opportunity to see it again—next time (or some time) possibly without so many commercials. Alan King, the comedian, swears that immediately after one scene, in which Kunta Kinte is dragged back into captivity with an iron collar around his neck, the sponsors cut in with the famous commercial about "ring around the collar"!

The other certainty about *Roots*, as we see it, is the healthiness of having an antidote to *Gone with the Wind*. Now, GWTW was grand entertainment which generations ahead will still enjoy, but its romanticized version of the Southern plantation life was, as they say, lacking in redeeming social value. Nobody should ever take GWTW seriously, even if so many Southerners *circa* 1939 did, thus extending both the myth and, incidentally, the popularity of those Greek columns for at least another generation in Southern architecture. (All white Southerners are in direct line of descent from Scarlett O'Hara, if not Marse Robert; does anyone know a Southerner descended from an overseer?)

The most delicious irony of all, indeed, was in the ratings *Roots* earned the last night, when finally it surpassed the previous all-time high earned by the televised GWTW! This symbolism was almost as rich as the triumph of the slave family itself at the end of the TV story in the successful exodus to a freeholding in Tennessee.

As for the power of television, as manifested in the ratings scored for *Roots,* we acknowledge that it is just a bit scary to think of a whole nation of people watching *anything,* (except possibly an inauguration) at one and the same time.

In any case, in the summing up, it is our thought that the televised *Roots* (as well as the novel) was good for the country. We think that it is historically valid, in essence if not in all details. Its villains on the slaveships and the plantations are so loathsome and the brutalization of slaves so vivid, indeed, that some resentment has been stirred a-fresh among black Americans, inevitably. Granted, there have been some incidents in the schools. Nevertheless, *Roots* never misses its moral—that racism is evil, whoever is the victim. And, in the end, the black descendants of Kunta Kinte emerge in freedom and in triumph after an ordeal that lasted for centuries. Possibly the most remarkable feature of the reaction to *Roots* is the great surge of pride experienced among black Americans. Such a swelling of pride makes *Roots'* best testimonial.

ARKANSAS DEMOCRAT

Little Rock, Ark., February 4, 1977

The recently-televised adaptation of Alex Haley's novel, "Roots," perhaps has had more national impact than any broadcast since 1938, when Orson Welles sent thousands into hysteria with his graphic depiction over radio of a Martian invasion of earth.

Many persons in 1938 had difficulty distinguishing Welles' fantasy from reality. Likewise, it's difficult for the 40 to 70 per cent of last week's nighttime TV audience who saw "Roots," to sort out historic fact from the product of the author's imagination.

There's no doubt "Roots" is a blockbuster of a 12-hour television movie. Its impact is said to have provoked racial flareups in Pennsylvania, Michigan and even at a Hot Springs school.

Haley wrote the novel after he spent 12 years tracing his ancestry forward from Kunta Kinte, an 18th century Mandingo warrior sold into slavery in Maryland. The film graphically depicts brutality and dehumanization of Kunta and his slave descendants.

Haley's novel should not be mistaken for history. It is based largely on the oral tradition, and the novelist has drawn heavily upon his imagination to fill holes in documentation.

But, if "Roots" has a conspicuous failing, it's only this one of perspective.

We tend to judge the novel's content by the values most of us now hold—not from within the milieu in which the events transpired. We see slavery from the vantage point of a mechanized age when virtually all menial toil is unnecessary. But then, slavery (while morally reprehensible) was an economically-expedient socio-economic system—the only one upon which large-scale agriculture could be based.

Furthermore, most slaveholders considered their slaves—not as humans perhaps—but as property, valuable chattels to be cared for, not abused.

"Roots" will be seen by many as an indictment of slavery and of the antebellum whites' attitude toward the black man. But Haley's subtitle indicates "Roots" goes deeper: It's the struggle of an American family upward toward self-realization and against seemingly insuperable odds.

In that context, "Roots" is a literary benchmark for us all. The struggle to be free — to discern one's identity and find one's place in the scheme of things — is not unique to Haley's ancestors. It's not just the black struggle, but also the human one and, as such, it should engender common understanding — not bitterness — among all those who read it.

The Evening Gazette

Worcester, Mass., January 31, 1977

First indications are that ABC's powerful, eight-part dramatization of "Roots" has had a landmark effect both on the American social conscience and on the coming of age of television.

Eighty million viewers — one of the largest audiences in history— followed this powerful adaptation of Alex Haley's best-selling novel tracing his own family's lineage from its African origins to the American post-Civil War period. The impact may have been as great as that of another tract on the horrors of slavery, "Uncle Tom's Cabin," 125 years ago.

It is easy to quibble that the black African society of 1750 may not have been as idyllic as portrayed, that all slaves were not as proud and sensitive and all owners not as cruel and unthinking as in "Roots." The anti-Christian flavor of the film has been noted. But this slaves'-eye account of the tragedy on which the early American South was built rings true in most essentials.

By all reports, this was a sort of traumatic experience for a great many Americans. It made blacks feel pride and anger. It made whites feel horror and guilt. And perhaps it brought to both races a new understanding of our shared heritage as, more than a century after the freeing of the slaves, we still grope for brotherhood and social justice.

The effect of "Roots" on future TV programming may also be significant. The drama's tremendous ratings success is another triumph for ABC, the "junior" network that has trounced its rivals with the Olympics, with a clutch of popular situation comedies and with its pioneering "novels for television."

ABC took several gambles with "Roots." It bet on an untried eight-successive-evenings format. It bet that times have changed since white Americans were noted for shunning serious drama with black protagonists. And it bet that a mass audience would respond to quality fare. All these bets paid off handsomely.

Television is the logical medium for adaptations of thick novels. With rare exceptions, the movies have been unable to do them justice because audiences won't sit still long enough. Now ABC has proved with "Roots," as with the original "Rich Man, Poor Man," that such extended works can be commercial blockbusters. The other networks are already trying to duplicate ABC's success in this form. More major efforts — including a continuation of "Roots" to the present — can be expected in coming seasons.

But even if "Roots" remains an isolated peak in TV programming, it will have served a very worthwhile purpose if it has eased, rather than exacerbated, racial prejudice in America.

The Charleston Gazette
Charleston, S.C., February 23, 1977

The television adaptation of the novel *Roots* incited black Americans to assault white Americans in scattered incidences, the Associated Press reports. We have one report, close to home, of an assault during which blacks chanted, ''Roots, Roots, Roots!''

The televised production of *Roots* was an enormously worthwhile undertaking and should have been beneficial to Americans of all hues. It is understandable that black Americans would feel rage as they watched a depiction of the systematic degradation which slaves endured, but ex post facto vengeance is irrational.

A few unfortunate side effects notwithstanding, we have no doubt that *Roots* deserved to be shown. We're not so sure, however, that a prevailing pattern of ethnic comedy shouldn't be discouraged by the networks and civil rights groups working in concert.

In their way, some black comedians may be polarizing American society as thoroughly as Earl Butz might have done. At any rate, we find ourselves experiencing similar reactions to Earl Butz jokes and ''Get Whitey'' jokes — a sick and uncomfortable feeling in both cases.

We refer to the humorous references by black comedians to what they portray as typical black activities — mugging, theft, and the like. Not long ago a popular black comedian got the laugh he wanted when he said he was an electronics expert — he dismantled burglar alarms.

At the risk of being a spoilsport, we suggest that some black comedians are doing a disservice to black citizens, creating mistrust among white citizens, and, at the same time, planting among impressionable young black people the idea that crimes against Whitey are justified.

Pittsburgh Post-Gazette
Pittsburgh, Pa., February 4, 1977

Commentators, both black and white, are still trying to sort out their explanations for the amazing, record-breaking success of the 12-hour television dramatization of Alex Haley's book, ''Roots.''

The infinitely detailed account of the enforced odyssey of Mr. Haley's ancestors from tribal Africa to life in post-Civil War America is, first and foremost, an engrossing saga of human suffering and ultimate triumph.

The fact that it is largely true and a genealogical tour-de-force added to the enthrallment of the immense audience.

★ ★ ★

Blacks could surely identify with the story in all its implications. White descendants of slave-owners were equally and personally involved.

But what about the millions of whites whose families came to this country after the Civil War? They, too, clung to their TV sets. Why?

Well, again, the phenomenon of Mr. Haley's resounding success probably isn't difficult to explain. The story he had to tell was real, and the characters in it were three-dimensional human beings.

★ ★ ★

To be sure, there was some oversimplification of mood and motive, and also some footnotes that might have been illuminating were omitted.

But basically it was controversial history, brought into the living room as never before. The fact that so enormously many viewers stuck with it all through the week is a happy omen for more mutual understanding in the future.

And then there's something else. Who needs soap operas and game shows when something like ''Roots'' is possible? Maybe the television programmers will take the hint.

TULSA WORLD
Tulsa, Okla., March 7, 1977

IF A TELEVISION network broadcasts material that puts slave-selling and lynching in a bad light, is the network required to provide equal time for ''the other side?''

This isn't exactly the question raised last week by the Grand Wizard of the Ku Klux Klan. But it's close.

The Wizard, DAVID DUKE of Jefferson, La., wants equal time under the Federal Communications Commission's fairness doctrine to respond to the ABC-TV dramatic series, ''Roots.''

''Roots'' was based on ALEX HALEY's best-selling book in which the author traced his ancestral history back through the American slave era to his family's roots in Africa. And it was pretty rough on slave traders, night riders and other mostly white participants in the Old South's ''peculiar institution.''

It was the sort of thing that, if repeated often enough, could give the whole institution of human bondage a bad name.

Grand Wizard DUKE's specific complaint is that it makes the white race look bad.

And indeed, although critics gave ''Roots'' universal praise, some suggested it could have been improved by adding one or two more sympathetic, non-brutish white characters.

But the question is this: If ABC-TV shows white people in an unfavorable light with regard to slavery, is ''the other side'' entitled to equal time?

If yes, then who should defend the white race's role in child-selling, torture and lynch law?

If, in fairness, slavery and racial brutality are entitled to equal time, the Grand Wizard is probably the man to speak for the defense. He seems to have the credentials.

In any case, his claim isn't too much more absurd than some others that have been made under FCC's unworkable ''fairness doctrine.''

The Des Moines Register
Des Moines, Iowa, February 1, 1977

The serialization of Alex Haley's epic novel, ''Roots,'' was a television landmark. Millions of Americans abandoned their ordinary routines to watch the series, which helped fill a large gap in the nation's understanding of its past.

Many Americans were taught a version of American history that largely ignored the black experience. The courses often failed to convey the horrors and impact of slavery upon the slaves, and almost never dealt with the African heritage that blacks brought with them to this country. Many Americans have been left with a ''Gone With the Wind'' impression of slavery: that it was often not all that bad, and that slaves generally were content with their lot.

''Roots'' has shattered, perhaps forever, this complacent view of slavery. ''Roots'' also conveyed the dignity that some blacks managed to maintain in spite of the horrors of slavery. Kunta Kinte and his descendants somehow preserved the unity of their family and an indomitable spirit.

This accomplishment, when added to the similar accomplishments of other slave families, must surely rank as one of the great lessons of history: that poverty and oppression do not always stamp out the spirit of a people. The lesson more often than not goes untaught.

History typically is written by the victors. In their attempts to justify the greatness and ''justness'' of what their people have accomplished, victors tend to skim over the miseries of those who lost.

The impact of ''Roots'' need not stop at the boundaries of slavery and the black experience. People who have understood Haley's message should now find it easier to take a similar approach toward the white man's treatment of Native Americans and other groups. ''Roots'' also should cause many Americans to take a fresh look at the legacies of slavery: the racism which still mars the nation, the poverty which still engulfs blacks in far greater percentages than whites.

The success of ''Roots'' contains a special message for the television networks. It should no longer be as easy to argue, as many have, that Americans are satisfied with the mindless cops-and-robbers shows which fill so much of television programming. ''Roots'' should serve as an inspiration to the networks to produce more programs of similar quality.

The Hartford Courant

Hartford, Conn., February 8, 1977

In one way or another, the recent production of "Roots" will change television. It depends on how producers and network executives view the show's success.

They could see it as an artistic success that personalized the experience of slavery from a black point of view, and which did so with unexpected impact. They might decide that good drama need not mean a small audience.

Or, the program can be viewed just as a commercial success in which it was perfectly natural for Lorne Greene to appear both as a hard-hearted slave owner and in a dog food commercial. Television might decide that "slavery sells" and bring us such spinoffs next fall as a Norman Lear comedy set on the old plantation, the adventures of an inept, but rocking, slave ship crew and a "Roots" sequel featuring a bionic blacksmith.

In which case, of course, television will have completely missed the point.

THE LOUISVILLE TIMES

Louisville, Ky., February 2, 1977

My wife sat at the breakfast table Monday morning. "Why does it have to be over?" she lamented. "It was so good. Wasn't it just fascinating?"

It was good. It had been fascinating. I don't believe, however, that it is over.

For the previous week my wife had done something she rarely does. She had sat glued in front of the television set while the 12 hours of *Roots* unfolded. She was not alone, judging from the many reactions I have heard to the shows. Nor were we all wasting our time.

For most stories on TV, an hour is too much. The dozen hours of *Roots* were hardly enough to tell its story and make its points. It was a drama peopled with slaves, but focused on freedom. It was a tragedy of the gulf between black and white, but it showed us all that what makes us human is what we have in common.

The gulf between black and white has narrowed in recent years. It is far from closed. But now in that gulf stand Tom Murray and Chicken George and Kizzy and Kunta Kinte, making it that much narrower yet. People may not understand history books or employment statistics or legal briefs, but they can understand living, and for 12 hours America has lived the lives of a family that kept its dreams alive.

The American Broadcasting Co. deserves great thanks. It can be proud of having stretched the medium of television toward its real potential: It carried an important story to a vast number of people, and did it with a regard for the quality of the story—and the quality of the audience.

Alex Haley, the author who turned his family's traditions, persistent research and emotional understanding into *Roots,* must be very satisfied Slavery, though it has been ended a century and more, is still a rankling scar. The physical deprivation it inflicted on blacks has been matched by a spiritual deprivation that yet afflicts the whole nation.

That is a truth dulled by repetition. Mr. Haley makes it sharp again: To the extent that any man would enslave another, limit him, denigrate him, hurt him, we are all enslaved a little, hurt a little. Mr. Haley, I believe, would have us accept healing.

I was getting a haircut, and the talk over the snip of the scissors turned, as most talk seemed to last week, to *Roots.*

"Have you seen all of it so far?" I asked.

"Oh, yeah," said one person, and after a pause, "I don't care much for the colored. They've gotten so arrogant. I don't think many of the ones nowadays would have lasted very long back then." I winced a little and kept quiet and then, amazingly, the thought was continued.

"Of course, I don't guess I'd have lasted very long either. They had a terrible hard time, didn't they, all the awful things done to 'em . . . cutting off that man's foot . . . .I may not care much for those people, but nobody should treat anybody like that. Whether he's white or colored a man's got some rights. . . ."

This is the seed that *Roots* has planted by the pale, dim light of a television screen. From this beginning may it grow in the mind of the nation so that someday every person in the land may taste its fruit—what Kunta Kinte was robbed of and his grandson lived to find again—sweet freedom, yes indeed.

St. Louis Globe-Democrat

St. Louis, Mo., February 5, 1977

The millions of Americans who let themselves become enslaved to television by watching the overblown production called "Roots" may dig out now and reflect on life as it is today.

No living American needs to feel guilty over the shame of slavery. No mentally healthy person broods over injustice of long ago. Every person has a right to take pride in one's heritage. No decent person glories over the degradation suffered by any human being anywhere at any time.

White will always be white and black will always be black. White does not make right. And all that is black is not beautiful.

Ambassador Andrew Young is the personification of a black man's rise to the pinnacle of prominence in the United States. He is on a mission for his government to black Africa amidst predictable grumbles from the white minority regime in Rhodesia.

Concurrently Ethiopia is in the throes of a violent upheaval, with one black Marxist-Leninist faction butchering another. Col. Mengitsu Haile Mariam, who came out on top, denounced as "reactionary" seven members of the ruling military council who were slain at government headquarters.

It's apparent that the safety of blacks who never left Africa is not guaranteed simply because their roots remain there. Nor has every black been demeaned because his ancestors were uprooted. Again, Andrew Young is the exemplification of this truth.

A person of any color who justifies racial hatred today on the basis of abuses committed centuries ago may be confusing roots with ruts.

Roots are a source of pride, nourishment and strength.

Ruts are a shallow grave, suffocating to the spirit.

The Providence Journal

Providence, R.I., April 21, 1978

The airing this past week of "Holocaust," NBC's four-day series on Nazi Germany's effort to exterminate the Jewish race, was a well-intended effort. Unfortunately, it did not, and perhaps for many reasons could not, accomplish all it set out to do.

Those old enough to have seen the documentary photographs and films of the Nazi death camps immediately after World War II were dealt a psychic blow at that time that remains indelible in memory. The reenactment of the horrors of Babi Yar, Buchenwald and Auschwitz in NBC's sanitized presentation did not wrench heart and mind as did that first terrible revelation of the depravity and barbarism that lies latent just below the veneer of civilization.

Not that anyone would wish to relive that pain, or to inflict it on a new generation that has since grown up. But explicit as the NBC cameras were in depicting the horrendous actualities of the death camps, even with the inclusion of some actual photos and film clips from the Nazi archives, the TV presentation failed to summon up the irresistible compulsion to shout "No!" and run from the room, as did those first showings after the defeat of Nazi Germany.

One must ask, why? Does this tell us something more profound and disturbing about the abuse of television's exploitation of sex, violence and nonsense for commercial gain, than the obvious fact of an opportunity lost for cultural gain? Does the clinical coolness of "Holocaust's" presentation suggest that our sensibilities have been dulled, our humanity deadened, by the cumulative exposure to murder and mayhem as a form of entertainment? And if so, where will a continued diet of the same lead?

As for "Holocaust's" ambitions to reawaken the American conscience to events of the past, like Hollywood's epic motion pictures of years gone by, it suffered from trying too hard to be all-encompassing. In art as in life, it succeeded best when the camera stopped trying to gather in too much and closed in an expressive face, or when a character voiced a rare insight into the lessons of the Holocaust.

One such scene occurred in the first sequence when Mrs. Weiss, mother of the Jewish family around which the story revolves, refused to accept the monstrous portents of the anti-Semitic incidents caused by Hitler's brown-shirts in the mid-1930s. Rejecting her husband's pleas to flee her beloved Berlin, Mrs. Weiss gave voice to the fatal denial that echoed mockingly through the film, as the Jews refused to believe what was happening even as it was going on. The barbarisms of a few Nazi thugs, she insisted, could not prevail in "in the land of Beethoven, Mozart and Schiller."

The irony of the Holocaust was that for reasons still not fully comprehended today — and on which the film sheds no light — genocidal madness did erupt "in the land of Beethoven Mozart and Schiller". The question "Holocaust" leaves poised is, Could it happen here in the land of Washington, Jefferson and Lincoln?

Recent events in Skokie, Illinois attest that the virus of anti-Semitism lies ready to break out in the heartland of America today as it did in sophisticated, cultured Germany four decades ago.

If there was valid reason to subject Americans to the painful reliving of the Holocaust this week, it must be the message that neither Jew nor Gentile dare say "It can never happen here." It can happen anywhere that racial intolerance and bigotry, fed by social unrest or economic hardship, are prepared to seek out scapegoats.

Only one response is acceptable to the question posed by "Holocaust," and that is the solemn vow of every American that "It *shall not* happen here."

Holocaust Drama Depicts Nazi Persecution of Jews

The original four-part television drama *Holocaust,* depicting the period of persecution and extermination of millions of European Jews by the Nazis, was aired April 16–19 by the National Broadcasting Company (NBC). The 9½-hour series, which told the story of two fictional German families during the 1930s and 1940s, was written by Gerald Green and produced by Herbert Brodkin.

The presentation coincided with the Jews' celebration of Passover, a holiday commemorating the deliverance of the Hebrews from slavery in ancient Egypt. The *Holocaust* broadcast also occurred during the same week that the National Socialist (Nazi) Party of America had scheduled a march through Skokie, Ill., a Chicago suburb where more than 5,000 concentration camp survivors lived. To date, the parade had been successfully blocked by locally passed ordinances, although the Nazis were winning court battles where they were defending their freedom of speech.

The controversial nature of the program's subject matter led to right-wing demonstrations in several non-Jewish communities. In four cities, groups charged NBC with anti-Christian bias, arguing that the show exaggerated the number of Jews murdered by the Nazis. Among Jewish leaders, there were allegations that *Holocaust* diminished the actual horror of genocide in order to make it palatable to a mass audience.

The program spawned a nationwide interest in reexamining the Nazi era and its ramifications. Beginning with the first Holocaust installment April 16, many American Christians wore yellow Stars of David, a Hebrew symbol, as a gesture of solidarity with the Jews. Donald W. McEvoy, senior vice president of the National Conference of Christians and Jews, explained that "the Nazis were making an appeal as Christians to other Christians. So we're approaching this as a Christian problem. I think 95% of Jews would feel there has been more anti-Semitism recently. We want to show the support of the vast majority of Americans."

Holocaust, seen in part or full by 120 million viewers, drew the second largest "entertainment" category audience in television history, according to NBC. In 1977, 130 million persons watched "Roots," a 12-hour series on a black man's search for his family's history.

Reprinted by permission of the Los Angeles Times Syndicate.

The Knickerbocker News
Albany, N.Y., April 20, 1978

Even when it was happening to them and their friends and family, some victims still could not believe it, so enormously terrible was this unprecedented government program to exterminate an entire people.

Today, there still are some adults who find it hard to believe that Adolf Hitler's Nazis murdered 6 million Jews (they probably also don't believe the U.S. sent men to the moon) and, more understandably, millions of young people who simply cannot conceive of man's inhumanity to man on such a broad scale.

Thus, "Holocaust," the compelling 9-hour-and-30-minute television special that was shown this week. While there were some uneven spots, including the kind of overdrawn stereotypes that inevitably seem to creep into such dramatizations, "Holocaust" was a chilling look back into history; a retrospective look we had to take.

In a way, "Holocaust" bears a thematic resemblance to the previous TV blockbuster, "Roots," in that it helps us understand the feelings, including the hopes and fears, of a people. In "Roots," it was the American blacks; in "Holocaust," it is the Jews.

At a time when attempts to achieve a lasting peace in the Mideast are undergoing complex and perplexing frustrations, "Holocaust" helps us understand the deeply-rooted feelings of our Jewish neighbors, particularly about prejudice and most particularly about Israel, their spiritual homeland.

Try as they might, even after viewing such a moving series as "Holocaust," many Americans still may not be able to understand how such a massive atrocity could have occurred. This is understandable. What is *is* important is that we never forget that it *did* happen.

The News and Courier
Charleston, S.C., April 19, 1978

Whether morbid interest, a desire to learn about a historic episode or some other reason drew the viewers, "The Holocaust" has provided a memorably dramatic review of Hitler's campaign to exterminate the Jews in Europe.

Some people are wondering why the gruesome story has been revived at this particular moment. We have no inside knowledge about the timing, any more than we knew about the production of "Roots," which stirred memories of slavery in the United States Nor do we compare these two episodes, and the respective qualities of the TV shows, as dramatic offerings or historic documents.

"The Holocaust" presents a version of inhumanity that still seems incredible, even to persons who remember the events as they unfolded in news of the 1930s and 1940s. Although the persecution of Jews in Germany was covered at the time, the full impact of the gas chambers and other mass extermination measures did not reach the outside world until after the defeat of the Nazis. So far as we are aware, the television production has reflected faithfully what the Nazis' own documents reported.

One may look back in history to other examples of brutality, such as the Inquisition, the persecution of Christians by the Romans, the slaughter by Genghis Khan and other conquerors and the Communist revolutions in Russia and China. Perhaps these themes also will be explored on the air waves

Adding poignancy to "The Holocaust" is the personal treatment of the Weiss family, focusing attention on characters with whom the audience can identify What may be accomplished by exposing the mass television audience to these somber tidings we do not know The world hardly needs more injections of bitterness. Rather we are moved to pray for forgiveness of evil committed by mankind of all ages and nationalities, and to hope that from these lessons in horror oncoming generations may learn to curb the murderous instincts of the human species.

St. Petersburg Times
St. Petersburg, Fla., April 21, 1978

NBC combined intolerable reality with television fantasy to present *Holocaust* this week. Whatever the faults of the three-night series, it brought home powerfully the message of man's incredible capacity for inhumanity.

As columnist William F. Buckley notes (opposite page), genocide is not a nightmare that ended with Hitler. Idi Amin in Uganda and the government of Nigeria have practiced it. The Cambodians ruthlessly pursue extermination as a government policy.

And in the realm of racial prejudice, who can forget that our own GIs often claimed the Vietnamese did not place the same value on life as we "superior" Americans? Jimmy Carter, before he became President, called the Vietnamese war a racist one, noting that America would not have been so willing to drop napalm and bomb the villages of white-skinned Europeans.

Yet Jews were not a separate race in Hitler's Germany or any other nation. They differed so little from the populations of Europe that they were ordered to identify themselves with armbands. Against these innocent people the most "civilized" country of the western world could commit unspeakable slaughter after slaughter. And many of those who knew did nothing.

NBC did not really explore why Germans created and tolerated this monstrosity. Although more time should have been spent on these questions, they are not really the kind the network should answer for us. It is for each individual to look inside and ask "Had I been one of the powerful, what would I have done? Would I bow to the call of prejudice now?"

If NBC has prompted Americans to examine their beliefs about Jews, about acquiescence and about power, then *Holocaust* was a valuable effort. Not too many years ago the poet e. e. cummings called us "manunkind." We have not yet unearned it.

NAZI GERMANY SPENT a decade (1935-45) systematically exterminating an estimated 6 million Jews. It took just four evenings of prime-time television drama to imprint the horror of the "Holocaust" on American minds either too young to remember or too centered on other things to care about one of the most infamous of 20th Century barbarisms.

It should not be forgotten. It cannot be ignored.

The world has been numbed by atrocities almost too great to comprehend in this century. Genocide is just one of them. But because genocide involves the deliberate, planned eradication of a specific group it is one of the most reprehensible.

"Holocaust," for all its trivialities, its documentary errors, its hokey story line and mind-boggling transitions from Auschwitz and Babi-Yar to yammering commercials, should serve a useful purpose. It succeeded in impressing this generation with a story that some find hard to believe. That is, that structured, civilized society can be so easily manipulated by prejudice and hate into accepting something so vile as the "death factory." And it reminded us of how little protest was raised from the outside.

THE COMMERCIAL APPEAL
Memphis, Tenn., April 21, 1978

FROM THE JEWISH standpoint, it is important to establish the Holocaust in history as firmly as the flight of Moses. The Holocaust is the crux of the forces which brought together enough international support to create the state of Israel after World War II. And Israel still fights for its right to exist.

The message of the television drama is important for non-Jews, also. For they, too, must be able to spot the traps of politics and nationalism which were used by a leader such as Adolf Hitler to proclaim a "new order."

The Turks gave Hitler an earlier example of the "final solution." It was they, in their hatred for 1,750,000 Armenians in Turkey at the time World War I was beginning, who decided to deport all of them. To be pushed into the desert march, as the Armenians were, was no different in outcome from being sent to the showers of Auschwitz. It was a death sentence. More than 600,000 Armenians died in 1915.

No real count exists of the millions exterminated by Stalin in the Soviet Union or Mao Tse-tung in Communist China. But they number in the tens of millions. Until Alexander Solzenitzyn wrote of the "Gulag Archipelago" and

"The Cancer Ward," few outside the Soviet Union were aware of the ghastly genocide there.

The grisly catalog is long. In Cambodia today, the Khymer Rouge has been ruthlessly wiping out lives — an estimated 1.2 million out of a 1974 population of less than 8 million.

HITLER DIED IN April, 1945, in the shattering climax of World War II. His memory is vivid but perhaps distorted today. It would be well to remember that he died still spouting the anti-Semitism that was the heart of his plan to set aside an empire for the "master race." In a will written shortly before his suicide, Hitler said: "Above all I demand of the nation's leaders and followers scrupulous adherence to the race laws and to ruthless resistance against the world poisoners of all people, international Jewry."

The Holocaust was real. And its fundamental sources are alive today, even here in America where neo-Nazis regurgitate the same old Hitlerian hate.

The sad thing is that we see the death marches, the massacres, the assembly-line slaughter, and having expressed renewed horror over the Holocaust ignore the genocide of this year — and next.

The Idaho STATESMAN
Boise, Idaho, April 19, 1978

The nastiest of organizations can lurk behind the noblest of names. A case in point is the Christian Defense League.

Sounds nice, doesn't it? What red-blooded, church-going American could fault a group with a name like the Christian Defense League? Unfortunately, the group's name and its behavior are a good distance apart. Christians, supposedly, love their neighbors.

The league is the group that is venting its spleen over this week's NBC presentation of *Holocaust*, a made-for-television movie depicting the horrors of Nazi Germany. League members have gone to great lengths to tell us all how horrible the film is. Local chapters are planning demonstrations in cities throughout the nation. Last weekend, members made the national wires by picketing an NBC affiliate. The league is demanding three hours of NBC's prime time to air its views and newspapers around the country have received league "news" releases.

The essence of all this breast beating is that *Holocaust* tends to make viewers sympathize with Jews. We couldn't agree more. There is something about watching people shot, gassed and otherwise murdered that does tend to evoke sympathy.

So what's the problem? What is un-Christian about sympathizing with a nationality that has suffered the misfortune of being slaughtered enmasse, be it Jews, Italians or Tasmanians?

The league assures everyone it is not anti-Semitic. We disagree. Finding fault with those who would arouse sympathy for Jews sounds a lot to us like anti-Semitism. So do the league's releases. We are among those who received them and read them with disgust.

But the most obvious indication of where the group is coming from came this weekend. In protesting *Holocaust's* imminent broadcast, the league claimed the film erred in saying 6 million Jews were killed by the Nazis. The league says the real total, according to *The Hoax of the Twentieth Century* by A.R. Butz, whoever he is, is only 1 million. Only a million. Hardly worth talking about. (Encyclopedia Britannica, by the way, places the total at up to 5.5 million.)

The leagues' argument seems to be that the film arouses sympathy for the Jews by distorting the facts. Hitler wasn't such a bad guy. He only killed a million. What are these Jews complaining about? Down with the network Zionists.

Locally, *Holocaust* has a lot of people talking. Many are saying it is one of the most powerful made-for-television movies ever. It isn't a pretty picture, but the Nazis did some very un-pretty things. It takes an occasional jolt like *Holocaust* to remind us how awful war is. Some of us need that. Our lives are too comfortable. We take too much for granted.

The league, in our opinion, has a warped view of sympathy. It should be freely extended to the unfortunate, including those whose prejudices make them incapable of feeling it.

THE BLADE
Toledo, Ohio, April 23, 1978

MANY Americans have found the television documentary-drama "Holocaust" both instructive and disturbing, though perhaps less revealing in its portrait of humanity at bayonet-point than the play and movie, "The Diary of Anne Frank."

Some critics have raised the question as to whether any television program can do anything to enhance our perception of one of the most ghastly acts in history — the extermination of millions of human beings in the Nazi death camps.

One point did emerge from the TV dramatization that too many people forget: It was not the Nazis exclusively who perpetrated this tragedy against Jewish and other people marked by a criminal regime for extinction. Some Europeans, either actively or by their indifference, were accessories in this policy of genocide — just as other Europeans, notably the Danes, did what they could to mitigate the horrors.

The indifference extended to this side of the Atlantic, too, although the civilized world was aware of the Nazi designs on the Jewish people. In July, 1938, representatives from 32 nations met at the French resort city of Evian-les-Bains at the invitation of President Franklin D. Roosevelt to discuss what might be done to find refuge for Jewish victims of Nazi persecutions.

Two days before the conference opened, Anne O'Hare McCormick wrote in the New York Times: "It is heartbreaking to think of the queues of desperate human beings around our consulates in Vienna and other cities waiting in suspense for what happens at Evian. But the question they underline is not simply humanitarian ... It is a test of civilization ... Can America live with itself if it lets Germany get away with this policy of extermination, allows the fanaticism of one man to triumph over

reason, refuses to take up this gage of battle against barbarism?"

But the depression-ridden America of 1938 was not prepared to make the gesture the moment seemed to demand — to throw our doors open to thousands of persecuted Germans and Austrians, Christian and Jewish people alike, who wished to emigrate to the United States. And even the quota — then 25,927 a year — had not been filled for the six preceding years.

France already had accepted 200,000 refugees. Other countries, notably the British Commonwealth and Latin American nations, were not willing to admit many refugees. There were only 570,000 Jewish people living in Germany and Austria at that time; that number could easily have been resettled in the 32 nations which took part in the Evian conference. A generation later, one writer noted, the United States accepted 585,000 Vietnamese refugees without severe economic strain.

The failure of Evian was followed a few months later by the infamous "krystallnacht" — the night of broken glass — in which state-organized looting, arson, and murder were committed against Jewish residents of Germany and Austria. Did Adolf Hitler interpret the failure of Evian as a tacit go-ahead for his policies of extermination? Hitler himself sneered at the western nations for their failure to provide refuge: "We, on our part, are ready to put all these criminals at the disposal of these countries, for all I care, even on luxury ships."

The thug regime of Nazi Germany is stained with one of the blackest marks in the long history of barbarism. But the failure of other nations to provide help to the victims at a crucial moment in history also provides food for thought by those who watched the compelling television series.

"What did you do in the Holocaust, daddy?"

THE SAGINAW NEWS
Saginaw, Mich., April 21, 1978

NBC television's "Holocaust" was brilliantly performed, but the story it told was not the kind that makes for easy viewing.

Entertainment it was not. Educational it was, particularly for a good many of the younger viewers.

More than anything, "Holocaust" was a stark reminder of one of the darkest chapters in human history.

From that standpoint, the sweeping narrative of the monumental tragedy that befell just one family in World War II Nazi Germany was, in its starkness, instructive.

Instructive to the extent it showed what can happen when any state embraces the single political ideology of "a man on the white horse." Or even worse, tumbles to the unholy promise of racism and racial superiority.

Some, no doubt, whose minds rebelled at the idea this could have happened, tuned out on "Holocaust" during its four-night run in search of escape to pleasanter things.

It did happen. It was real. And the very reality of methodical Nazi extermination of six million Jews still shocks the civilized world.

It's a message to those fools who parade in Skokie under the protection of Constitutional rights.

And a reminder to the rest of us who live in freedom under the same Constitution, that it must never ever happen here.

The Wichita Beacon
Wichita, Kans., April 21, 1978

In shocking, depressing detail, the story was told. It was the story of how a great nation destroyed six million men, women and children for no reason other than that they were Jews. More than five million other minority members were slaughtered at the same time.

Every viewer of NBC-TV's film presentation, "Holocaust," must have felt the universality of the blame. All the supposedly civilized world shared in it, if only by failure to raise a protesting voice.

Well-meaning but misguided people have raised the question: "Is it not a mistake to show a program like this? Won't it cause more trouble than good? Why stir up these unpleasant memories?"

The answer is simple: It is because the memories are so unpleasant that we must not forget. Those who ignore the unpleasant, or who hide from it, are in danger of making the same mistakes — and of making them over and over.

It may not be realistic to compare the audience attracted by "Holocaust" with that drawn by "Roots". "Roots" dealt with ancient cruelties. Its characters had hope and a future. It had an entertainment factor. "Holocaust," which had a considerably lower viewer attraction, was consistently grim. The situation it described was utterly hopeless.

Or was it? It will be hopeless only if we do not learn from the lessons it taught. One way of helping that happen would be to show "Holocaust" again — next year and at regular intervals. Perhaps next time it should be shown on public TV, without commercial announcements.

The vital subject of the Holocaust also should be added to the public school curriculum.

We must not, cannot, forget. Buchenwald and Auschwitz are more than aberrations from the past. Forgotten, they are grim harbingers of what could happen again.

The Cincinnati Post
Cincinnati, Ohio, April 22, 1978

We can think of only one thing more obscene than the obscenity of the Nazi-engineered Holocaust itself.

That would be for the world to forget the deliberate murder of 6 million human beings during World War II — mostly Jews but also gypsies, Slavs and other ethnic or political "undesirables" — and to leave unchallenged those who, for whatever reasons, pretend that one of history's most monstrous crimes did not really happen.

The NBC television network is to be commended for its four-evening dramatization, "The Holocaust," the fictional story of one German-Jewish family against the larger background of true events in Germany and Europe in the late 1930s and early 1940s.

Despite minor artistic flaws, this series brought home to millions of Americans, especially young people, the horrors of that period with an immediacy and impact no book or film documentary could match.

It is also gratifying that many schools are using the program as a teaching tool. Too many history texts gloss over the Holocaust, if they do not ignore it entirely.

The Holocaust was not just a crime perpetrated by evil men. It was a crime good men permitted to happen. It was a crime that sprang from a dark strain of anti-Semitism that persists in some Christian societies even today.

Remembering the Holocaust is painful. But it is one method of insuring that free men will remain alert to the constant threat of man's inhumanity to man.

The Providence Journal

Providence, R.I., January 27, 1979

In an experiment as courageous as it was painful, West German television stations offered their audiences this week an exposure to the terror of the Nazi past. The American-produced series "Holocaust," dramatizing the extermination of European Jews under Hitler, was aired in West Germany amid currents of hesitation and anxiety. But it drew a far larger viewing audience than expected, suggesting that many Germans today feel it possible, and important, to confront the facts of the Nazi era with honest appraisal.

For older Germans, "Holocaust" inevitably became a searing episode of forced remembrance; for a younger generation, it perhaps became something of an education. Chancellor Helmut Schmidt told parliament that the series promoted "critical reflection" on the Nazis' atrocities. This brave and honest statement suggests that many thoughtful Germans are becoming able and even determined to keep an awareness of Nazism from being sloughed off and discarded.

The fact that many West Germans resented the showing of "Holocaust" makes the decision to broadcast the four-part drama all the more remarkable. The film, flawed though it is, offers a unique vehicle to Germans (as it did to Americans) for encouraging an honest awareness of a black period that it would be more comfortable to forget. Screened without the commercial breaks that so jarred American viewers, and with the sound-track dialogue dubbed into German, the "Holocaust" telecast appears to have had a surprisingly wide impact. More than one-third of the possible viewing audience — twice what was expected — watched the programs.

Curiosity doubtless prompted some of the German viewers' interest, but there was something deeper. By offering a powerful perception of Nazism that may not be widely shared in modern Germany, the series, noted *Bild Zeitung*, the country's largest daily newspaper, "has touched the soul of the Germans." In this lies its value, instructive and even therapeutic. A refusal to remember would be unconscionable — even if the act of remembering is undertaken at a distant remove from the event, through the scrim of a television play.

San Francisco Chronicle

San Francisco, Cal., January 30, 1979

WEST GERMANS WERE quite evidently caught up in the showing of "Holocaust," the American television series about the Nazi extermination of Jews. Even though the drama was presented on that country's Third Channel, which is regularly used for regional-interest programs, and attracts a much smaller audience than the two national channels, the viewer response was formidable.

There's no denying that valid criticisms may be made of the series. They were thoroughly aired when it was shown here last year, and some bear on the nature of the media. The more substantial hold that an epic human chapter was essentially trivialized by reducing it to standard drama for the electronic box.

But a 34-year-old West German tax consultant, who tuned in last week, was quoted in The New York Times as saying: "It's surprisingly right. I feared it would be one of those television monsters, but it has something more." And his wife put it this way: "It was really quite good, you know. Things were a millimeter off for the German audience every now and then, but your intelligence was never insulted. And it did get to your emotions — mine, at least, and that is terribly important."

GIVEN THE DRAWBACKS inherent in this situation: no television drama can do justice to, or really evoke, the appalling fact of the holocaust, still some satisfaction may be found in these reactions and this audience response. If the series can invade the national emotions to this degree, it has performed a valuable function. By this very token, one wonders just how many citizens of the East German Republic heard about the program and dared to have their emotions lanced by listening in.

Democrat ⬛ Chronicle

Rochester, N.Y., February 7, 1978

ABOUT HALF the people of West Germany were born after the Holocaust took place, and there's apparently been no very full treatment in the schools of the horrors of those days.

So the recent showing of the American television drama, "Holocaust," had more significance for that reason.

Despite several angry protests, it's estimated that at least one-third of the West German television audience tuned in to the show, carried only on regional channels.

And the reaction seems to have been basically a healthy one, with many of the people facing up to the painful fact of Nazi Germany's systematic slaughtering of the Jews.

Even as it was here, "Holocaust" was criticized for its soap opera qualities. There was debate for example, over whether the series' SS officer, Erik Dorf, was a credible figure or only a stereotype.

But in the final analysis, the quality of the show perhaps wasn't very important.

Commented Der Spiegel magazine:

"An American TV series of a trivial sort, produced more out of commercial than moral motives, more as entertainment than as enlightenment, has done what hundreds of books, plays, films and TV broadcasts, thousands of documents, and all the concentration-camp trials and more than three decades of postwar history never succeeded in doing:

"It presents to the Germans so strong an image of the crimes against the Jews performed in their name that millions were shocked."

"Holocaust," then, turned out to be something of a catharsis.

And it's significant that Nobel laureate Heinrich Boell and six other authors have declared themselves ready to help in a German television series on the Nazi extermination of Jews.

A crust has been broken, and the democratic institutions that now exist in West Germany will surely be strengthened by new honesty about the past.

The Evening Bulletin

Philadelphia, Pa., January 28, 1979

Any American who watched the four-part "Holocaust" television series last year will remember it as high-impact drama. It didn't evoke every last horror of the Nazi extermination of six million Jews. But, certainly for TV, it was strong stuff indeed.

It would be, obviously, a much stronger dose for Germans. Some credit should be given, therefore, to the West Germans for putting the series into their own living rooms, for turning it on in large numbers and for a generally favorable response. Credit also Chancellor Helmut Schmidt for his support of the telecast.

True, the series was not carried on one of West Germany's two national networks. It was aired instead on a regional network of five stations. Still, it won an estimated 34 percent of the viewers and, of those who called in, about two-thirds responded "positively."

On grounds that those who forget history may be doomed to repeat it, we find that encouraging. Especially since half the present German population was born after Hitler and has some sense of unreality about his works and much of the older half would prefer to forget those ghastly days.

Not that the nation has really swept the attempted "final solution" under the rug; over the past 20 years other documentaries on the war and the massacre have been aired.

But the special power of "Holocaust" was in telling the story in human-scale terms, what happened to the fictional Josef Weiss and his wife, Berta, and their kids, Karl, Rudi and Anna — and also to SS officer Erich Dorf. Dorf's transformation from a human-enough functionary to a ruthless instrument of death apparently hit home to German viewers in particular.

Some who saw the show were annoyed at the American export, feeling that they were blameless and didn't want "our noses rubbed in it."

The reaction is understandable. But what Germans, Americans — everybody — would do well to remember is: if a developed, educated, cultured nation like Germany can perpetrate a holocaust in the middle of the 20th Century, it can happen anywhere.

MANCHESTER NEW HAMPSHIRE UNION LEADER
Manchester, N.H., April 23, 1978

NBC-TV's recently-concluded series on Nazi Germany's mass murder of European Jews has caused much comment in New Hampshire and throughout the nation.

The series was quite effective, very moving and very powerful.

There have been objections to it, some of which are ridiculous—"why bring all that unpleasantness up again?"—and others quite valid—by those who suffered and survived.

One of the latter group, writing in a New York paper, objected to the superficiality of the programs, insisting there was no way to adequately tell this horror story and that making it into a television show, complete with commercials, gave it a dangerously fictional quality.

Perhaps this story can never be told adequately, no matter the medium. But what we hope all those who were involved in this period bear in mind now is that there are entire new generations of Americans who know little or nothing about that most atrocious time.

And it's a sad but true commentary that the only way many of these younger Americans will ever be exposed to it is through a TV show.

Put in that light, we think NBC has done a credible job of telling the incredible story of the extermination of six million Jews and another five million non-Jews by the Nazis and their helpmates in World War II.

It's a story that needs telling and repeating, lest we forget.

The Detroit News
Detroit, Mich., April 19, 1978

Rather than watch the four-day NBC television special, "Holocaust," the American people might be better advised to read — or reread — "The Diary of a Young Girl."

Anne Frank, a Jewish girl who hid from the Nazis in Amsterdam during World War II, wrote an enduring tribute to the indomitable human spirit: a diary of humor, poignancy and insight against a background of humiliation and horror.

No creative work — movie, novel or play — can adequately present the monstrosity of exterminating six million Jews. Should we really expect a docu-drama, that sham TV form, to do so?

One TV critic savaged the production as "a stereotypical collection of wooden characters and impossible coincidences." The result: a fatal trivialization.

Elie Wiesel, a Boston University professor and historian who himself survived the holocaust, described the TV production as "an insult to those who perished and to those who survived."

Yet, while we make no brief for "Holocaust" as art, the nine and one-half hour television drama is an important reminder and a consciousness raiser.

For a younger generation, the production is an education. That generation has not fully realized the inhuman depths man is capable of reaching.

For those who need no reminder of Nazi enormities, the production should underscore a concern for human rights. Regrettably, worldwide anti-Semitism has revived.

The stench of the American Nazi Party is so great, in fact, that some would bar a uniformed Nazi march in Skokie, Ill., a Chicago suburb with 40 percent Jewish population.

The issue has split the American Civil Liberties Union. ACLU support for civil rights, even for the detested Nazis, has caused it to lose 15 percent of its membership and more than $500,000.

Yet as paradoxical as it may seem, the ACLU position is precisely the kind of vigilance that America needs to assure that a holocaust will never happen in America.

In any case, the trauma of the European holocaust for Jews should not be forgotten.

As Israel Shenker, a feature writer for the New York Times, wrote:

From the weeping, from the ashes, from the abyss, Auschwitz and the final solution speak of the hazards of Jewish existence.

THE BLADE
Toledo, Ohio, February 2, 1979

ONE would hardly have expected the television series "Holocaust," the depiction of Nazi persecution of Jewish victims, to be a big hit in West Germany. And yet, surprisingly, the four-part drama drew an audience of more than one-third of the potential viewers in that country, double the number that had been anticipated.

Moreover, there was a substantial telephone response to the series, the majority of which was favorable to the broadcast. These two factors — viewership and reaction — are indications that there may finally have been a fundamental change in the way West Germans today perceive that dark chapter of their history.

Generally in the past, any reminders of Nazi atrocities have been met with almost sullen diffidence — the why-bring-that-up-again syndrome. And this in turn has led to a tendency for others to regard the German people as permanently stigmatized. There are, to be sure, still those Germans who refuse to recognize any national guilt in respect to the Nazi past. But the largely positive reaction to "Holocaust" should go a long way toward dispelling the temptation to assign that guilt to the German people as a whole.

The real hope that the horrors of the past will not be repeated, however, lies in the governmental structure of West Germany, a parliamentary system under which genuine democratic institutions have developed since World War II. And, in that context, it is not surprising that Chancellor Helmut Schmidt endorsed the television series, noting that it encouraged "critical reflection." It was not amiss either that Mr. Schmidt called for the program to be broadcast to East Germany because "they also have reason to reflect on our common heritage."

As superficial as "Holocaust" undoubtedly was in many respects, it has apparently operated as a catharsis for many citizens of West Germany. That dismal period of German history will probably never disappear completely from the consciousness of the world, but the fact that Germans can talk about and question the Nazi excesses is a sign that they are placing them in a healthier perspective.

Pittsburgh Post-Gazette
Pittsburgh, Pa., February 7, 1979

The television film, "Holocaust," had considerable impact in the United States when it was shown last year. But what about showing in Germany itself the film dramatizing the Nazi genocide of the Jews?

That question created much soul-searching among West Germany's television executives. Would showing the NBC series simply reopen old wounds, divide the generations, and demonstrate that Nazi persecution of the Jews was too grim a subject for television? In the end a compromise decision was made — to show it on regional networks rather than nationwide.

Yet even with this limited circulation the impact has been tremendous. Although over the past 20 years German TV had presented 156 documentaries, films and plays depicting the Nazi era, the January airing of the NBC series received an overwhelming response. A record 15 million (41 percent of German sets) tuned in the last day of the four-part series.

While there were criticisms in America that the story of a fictionalized family from Berlin was marred by soap-opera melodramatics, that was not the reaction in Germany. More than 30,000 viewers called WDR studios in Cologne, and although many said that after more than 30 years the past should be left alone, the majority were positive and intensely interested.

The newspaper Frankfurter Allgemeine editorially questioned the use of the "hot" television medium for subjects such as the genocide of the Jews in Germany, black slavery in America or the Emperor Claudius in Rome, contending such TV series do not enlighten the viewer but merely create emotionalism. But other newspapers commended the effort. The Stuttgarter Zeitung hit the subject the hardest under a headline, "'Holocaust — a Breakthrough," with these words: "The German population is agitated. For the first time since the war millions of Germans seem to have acknowledged that German National Socialists . . . systematically . . . murdered six million Jews."

The awful story of the Holocaust should never be forgotten, least of all in Germany. But it is heartening that this generation of Germans was willing to respond, to have its conscience stirred as never before.

THE ARIZONA REPUBLIC
Phoenix, Ariz., January 31, 1979

WEST GERMANS apparently are coming to terms with their past. Until recently, the vast majority of them were reluctant to face the facts about the Nazi era, the concentration camps, the gas chambers, the extermination of 6 million Jews.

This was understandable. The Germans felt very much as Americans do today who want to wipe the memory of the war in Viet-

nam from their minds, and who act as though it never happened.

The enormous and unexpected success of the telecasts of *Holocaust* in West Germany last week would seem to indicate that the German attitude is changing.

The major networks refused to show the series on the pretext that it would disrupt their regular programs. Actually, it was because they feared a backlash.

A group of regional stations finally agreed to put the series on.

Hor Zu, the West German equivalent of *TV Digest*, gave the program a small notice on page 50 in the kind of type normally reserved for lost-and-found ads. The rest of the page was devoted to the competing network programs, a serial called *The Loves Of Lydia*, a variety show, and a movie about a dubious religious sect.

Programs shown on regional stations usually gain a rating of between 1.5 percent and 3 percent. *Holocaust* won 34 percent the first night, and 36 percent the next, twice as much as the major networks combined.

Like the response to *Roots* in the United States, the success of *Holocaust* in West Germany was a sign of growing maturity. For, to face the future, a nation must be able to face the past.

THE MILWAUKEE JOURNAL
Milwaukee, Wisc., April 20, 1978

The atrocities of Nazi Germany have been depicted forcefully many times — in the hideous newsreel footage at the end of World War II, in the Nuremberg and Eichmann trials, in novels, historical works, screen plays and documentary films. Yet the story of unequaled genocide cannot be told too often or emphasized too strongly because it contains so many grim lessons for the human race.

Television's latest contribution, the epic series "Holocaust," impressed us as particularly valuable. It was wisely tailored to TV's mass audience, permitting maximum impact. It was partly fictionalized, but it remained faithful to the essential historical facts. Furthermore, it wasn't the story of a few demented monsters committing psychopathic crimes. No, it was much more disturbing and realistic than that because it showed how many fairly normal people — immersed in a national campaign of racism and prompted by the desire to get ahead or just get by — can drift into passive and active roles in a campaign of wanton extermination.

Viewers are left with an uneasy reminder that mankind's veneer of civilized conduct is very thin, that many people can acquiesce in a program of mass murder once it is condoned by the state, that few will stand against it, and that those who actually take part in the killings quickly become inured to their gruesome work.

Likewise, there is the morbid lesson that the sanctioned killing of one category of persons can spread to others. It was "mercy killing" of the mentally defective that provided the model and technology for

destroying millions of others whom bigotry decreed to be undesirable — Gypsies, Slavs and, most of all, Jews.

Although the crimes committed against Jews in the concentration camps and ghettos were singularly ghastly in scale, and although they were unbelievably senseless in that they didn't even serve a military purpose, they were still far from unique. To a lesser degree, mass murder has been practiced against many populations throughout history.

Of course, Americans can be grateful that our history has no blot to match the magnitude of Germany's onslaught against minorities, but we cannot ignore the sorry chapters in this nation's record — slavery, Jim Crow, devastation of the Indians, detention camps for Japanese Americans, political persecution in the McCarthy era.

And of course, there is good reason to hope our system of democratic government and tradition of civil liberties will keep the US from the demoniac road that Germany traveled. Yet, in times of crisis, anxiety and social upheaval, Americans have had recurring reminders that democracy, liberty and tolerance are fragile. Those vital qualities have to be shielded constantly if they are to prevail when severe tests come.

Thus any country that aspires to preserve a free and humane society must heed a central lesson of the holocaust: Never become complacent, never condone infringement of any basic right, never assume that "it can't happen here."

THE ☼ SUN
Baltimore, Md., April 24, 1978

NBC's telecast of "Holocaust," a docu-drama of the Hitlerian horror that befell six million Jews, is above all a political event. Just as the ABC presentation of "Roots" forced white America to think upon the abomination of black slavery, so "Holocaust" should remind gentile America of the evil of anti-Semitism. It was this impulse run rampant that led to mass murder worse than nightmare, that (in Willy Brandt's words) betrayed the German nation and that created the moral basis for the state of Israel.

Neither telecast may have been good drama or even good documentary. But the fact that tens of millions of Americans watched both cannot help but temper the political mood of our times. Tonight, as the Passover commemorates the Biblical flight from Egypt, Jewish children will not be the only young Americans mindful that the Warsaw ghetto uprising also began on this night. In many schools, youngsters were told to stay up late to learn vividly the history their parents and grandparents lived through.

It is a coincidence, but an important one, that the presentation of "Holocaust" has come at a moment of declining American support for the policies of the present Israeli government. The Jewish nation is today headed by Menachem Begin, a man uprooted and shaped by the Hitler catastrophe into what he has described as "a new specimen of human being, a specimen completely unknown to the world for over eighteen hundred years, the Fighting Jew." Mr. Begin is neither as adaptable to political exigencies as

his predecessors nor as beguiling as Egypt's Anwar Sadat. A CBS-New York *Times* poll reports that U.S. support for Israeli policies dropped from 54 per cent last October to 43 per cent in early April. The period coincides with Mr. Sadat's emergence as a U.S. media idol, with President Carter's preference for Mr. Sadat's policies and with growing apprehension among American Jews.

These various developments may soon come to a head when the President submits to Congress his proposed "package" aircraft deal for Israel, Egypt and Saudi Arabia. The President seems ready to insist that if Congress disapproves planes for the Arabs he will cancel planes for Israel; Jerusalem is counting on pro-Israel legislators to block a deal it fears will menace Israel militarily. One has to hope a Carter-Begin clash can be avoided, because it is a clash the Israeli prime minister cannot win, even if his cause triumphs momentarily on Capitol Hill. Israel's need is flexibility, not the reverse. But Mr. Carter, too, is obligated to restore a sense of balance in Middle East negotiations.

It would be stretching a point to suggest that the telecast of "Holocaust" will cause more than a flutter in the coming congressional debate or in Israel's poll ratings. Nevertheless, America's sharpened remembrance of the tragedy that befell the Jewish people should make this nation doubly cautious of any policies that could make Seder herbs more bitter at future Passovers.

Oregon Journal
Portland, Ore., April 25, 1978

Although countless thousands of books, pamphlets, articles and films have been circulated about the horrifying mistreatment of Jews by Nazi Germany and the ways in which most of the world ignored their fate, it took a television series last week to reawaken Americans to the "Holocaust."

The genocide perpetrated by the Nazis beginning more than four decades ago was one of history's darkest hours because of its magnitude. It was made all the worse because the civilized world did nothing to prevent it. The war against Germany was not carried out primarily because of the murder of Jews, but to stop territorial invasions.

There are cases of genocide being perpetrated today, with little or no willingness on the part of politicians, religious leaders or the general public to become involved.

Much of the murder involves minority groups, as was the case with European Jews.

Brazil has systematically obliterated Indian tribes deep in its Amazon forests in order to lay claim to jungle lands rich in minerals and other resources.

Uganda's Amin regime with some design and with great abandon is slaughtering people along tribal lines to insure the perpetuation of government.

Cambodians are carrying out a form of "self-genocide," not in a civil war but rather an enforcement of tough government policies which apparently are aimed at eliminating the weak and protesting.

Vietnamese and Laotians have murdered along racial lines isolated mountain tribes.

Politics decrees that nations do not intervene, as was the shameful case in Hitler's time, when not even peaceful, non-militaristic aid came to the rescue of Jews.

It will take more than a television series 40 years after the fact to deal with these sad cases.

If ever there were a case for stepping up the White House's human rights campaign, these genocidal acts provide ample opportunity. Presidential statements last week about Cambodia could help spur international action.

International opinion needs even stronger prodding, since there is a tendency to consider these cases merely untouchable "internal politics."

Waiting 40 years is simply and plainly too long.

Los Angeles Times

Los Angeles, Calif., January 28, 1979

West German television critics and other commentators had made their soundings, and were convinced that only a small audience would watch the airing of "Holocaust," the American TV dramatization of the Nazi extermination of the Jews.

The signs were not auspicious. A television guide with the largest magazine circulation on the continent printed the listing of the program in small type. "Holocaust" was assigned to regional TV channels rather than to national network stations. Even the producer who bought the four-part film estimated that it would be seen by no more than 15% of the West German television audience.

The number of viewers was a critical element for a TV critic of a major West German paper who said, "Every means is right that disturbs and weakens the suppression mechanism that the majority of Germans have so perfectly mastered till now in relation to the mass murder of European Jewry."

The critics underestimated the appeal of the program. The two segments of the four-part series dominated West German viewing, and the percentage of the TV audience attracted by the film more than doubled the 15% prediction.

Chancellor Helmut Schmidt interrupted a speech in parliament to say that the series "compels one to critical and moral reflection." Mildred Scheel, who watched the program with her husband, President Walter Scheel, said, "I was deeply touched. Young people in particular should see this film."

A television station reported that two-thirds of the response to the film was "positive," but about one-third of the station's callers opposed the program, mainly on the basis that it opened old wounds and hurt Germany's image abroad.

One viewer—not a critic, not a public official, not a person of any prominence at all, but a 16-year-old student—made the essential point about "Holocaust" and its showing in West Germany: "We can never get too much information about the Nazi era. Otherwise, the danger would exist that such a thing could happen again."

The Charlotte Observer

Charlotte, N.C., April 28, 1978

Elie Wiesel, a survivor of Buchenwald who teaches at Boston University, thinks the TV broadcast "Holocaust" was "untrue, offensive, cheap." We thought it was great television.

"Holocaust" had to succeed as mass entertainment while trying to tell the story of what happened to Europe's Jews under the Nazis. Those who lambast the nine-and-a-half-hour broadcast have often done so without considering the environment in which it had to operate.

Commercial TV is not a theater for art films; it is *mass* entertainment. So even at its best, it enrages those like Mr. Wiesel, who wish American commercial television to be something it is not.

Mr. Wiesel writes of one particularly anguished scene: "We see naked women and children entering the gas chambers; we see their faces, we hear their moans as the doors are being shut, then — well, enough. To use special effects and gimmicks to describe the indescribable is morally objectionable. Worse, it is indecent."

Wiesel

But it is not physically impossible to describe what Adolf Hitler did to Europe's Jews. He exterminated most of them. He did so with ordinary means; machine guns, starvation, poison gas, tools that lie at hand today. "Holocaust" showed those tools at work.

Perhaps those who decry "Holocaust" are saying that *no* television program that attempts a realistic video description of a piece of history so obscene can ever do more than make it trivial; that by the fact of its appearance on prime-time TV, the central tragedy of the century has been made shiny and plastic.

If you watched it all four nights, you inflicted a painful experience on yourself. If the commercials seemed in dreadful taste, it was because the drama took you far beyond the usual massage-the-viewers-so-our-commercials-will-sell philosophy of TV programming.

We thought Tom Shales, television critic for the Washington Post, had a point. "Expatriate viewers," he wrote, "who drop in on television only to witness a rare special event — and then find the event an enormous disappointment — are like citizens of a republic who haven't voted in 30 years and then, upon entering the voting booth, become horrified by the caliber of the candidates. They have a right to complain but their previous abstinence makes their objections irrelevant."

"Holocaust" did not surrender its basic honesty, which means it was no fun to watch. And an estimated 120 million people — a near-record for a mini-series — saw at least part of it. Would it have been better if commercial television had attempted nothing, sticking instead with the usual pablum?

THE BISMARCK TRIBUNE

Bismarck, N.D., April 21, 1978

While we live in a fairly well educated society, a sizable number of Americans rarely read anything more informative than the latest paperback novel. Sometimes even those who finish college.

Such reading habits make it all the more important when television comes up with an informative program. NBC estimates 120 million viewers in this country saw the four-part docu-drama "Holocaust." The program conveys some of the reality of the Nazi extermination of nearly six million Jews during World War II.

Discussions spurred by the series have added some awareness to similar plights such as the ongoing Cambodian "resettlement." The program also gives younger people a graphic example of the possible consequences of domination by a militaristic society.

Those of us who lived through World War II presumably realize Americans are not automatically immune from similar treatment. There's no magic circle around our shores to ward off demons.

The program makes it easier to see why Israelis, who have lately gained some cluster bomb infamy of their own, remain reluctant to grant substantial concessions in exchange for promises of peace.

Surrounded and badly outnumbered, Israelis can't feel very distant from the holocaust. Russian Jews have no less reason to feel insecure. Outsiders, conscious of growing hatred festering in Palestinian refugee camps, may see concessions as the only real hope Israelis have for long-term peace and survival in the Middle East.

Such judgments won't come as easily for Jews, little more than three decades distant from Buchenwald. A visit to the barracks, showers and ovens at that camp make it easier to see the Jewish point of view. "Holocaust" does too.

The validity of Jewish fears doesn't mitigate the real suffering of Palestinians. This confrontation of the displaced isn't the same as the ideological Russian-American stand-off because it won't dissolve with time.

The first message of the television program is the possibility of slaughter as well as the reality of killing. If killing remains an inseparable aspect of man, perhaps the best we can do is prevent the slaughter — another holocaust.

If another holocaust begins, this one by nuclear fires, the technology of weapons will encompass everyone in the world. Prevention won't be found by divorcing ourselves in disgust from weapons and trying to reason by our peaceful intentions toward our enemies.

As the Jews found out, reasoning with Nazis who carry guns won't stop the reality of family camp trains leaving for Auschwitz.

When we meet a viper on the trail, the wisest course is to hold a big stick and try to work around it. Not the perfect solution, but probably the only one that works at this stage of the game.

Bitten once, Israelis cling even more strongly to this strategy, whether it's the answer or not.

Public Broadcasting: At Whose Expense?

In 1967, Congress set up the public television structure on the basis of a blueprint designed by the Carnegie Commission on Educational Television. The commission, sponsored by the Carnegie Corporation of New York, urged "immediate action to extend and strengthen educational television." It proposed the formation of the Corporation for Public Television, a federally chartered, non-profit, nongovernmental organization. It placed the power to receive and disburse funds and to control programming in the hands of this corporation. It also stressed the equal importance of national and local programming.

In 1979, the Carnegie Commission on the Future of Public Broadcasting proposed a complete reorganization of the public television structure the original Carnegie Commission had recommended twelve years earlier. After an 18-month evaluation of public broadcasting, the commission declared the noncommercial system "fundamentally flawed" and unable to sustain programming excellence. They found the original structure of the PTV system had become a bureaucracy sensitive to political and corporate interference and hostile to diversity and innovation in programming.

The second Carnegie Commission, therefore, proposed the elimination of the Corporation for Public Broadcasting and its replacement by a new Public Telecommunications Trust. The trust would be the fiduciary agent for the system and have no say at all in programming selection. Programming would fall under the auspices of a semiautonomous division of the trust, the Program Services Endowment. This division would develop and underwrite a broad range of national television programming and serve as a "safe place for nurturing creative activity." To prevent the two organizations from becoming "repositories for political patronage," a new and elaborate selection and renewal process for organization members would be delineated.

The Carnegie Commission also proposed inflating the annual financing of PTV to $1.2 billion per year. One-half of the total funds would be raised by the station from non-federal sources: state and local governments, public contribution, foundation grants and corporate underwriting. The federal government would allocate $590 million. It would also distribute additional funds according to a matching formula of two federal dollars to every $3 raised by a local station; this money would be designated strictly for programming and not for the improvement of facilities. Additional funds would come from a fee to be imposed on users of the public airwaves, principally commercial broadcasters.

The committee's report emphasized the need to insulate public broadcasting from control by the federal government and to insure freedom of programming. During the seventies, local PTV stations were often frustrated by the federal emphasis on the mass national audience, wary that the needs of local station audiences would be overlooked.

The Dallas Morning News

Dallas, Tex., June 29, 1978

Inherently there are philosophical problems with the concept of a television network financed in large part with public money. At least with Ralph Rogers at the helm of the Public Broadcasting Service, one knew PBS would never degenerate into a government propaganda organ or an outlet for cultural snobbery or populistic reverse snobbery.

Rogers, the Dallas business executive who chaired PBS from 1973 until this week, has served ably and well. He deserves the rest he's getting, but in truth he will be missed. (His successor is former Federal Communications Commission Chairman Newton Minow.)

PBS has more money than ever before—thanks in part to Rogers, Congress in 1975 was persuaded to grant public broadcasting long-range financing.

But what of the local control that Rogers so assiduously battled for? This is much chancier. HR 13015, a proposed mammoth overhaul of the communications industry, would abolish the Corporation for Public Broadcasting, which funnels federal money to PBS, and replace it with a Public Telecommunications Programming Endowment to make discretionary grants to stations.

The endowment would forbid such stations from accepting outside contributions for specific programs (like Mobil Oil's "Masterpiece Theater"); it would also mandate "community advisory boards," open meetings and, in effect, job quotas for women and blacks. "The Reich Broadcasting System," wags within FCC have nicknamed the proposed new dispensation.

Great battles loom ahead. Would that Ralph Rogers' strong right arm were available for them. As it is, we shall have to hope that Minow proves himself as big a fish as his predecessor.

The Kansas City Times

Kansas City, Mo., December 20, 1978

Legislation in Congress that would provide funding for the Public Broadcasting Service has PBS officials upset. A bill, which already has won approval by voice vote in the House, calling for subjective judgment by PBS in awarding matching funds to local stations, treads dangerously close to a government agency controlling local programming.

Already the broadcast industry, under the control of the Federal Communications Commission, is heavily regulated. Despite its overall shelter under the First Amendment, broadcast — because of its technology — comes under close scrutiny. Public broadcasting affiliates are subjected to the FCC regulations and must seek the same important goals . . . access, affirmative action and excellence in programming . . . as prescribed by the FCC.

The House bill, by its language, mandates these subjective goals as requisite for funding. We have no doubts about the intent of the bill, but its application would be extremely faulty. From funding formulas, to deciding the composition of station boards of directors (which vary according to the affiliation of the outlet, for example some stations are still linked to school districts), to pursuing "excellence" in programming. How can these criteria be met according to federal law?

A similar bill in the Senate, which has not come to the floor yet for a vote, would provide renewed appropriations for PBS stations. The measure is worded more carefully and does not have as much potential for abridgement of free speech. That bill should be adopted by Congress.

There is much to debate on the philosophy of media, in this case PBS, accepting operating funds from the federal government. The implied obligation for editorial independence to yield to government propaganda has been avoided in the award of Community Program Grants. General guidelines, which would prohibit the misuse of tax dollars on broadcasting, must apply, but the House bill gets specific to a point of confusion and possible misrepresentation. The Senate version should prevail.

DENVER POST

Denver, Colo., August 10, 1978

CAN THE FEDERAL GOVERNMENT increase funding for public broadcasting without exerting unwarranted controls?

That is the question before Congress now as both the Senate and the House consider bills extending funding into the 1980s.

Officials of the Public Broadcasting Service (PBS)—the independent agency created by the Public Broadcasting Act of 1967 to disburse federal funds—are worried about the mood of Congress. And for good reason.

The two funding measures fall short of goals for public broadcasting set by the Carter administration and applauded by PBS.

President Carter in a 1977 message had called for legislative action to provide public broadcasting with greater financial stability, increased isolation from possible political interference and greater editorial independence.

Both measures in Congress provide authorization for federal funding through 1983; Mr. Carter had asked for funding through 1985.

And both measures call for tighter public accountability requirements for national broadcasting entities—such as PBS, the Corporation for Public Broadcasting and National Public Radio—as well as for individual public stations such as Denver's KRMA and KCFR.

The proposed regulations reflect concern in Congress that federal funds are not being wisely spent. That, of course, is a legitimate concern. Certainly, uniform auditing requirements—not now the case—ought to be implemented for proper accountability.

But Congress should be careful not to overstep the line into the area of unwanted interference in the operation of public television and radio.

Both the House and the Senate bills contain provisions which virtually recast the Corporation for Public Broadcasting into a quasi-governmental agency whose decisions on programming would be subject to scrutiny by an arm of the federal government.

The House bill also provides for overly subjective criteria, such as cost efficiencies in disbursing community service grants, heretofore unrestricted money for public television stations.

In determining if a station is operating on a cost efficient basis, will federal officials begin to question whether funds should be risked on controversial or unusual programs? Or on programs for small specialized audiences? Or limited to general audiences?

There is still time for Congress to avoid such potentially harmful action.

Whatever changes are undertaken in the structure of the public broadcasting system, they ought to be within the spirit and intent of the 1967 act, which overall has worked remarkably well in separating government assistance from government control.

THE MILWAUKEE JOURNAL
Milwaukee, Wisc., October 18, 1977

Many fans warmly praise public television as a short trip around the dial from excessive violence and other low grade offerings on commercial TV. But other viewers continue to feel frustrated when they think about what public stations could be: not just a medium for art forms and innocuous documentaries but aggressive public affairs forums.

Public broadcasting leaves a lot to be desired for several reasons — inadequate public funding, bickering among controlling agencies and a legacy of government interference and distrust left by the Nixon administration. Now the Carter administration has offered legislation that would help remove some of these obstacles. The proposal deserves a warm reception in Congress.

The proposal would: (1) appropriate $1 billion to public broadcasting over the next five years, nearly doubling the current annual appropriation; (2) earmark $50 million of that annually for national programing, enough to give some respectability to this activity; (3) restructure the roles of the bickering Public Broadcasting Service (the public programing network) and the Corporation for Public Broadcasting (the distributor of funds that was used by the Nixon administration to squelch criticism and independence in public broadcasting); and (4) increase the number of public stations and permit all stations to air editorials.

Local stations still would have to raise most of their operating funds locally, but the legislation would give them more freedom and resources to improve their programing and play a more stimulating role in the often vapid video world.

Pittsburgh Post-Gazette
Pittsburgh, Pa., October 8, 1977

PRESIDENT CARTER'S funding request for public television is disappointing in one respect. He proposes $1 billion over five years, a trimmer Corporation for Public Broadcasting and a more vital Public Broadcast System. But he has not taken into account the special needs of children.

The Administration's proposals should give public television a morale boost that has been needed ever since the system's independence was undercut by presidential politics during the Vietnam war, but the network's youngest audience also needs special attention.

Television producers estimate that children spend 25 to 30 hours in front of the TV tube each week, and public policy can no longer afford to treat this mass of the viewing population indifferently. In the preoccupation it provides and by its often negative effect, television exerts more influence upon children even than schools.

To assure that this influence has basis and focus, public television should provide programming which combats an excessively banal and distorted view of life fostered by the need of the commercial networks to have mucilage for candy and cereal advertisements.

Several programs developed for the Public Broadcast System, such as Sesame Street and Misterogers Neighborhood, have challenged the prevailing values of commercial children's television. But these sometimes brilliantly inspired efforts have been limited by other demands upon public television's insufficient budget.

In introducing a measure which recognizes that the system should have more money, Mr. Carter nevertheless has not proposed to cure this special problem. Either special legislation or congressional mandate is needed to safeguard the interests of children whose needs are too often absorbed, then dissipated in the existing system.

Whether these safeguards around children's television are provided through the Public Broadcast System, which seems like the most probable means, or through a special agency such as the National Endowment for Children's Television proposed by Sen. H. John Heinz of Pennsylvania ought to be decided by a simple rule. Which agency will generate the greater volume of new programming for the same amount of money?

THE SUN
Baltimore, Md., October 4, 1977

President Carter's plan for revamping public television and radio would more than double federal expenditures in this area and might even stop the feuding between the Public Broadcasting Service and the Corporation for Public Broadcasting.

But the President's plan might do very little for the local stations, which are—or should be—the backbone of the public system. Under the President's plan, CPB would be stripped of programming authority and would return to its original, smaller role as a distributor of funds appropriated by Congress. But the local stations apparently would not be given more programming authority. Rather, there would be a kind of fourth network on the order of the British Broadcasting Corporation, with PBS very much in charge.

PBS, originally a national membership body for the local stations, has grown to the point where it now often dictates local programming. Local station officials argue convincingly that this is contrary to the original purpose of public television, which was to meet local needs as these needs were perceived locally. Some of these programs, including a number produced by the Maryland Center for Public Broadcasting, have been suitable for national distribution. But some smaller local stations on barebones budgets are hard put to produce shows good enough for local airing.

Turning PBS into a "fourth network" for the production of major works may be a good idea, but only so long as it does not starve local stations of the funds needed for shows worthy of national distribution. Equally important, public stations on shoestring budgets in smaller cities must be assured the financing to offer the local public affairs programming that commercial television so often fails to provide. The President's proposals give too little attention to the needs of local public stations.

The Washington Post
Washington, D.C., October 27, 1977

WHILE THE HIGH-POWERED network-television executives have been agonizing over the ups and down of another fall season, their colleagues in public broadcasting have won some important support for better noncommercial programming. In a comprehensive set of proposals sent to Congress this month, President Carter has moved to strengthen the state of public broadcasting through reorganization, better financing and a commitment to "increase public broadcasting's insulation from inappropriate political influence." If enacted, the White House legislation could do much to encourage the kind of talented, imaginative personnel—at local stations and on a national level—that the public system deserves.

In particular, the President's emphasis on increased programming independence for the public system is a welcome, formal shift from pressures that were brought to bear on public broadcasting during the Nixon years. Then, though it didn't show up directly on your screens, there was a bitter internal conflict over control of the nation's public-television hookup of stations under the Public Broadcasting Service. When the Nixon White House expressed displeasure at the way public television was being run and at the content of public-affairs programs, the presidentially appointed Corporation for Public Broadcasting—which receives money from Congress and distributes it to National Public Radio and PBS for a matching at the local level—fought to take over all programming and scheduling of TV.

The battle eventually ended in a delicate truce between CPB and PBS. But now President Carter is seeking an increase in federal funds to be appropriated under an advance five-year congressional authorization totaling nearly $1 billion—which is as much as has gone into the system since the federal government started putting in money 10 years ago. The Carter plan also could double the money for improved equipment at the local level, which is a key to any increase in local stations' initiative and independent operation.

As the President noted, "Because it is free of the scramble for ratings, public broadcasting has room for experimentation and risk-taking. . . . It can meet the needs of audiences that number in the millions but are seldom served anywhere else." To reduce the opportunities for political interference by the government in programming, the White House measure would 1) phase out four presidentially appointed members of the 15-member CPB board and replace them with members chosen by public-television and -radio licensees and 2) remove CPB from decisions on individual programs.

Thus, PBS would have control of national public-television programming, and there would be a "substantial reduction" in the CPB's current staff and any overlapping duties it now performs.

There are some doubters, of course, who see the plan as a way of turning public television into a "fourth network" fully competitive with commercial television. While we don't think that's necessarily bad, the existence of a strong, independent PBS network can also set some glittering examples for commercial television as it has already with programs such as "Sesame Street," the "MacNeil-Lehrer Report," coverage of congressional hearings and the past interpretive efforts of William Buckley, Bill Moyers, Elizabeth Drew, Paul Duke and many more.

Obviously no legislation can guarantee viewers and listeners a permanent season of high-quality, stimulating, controversial and innovative programming on their local stations, but with approval of President Carter's sensitive proposals, a much healthier public-broadcasting environment could surely foster a constructive (and instructive) alternative use of the public airwaves.

EVENING JOURNAL

Wilmington, Del., Setpember 12, 1977

It's time we stopped thinking about public television as something like castor oil — a little ough to take but in the long run good for you.

This attitude is a disservice to public television and to the television viewers themselves. n the 20-odd years that publicly supported elevision has operated in this country it has mproved significantly. Just as the commerial networks, whose programing it supplenents, have done, public television has masered its craft. No longer simply an "educaional" operation that presents stiff and stuffy liscussions on "important" (but often boring) ubjects, public television today offers first lass entertainment along with its fare of ublic service programs. Often it combines oth as in the children's shows like Sesame Street and The Electric Company.

A significant problem with public television s its reliance on government support and rivate donations for its existence. It is the ublic tax support that concerns us here. Year after year, the Corporation for Public Broadasting (CPB) must turn, hat in hand, to Congress for support. Support is given, but in a manner more like giving to a worthy cause han providing the viewing public with a responsible vehicle for the airing of alternative views and presenting entertainment that would not survive the mass appeal demands of commercial network. It seems to us that alternaive programing like opera, William F. Buckey's "Firing Line", and drama uninterrupted by advertisements is worthwhile and should be encouraged.

An excellent example of the service public television can provide is the current live broadcasts of Senate hearings into the affairs of Bert Lance, the Carter administration's director of the Office of Management and Budget.

A serious difficulty in television production comes when long-range financing is absent. The commercial networks, assured of money (without end, it seems) spend months, if not years, developing shows. Public television, if it is to continue to mature, produce quality programs, and cease its reliance on British imports for drawing larger audiences, should enjoy a similar capability.

Congress, however, seems to want to keep a **tight rein on public television.** Whether Congress is motivated by a desire to reward or punish programing or by some sense of fiscal restraint no one really knows. The fact is, that forcing those who run public television to make an annual pitch for support defeats any long-term growth and improvement in the industry.

With proper long-term financing, public television could provide American-made programs equal to the British ones that now seem to dominate.

Long range funding could be achieved in a number of ways. In Great Britain, a small annual tax is levied on each television set. The approach used by Congress is funding a num**ber of education programs through multi-year money guarantees requiring little more than token annual approval**—would be another way. There must be others.

What's important is that Congress recognize the value of public television and support it in a way that makes it a real alternative to commercial broadcasting and not just another bit of "good medicine" to be prescribed for constituents.

Denver, Colo., January 29, 1977

THE GENIUS OF America manifests it self in many ways. One of its least admirable aspects is our towering talent for creating instant bureaucracies.

Public television is an immediate case in point. Public television is relatively new, but at this early date in its history it's already bowing beneath the weight of its bureaucratic superstructure.

More than eight of every 10 federal dollars appropriated for public broadcasting go to the support of its own bureaucracies. This fiscal year, of the $103 million in matching funds authorized for public television, only $13.3 million has been budgeted for national programming.

Last year's authorization was $78 million, of which $9 million went for programming. Thus, an increase in federal spending of $25 million produced only $4.3 million more for building shows.

That's nothing more nor less than outrageous budgeting. And it's certainly part of the reason that many of the best shows on public television are products of the British Broadcasting Corp.

One of the problems is that U.S. public television is a two-headed monster. There's the Public Broadcasting Service (PBS) which is charged with developing programs, and the Corporation for Public Broadcasting (CPB), whose board is politically appointed and mainly responsible for distributing the federal funds.

Both organizations have large and highly paid staffs by government wage standards. In many instances their jobs overlap. And each time the federal appropriation has been increased, the bureaucracies have increased disproportionately, as is, alas, always the case.

Surely, public television in this country needs help if it is to become the important factor in American home entertainment and enlightnment that it can and should be

The first step toward wiser use of public money should be to eliminate the costly overlaps between PBS and CPB, and pour the money where it belongs — into the development of more and better original shows.

President-elect Carter has pledged himself to eliminate waste in the whole federal bureaucracy. A good place to begin would be in this bureaucracy before it becomes as ingrained as it is in the older departments of the government.

The Boston Globe

Boston, Mass., May 29, 1978

When American audiences assess public television six years from today, they should look back on diverse, controversial, high-quality programming that served a broad range of people and interests, particularly those ignored or shortchanged by commercial broadcasters. Whether this will be the view from 1984 will be determined this year by the long-range direction Congress gives to public broadcasting.

Three proposals are before Congress concerning the next phase of public radio and television.

The Carter Administration's plan proposes five-year funding beginning in 1980, and is regarded as more responsive to the complaint of minority groups that public broadcasting has not served them adequately. And it would establish a fund for national programming that would imitate the centralized system of the commercial networks.

The House proposal is regarded as weaker on guarantees for minority participation throughout public broadcasting, but includes a set-aside for national programming. In addition, the House version allocates a specific amount for public radio and directs the Corporation for Public Broadcasting (CPB) to get outside help for better financial accountability.

None of these provisions is in the Senate version, which, like the House proposal, is a three-year funding bill to begin in 1980.

In the next month, the three versions will have to be reconciled. The congressional committees that devised the House and Senate versions were probably right in limiting their bills to three years, since the Carnegie Commission and Congress itself are both in the middle of studies bound to have a lasting effect on public broadcasting's future. Their reports are due next year.

But whatever the reports recommend, it is clear that public television will best be served by encouraging the diversity and sensitivity to public affairs that viewers and listeners of WGBH have become accustomed to in Boston.

It is also clear that when Congress finally tackles the problem of long-range, politically independent funding for public broadcasting, the debate will be better focused if there is confidence beforehand that public stations have used their funds wisely and responsibly. An unpublished but leaked report from the General Accounting Office reportedly indicates that this is not now the case at many stations.

Public broadcasting has been criticized for being "elitist" because it plays to a limited audience. But the real mission of public television and radio is to speak to audiences with special needs not served by commercial networks.

At its best, public broadcasting is a countervailing and dissenting force from what is offered to mass audiences. Whatever emerges from Congress should reinforce this function by combining President Carter's approach to allocating funds for specific purposes with short-term funding and the House requirement for better financial accountability.

The Oregonian
Portland, Ore., December 25, 1977

Public television has been increasing its audience (up 11.4 percent since last March), but the number of Americans who watch commercial television has been dropping by the millions (ranging from 1 to 6 percent a month), according to polls done by A.C. Nielsen.

But among those who support public television, there is the feeling that the shift is due more to a decline in interest in the commercial fare than any increase in the quality of public programs.

At least one critic, Andrew A. Stern, a producer of TV shows in San Francisco, believes that public television has become the victim of the "tyranny of the majority," resulting in bland, conservative programming, particularly in the areas of news and public affairs.

When the Congress set up public television in 1967, it hoped to see an alternative to commercial TV develop. That has not happened. Public television is much too prone to copy or actually use commercial programs or well-known performers. It should be developing new faces and avoiding the stereotypes seen on the commercial stations.

But instead of new faces, network news programs have been run on public television stations with only the commercials deleted; Dick Cavett is now performing on the public tube; local sports and other TV personalities are used, while uninspired formats representing the worst of commercial TV too often are accepted.

President Carter has offered public television more money so that a secure future will provide adequate lead time to produce high-quality productions. The funds would increase from $152 million in the current appropriations to $180 million in 1981 and to $200 million in the four succeeding years. But more money will not help if it is used to produce only the same old things done by the commercial stations — warmed-over sports, tedious interviews that produce no new information and uninspired cultural events that are hardly above the level of daytime radio.

Lawrence Grossman, the president of the Public Broadcasting Service, has said that $1 billion is needed to adequately finance the programs PBS distributes. However, it is not the amount, but how it is spent that counts. CBS spends only $3.6 million, Stern pointed out, in producing its highly regarded news anthology, 60 Minutes. But the Corporation for Public Broadcasting spent $6 million on the Best of Families and $1.2 million on The Dick Cavett Show. The McNeil/Lehrer Report cost $3.6 million, and although it was an Emmy award winner, it was not even carried this season in Oregon.

Unless comprehensive reform is undertaken, Carter's plan to throw more money at public television will succeed only in making it more like a poor relative of the commercial networks. After warmed-over Cavett will we get souped-up Mary Hartman?

St. Petersburg Times
St. Petersburg, Fla., October 7, 1977

Jimmy Carter is proposing a $1-billion invigoration for public broadcasting in the United States.

If that sounds extravagant, consider that the appropriation would help fund public radio as well as television and would be spread over five years beginning in 1981.

MORE IMPORTANT, consider the purposes of public broadcasting, as outlined in a speech at St. Petersburg Beach in June by Larry Grossman, president of the Public Broadcasting Service:

✔ "To foster American creative talent;

✔ "To reach out to the underserved minorities with programs of interest to them;

✔ "To portray a diversity of American culture;

✔ "To provide education;

✔ "To investigate the problems of our communities, our country and our planet;

✔ "To enrich the educational process and learning of our people;

✔ "To reach out into the community and reach a big enough audience to justify the funds we receive."

THAT'S A tall order, but one fully in keeping with this nation's commitment to democracy, and to equal opportunities for all its citizens. Public television has the potential to bring life-long learning opportunities, superb cultural offerings and outstanding public affairs programs into American homes and schools. Neither Grossman nor anyone else claims that it fully is living up to its potential today.

Certainly there have been some first-class American productions, such as *The Adams Chronicles*. But major domestic productions again are sparse this year. As usual, some of the best programing is being furnished by the British Broadcasting Corporation. In public affairs, national productions like the *MacNeil/Lehrer Report* and such Florida standouts as *Today in the Legislature* show what noncommercial television can do and whet the appetite for more.

A new Carnegie Commission on Public Broadcasting is examining public TV and will make recommendations in 1978 on such matters as creative programming, the impact of new technologies and the sources of operating funds. No doubt the commission will find that federal neglect largely is responsible for the system's shortcomings.

THE NIXON years dealt severe setbacks to public television, curtailing both its funding and its journalistic independence. In marked contrast to those policies, Carter's proposal for the next 5-year funding cycle would exceed the government's total support over the last 10 years. In addition to strengthening national programing, the increased funding is designed to ease local matching requirements, to encourage greater minority participation and to expand the public TV system, which now reaches only half of the country.

Other recommendations that the President made to Congress Thursday include greater journalistic and editorial independence for community-based stations. To shield the system itself from government interference, Carter is offering to relinquish some of his own appointive power over the Corporation for Public Broadcasting. And to settle long-running jurisdictional disputes between the corporate board and the Public Broadcasting Service (PBS), Carter recommended that the corporation concentrate on funding decisions and leave programing to PBS.

DURING HIS presidential campaign, Carter promised to give public broadcasting a boost. We're glad to see he meant it.

Newsday
Garden City, N.Y., October 20, 1977

In most countries with both public and commercial television, the public channels offer strong competition to those that accept advertising. Not so in the United States, where public broadcasting has lacked the means and the outlets to compete successfully with the commercial kind.

Funds have been a major problem. Since government contributions have always been too skimpy to allow for much independent programing, public television has had to rely increasingly on foundations and business sources.

Corporations have found it to their advantage to sponsor public television programs. The brief mention at the beginning or end of a show—e.g., "This program was made possible through a grant from the Mobil Oil Corporation"—has been recognized as a great prestige-enhancer, and businesses are lining up as sponsors. The danger lies in public television's losing its programing independence as it becomes increasingly dependent on funds from private corporations. The practice is also blurring the line between public and commercial television.

Richard Nixon distrusted educational television and tried to tie its hands. Continuing squabbles between the parent company, the Corporation for Public Broadcasting, and the network, the Public Broadcasting Service, didn't help either.

But now President Carter, in line with a campaign promise, has sent Congress a request for $1 billion for public television over a five-year period. His proposal also attempts to give greater power to independent producers and individual stations and allow them greater journalistic latitude to broadcast editorial comment.

At a time when commercial television is under increasing—and justified—attack over program content, Americans certainly need an alternative. It's up to PBS to furnish it, and it's up to Congress to make that possible.

Arkansas Gazette.

Little Rock, Ark., December 6, 1976

Once again we have a flurry of conflict in the field of public television, but it probably amounts to nothing that will work to the detriment of this important and advancing medium. Certainly the current hassle contains none of the acrid portents of repression which cropped up during the Nixon administration, and indeed it may point to just the opposite: A period of fermentive argument which will lead to greater excellence in public broadcasting.

The argument is familiar and may go on forever in one degree or another. At odds are the Public Broadcasting Service, an organization of the 265 member stations, and the Corporation for Public Broadcasting, the central Washington authority, run by 15 presidential appointees, which hands out the federal money to those stations. Some dispute, we suppose, is inevitable between the people who disburse it and those who receive it; the former rarely if ever are willing to give up all their say over how it's spent. So the PBS is complaining again (after three years of relative truce) that the CPB is trying to dictate the kind of programs which the public TV network will carry, and that this should be left altogether to PBS discretion, which is to say, to the station managers consulting among themselves. In a recent resolution of annoyance, the PBS insists that the corporation's role should be strictly limited to disbursing federal funds, assisting the public stations, and insulating them from politics.

Well, such a view certainly could be appreciated—as to the latter point—during the Nixon years, when Spiro Ted Agnew was terrorizing *all* TV, both public and private, and the White House Office of Telecommunications wasn't far behind in trying to dampen public affairs commentary and analysis. If this had continued, there might have been little left on public TV any more controversial than body-building exercises and Sesame Street, but of course it did not continue, any more than Mr. Nixon continued. His pitch in these matters was, however, similar to that of the PBS at present, in one particular, though for a different reason, no doubt. It was against centralized network program planning in Washington for public TV. Let the individual stations, which are closer to the people, have a bigger say in choosing, his people argued. Of course the stations themselves have no great analytical resources on a national scale, and some of those brainier public TV analyses of the Nixon administration had incited the furies at the White House.

There is none of that now, we can say thankfully. Indeed, the glories of public TV now include, most notably, the searching analysis, the expansive documentary, the long and varied panel discussion in which each expert has time to say his say, the many long interviews which commercial TV would not accommodate in prime time, and which develop and illuminate the main issues before the country in marvelous detail. If there is any effort at political intimidation of such free discussion nowadays, we haven't heard of it, nor do we expect to hear of it during the Carter administration. The dispute now is not over any political or ideological intrusion, apparently, but over the CPB's intent to plough some large sums into high-quality national productions for the public network.

It has, for example, set up a $1 million revolving fund to produce documentaries, and committed $1.2 million over six years to acquire the British Broadcasting Corporation's Shakespeare series. We deem these excellent investments, but PBS folks reportedly are rankled at such central decisions by the money-giving body. They'd prefer instead to let local stations make more of the monetary decisions so as to satisfy what they consider local viewing needs.

★　★　★

Certainly a balance must be struck between national and local values in disbursing the funds, but we believe the CPB has to retain a role in preserving and enhancing quality on the network. Local programming is important, all right, but what comes in on the national public network—in children's and cultural programming, in great drama and music and public affairs productions, is what provides the indispensable alternative to commercial TV in the evenings. It gives the needed escape, often of supreme quality, from the increasing violence and salaciousness on the commercial waves on which, Nicholas Johnson informs us, the average child has seen 11,000 murders by the time he or she reaches age 14.

In any case, things should be improving, for the American families who are depending more and more on public TV for these reasons. Congress finally has voted the necessary, heavier funding for the public medium, on a long-term basis. And here in Arkansas, we have seen splendid technical results just recently, in extending public TV coverage to most parts of the state, so that people who move here from other regions sometimes are amazed at the scope and excellence of it. But all of us should be determined, as the funds are spent, not to let a temptation toward localism sap the quality of national programming, which is what most Arkansans, we expect, appreciate and profit from the most.

Detroit Free Press

Detroit, Mich., February 13, 1978

PRESIDENT CARTER'S proposals for increased support of public broadcasting are too little of a good thing; they leave us grateful for what has been offered, but wondering if he couldn't scrape up a little more from the bottom of the pot.

The president has proposed a rather niggardly increase in federal support, to $180 million in fiscal 1981 and a flat $200 million a year for the four years thereafter. He has also proposed a change in the matching funds formula to give the stations one federal dollar for every $2.25 they raise from non-governmental sources, compared to every $2.50 at present.

Surely public broadcasting deserves better. Although it is the only alternative to the numbing mediocrity and sugar-coated materialism of commercial TV, for lack of funds its potential has barely been scratched.

Public television still reaches only 60 percent of the TV receivers in the country. And it remains almost completely dependent upon the largess of corporate donors for program development.

The congressional committees that will take up the broadcast bill later this month could ease the burden of public radio and TV by lowering the matching formula even further, to one federal dollar for every $2 in contributions.

Another important step Congress could take is to approve outright a five-year appropriation for public broadcasting. The Carter bill contains a five-year authorization for funding—which means it promises the funding in principle. The actual appropriation, the handing over of the money, is done no more than two years in advance. That's the way suspicious congressmen make sure public broadcasters aren't going to run off with the money and air something controversial. Their tight hold on the purse strings has the intended chilling effect, of course, and it also makes long-range planning difficult for the stations.

Finally, Congress should insist that at least 50 percent of the funds appropriated be distributed to the local stations, to insure that the bulk of the funds are not drawn off at the national level for the Public Broadcasting System.

Here in Detroit, federal funds provide only $334,000 of the $2.8 million budget of Channel 56 this year. No one, especially the broadcasters, wants the federal government to pay much more than a third of public TV's budget—for fear that he who pays the bill will try to call the tune—but that still leaves a lot of room for improvement.

Michigan's Sen. Robert P. Griffin, who sits on the Senate communications subcommittee, should use his influence to win more generous, long-range funding for public broadcasting. It would be an excellent way for Congress to boost its own ratings with the viewers back home.

THE CHRISTIAN SCIENCE MONITOR

Boston, Mass., October 26, 1977

American families take it for granted now. Almost any night of the week they can turn on their TV sets and find Beverly Sills performing live at Lincoln Center, or see history being made as a congressional panel interrogates a public official about alleged wrongdoing, or watch the Cookie Monster, Bert, or Big Bird make children's eyes light up with their Sesame Street antics.

Public broadcasting has become an integral part of American life in the past 10 years, and recent nationwide surveys indicate more people than ever are tuning in and enjoying the 10-year-old public broadcasting system.

Thus it was good news indeed when President Carter announced he is submitting a bill that would strengthen public broadcasting and authorize more than $1 billion over a five-year period to keep public radio and TV broadcasts beaming into American homes.

Not only would the President's plan increase national programming, specifically allocating funds for production of quality programs comparable to those now imported from the British Broadcasting Corporation, the President's bill would resolve the organizational and jurisdictional conflicts that have marred the system in the past, trim down its bureaucratic structure, encourage journalistic independence and editorializing on issues of public importance, and enlarge the role of independent producers and the public in its overall operations.

Mr. Carter also proposes lowering the amount of private matching funds the 271 public TV stations and 203 public radio stations must raise. Current law requires that they raise $2.50 for every $1 received in federal funds. The President would reduce that to $2.25 for each $1. Therefore, viewers and listeners, it appears, will have to continue suffering through those long, fund-raising appeals sandwiched between their favorite programs. But for a chance to hear Beverly Sills or watch the Cookie Monster, we'll gladly endure.

THE TENNESSEAN

Nashville, Tenn., October 17, 1977

INSOFAR as the government is concerned there is some good news and some bad news for public broadcasting.

The good news is that President Carter says $1.04 billion should be spent over the next five years for public broadcasting. That is more than was spent in the last 10 years.

The bad news is that there is strong opposition on Capitol Hill. Some are in favor of trimming that considerably, and the argument is that the system has become top-heavy and wasteful and that too little is going for TV and radio programming.

Still, if Mr. Carter is willing to push for the money, he might get most of it and assuredly there are ways in which to change programming for the better.

Mr. Carter proposed one. He wants to change the idea that a public broadcasting system receiving federal money should not engage in news and public affairs programming.

The idea, Mr. Carter said, is to "insulate it from political manipulation" and press for greater "journalistic independence," encouraging public broadcasting at all levels "to engage in active news reporting and public affairs programming."

That's a welcome approach. During the Nixon administration and to some extent during the Ford administration, the idea seemed to be that of setting strict limits on public affairs reporting.

Public broadcasting has a key role to play in many areas of communication and it can play that role well if it has the means and independence to do so.

Los Angeles Times

Los Angeles, Calif., October 13, 1977

The Carter Administration's proposals for expanding and streamlining public broadcasting open the way for better programming.

The proposals, submitted to Congress last week, call for needed bureaucratic reforms and $1 billion in federal funds for public radio and television broadcasting over a five-year period starting in 1981. The outlay would be more than the government's total support during the past 10 years.

Among the innovative features of the proposals are calls for expanding public-service programs and lifting the ban on editorials by community-supported stations. The ban resulted from fears that, because these stations were supported in part by public funds, they could become propaganda mouthpieces for the government.

We think these fears are overdrawn. Like their commercial counterparts, the stations are licensed by the Federal Communications Commission, and are subject to the same FCC regulations covering equal time and fairness in news and public-affairs programming.

To further minimize the possibility of government interference, the Administration proposed that 8 of the 15 appointees who make up the governing board of the Corp. for Public Broadcasting, public broadcasting's oversight agency, be appointed by other agencies in the field. At present, all 15 are named by the President.

The extra money in the Administration's proposals would be used in part to beam service into areas that do not now receive public broadcasts. Other funds, along with proposed changes in disbursement requirements, would provide a welcome incentive for greater domestic production of high-caliber programs.

The Administration has conceded that money alone will not improve public broadcasting, and therefore has advocated an overhaul of its bureaucracy.

It has proposed that the broadcasting corporation be limited to the chore it was originally set up in 1967 to do—provide general oversight and block grants to the agency responsible for specific programming, the Public Broadcasting Service.

PBS, which represents the stations, and the corporation have engaged in a long jurisdictional feud over the control of programs that has resulted in waste, inefficiency and overlapping activities.

The Administration should seek to have such faults corrected immediately rather than have them wait until 1981.

The Topeka Daily Capital

Topeka, Kans., November 19, 1977

Thanks, but no thanks, public broadcasters told President Carter this week.

They object to his plan requiring a percentage of federal funds given to public broadcasting be devoted to "national programming."

Frederick Breitenfield Jr., director of the Maryland Center for Public Broadcasting (which originates Louis Rukeyser's popular "Wall Street Week" program), objected.

No matter what "national programming" means, he implied, Carter proposed a remarkable precedent — a "legal quota on broadcasting "

In short federal government would tell public stations they must devote so much time to certain types of programs. That is a dangerous precedent.

A few other governments have consolidated power by seizing stations and broadcasting the information they want people to receive.

President Carter, a believer in democracy, certainly does not intend anything like this.

But once the precedent that stations must take government orders about programs is set, the door will be open to possible domination.

"Yes, we want the money, but no, we don't want official qualifications on programming. The money is critical, but we can't relinquish a principle to get it," said Breitenfield.

Public broadcasters should not back down. Government has a bad record for dominating programs it "aids" with tax money — school busing, 55-mph speed limits, motorcycle helmets.

The President's plan for national programming could be the first step toward added control of the Public Broadcasting System.

The Charlotte Observer

Charlotte, N.C., November 4, 1977

Have you been watching public television's new offering, "The Best Of Families," being shown on WTVI and WUNG at 9 p.m. Thursdays? It is a wonderful piece of work, television for grownups by the people who do "Sesame Street" for kids. The fact is, though, that public television is only a fraction as good as it could be.

The reasons are money, political interference and bureaucratic disputes. A piece of legislation the Carter administration has sent to Congress goes a good distance toward resolving those problems. The bill is intended to protect public television from political pressure, to give stations like Charlotte's Channel 42 (WTVI) a slightly more reliable source of funding and, at long last, to decide who will be public television's boss.

There has been a major tug-of-war going on between the presidentially appointed Corporation for Public Broadcasting (CPB) and the Public Broadcasting Service (PBS), which actually distributes programs. The Carter legislation would gut the 15-member CPB board of four presidentially appointed members. CPB would also lose its authority to make decisions on individual programs.

The new legislation would authorize an advance five-year congressional appropriation of nearly $1 billion, about equal to all the federal money that has ever gone into public television. Moreover, it would lower the matching requirement for local stations from $1 in federal funds for every $2.50 raised locally to $1 for every $2.25. That would mean that when WTVI seeks viewer contributions, which it will do later this month, fewer viewer dollars would be needed to produce a given amount of federal dollars.

This legislation is not the final answer. It does not deal with the logically attractive but politically touchy concept of financing public television with a slice of the enormous profits commercial broadcasters earn through their licensed privilege to broadcast. (Profits last year topped $1.2 billion, up 60 per cent from 1975.)

But it could prove an important step in allowing public broadcasting at least to do a larger fraction of what it is capable of doing. Someone in the administration has taken the trouble to understand a complex situation and write a sensitive piece of legislation for it. It deserves to pass.

The Birmingham News

Birmingham, Ala., October 6, 1977

The observation that "no one ever went broke underestimating the taste of the American people" preceded television, but sadly, is proven daily in the quality of network programming.

In a recent debate with Birmingham television executives, Rabbi Milton Grafman argued that the mission of the religious community often comes in direct conflict with TV's message of sex and violence.

The television programmers responded by saying they are only trying to give people what they want. And in many cases it turns out to be the murder and mayhem of "Baretta" and "Starsky and Hutch."

While trying to persuade the networks to change a success formula toward more "wholesome" and diverse programming may be hopeless, some help may be coming from the outside.

President Carter has introduced a bill this week that would authorize more than $1 billion for public broadcasting over a five year period.

The proposed federal contribution is the largest ever and is tied to wide-ranging proposals aimed at resolving the organizational conflicts within the public broadcasting system.

The goal is also to trim the bureaucratic structure surrounding public TV, eliminate fiscal waste and enlarge the role of independent producers and members of the public in the overall scheme.

The plan will attempt to give public television greater artistic and editorial independence.

In contrast to the Nixon Administration's prescription for public broadcasting, which deemed it inappropriate for a broadcast system receiving government funds to engage in news and public affairs programming, the President will encourage greater journalistic independence, including the right of community-based stations to editorialize.

The plan, moreover, contains mechanisms intended to shield public broadcasting from attempts at Government interference with program content.

A key feature of the President's plan will be a provision for an increase in national programming.

The new authorization, which will become effective in 1981, would provide for 25 per cent of the total federal contribution to be allocated specifically for programs on a national scale. Thus public television will have greater ability to create programs comparable to those of the British Broadcasting Corporation.

Local stations collectively will be asked to match that amount — $45 to $50 million — so the national programming fund might be maintained at a $100 million level during the 1980s.

Public broadcasting may not be the salvation of network programming, but, when properly managed and funded, it is capable of rising above the tendency to appeal, as Rabbi Grafman put it, "to the lowest common denominator."

THE SACRAMENTO BEE

Sacramento, Calif., July 5, 1977

Public broadcasting, as the Carnegie Corporation observed in 1967, exists to narrow "the gap between the knowledge of the few and the understanding of the many."

The gap appears to be narrowing as the number of noncommercial public television stations increases, programming improves and the stations continue to perform an invaluable public service.

An appropriation measure to increase the amount of federal funding is making its way through Congress.

Public television funding works on a two-year advance timetable, so the bill before Congress would help finance the stations in fiscal 1980.

About $160 million is authorized but the House of Representatives has only appropriated $145 million. This is better than the $120 million for 1979 but not enough.

We would like to see the Senate increase the appropriation to $160 million. The Corporation for Public Broadcasting could make good use of the money. The result would almost certainly mean better programs for the viewer.

Public broadcasting's income from all sources amounts to only $400 million, a fraction of the operating budget of a commercial network. Commercial broadcasting profits are around a billion dollars a year.

The public broadcasting stations get money from several sources: 27.7 per cent from the federal government; 41.6 per cent from state and local governments and 30.7 per cent from private donations and membership fees.

The federal government should increase its contribution. Public television is an important national asset to be preserved and strengthened.

ST. LOUIS POST-DISPATCH
St. Louis, Mo., October 10, 1977

In a message to Congress on federal support for public broadcasting, President Carter, without specifically saying so, has set out to both undo organizational damage done by the Nixon Administration and to substantially increase the resources of public television and radio.

As part of a vendetta against the news media, which he envisioned as his enemy, Mr. Nixon undertook to eliminate public affairs and other supposedly controversial programing from the public network. He eventually succeeded for the most part when a reorgan- ized, Nixon-appointed board of the Corporation for Public Broadcasting dismantled the Public Broadcasting Service as a central programing agency (leaving it only as a distribution mechanism) and transferred the programing function to a new "Station Program Co-operative" which left to local television station managers the choice of what to put on the PBS network. The result, whether by conscious design or not, was a rejection of many of the potentially controversial programs offered by the National Public Affairs Center for Television.

Now Mr. Carter has proposed to reverse the trend by strengthening the ability of public broadcasting to do national programing in news and public affairs, by encouraging community-based stations to editorialize and by promoting journalistic independence through mechanisms intended to shield public broadcasting from attempts at government interference with program content. Under the Carter proposals, the PBS would be designated as the central programing authority; the Corporation for Public Broadcasting would function as the overseer of the system and would make bloc grants to producing organizations but would not produce pilot programs or provide backing for specific shows.

To make the CPB responsive to varying interests, four of its 15 presidentially appointed board members would be replaced by two chosen by the PBS—representing 271 public television stations—and two chosen by Nation- al Public Radio—representing 203 public radio stations. The proposed organizational revamping is intended to trim the bureaucratic structure, help eliminate fiscal waste and help end the long-running jurisdictional disputes between the CPB and PBS.

A key provision in the Carter message called for 1 billion dollars in federal funds to be spent over a five-year period—more than was spent in the last 10 years. For fiscal 1981, when the current five-year authorization ends, the appropriation would be $180,000,000, and for each of the succeeding four years it would be $200,000,000. Instead of having to match each federal dollar with $2.50 from nonfederal sources, as is now the case, public broadcasting would have to raise $2.25 in matching money. One objective would be to create a $100,000,000-a-year fund for national programing, compared to only $13,000,000 from federal funds this year for national television programing and $4,000,000 for national radio programing, plus an additional $19,000,000 pooled by local stations for the production of the system's basic weekly series of national programs. Under the present arrangement, major productions have been sparse.

If public broadcasting's structure is strengthened and its resources greatly increased, as proposed, the time may finally be ripe for the creation of a noncommercial network that can provide solid public affairs programing as an alternative to the vacuous fare so often offered by the commercial networks.

DAYTON DAILY NEWS
Dayton, Ohio, October 4, 1977

President Carter's reported intention of doubling federal support for public television and of cleaning up public TV's bureaucratic act comes just in the nick of time, when public TV's genteel poverty is letting cynical ABC define the nature of television competition.

Some competition. ABC's crude pursuit of ratings has lowered programming standards to a point where they are hardly identifiable, a combination of snickering sex, amok cops and assorted bionic things. (And if you have not seen *San Pedro Beach Bums,* do at least once. Here, witlessness has won utterly.)

NBC and CBS have not, at least so far, given into ABC's technique of undercutting the lowest common demoninator but, disoriented, they have compromised with the threat by risking little on new, quality programs.

And while all this is happening, public TV is unable to prove the alternative, partly because it is underfunded and partly because it is locked in an internal bureaucratic stalemate.

The first problem will be solved if Congress appropriates more money; it should. The second Mr. Carter would end, properly, by assigning more programming authority to the network, the Public Broadcasting System, and less to its overseer, the Corporation for Public Broadcasting. He also wants to cut the number of presidential appointees on the corporation board, thus insulating the network from political pressures of the sort the Nixon administration applied and whose consequences include the current funk in program development.

Public television has shown that when it has adequate funds and is free to follow its own instincts, it can attract an audience large enough to make the commercial networks take at least peripheral notice.

The public — especially, though roundabouty, the public least likely to watch public TV — needs a strong public network. Otherwise, impulses of the sort that govern ABC currently will drag the other networks toward competition solely on ABC's terms and eventually could excite direct federal intervention in programming, something no one should want.

The choice is between limiting commercialism's potential excesses by quality competition or by government fiat. It should be clear which is preferable.

The Philadelphia Inquirer
Philadelphia, Pa., October 4, 1977

Later this week, President Carter is expected to submit to the Congress a long-range proposal for the funding and organization of public television and radio broadcasting in the United States. The broad intentions of the plan — substantial increases in funding, streamlining administrative control, and further insulating programming from political influence — are sound.

There can be no question in reasonable minds that public broadcasting in America has demonstrated its irreplaceable value. Educationally, culturally, and importantly in volatile areas of public affairs, publicly supported television and radio broadcasts have made and continue to make major contributions to American awareness in every area of the country in which they can be watched and heard (though, sadly, that is only about half the nation's population for public television and about 60 percent for public radio).

Commercial television, for all its strength, variety and sometimes healthy competitiveness, is severely limited by the inescapable rush for short-term public approval. It is and, so long as it is commercial, will remain dependent on advertising revenue and thus upon the whims and fickleness of mass-audience response. Public broadcasting has clearly demonstrated its ability to rise valuably above those limitations.

If there were a legitimate argument that public broadcasting, supported as it is by major tax money, threatened privately owned broadcasting within any significant terms of commercial competition, there might be reason for misgivings about expanding its tax-support base. This year's federal appropriation, however, is $103 million, nationwide; in contrast, the three main commercial networks will have revenues of $2 billion and will show combined profits substantially more than $200 million

Mr. Carter's plan proposes increasing the federal contribution to public broadcasting to $180 million annually in 1981, when the current five-year authorization has run its course, and then to an annual level of $200 million for each of the four subsequent years. Each dollar of those funds which go to supporting programming must now be matched by $2.50 from non-government sources; under the new proposal that matching formula would be relaxed to $2.25.

Lurking beneath the extension, or the very existence, of a national public broadcasting institution is the danger of misuse. It is not mad to imagine a powerful influence being exercised by power-corrupt public officials to propagandize. The beginnings of such an effort were clear in the Nixon Administration.

Preventing the possibility of such a development will be of vital concern as the Carter proposal is put forward and examined by the Congress. On first blush, the administration's suggestions for revising jurisdiction and for reducing the force of presidential appointments in the management of the system appear to be constructive steps in that direction.

Public broadcasting is here to stay, and Americans are better off for it. President Carter's initiative to extend it in strength and vigor is on firm ground.

The Hartford Courant

Hartford, Conn., October 9, 1977

With public television about to start its 25th year of broadcasting, the medium is having an increasingly important — and admirable impact — on American communications. Still, its full potential for top-quality programming has yet to be realized.

Fortunately, the Carter Administration is most sympathetic to public TV's problems. The President is proposing to Congress a measure that would increase federal financial support and reduce bureaucratic bickering within the industry. Both steps are urgently needed.

Currently, the total budget of the nation's 272 noncommercial stations adds up to only $400 million a year. By comparison, the combined revenues of the commercial networks and stations come to a whopping $6.5 billion.

The Federal Government now provides about one quarter of the budget of the noncommercial system, with the rest coming mainly from state and local school systems, philanthropic organizations, private corporations and gifts from individuals. Under the Carter proposal, Washington would put almost $1 billion in public television and radio during the next five years, a welcome increase over the present allocation — about $103 million this year and slated to rise to $152 million by 1980. The government underwriting will mean more work for the stations, however. Every federal dollar would have to be matched by $2.25 from the broadcasters.

Red tape also is hindering the industry. Congress could ease that problem by streamlining the two large organizations that oversee much of public TV's operations. Both the Corporation for Public Broadcasting, which disburses federal funds to noncommercial broadcasters, and the Public Broadcasting Service, which distributes programs nationally, have rightly been charged with wasteful duplication of each other's functions.

There is ample impetus to overcome the financial and bureaucratic hurdles. A recent Neilsen survey showed that well over half the nation's TV households — 60.1 per cent — viewed noncommercial television at least once a month, compared with only 14 per cent in 1970. While the increase in audience is impressive, a vast number of viewers have not yet been won over.

Congress should recognize that potential by solidly endorsing Mr. Carter's public TV proposals.

DESERET NEWS

Salt Lake City, Utah, October 24, 1977

For television watchers, public TV is often an oasis in a desert of violence, sex, inanity, and a word from the sponsor. But public television has two besetting problems:

First, no ads means no ad money, leaving public TV often short of cash.

Second, because government pays most of the bills for public TV, there is a threat that politicians or bureaucrats will control programs.

KUED, Utah's public television station, has been spared the second problem. But currently the station is particularly short of money.

The $1.2 million annual budget is barely adequate for programming and operations. There are no funds to replace worn out equipment. And after 20 years of tight budgets, the station might not be able to broadcast if some of its equipment is not replaced.

University of Utah President David P. Gardner and the Board of Regents, who control KUED, recently approved a request for the Legislature to raise the station's budget over 25 percent. The increase would contain some $200,000 to replace worn out equipment, and should be considered favorably by the lawmakers.

In the long run, help might be on the way from Washington, too. President Carter recently proposed increasing the federal subsidy for public TV by one-third. But the increase, even if Congress approves, won't begin until fiscal 1981.

The President also made some sensible suggestions to remove programming even further from bureaucratic and political interference.

Yet even with the proposed safeguards, the federal largesse should be viewed suspiciously.

Increased federal money can help KUED continue to provide good viewing. But the best way to insure that Utah's public television meets Utah's needs is for Utahns to continue to pick up most of the costs themselves.

THE LOUISVILLE TIMES

Louisville, Ky., Ocotber 13, 1977

Even our friends who claim they never, ever watch television may be tempted to sneak a peek or two if the Carter Administration's ambitious five-year-plan for public TV and radio is approved by Congress.

The plan is controversial, because it's expensive—$1 billion for 1980 through '85. A lot of taxpayers think this is too much to spend for a network that is misconceived as a caterer to eggheads and Anglophiles.

Even if the measure passes, as it should, opposition could be fairly stiff from the commercial networks, which could be faced by the first serious non-commercial competition for their viewers since the Corporation for Public Broadcasting was established in 1967.

The Carter proposal indicates an unequivocal desire to allow public television the freedom to explore ideas, even controversial ones, without interference from the White House or the Federal Communications Commission. That's a radical departure from the philosophy that has generally prevailed since Richard Nixon put public television on his enemies list because it was too probing, too controversial.

Some fine programs bit the dust—notably Bill Moyers' *Journal* and *The Great American Dream Machine*—in the wake of the drive for mediocrity that was urged on an unsure public broadcasting corporation.

The Carter Administration's plan would attempt to prevent any similar action in the future by stripping the Corporation for Public Broadcasting of its programming responsibilities, leaving it to dispense federal dollars to local stations and the Public Broadcasting Service. PBS, the loose network of local stations, would take a more active role in programming.

The amount of money that the local stations—or PBS or National Public Radio, the noncommercial radio network—would have to put up to obtain federal grants would be reduced from a $2.50 local contribution for every matching dollar to $2.25. Although still a burden, it would be a step toward curbing the seemingly endless fund-raising drives on noncommercial stations.

The plan would not guarantee improved programming on PBS and, particularly, local stations. But the availability of additional funding seems to boost the prospects for more expensive and ambitious ventures.

There is also no indication that the $1 billion would be enough money to reduce public television's reliance on major corporations' support. Were it not for the controversial big oil companies, some large photocopying and equipment concerns and the major foundations, few quality programs now being produced would be financially possible.

The administration is selling the public broadcasting plan as a method to encourage more home-grown, domestic offerings. In reality, there's a lot of silly jingoism in the arguments of those who contend that PBS relies too heavily on British-made television series. If you run over the weekly TV listings, it's obvious that British-made series occupy relatively few hours of PBS time. And the conspicuous success of *Masterpiece Theater* (compliments of Mobil Oil) has lately been challenged by some splendid domestic efforts.

One of them, *The Great American Short Story*, has been purchased by British Broadcasting Corporation—the first time a series produced by American public TV has stimulated any interest in Britain. This fall's PBS schedule seems to have a distinctly American accent, led by Dick Cavett, and bolstered by the perennially popular Louis Rukeyser, Tom Lehrer and William F. Buckley Jr. But we'd predict a civil war before some folks would allow nationalists to deprive us of Alistair Cooke.

Fresh ideas, particularly at some of the larger stations like WNET in New York and WGBH in Boston, are setting a course for the rest of the country. They provide proof that public television can shed the dowdy image of "educational TV." But only if it gets the kind of money and independence it needs.

EDITORIAL

2

WCBS-TV
NEW YORK

A VOICE FOR PTV

Public broadcasting has come a long way since it was first promoted by Congress 10 years ago. But it is still beset by funding problems and still searching for independence.

Increasingly, Congress has been supplying more generous support; but as government funding rose, so did the concern that government would try to influence public broadcasting politically.

For the next five years, President Carter is trying to address this dilemma by giving public broadcasters more funding, up to $200 million a year.

While this increase in government support may look good to public broadcasters over the short run, we wonder whether ever-increasing government funding for public television will eventually jeopardize its ability to be truly independent.

What's needed is a thorough study of the issue, one that seeks to determine how the public and not the government can best support public television. Fortunately, a new Carnegie Commission on the Future of Public Broadcasting should be giving this issue the kind of study it needs.

Another part of the Carter proposal, however, gains our enthusiastic support. The President's plan would allow editorializing in public broadcasting, which is now prohibited by federal law. The plan would not allow editorials by government operated stations, and that makes sense to us. But it would let non-government public stations, like Channel 13, editorialize if the station chose to do so.

At Channel 2, we think that idea is great. Editorializing is a first amendment right. But more than that, the editorial process provides a forum for ideas, and carries with it, the obligation to present differing views.

Editorializing isn't something to be prohibited. As the Carter proposal recognizes it's something to be encouraged in public broadcasting as well.

Presented by Peter Kohler, Editorial Director
November 1, 1977 at 6:55 PM.

The Courier-Journal
Louisville, Ky., June 24, 1977

THE CARNEGIE CORPORATION, which a decade ago sponsored a study that became pretty much the blueprint for public television in America, is at it again. The non-profit foundation has established a new commission to review what has happened in public broadcasting since 1967 and to suggest ways of strengthening it.

The commission, which is private but has the blessings of President Carter, will be studying the financing, organizational structure and goals of public broadcasting and the possible impact of such new technologies as communications satellites, cable TV and video discs.

This is a fine idea, and the folks at the Corporation for Public Broadcasting, the Public Broadcasting Service and National Public Radio reportedly are delighted that the study is in the works.

But viewers doubtless are less interested in the structure and funding of public broadcasting than in finding out why so many local public TV programs are so downright awful and why PBS, for all its noble efforts, never seems quite able to match the high quality of many British imports.

The original Carnegie Commission report, alas, was long on idealistic abstractions and short on specifics. Largely because of the original report, public TV in this country has been operating on the assumption that the public can be better served by a loose federation of strong local stations than by a strong centralized network.

It hasn't worked out that way. Most local public TV stations, Louisville's included, produce programs almost guaranteed to send viewers switching to even the worst competing commercial fare. Meanwhile, PBS, perhaps for lack of funds, has yet to live up to what many believe is an enormous potential.

In establishing the new commission, the Carnegie Corporation conceded that many of the promises of public broadcasting envisioned by the original commission haven't been fulfilled. Perhaps with this in mind, those appointed to the commission are mostly people active in various aspects of public broadcasting, rather than the academic types who dominated the original group.

Every viewer who yearns for an alternative to the game shows, police dramas and sitcoms of the commercial networks will wish them success.

THE CHRISTIAN SCIENCE MONITOR
Boston, Mass., May 16, 1978

Unless something happens to change the picture, public television in the United States faces some difficult days. Congressional hearings and an investigation by the General Accounting Office have produced reports of mismanagement, internal dissension, and waste that could prompt many TV viewers to turn off public television – particularly those long on-the-air appeals for financial support so crucial to its survival.

Monitor television critic Arthur Unger reported last week that GAO audits are disclosing that some Public Broadcasting Service (PBS) stations indulge in slipshod bookkeeping, spend excessively on public relations, and misuse grants for programming.

Public broadcasting also has come under fire for failing to provide enough high-quality programs as an alternative to the pap too often offered by commercial television. There are occasional high points, such as live opera broadcasts from Lincoln Center, as well as fine continuing music and public affairs shows, not to mention children's programming the likes of Sesame Street and Zoom. But in the dramatic field PBS is rightly criticized for relying too heavily on British imports instead of backing more original dramas produced at home.

The future of public broadcasting is expected to be shaped by the nine-member Carnegie Commission on Public Broadcasting which will issue a definitive report and recommendations in early 1979. Congress currently is weighing what is generally considered an interim proposal by the Carter administration for a five-year, $1 billion financing plan for public TV. It also is in the midst of rewriting the master communications law, with the House communications subcommittee scheduled to present a draft in June.

Considering the Carnegie commission's potential influence, it is regrettable that commission chairman William McGill appears to be calculating what will be politically acceptable to Congress as much as seeking out the best possible restructuring and funding for public TV. As a privately funded independent group, the commission ought to leave the political compromises and negotiations for Congress to work out later.

The commission now has under consideration several proposals that would appear to go a long way toward resolving many of public TV's basic problems. On the funding question, one particularly intriguing plan would tax commercial networks to help support public broadcasting. Another would tax television advertising. Both would provide commercial networks a means for repaying viewers for the use of the public airwaves. They would also give network programmers convenient ways to fulfill some public-responsibility requirements for licensing. These plans would seem preferable to imposing a tax on television sets, as is done in Britain and Germany.

The commission also is weighing the possibility of recommending increased funding from the current $200 million level to more than $1 billion a year. Such an increase would do much to stimulate more quality programming. But in view of the allegations of station mismanagement now being made it is essential that the confusing two-tiered organization with responsibilities divided between PBS and the Corporation for Public Broadcasting be simplified and restructured to include safeguards against management abuses. Equally important is the need to keep programming free of political or governmental censorship; stations should be allowed to develop creative talents and pursue controversial subjects without fear of funding cutoffs or other reprisals. Picking its way through such potentially explosive issues will be no easy task for the Carnegie commission. But public TV's unique role is too important to allow political considerations to stand in the way of recommendations for the best possible system.

Los Angeles Times
Los Angeles, Calif., June 27, 1977

A private commission has been established to take a careful and independent look at the future of public television. That could prove to be a most useful exercise.

Money for the 18-month study will be provided by the Carnegie Corp., which also financed the study a decade ago that led to the creation of the Corp. for Public Broadcasting and a growing commitment of federal support.

Despite growing support, however, public broadcasting remains the center of uncertainty and controversy. Some of that is inevitable. But a fresh look at this time may help resolve some of the controversies, including those centered on the way public funds are shared, program selection, program production and the impact of new technologies.

Last year, public broadcasting had a total revenue of $412 million—miniscule alongside the revenues of commercial radio and television stations, but important in terms of impact. That revenue was divided into $361 million for television, $51 million for radio. About 70% of the money came from government diversion of tax funds, a fact that alone requires a careful look to be sure that the money is being used in a way responsive to the public interest.

Involved in this, then, are various problems: Will the spread of cable television affect public broadcasting? Can television disks be utilized as a new tool that will broaden access to better programs? What can be done to increase the number of high-quality programs produced in the United States to balance the Upstairs, Downstairs tilt that has given British programs domination among quality programs? How should federal funds be divided, and what influence does this imply on program selection?

The new commission will be headed by Dr. William J. McGill, president of Columbia University. Among its 20 members will be Dr. John W. Gardner, former head of Common Cause; Bill Moyers, the CBS news reporter who previously worked for public television; Beverly Sills, the singer; Bill Cosby, the entertainer; Dr. Walter Heller, the economist, and Carla Hills, former secretary of housing and urban development.

An indication of the seriousness of their intentions is a commitment of 18 months of work, and an initial grant of $1 million to finance it.

Alan Pifer, president of the Carnegie Corp., expressed a hope that the continuing study would not become an excuse for inactivity in Congress, where a five-year extension of public-broadcasting legislation will be coming up later this year. He is right in urging that there be no delay on that legislation.

We are encouraged by the reception already given the commission by President Carter's special assistant for radio and television. It is evident that the Administration will be receptive to any good sense that the commission can come up with. That makes it more likely that there will be additional rewards for all who have already discovered the considerable merits of public radio and television.

DESERET NEWS

Salt Lake City, Utah, February 6, 1979

The Carnegie Commission on the Future of Public Broadcasting has just issued wrongheaded report on what should be done with public television.

Much of the best fare on television is now to be found on the public channels. The Deseret News is proud of its participation over two decades on the discussion program Civic Dialogue on KUED Channel 7.

So we share with the authors of the report the desire to improve and strengthen public television.

But the Carnegie Report suggests that federal funding for public television should be raised from the present $485 million to $1.2 billion by 1985.

The public mood is now for government austerity, and such a sharp increase would be hard to obtain. But even if the money were available, it might do public TV more harm than good.

Many good programs come through the national Public Broadcasting System. But now, some 60 percent of the shows on public TV are locally produced. Public stations obtain a large portion of their funding locally, and are thus responsive to local needs and tastes.

A sudden large infusion of federal money could diminish the voice of local communities in public television.

Such fears are increased by other proposals made in the report. Most of the new money would be used for national programming. This programming would be controlled by a national board "insulated" from politics—that is to say, beyond the public's control.

According to the report, the new national programming would "have a strong editorial purpose." The system would "have the complacent views of its audience shaken occasionally by programs that it finds disturbing." And all this is founded on the Commission's view that radio and television are "social tools of revolutionary importance."

The Carnegie report raises the spectre of an elite and irresponsible board using taxpayers' money to propagate views the taxpayers don't share.

Congress should reject this report. Some increase in federal funding is justified. But such increases should be matched by corresponding increases in state, local, and private contributions.

No more control over public television should pass to any national board. And public television should stick to its job of providing quality entertainment and even-handed explanations of public issues. Elitists should be told to look elsewhere for a propaganda vehicle.

THE INDIANAPOLIS NEWS

Indianapolis, Ind., February 9, 1979

If it doesn't work, throw money at it.

That's a favorite recommendation of all blue-ribbon panels and *A Public Trust: The Report of the Carnegie Commission on the Future of Public Broadcasting* sticks to that tried-and-true formula. The commission's recently issued report recommends tripling the money currently available for public broadcasting to $1.2 billion by 1985.

Why? "We find public broadcasting's financial, organizational and creative structure fundamentally flawed . . . it suffers from chronic underfunding, growing internal conflict and a loss of a clear sense of purpose and direction." Those findings, while accurate, constitute a surprising admission. An earlier Carnegie commission report was the blueprint for the Public Broadcasting Act of 1967 — the act that set up the flawed system now being reviewed.

Underfunding: The commission recommends increased funding, in part with a system taxing commercial broadcasters. A "spectrum fee" would require licensed users to pay for use of the broadcast spectrum. We are sympathetic to the plea for more funds and to the spectrum fee. The quality of commercial programming is abysmally low. The violent, vapid, pointless fare offered by networks that have totally abdicated their responsibility to quality programming is reason enough to call for a stronger public broadcasting system.

Internal conflict: The commission recommends a structural reorganization creating a private, non-profit Public Telecommunications Trust to replace the current Corporation for Public Broadcasting and establishing a Program Services Endowment to underwrite radio and television productions. The reorganization would re-

solve current conflicts between the Corporation for Public Broadcasting and the Public Broadcasting Service over control of programming. That step also seems necessary to strengthen the public broadcasting system.

Purpose and direction: Finally, in grand, grander and grandiose language, the commission paints its vision of the future of public broadcasting. "We remember the Egyptians for the pyramids, and the Greeks for their graceful stone temples. How shall Americans be remembered? As exporters of sensationalism and salaciousness? Or as builders of magical electronic tabernacles that can in an instant erase the limitations of time and geography, and make us one people?"

The commission believes that public broadcasting is a social tool of "revolutionary importance." Hopeful passages about the future of public broadcasting call for "a strong editorial purpose . . . We believe for example, that a mature journalistic role for public broadcasting will require the institutions speak out on matters of public policy, attempt to uncover wrongdoing and occasionally criticize those in high places."

Far be it from us to suggest that those in high places never merit criticism or that public policy shouldn't be discussed. But increased Federal financing, called for in the report, and increased editorial freedom are contradictions in terms. There is no way to editorialize "fairly" when tax dollars pay the power bills. Any forum with Federal strings attached is going to have a difficult time presenting all points of view. Public broadcasting should steer away from editorializing. Public broadcasting can be and should be greatly improved. But disseminating opinion is not its primary direction or purpose.

The Washington Post

Washington, D.C., February 9, 1979

PUBLIC TELEVISION and radio have come a long way since the first Carnegie Commission report a dozen years ago. That commission's recommendations, with one key exception, became the base of the legislation that changed public broadcasting from a local affair into a national institution. Congress adopted its proposals to create a Corporation for Public Broadcasting, insulate it somewhat from political pressures and provide it with federal funds. But Congress rejected the idea that it place a tax on the sale of television sets and dedicate the revenue from it exclusively to public broadcasting.

The second Carnegie Commission, which released its recommendations last week, is still trying to fill that gap. While it wants to reorganize the existing public-broadcasting bureaucracies and to protect them better against political interference, its key recommendation is that Congress levy a fee on those who now use the public airways as a way to provide the additional funds it says public broadcasting should have. The biggest fees would be imposed on those who make a profit out of that use—commercial television and radio stations, like those owned by this newspaper. Fees would also be imposed on other users of the radio spectrum, such as citizens' band and mobile radio operators.

The idea of these user fees is not new. Rep. Lionel Van Deerlin (D-Calif.), who heads a House subcommittee that is attempting to rewrite the communications act, has already drafted legislation to levy them on commercial broadcasters. Given the strong opposition of most broadcasters to such proposals, it is not clear whether they will fare better in Congress than did the original proposal for an earmarked tax on the sale of television sets. Congress refused then and chose to provide federal funds through direct appropriations.

It is clear that the new commission would prefer for Congress to dedicate a tax, any tax, to public broadcasting. That's because a guaranteed source of income would permit better long-range planning and help free public broadcasters from political pressure. But the commission shied away from making such a recommendation to avoid the old argument about whether any public institution, particularly one involved in forming public opinions and attitudes, should have so large a measure of financial independence.

If the commission can persuade Congress to appropriate more money for public broadcasting and impose the spectrum fees to raise at least part of the additional funds, it may succeed in doing indirectly what Congress refused to do directly a decade ago. An appropriation with such an offset might soon come to be regarded as a fixture rather than a continuing item in each year's budget.

We would prefer not to see these matters so closely linked. If public television needs more money from the federal government—and there is a substantial argument that it does—the case for that should be made without regard to where the money will come from. If it is in the public interest to impose license fees on users of the airways, they should be imposed without regard to where the money will go. By tying the two together, the commission has deflected attention somewhat from the key questions in public broadcasting's future: What changes are needed in its bureaucracies and what, besides just more money, does it need to improve its programming as much in the next dozen years as it has in the last dozen?

Pittsburgh Post-Gazette
Pittsburgh, Pa., February 5, 1979

In most respects, the American experiment with government-owned television and radio has never quite emerged from the laboratory. Columbia University President William McGill underscored this reality the other day when presenting the Carnegie Commission's report on the future of public broadcasting. He described it as "a radical idea whose time is at hand." The truth is that the idea of public broadcasting was at hand 12 years ago. The question really is whether Congress will extend more than half a hand to support the very urgent and important recommendations by the commission.

In the forward to its findings, the commission pleads a somewhat tendentious case for public television as the appropriate means to bind the nation's wounds in the social reformation which has followed upon the war in Vietnam and Watergate. With luck such an inflated sense of mission will not distract from the recommendations. Public television and radio can fulfill unique services as a non-commercial network. It is doubtful that the message will be heard if the tone is messianic.

From its legislative origins in 1967, the Corporation for Public Broadcasting has been governed by a political dilemma. As an entity of the government, public radio and television remain uniquely susceptible to congressional and presidential pressure; a pressure which became especially evident when President Nixon applied a punitive veto to CPB funds in 1972. Such pressures have not always prevailed of course. The public network offers many programs which display independence and thoroughness. But whether seen through the eyes of the programmer who wants independence but needs federal revenue or of the member of Congress who extends revenue but expects some political accounting for its use, the relation has been flawed and imperfect.

On this account, the commission's recommendation to restructure the public networks ought to be heeded by the Carter administration and Congress. Of utmost value is the proposal to place public broadcasting under a nongovernmental trust whose members would be appointed for staggered, nine-year terms by the president, upon the recommendation of the librarian of Congress. This approach respects the federal character of public broadcasting while providing it with a maximum of political insulation.

Then, to free public broadcasting from the whims of congressional budget committees and presidential vetoes, a broader base of revenues is proposed. To this end, the commission properly emphasizes the public network's own role in raising at least half of its operating revenue from individuals, other private sources, and state and local governments. This approach pledges the public network to strive for its own independence. But the federal government nevertheless would retain responsibility for about half of $1.2 billion, total revenues which the commissioners hope to see allocated to public broadcasting by 1985. Since an important part of the federal share would be underwritten by a spectrum tax upon citizens' band and commercial airwaves, the increase in the federal commitment would not create any real strain upon federal revenues. Both features of political and fiscal reorganization represent a resourceful answer to a troubled relation.

The commission expresses the further hope that, once reorganized, the public broadcast service will be better able to resolve the many tensions between the system's national and local purposes. A general estimation of the system to date suggests that national programming goals have most often prevailed. Even the larger metropolitan stations, such as Pittsburgh's WQED, have developed remarkable strength mostly on the basis of their commitment to national programming. While striving for an optimal balance between two missions, the public system should outline as its most immediate goal greater creativity and seriousness for local programming.

The TENNESSEAN
Nashville, Tenn., February 7, 1979

AFTER 18 months of study on the role of public broadcasting, the Carnegie Commission has presented a somewhat glowing picture of its potential.

It noted that public broadcasting is now firmly embedded in the national consciousness and that in less than a dozen years has managed to establish itself "as a national treasure."

After having said this, however, the commission had an indictment of both commercial and public broadcasting for failing to live up to their potential. It jabbed commercial TV for concentrating its wares in terms of the lowest common denominator and said that public broadcasting has reached its potential only occasionally. It said that public broadcasting hasn't been able to resolve the dilemma posed by its own structure.

The commission made a number of major recommendations. These included: structural reorganization; increased government funding, plus a fee from licensed users to augment that; greater stress on programs and services to assist in the education of all Americans; and the creation of a program services endowment whose sole purpose would be supporting creative excellence.

Some of the suggestions are likely to draw strong opposition. Some of them raise questions. The "use of the spectrum fee" is not clearly set out in terms of application or end result.

Would commercial stations paying such a fee then be exempt from public service requirements? If so, that loss would be keenly felt. Is the "use of the spectrum fee" really a direction in which the nation should be headed?

And as far as financing is concerned, is it reasonable to expect that the Carter administration and the Congress, both concerned with tightening spending, will look favorably toward a $500 million spending goal by 1985?

These are questions for which there are no immediate answers. But that should not deter the Congress or the Carter administration from studying and absorbing the commission recommendations in trying to hammer out legislation to guide communications in the future.

The commission spoke of the many who expressed their views on public broadcasting and of the great diversity it found. "The true greatness of America," the report said, "lies in the strength that emerges from this kind of diversity of religious, racial and cultural heritage. Public broadcasting must create an enterprise that attracts their continuing ...support."

There was this notable paragraph: "The revelation of diversity will not please some, notably the book burners and the dogmatists among us. It will startle and anger others, as well it should. But we have discovered in our own time that anger yields to understanding. America needs, perhaps even more than healing, a sense of understanding, something that is impossible if we each continue to wall ourselves within the corner of society that we find safe, appealing and comfortable.

"Unless we grasp the means to broaden our conversation to include the diverse interests of the entire society, in ways that both illuminate our differences and distill our mutual hopes, more will be lost than the public broadcasting system."

Those thoughts catch something of the vision of the commission of a non-commercial system dedicated to excellence, aware of diversity and committed to bringing greater understanding. It is not an impossible dream to pursue.

The Oregonian

Portland, Ore., February 4, 1979

Can public broadcasting become a "free press sponsored in part by the government?" is one of the fundamental questions raised by the Carnegie Commission's 401-page report, "The Public Trust." The report calls for a new structure and a new commitment by the federal government to help finance non-commercial radio and television.

The early response to the commission's sweeping recommendations was generally favorable. Commercial broadcasters, of course, couldn't be expected to warmly endorse a "spectrum fee" tax, which would be levied against radio, television and various others who use the public's airways for profit, including citizen-band and mobile-radio operators.

A key element in the Carnegie recommendations is the proposal for an annual radio and television budget of $1.2 billion, a giant leap from this year's $500 million budget from all sources. Under the new budget, about half of the total would come from the federal government, compared to 30 percent now paid from federal funds.

The proposal would eliminate the Corporation for Public Broadcasting and replace it with two organizations. One, the Public Telecommunications Trust, would set goals and evaluate performances, serving as a fiduciary agent but would not influence programs. The Program Services Endowment would be created to underwrite a broad range of programs. The idea is to free programs and news from political or other influences caused by the need for federal and private funding.

The report found that the present system is "fundamentally flawed" and is incapable of consistently achieving excellence. We agree. Public television has indicated by its occasional brilliance its capabilities. But too often it flounders, both at the local and national levels, failing to set standards for excellence. Often, its finest programs speak with a British accent, having come from the BBC.

Public television in Oregon is under attack at the Legislature where an effort is being made to divorce it from the control of Higher Education and set it up as an independent service. Earlier expectations that the service would set standards for excellence and provide a place where program innovations might take place have not been realized. Instead, local programs are often the dismal products of an untalented lot of amateurs. Unless skilled direction and talent are sought out, tossing more money at the present system may not improve it.

The Carnegie report recognizes that reorganization is needed to eliminate bureaucratic barriers, particularly if first-rate public affairs and news programs are to be developed.

Public broadcasting, as the report notes, has become an "indispensable tool for our people and our democracy." It must be improved, matching and exceeding the quality of other public broadcast services that are well-financed in nations like Japan and Britain.

The Washington Star

Washington, D.C., February 5, 1979

It probably is too much to call the new Carnegie Commission vision of the future of public broadcasting utopian. Its recommendation of a $1.2 billion annual budget, with a $590 million federal contribution, is relatively modest compared to the billions generated every year by commercial television.

Television and radio, the report says, are "social tools of revolutionary importance." That is arguable, even in a time when a word like revolutionary is used too casually.

"If those media are permitted to assume a wholly commercial character," the Carnegie report warns, "the entire cultural and social apparatus of the nation will become transformed by what may already have become the dominant mode of the electronic media in the United States: the merchandising of consciousness."

Patches of piffle such as that — whatever it means — do not seem altogether sober. But similar passages are disconcertingly plentiful in the Carnegie report.

Public broadcasting plays a useful countervailing role to the mediocrity and preoccupations of commercial television. It has shown from time to time that television need not be an exercise in unrelieved passivity, that it can provide a sense of a wider world, of intellectual elbow room. Public broadcasting has improved year by year; it will continue to improve, as it is challenged and instructed and supported by — the public.

But can it, or should it, aim for the cultural mountaintop envisioned by the Carnegie Commission — ". . .To bring us together through the teaching and inspiration possible in a noncommercial telecommunications alternative"?

Should public broadcasting be conceived as "increasingly indispensable during the next decade as our fragmented and troubled nation attempts to rebuild its self-confidence, to heal its wounds, and to discover the strength that emerges in the wake of a shared ordeal"?

The commission seems anxious to make public television an Archimedean lever of social uplift. The means to this vast end are a great many new dollars and an "insulated" freedom of action — a freedom to take artistic and journalistic "risks" through innovative programming, to strive toward "creative excellence" as an "alternative to the increasingly vulgarized commercial fare." Admirable, to be sure.

But the vigorous shaking of the public broadcasting structure recommended by the commission could centralize it more than might be good for any of us, grand intentions for the common weal notwithstanding. The commission notes the danger that public broadcasting might become in effect a "ministry of culture" and a purveyor of propaganda; but it dismisses the possibility rather too easily, it seems to us. The coalescence of a kind of centralized electronic bureaucracy, oiled with tax dollars and fortified against outside influences, is not pleasant to contemplate.

The commission's financial recommendations are a curious blend of the dreamy and the practical.

A tripling of federal appropriations by 1985 is unlikely and implies a dubious cause-and-effect relationship between financing and results. The report does suggest — sensibly, we think — that new revenue for public broadcasting could be raised by a "spectrum fee," a fee charged to all users of the electromagnetic spectrum, including such air-wave consumers as CB radio operators. The commission then cannily slides around that volatile prospect: Should Congress not think it "appropriate" to establish use rates across the spectrum, "it may wish to designate the proceeds from fees charged to commercial broadcasters for financing the public system."

It would, we agree, be "equitable and proper" to charge commercial broadcasters for their dominance of and profit from a public resource. Public television needs and deserves greater funding, if not the boarding-house reach suggested by the Carnegie Commission.

It is too bad that commercial television is allowed to pay so little due to creative excellence. Even so, a public broadcasting service summoning us toward a New Jerusalem it deems intellectually proper and culturally beneficial may not be much of an improvement.

The second Carnegie Commission report, like the first in 1967, offers a forum for useful discussion and reflection. But it is strained, and possibly even dangerous, to inflate public television and radio to the level of "magical electronic tabernacles."

The Hartford Courant

Hartford, Conn., February 3, 1979

The Carnegie Commission's new report on public broadcasting is as predictable as it is wise.

No blue-ribbon study commission could resist an opportunity to reorganize that which it is studying; thus, the report recommends a reorganization of the public television and radio administrative apparatus. At first glance, the reshuffling makes sense — the present system has been marred by some bureaucratic and political guerrilla warfare that can perhaps be eased through structural change.

And, as expected, the commission also recommended a massive infusion of new dollars into the public broadcasting system. The recommended budget would reach $1.2 billion per year by 1985. The federal government's share would eventually rise to $640 million a year, with most of it in the form of matching grants. The expected resistance to an almost 400 percent increase in federal expenditure is to be bypassed with a fee on commercial broadcast licenses to pay for most of the government's share.

Billion-dollar budgets for this 10-year-old national experiment seem awesome, but the public broadcasters must be guaranteed a reasonably stable source of substantial income if they are to truly create a nationwide alternative to commercial broadcasting. The present system of congressional appropriations is filled with uncertainty, and leaves the public broadcasters open to political pressures.

The gradual nature of the funding increases is important, for public broadcasting still has administrative and policy flaws that should be resolved before it is showered with dollars. Culture versus news, imports versus home-grown programs, the wisdom of editorials on public stations, the unresolved conflict between those who want a strong national network and those who emphasize local programming — these are a few of the nagging issues that should be settled before the nation commits large amounts of money to the cause.

Public broadcasting has proven itself as a valuable, often-creative alternative to its commercial competition. The challenge of the next 10 years will be to accept significant new funding, without succumbing to the sluggishness and lack of responsiveness that large amounts of government money can create.

Congress should take its lead from the Carnegie study, and approve a long-term funding system for public broadcasting. The results should be worthwhile.

The Miami Herald
Miami, Fla., February 1, 1979

PUBLIC broadcasting has come of age at last in the United States. By recent count there were 260 noncommercial television stations and 982 noncommercial radio stations on the air. They serve almost every part of the nation.

Because public broadcasting has grown to maturity as a social institution, its organizational needs have changed. Where once the chief concern was the expansion of facilities and programming, now a major concern is improving the quality and insuring the independence and integrity of these powerful media.

It won't be easy to reach a consensus. Broadcasting in the United States traditionally has been owned and managed by private enterprise and supported by advertising. Many Americans still get nervous — and with some reason — at the thought of paying taxes to provide a potential outlet for government propaganda. That danger would be exacerbated if programming decisions became unduly centralized and politicized.

Equally undesirable would be a situation in which public broadcasting reflected the views and served the interests of the corporate giants and elite foundations whose largesse sustains it.

To avoid those pitfalls, care must be exercised when any change or reorganization is contemplated in the carefully balanced structure of public broadcasting.

Fortunately, the Carnegie Commission on the Future of Public Broadcasting has shown such care. Its report, released Tuesday, suggests ways to improve the financial support for public broadcasting while preserving necessary checks and balances between local control and centralization, between political interference and reasonable accountability.

One Carnegie recommendation is that larger fees be charged commercial broadcasters for their Government licenses. The funds, which could amount to as much as $1 billion a year beginning in 1981, would be allocated to public broadcasting. Stations could still solicit additional donations from viewers and listeners.

Such a plan would provide a strong, dependable source of funds. It would also protect public broadcasting from the whims of congressmen offended by any program meatier than *Sesame Street*.

The Carnegie report recognizes, however, that more money alone won't guarantee better programs. The commission recommends that a larger share of public television's money go into programming, less into overhead. In particular, says the commission, the national Corporation for Public Broadcasting has failed and needs to be re-examined.

In making these recommendations and others, the Carnegie Commission has addressed its report to the general public and is inviting public response. To facilitate it, the commission will publish its findings in paperback and seek wide distribution of them.

That is as it should be. The Carnegie Commission has performed a real service by examining the serious questions surrounding the future of public broadcasting. In the end, however, only the public can decide the answers to those questions.

The Virginian-Pilot
Norfolk, Va., February 6, 1979

The Carnegie Commission on the Future of Public Broadcasting took a long and tough look at public radio and television and found them falling far short of their vast potential. The commission's report, released last week, deserves thorough consideration.

The commission views public broadcasting as underfunded, subject to political and financial pressures, and governed by a public corporation whose members are chosen more for their political connections than their commitment to excellence in the art.

The commission recommends sweeping changes, including greatly increased funding, and the creation of two new organizations to oversee this awesomely important realm of public life.

It calls for establishing one organization that would raise and disburse money, set standards, and evaluate performance, but have no say in programming. The other would develop and underwrite a broad range of programming, and experiment with new technology as well as new ideas.

Congress, which will have the final say, would have to take care that the two organizations would work more effectively together than have the present Public Broadcasting System and Corporation for Public Broadcasting. Congress would also have to ensure that the suggested methods of appointing board members would not permit either self-perpetuation by the boards or political patronage.

Overtaxed taxpayers understandably may wince at the commission's suggestion that the government contribute some $590 million a year to a broadcasting system. But television must be viewed for what it is,

the most pervasive influence of our time, one that reaches virtually every citizen.

In a country where daily television viewing averages six-and-a-half hours per household and daily radio listening averages three hours per person, the importance of the media must not be underestimated.

The commission views television as our common bond, a force for bringing citizens together. Its report suggests that our age might be remembered as "builders of magical electronic tabernacles that can in an instant erase the limitations of time and geography, and make us into one people."

The commission is correct in its perception of the importance and potential of public broadcasting, and the need for well-financed, independent, and imaginative public programming.

It is dead right in wanting to ensure that we will have a public system as opposed to a federal one. Perhaps one of the greatest services that public broadcasting can render is to broaden its reporting of governmental affairs and other public concerns.

Television has brought us magnificent moments, and given us front-row seats on history in the making. What but television could fly us to the moon, right along with the astronauts? But mediocrity more than magnificence has most often been the medium's stock-in-trade.

The commission's report deserves the careful consideration that is granted to matters of great importance to the country. President Carter has pledged his commitment to public broadcasting. Congress should do likewise.

THE WALL STREET JOURNAL
New York, N.Y., February 2, 1979

When you steam all the purple prose out of "The Landmark Report of the Carnegie Commission on the Future of Public Broadcasting," you come up with something fairly simple: The cure for whatever ails public broadcasting is more money.

In addition to giving new names to the Commission for Public Broadcasting and the Public Broadcasting Service, and proposing to further "insulate" these bodies from the real world, the commission would like to triple federal dollar support. The money would come partly from a levy on commercial broadcasters. An attempt would be made to insure that most of this money be used for national programming.

The commission lays out this proposal with some of the most passionate rhetoric we've ever heard outside a revival hall—for a sampling we recommend Mr. Henninger's article on the page opposite. It sounds as if we haven't been through all this before. But in fact we have been.

The system that the Carnegie Commission would like to overhaul was ordered along lines recommended by a similar Carnegie Commission in 1967. Since then, we've been hearing complaints that CPB-PBS is too bureaucratic, that it doesn't spend enough of its funds on programming, that the whole public broadcasting enterprise suffers from the lack of a strong central network core. The new Carnegie Commission wants to fix all that with more money and new rules.

As Les Brown of The New York Times observes, the commission has seemingly tailored its recommendations with influential politicians in mind, which suggests it wasn't as politically naive as a reading of the report would suggest. There's a nod to Jimmy Carter, who has talked much about "insulating" the system from political interference—although at the same time saying, contradictorily, that there should be better means of "judging" its performance. The tariff on broadcasters comes from Lionel Van Deerlin, chairman of the House

Communications subcommittee, although Mr. Van Deerlin seems to have been mainly interested in insulating commercial broadcasters from the political strings attached to free-of-charge licenses. There is even a bonbon for Ernest Hollings, head of the Senate communications subcommittee and former governor of South Carolina—in the form of praise for his state's educational TV system.

But we are not much persuaded by the commission's belief that a new structure will somehow make for strong national programming. Public broadcasting has evolved along lines that suggest the greatest impetus for creativity comes from the local stations, where program directors are faced with the daily challenge of finding something to put on the air. As the report notes, some 60% of the programs broadcast by public stations in 1976 were locally produced. A good many such productions are picked up by other stations when they see merit and interest in them.

This localized, decentralized approach may offend high-powered national commissions, but we can imagine much worse. The local stations have often simply drawn on high-quality cultural institutions, such as the Boston Symphony, that exist independently of TV. The quality of those famous BBC series, we would argue, derives mainly from something that can't be built in a day, the long theatrical tradition in England. The solid public affairs coverage of the Mac-Neil-Lehrer Report is nothing more than intelligent interviews of public figures in the news.

Such creativity involves more than money. We of course recognize that all enterprises need funding, but a tripling of federal support suggests to us the kind of "big bucks" psychology that public TV's fans so often deplore on the commercial networks. And anyone who thinks you can get more federal dollars and at the same time be better "insulated" from government influence hasn't been reading the newspapers much these last 20 years.

THE CHRISTIAN SCIENCE MONITOR

Boston, Mass., February 2, 1979

The Carnegie Commission has presented Americans with a grand vision of what public broadcasting has the potential to become. Whether its major recommendations — i.e. that government funding be tripled and that commercial broadcasters, in effect, be taxed to support public radio and TV — are the proper way to achieve the commission's bold and idealistic goals remains to be seen. Some of its suggestions are almost certain to draw strong opposition and all of them ought to be closely scrutinized as Congress and the Carter administration hammer out legislation that will affect US communications for years to come. Yet it would be a pity if lawmakers, in focusing on the commission's individual recommendations, were to lose sight of its broad, forward-looking concept of public broadcasting as a powerful force for good in helping shape tomorrow's literary and artistic tastes and standards.

The commission delivered a stern indictment of the failures of commercial and public broadcasting to live up to their potential. It hit commercial TV in particular for concentrating only on "audience maximization." And it issued an eloquent plea for a public broadcasting system that "can help the creative spirit to flourish." A system that "can reveal how we are different and what we share in common. . . . It can illuminate the dark corners of the world and the dark corners of the mind. It can offer forums to a multitude of voices. . . . Above all, it can add to our understanding of our own inner workings and of one another."

Moreover, the commission said, "Public broadcasting must be able to find and sustain the inventive and inspired people who are capable of making the American scene into a hallmark of excellence acknowledged by the rest of the world." Noting that the average American spends 6½ hours a day before a TV set, the 17-member commission warned, "Many of us spend more time with the elec-

tronic media than we spend with other human beings, much less reading or learning."

The major impact of the recommendations would be to encourage more original American programs, to shield public broadcasters from political and commercial pressures that inhibit them from tackling controversial or experimental projects. To provide the far greater financial resources public broadcasting would need to fulfill such a mission, the Carnegie Commission would charge commercial broadcasters, "CB" operators, land-mobile radio users, and others a fee for use of the public airwaves. It would also continue to rely on private and corporate contributions and matching government funds.

A host of questions are raised by the "use of the spectrum" fee in particular. Would that fee exempt commercial stations from their current obligation to broadcast in the "public interest, convenience, and necessity," a requirement that encourages the airing of controversial topics and at least some public-affairs programming? Or could the government make any programming demands at all if such a fee is charged?

In this current period of inflation, is it realistic to ask the government and taxpayers to spend $590 million a year?

The commission proposes increasing the number of public radio stations. But it would also require public radio stations for the first time to compete with public TV in soliciting private contributions. Some public radio officials doubt that their stations could survive under such circumstances.

Concerns such as these will need to be addressed before public broadcasting can hope to become the pioneering medium the Carnegie panel foresees. Public broadcasting leading the way with technological innovations and original and experimental programming into a new era of electronic communications. An impossible dream? The Carnegie Commission thinks not.

The Boston Globe

Boston, Mass., January 4, 1979

The Carnegie Commission has charted an ambitious course for public broadcasting, calling for substantially increased funding and greater insulation from political influence on journalistic and artistic decisions. But the emphasis of the report, which was issued this week after an 18-month study by an elite panel serving the Carnegie Foundation, is not placed on catching up with commercial broadcasting. To the contrary, the commission's assessment of commercial broadcasting suggests that privately owned radio and television companies have been driven toward excesses in entertainment by ratings wars. In that withdrawal from artistic and informative programming, the commission sees a crying need for public broadcasting to step up its role.

The report virtually rhapsodizes about the potential for public broadcasting, at the same time taking accurate note of America's inattention to the quality of radio and TV. In the average household, television is watched 6½ hours daily; radio heard 3½. Within that framework the commission says, "The United States is the only Western nation relying so exclusively upon advertising effectiveness as the gatekeeper of its broadcasting activities."

The dilemma public broadcasting faces is how to increase the federal contribution in funding, yet prevent government interference and influence on programming.

Public broadcasting never will seriously challenge commercial networks in the current system of audience ratings, but it should improve on the number of households reached. Now 65 percent of the nation's TV audience tunes in a public broadcast about once a month. To boost that figure to 100 percent, at least once monthly and ultimately once weekly, public broadcasting must be financially able to produce quality programs.

The commission recommends total funding for public broadcasting at $1.2 billion by 1985, about double the cur-

rent level. Half of that would come from federal contributions, which includes an estimated $200 million from proposed charges for all commercial uses of broadcasting and satellite communications. Since commercial television is the largest user of the broadcast spectrum, a tough battle could develop over the proposed fees.

But public broadcasting will have some tough battles on its own in raising local contributions to take advantage of the suggested $3-for-$2 ratio of federal matching contributions. Thus public broadcasting will not be freed completely of its hand-to-mouth struggle for existence.

To remove public broadcasting further from governmental influence, the commission recommends that the Corporation for Public Broadcasting (now appointed by the President with members approved by the Senate) be replaced by the Public Telecommunications Trust. The trust would be comprised of presidential appointees nominated by a special committee chaired by the Librarian of Congress. The trust would appoint a committee, the Public Services Endowment, which would award programming grants. Instead of political appointees making programming grants, the endowment would be responsible. The trust would coordinate broadcasting stations' planning and facilities. That alleviates the current procedure of stations and producers having to go through a maze of federal agencies for program funding. The overall increase in funding also would reduce dependence on corporations to sponsor individual programs.

The logical role for public broadcasting is to present high quality programming. But that requires significant financial support from a variety of sources — federal, state and local government, public contributions, foundation grants and corporate donations. At the same time, public broadcasting must be shielded from government and corporate intimidation. The Carnegie report suggests feasible steps for accomplishing this.

The Evening Gazette

Worcester, Mass., February 9, 1979

An aphorism for our time: Money is the root of all good.

That seems to be the gist of the 400-page Carnegie Commission report on the Future of Public Broadcasting. The commission holds that the "fundamentally flawed" state of public television and radio can be greatly eased by massive injections of money. The commission would have the federal government quadruple its 1980 public broadcasting appropriation to $590 million by 1985. Revenue from other sources — audiences, foundations, corporations and state governments — would bring the total to $1.2 billion a year.

Theoretically, the onus of the quadrupled federal share will be lessened by imposition of so-called spectrum fees on users of the airwaves, particularly commercial television and radio. Or, in other words, by another tax.

For unconvincing reasons, the commission believes that more federal money and an organizational shuffle will create a broadcasting system more independent of political influences. Under the new system, the Corporation for Public Broadcasting would be scrapped for a Public Telecommunications Trust to allocate federal funds and do long-range planning and a Program Services Endowment to underwrite productions.

But whether new titles on the doors and new faces behind the desks of the public broadcasting bureaucracy will make any difference remains to be seen.

Perhaps the commission should face up to the fact that public broadcasting is "public" only in the sense that its programming is aimed at a variety of elites whose interests are not prime commercial soil for the major networks. On public television, for example, there are programs for ballet aficionados, symphony fans, gardening buffs and stock market investors. All important subjects, but not real Nielsen territory.

Public television does what it does quite well. It may need and deserve increased financial support. But one of the more perceptive comments in the Carnegie Commission report is: "Perhaps as acutely as any other American institution, the system of public broadcasting was caught in the transition from an American outlook that we could do anything we chose, to today's anxiety that we may have chosen to do too much."

There are bound to be some tough questions about where public broadcasting fits in with the rest of the special interest demands for federal money. How high is public broadcasting in the list of national priorities? How much can we make it better? And what degree of improvement — if more money does in fact guarantee excellence — is simply too expensive to contemplate?

DESERET NEWS

Salt Lake City, Utah, February 21, 1978

Should public television and radio stations be free to editorialize and endorse political candidates?

The Carter administration says they should, with certain limitations. An administration proposal is now before Congress to remove the present ban on these activities.

Excluded from such privileges under the bill would be stations run by tax-supported colleges and by state and local governments. The reasoning is that those stations are not properly insulated from the influence of state and local governments.

That's a sound approach. But it also raises another question: If some public broadcast stations are allowed to editorialize while others aren't, won't that split the broadcast community worse than it's now split? Already there's considerable disaffection among broadcasters themselves on the matter. Some adherents of a freer editorial license complain that instead of being just second-class citizens, now they'd be third-class citizens if the bill passed to permit some but not others to editorialize.

That split was evident in a recent meeting of public TV and radio executives in San Diego. Of 40 present, 35 indicated they would favor editorializing. But when asked how many would editorialize if given the permission, the number dropped sharply. And only five thought their governing boards would permit editorializing even if Congress gave its consent.

The Public Broadcasting Act in 1967 required "strict adherence to objectivity and balance" in all controversial programming for public stations. Language of the law prohibited both editorials and endorsements.

That still seems like a good policy — particularly when much of the broadcast community itself is reluctant to change the rules at this stage.

THE BLADE

Toledo, Ohio, February 6, 1978

IT was expectable that President Carter's proposal to allow some public television and radio stations to editorialize and to endorse political candidates would run into congressional opposition. Highly significant, however, is that public broadcasters themselves are by no means universally enamored of the idea.

The skepticism — both on Capitol Hill and among the broadcasters — is well founded. A basic argument against the proposal was expressed by key congressional leaders from both parties. It would be inappropriate, they said, for stations financed in part with public funds to push the candidacies of persons who could wind up in a position to influence the allocation of those funds.

As for the public broadcasters, one noted that the proposal would give "people who think public broadcasting already isn't fair and objective a chance to chomp down on us." That statement acknowledges the fact that public broadcasting still has not achieved — either in principle or in practice — the acceptance that was envisioned for it when the present system was established a decade ago.

There are several reasons for that. Some are attributable to conflicts within the public-broadcasting system itself. Others are the result of a chronic unwillingness on the part of some politicians to give public broadcasting the leeway as well as the money to do the kind of job the system supposedly was created to do.

Obviously, then, the most important task ahead for the national public-broadcasting structure and for its components is to try to work out the problems, seek greater confidence in its performance from the public in general and politicians in particular, and thereby reduce its vulnerability to criticism.

Until that can be accomplished, at least to a substantial degree, public broadcasters would simply be inviting more trouble for themselves and for the cause of tax-supported, noncommercial radio and television by venturing into the inherently controversial realm of editorial comment and political endorsements. The privilege of doing so is one right advanced by Mr. Carter that the prospective beneficiaries are understandably willing to forgo.

The ⚘ State

*Columbia, S.C.,
February 3, 1978*

IN A MESSAGE to Congress last fall, President Carter proposed that certain public broadcasting stations be permitted to editorialize and endorse political candidates.

Proponents of the idea argue that public stations should have protection under the First Amendment equal to that offered conventional broadcast media.

About a third of the country's public television stations and about a quarter of the public radio stations would be free to editorialize under the proposal. The ban against editorials on stations run by tax-supported colleges and by state and local governments would continue. (Included in this category is SCETV, which is operated as a state agency.)

But even public stations that are not associated with state or local governments receive substantial federal funding — made possible by tax dollars extracted from citizens of every political outlook. In the interest of fairness, public stations should not editorially favor one party or candidate or political philosphy.

The Public Broadcasting Act of 1967 required "strict adherence to objectivity and balance." It would be unwise for public television to stray from that policy and be buffeted by the currents of partisan politics.

THE CHRISTIAN SCIENCE MONITOR
Boston, Mass., May 3, 1977

He got a busy signal, so he went to bed. We refer to a friend who phoned to pledge a donation to the "Upstairs, Downstairs" million-dollar fund-raising party on public television Sunday night. Though the goal was comfortably passed (beyond $1.3 million), our friend had not contributed to it. But, don't worry, his local public television station will still accept the money from him. And from all those who have the impulse to support a channel that has enriched their lives — but who then, in effect, lie down until the feeling passes.

Such people ought to know that for each $2.50 they do not send, the station loses the $1 it would have received in matching federal money. Individual Americans and families fortunately do seem to be getting the idea. For the year ending June 30, some 2½ million of them are expected to have contributed some $55 million, a welcome if not luxurious boost over a figure of $40 million for the previous year.

Not often, of course, is there such a gala reminder of the public's debt to public television as the party bringing together "live" so many familiar faces from the four years of Britain's ineffable version of soap opera. The "upstairs" masters and the "downstairs" servants may have been competing as on-camera fund-raising teams. But the winners were the public TV stations across the country that received contributions — and the public which, in turn, benefits from the alternative they provide to commercial fare.

Continuing controversy over the question of overlapping bureaucracy involved with government funding suggests that public television ought to be sure that it is efficiently organized to make its public support count as much as possible.

But no true friend of the Bellamys and their faithful retainers is in a mood for carping after sharing that final tear on Rose's cheek as the ménage in Belgravia — and the series — came to an end. There had been marriages both upstairs and downstairs in the satisfying symmetry of classic comedy. The sense of an era ending was enhanced by the authentic sense of period in what had gone before, redeeming the occasional narrative lapses of an always deftly acted series. An American public that coughs up to support such television can't be all bad.

By commercial standards, the American millions viewing "Upstairs, Downstairs," have compared to only a fraction of those watching, say, "Laverne and Shirley." But there is such a thing as loyalty. And the people of Eaton Place have developed it to an extraordinary degree in the hearts of many Americans, not to mention many of the billion viewers estimated for the series in some 40 countries around the world.

One measure of this loyalty may be the fact that Boston's WGBH, which presented the series in the U.S. and put on the final party, had pledge figures of $154,400 for this channel alone, more than twice as much as the previous high for a single evening, which was itself considered remarkable. All the funds pledged Sunday go to the individual stations to which they were sent, with no percentage going to WGBH or the Public Broadcasting Service.

Stations have a growing need for such funds, not only for transmitting such programs as "Upstairs, Downstairs," which are provided through corporate funding, but through paying a share of the production costs of programs that are not underwritten. Though the number of contributing viewers is growing, it is still a small percentage of viewing households. We hope our friend, after a good night's sleep, sent in that pledge after all.

Pittsburgh Post-Gazette
Pittsburgh, Pa., May 5, 1977

UPSTAIRS, DOWNSTAIRS, the television series that has enchanted Public Broadcasting System television audiences for four seasons, is ended. Its death, while poignant, was inevitable and right, much like that of Maj. James Bellamy, one of the series' principal protagonists.

These programs, honored as they have been, are one of the modern achievements in the performing arts, certainly among the best original material ever produced for television.

But Upstairs, Downstairs was not merely first-class entertainment, it was also good history, both social and political. Hypocrisy, dignity, frailty, solidity: the full range of human character was laid out in this rich tapestry.

"Mellow"-drama? Yes. Mannered romance? Sometimes. But, as the program's host, Alistair Cook, pointed out at the end of the next-to-last episode, the series held its audience because its characterizations and plot always rang true. That is the essence of good art. And its very rarity makes all the more exciting its discovery, particularly on television.

The Evening Bulletin
Philadelphia, Pa., May 4, 1977

This week millions of Americans sadly said goodby to a cast of television characters who were like near and dear neighbors. After 68 episodes the Public Broadcasting Service's British import "Upstairs, Downstairs" came to an end.

There have been numerous attempts to account for the enormous popularity of "Upstairs, Downstairs." Contemporary man longs for the sense of order created by the social class system portrayed in the series, some said. Americans, particularly, it is thought, were fascinated by the proprieties and improprieties of class interaction in early 20th-century England.

As much as anything else, the sheer excellence of the acting won accolades for the series. Also, "Upstairs, Downstairs" gave us characters we could care about. Eaton Place was populated with individulals who behaved with dignity and who tried to treat each other decently. Unfortunately, that's not usual television fare.

Sunday night performers from "Upstairs, Downstairs" joined in a telethon to raise money for public television in this country. A spokesman for the Public Broadcasting Service tells us about $1.7 million was pledged.

We hope the money helps American public television develop programs that approach the quality of "Upstairs, Downstairs." Meanwhile, a reluctant and fond farewell to Hudson and Rose, Georgina and James, and the entire Bellamy household.

BUFFALO EVENING NEWS
Buffalo, N.Y., May 3, 1977

Perhaps not since the creation of Sherlock Holmes have fictional characters taken on such a sense of reality as those in "Upstairs, Downstairs," the fine public-TV series whose final episode is being shown this week.

Just as Sherlock Holmes fans still go looking for Holmes' lodgings at the nonexistent address, 221B Baker St., "Upstairs" addicts will continue, we imagine, to seek out Eaton Place, the street in London where the series was filmed. One such addict, back from London, demonstrated the extraordinary triumph of fiction over reality when, on viewing an episode with a glimpse of the street, he exclaimed: "It's just the same today!" — as if he had been looking at an actual film of the 1920s.

An estimated billion people in 50 countries have shared in the tears and joys of the Bellamy family and their servants through a quarter of a century. What is the secret of the program's success?

Many observers cite the interest and nostalgic appeal of the well-ordered Edwardian period and the event-filled years up to 1930—years that have just passed into history. And then there is the undoubted excellence at every level of production. These factors alone probably would have been enough to guarantee success. The earlier series, "The Forsyte Saga," demonstrated that.

But "Upstairs" is much more. It is a subtle study of class, a story not of upstairs or downstairs but of the interplay between them. By combining two stories in one, it creates an additional dramatic dimension, one that "The Forsyte Saga," fine as it is, does not have.

And so the Bellamys are gone— at least until the next rerun (which we hope will be soon)—but this splendid series lingers in the memory as a credit to all who took part in it, to public-TV for presenting it and to all those who support public-TV with their contributions. As Meg Wynn Owen, who played Hazel Bellamy, put it: "It was the most lovely creative thing."

The Des Moines Register

Des Moines, Iowa, May 3, 1977

Occasionally a program comes along to challenge the "vast wasteland" theory of television. Such a program was "Upstairs, Downstairs" on public TV's "Masterpiece Theater." The final episode in the British series was broadcast Sunday night.

Faithful viewers grew fond of the members of the two-tiered Bellemy family, whose comings and goings, successes and failures they monitored from before World War I to 1930. In life, the high points and low points usually come at emotionally manageable intervals. "Upstairs, Downstairs" so compressed the hills and valleys that watchers often felt drained at the end of an hour. Yet we will miss being wrought up on Sunday nights.

The series was a history lesson, too, one made the clearer by Alistair Cooke's opening and closing remarks. It gave us glimpses of wartime hardships and the difficult adjustments of the Twenties; of the strength of the lower classes and the limitations of the upper. (Never mind that real-life servants probably never had it so good.)

"Upstairs, Downstairs" met many of the criteria of good television. It informed, entertained and moved us. It was a lush oasis in the "wasteland."

WINSTON-SALEM JOURNAL

Winston-Salem, N.C., May 4, 1977

Running a British social drama opposite a John Wayne movie and a rerun of "Airport" might seem a surefire way to hit bottom in television's Nielsen Ratings. But the Public Broadcasting Service did just that Sunday night, even throwing in a plea for money to meet ever-rising operating costs. The results merit some contemplation about the PBS role in television.

In short, the service did very well. It expects to surpass the national goal, $1 million, by as much as 50 per cent. In this state, University of North Carolina television had set a goal of $50,000, half of what is needed to fill out the new budget. National officials said the $50,000 goal was high, but by Tuesday, the network was reporting more than $55,000 in pledges. "Upstairs, Downstairs," the much-acclaimed drama of early 20th Century England, probably was last in the ratings Sunday night. But it clearly was first with the people who were watching it.

All that isn't final proof that PBS has shed the elitist image for which it has been criticized from time to time. But response to the appeal does seem to offer evidence that a large number of people are attracted to good drama no matter what is on other channels. The General Assembly and the Congress, which allocate money to the service, should take notice. So should other broadcasters.

DESERET NEWS

Salt Lake City, Utah, February 25, 1977

When and if "Roots" is televised in England, suppose some British labor leader insists the production be made only with British actors.

If that ever happened, the reaction of the American public — not to mention that of government and the U.S. entertainment industry — would not be hard to imagine.

Well, that must be the reaction of the British to the latest brainstorm of that eminent connoisseur of the arts, George Meany, who's demanding that if Shakespeare's works are to be shown on American public television, then the actors should be American.

George Meany an authority on matters cultural? The AFL-CIO boss evidently must be, since he insists the decision to use public and private U.S. funds for a series of Shakespearean plays on PBS using British actors cannot be justified artistically, let alone economically.

The Meany proposal is protectionism, pure and simple. Like any other barrier to international trade, it invites retaliation in kind.

Even if it didn't, suppose that such popular British productions as "Upstairs, Downstairs" or the "Forsyte Saga" had to be re-made with American actors in order to be shown on American public television. Then Americans might never see such shows — or might not want to.

Syndicated columnist George Will recently suggested that anyone responsible for a demand like Meany's be chained to a chair in front of a set tuned to commercial television's routine offerings.

The trouble, aside from the Constitution's ban against cruel and unusual punishment, is that his fuzzy-minded notions on how to produce Shakespeare sound like the result of George Meany's already having served just such a sentence.

MANCHESTER NEW HAMPSHIRE UNION LEADER

Manchester, N.H., December 26, 1976

We don't always like or agree with the American-made programs shown on what is called "public television." And we are great fans of several of the British imports aired on public TV, particularly the Masterpiece Theatre presentations. Still, we find it impossible to understand the latest public TV arrangement with its British counterpart.

The Corporation of Public Broadcasting, distributing agent of federal monies to the Public Broadcasting System, has proposed granting the British Broadcasting Corporation $1.2 million so BBC can produce all 36 of Shakespeare's plays. Presumably, the series would eventually be shown on American PBS stations.

It's too bad Britain is having such economic troubles these days, but that's no cause for American dollars to underwrite BBC television enterprises at the expense of our own productions. Perhaps the public broadcasting corporation believes that, if it doesn't underwrite the BBC now, we may one day see an end to all high-quality British programming.

If this is the thinking, then we see nothing but gloom for the future. BBC requests for more U.S. television dollars will continue — and increase — until such time as the U.S. must finally say, "no more." And when that happens we will have to rely solely on "home-grown" artists and programs which will have suffered in the interim due to a lack of funding.

Critics of the current proposal say the U.S. should wait until the BBC series is completed and then purchase the programs for airing here. The corporation, however, says BBC won't be able to make the shows without our money. That's too bad. But we agree with AFL-CIO president George Meany who protested the proposal earlier this month saying, "We object to an organization funded by the government using taxpayers' dollars to create jobs in other countries."

Spend the money at home. Continue to fund such American-made efforts as the "Adams Chronicles" which showed that U.S. public television programming can be of as high a quality as that of our British cousins.

THE BLADE

Toledo, Ohio, August 3, 1978

WHETHER a publicly supported television network can remain free of government influence has been long debated, especially during the administrations of former President Nixon who frequently betrayed his annoyance at the liberal tinge of some public-television commentators.

This question can properly be raised again in light of the Public Broadcasting Service's effusive — one commentator called it "groveling" — documentary on House Speaker Thomas (Tip) O'Neill entitled "Mr. Speaker." The program was not, thankfully, aired on Toledo's public television outlet.

The documentary showed Mr. O'Neill at home, on the golf course, singing with his buddies, and charming his staff in Washington. There was only brief reference to the Korean bribery scandal which has implicated several leading members of the House, including some prominent Democrats. Mr. O'Neill himself has been a beneficiary of South Korean moneyman Tongsun Park's largess.

One critic summed it up: "Instead of showing us Tip O'Neill as the backroom pol who kept the lid on a scandal that could have blown the Democratic party out of the water, the program gave us Tip O'Neill as the nice grandfather from Boston who works so hard in Washington."

Mr. O'Neill, it may be remembered, was one of the most vigorous pursuers of the Watergate scandal, and he played a leading role behind the scenes in bringing about the Nixon impeachment proceedings. But his zeal to ferret out wrongdoing involving his own party has not been nearly as noticeable in the Koreagate scandal, the full proportions of which may never be known.

Such documentaries do not enhance the image of public-television broadcasting which has produced some notable fine-arts triumphs but has virtually abandoned its hard-hitting public affairs documentaries of earlier years.

It is outrageous that the nation's public-television service should kowtow to the party in power or to powerful politicians of either party. There is a proposal, as yet not enacted, to permit public television to broadcast editorial commentary. In one sense, at least, it would seem that PBS has jumped the gun.

The Birmingham News

Birmingham, Ala., January 26, 1977

The Corporation for Public Broadcasting recently was voted an authorization by Congress of $634 million. That figure was above 40 per cent more than President Ford's budget request.

CPB distributes the sizeable funds for programming, some of which clearly mirrors a radically liberal point of view. One example was "A China Memoir," based on a tour by actress Shirley MacLaine. The program was slavishly laudatory of that Communist society. Another example was "The Unquiet Death of Julius and Ethel Rosenberg," which sought to rehabilitate the convicted spies and which was designed to show that they were the victims of a frameup.

When funding for "educational" television began, Congress wanted to make sure that funds would not be used to finance programs on controversial issues that would favor one side or the other.

The Public Broadcasting Service "Document of Journalism Standards and Guidelines" says, "We pledge to strive for balanced programming... We recognize the obligation to strive for objectivity." Further, the Communications Act requires that programs financed with federal money be balanced and objective in dealing with controversial issues.

Yet, Congress has passed and the President has signed an authorization for more funds to allow the CPB to continue to present a one-sided, distorted viewpoint through public television programming.

Although the funds have been authorized, the money still has to be appropriated. Those who disagree with programming such as "A China Memoir" and "The Unquiet Death of Julius and Ethel Rosenberg" should contact their senators and congressman and urge that Congress give some thought to this problem of bias. Safeguards should be written into the legislation which would correct the abuses which now are all too apparent.

The Times-Picayune

New Orleans, La., July 13, 1975

The shining promise of public television a few years back rested largely upon the proposition that it would be free of the whims and fears of sponsors. Art and truth would be offered as an alternative to the cultural "wasteland" of commercial television.

To the contrary, today's danger is that public television could become subject to the whims of politicians and special interest groups. Consider, for example, the recent "Cajun controversy."

Last week, the WNET production, "The Good Times Are Killing Me," drew fire from James Domengeaux, head of the Council for the Development of French in Louisiana (CODOFIL), who said it depicted Cajuns in "a false, vulgar and unrealistic role."

Whether the program was as Mr. Domengeaux claimed is best left to individual judgment. After all, he objected to the term "Coonass," while Gov. Edwin Edwards has referred to himself with some pride as "the state's Number One Coonass."

More important was Mr. Domengeaux's demand that the Congress investigate public television and "bring this improper expenditure of funds" to the attention of President Gerald Ford.

In fact, the Congress is not likely to act just because Mr. Domengeaux demands it — sometimes it is hard to get the Congress to act no matter who demands it — but just in case some congressman is tempted to bring it up, we should like to point out a few dangers.

They are, simply stated, the dangers of government censorship, the draining of any substance from educational programs, an exodus of talent from public television and the reduction of the medium to a quivering echo of unscrupulous politicians — those who would have the most to gain by control of the airwaves.

It is regretable that some people were offended by a particular program (whether the offense was justified is not the subject of this edtorial) but the demand for an investigation of public television in general is an overreaction that should be ignored by Congress.

The Standard-Times

New Bedford, Mass., July 24, 1977

Back in 1960, Groucho Marx observed, "I read in the newspapers they are going to have thirty minutes of intellectual stuff on television every Monday from 7:30 to 8. They're going to educate America. They couldn't educate America if they started at 6:30."

This year marks the 25th anniversary of noncommercial, educational television in the United States. Today, there are 272 educational television stations in the country.

In the early days, much emphasis in this field was placed on instructional programs. The effectiveness of TV as a teaching tool was widely heralded. Harold Hunt, a professor of education at Harvard, said seventeen years ago that, "Television is our best hope for bringing today's outworn, restrictive and unimaginative educational system out of the oxcart age and into the 20th Century."

Throughout the 1950s, supporters of educational television recognized that programs — if they were to become "the most dominant force in the classroom next to the teacher" in the words of one observer — would have to be entertaining as well as instructive. Lynn Poole, producer of the Johns Hopkins Science Review, one of the most successful educational programs commented, "If informational programs are to survive, they must be planned and presented in such a way that they can hold their place in competition with the mystery drama, variety show and quiz program."

In essence, that is what has happened. During the last decade, noncommercial, public television has continued to combine its educational and entertainment functions. Programs such as Sesame Street, The Electric Company and Civilization have shown children and adults alike that learning can be fun.

Groucho Marx notwithstanding, educational television has taught Americans a lot.

THE MILWAUKEE JOURNAL
Milwaukee, Wisc., January 19, 1978

Needless use of foul language, nudity or violence is no more palatable on public television than it is when sandwiched between shampoo ads on commercial TV. But ridding public TV of truly objectionable material is a considerably more touchy issue, for it skirts the edges of government censorship.

The question is heating up. At a meeting last week, officials of public TV stations from throughout the South called on the nationwide Public Broadcasting Service to take a tougher stand against objectionable program content. The group cited examples of what it considered bad taste and obscenity.

PBS properly seems reluctant to turn censor. It notes that most of the programs it distributes are produced by local member stations. Moreover, law and court precedent regarding obscenity put responsibility on local stations to determine what is acceptable to their own viewers. Finally, PBS officials say, the goal of "tasteful national programming" must be pursued "without compromising the creative process." That means wielding the censor's scissors with great restraint, especially when "bad taste" can be highly subjective.

PBS does try to accommodate local stations by giving advance warning of potentially objectionable programs (most of which are recorded and thus available for preview). But the Southern broadcasters complain about the workload of previewing so many shows.

Sorry about that, but we think PBS is right. Commercial television, with its inherent need to satisfy a truly mass audience, almost inevitably tends to reflect something close to a national consensus on acceptability. One of the most valuable aspects of public TV is that it can be a broader and more daring forum for expression.

Thus, a national norm of "good taste" should not be set for public TV by whatever part of the country complains the most. Individual stations should be concerned about their own viewers' sensibilities, but it would be dangerous to buck that responsibility to a government-like central agency such as PBS.

The Burlington Free Press
Burlington, Vt., November 29, 1979

THE ROLE of public television as an alternative to the commercial networks has been defined as an attempt to bring to audiences the cultural, educational and public affairs programs that commercial television cannot, or will not, offer to its viewers.

Funded by the government through the Corporation for Public Broadcasting and by private donors, public television has won a large and appreciative audience for its varied programs. The absence of periodic commercials that break up the continuity of programs has been another large plus for the public stations.

But the heads of public stations must assume a weighty obligation in seeing to it that some of their programs do not stray from the informative into the area of political advocacy. During the political campaign this year, Vermont Educational Television fulfilled that responsibility by bringing to viewers the opinions of all candidates for state and national offices.

Questions, however, must be raised about a series of recent programs that originated in the Senate television studios in Washington. Sen. Patrick Leahy, D-Vt., interviewed federal officials on various aspects of government.

That Leahy, who is expected to seek reelection in less than two years, should be given this kind of exposure as interrogator of public officials on a 10-part series certainly represents a significant departure from the non-partisan role that public television should play in dealing with political matters. His appearance on the series, no matter how it might be interpreted by local ETV officials, was an opportunity for political image-polishing that other politicians would envy. As an incumbent who no doubt will seek reelection to his Senate seat, he was given yet another advantage over potential challengers by being selected to serve as host on the programs.

If public television is to retain its credibility with its audiences, it must steer a careful course through the shoals of political involvement. It should be cautious about presenting programs that might raise the eyebrows of its viewers.

In the future, officials of the state's public television network must weigh carefully their decisions to present programs of this nature to determine whether they violate the non-partisan guidelines that have been marked out for public television.

The Washington Star
Washington, D.C., April 22, 1976

In its Tuesday evening "report" on the youthful struggles of American public television, CBS hit upon a promising idea. One of the familiar failings of the press, newspapers and television alike, is that despite high visibility it is an underreported institution.

Things are improving, gradually. There was a time, within recent memory, when the only consistently probing reportage on the press was A.J. Liebling's "Wayward Press" column in *The New Yorker*. Despite its classic excellence, Mr. Liebling's column enjoyed only a modest audience. Now newspapers, especially in this city, write about one another (and even themselves) bluntly and often informatively.

The television networks, by contrast, respect one another's privacy to a fault — one hesitates to suggest that there is a conspiracy of silence. Oh, we suppose that NBC would put it on the evening news if the president of CBS should be levitated above the streets of Manhattan — and vice versa — but of the internal intrigues of commercial television we see very little on the tube itself.

It was natural, we suppose, for the ice to be broken by the faintly condescending CBS take-out on public television, which is struggling and vulnerable and lacking in the investigative resources and audience to strike back very hard.

It was also natural for CBS to tease public broadcasting's fund-raising techniques, the influence of big financial contributors, the cost overruns on "The Adams Chronicles" and the political atmosphere that constrains the freedom of state-owned and operated public television channels. It was a good story, although it seemed a bit inconsistent to belabor PBS for the cost of filming "The Adams Chronicles" while in the next breath deploring its reliance on the inexpensive dramatic productions of British television.

CBS even noted the technical difficulty that most public television stations depend on ultra-high frequency channels so that one needs "the fingers of a safe-cracker" to tune them in sharply. (It notably omitted, however, to say that a ready solution lies in lifting some of the FCC restrictions on cable technology which the commercial networks like so much.)

In any case, now that CBS has broken the ice, we trust that it plans to follow with a close look at the internal operations of the commercial networks, with at least equally close attention to the pressure of sponsors and the preoccupation with audience ratings. If we have a CBS report on NBC and ABC, no doubt the favor will be returned. And a large and curious audience will be waiting.

WORCESTER TELEGRAM.
Worcester, Mass.,
June 15, 1978

The audience for public television — Channels 2 and 44 in this area — is widely thought to be limited to the affluent and well educated.

But this is not so, according to a recent Nielsen ratings report to the Public Broadcasting Service.

Nielsen says 61 percent of the heads of household watching PBS have no formal education beyond high school, and more than a quarter aren't even high school graduates.

About half are employed in clerical or sales jobs or at skilled or unskilled labor. Twenty-five percent are unemployed or retired. The other quarter are indeed professionals or owners or managers of businesses, but that is about the same percentage as in the American population as a whole.

Some 53 percent of families that watch public TV have incomes of $15,000 or less. Only about 31 percent earn over $20,000.

The report also dispels another myth — that public TV devotees "never watch anything but PBS." Some may say that, thinking to impress people. But in fact, the average family that watches any public TV sees only three hours of it a week, and this makes up a small part of the total household TV diet. This same family's TV set is tuned to commercial channels a total of three to six hours a day.

PBS children's programming is especially popular. So are costume dramas and, to a lesser extent, news and documentary shows. Classical music outdraws popular on PBS.

By commercial network standards, the public TV audience is still tiny. Except when public channels run such heavily advertised blockbusters as the National Geographic specials, they get no more than 6 percent of the prime-time audience. Yet more than a third of the nation's households watch some public TV. And in the Boston viewing area, where public TV got an early start and has been especially successful, more than half do.

The Nielsen report gives strength to the PBS claim that its programming is an alternative to commercial fare that can be enjoyed by all Americans, not just an elite. We may be sure that this report will be used in public TV's ongoing struggle to wrest more tax funds from Congress.

The thought of Joe Sixpack settling into his recliner for Masterpiece Theater or Evening at Symphony may seem incongruous, but it apparently represents the encouraging truth of the matter for public TV today.

HOUSTON CHRONICLE

Houston, Tex., July 25, 1978

An attempt to use the Public Broadcasting System as a forum for the president would in our opinion be most unwise.

The man President Carter has called in to shore up his frayed image, Jerry Rafshoon, says he is exploring ways to get greater exposure for the president on PBS' television network. This is apparently linked in some degree to reluctance of the three commercial networks to grant air time to the president for what they don't consider particularly newsworthy or perhaps consider more political and/or image-making than news.

Using PBS in this manner would be quite troubling. It is a taxpayer-supported institution and any hint that it might be being used as a vehicle for propagandizing whatever president or party is in office would be destructive of the whole PBS concept. PBS only manages now to stay one jump ahead of controversy about its political and ideological balance and neutrality.

Such an idea would not just be harmful to PBS. We think it would backfire on the White House for the same reasons it would damage PBS.

The Charleston Gazette

Charleston, S.C.,
January 30, 1978

At a professional gathering, officials of public television stations throughout the South approved a resolution calling on the Public Broadcasting Service (PBS) to turn censor.

That wasn't the language of the resolution, but that's what it meant when it asked PBS to take a tougher stand against "objectionable program content."

We're ready to agree that needless use of foul language, pointless nudity and violence not necessary to the telling of a story are no more palatable on public television than on commercial television.

But government censorship is far less palatable. We are pleased to observe that PBS is resisting the local member stations which, after all, already have the power to determine what their viewers may see.

This option of local stations was pointed out in the PBS response to the resolution, a response that also said national programming must be pursued "without compromising the creative process."

What is in "bad taste" can be highly subjective, and PBS already tries to accommodate local stations by giving advance notice of programs which local stations might find objectionable. To this, the Southern broadcasters say it is inconvenient to preview shows.

We think PBS is right. Commercial television has a financial stake in satisfying a mass audience, and it takes pains to drive away no viewers. But the whole idea of public television is that it provides a broader forum for expression.

We think it would do great damage to that freedom of expression if a standard of "good taste" were to be imposed on public television by that part of the country which complains the most.

Arkansas Gazette.

Little Rock, Ark., December 18, 1977

Various complications have prevented the initiation of news broadcasts on Arkansas's educational television network, and the plan advanced by Governor Pryor now is consigned to the wastebasket. It envisioned the rebroadcast of commercial news programs (minus the commercials) from Little Rock's three network television stations on a delayed basis over the ETV channel.

Though the executives of the three commercial stations did, to their credit, get together on this plan, there was static from other segments of both commercial and public broadcasting. As a major example, the National Broadcasting Company objected to rebroadcast of its taped national news on the public system. Also, the Arkansas Broadcasters Association, which has some influence in the commercial airwaves sector, passed a resolution against the idea. So Mr. Pryor, whose motivation was commendable, has seen his proposal go down the drain, irretrievably, perhaps, and the people he was hoping to serve the most — those Arkansans on the fringes who cannot get Arkansas television news on their sets — still won't be able to.

The matter assuredly should not be dropped at this point, however. Some ideas looking toward a remedy in the longer run need to be developed. We think that not only the people on the extremities and in the deepest hollows of Arkansas should be considered, but that *everyone* in the state is entitled to expect some sort of scheduled news reportage on public television. It need not be elaborate, but it could be quite abundant, given the lack of time-consuming commercials on the public ETV system. An announcer simply reading, quickly and seriously, the output of a news wire-service teletype could put out a lot of news in five or ten minutes, without interruptions or distractions. Nor should the ETV people hesitate to think about attempting, someday, the lengthy and high-quality interview- and analysis-type programs, in the state context, of which, in the national context, the MacNeil-Lehrer Report and two or three others provide excellent examples.

Of course public television always has money problems and these things might not be possible in the near future. But almost by definition public broadcasting is supposed to be concerned with public affairs, in the illumination of which there is nothing more basic than the news. President Carter, in fact, proposes a heavier outlay for public affairs programming in his recommendation of a vastly expanded federal contribution to the public media. Still, rather than waiting for added help from that quarter to arrive, might not the Arkansas network take some modest steps of its own toward the news function? The public might be quite appreciative — even supportive with a few additional contributions to ETV.

The Washington Spectator®

and

BETWEEN THE LINES

ISSN: 0145-160X

nuary 15, 1979   **Tristram Coffin, Editor** © 1979 The Public Concern Foundation, Inc.   Volume 5, No. 1

Television, the Great Debate

A decision that could cut deeply into America's future will be made by the 96th Congress.

Congress will make a choice in a debate raging between the roadcast industry and its critics, whether to free TV from overnment control. The industry claims it is unduly shackled y the Federal Communications Commission. For the opposition, Everett C. Parker of the United Church of Christ states: "The American people are not just a hapless audience to be elivered by the Congress to advertisers, broadcasters and ommon carriers for their enrichment."

The importance of the decision is stressed by the influence of V on modern life. In ages past, religion was the major source f truth, culture and knowledge. The faithful looked to it for uidance and lived by its precepts. Today, says the religious nonthly, *Eternity,* TV has taken over this role; it is "in many ays a parent, a teacher and a priest" and is "the new religion . . , a momentous and unprecedented force in shaping our uture." George Gerber, dean of the University of Pennsylvania chool of Communications, states, "Television has profoundly ffected the way in which members of the human race learn to ecome human beings."

The *Saturday Review* calls TV an "awesome medium" and otes "the millions the medium manipulates, . . . the endless earch for the sensational to attract the audience whose truth and eality comes from the tube." Marshall McLuhan states: "The V experience is an inner trip and is as addictive as any known rug. The discarnate TV user lives in a world between fantasy nd dream and is in a typically hypnotic state which is the ltimate form and level of participation. . . . Death on TV is a orm of fantasy, and all the fantasy violence of TV is a reminder nat the violence of the real world is motivated by people uesting for lost identity." (*New York* magazine)

According to the *Washington Post,* broadcasters boast that 'television is the most potent mind-altering medium available or advertising dollars.''

Commercial TV is, of course, not all wasteland. There have een some magnificent documentaries, useful investigative re-orting, as in "60 Minutes," and great drama and opera.

THE WASHINGTON DEBATE—Under present law, TV nd radio stations are considered by law as trustees of public roperty, the airwaves. They are licensed to use the airwaves 'in the public interest, convenience and necessity." The estraint by the Federal Communications Commission, how-ver, has been progressively weakened over the years by politi-al pressure.

Today the industry wants the restraints removed, and reform roups generally ask for tightened controls, particularly against iolence. The industry-backed plan would diminish the regu-latory powers of the FCC, phase out the regular review and renewal of station licenses, and eliminate the "fairness doc-trine" which requires a balanced treatment of opposing views.

The *New York Times* in support of relaxed control calls it "a fresh approach to an unsatisfactory situation." The plan "is designed to encourage diversity and let the market work its will." *Christianity and Crisis* argues the plan would turn the medium over to "the hands of industrial giants whose primary motivation is to make profits, not to maximize the free flow of information." The National Radio Broadcasters Association "heartily endorses the philosophy under the proposed rewrite."

"Massacre of the Innocents"

"We are no more prepared to encounter radio and TV in our literate milieu than the native of Ghana is able to cope with the literacy that takes him out of his collective tribal world and beaches him in individual isolation. We are as numb in our new electric world as the native involved in our literate and mechanized culture.

"Electric speed mingles the cultures of prehistory with the dregs of industrial marketeers, the nonliterate with semi-literate and the postliterate. Mental breakdown of varying degrees is the very common result of uprooting and inundating with new information and endless new patterns of information. Wyndham Lewis made this a theme of his group of novels. . . . *The Childermass* is concerned precisely with accelerated media change as a kind of slaughter of the innocents."

—Marshall McLuhan in *Understanding Media*

A CRITICAL VIEW—Critics believe that the risk in TV is that the conduct seen there is so often imitated. The Eisenhower Commission and the Surgeon General's report have linked vio-lence on TV to the rising tide of violence in America. In his book, *The Pentagon Propaganda Machine,* the former Foreign Relations Committee chairman, J. William Fulbright, suggests militarism in America is related to the way TV pictures violence and force as the only way to overcome opposition.

OTHER EFFECTS OF TV CITED—Two legal researchers believe that "an endless stream of television police dramas" glorify "the most blatantly illegal and unconstitutional behavior of police officers. . . . Those principles include the notions that the end justifies the means, and that violence is perfectly accept-able when resorted to by the right people." (Stephen Arons and Ethan Katsch in *Saturday Review*)

In a recent Supreme Court brief, the question is asked: "What is really wrong with tricking a man into telling the truth?

That is one of the goals of a good Perry Mason-type cross-examination.'' The authors point to a "blindness to individual liberty" in TV shows.

TV has become a serious weapon in American politics and enables a candidate to present a superficial view avoiding major issues. Erich Fromm is concerned that "American voters know their candidates only by the artificial image created by public relations specialists." The technique of using TV for the "image" was developed particularly well by Richard Nixon, as in his "cloth coat" speech which so moved General Eisenhower he decided to keep him on the ticket.

"Television dulls sensitivity and creates a tendency to detachment from the consequences of one's acts," says former FCC Commissioner Nicholas Johnson. "It produces an erroneous set of factual assumptions about the real world in heavy viewers regardless of their educational level."

Children under five watch TV an average of 23.5 hours a week, according to the Nielsen surveys.

A Child's World

"His first polysyllabic utterance was "Bradybunch.' He learned to spell Sugar Smacks before his own name. He has seen Monte Carlo, witnessed a cocaine bust in Harlem and already has full-color fantasies involving Farrah Fawcett-Majors. Recently, he tried to karate-chop his younger sister after she broke his Six Million Dollar Man bionic transport station. (She retaliated by bashing him with her Cher doll.) His nursery-school teacher reports that he is passive, noncreative, unresponsive to instruction, bored during play periods and possessed of an almost nonexistent attention span—in short, very much like his classmates.

"Next fall, he will officially reach the age of reason and begin his formal education. His parents are beginning to discuss their apprehensions—when they are not too busy watching television."

—*Newsweek*

WHO SHOULD CONTROL THE MONSTER? Should TV be controlled, by whom, and with what guidelines?

Marshall McLuhan, in *"Understanding Media,"* wrote: "The threat of Stalin or Hitler was external. The electric technology is within the gates, and we are numb, deaf, blind and mute about its encounter with the Gutenberg technology. . . . I am in the position of Louis Pasteur telling doctors that their enemy was quite invisible, and quite unrecognized by them."

Complete government control of TV, as in totalitarian lands, gives the state a masterful weapon to load up the public mind with half-truths and lies and to erase the concept of liberty. This is the Orwellian world that Erich Fromm describes: "The world becomes a sum of lifeless artifacts. Man has no plan, no goal for life, except doing what the logic of technique determines him to do."

Complete control of TV for private profit might bring an almost hysterical level of sensationalism and voyeurism, in order to gain the mass audience to please the advertiser and bring in larger profits. Advertising would presumably take an increasing share of viewing time.

Most critics of TV programming agree that either complete freedom or government censorship would be unfortunate. They suggest alternatives.

• The Public Broadcasting Service, which does not use commercials, pays its way by listener memberships, foundation grants and government funds. Its programs for children, such "Sesame Street," are outstanding; and its format is general cultural, educational and of community interest.

• The BBC is a model for a government-operated TV ne work. A Board of Governors provides policy guidance. BBC gives general programming, and BBC 2 offers more education programs, and those of minority, special and local interest. BB is financed by a tax on TV sets.

USEFUL SERVICES OF TV—Rather than serve as simply medium of crude entertainment and profit, TV can become useful tool of society. It could, for example, increase literacy The US Office of Education estimates there are 23 millio American adults who cannot perform such a basic skill reading a train schedule. A study by the National Assessment Education Progress, watching 7,500 students, "concludes th only 10% of 9-year-olds, a third of 13-year-olds and half 17-year-olds showed the capacity to organize ideas on paper. One in seven Philadelphia high-school seniors who took a lite acy test could not fill out a job application; 7.2% could not read newspaper; 8.3% did not know the meaning of such words "deposit . . . credit . . . beware."

More than half the 17-year-olds did not know the Fif Amendment's protection against self-incrimination. One every eight thought the President was not required to obey th law. Few know what steps Congress can take to halt a Pres dent's march to war. One or two thought the President cou appoint Congressmen.

And "by the time the average American youngster graduate from high school he has spent more time watching the televisio screen than he has spent in school, or in any other activity exce sleeping." *(Washington Post)* Thus, the opportunity for educ tional programming to reduce illiteracy is almost limitless.

TV also can be of great service in informing the electorate issues. This promise has not been fulfilled, says the *Columb Journalism Review;* it states, "Television, despite all its ma velous capacity to advance communication, is a graveyard f substantive issues in a political campaign." In his book, *Th Manipulators,* Robert Sobel declares, "Television and motio pictures have accomplished what no other forces could ha done—they have helped shatter the American political proce and cripple the party system, replacing them with a plebiscitor democracy, run more by polls than election."

POLITICAL IMPACT OF TV—Erich Fromm finds th "American voters know their candidates only by the artifici image created by public-relations specialists." The *Washingto*

𝕎𝖆𝖘𝖍𝖎𝖓𝖌𝖙𝖔𝖓 𝕾𝖕𝖊𝖈𝖙𝖆𝖙𝖔𝖗® & **BETWEEN THE LINES**

Copyright © 1979 The Public Concern Foundation, Ralph E. Shikes, President.

Editorial Board: Tristram Coffin, Carey McWilliams, Ralph E. Shikes, Alden Whitman.

| Address subscription corre-spondence to P.O. Box 32280 Washington, D.C. 20007 | Address editorial corre-spondence to P.O. Box 9965 Washington, D.C. 20015 |

Published the 1st and 15th of each month at 1701 N. Fort Myer Drive, #602, Arlington, Va. 22209.

Your dues payment to The Public Concern Foundation is used entirely to forward the task of sharing information and stimulating discussion. Your $10 dues are divided between publishing the *Washington Spectator* and sponsoring research, symposia, and other Foundation activities. Seventy percent of your membership dues is used for publishing the *Washington Spectator.* The *Spectator* is available only to members of the Foundation.

Post adds: "Political TV commercials have reached a frightening sophistication. . . . Four years from now [1980] we can expect even cleverer use of the media. It may reach the point where candidates . . . concentrate almost entirely on controlled media presentations." President Ford's astonishing comeback from a low point in the polls to a photo finish in 1976 was accomplished by 130 adroit TV spots, according to advertising consultant Malcolm MacDouglas.

Politics and the TV

"We just can't handle [political] issues the way a newspaper can. A writer can go into all kinds of detail to explain things. We have to have something on that film. And you've got 90 seconds to tell it."
—Richard Kaplan, writer of the Cronkite evening news

"In the recent election the media, and particularly radio and television, reported the whole thing as a sporting event, a horse race and avoided issues."
—Richard Strout, *Christian Science Monitor*

MARKETING GOODS—TV could be of great help to the consumer in selecting his purchases. Instead, it has become the most successful seller of junk merchandise since the medicine man. This is because loading up the airwaves with advertising has made TV stations the golden calf. The *New York Times'* Les Brown points out, "Economics serves as aesthetics in commercial broadcasting. Every rating point gained or lost by a show represents about 700,000 television households on a national scale. After costs are met, a single rating point in a network's weekly average, over the course of a season, comes to represent $20 million or more in profits. Getting these rating points is the art of television."

Producer Norman Lear explains, "The programming department is responsible for ratings, and ratings are responsible for network income, dollars."

TELEVISION AND THE NEWS—TV could become the most important source of accurate, balanced news. The *Columbia Journalism Review* does not think it has done the job and states: "With one or two exceptions, at no time during the period of major American involvement in Vietnam did the television networks employ their vast resources in an honest effort to discover the actual reality of the Vietnam situation. . . . In 1967-68, the networks glamorized the air-bombing of North Vietnam while noticeably refraining from following up reports of the wasteful and pointless destruction of South Vietnamese land and life that was then taking place as a result of American military policy."

Michael Arlen, TV critic for the *New Yorker,* commented: "For roughly the past 10 years—a period dominated by the Vietnam war—the lenses through which so many Americans scanned the landscape of their nation and the world proved to be so shortsighted and out of focus that tens of thousands of American lives were lost in Asia, apparently to no purpose, and a poisonous and highly unstable division was allowed to appear in American life; and on top of that, as a result of the inflationary armament expenditures under two Presidents, the once-vaunted American economy was seriously weakened and propelled into a decline." ("The View from Highway 1")

President Nixon was able to manipulate TV and cast himself in the role or hero and benefactor. His trip to China was treated as a TV spectacular with Nixon as the guide. President Carter moved the emotions of a nation by getting out of his limousine and walking part of the way during the Inaugural parade. John Kennedy's press conferences were a TV event, not so much for what he said as for his lively manner.

PROTEST AND REFORM—Citizens groups, such as the National Citizens Committee for Broadcasting and the Parent-Teacher Association, have discovered an effective weapon, when neither the FCC nor the broadcasters heed their alarms. They bombard advertisers with complaints. After the Committee cited McDonald's for having the most ads on violent shows, it switched and sponsored "The Sound of Music" and "Snoopy" cartoons.

What has been suggested is a series of guidelines which might govern commercial TV.

● TV should be required to set aside good time for children's programs not laden with demanding advertising and for cultural affairs such as good music and drama. Theater critic John Simon would like "some time—not necessarily prime time—reserved for the concern of intellectuals. As it is, intellectuals are television's only despised and ignored minority."

● TV should offer time for public issues, minority opinions and, as Studs Terkel puts it, "the real world as real people live it, . . . non-celebrated people telling us their lives, their hopes, their fears."

● TV advertising should be keyed in to national economic policy, and not try to sell gas-guzzlers when we are trying to save fuel.

● TV should offer free time to political candidates to discuss public issues, and political advertising should be banned.

● TV should use restraint in showing violence and criminal acts. Rep. Paul Simon (D-Ill.) writes: "While they were growing up—from the ages of 5-15—these young people probably watched 13,000 people killed. And they spent more time being 'taught' on television than being taught in the classroom. Eight out of ten TV programs contain violent behaviour. Our children are still getting high doses of switch-blade knives, kicks in the groin and 'Saturday-night specials.'"

● TV should be used to encourage local musicians and dramatists, and local self-help projects.

Index